If you're wondering why you should buy this new edition of *Case Histories in International Politics,* here are ten good reasons!

1. "Anarchy: The League of Nations" is a new case that helps you understand the history of international organization and the concept of **anarchy**.

2. "Economic Interdependence: North–South Trade" is a new case that will give you the background to understand **economic globalization**.

3. "Decolonization and Development: India Rising" is a new case that will improve your understanding of **development** and India's economic power.

4. "Global Governance: The Asian Financial Crisis" is a new case that will familiarize you with the nature

of **fina**
global

D1039779

5. "In
new case tha...
ments train for and respond to threats to **national security**.

6. "International Law: The Nuremberg Trials" is a new case that will provide you with a foundation in international law and **human rights**.

7. Connections between historical events and **recent world affairs** are made in every case.

8. Each case study illustrates the application of **core concepts** covered in your course.

9. **Timeline** and **Key Figure** boxes make it easier to follow the main actors and events.

10. **Discussion questions** help you critically engage the cases and explore them in greater depth.

Case Histories in International Politics

Sixth Edition

Kendall W. Stiles

Brigham Young University

N
London   Tor
Mexico City   Mu

Acquisitions Editor: Vikram Mukhija
Editorial Assitant: Toni Magyar
Marketing Manager: Lindsey Prudhomme
Production Manager: Frances Russello
Project Coordination, Text Design, and Electronic Page Makeup: Yasmeen Neelofar/GGS Higher
    Education Resources, A Division of Premedia Global, Inc.
Senior Cover Design Manager: Nancy Danahy
Cover Illustration/Photo: © Veer, Inc.
Printer and Binder: Courier Companies, Inc

Library of Congress Cataloging-in-Publication Data

Stiles, Kendall W.
    Case histories in international politics / Kendall W. Stiles. — 6th ed.
        p. cm.
    Includes bibliographical references and index.
    ISBN-13: 978-0-205-73995-0 (alk. paper)
    ISBN-10: 0-205-73995-4 (alk. paper)
    1. World politics—20th century—Case studies.   2. World politics—21st century—Case studies.
I. Title.
  D840.S68 2010
  327.09'04—dc22

                                                                                2009020670

Longman
is an imprint of

www.pearsonhighered.com   ISBN-13: 978-0-205-73995-0
                                 ISBN-10:   0-205-73995-4

Brief Contents

Detailed Contents   vi
Preface   xii

PART 1   FUNDAMENTAL CONCEPTS   1
 1 Levels of Analysis: The Camp David Accords   2
 2 Anarchy: League of Nations   24
 3 Balance of Power: Sino–Soviet–American Relations   41
 4 The National Interest: 9/11   62
 5 Rationality: The Cuban Missile Crisis   81

PART 2   INTERNATIONAL SECURITY   95
 6 Nationalism: The Russian–Chechen Conflict   96
 7 Collective Goods: The Kyoto Protocol   110
 8 Military Power: The Persian Gulf Wars I and II   125
 9 Terrorism: Al Qaeda   143
10 Intervention: Bosnia   162
11 Intelligence: Pearl Harbor   185

PART 3   INTERNATIONAL COOPERATION   201
12 Democratic Peace Theory: Vietnam Homefront   202
13 Human Security: The HIV/AIDS Pandemics   220
14 Economic Interdependence: North–South Trade   235
15 Decolonization and Development: India Rising   251
16 Globalization: Sweatshops and Outsourcing   269
17 Economic Regionalism: Europe Uniting   282
18 International Law: The Nuremberg Trials   301
19 Human Rights: Apartheid in South Africa   317
20 Global Governance: The Asian Financial Crisis   338

Index   355

Contents

Preface xii

PART 1   FUNDAMENTAL CONCEPTS   **1**

1 Levels of Analysis: The Camp David Accords   **2**

Introduction   2
Henry Kissinger and the 1973 War   3
Camp David   9
Middle East Peace since Camp David   16
Conclusion: Assessing the Levels of Analysis Approach   17
Key Figures   20
Chronology   21

2 Anarchy: League of Nations   **24**

Introduction   24
Origins of the League of Nations   25
League Decision-Making Structures   26
League Politics   27
Manchuria   30
Danzig   32
Abyssinia   33
Was WWII a League Enforcement Action?   36
Conclusion: The Power of Anarchy?   37
Key Figures   38
Chronology   39

3 Balance of Power: Sino–Soviet–American Relations   **41**

Introduction   41
The Superpower "Triangle" and Alignments   42

Major Incidents 43
The Balance of Power Triangle 54
Conclusion: Still a Triangle? 56
Key Figures 57
Chronology 58

4 The National Interest: 9/11 62

Introduction 62
September 11 and the Great Debate 67
Conclusion: Aftermath and Debate 75
Key Figures 77
Chronology 78

5 Rationality: The Cuban Missile Crisis 81

Introduction 81
Rationality and the Cuban Missile Crisis 82
The Cuban Missile Crisis 83
Analysis of the Decision to Blockade Cuba 86
Response to the Soviet Offers 89
Conclusion: Rationality Tested 91
Key Figures 92
Chronology 93

PART 2 INTERNATIONAL SECURITY 95

6 Nationalism: The Russian–Chechen Conflict 96

Introduction 96
"Civilization" as an International Relations
    Concept 97
A Thumbnail Sketch of the Chechen People 98
History of Chechnya's Conflict with Russia
    since 1990 99
The First Chechen War: 1990–1996 100
The Second Chechen War: 1997–2000 102
The History since 2000 102
Conclusion: Nationalism or Sovereignty? 104
Key Figures 105
Chronology 106

7 Collective Goods: The Kyoto Protocol   **110**

    Introduction   110

    Global Warming   111

    Creating Rules on Global Warming Gases   114

    Impasse at the Hague   119

    The Current Situation   120

    Conclusion: The Challenge of Providing Collective Goods   121

    Key Figures   122

    Chronology   123

8 Military Power: The Persian Gulf Wars I and II   **125**

    Introduction: Power   125

    The First Persian Gulf War   126

    The Inter-War Period: March 1991–March 2003   131

    Enter the Vulcans   132

    The War in Iraq   134

    Conclusion: The Limits of Military Power   137

    Key Figures   138

    Chronology   139

9 Terrorism: Al Qaeda   **143**

    Introduction   143

    Islamic Fundamentalism   144

    Osama bin Laden and the Founding of al Qaeda   146

    Describing al Qaeda   148

    Al Qaeda after September 11   154

    Conclusion: The Lessons of the War on Terror   156

    Key Figures   157

    Chronology   158

10 Intervention: Bosnia   **162**

    Introduction   162

    History to 1918   164

    1918 to 1980   167

    After Tito   170

    Warfare in Slovenia and Croatia   171

    Warfare in Bosnia   173

    Warfare in Kosovo   177

War Crimes Tribunal   178
Conclusion: Whither Yugoslavia?   179
Key Figures   181
Chronology   181

11 Intelligence: Pearl Harbor   185
Introduction   185
Prologue   186
Pearl Harbor: The Controversy   186
Conclusion: The Lessons of Pearl Harbor   196
Key Figures   196
Chronology   197

PART 3   INTERNATIONAL COOPERATION   201

12 Democratic Peace Theory: Vietnam Homefront   202
Introduction   202
Public Opinion and Vietnam   204
Tonkin Gulf and Rally 'Round the Flag   204
Growing Skepticism   205
Tet Shock and Johnson's "Resignation"   207
The Peace Movement   209
The Nixon Era and Congressional Reassertion   211
Conclusion: Did Democracy Bring Peace?   212
Key Figures   214
Chronology   215

13 Human Security: The HIV/AIDS Pandemics   220
Introduction   220
History of Recent Pandemics   221
HIV/AIDS   223
The International Response to HIV/AIDS   225
Alternative Strategies   227
Conclusion: Achieving Human Security   232
Chronology   233

14 Economic Interdependence: North–South Trade   235
Introduction   235
Basic Concepts   236

Conditions After World War II 237
The Creation of UNCTAD and the NIEO 238
The Collapse of the G-77 and NIEO 242
Agriculture in Uruguay and Beyond 243
Conclusion: Interdependence or Dependence? 247
Chronology 248

15 Decolonization and Development: India Rising 251

Introduction 251
India before Independence 253
India under Nehru 256
India under Indira 259
Indian Economic Liberalization 260
Conclusion: India Today 264
Key Figures 266
Chronology 266

16 Globalization: Sweatshops and Outsourcing 269

Introduction 269
The Sweatshop Phenomenon 271
The Outsourcing Phenomenon 272
Competing Perspectives 273
Conclusion: Globalization 279

17 Economic Regionalism: Europe Uniting 282

Introduction 282
The Emergence of the Common Market: 1945–1957 283
The EEC at Work: 1957–1973 286
The European Community under Stress: 1973–1985 288
Renewal 1986–2006 290
Conclusion: Regionalism and Europe 296
Key Figures 297
Chronology 298

18 International Law: The Nuremberg Trials 301

Introduction 301
Organizing the Trials 302
Courtroom Drama 307
The Judgment 309

Implications of the Nuremberg Trials   310
Conclusions: International Law and Justice   312
Key Figures   314
Chronology   315

19 Human Rights: Apartheid in South Africa   **317**
Introduction   317
Origins of South Africa: 1652–1910   318
Establishment and Consolidation of Apartheid: 1910–1965   321
Stalemate: 1965–1988   326
Dismantling Apartheid: 1989–1994   329
Postapartheid South Africa   331
Conclusion: Promoting Human Rights   332
Key Figures   333
Chronology   334

20 Global Governance: The Asian Financial Crisis   **338**
Introduction   338
A Primer on International Finance   340
Asian Finances in the 1990s   343
The Crisis Erupts   345
Russia Next   347
Brazil and Others   348
Management of the Crisis   348
Conclusion: Global Governance?   351
Chronology   352

Index   **355**

Preface

As the reader considers each new day's headlines, the breathless language often instills fear and confusion. We learn that Russia and Georgia are at war; does this mean the same thing as when Germany and France were at war? We read that the world economy is in a meltdown; have we ever survived anything like this before? We are warned of global warming; is this part of a natural cycle or the result of something we did? It is best not rely on headlines to provide the necessary context and historical perspective, of course. Television news devotes only a few minutes each day to world affairs, and we should not forget that most news organizations are in the business of selling the news. And any salesman will tell you that much depends on eliciting an emotional rather than an intellectual reaction in the consumer.

Showing how the academic study of international relations offers a systematic way to interpret new developments, *Case Histories in International Politics* provides an opportunity to more critically reflect on the events and issues of our time. The twenty chapters in this book present essential concepts in the field. One could easily cover more (some might take out a few), but the list is a good start. The "state," the "nation," "power," the "balance of power," "levels of analysis," "international law," and so forth are defined to help readers understand the material found in other readings and their instructors' lectures.

But since the concepts are derived from observing history and since history becomes understandable through the concepts, I feel the best way to understand abstract ideas is to present an illustration in the form of a historical case study. The cases are mostly stories of important events in the 20th and 21st centuries; most took place after the end of the Second World War and several are quite recent. But in order to make sure the cases are significant and are likely to be meaningful for years to come, I focused on material that has its roots in decades-old and even centuries-old antecedents. Thus the case on the situation in the former Yugoslavia begins with a description of the region in the Middle Ages. The case on sweatshops describes the dawn of the Industrial Revolution. The discussion of the League of Nations takes readers back to the dawn of parliamentary diplomacy.

The material, however, is more than a mere compendium of facts and figures. It offers the ingredients to create theories and to test hypotheses. Readers will see enough different events and developments that they can begin developing their own generalizations. By looking at cases and concepts, they will be engaged in the most fundamental activity of the profession. They may even develop new theories and generalizations that will allow us to better understand some new event that no one has yet foreseen.

Like readers of previous editions, readers of this new edition will find a useful introduction to the field in these pages as well as a useful reference beyond the classroom. The historical background provided here does not change, although its interpretation naturally does. As new problems emerge in new parts of the world, my hope is that this background will give readers an advantage in understanding world problems that endure and emerge in their lifetime.

FEATURES

Each case is written with both the student and the teacher in mind. It begins with the description of a key concept in the field of international affairs. This will allow the instructor to link the case to the more theoretical material in the course. The concept provides a window to understanding the subsequent material, which is presented chronologically in most cases. Essential background information is followed by details of the event or development itself, followed by a discussion of its implications and ramifications. In presenting the material this way, students can not only see the relevance of the concept for the case, but can also begin to engage in some "process tracing" analysis of their own in order to begin to explain how certain antecedents brought about certain outcomes.

In each case, helpful pedagogical features are incorporated. Timelines orient the reader to the sequencing of events and allow them to compare patterns in other cases. It's useful to note, for instance, that India's move to economic liberalization coincided with the collapse of the Soviet Union. Whether the two are related is up to the reader to consider. Brief descriptions of key individuals involved in the events are provided to help the reader appreciate the impact they had on their world. Maps and figures add a visual dimensions to the conceptual and historical materials covered. Finally, because the cases are intended for classroom use, provocative end-of-chapter questions about how the concepts apply to the histories, the wisdom of the decisions made by the actors, and the implications of past events for today are included.

Case Histories in International Politics is organized around three key sections: "Fundamental Concepts," "International Security," and "International Cooperation." This follows the standard structure of most introductory courses on international relations and has the virtue of preparing the student with some basic theoretical material before launching into a more systematic review of the two principal subfields of the discipline.

Several alternatives to this organization are available, however. First, one could review the cases chronologically in the following sequence:

Pre-1960: Chapters 2, 11, 14, 15, 18
1960–1980: Chapters 1, 5, 12, 17, 19
1980–2009: Chapters 3, 4, 6, 7, 8, 9, 10, 13, 16, 20

One could also focus on particular regions to make comparisons. Although some cases cover more than one region, they could be organized in this sequence:

U.S. Foreign Policy: Chapters 1, 3, 4, 5, 8, 11, 18
Europe: Chapters 2, 6, 7, 10, 17
Latin America: Chapters 5, 14, 16, 20

Asia: Chapters 2, 3, 11, 12, 14, 15, 16, 20
Africa: Chapters 2, 13, 14, 16, 19
Middle East: Chapters 1, 4, 8, 9, 14

Certain issues and events can be understood by looking at particular groupings of cases. For example, the problem of international terrorism is addressed focused on in Chapter 9 and discussed in Chapters 4, 8, 10, and 15. Likewise, the question of economic integration is addressed not only in Chapter 17, but is also prominently featured in Chapters 7, 14, 15, 16, and 20.

NEW TO THIS EDITION

This sixth edition brings greater focus to long-term historical developments as well as greater attention to economic issues. New cases include the League of Nations and anarchy, the North–South debate and the rise and fall of the NIEO, the emergence of India from colonialism to world prominence, and the Asian financial crisis of 1997–1998.

The League of Nations was the first global institution of its kind. Its purpose was nothing less than the abolition of war at a time when governments still imagined that invasion and conquest were their birthright. It is astonishing to think that such an institution was ever invented, and its story allows us to see clearly the power of anarchy in international affairs. By inference, the story of the League helps to explain the obstacles facing international cooperation, as described in Chapters 7, 13, 14, 17, 18, and 20.

This edition also includes several new studies of economic development, conflict, and cooperation. Chapters 14, 15, and 20 can be read in combination, as they all tell the story of Asia's economic emergence in a global economy. The story of the North–South debate shows the importance of economic power in relation to global negotiations on economic rules. Likewise, the troubles facing countries in financial collapse show the need for global governance in an age of interdependence—a lesson that contemporary world leaders would be advised to learn. Finally, the rise of India shows how one country tried to decide between the competing views of development and manage its relationship to the rest of the world.

Further, cases on Pearl Harbor and the role of intelligence as well as the Nuremberg Trials and international law have been restored to this edition, allowing us to more clearly see the evolution of the use of intelligence as well as the role of international law historically. These cases can be used in tandem with others in the text to show the overall evolution of these phenomena. For example, one could pair the story of Pearl Harbor with Chapter 4 on 9/11 to show how the nation prepares for and responds to "bolts from the blue." Likewise, the story of the Nuremberg Trials can be paired with Chapter 19 on Apartheid to show some of the ways the international community has addressed grow violations of basic human rights.

Most of the cases have undergone significant revision in light of recent developments. New developments in Iraq have been described in Chapters 8 and 12, making them current through late 2008. This allows us to discuss some of the effects of the "surge" and the implications of President Barak Obama's anticipated draw-down of forces. Likewise, recent events surrounding the fighting in Georgia between Russian and Georgian forces have been included in Chapter 6. This material can be combined with the broader perspective on Russian foreign relations generally presented in Chapter 3. In all of these updated cases, new characters are introduced and discussed, timelines are updated, and new concepts and questions frame the discussion.

Perhaps most important, each case was re-worked to illustrate concepts that are more central to the discipline of international relations. Camp David is now used to explain levels of analysis. Pandemics are juxtaposed to the concept of human security. And the Vietnam homefront case is used to illustrate the democratic peace theory, among other examples. Taken together, the text provides numerous resources for faculty to help students think critically and creatively about world events, international relations theory, and policy making. Whatever your emphasis in the classroom, you will find this text will complement and enhance outcomes.

SUPPLEMENTS

Longman is pleased to offer several resources to qualified adopters of *Cases in International Relations* and their students that will make teaching and learning from this book even more effective and enjoyable.

For Instructors

MyPoliSciKit Video Case Studies for International Relations and Comparative Politics   Featuring video from major news sources and providing reporting and insight on recent world affairs, this DVD series helps instructors integrate current events into their courses by letting them use the clips as lecture launchers or discussion starters.

For Students

Longman Atlas of World Issues (0-321-22465-5)   Introduced and selected by Robert J. Art of Brandeis University and excerpted from the acclaimed Penguin Atlas Series, the *Longman Atlas of World Issues* is designed to help students understand the geography and major issues facing the world today, such as terrorism, debt, and HIV/AIDS. These thematic, full-color maps examine forces shaping politics today at a global level. Explanatory information accompanies each map to help students better grasp the concepts being shown and how they affect our world today. Available at no additional charge when packaged with this book.

New Signet World Atlas (0-451-19732-1)   From Penguin Putnam, this pocket-sized yet detailed reference features 96 pages of full-color maps plus statistics, key data, and much more. Available at a discount when packaged with this book.

The Penguin Dictionary of International Relations (0-140-51397-3)   This indispensable reference by Graham Evans and Jeffrey Newnham includes hundreds of cross-referenced entries on the enduring and emerging theories, concepts, and events that are shaping the academic discipline of international relations and today's world politics. Available at a discount when packaged with this book.

Research and Writing in International Relations (0-321-27766-X)   Written by Laura Roselle and Sharon Spray of Elon University, this brief and affordable guide provides the basic step-by-step process and essential resources that are needed to write political science papers that go beyond simple description and into more systematic and sophisticated inquiry. This text focuses on the key areas in which students need the most help: finding a topic, developing a question, reviewing literature, designing research, analyzing findings, and last, actually writing the paper. Available at a discount when packaged with this book.

Study Card for International Relations (0-321-29231-6)   Packed with useful information, Allyn & Bacon/Longman's Study Cards make studying easier, more efficient, and more enjoyable. Course information is distilled down to the basics, helping students quickly master the fundamentals, review a subject for understanding, or prepare for an exam. Because they're laminated for durability, students can keep these Study Cards for years to come and pull them out whenever they need a quick review. Available at no additional charge when packaged with this book.

Careers in Political Science (0-321-11337-3)   Offering insider advice and practical tips on how to make the most of a political science degree, this booklet by Joel Clark of George Mason University shows students the tremendous potential such a degree offers and guides them through: deciding whether political science is right for them; the different career options available; job requirements and skill sets; how to apply, interview, and compete for jobs after graduation; and much more. Available at a discount when packaged with this book.

ACKNOWLEDGMENTS

I would like to extend thanks to a number of individuals who helped bring about this sixth edition. I would like to thank my editor, Vikram Mukhija, who contributed significantly to the re-working of this edition, along with the staff at Longman. I would also like to thank the reviewers of this edition: Russell Crandall, Davidson College, Timothy Hellwig, University of Houston; and Andrew P. Miller, Wilkes University. Here at Brigham Young University, I would like to thank W. Chris Harvey for his able research assistance without which the manuscript would have been many months behind schedule. And finally, I thank my wife Rebecca for putting up with all the work I brought home in connection with this project.

KEN STILES

Fundamental Concepts

1

. . .

Levels of Analysis: The Camp David Accords

INTRODUCTION

Every four years, Americans are urged to select the individual who will best lead the country as it faces a multitude of international problems. The year 2008 was no different: a month before the Presidential election, *Newsweek* featured a cover story that compared Barack Obama's approach to world affairs with that of John McCain—"Mr. Cool vs. Mr. Hot" (Meacham & Thomas 2008). The operating assumption is that the individual in the White House will indeed make a big difference (Hermann 1972; Holsti 1989; Hermann & Hermann 1989).

But there is another perspective—namely, that individuals are constrained by a wide array of forces (Hermann & Hagan 1998, 124). To begin with, presidents must operate within fairly clear constitutional parameters. Anything involving money will need the approval of Congress. Any decision to stage a military assault will require the willing compliance and effective operations of troops, sailors, and their commanders. Any effort to negotiate a new treaty or send economic aid to a disaster zone will have to be carried out by foreign service officers, aid officials, and a variety of other bureaucrats and contractors, all of whom will have their own agendas—which may or may not match up with the president's. These actors and the forces that cause them to act make up what is known as the "governmental level of analysis" and require serious attention on the part of any thorough scholar.

*This chapter includes substantial portions reprinted from Linda B. Miller, "Shadow and Substance: Jimmy Carter and the Camp David Accords," #433R Pew Case Studies in International Affairs, © 1988 by the Pew Charitable Trusts, revised 1992 by the Institute for the Study of Diplomacy, Georgetown University.

On the other hand, even the government exists within constraining institutions, known as the "society." This includes all those actors and factors that make up a country's society, character, history, and traditions. For example, no presidential candidate who wants to win the New York primary will announce opposition to the state of Israel. Likewise, those in government learn early on that eliminating farm subsidies is not an option if one wants to avoid open rebellion in the Great Plains. Americans tolerate a wide range of policies, but the toleration has its limits. Furthermore, those who work in government are themselves products of American culture and attitudes, and so it would likely not occur to them to do outrageous things by American standards. Promoting polygamy, sponsoring terrorism, attacking Christianity, shutting down newspapers, and imprisoning political opponents generally don't come to the minds of most government officials in the United States—contrary to those in some other places.

Finally, states, governments, and individual leaders operate within a global environment that is often very inflexible. The individual leader cannot relocate his or her country, suddenly make it a major (or minor) power, sever ties with historic allies, or bomb the United Nations (UN). Countries have certain roles to play in the international system that stem from their capabilities, relationships, and the system of rules they inherit. The United States is one of the few countries that is criticized for failing to take a "leadership" role, for example—something no one expects of Sierra Leone. Likewise, the world would have a hard time adjusting to an anti-Europe, anti–free trade, anti-capitalist America, and taking such positions would likely prompt a drastic restructuring of the world, much as when the Soviet Union broke up in 1991. Naturally, things can change, as we see in Chapter 4 on the September 11, 2001 attacks, but generally speaking, the world environment is relatively stable and also rather demanding of its members.

The story of the Camp David Accords is largely a story of several strong personalities taking advantage of historic opportunities involving changes at different levels of analysis. Henry Kissinger, Jimmy Carter, Anwar Sadat, and Manachem Begin each enjoyed considerable formal power (enhanced by a proclivity for secrecy), relatively strong personalities and visions for the future, and a crisis atmosphere in which to operate.

HENRY KISSINGER AND THE 1973 WAR

Israel's lightning strike into Jordan, Syria, and Egypt in 1967 left Israeli troops and a growing number of settlers in power in the Golan Heights, the West Bank, the Gaza Strip, and the Sinai to the Suez Canal. None of these actions were recognized by the diplomatic community, and certainly not by the Arab states, which were determined to reverse Israel's gains. The Arab states seized their opportunity on October 6, 1973, during the Jewish Yom Kippur feast in Israel, when Egyptian and Syrian troops launched a coordinated surprise attack on Israel.

Unlike earlier Arab–Israeli wars, this battle did not produce a classic victory of the West over the East. To begin, Egypt had previously expelled its Soviet advisors in an ongoing effort to improve relations with the United States. ("Why has Sadat done me this favor?" Kissinger asked his aides; Sheehan 1981, 49.) Egypt was thus not acting as a Soviet surrogate. More importantly, the war did not go well for Israel. By the third day, it was clear that the Arab forces were well organized, were well armed, and were having moderate success. The Egyptians had reclaimed the Suez and a roughly ten-mile-deep adjacent strip in the Sinai. The Syrians reclaimed as much as one third of the Golan, and the Syrian forces pushed to within five miles of the Israeli border (Dockrill 1991, 109). Henry Kissinger took note of this rather unusual situation by endeavoring to "consolidate the stalemate":

> I believed that only a battlefield stalemate would provide the foundation on which fruitful negotiations might begin. Any equilibrium—if only an equilibrium of mutual exhaustion—would make it easier to reach an enforceable solution. (Kissinger 1982, 496)

From October 10 to November 9, 1973, Kissinger exerted considerable pressure on Israel to accept a ceasefire and a negotiated settlement. On October 11, President Richard Nixon accepted Kissinger's recommendation to send an airlift of military supplies to Israel, having failed to secure Egyptian acceptance of an immediate cease-fire. Shortly afterward, Arab members of the Organization of the Petroleum Exporting Countries (OPEC) imposed an embargo on the export of oil to the United States, along with a unilateral quadrupling of crude oil prices.

The oil embargo intensified Kissinger's efforts to reach a negotiated settlement of the war, and he sought the support of the Soviet Union. On October 22, the UN Security Council Resolution 338, cosponsored by the two superpowers, demanded the immediate cessation of hostilities and the beginning of a peaceful settlement (along the lines of a two-state solution called for in the UN Security Council Resolution 242). The resolution did not stop the fighting, and Israeli armies swarmed across the Suez, effectively cutting off Egypt's Third Army on the eastern bank. The Soviet Union came close to intervening directly to support Egypt, but America's warnings and a dramatic rise in its nuclear preparedness (DEFCON) caused the Soviets to refrain. The United States simultaneously exerted pressure on Israel to pull back from the Egyptian front to allow Egypt's forces to be re-supplied. Israel was reluctant to agree, given the considerable diplomatic leverage on Egypt this military posture commanded.

With each passing day, Kissinger became more and more directly involved in negotiating a peaceful settlement of the Suez dispute. On November 7, while in Cairo, he secured the support of President Anwar Sadat of Egypt for a six-point program that provided for Third Army relief, prisoner exchange, and a future peace conference in Geneva. This has been considered a major turning point in Egyptian policy because it was the first time Sadat was willing to accept something less than full Israeli withdrawal to the 1967 lines (Kalb & Kalb 1974, 510). It was also the beginning of a break in the Arab alliance, although this outcome was more unintended than deliberate. On November 9, Israel agreed to the plan after the United States gave assurances that it would monitor the re-supply effort for the Third Army. The model of Israeli concessions conditional on major guarantees by the United States was repeated again and again during later talks.

Israel and Egypt were still far apart on two main issues: "nonbelligerency" and exchange of prisoners. The Israelis sought from Egypt a firm commitment to peaceful relations, whereas Egypt wanted to maintain strong ties with other Arab states. Egypt was also reluctant to engage in a full-scale exchange of prisoners until it could be assured that Israeli forces would withdraw from Egyptian territory west of the Suez Canal.

A third issue that still divided Israel and Egypt involved Palestinian rights and self-determination. Kissinger hoped to set this problem aside and move forward instead on bilateral arrangements between Israel and each of its enemies. Nonetheless, a conference was organized to study the general problem of the occupied territories as well as to finalize plans for troop disengagement in both the Sinai and the Golan. In this context, Kissinger sought the participation of Syria, Jordan, and Saudi Arabia, as well as Israel and Egypt.

The December Geneva conference met with little enthusiasm. Although Israel, Egypt, and Jordan accepted invitations delivered jointly by the Soviets, Americans, and UN, Syria and Saudi Arabia declined on the grounds that Israeli withdrawal should precede any conference. Israel opposed UN participation, but the United States insisted, so Kissinger agreed to lessen the secretary general's role to that of a symbolic figurehead. Israel refused to permit Palestinian representatives at the conference, which Egypt regretted but accepted. Throughout the preliminaries, all the Arab nations except Egypt seemed to assume that the United States was able to change Israeli attitudes with the wave of a hand—in reality, it seemed at times that the reverse was more accurate. Nevertheless, running throughout this process as a subtle prod to Arab attentiveness and flexibility was the implicit threat of U.S. military intervention.

The conference itself was largely symbolic rather than substantive, and it did not lead to any larger negotiations or even to talks between Israel and Jordan. In fact, by January what Kissinger hoped would become an ongoing negotiation process in Geneva was superseded by what became "shuttle diplomacy." On January 12, while meeting with Sadat in Cairo, Kissinger accepted Sadat's invitation to act as a go-between to Israeli Prime Minister Golda Meir. The arrangement suited all the parties: not only did it give Sadat a superpower in Egypt's camp, but it also calmed Israeli fears that its concessions would make it more vulnerable. Kissinger himself received extraordinary publicity from the process.

The process of diplomacy led to a rather rapid reconciliation of the conflicting demands of the major parties. By mid-January, an agreement was reached on an immediate Israeli troop withdrawal and Egyptian troop redeployment. On January 17, 1974, the agreement was signed, providing for a thin line of Egyptian forces on the east bank of the Suez Canal, while Israeli troops withdrew to a line roughly six miles to the east. Following a proposal by Israeli Defense Minister Moshe Dayan, a UN contingent was deployed in the narrow buffer zone between the forces, and troops near the buffer zone were lightly armed (Sheehan 1981, 65–66). This "five-zone" approach proved to be the recurring theme in all of the 1974–1975 disengagement talks involving Israel (see Map 1.1).

What role did Kissinger play in these negotiations? According to Touval, he was able to induce concessions without resorting to pressures. The incentives that the United States offered—economic aid to Egypt and economic and military aid to Israel—do not appear to have been important causes for the parties' flexibility either.

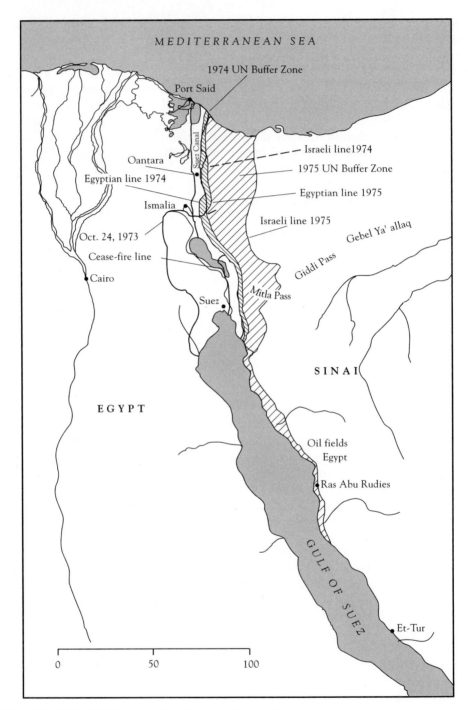

Map 1.1 1973–1975 Egyptian–Israeli troop withdrawal agreements
Source: Lester Sobel, ed. *Peace-Making in the Middle East* (New York: Facts on File, Inc., 1980).

It was rather the pressure of the circumstances in which Egypt and Israel found themselves that made them eager to conclude a disengagement agreement rapidly. The mediator's contribution was, however, essential in suggesting compromises and in arranging the indirect transaction of commitments. This procedure helped to reduce Sadat's vulnerability to criticism from the opponents of the agreement, which a direct commitment to Israel might have entailed. And finally, by providing both parties with implicit and explicit guarantees, the mediator encouraged them to feel protected from some of the risks that they believed their concessions entailed (Touval 1982, 248).

After this relatively easy success, Kissinger was drawn into two much more contentious processes: disengagement in the Golan and a second permanent Egyptian–Israeli disengagement in the Sinai. Because Syria simply did not trust the United States, Kissinger found it far more difficult to establish warm relations, unlike the rather easy warmth that developed between Kissinger and Sadat on the one hand and the near-infatuation between Kissinger and Meir on the other (Sheehan 1981, 72). Kissinger's first major contribution involved conveying prisoner lists to each party in late February and privately assuring King Faisal of Saudi Arabia that he would quietly work for Syria's interests. Formal talks were opened on March 18, the same day the oil embargo was finally lifted (over Syrian objections).

The key issues in these talks were rather simple. On the one hand, Israel did not want to withdraw its forces, which at the time were deep in Syrian territory— twenty-five miles from Damascus—beyond the territory it had occupied since 1967. On the other hand, Syria insisted on gaining considerable territory to prove that its war effort had been at least somewhat fruitful. The debate focused on the eastern town of Kuneitra (El Quneitra), which Israel firmly controlled but which was once a regional administrative center for Syria. Kissinger urged Israel to concede the city, or at least a sizable portion of it, and Israel relented. When it came to determining precisely where the Israeli troops would be deployed, the talks nearly broke down, because Israel insisted, to Syria's dismay, on occupying three overlooking hills. Israel also insisted on allowing settlers to harvest their crops around the town. Eventually, after Kissinger repeatedly threatened to walk out, the two parties settled on slightly deeper Israeli withdrawals in exchange for harvesting rights and a fairly strong UN presence in a buffer zone around the town (see Map 1.2).

On other issues, Syria refused to inhibit clandestine Palestine Liberation Organization (PLO) raids into northern Israel, even though Israel refused anything less than a guarantee that such attacks would cease. Kissinger intervened by pledging U.S. guarantees that any such attacks would be interpreted as a violation of the agreement, to which Israel could respond with all necessary means. The United States also provided considerable aid as an inducement (converting a $1 billion loan to a grant and sending military hardware).

Perhaps most interesting in these talks is how Kissinger made himself indispensable. He made the point that Israel would have a difficult time finding a better interlocutor than a Jew from the United States. He demonstrated even-handedness with Syria to prove to Damascus that he was the best available spokesman to Tel Aviv. He was able to keep the talks moving forward simply by threatening to go home. On May 25, 1974, he went so far as to coauthor with President Hafez

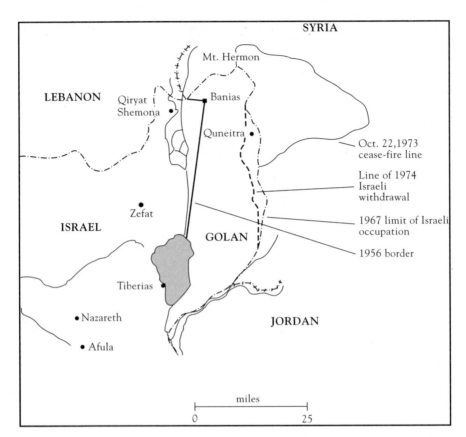

Map 1.2 1973–1975 Egyptian–Israeli troop withdrawal agreements
Source: Lester Sobel, ed. *Peace-Making in the Middle East* (New York: Facts on File, 1980).

al-Assad of Syria a communiqué announcing the collapse of the talks and laying the blame on Israel (an important threat for Tel Aviv) when, on his way out the door, Assad said to him, "What a pity. We've come so far and not succeeded. Can't anything be done . . . ?" and urged him to try once more with the Israeli leadership (Sheehan 1981, 71). On May 29, Israel and Syria signed their disengagement treaty under Kissinger's watchful eye.

The second disengagement talks between Israel and Egypt stumbled from the start. The new government of Prime Minister Yitzhak Rabin was adamant about a peace treaty with Egypt, while Kissinger tried to convey the political dangers that such a move posed for Sadat vis-à-vis his Arab counterparts. Israel refused to abandon the strategic mountain passes Giddi and Mitla without guarantees. It sought access to Egypt's oil, U.S. aid, and U.S. weapons. Israel also wanted more participation in the rules surrounding the UN buffer troops. Israel's demands were so extreme and its position so obdurate that by the spring of 1975, Kissinger and other senior officials had concluded that the negotiations were dead. In a highly publicized "reassessment" of the U.S. policy, Kissinger and President Gerald Ford implicitly accused Israel of stonewalling and threatening the talks. This ambivalence precipitated a "full-court press" by the Israeli lobby in the U.S. Congress, culminating in a letter signed by seventy-six members of Congress urging the Ford administration to maintain its commitment to Israeli security.

In this context, Israeli demands ultimately softened. Tel Aviv accepted the Egyptian offer of a "functional equivalent" to a peace treaty by pledging to solve all disputes by peaceful means. Egypt offered its oil to Israel at world market prices, and Israel was allowed a voice in decisions relating to the UN troops (particularly regarding their withdrawal, which in 1967 had been done unilaterally by Egypt). Israel also agreed to withdraw completely from the passes and allow U.S. and UN inspection of its deployment on the ground. Egypt explicitly (and Israel implicitly) agreed to abide by this treaty for at least three years, subject to annual review, thus creating de facto the Geneva conference arrangement Kissinger had originally hoped for. On September 1, 1975, the documents and corollary agreements were formally signed, and Kissinger was hailed as a miracle worker.

In exchange for these agreements with Israel, the United States made what Sheehan describes as a "marriage": It promised to protect a wide range of Israeli interests, guarantee the security of Israel, and verify compliance with the treaties. The United States also promised to have no contact with the PLO so long as it did not renounce terrorism. Finally, the United States promised to veto any UN Security Council resolution that might undermine these various agreements. United States' aid to both Israel and Egypt increased dramatically and proportionally.

CAMP DAVID

On September 5, 1978, President Anwar Sadat of Egypt and Prime Minister Menachem Begin of Israel and their delegations arrived at the U.S. presidential retreat in Maryland, Camp David, for a series of fateful meetings with President Jimmy Carter and his entourage. On March 26, 1979, the three leaders met on the front lawn of the White House to sign a peace treaty between Egypt and Israel. In the months that separated these widely publicized events, numerous obstacles between the countries arose and intensified; some crucial issues remained unresolved until the actual day of the signing. The entire undertaking was precarious at the time Carter reactivated his peacemaking initiative in August 1978 and remained so even after the documents were initialed and exchanged the next year. The story of these hopeful yet frustrating months is full of twists and turns that kept participants on the edge of failure and observers on the edge of their seats.

From the perspective of more than two decades after the accords were negotiated, the central issues that dominated the talks and their aftermath are clear. Would there be a bilateral accord between Egypt and Israel, linked vaguely (if at all) to an accord on the future of the West Bank and Gaza? Or would a comprehensive settlement address all facets of the Arab–Israeli conflict, from the status of Jerusalem and the Palestinians to elaborate security arrangements and normal relations among all the players (the approach that Carter's advisors favored)? Furthermore, what should the United States offer and when should it secure the allegiance of Sadat and Begin to any agreements, as the two local leaders manipulated their own domestic constituents and the American public to gain better terms for themselves and their countries?

In November 1977, President Sadat paid his unprecedented visit to Jerusalem. His bombshell undercut U.S. plans for an international conference in Geneva. Carter was in danger of losing control over a process that had already aroused concerns in segments of the U.S. Congress and the American Jewish community. Some worried that Israel would be compelled to deal with the PLO or with a Palestinian state, and others were anxious about Syrian or Soviet meddling in the diplomatic process.

In the months of reassessment that followed Sadat's breakthrough trip, U.S. efforts concentrated on getting the Israelis and Egyptians to clarify their demands after bilateral talks at Ismailia stalled. Several of Carter's closest advisors "suggested moving toward a strategy of collusion with Sadat to bring pressure on Begin" (Quandt 1986, 163). Although Carter and U.S. Secretary of State Cyrus Vance flirted with this idea as a way of preventing the collapse of bilateral talks in the atmosphere of ill will and hostile rhetoric, they understood that it would not produce a lasting agreement and might worsen administration relations both with Begin and with the American Jewish community. Later, as America grew exasperated with Begin's rigidity, variations on this theme of U.S.–Egyptian collaboration reappeared in administration memos and dialogue. As 1978 proceeded, American officials became aware of the differing style of the two leaders: Sadat was eager for the dramatic gesture but not for the tedious details of negotiations. Begin was insistent on dotting every *i* and crossing every *t* while lecturing his fellow politicians on Israel's security needs, its territorial claims, and the virtues of "autonomy" for the Palestinians rather than an independent Palestinian state or some form of federation of the West Bank and Gaza with Jordan.

Thus in the second year of his administration, Carter, known for his own meticulous attention to detail, faced the choice of continuing to search for Israeli concessions on the West Bank and Gaza, perhaps more vigorously than Sadat himself would do, or striving to arrange a bilateral Egyptian–Israeli peace treaty based on the trade of Sinai for an end to belligerency. In seeking the second course—in deciding to work with Begin rather than against him—Carter adopted a posture consonant with the national objectives of Sadat and Begin and with public opinion on Resolution 242. When Carter issued his invitations to an unusual three-way summit in September 1978, he knew that he would have to promote interim arrangements for the thorniest issues—Jerusalem and the occupied territories.

Carter also knew that engaging the prestige of the U.S. presidency in such a venture was a high-risk enterprise that could backfire both domestically and internationally and might endanger other initiatives such as the Strategic Arms Limitation Talks II agreement with the Soviet Union or the congressional approval of the Panama Canal treaties. Stresses and strains with Egypt and Israel mounted as Sadat and Begin pressed their respective cases with the White House, Congress, the press, and U.S. public opinion (Spiegel 1985, Chapter 8). Keeping the diplomatic game going as the administration prepared to submit a Middle East arms package to

Congress was the biggest challenge, especially because Carter was also working on relations with China. The president's growing involvement with the minutiae of diplomacy meant that Middle East political figures would not be satisfied dealing with lesser U.S. officials. Each complicated exchange of questions and answers among Washington, Cairo, and Jerusalem seemed to offer Washington two choices: either confront the parties by submitting American-drafted texts or retreat from an active role, with the possibility that the enterprise would bog down and Carter personally would be blamed.

Inviting Sadat, Begin, and their closest advisors to Camp David to explore the possibilities of an accord was one thing; keeping them there long enough and secluded enough to develop a general formula or framework for negotiations together with supporting details was quite another. Although Carter believed that gaining and keeping the trust of the two leaders and their negotiating teams were crucial, he did not anticipate that moving beyond opening positions would take a full ten days or more, far longer than the initial three days, or at most a week, that he had planned to devote to the summit. One reason for the length of the negotiations was the expressed desire of both Begin and Sadat to structure agreements with the United States before or, at the very least, alongside any they might conclude with each other. As Carter reports in his memoirs:

> I knew it was a good negotiation tactic by either Sadat or Begin first to reach agreement with me and then to have the two of us confront the third . . . I must admit that I capitalized on this situation with both delegations in order to get an agreement; it greatly magnified my own influence. (Carter 1982, 366)

After ten days of successive one-on-one meetings with Begin and Sadat, Carter began to develop the essential feature of an agreement that would leave the Gaza and West Bank issues largely unresolved at Sadat's suggestion. On the eleventh day, Sadat threatened to leave—on the grounds that Israel would sign no agreements despite the tedious days of discussion and refining of terms. Impressed as he was with the efforts of two Israelis, Moshe Dayan and Ezer Weizman, to help bridge the gaps, Sadat nonetheless insisted that his advisors now counseled against signing an agreement with the United States alone if Israel could not be brought along. According to Carter's recollections, he approached Sadat, who was preparing to leave:

> I explained to him the extremely serious consequences of his unilaterally breaking off the negotiations: that his action would harm the relationship between Egypt and the United States, he would be violating his personal promise to me, and the onus for failure would be on him. I described the possible future progress of Egypt's friendships and alliances—from us to the moderate and then radical Arabs, thence to the Soviet Union. I told him it would damage one of my most precious possessions—his friendship and our mutual trust. . . . I told Sadat that he simply had to stick with me for another day or two—after which, if circumstances did not improve, all of us simultaneously would take the action he was now planning. (Carter 1982, 392)

The experience was most likely more jarring for Sadat than Carter presents it here. National Security Advisor Zbigniew Brzezinski remembers Carter explaining that he told Sadat his departure would mean "an end to the relationship between the United States and Egypt" (Brzezinski 1983, 272). In the end, Sadat agreed to stay, in part because Carter assured him that any tentative concession he might offer at Camp David, if not part of a treaty agreement, would not be taken as a starting point for future talks with Israel.

Significantly, neither Carter nor Brzezinski mentioned any promises of massive U.S. economic aid or military assistance to Egypt that may have induced Sadat to stay at Camp David. The practicality of such a pledge would become clearer in the future. Carter next turned to Begin and the Israelis to try to resolve the remaining differences. As the talks neared the crucial phase on such issues as Sinai settlements, oil resources, and the demilitarized zones, together with the connections between Sinai and the West Bank or Gaza, Begin's stage presence, frequently overshadowed by Sadat's flair for surprise and presumed outrage, emerged.

The Likud Party leader, whose ideological predilections differed from those of the Israeli Labour Party leaders with whom U.S. officials were accustomed to dealing over the years, was careful to leave himself a loophole on the issue of removing Israeli settlements from Sinai by stating that he would submit the matter to the Israeli parliament (Knesset) for a vote. In view of what would happen in the later phases of interpretation and implementation, Carter was perhaps too persuaded of his own skill as a mediator at this stage: "I told him again and again that this proposal was totally unacceptable to Sadat, who insisted on a commitment to remove all Israeli settlers from his territory before any other negotiations could be conducted" (Carter 1982, 396).

Begin finally agreed to an accelerated Knesset review without the requirement of party loyalty, thus freeing Knesset members to simply vote their conscience. This commitment was enough for Sadat, who tended to lack interest in other details of the agreement. The issues of the West Bank settlements and the status of Jerusalem were addressed with an oral agreement on Israel's part to halt the construction of new settlements until a more formal resolution could be reached. As Carter put it after the talks were through:

> After the Israelis left, Vance and I agreed that we had a settlement, at least for Camp David. There was no doubt that Sadat would accept my recommendations on the issues we had just discussed with Begin. What the Knesset might decide was uncertain, but I was convinced that the people of Israel would be in favor of the overall agreement, including the withdrawal of the settlers from the Sinai. . . . I intended to try in every way possible to shape world opinion and to get the American Jewish community to support this effort. (Carter 1982, 397)

Carter's persistence paid off. An agreement was reached, even though the final tradeoffs were specific only with reference to the Sinai, and they downgraded the link between the bilateral accord and the future of the occupied territories, including Jerusalem. Begin could take pride in the arrangements calling for normalization of relations with Egypt. Sadat had attained what no other Arab leader had the courage to seek—the return of occupied territory through negotiations with Israel, even though the basic formula guaranteed Egyptian national aims at the expense of wider Arab demands concerning the Palestinians. Furthermore, Sadat had succeeded in having the United States play the role of "full partner." Ironically, the price he would pay for that accomplishment would be additional demands for concessions (see Map 1.3).

The thirteen days at Camp David had produced a framework outlining transitional arrangements for the West Bank and Gaza, an agreement by Egypt and Israel to sign a peace treaty within three months, and a specific plan for the return of the Sinai to Egypt with demilitarized zones and international policing of strategically sensitive areas. The issue of linkage might arise again, but for the time being, Begin's loose formulas had prevailed.

The post-conference haggling over who agreed to what, though predictable, threatened to heighten misunderstandings. Trust began to dissipate as the conflicting positions of Egypt and Israel hardened on the settlements and on linking a bilateral treaty to prospects for the West Bank and Gaza. Carter, sensing urgency, found it difficult to comprehend the domestic political problems that Sadat and Begin faced. He was well aware of his own problems, with the midterm elections scheduled for November 1978. He was also aware that Begin was a master at using Israeli domestic constraints as a way to drag out the negotiations. Begin was often tougher than his advisors, whereas Sadat was often more accommodating. American policymakers openly considered an overture to the PLO as a way of pressing Israel harder, but Carter demurred, citing the 1975 U.S. pledges to Israel on the subject as a test of American credibility.

Perhaps more important as the months passed after Camp David, both Begin and Sadat knew that Carter's influence had peaked in 1978 and that as the 1980 U.S. presidential election approached, he would be entangled elsewhere. Begin sought a deceleration of the process to avoid granting Palestinians any additional rights, while Sadat hoped for a measured pace toward eventual linkage with independence for the occupied territories. Cyrus Vance approached Jordan and Saudi Arabia to enlist their support for some eventual Palestinian autonomy accord, although he was also aware that this had not been made explicit in the Camp David language.

In the context of these conflicting interpretations and hidden agendas, Carter learned of Israel's intention to increase the number of settlements in the West Bank, in violation of the oral agreement at Camp David:

It [was] obvious that the negotiations [were] going backwards. . . . I told Cy [Vance] to withdraw from the negotiations at the end of this week, to let the technicians take over, and let the leadership in Israel and Egypt know that we are through devoting full time to this nonproductive effort. It [was] obvious that the Israelis [wanted] a separate treaty with Egypt; they [wanted] to keep the West Bank and Gaza permanently . . . and they [used] the settlements (on the West Bank) and East Jerusalem issues to prevent the involvement of the Jordanians and the Palestinians. (Carter 1982, 409)

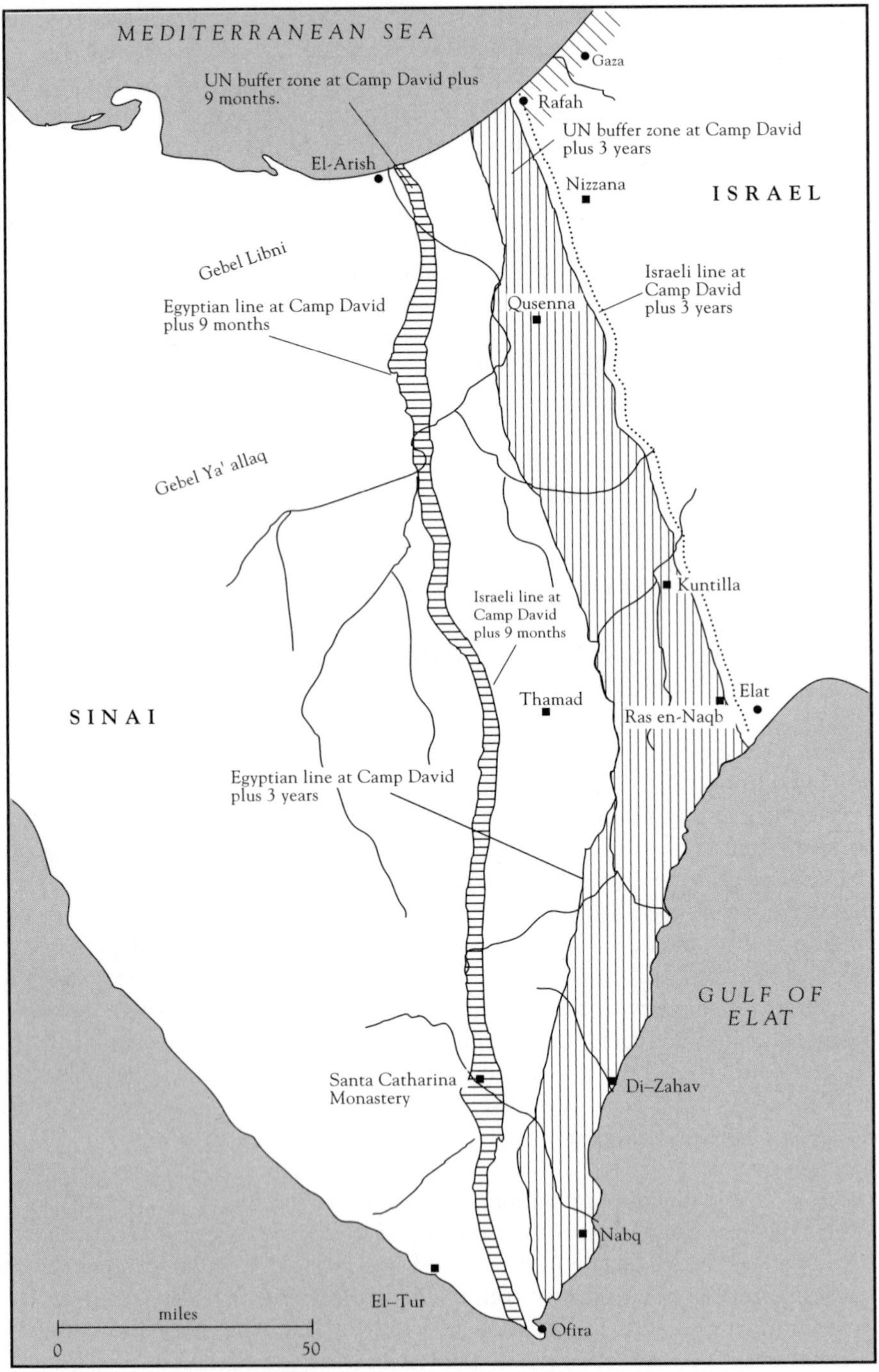

MEDITERRANEAN SEA

Gaza

UN buffer zone at Camp David plus 9 months.

Rafah

UN buffer zone at Camp David plus 3 years

El-Arish

Nizzana

ISRAEL

Gebel Libni

Egyptian line at Camp David plus 9 months

Qusenna

Israeli line at Camp David plus 3 years

Gebel Ya' allaq

Israeli line at Camp David plus 9 months

Kuntilla

SINAI

Thamad

Elat

Ras en-Naqb

Egyptian line at Camp David plus 3 years

GULF OF ELAT

Santa Catharina Monastery

Di–Zahav

Nabq

miles

0   50

El–Tur

Ofira

Map 1.3 1979–1982 Egyptian–Israeli troop withdrawal agreements
Source: Lester Sobel, ed. *Peace-Making in the Middle East* (New York: Facts on File, 1980).

By December 1978, Carter was close to throwing in the towel. The three-month deadline for an Egypt–Israel peace treaty set at Camp David would not be met. For Carter, the confluence of U.S. domestic politics—the 1980 election—and international politics—the tumultuous Iranian revolution then unfolding—meant that an Egyptian–Israeli peace treaty must come soon, if at all. "I decided to pursue with my top advisers the possibility of my going to Egypt and then to Israel—getting together with Sadat and making my strongest appeal to the Israelis. My main purpose would be to remind them what they would be giving up if the treaty were lost" (Carter 1982, 415).

Prior to the trip, Carter met with Begin in Washington and managed to create a treaty text that was "barely acceptable to the Israelis but did not quite comply with the key points on which Sadat was insisting. . . ." Upon hearing news of the treaty and Carter's upcoming trip to the Middle East, Sadat "was overjoyed" (Carter 1982, 416). Before leaving Washington, Carter was careful to prepare Sadat, who was delighted to welcome the president to Egypt. Carter warned him that additional concessions would be needed:

> The language may not be exactly what you want, but the target date issued and the "priority of obligations" issue are such that you can accept them and legitimately claim victory. You may or may not completely agree with me on the nuances of the exact words but, in any case, the differences are minimal when compared to the overall strategic considerations which you and I must address together. (Carter 1982, 417)

If the Camp David formula could be preserved, the details might be completed quickly while Carter was on the scene in the region. When Sadat did accept what the Israeli cabinet had approved, Carter was encouraged, yet Begin, in keeping with his previous modus operandi, told the president on his arrival in Israel that "he [Begin] could not sign or initial any agreement." As Carter wrote:

> I would have to conclude my talks with him, let him submit the proposals to the cabinet, let the Knesset have an extended debate, going into all the issues concerning the definition of autonomy, East Jerusalem, and so forth, and then only after all that would he sign the documents.
>
> I couldn't believe it. I stood up and asked him if it was necessary for me to stay any longer. We then spent about 45 minutes on our feet in his study. I asked him if he actually wanted a peace treaty, because my impression was that everything he could do to obstruct it, he did with apparent relish. He came right up and looked into my eyes about a foot away and said that it was obvious from the expression on his face that he wanted peace as much as anything else in the world. . . . (Carter 1982, 421)

The final breakthrough that permitted plans for signing of the treaty to go forward came when Carter returned to Cairo from Israel with agreements in hand that committed him to asking Congress for substantial aid in relocating Israeli bases from Sinai and provisions for the United States to compensate Israel for giving up Sinai oil. Also spelled out were steps to be taken if Egypt violated the treaty.

After Carter's return to Washington, amid preparations to receive Sadat and Begin in triumph, Vance, Dayan, and others strove to wrap up all the details in time for the signing. As Vance recalls, it was a close call:

> Inevitably, there were last-minute hitches. For several days prior to Begin's arrival I had discussions with Dayan on the U.S.–Israeli memorandum of agreement, as well as on the oil supply agreement and the U.S. financial and military assistance package that had been agreed to in Jerusalem. The President also met Sadat and Begin to work out the precise details of the accelerated Israeli withdrawal from that portion of the Sinai containing the oilfields. The final details concerning Israeli access to Sinai oil remained an issue right down to the end. They were not finally resolved until Sadat and Begin agreed in a meeting in the residence of Ashraf Gorbal, the distinguished and extremely able Egyptian ambassador in Washington. At that time Sadat guaranteed to the Israelis the right to bid for Egyptian oil at the world market price on a permanent basis, thus removing the last major stumbling block to the signing ceremony. We did go down to the wire on one or two minor details. . . . (Vance 1983, 252)

On March 26, 1979, then, the signatures were placed on the document and an arduous process, begun by Henry Kissinger in 1973, was completed. The implementation of the agreement, including the continuation of discussion on Palestinian autonomy, was spotty. The Israeli army left the Sinai within the prescribed deadline—a remarkable example by Egypt of winning back territory through the pen rather than the sword. Autonomy talks for the Palestinians, however, were almost immediately overwhelmed by nationalist pressure in Israel and the revolution in Iran. More than a decade later, Camp David may seem to be less of an achievement than it was. If so, it is because Egyptian–Israeli peace is now taken for granted in the midst of rising political extremism in the region as a whole. That peace is perhaps the finest tribute to the thirty-ninth president: other politicians come and go with less to show for their labors than Jimmy Carter.

MIDDLE EAST PEACE SINCE CAMP DAVID

With Carter voted out of office in November, the Middle East peace process halted. Egypt paid dearly for its peace with Israel. It was castigated by other Arab states. Sadat was assassinated in 1981, thus removing one of the most conciliatory Arab leaders in history. Israel invaded Lebanon in 1982, which precipitated the deployment of peacekeeping troops in Beirut by President Ronald Reagan, the evacuation of PLO headquarters, and the movement of thousands of troops across the Middle East. The PLO initiated the bloody "intifadah" in 1987—a mass uprising that continues to this day and in turn has spurred increased Israeli repression in the West Bank and Gaza. In 1988, the PLO renounced terrorism and quietly recognized Israel's right to exist, thus allowing the United States to undertake direct talks with PLO representatives. Throughout the 1980s, however, the Israeli position hardened, and the United States found itself more and more at odds with Tel Aviv over everything from Israeli police repression in East Jerusalem to increased Soviet Jewish settlements in the West Bank.

It was not until the Persian Gulf War in 1991 that major shifts occurred in Middle East political alignments. During the war, many Arab countries sided with the United States and therefore implicitly with Israel. Israel also broke with precedent by not retaliating against Baghdad after repeated Scud missile attacks. Within a year of the war, the United States and the Soviet Union, under the leadership of U.S. Secretary of State James Baker and Foreign Minister Eduard Scheverdnadze, organized a new multilateral Middle East peace conference amid skepticism, ambivalence, and only a modicum of hope. The seating at the conference of a joint Jordanian–Palestinian delegation made possible the first direct talks between Israelis and Palestinians in forty-three years. In spite of this historic breakthrough, however, the negotiations plodded along unsuccessfully for nearly two years. Even the election in June 1992 of Yitzhak Shamir's Labour Party—traditionally more flexible on the issues of land for peace and Palestinian rights—had little effect.

On August 31, 1993, in the eleventh round of what seemed to be almost pointless negotiations, Israel and the PLO announced a surprise. As a result of extended secret talks, they had concluded a deal that provided for mutual recognition and self-rule for Palestinians in parts of the West Bank and Gaza. Within two weeks, Shamir and Arafat were shaking hands in front of the White House and American senators were dining with a former terrorist. President Bill Clinton was quick to take credit, if only by virtue of his intentions, even though the Norwegian government had a more direct role in facilitating the secret talks by discreetly providing good offices. More agreements signed in May and September of 1994 sealed the progress achieved. In October 1994, Jordan and Israel signed a peace agreement settling numerous outstanding issues.

CONCLUSION: ASSESSING THE LEVELS OF ANALYSIS APPROACH

The assassination of Yitzhak Rabin in Israel in 1995 and the subsequent election of Benjamin Netanyahu in mid-1996 derailed the peace process for another two years. Ultimately, in October 1998, at the Wye River complex near Washington, under the guidance of U.S. Secretary of State Madeleine Albright and President Bill Clinton, the Israelis and Palestinians committed to a timetable to complete the peace process—the withdrawal of Israeli forces from the West Bank and Gaza, the sovereignty of Palestine, and the disposition of Jerusalem. The process moved slowly until the election of Ehud Barak as Israel's prime minister in May 1999. He won on a campaign of bringing peace to the region and immediately began settling differences with his neighbors to the north (Israel withdrew its forces from Lebanon after an eighteen-year occupation and began peace talks with Syria) and his Palestinian rivals. Although an intense round of negotiations at Camp David in July 2000 (dubbed Camp David II) ended in failure, the process clarified what elements are needed for a final settlement—namely, resolution of the status of Jerusalem, compensation and repatriation of refugees, Israeli recognition of Palestinian statehood, and Palestinian security guarantees for Israel.

Today, the situation in the Middle East is as tense as ever. On September 28, 2000, Ariel Sharon, an Israeli leader much despised in the Palestinian community, paid a visit to the al-Aqsa mosque on the Temple Mount. The next day, Palestinians began systematically rioting and attacking Jewish targets, using both rocks and rifles. The Israeli government responded with rockets and missiles. In spite of intervention by Bill Clinton, the violence continued throughout the month of October until more than 300 Palestinians and Jews had been killed in what was dubbed the "al-Aqsa intifadah." By early November, the violence had begun to subside and Arafat and Barak were attempting to cement a cease-fire with President Clinton's help. Ehud Barak's failure to stem the violence or reach a settlement with the Palestinians contributed to his resounding defeat in the elections in February 2001. The new prime minister, none other than Ariel Sharon, promised a hard line in talks.

Since the terrorist attacks on September 11, 2001, conditions in the Middle East have worsened considerably. Although Arafat was quick to condemn the attacks and continued to renounce terrorism, an increasing amount of violence was perpetrated on the Jews in Israel and the West Bank. Suicide bombings became the favored tactic and cost hundreds of Israeli lives. With each attack, reprisals were administered by an increasingly belligerent Israeli government. The George W. Bush administration supported Sharon's policy as part of the war against global terrorism.

In March 2002, the Israeli government invaded Arafat's compound in Ramallah and proceeded to seize control of numerous Palestinian towns in the West Bank that had previously been turned over to the Palestinian Authority. Arafat remained holed up in his offices for days while Israeli soldiers swept the region for suspects. At roughly this time, the United States, Russia, the European Union, and senior UN officials (dubbed the "Quartet") began meeting regularly to plot a course for peace in the Middle East.

In 2003, Ariel Sharon was re-elected as prime minister and instituted plans for a unilateral withdrawal of Israeli settlements from the Gaza Strip and the West Bank. Although the announcement could have been seen as a step forward in the peace process, it was widely criticized as a repudiation of the Oslo Accords and the legitimacy of the Palestinian regime. At the same time, in an effort to curtail suicide bombings in Israel, the Sharon government began building a wall around the West Bank territories—a move that was condemned by the International Court of Justice in late 2004. On the other hand, the question of Palestinian governance was thrown into disarray with the death of Yassir Arafat in November 2004 after an illness. Ultimately, Mahmoud Abbas, a pro-Western moderate, emerged as the leader of the PLO and the Palestine Authority. Throughout this period, the United States was virtually mute (Jimmy Carter's receipt of the Nobel Peace Prize in 2003 was probably intended as a criticism of the U.S. role in the Middle East under Bush).

Since 2004, negotiations have continued to face impediments. Israel has proceeded with unilateral withdrawal from Gaza as a signal that it considered negotiations with Palestinians futile. This view was validated to some extent with the election by Palestinians in January 2006 of the radical Hamas party. Its denunciation of Israel and past support of terrorism made it an unlikely candidate for talks and instead made it the target for economic and diplomatic sanctions by Israel and most Western governments. Finally, the incapacitation of Ariel Sharon in the same month (he was comatose after a stroke) left the country essentially leaderless—a problem that was partly remedied by the victory of Sharon's newly founded Kadima party in the March elections and the assumption of power by Ehud Olmert. In 2007, former British Prime Minster Tony Blair began shuttle diplomacy as the special representative of the Quartet, but his efforts were disrupted by the electoral victory of Hamas in the Palestinian elections. The Gaza Strip falls under Hamas control, while Al Fatah retains control in the West Bank. The Quartet announced its support of Mahmoud Abbas and its intent to isolate the Hamas government, culminating in a large-scale meeting in Washington in November 2007. Efforts by the Bush administration to resolve the issue before the end of the term appeared unlikely to succeed at the time of writing (November 2008).

What does this story tell us about the power of individuals and the levels of analysis approach generally? It is clear that had Kissinger not applied his ample diplomatic skill to freeze the military stalemate in 1974, there would have been no reason for a peaceful settlement in 1979. Likewise, without Anwar Sadat's heroic initiative toward Israel, the peace process would not have occurred. And finally, Jimmy Carter's vision and tolerance were essential to the successful conclusion of the talks. As predicted, strength of personality, crisis conditions, and substantial power and authority combined to increase the significance of the actors' personalities in the outcomes.

Or did they? The fact of the matter is that although personalities appear to have mattered, this was true only to an extent. They were also constrained by domestic politics and other conditions. Anwar Sadat paid for his daring move with his life. And although his successor, Hosni Mubarak, was able to continue his work, he was not able to expand upon it to any great extent and has struggled to contain the fundamentalism that took Sadat's life. Manachem Begin left office shortly after Camp David, the breakthrough notwithstanding. And subsequent Israeli prime ministers have had to walk a fine line between confrontation and appeasement due to conflicting domestic pressures. Yasser Arafat and his Fatah party found their popularity plummet among Palestinian voters as they reached out to Israeli leaders. Needless to say, it is doubtful that the new Hamas government will come forward with new peace initiatives in the near future. Even Jimmy Carter found that his Camp David success did little to prevent his electoral defeat in 1980.

Futhermore, these actors functioned within an international context that was not of their creation. It is clear that Jimmy Carter could not have performed his role had he presided over a country other than the United States. No other state had a record of support to Israel—a key to bringing Begin on board—or the military and financial resources to guarantee the agreement. Likewise, Israel and Egypt were uniquely positioned as relatively equal rivals, each with the capacity to launch devastating attacks against the other—and to repel them. Had Israel entered into talks with Lebanon, the outcome would have no doubt been very different due to the power imbalance. And so, although it is clear that personalities mattered in this account, the reader should also ask whether they would have mattered as much had domestic and international conditions been significantly different.

QUESTIONS TO CONSIDER

1. To what extent were the individuals interchangeable? Does this story provide clear evidence that personality matters more than other factors?

2. In your view, how much difference did it make that it was the President of the United States (as opposed to, say, Malawi) who hosted the Camp David Accords? Was the story more about the balance of power than diplomacy?

3. How has the international situation in the Middle East changed since 1979? Does the US still play a leadership role? Why or why not?

KEY FIGURES
THE CAMP DAVID ACCORDS

Henry Kissinger   National Security Advisor, 1969–1975; U.S. Secretary of State, 1973–1977. He played a pivotal role in creating a stalemate between Egypt and Israel after the Yom Kippur/Ramadan War.

Jimmy Carter   U.S. President, 1977–1981. He is credited with bringing Sadat and Begin together to work out a settlement to the Egyptian–Israeli conflict.

Menachem Begin   Prime Minister of Israel, 1977–1983. A conservative who fought with Jewish guerrillas in the 1940s, his nationalist credentials made it easier for him to persuade the Israeli people of the benefits of the Camp David Accords.

Anwar Sadat   President of Egypt, 1970–1981. He reversed the pro-Soviet policies of his predecessor and made overtures to the West and to Israel. He was assassinated by Muslim fundamentalists in 1981.

Golda Meir   Prime Minister of Israel, 1969–1974.

Yitzhak Rabin   Prime Minister of Israel, 1974–1977, 1992–1995. He reached a preliminary agreement with Yasser Arafat on Palestinian control of the occupied territories. He was assassinated in 1995 by Jewish nationalists.

Yitzhak Shamir   Prime Minister of Israel, 1986–1992.

Shimon Peres   Prime Minister of Israel, 1984–1986, 1995–1996. He served in numerous capacities in the Israeli government and repeatedly negotiated with its adversaries.

Yasser Arafat   Leader of the Palestinian Liberation Organization (PLO) and later the Palestinian Authority.

Benjamin Netanyahu   Prime Minister of Israel, 1996–1999.

Ehud Barak   Prime Minister of Israel, 1999–2001.

Ariel Sharon   Prime Minister of Israel, 2001–2006.

Hosni Mubarak   President of Egypt, 1981–present.

Bill Clinton   U.S. President, 1993–2001. He helped sponsor the Oslo and Madrid Accords between Israel and the PLO and hosted Camp David II.

CHRONOLOGY
THE CAMP DAVID ACCORDS

1948
The State of Israel is declared. A war almost immediately ensues between the new Jewish government and the surrounding Arab states.

1956
The Suez War pits Israel against Egypt over control of the Suez Canal.

1967
The Six-Day War takes place between Israel and its Arab neighbors.

1973
The Yom Kippur/Ramadan War between Israel, Egypt, and Syria ends in a stalemate. Henry Kissinger intervenes to negotiate a cease-fire and deployment of troops in a buffer zone.

1974
A cease-fire agreement between Israel, Egypt, and Syria is accepted by all parties.

1975
Preliminary and temporary agreements are signed by Egypt and Israel.

1977
Anwar Sadat meets Menachem Begin in Jerusalem.

1978
The Camp David negotiations begin. The apparent progress made earns Begin and Sadat the Nobel Peace Prize.

1979
Begin, Sadat, and Carter shake hands on the White House front lawn to celebrate the signing of the Camp David Accords, which provide for the gradual return of the Sinai peninsula to Egypt and the guarantees of peace between Egypt and Israel.

1981
Anwar Sadat is assassinated. Hosni Mubarak succeeds him as president of Egypt.

(*continued*)

(*continued*)

1982
Israel invades and occupies southern Lebanon.

1987
The intifada (Palestinian uprising) begins.

1988
The PLO renounces terrorism.

1991
The Persian Gulf War creates new alignments in the Middle East.

1992
Yitzhak Rabin is elected prime minister of Israel.

1993
The PLO and Israel accept the Oslo Peace Accords, which provide for a form of mutual recognition and a phased transfer of land then under Israeli control to the new Palestinian Authority.

1994
Shimon Peres, Rabin, and Arafat are awarded the Nobel Peace Prize.

1995
Yitzhak Rabin is assassinated.

1998
The Wye River Accords are signed in Washington.

1999
Camp David II ends in deadlock.

2000
The second intifada begins. Palestinian suicide bombers attack Israeli cities.

2001
Islamic fundamentalists attack the World Trade Center in New York and the Pentagon in Washington, D.C., creating a shift in Middle East alliances.

2002
Israel seizes control of large segments of the West Bank that had been ceded to the Palestinian Authority, including Arafat's presidential compound. Jimmy Carter receives the Nobel Peace Prize for his years of peacemaking and election monitoring.

2003
Ariel Sharon is re-elected prime minister of Israel.

2004
January   Sharon announces his plan for unilateral withdrawal from the Gaza Strip. The controversial decision is ultimately approved by the Cabinet and the Bush administration.

November   Yasser Arafat dies in Paris following an illness.

2005

January   Elections in Palestine keep Fatah in power under President Mahmoud Abbas.

August   Israel completes pull out of troops and settlers from the Gaza Strip.

2006

January 5   Ariel Sharon has a stroke that puts him in a coma. Deputy Prime Minister Ehud Olmert assumes power.

January 26   Hamas wins parliamentary elections in Palestine. Western states begin applying for economic and diplomatic sanctions against it.

March   Elections in Israel bring a victory for Kadima, the party founded by Ariel Sharon.

REFERENCES

Brzezinski, Zbigniew. *Power and Principle* (New York: Farrar, Strauss and Giroux, 1983).

Carter, Jimmy. *Keeping Faith: Memoirs of a President* (Toronto: Bantam Books, 1982).

Dockrill, Michael. *Atlas of Twentieth Century World History* (New York: Harper-Perennial, 1991).

Hermann, Charles. *International Crises: Insights from Behavioral Research* (New York: The Free Press, 1972).

Hermann, Margaret, and Charles Hermann. "Who Makes Foreign Policy and How: An Empirical Inquiry." *International Studies Quarterly* 33 #4 (December 1989): 361–387.

Hermann, Margaret, and Joe Hagan. "International Decision Making: Leadership Matters." *Foreign Policy* #110, Special Edition: Frontiers of Knowledge (Spring 1998): 124–137.

Holsti, Ole. "Crisis Decision Making." In Philip Tetlock, Jo Husbands, Robert Jervis, P. Stern and Charles Tilly, eds. *Behavior, Society, and Nuclear War* (New York: Oxford University Press, 1989): 8–84.

Kalb, Bernard, and Marvin Kalb. *Kissinger* (Boston: Little, Brown, 1974).

Kissinger, Henry. *Years of Upheaval* (Boston: Little, Brown, 1982).

Meacham, John, and Evan Thomas. "The Vices of Their Virtues." *Newsweek* 152 # 14 (October 6, 2008): 22–23.

Miller, Linda B. "Shadow and Substance: Jimmy Carter and the Camp David Accords." #433R Pew Case Studies in International Affairs, 1992.

Quandt, William B. *Camp David: Peacemaking and Politics* (Washington, DC: Brookings Institution, 1986).

Sheehan, Edward. "How Kissinger Did It: Step-by-Step in the Middle East." In Jeffrey Z. Rubin, ed., *Dynamics of Third Party Intervention: Kissinger in the Middle East* (New York: Praeger, 1981): 44–93.

Sobel, Lester, ed. *Peace-Making in the Middle East* (New York: Facts on File, 1980).

Spiegel, Steven. *The Other Arab–Israeli Conflict* (Chicago: University of Chicago Press, 1985).

Touval, Saadia. *The Peace Brokers: Mediators in the Arab-Israeli Conflict, 1948–1979* (Princeton, NJ: Princeton University Press, 1982).

Vance, Cyrus. *Hard Choices: Critical Years in America's Foreign Policy* (New York: Simon & Schuster, 1983).

2

...

Anarchy: League of Nations

INTRODUCTION

Anarchy means the absence of a central, controlling authority and describes prevailing international order, according to most international relations and international legal scholars. Although there are tremendous differences in the capabilities of various states and other international actors, at present, no state has either the legal authority or the physical ability to control or protect the rest of the world. Anarchy implies that if a state is to be safe, it must seek out its own allies, build up its own armies, and play the diplomatic game carefully. No one can be depended upon to rescue it from attack. Thus the key implication of anarchy is "self-help."

Contrary to common usage, anarchy is not necessarily equivalent to chaos or violence. Peace and anarchy may exist simultaneously, which is generally the case in the international system. This can result from states voluntarily choosing to respect each other's independence or from the emergence of dominant states that create "spheres of influence" that discourage aggression or interference. These are the solutions to anarchy proposed by liberal and realist thinkers, respectively. Historically, the "balance of power" that emerges when the major powers in the international system build competing and offsetting alliance networks has been the natural mechanism to promote peace and stability. However, from time to time, states have endeavored to craft global agreements aimed at mutual respect and barring aggression, conquest, or other forms of intervention and interference.

It is when states have worked to build such global compacts that the forces of anarchy often become more apparent. The United Nations (UN), for example, was essentially a compromise between anarchy and the rule of law. The UN Charter calls for states to take military action to protect any country that is under attack, but the responsibility to determine whether an attack is under way is left to the Security Council. Because the key body within the Security Council provides a "veto" to the most powerful states in the system (as of 1945, when the organization was founded), this meant that the UN would never take action against aggression by the United States, the Soviet Union (now Russia), China, France, or Great Britain. The UN is not really a world government at all because the major powers can still act with relative impunity. The balance of power still does more to maintain peace and order than the UN's rule of law.

A key reason for this compromise was the experience of the League of Nations. In some respects, the League was more ambitious than the UN because it did not provide major powers with a veto. But, as we will see, it is one thing to grant an international agency sweeping powers—it is another to actually make use of them. Anarchy proved to be an extremely potent force during the League's existence from 1919 to 1946.

ORIGINS OF THE LEAGUE OF NATIONS

World War I resulted in roughly 16 million deaths between 1914 and 1918. It was considered by some to have been an "accidental" war (Tuchman 1963), in that no one government sought the conflagration that ultimately occurred and engulfed roughly fifty countries on six continents, or about three of four nations in the world. With the entry of the United States in the war in April 1917, President Woodrow Wilson and his idealist philosophy altered the aims of the allies (Bern 1975, 8). Although France and Britain were mostly interested in beating back German incursions into Northern Europe and restoring the European status quo (and preserving their empires), Wilson saw the need to take definitive actions to make war obsolete. Many other liberals and idealists across Europe agreed that because the death toll of World War I so far exceeded that of ordinary continental actions, that the only way to ensure that those who died had not done so in vain was to elevate the aims of the war to something truly historic (Egerton 1983, 98). Wilson argued that states must "make the world safe for democracy" and achieve "peace without victory," thereby making this a "war to end all wars" (Jones 2001, 83). The world's leaders owed it to future generations to ensure that war on this scale would never occur again, Wilson argued, and proposed as one of his Fourteen Points to establish an international institution that would enforce "collective security." He imagined that states would "enter into a solemn promise to one another that they will never use their power against one another for aggression; that they never will impair the territorial integrity of a neighbor; that they never will interfere with the political independence of a neighbor . . ." (Wilson 1919/1989).

Specifically, this involved especially (1) disarmament and (2) collective security. The League sponsored a series of disarmament talks with the aim of reducing national militaries to defensive proportions, such that states would not have the wherewithal to engage in aggression. More importantly, states would agree to denounce war and pledge to defend any state under attack. Clearly this represented a repudiation of the balance of power in that states would not enter into alliances to defend spheres of influence or national territory but rather would agree in advance to defend a principle against any state that might violate it—even if the culprit were a friend. The hope was that by entering into such a pledge, states that might otherwise be tempted to commit aggression would be deterred. Thus peace would prevail. The danger, perhaps optimistically downplayed, was that a major power would emerge to challenge the world's resolve—and succeed in paralyzing other states as it conquered its neighbors one by one. The bargain was essentially a gamble that only weak states would threaten the new order. Should a powerful state defy the rules, states would have to decide whether defending the order was worth risking global war. But this is precisely what happened. As we will see, states had to decide whether defending Manchuria or Abyssinia or Poland from aggression was worth starting World War II.

LEAGUE DECISION-MAKING STRUCTURES

The structure of the League was relatively simple, based on the notion that every state should have an equal opportunity to express itself, while at the same time, a more limited number would have regular duties of management and greater decision-making powers. The result was an Assembly that met once a year for a few weeks and a Council that met more or less continuously (about five times each year). The scope of each body's responsibilities were similar in that they were to deal with "any matter . . . affecting the peace of the world" (Article 3). The Assembly members each had one vote, although they could send as many as three members. The peak membership of the League was fifty-eight in 1934 (about 90% of the eligible countries in the world), although its membership varied considerably, from forty-two original members in 1920 back to only forty-three during World War II. The Assembly made decisions on the basis of majority vote.

The Council was composed of eight states initially, although the number eventually grew to fifteen in 1926 and included the major powers as permanent members and lesser powers on rotating, three-year terms (elected by the Assembly). The number of non-permanent states increased as the number of great powers declined. The Council made decisions on the basis of unanimity, meaning that any state on the council could veto almost any action. This naturally led to some very tentative and slow decision making, as we will see below, but was considered an essential provision to reassure American legislators (in vain, as it turned out) that each major power would be able to protect its interests (Wilson 1919/1989). As stated by British diplomat Sir Alfred Zimmern:

> . . . The League of Nations was never intended to be, nor is it, a revolutionary organization. On the contrary, it accepts the world of states as it finds it and merely seeks to provide a more satisfactory means for carrying on some of the business which these states transact between one another. It is not even revolutionary in the more limited sense of revolutionizing the methods for carrying on inter-state business. It does not supersede the older methods. It merely supplements them. (Zimmern 1936, 4, in Goodrich 1947, 4–5)

The League was supported by a Secretariat of several hundred individuals in Geneva, Switzerland, and a Secretary-General, whose role was primarily clerical, although he had senior diplomatic standing. The staff provided some limited analysis and documentation for the various governments and also worked with various other ancillary bodies (some of which, like the International Labour Organization, have survived till today). Also important was the Permanent Court of International Justice, now known as the International Court of Justice, which served governments as a place to resolve disputes according to international treaty and customary law. The Court heard twenty-nine formal cases and delivered advisory opinions in twenty-seven more, including disputes involving major powers (International Court of Justice 2008).

LEAGUE POLITICS

The British government quickly emerged as the dominant voice in the League, supported initially by the British public that was weary of warfare (Birn 1975, 6). Many in the British government were sceptical of the League's potential. Winston Churchill in 1926 lamented the naiveté of many League supporters "who intended it to create a heaven upon earth, provided human beings and events would allow an interval of fifty years, say, to occur in which to build this wonderful edifice" (Birn 1975, 94). In other words, even the nation that was the League's most ardent supporter was ambivalent about its basic mission. This contributed to its subsequent hesitancy to act forcefully when faced with a crisis.

A key problem for the League of Nations was how to attract the support of the major powers. In 1919, the major powers were France, Germany, Italy, Japan, the United Kingdom, the United States, and the Soviet Union. The status of Germany was resolved in 1926 with its admission after the council determined that it had again become a "peace-loving" nation. The Soviet Union did not want to belong to the League so long as Germany was a member, among other reasons. The United States never joined the League because of opposition from a Republican-controlled Senate which suspected membership in an international organization would too seriously restrain American foreign policy choices (Jones 2001, 98–100).

The result was that only for about seven years did the League's membership include the bulk of the major powers. In 1933, as a result of the Manchurian crisis (see below) and its unwillingness to comply with the League ideals, Japan withdrew from the organization. Germany's new Nazi regime likewise repudiated the League and left in the same year, leaving just the United Kingdom, France, and an increasingly belligerent Italy under Benito Mussolini. The only benefit of Germany's departure was the Soviet Union's decision to join, partly for spite, in 1934. After the Abyssinia crisis (see below) and the sanctions regime imposed by the Council, Italy withdrew in 1937, and the Soviet Union was expelled forcibly in 1939 after its attacks on Finland. By this point, the League ceased to be an active member of the international community, although it did not officially close its doors until 1946.

Add to this the various strategic machinations taking place between the major powers. Britain's concern was primarily with avoiding another global war while at the same time maintaining control of its far-flung empire. Britain's status as the world's financial center was also under siege during the inter-war period, especially because the United States was generally unwilling to provide it a bail-out. During the 1930s, Britain generally played an increasingly accommodating role toward Germany, mostly out of fear of provoking war, but also in part because of second thoughts about the more punitive aspects of the Versailles Treaty that ended World War I.

France took a somewhat harder line toward Germany, building substantial defences, rebuilding its military, forging an alliance with Poland, and hoping to establish closer ties with Italy and the Soviet Union as a bulwark against German expansion. It also experienced economic and political turmoil during the 1930s, including electoral successes for communist and fascist parties.

Germany, Italy, and Japan each experienced a right-wing shift of leadership during the inter-war period, with Mussolini coming to power by a coup in 1922 (he used his party members to intimidate the King into giving him power by staging a coup attempt) and Adolf Hitler by election and pressure (he gradually secured the support of various parties for his plans for absolute power). In Japan, after the largely unplanned invasion of Manchuria (see below), various military commanders accrued increasing influence, culminating in the militarization of virtually all aspects of Japanese foreign policy. In the Soviet Union, Josef Stalin took control after Lenin's death and transformed the communist experiment into a ruthless autocracy—mostly through a series of "purges" that left millions of senior government officials, wealthy landowners, intellectuals, and other would-be opponents of the regime impoverished, in prison, or dead.

Each of these four regimes had imperial designs on their neighbors and beyond. As "late developers" on the international stage, they were less active in the colonial expansions of the 19th century and naturally felt resentful of what seemed to them as second-class status. The Germans were deeply angered by what they perceived as unfair treatment at Versailles, and the Soviet Union's government was based on a radical view of the world economy that called for global revolution to resolve class conflict. Mussolini sought to bring Italy to the level of Britain, and Japanese militarists wanted to secure raw materials for the resource-poor country by conquering much of Asia and the Pacific. Needless to say, the pacific principles of the League—as a "status quo" agency—did not mesh well with these territorially ambitious states. Their support ran from tepid to hostile.

The Soviet leaders were also concerned about German expansion and made overtures to France and Italy during the 1930s (Hardie 1974, 69), only to sign a secret non-aggression pact with Germany in 1939 in which the two countries agreed to divide Eastern Europe among them. Germany and Italy were also at times hostile and at times friendly during the 1930s, creating uncertainty in Europe and a strong incentive to forge secret alliances with other European powers from time to time. It is important to remember that the World War II alliances did not seem as inevitable to those then alive as it may now seem to those of us looking backward through history.

The net result of this was that the League of Nations was primarily a Franco-British institution in both membership and philosophy. The staff was predominantly

British and French, although dozens of nationalities were represented, and the principles undergirding the institution were decidedly liberal and socially progressive. This came across in the League's promotion of conciliation and mediation, as well as court involvement in the peaceful settlement of disputes. But it was also expressed in advocacy for human rights (including those of refugees and slaves), disarmament, economic development, self-determination, and women's rights (Birn 1981).

This meant that, for all its idealism, once the autocratic regimes took power in the capitals of the most powerful states, the League was generally unable to promote cooperation. Stalin's regime was never fully committed to the League principles, and the replacement of liberal regimes in Japan, Italy, and Germany in the early 1930s also put them out of step. Although Britain and France remained committed, they also feared the more violent implications of their own ideals—namely the need to carry out full-scale war against a major power should that country violate fundamental League norms. The 1935 British Cabinet "has been described as 'full of mild men'." (Hardie 1974, 41) They were still concerned about balance of power questions and weighed the costs and benefits of military engagements, including the very real risk of defeat. The only other major power that might have sustained them, the United States, was struggling with its isolationist identity and would not take a significant international leadership role until the early 1940s. France felt especially alone on the continent and was willing to entertain a wide array of dubious alliances for the sake of its survival against an expansionist Germany. As we will see, more often than not, France and Britain were unable and unwilling to defend abstract ideals when doing so risked all-out world war.

One might fairly ask whether this historical development was inherent in the League's structure and law. As we will see, the League was in some respects merely an amplifier for international politics. After all, within very broad parameters, the states that joined the League could say and do what they wanted. They could form alliances, build up armies, and issue threats. Although they promised to protect the world from aggressors, these other more traditional balance of power policies were still permissible. They were even permitted to go to war with each other, so long as they submitted their disputes for debate and settlement first. If, after the decision by the League is rendered, the problem is not resolved to the parties' satisfaction, "they agree in no case to resort to war until three months after the award by the arbitrators or the judicial decision, or the report by the Council." (Article 12) Add to that a six-month delay for the court/council to deliberate, and the net effect is simply a nine-month delay of war. Further, any decision by the Council had to be unanimous, which would be unlikely if the two beligerents (or their allies) happen to be sitting on the Council at the same time.

The structures of the League, then, boded poorly for changing the fundamental nature of world politics, although they would help to dramatically decrease the likelihood of accidental, precipitous, or aggressive war, because the world would have to know what was going on and take some time to talk it over first. Naturally, the League did not have the capacity to investigate problems that were brought to its attention, meaning that a secret military build-up and a surprise attack could occur even if the organization were fully functional.

We will now take a closer look at a number of crises and disputes that came before the League to understand better the institution's ability to constrain international anarchy. These three cases—Manchuria, Danzig, and Abyssinia—illustrate a range of League actions. The League Council dealt with more than a dozen serious international crises involving major powers as well as lesser powers. In six cases, the League played a pivotal role in facilitating the peaceful resolution of such issues as territorial disputes, human rights, and even open warfare. At the same time, the League was unable to prevent a number of disputes from being resolved without resort to violence. This was true even when the parties were relatively weak states, such as Bolivia and Peru during the Chaco War of 1932. The three cases below illustrate a broad range of League actions.

MANCHURIA

In September 1931, local Japanese commanders based in northern China to protect Japanese assets won after a war with Russia conspired to provoke a war. Knowing that senior officers were on their way from Japan to rein them in, the local colonels planted a bomb near a Japanese-controlled railway in the hope that they could claim that local Chinese soldiers had done it. With feigned outrage, the Japanese forces attacked numerous Chinese installations and quickly overran the whole of Manchuria (see Map 2.1). Presented with a victory, the government in Japan decided not to reprimand the commanders but instead ratified the event by recognizing the "autonomy" of the region and making it an economic colony.

As the initial attacks commenced, China's government appealed to the League to pressure Japan to cease and withdraw. The Council responded with repeated resolutions chastising the Japanese for their incursion, although several of the major powers also reassured Japan privately that they had no intention of doing anything to block its moves. The British Foreign Secretary said as much to the Parliament. The British ambassador in Tokyo even signalled his approval of the invasion (Rappard 1933, 730).

As the events of Manchuria began to unfold, the British Foreign Secretary asked for advice from the UK's League representative in Geneva. He recommended sanctions under Articles 15 and 16 and was promptly told to "drop this line" (Birn 1975, 96). The problem resided in the fact that any strict sanctions would never work unless the United States was willing to go along with them—which it was not. A year later, once a puppet regime was in place in Manchuria, the British government was still not interested in military action of any kind, and further "doubted that 'concerted economic pressures will be brought to bear'." (Birn 1975, 103)

In its defense, Britain did not have the resources to move unilaterally against Japan, whom it considered an ally at any rate (Japan fought with Britain during World War I). Although the United Kingdom had interests in Asia, it was only indirectly involved in China (in Hong Kong). France likewise considered the League mostly for Europe rather than Asia. Asia was a problem for Japan, the Soviet Union, and the United States. But because the latter were not even

Map 2.1 Manchuria, mid-1930s
Source: http://www.asia-wwii.org/history.html

members of the League in 1931, it was clear early on that it would fall entirely to the British Navy to defend China. No British ship was mobilized (Rappard 1933, 730). To make matters worse, China lacked a central government capable of defending itself or supporting an international force. And finally, it should be remembered that most of Europe was reeling from the 1929 financial crisis and standing on the precipice of the Great Depression. A major war in Asia was simply not feasible (Rappard 1932, 490).

Japan announced in March 1932 that it was leaving the organization and the inconvenient attention it was receiving. Ultimately, the League was able to do little more than lament the resort to force. It did not impose sanctions or threaten military actions (Joyce 1978, 173). This stemmed in large part from an unwillingness of Britain and France (and the United States) to directly challenge Japan and make use of the League's tools. At the same time, it is doubtful that even relatively forceful action would have made any difference.

The inaction of the League brought withering criticism. League members, especially Britain, were charged not only with betraying China, but also with betraying the League's principles themselves (Rappard 1933, 727). There were no sanctions, no threats, and ambiguously worded disapproval. As put by William Rappard, senior official at the League, the great powers gave a clear signal to the rest of the world — especially weak states threatened by powerful ones—that the League "can under no circumstances be looked to as a protector of the victims of any aggression that may take place in the future" (Rappard 1933, 729).

DANZIG

At Versailles, the important port of Danzig (now Gdansk; see Map 2.2) was claimed by Poland and Germany, so to settle the matter, the victors agreed to allow the citizens of Danzig to draft a constitution, provide an international administrator, and declare it a "free city." This allowed Poland access to the sea without having direct control over the territory. The League's job was to maintain this equilibrium against formidable opposition from within and without.

The most serious threat came from Berlin. Beginning in 1934, the new Nazi regime in Germany sought means to regain control over the territory (Gageby 1999, 54). That many citizens of Danzig were also Nazis seeking unification with Germany did not make the League's task any easier. In 1935, Nazis won 57% of the vote thanks in part to the campaigning in the region by senior German propagandists, although the total came short of the three-fourths majority required to re-make the Constitution (Gageby 1999, 79).

That the League had no military forces at its disposal made its task virtually impossible. Instead, challenges to Nazi actions within Danzig by the minority could only be done through legal channels to the League council. In May 1935, for example, appeals were made against Nazi efforts to monopolize the enforcement of criminal law (making it possible for them to imprison political opponents). For their part, Nazis challenged the League's local representative's closure of certain Nazi newspapers. The League, treading a careful line, ruled in favor of both petitions (Gageby 1999, 85). Danzigers even requested the deployment of international peacekeepers and election monitors for future purposes, but were rebuffed.

Over time, the leaders of the Nazi majority in Danzig worked consistently to undermine the constitution and repudiate the powers of the League. The anti-Nazi opposition was increasingly frustrated and unable to block these assertions of power.

Map 2.2 Danzig, mid-1930s
Source: http://www2.bc.edu/~heineman/maps/Danzig.jpg. Used by permission of John Heineman.

They succeeded in passing laws prohibiting newspapers that jeopardized public safety—which is to say that opposed Nazi programs—and beginning in mid-1936, many major opposition newspapers were shuttered. At roughly the same time, Nazis attacked the offices of the opposition political parties. Victims streamed into the local League office, where they were told to abide by the law and rely on the courts for their protection (Gageby 1999, 120).

By the end of 1936, the Nazi-dominated Danzig government refused any dealings with the League representative, and the territory became a de facto extension of Nazi Germany, in open defiance of its constitution. The League representative was ultimately ushered unceremoniously out of the city on September 1 when bombs began to fall as World War II broke out.

It seems clear in retrospect that Germany sought to dominate Danzig throughout the Nazi era. The League could take credit for at least discouraging the German government from invading and annexing Danzig for a time, so that it did not succumb to the fate of Austria and other German neighbors. It is possible that the physical presence of a League official made it more difficult for Germany and the Danzig Nazis to act with impunity, but instead pressured them to at least justify or conceal their actions. The League's resolve can be attributed in turn to France and Britain taking a united anti-Nazi position for much of the period in question.

ABYSSINIA

Italy began to have territorial designs on the independent state of Ethiopia since the turn of the century. Controlling the area would allow it to unite three provinces: Eritrea, Abyssinia, and Italian Somaliland (see Map 2.3). Italy began to deploy troops inside Abyssinia during the 1920s and made public claims on certain regions, such as the city of Walwal (well inside southern Abyssinia and beyond the line demarcated in a 1928 treaty). Skirmishes took place between Italian and Ethiopian forces in December 1934, leading to roughly 200 deaths in total. Ethiopia demanded that the League provide a legal ruling regarding Italian territorial claims, confident that justice would prevail and the Italians would be forced to retire. But instead, the French and British governments applied pressure to Emperor Haile Selassie of Ethiopia to accommodate many of Italy's demands (Hardie 1974, 88). The League investigation dragged on for months, culminating in a finding in September 1935 that the incident was an "accident" and that neither party was culpable (Hardie 1974, 93).

Italy largely ignored the generally favorable ruling and continued a significant military build-up on Abyssinia's borders. By the end of September 1935, Britain and France were growing deeply concerned that Italy was planning a full-scale invasion and began issuing strongly worded warnings. The message may well have been lost on Rome, as several months before the French had apparently negotiated a secret arrangement that ceded Abyssinia to Italy in exchange for its help against Germany (Hardie 1974, 61). In fact, throughout the crisis, Italy took advantage of Britain's and France's clearly expressed desire to keep Italy in the anti-German camp (Baer 1973, 166). In early October 1935, Italy launched a full-scale invasion of the region, attacking from the north and the south with more than 300,000

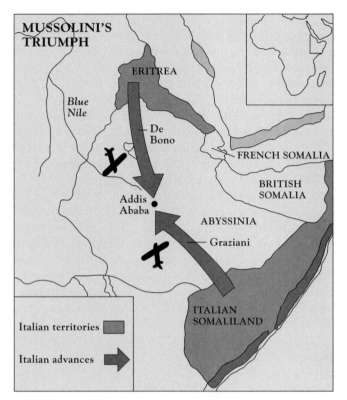

Map 2.3 Abbyssinia, mid-1930s

Source: http://www.warchat.org/history-world/second-italo-abyssinian-war-1935-1936.html

troops (not including the several hundred thousand already in Abyssinia). The advance was slower than might have been expected, given Italy's considerable technological advantage. But by April, Ethiopian resistance had been broken and the Emperor was in exile. On April 7th, Italy officially announced the annexation of Ethiopia, marking the event as the beginning of a new Italian empire.

As the events unfolded, the League took unusually assertive action, although it would prove to be too little, too late. On October 7, 1935, the Council voted to condemn Italy's invasion and impose a series of economic and political sanctions against the country. This was done under the authority of Articles 11, 15, and especially 16, which states:

> Should any Member of the League resort to war in disregard of its covenants . . . it shall . . . be deemed to have committed an act of war against all other Members of the League, which hereby undertake immediately to subject it to the severance of all trade or financial relations. . . . [The Council shall] recommend to the several Governments concerned what military, naval or air force the Members of the League shall severally contribute to the armed forces to be used to protect the covenants of the League.

Virtually all League members, and even several non-members, agreed to cut off almost all trade relations with Italy, including arms sales. The result was rather impressive, as many states reduced trade by more than half. The toughest sanctions were imposed by Britain, and important members of its Empire (Australia, Canada, India, South Africa, New Zealand) (Welk 1937, 106). United Kingdom exports to Italy fell by 95% from January 1935 to January 1936, when the sanctions were in full force. Imports from Italy dropped by 96%. France and the Soviet Union were the most ambivalent, cutting their exports by 45% and 25%, respectively, during the same period (Tillett 1956, 13).

At the same time, however, the government stopped short of doing everything that was listed in Article 16. No effort was made to provide troops to Ethiopia, and although it was debated for months in Paris, London, and Washington, D.C., no effective oil embargoes were imposed. Likewise, bans on exports did not include iron ore and scrap iron, which meant Italy still had the means of producing steel and running war machines. On the contrary, the League pressed both countries to achieve an "amicable settlement of the dispute," as put by French Foreign Minister Pierre Laval (Hardie 1974, 103). In fact, no other League member declared war on Italy or severed diplomatic relations, and little effort was made to impede economic transactions between private citizens and Italy.

Several months into the war, French and British diplomats negotiated a peace package they hoped might bring an end to the war. Its substance helps us better understand what the two major powers hoped for and feared. France was deeply concerned that imposing oil sanctions would anger Italy to the point that it would form an alliance with Germany. Britain feared that do-gooders and League supporters might force it into a land war in Abyssinia. In December 1935, the two presented their plan for peace that included the following:

1. Ethiopia would get some territory—preferably with access to the ocean through Italian-controlled Eritrea—in exchange for ceding considerable territory to Italy, more even than the country had thus far conquered.
2. Italy would have exclusive economic rights in much of Ethiopia. (Hardie 1974, 169–170)

The implications of the deal were clear to Ethiopia: Europe was essentially sacrificing the country's independence for the sake of preventing an Italy–Germany alliance. Advocates for the plan conceded that the proposal betrayed League principles since it gave so much to an aggressor, but they argued that it was the only deal that had a chance of being accepted in Rome. Ironically, because League sanctions were in place at the time, one could argue that entering into negotiations was inherently at odds with the principle of collective security (Baer 1973, 174). But imposing sanctions and negotiating at the same time was perfectly consistent with the balance of power politics. The proposal was met with dismay in London and led to the resignation of the Foreign Secretary, who had negotiated the deal, and inflicted severe damage to the reputation of the Prime Minister, who had just won election on a pro-League platform (Hardie 1974, 195). But neither did London come up with a more forceful counter-proposal. Instead, British policy languished in ambivalence. At any rate, Italy rejected the proposal and renewed its offensive, ultimately conquering the territory in April. Once the war was over, the League quickly suspended the sanctions program.

At roughly the same time as the League was debating the end to the sanctions, they received Emperor Selassie, who addressed the Assembly. He lamented the League's ineffectual performance and chided the great powers for failing to protect a weaker power against aggression:

> If a strong government finds it can destroy a weak people, then the hour has struck for that weak people to appeal to the League of Nations to give judgment in all freedom. God and history will remember your judgment. . . . It is us today. It will be you tomorrow.

The Abyssinia crisis is perhaps the clearest case of a direct confrontation between the League ideals and the balance of power realities. Everything about the crisis was influenced by calculations of European strategy, particularly with respect to France's desire to secure an alliance with Italy against Germany. As put by Baer:

> No official, political or professional, advocated abandoning the League. It was just that the French, like the professional foreign office men and military leaders in London, thought that from a nationalist perspective a full-fledged enforcement policy would, in this case, be unduly and immediately dangerous and this restrained them from taking risks for the Covenant. (1973, 170)

This gave Italy almost limitless freedom to engage in actions that clearly violated the most fundamental and sacred principles of the League. Britain, for its part, was the picture of indecision, torn between a commitment to the League's norms and the balancing of strategic interests between France, Germany, and Italy. Had the United States been an active member of the League, it is likely that Britain would have been emboldened. After all, in a national referendum on the League in the summer of 1935, nearly 60% of Britons said that nations of the world should use force to stop international aggression, consistent with League principles (Hardie 1974, 55). The government's leadership in condemning the invasion and imposing sanctions in October 1935, as well as its rejection of the December 1936 peace proposal, were indications of its commitment to League norms. But it was unwilling to go it alone in providing Ethiopia with military support, since doing so risked not only British lives and treasury, but also a European-wide war as Italy sought assistance from Germany and so forth. Britain did not want to be responsible for such a conflagration.

WAS WWII A LEAGUE ENFORCEMENT ACTION?

An argument might be made that by declaring war on Germany on September 3, 1939, two days after its invasion of Poland, France and Britain were promoting the principles of the League. But the fact is that by this point, the League had largely ceased to function. It did not even address the German incursion, but instead devoted its last full meetings to expelling the Soviet Union for its invasion of Finland (Gageby 1999, 184). Britain and France defended Poland largely because of treaty commitments both had made under military alliances (Joyce 1978, 195). The war Britain had hoped to prevent had finally begun. Perhaps it was inevitable, as Italy, Germany, and Japan had all determined long before that they were dissatisfied with the distribution of land and power on the European and Asian continents. Satisfying their territorial ambitions could only happen at the expense of other great powers, which would naturally be expected to resist at some point.

Sean Lester, the last Secretary General of the League, was relegated to the role of lonely observer after the outbreak of World War II. The League did not officially close its doors until it was formally replaced by the UN in April 1946. The term "united nations" was in fact the informal name of the World War II anti-Nazi alliance under the leadership of the United States and Great Britain, rather than a carry-over from the League days.

CONCLUSION: THE POWER OF ANARCHY?

Gageby asks the key question:

> Looking back on the events in Danzig and Germany [and Abyssinia] in general, today, the reader must ask how could it be that the dictators, Hitler and Mussolini, could get away with so many acts of aggression, often with hardly a protest from the League. One of the answers is that no one quite realized to what excesses Hitler could lead not just his own Nazis but also the vast majority of the German people, including its disciplined army. But the major powers in the League of Nations were divided and irresolute. France and Britain were strongly for the League when it suited their own national policy." (1999, 105–106)

In a statement made shortly after the Abyssinian crisis, Fenwick offered an anticipatory epitaph:

> In a loose confederation which can only act with the unanimous consent of the individual governments, the failure of the leading members of the confederation to agree is likely of itself to be fatal; and this probability is all the greater when important States are outside the confederation . . . (1936, 508)

Anthony Eden, the advocate of what would be later disparagingly called "appeasement," was under great pressure from British citizens not to provoke war for the sake of idealist principles. An editorial in the *Evening News* declared in 1936: "Membership in the League of Nations is, short of actual war, the most dangerous luxury that this country has ever indulged in . . . Danzig means nothing at all to this country." (Gageby 1999, 106–107)

It is interesting to note that in forming the UN, rather than resurrecting all of the League's idealism and structures, the founders were more willing to incorporate realist notions of balance of power into the Charter directly. In fact, they were eager to present the UN as an entirely new institution, even though it represents in many ways a carry-over (Goodrich 1947, 4). For example, the five Permanent

Members of the Security Council enjoy a veto over all questions—including those in which there is a disputant. This meant that never would the UN impose sanctions on a major power—something that the League experience taught was unrealistic and ineffective anyway. Likewise, the UN Charter explicitly provides for military alliances and the right of self-defense without the approval of other member-states. And although the Charter still included detailed provisions for collective security, because any such operation would be decided by the Security Council, there would never be any question of the UN approving full-scale military action against a Permanent Member. Thus the practical reality that the major powers cannot be constrained by law was incorporated in a far more pragmatic—and longer lasting—UN Charter.

QUESTIONS TO CONSIDER

1. What best describes the motives of the various actors during the 1930s? Peace? Power? Security? To what extent was this typical of what motivates all countries?

2. What else could the League of Nations have done to prevent war? What powers could it have used? What resources were at its disposal?

3. To what extent did the quest for power trump the quest for peace? To what extent is this true today?

KEY FIGURES
LEAGUE OF NATIONS

Benito Mussolini   Leader of Italy, 1922–1943.

Adolf Hitler   Chancellor of Germany, 1934–1945.

Emperor Hirohito   124th Emperor of Japan, 1926–1989.

Anthony Eden   British Foreign Secretary, 1934–1938.

Sean Lester   Prominent Irish diplomat and last Secretary-General of the League of Nations.

Emperor Haile Selassie I   Leader of Ethiopia, 1930–1974.

Neville Chamberlain   British Prime Minister, 1937–1940.

Pierre Laval   French Foreign Minister, 1934–1936.

Josef Stalin   Leader of the Soviet Union, 1922–1953.

Woodrow Wilson   President of the United States, 1913–1921.

CHRONOLOGY
LEAGUE OF NATIONS

1919
April 18   Woodrow Wilson's draft of the League of Nations Covenant is approved.

June 28   Treaty of Versailles is signed, including the League Covenant.

1920
January 10   League Covenant enters into force. The Council holds its first session a week later.

November   The League moves its headquarters to Geneva, Switzerland.

1922
May 15   Germany and Poland reach a settlement on Upper Silesia.

September 8   Germany is admitted to the League and becomes a permanent member of the Council.

1931
September   Japanese forces attack Chinese targets in Manchuria.

1933
March 27   Japan announces its intention to withdraw from the League.

October 21   Germany announces its intention to withdraw from the League.

1934
September 17   The Soviet Union joins the League.

December   Italian forces clash with Ethiopian forces.

1935
October 3   Italian forces launch a full-scale invasion of Ethiopia. The League Council condemns the invasion on October 7.

1936
October   The Council increases its membership from ten to eleven.

1937
December 11   Italy announces its intention to withdraw from the League.

1939
September 1   Germany invades Poland.

November 30   The Soviet Union invades Finland.

December 14   The Soviet Union is expelled from the League after its invasion of Finland.

1946
April 18   The League transfers its assets to the United Nations and ceases to exist.

REFERENCES

Baer, George W. "Sanctions and Security: The League of Nations and the Italian-Ethiopian War, 1935–1936," *International Organization* 27 #2 (Spring1973): 165–179.

Birn, Donald. *The League of Nations Union, 1918–1945.* (Oxford: Clarendon Press, 1981).

Egerton, George. "Great Britain and the League of Nations: Collective security as myth and history." In United Nations University and Graduate Institute of International Studies, eds. *The League of Nations in Retrospect* (New York: Walter de Gruyter, 1983): 95–117.

Fenwick, C.G. "The 'Failure' of the League of Nations," *The American Journal of International Law* 30 #3 (July 1936): 506–509.

Gageby, Douglas. *The Last Secretary General: Sean Lester and the League of Nations* (Dublin: Town House, 1999).

Goodrich, Leland M. "From League of Nations to United Nations," *International Organization* 1 #1 (February 1947): 3–21.

Hardie, Frank. *The Abyssianian Crisis: Le relais où les destines changèrent de chevaux* (London: B.T. Batsford, 1974).

International Court of Justice. "Publications of the Permanent Court of International Justice (1922–1946)", available at http://www.icj-cij.org/pcij/index.php?p1=9&p2=1&p3=0&co=A10. Accessed September 8, 2008.

Jones, Howard. *Crucible of Power—A History of the U.S. Foreign Relations Since 1897* (New York: Rowman and Littlefield, 2002).

Joyce, James Avery. *Broken Star: The Story of the League of Nations, 1919-1939* (Swansea, UK: Christopher Davies, 1978).

Rappard, William E. "The League in Relation to the World Crisis," *Political Science Quarterly* 47 #4 (December 1932): 481–514.

Rappard, William E. "Nationalism and the League of Nations Today," The *American Political Science Review* 27 #5 (October 1933): 721–737.

Tillett, Lowell R. "The Soviet Role in League Sanctions Against Italy, 1935-36," *American Slavic and East European Review* 15 #1 (February 1956): 11–16.

Tuchman, Barbara. *The Guns of August.* (New York: Dell, 1963).

Welk, William G. "League Sanctions and Foreign Trade Restrictions in Italy," *The American Economic Review* 27 #1 (March 1937): 96–107.

Wilson, Woodrow. "Final Address in Support of the League of Nations," delivered September 25th, 1919 in Pueblo, Colorado, from James Andrews and David Zarefsky, eds. *American Voices: Significant Speeches in American History, 1640-1945* (White Plains, NY: Longman, 1989).

Zimmern, Sir Alfred. *The League of Nations and the Rule of Law, 1918–1935* (London: Macmillan, 1936).

3

∎ ∎ ∎

Balance of Power: Sino–Soviet–American Relations

INTRODUCTION

As major powers seek security in international affairs, they have several options: increase their military capability beyond the level of any potential adversaries, declare neutrality, or align with other countries to combine their military strengths. The last option is the essence of the balance of power: As nations seek security by forming alliances, the international system will be composed of coalitions that balance one another. This is not to say that every state will remain in a given coalition, but that overall, the arrangement of alliances will tend toward a stalemate. Advocates of the balance of power emphasize that this arrangement is both inevitable and beneficial, because it prevents any one state from conquering the world. Opponents point out that the balance of power has failed to prevent world wars in the past and that it is based on the amoral principle that "might makes right."

In the past, the story of world affairs has often been told as the story of great power alliances. European history, in particular, consists largely of a string of strategic and tactical agreements between monarchs and emperors, cemented through treaty, marriage, territorial transfers, and so forth. Rarely did any question of whether a particular alliance was "moral" or "right" arise—just whether it was advantageous or prudent. The result has been a string of strange pairings between democracies and dictatorships, kingdoms and republics.

This situation began to change at the beginning of the 20th century, when ideology began to emerge as an important defining trait of states. With the entry of the United States into World War I, President Woodrow Wilson could claim (however speciously) that the struggle pitted freedom against oppression (he conveniently ignored the fact that Great Britain, France, and the United States were on the same side as the despotic Tsarist Russia). Since then, it has become increasingly important for alliances to have a greater purpose than to merely offset the power of a threatening state. Rather, they must also advance some overarching cause, such as democracy, socialism, or divine destiny. Pragmatic realists seem to be on the defensive in their advocacy of alliances of convenience.

Throughout the Cold War, the three major powers—the United States, the Soviet Union, and the People's Republic of China (PRC)—were often torn by the desire to make alliances meaningful while at the same time behaving pragmatically to defend against would-be enemies. The result has been a series of often-surprising alignments.

THE SUPERPOWER "TRIANGLE" AND ALIGNMENTS

John Stoessinger opined:

> Machiavelli would have taken considerable pleasure in the dynamics of Sino–Soviet–American triangular relations in our time. During the 1950s, China and the Soviet Union were allies, and the United States feared the menace of a monolithic Sino–Soviet threat. In the 1960s, after the Cuban missile crisis had ushered in a détente between the Soviet Union and the United States, China began to fear the specter of Soviet–American collusion. And in the 1970s, the Soviet leaders began to worry that the Chinese and Americans might be getting along too well. Each of the three powers has had its turn at being frozen out by the other two. (Stoessinger 1990, 257)

The tenuousness of superpower relations is symptomatic of the balance of power. To understand the changes in relations among these countries, it is not enough to know the ins and outs of diplomatic language, protocol, and individual personalities. It is also not enough to understand the cultural heritage, historical habits, and ever-changing perceptions of world leaders. Instead, one should focus on how each nation has tried to increase its security by adjusting its relations with a pair of enemies. This adjustment is the essence of the balance of power.

Little naturally links the United States, the Soviet Union, and the PRC. In fact, it was not until the 20th century that meaningful contacts developed among the three nations, at a time when each was already a major global power. The historical circumstances that have forced these three nations to take on the burden of world leadership seem to have been largely beyond their control. Because of this fact, the response of the countries' leaders to these political choices can be more clearly attributed to strategic concerns than to habit, tradition, or heritage.

Each of the three nations has viewed itself as a model for the rest of the world. China's sense of cultural superiority was boundless until the 20th century, when Western barbarians began to exact humiliating concessions for trade. The Russian empire has consistently viewed itself as a model of efficiency and sophistication, although its views of the West have been generally sympathetic. The United States, with its feelings of "Manifest Destiny," has long considered its role as a model of democracy and scientific progress to be unquestioned. The Communist revolutions in Russia and China had the effect of accentuating ideological differences and feelings of uniqueness and superiority.

At the turn of the century, the United States attempted to mediate a dispute between Western powers intent on trading with China and anti-Western Boxers with its "Open Door" policy, but in the end it sided with the Westerners (Stoessinger 1990, 25). The United States refused to accept the outcome of the October 1917 Bolshevik Revolution and joined an international force to overthrow the new Russian regime in 1919. The Chinese were largely uninterested in Russia, although the Great Wall provided little insurance that the influence of the northern barbarians could be contained for long.

By the 1930s, however, relations among the three nations had grown generally warm. The Soviets provided support for both the Nationalist government in Beijing and the Communist Party forces under Mao Zedong. In 1933, since the Soviet Union had demonstrated political and economic resilience through the Great Depression and America had not, the United States was more favorably disposed toward working with the socialist behemoth on equal terms. Their budding friendship was temporarily strained by Stalin's decision to sign a nonaggression pact with Hitler in 1939. Americans actively supported the beleaguered Chinese National government in its failed efforts to prevent the conquest of Manchuria (northern China). When Hitler invaded Russia in 1941 and Japan attacked Pearl Harbor a few months later, the three superpowers-to-be suddenly and quite unexpectedly found themselves on the same winning side in World War II.

The story of how these three World War II allies evolved into a nuclear triangle is the great diplomatic saga of our time.

MAJOR INCIDENTS

Outbreak of the Cold War and U.S.–PRC Tensions

On March 12, 1947, President Harry Truman addressed a joint session of Congress and requested $400 million to support regimes in Greece and Turkey against Soviet-backed insurrections. Without explicitly naming the Soviet Union, Truman declared:

> It would be an unspeakable tragedy if these countries, which have struggled so long against overwhelming odds, should lose the victory for which they sacrificed so much. Collapse of free institutions and loss of independence would be disastrous not only for them but for the world. Discouragement and possibly failure would quickly be the lot of neighboring peoples striving to maintain their freedom and independence. (McCormick 1986, 59)

With that statement, all pretense of cordial postwar relations with the Soviet Union was dropped, and the Cold War began in earnest. The 1945–1947 period had witnessed the "gradual disengagement" of the Soviet Union from its Cold War alliance with the United States (Ulam 1971, 102). Fueled by a persistent fear of invasion from Europe, Soviet leaders acted to consolidate control over the Eastern European territories liberated by the Red Army in the closing months of World War II. The response from the West was slow; the Truman administration held out a great deal of hope for the United Nations (UN) to act as a vehicle for restoring postwar order.

Soviet attitudes toward the UN were disturbing. The "Baruch Plan" to bring all nuclear weapons under international control was rejected by the Soviets in 1946, as were countless resolutions in the Security Council, where the Soviet veto prevented action. Americans deeply resented this frustration of a great cause and began to question Soviet commitment to peaceful coexistence. The fact that Stalin was carrying out an extraordinarily intense re-industrialization program at the time did little to comfort the West.

Soviet forces and pro-Soviet leaders in East Germany became alarmed during 1948 at the collapse of the East German mark specifically and the vulnerability of the economy generally. In response, Soviet forces were dispatched to seal off West Berlin from Western products and prevent emigration by rail or road. The United States then embarked on an eighteen-month airlift that supplied so much food and other materials that prices for the goods fell below East Berlin levels. The worst fears of Soviet intentions were confirmed, and events demonstrated the importance of American leadership, technology, and boldness. The Soviet decision not to shoot down the aircraft also illustrated the limits to Soviet power and belligerence.

At that time, U.S. policy was heavily influenced by the thoughts of George Kennan, a senior expert on Russia, who coined the word *containment*. Kennan's call for diplomatic maneuvering to undermine the Soviet bloc suggested ways to pull apart the East European coalition through selective pressure, enticements, and determined resoluteness. He added the recommendation to act quickly to shore up collapsing pro-U.S. governments in Western Europe by providing massive economic aid and a strong military presence. In 1948, the Marshall Plan aid from the United States, which amounted to some $12 billion over five years, became available to Western Europe. In 1949, the United States helped to form the North Atlantic Treaty Organization (NATO), a military alliance aimed at preventing further Soviet expansion in Europe. NATO members moved quickly to restore German sovereignty and military might, and thousands of American soldiers were deployed to Germany. The Soviets responded by organizing the Warsaw Pact and maintaining a large military force in the East European theater.

In September 1949, the Soviet Union detonated its first atomic weapon, thereby ending the U.S. nuclear monopoly. The effect of this event was primarily psychological, in that the Soviets then lacked the means to deliver the weapon to a target. It was at this time that the U.S.–Soviet nuclear arms race began, however.

The Chinese Revolution in 1949 represented the culmination of a fifteen-year Communist insurrection that had weathered assassinations, mass arrests, a "Long March" to regroup forces, and Japanese invasion. Mao Zedong received Soviet support, although he had sought American backing, and almost immediately turned to the Soviet Union once victory was achieved. The Soviets responded by providing large numbers of military, economic, and industrial advisors, whose aim was the establishment of a large-scale industrial plant in China and the inclusion of the Chinese Communist Party in the Soviet-dominated Comintern—the umbrella organization of all Communist parties worldwide. Mao was quick to embrace Soviet support and formed what appeared to be a united front against imperialist capitalism. For its part, the United States denounced the Cultural Revolution and preserved formal diplomatic ties with the exiled Nationalist government, now based on the island of Taiwan.

The formation of what appeared to be a united Communist bloc covering the entire Eurasian continent from Warsaw to Beijing gave a special urgency to the U.S. containment strategy. The document designated NSC-68 took the original ideas of Kennan and tilted them toward a blatantly military strategy of direct confrontation (Gaddis & Diebel 1987, 6). The result was a readiness on the part of the United States to respond to Soviet "mischief" with proportional force. This primarily reactive policy prompted U.S. interventions in Korea, Vietnam, and Cuba over the next fifteen years.

The jury is still out on the question of who started the Cold War. Soviet behavior in Eastern Europe can easily be interpreted as aggressive, especially when combined with Soviet support for the Western European Communist parties that came close to taking power in the late 1940s. Given Soviet apprehensions about the vulnerability of its western borders, however, the policies are easy to explain and even justify. From the Soviet perspective, U.S. attempts to shape the world through the UN, the Marshall Plan, and the rearming of Germany seemed no less threatening. After all, the United States had delayed its entry into the European theater by two years in World War II (Soviets expected an American landing by 1942); it had detonated an atomic weapon and in the process cut the Soviets out of the peace process in the Far East, and it had participated in an invasion of the Soviet Union in an attempt to reverse the Bolshevik Revolution.

Much as in a family feud, the question of who started the conflict may be immaterial once the fight is on. We can, however, gain some interesting insights into the nature of the balance of power. One can easily argue that when two powers exist on the world stage without a rival, they will tend to fear each other and therefore each will protect itself against the other (Waltz 1979). Once this process has begun, it is nearly impossible to distinguish "prudent preparations for potential conflict," on the one hand, from "openly hostile actions" on the other. One cannot tell by looking at it whether a nuclear missile is "offensive" or "defensive" after all.

Cold War I: 1949–1962

With the stage set for an enduring three-way conflict among the United States, the Soviet Union, and China, all three nations were preparing for a possible outbreak of hostilities. On June 25, 1950, equipped with Soviet-made weapons and supported politically by China, North Korean forces crossed the postwar dividing line of the 38th parallel to invade and ultimately annex the United States ally South Korea.

The United States called for multilateral action against the North Koreans, which was organized in the UN (the Soviet delegation was boycotting the Security Council to protest the continued occupation of the China seat by the Taiwanese Nationalists and so was not able to veto the proposal). American ships were already on their way and within days began pushing back North Korean forces, which had taken control of roughly seven eighths of the total South Korean territory. General Douglas MacArthur led the counteroffensive and, with the dramatic invasion at Inchon behind the front lines, succeeded in pushing back the invaders to the original frontier by late September. After MacArthur's demand for surrender went unheeded, the General Assembly authorized the invasion of North Korea by UN forces.

With the tables turned, the North Korean forces quickly fell back until the UN armies threatened to enter China, Korea's neighbor. Despite Chinese threats not to approach the border, UN forces came within miles of China and prompted the People's Liberation Army to enter the fray. Chinese intervention in the Korean War raised the very real possibility of a full-scale world war in late 1950. MacArthur was sacked by President Truman precisely because he had ignored Truman's warnings to avoid accidental escalation. The front moved back into South Korean territory and eventually stabilized near the 38th parallel. Peace talks dragged on as both sides hoped for a military breakthrough. An armistice was eventually signed on July 27, 1953, after some 450,000 casualties on the South Korean side, of which 150,000 were Americans, and an estimated 2 million casualties on the North Korean/Chinese side (Chai 1972, 86).

In the beginning of the Korean War, U.S. ships were maneuvered into the Formosa Straits between mainland China and Taiwan to discourage would-be aggression by the PRC against the Nationalist government on the island. Throughout the 1950s and 1960s, both governments remained adamant in their claims that the other side had no right to govern any part of China. The United States repeatedly acted to prevent aggression, but by doing so precipitated belli-cose responses from Beijing. The U.S.–Taiwan Mutual Defense Assistance Agree-ment of 1951 confirmed China's fears that the United States sought domination of the entire Asian continent from this foothold (Camilleri 1980, 32). With the formation of the South-East Asian Treaty Organization (SEATO), which encir-cled China, Beijing had sufficient evidence to seek a preemptive strike to reassert its control over the region.

China began shelling some of the Taiwanese fortresses on the islands in the Formosa Straits in late 1954. In response, the United States demanded a cessa-tion of hostilities, implicitly threatening U.S. intervention with atomic weapons. This U.S. policy of "brinkmanship" surfaced again in 1958 after Chinese shelling was renewed. The Chinese, meanwhile, were ambivalent. In 1956, China declared its interest in improved relations with the West in the context of the Third World Bandung Conference. The goal of disengaging the United States from the region had clearly failed, but concerns about precedents and appearances prevented a public capitulation on the issue. The result was simmering Sino–American hostility, which was exacerbated by the U.S. entry into the Vietnam War in the mid-1960s.

During the 1950s, the U.S.–Soviet Cold War was in full swing. Although the Eisenhower administration offered tentative olive branches (his "Open Skies" proposal would have permitted free access by each nation's reconnaissance aircraft to the other's airspace), confrontational rhetoric dominated the debate. John Foster Dulles, the U.S. secretary of state, strongly advocated a "perimeter containment" strategy, which led to the formation of numerous regional alliances (containment) in areas surrounding the Soviet Union. Minor skirmishes were to be treated as major tests of resolve. The enemy was seen as an insidious, pervasive, single-minded force bent on world domination. This perspective was codified in the 1957 "Eisenhower Doctrine" declaring U.S. support for any victim of "armed aggression from any country controlled by international Communism" (Spanier 1988, 101). We should note, however, that U.S. intervention stopped short of helping nations already within the Soviet sphere, such as Hungary in 1956, where an anti-Soviet uprising was quelled with tanks.

The Soviets, on their side, viewed any American efforts at self-defense as inherently provocative. The rearmament of Germany beginning in 1950, the establishment of anti-Soviet alliances, the dramatic era of the Korean War–U.S. military buildup, and the detonation of the hydrogen bomb in 1952 all seemed to convey the attitude that the United States was preparing to conquer the world. With the economic aid provided to Western Europe in the context of European integration and the isolation of the Soviet economy, Moscow had evidence that the United States also aimed to cripple the socialist world financially.

By 1960, Americans were close to panic after a chain of Soviet achievements: the Soviet detonation of a hydrogen bomb in 1953, the test of the first intercontinental ballistic missile in 1957, and the shocking success of the Sputnik satellite in 1957. Fidel Castro's successful revolution in Cuba in 1959 prompted the United States to intervene in what would be later called the "perfect failure"—the Bay of Pigs. A group of U.S.-backed Cuban exiles attempted an amphibious invasion to overthrow Castro's regime, only to be captured at great public embarrassment to the Kennedy administration (Higgins 1987). The downing of a U–2 reconnaissance aircraft in 1960 scuttled an important peace conference being planned at the time, and the Berlin Wall crisis of 1961 severely tested the mettle of the newly elected President John F. Kennedy.

This is not to say that the entire period was a catastrophe. On the contrary, many felt that with the death of Joseph Stalin in 1953, his successor Nikita Khrushchev would bring a new warmth to U.S.–Soviet relations. A number of early summits and agreements confirmed this hope. Khrushchev became the first Soviet leader to visit the United States when he attended a summit there in 1959. Talks concerning the disposition of Germany continued throughout the decade, albeit with no resolution. American intervention to prevent the fall of Egypt's left-leaning Gamel Nasser during the 1956 war with Israel did much to convince Third World revolutionaries that the United States was capable of impartiality.

The culmination of these Cold War tensions was also the crucible for change. The Cuban Missile Crisis, which took place over a two-week period in October 1962, brought the two superpowers to the brink of full-scale nuclear confrontation (see Chapter 5). Kennedy estimated at the height of the crisis that the chances of all-out war were "between one out of three and even" (Allison 1999, 1). Ostensibly an attempt by the Soviet Union to offset the tremendous American advantage in nuclear weaponry, the deployment of Soviet medium-range nuclear missiles in Cuba was deemed provocative by the Kennedy administration, and their removal became the object of a tense confrontation. The Soviets demanded, after stonewalling for a week, U.S. assurance that Cuba would never again be attacked and that U.S. weapons deployed in Turkey would be dismantled. Kennedy placed a naval blockade around the island in an attempt to buy time and prevent completion of the missile project, only to find that by day 13 the missiles were apparently operational. An American reconnaissance aircraft was shot down over Cuba, and the United States prepared to implement plans for an all-out attack and invasion against Cuba. Only at the last moment did word come from Moscow, in the form of conflicting cables, that the Soviets would accept a settlement.

While the world breathed a sigh of relief, the immediacy of nuclear war led leaders on both sides of the Cold War to seek new arrangements and agreements to prevent a serious confrontation from happening again. From 1963 through 1979, the United States and the Soviets (later joined by the Chinese) entered a period of relative "détente," or relaxation of tensions. Although the Vietnam War interrupted this trend, the pattern is nonetheless visible (Stoessinger 1990, 207).

Détente I: 1963–1979

Almost as soon as the Cuban Missile Crisis was over, Kennedy and Khrushchev (soon to be replaced by Lyndon Johnson and Leonid Brezhnev) began to build bridges. The "hotline" was established in 1963 as a permanent communication link between the United States and the Soviet Union (although a Norwegian's plow once severed it!), and the problem of rapid communication in times of crisis was essentially solved. An above-ground nuclear Test Ban Treaty was also signed, ending the environmentally catastrophic practice of testing nuclear weapons in the atmosphere.

Perhaps the most significant development during this period, aside from the gradual rapprochement between East and West, was the severing of relations between erstwhile comrades in the Soviet Union and the PRC. Although the Sino–Soviet alliance had clearly been as much a marriage of convenience as an ideological alliance, the breakup largely resulted from differences in philosophy and priority. Mao's revolutionaries had long placed Third World liberation ahead of all other international objectives and did not hesitate to burn bridges with the United States in their efforts to liberate colonies and spread socialism. The Soviet Union, on the other hand, had learned that it was partly dependent on Western support and goodwill to succeed in the world and was inclined to favor warmer relations. This difference in attitude became more pronounced after the Cuban Missile Crisis, when China found itself allied with more and more radical regimes in the Third World as decolonization moved into full swing and as the Soviets mended fences with the West.

Another key factor in the rupture was China's resentment of the influence exerted on its political and economic life by a Soviet Union long intent on reproducing itself. Soviet economic advisors urged Chinese leaders to implement a full-scale industrialization program based on steel, machines, and other heavy industry. This plan collided with the largely agrarian context in which the Chinese Revolution had flourished. The Great Leap Forward, a program of intense modernization of the Chinese economy, was initiated as much to achieve economic objectives as to assert Chinese autonomy. Furthermore, Mao objected to the rather tentative Soviet reforms under Khrushchev, which introduced more market-oriented policies. Chinese leaders felt that the Soviets had essentially sold out the revolution and that China alone held the torch of true socialism.

In 1962, Mao declared that the leaders of the Soviet Union were now "revisionists"—a withering attack from an ideological perspective that aimed at undermining Soviet leadership of international communism. In 1963, China condemned the Test Ban Treaty, which pointedly left it out as a "non-nuclear power." In 1964, the country tested its first atomic weapon, as if to thumb its nose at what it saw as a U.S.–Soviet alliance forming against it (Yahuda 1982, 30). By the late 1960s, the Soviets and Chinese engaged in border skirmishes that threatened to escalate as the Soviets spoke of preemptive strikes against Chinese nuclear installations. Ultimately, it was the United States that intervened to defuse the conflict.

The Vietnam War created new tension in what by the mid-1960s was clearly a three-way relationship. American support for the South Vietnamese government deeply troubled China, although China's relations with the North Vietnamese were cool at best, stemming from Hanoi's rejection of Chinese claims on Vietnamese territory. The Soviet Union, having supported Ho Chi Minh and the North Vietnamese revolution, was forced to provide support for China again throughout the Vietnam War. China was thus in the enviable position of watching its two enemies fight it out with each other, all the while hoping that the violence could be contained to a modest level. During this period of relative security, the Cultural Revolution was begun to purify China's society of Western influences, although the result was the elimination of many of the nation's most accomplished intellectuals. The events so disgusted Western observers that Chou En-Lai felt forced to render a weak explanation six years later on the occasion of Henry Kissinger's first visit to China (Kissinger 1979, 751).

The escalation of U.S. involvement in Vietnam from a handful of troops and advisors in 1964 to more than 500,000 personnel by 1969 was so gradual that it never, in and of itself, constituted a serious threat to global stability. It was not until the war began to wane, after Lyndon Johnson's decision in 1968 to begin troop withdrawals, that uncertainty entered the picture. Richard Nixon's attacks on Cambodia; the "Vietnamization" of the war, through which poorly motivated South Vietnamese soldiers were put in charge of the fighting; the popular unrest at home; and the on again–off again peace talks in Paris combined to give the closing years of the Vietnam War an unreal dimension that was separate from the "real" world of superpower diplomacy. An illustration of this was Beijing's crucial invitation to the United States to send a high-level representative in 1971. Henry Kissinger went to

Pakistan and secretly on to China (absent on the pretense of catching the flu!), where preparations were made for Nixon's historic trip. All of this activity took place against the backdrop of intensified American air attacks in North Vietnam and a secret invasion of Cambodia.

Nixon's visit to China came in late February 1972 and resulted in a rather ambiguously worded statement known as the Shanghai Communique. The statement pledged an effort toward normalization of relations and supported the notion of "One China," although it left unclear who should govern this entity—the PRC or Taiwan (Kissinger 1979, 1085). Nixon's visit to China was followed in May by the first-ever visit by an American president to Moscow, where the Strategic Arms Limitation Talks (SALT I) were accepted in principle. Each of these agreements came in spite of ongoing disputes between the superpowers over conflicts with China, India, and Pakistan; between North and South Vietnam (although the Paris Peace Accords ended U.S. involvement in the war in January 1973); between Israel and Arab nations (Anwar Sadat expelled Soviet advisors from Egypt in July 1972, five years after they had supported his country during the Six-Day War); and in Cambodia and elsewhere.

The period of détente was perhaps best known for the general warming of relations between all Western nations and the East. Willy Brandt, Chancellor of West Germany during the mid-1970s, established solid ties with the German Democratic Republic to the East. The Helsinki Accords were signed in 1975 and pledged all European nations, East and West, to safeguard human rights and civil liberties. The United States, under Jimmy Carter, continued these trends by strengthening the arms control agreements made under SALT I and extending full diplomatic recognition to the PRC, now under the leadership of Western-oriented Deng Hsiao Ping in 1979. In short, there seemed to be every reason to hope that the United States had established an era of understanding and cooperation.

Cold War II: 1979–1985

The year 1980 stands out as a critical turning point in the Cold War because it was in January of that year that the Soviet Union for the first time invaded a neutral country with its own troops. It would be another nine years before the troops were withdrawn, and during this period, East–West relations slipped back into Cold War patterns.

After the Afghanistan invasion, Jimmy Carter declared, "My opinion of the Russians has changed more drastically in the last week than in the previous two and a half years" (Stoessinger 1990, 232). Soviet motives for the invasion remain difficult to understand, although the immediate reason was to shore up an embattled ally in a strategic region. The fall of the Shah of Iran in 1979 had facilitated the spread of radical Islamic fervor throughout the region and jeopardized Russia's long-term quest for a warm-water port, access to oil reserves, and proximity to Pakistan and India. Perhaps also the Soviets estimated that the benefits of U.S. rapprochement were at a zenith and could only go downhill. The Soviet Union imposed martial law in Poland in response to worker unrest, and with the election of President Ronald

Reagan in late 1980, détente was over. The Carter Doctrine, which pledged U.S. action against any attempt by an "outside power" to control Middle East oil, was the new agenda. (The Carter Doctrine later formed the basis for George H. W. Bush's Gulf War actions.)

The Reagan administration chose this time to strengthen U.S. power at home and to improve ties with Beijing abroad. Sino–American relations were never better. China imposed diplomatic sanctions against Moscow and joined the United States in its containment of Soviet expansionism (Stoessinger 1990, 106). Reagan expanded the arms buildup begun by Carter, even at the cost of an overwhelming fiscal deficit, and engaged in military interventions in Nicaragua, Lebanon, and Afghanistan. SALT II was abandoned, and Reagan's aggressive rhetoric ("evil empire," "plan for Armageddon") alarmed Europeans without chasing away their support. Margaret Thatcher and Helmut Kohl were united in condemning Soviet aggression and, acting against extraordinary public pressure, permitted the deployment of a new generation of medium-range nuclear missiles in Europe.

Reagan offered rather unrealistic arms control proposals, which resulted in a stalemate and ultimately a Soviet walkout at the Strategic Arms Reduction Talks (START) and Intermediate-Range Nuclear Forces (INF) talks. The Strategic Defense Initiative (SDI) was proposed in 1983 with the goal of enveloping the United States in a protective shield of high-tech weapons aimed at incoming Soviet missiles. Reagan proposed repeatedly to abandon the research program in exchange for deep unilateral Soviet arms cuts.

It was not until the emergence of Mikhail Gorbachev on the world scene that Cold War II began to change course.

Détente II: 1985–1991

The story of the second wave of détente, culminating in the collapse of the Soviet Union itself, is probably familiar and so bears only a cursory review. Suffice it to say that Reagan embraced the new, youthful, and apparently open-minded Soviet leader with open arms. He noted that Gorbachev was not a typical Communist, but rather someone with whom the United States could work (Nathan & Oliver 1989, 483). A number of summits were arranged, and by 1987, the INF Treaty, the first-ever arms reduction agreement, was signed.

Strategic arms talks took much longer to resolve, with Gorbachev repeatedly asking the United States to abandon SDI unilaterally. It was not until the Soviet empire was crumbling during the Bush administration's watch that a far-reaching strategic arms reduction treaty was signed. Before the ink was dry (and prior to ratification by the Senate), a new, more profound agreement was signed with the new Russian Republic under the leadership of Boris Yeltsin. Other agreements to dramatically cut chemical weapons stockpiles and ban their production, implement significant cuts in conventional (nonnuclear) weapons deployed across Europe, and form an eventual U.S.–Soviet "alliance" against Iraq in the Persian Gulf War of 1990–1991 demonstrated an entirely new era of cooperation. With the Soviets leaving Afghanistan and releasing control over all East European states in 1989, thereby permitting the reunification of Germany in 1990, the Cold War was well and truly over. Rehabilitation of the defeated erstwhile enemy became the pressing issue of peacetime, much as it was after the defeat of Nazi Germany and Imperial Japan in 1945.

What was the Chinese orientation to the Americans and Russians in this new context? The well-known Tienanmen Square massacres of 1989 dealt a serious blow to the emerging democracy movement that had swept across China under Deng. The immediate result was the imposition of sanctions against China by the United States and Western Europe, although most of these were either allowed to lapse or reversed by 1992. Chinese relations with the Soviet Union improved significantly during the Gorbachev era. The Soviets supported a UN-mediated withdrawal of Soviet-backed Vietnam from China-backed Cambodia—a process that has not entirely succeeded at this writing. A Sino–Soviet summit took place in 1989 (the first since 1956) as "Russia wooed and China cooed" (Rourke 1990, 44). China became concerned about the closeness of U.S.–Soviet relations during the Gulf War, but stopped short of vetoing a critical UN resolution permitting armed intervention against Iraq.

Post–Cold War Era: After 1992

Since the breakup of the Soviet Union in 1991, the strategic triangle has been far more difficult for analysts to understand. Economic factors seem to predominate now. It is thus increasingly difficult to know which pair of countries is experiencing strain or harmony, because trade and investment not only serve as indicators of good relations, but also generate friction and can be used as potential weapons. Russia received billions in aid from the West, particularly through the International Monetary Fund (too much, according to both Russian and IMF accounts). This largesse generated considerable resentment, however: In Russia, nationalists and Communists objected to the "neoimperialism" implicit in this economic dependence; in the West, officials grew increasingly impatient with the inefficiencies and corruption of the Yeltsin regime. For China, economics has become the focal point of national planning, which has produced annual growth rates of close to 10% for much of the 1990s. Maintaining a strong trade relationship with the United States has significantly helped China control its balance of payments. Americans have shown increasing resentment of the unbalanced trade relationship with China, and Congress resisted granting the country "normal trade relations" status until 2000. Considerable doubt remains as to whether China will become a full-fledged member of the World Trade Organization. China's mixed record in human rights further complicates U.S. willingness to work closely with Beijing.

On the security front, the relationship among the three countries is also ambiguous. Officially, relations are good, but at the same time, each country is acutely aware of the potential threat that the others pose. Consequently, the game is more "shadow boxing" than outright rivalry. Each country is engaged in efforts to enhance its military preparedness, although Russia is clearly lagging in this regard. During the 1990s, China detonated a number of nuclear warheads, resisted cooperating in the nonproliferation regime, openly threatened Taiwan's election campaign in 1999 (to which the United States at times responded with military deployments of its own), and was involved in illicit military technology transfers—both by spying on U.S. nuclear facilities and by selling technology to Pakistan and other Asian countries. The United States has maintained high levels of defense spending in the past ten years, although it has also dismantled a number of bases and units and has moved forward to implement START II nuclear weapons reductions (along with Russia, although both have encountered resistance in their respective legislatures). In addition, the United States has continued to improve weapons based on stealth technology and has undertaken a new initiative to improve its antiballistic missile defense capability, purportedly to protect against isolated attacks from rogue states such as North Korea. Dramatic U.S. support of regional military intervention, particularly in Yugoslavia (both Bosnia and Kosovo), was resisted by Russia. Perhaps most directly threatening was the decision taken by the United States in 1995 to expand NATO by including Poland, Hungary, and the Czech Republic, a move that met with considerable Russian opposition ("Eastern Cheers" 1997, 5). Yeltsin spoke of a "cold peace," and at a summit meeting in mid-2000, both Russian and Chinese leaders warned the United States of the dangers of generating tensions through its antiballistic missile defense plans ("At CSCE Summit" 1995, 8).

Although it is too early to say that the United States is becoming isolated by Russia and China and that the latter are forging a strong alliance, those developments would hardly be surprising. Realists would predict that the second- and third-ranking powers in any international system would naturally unite to offset the power of the preeminent state. As China becomes more economically powerful and Russia regains its financial footing, we can expect to see both act with considerably less deference to Washington's wishes. In the spring of 2001, for example, the United States deployed one of many spy planes along the Chinese coast to intercept various electronic communication signals. Unlike in past incidents, the Chinese air force intercepted one plane and accidentally made contact, forcing it to land in Chinese territory. Rather than return the plane and simply write off the incident, Beijing opted instead to castigate the United States for recklessly violating its territory and proceeded to detain the crew and dismantle the aircraft. After weeks of negotiation, the United States agreed to issue a "quasi-apology" for the incident and the crew was released. The plane was later returned—in several crates.

The September 11, 2001 terrorist attacks altered the superpower relationships, at least temporarily. Both Moscow and Beijing made it very clear that they viewed the attacks as a threat to civilization itself and pledged unlimited support for the United States. They all joined in the war against terrorism, with the United States leading the way in Afghanistan. Except for a U.S. decision to withdraw from the Anti-Ballistic Missile (ABM) Treaty, which was greeted with dismay by Russian President Vladimir Putin in early 2002, there are few signs that the latest era of good feelings has diminished significantly. The decision in early 2003 to invade Iraq damaged U.S. relations with Russia and China, both of which blocked a resolution approving the action in the UN Security Council. The result was a clear rapprochement between Moscow and Brussels, which followed a very friendly meeting between Vladimir Putin and Hu Jintao, the new Chinese premier. China, for its part, has continued to object to U.S. support for the Taiwanese government—particularly military assistance. This said, China's membership in the World Trade Organization, beginning in 2001, along with Russia's imminent membership, are indicative of a generally positive relationship between the three major powers (*China Daily* 2004). They are further united on fighting terrorism (the Bush administration has given Moscow considerable leeway in its war in Chechnya) and limiting nuclear proliferation (China has actively worked to persuade North Korea to halt its drive to possess nuclear weapons—although there are rumors that it helped Pakistan and others obtain nuclear technology).

One could argue that the most serious threats to the relationship today are economic. Russia's economic weakness continues to be a drain on the world economy, and its indebtedness threatens to strain relations. Although its oil reserves have given it leverage and what might prove to be short-lived prosperity, the fact remains that the Russian economy is still fundamentally weak. Its economic success in 2007 has been largely swallowed up by the 2008 international financial crisis. At the same time, Russia's military action against Georgia in August 2008 (See Chapter 6) left many in the West wondering whether the country was attempting to restart the Cold War.

For its part, China's remarkable economic growth is seen as both a serious challenge and an irresistible opportunity by Westerners in general and Americans in particular (*New York Times*, December 6, 2004, special Business Day issue). The United States has expressed its concern about the undervalued Chinese currency, which artificially lowers the price of its exports, calling upon the government to set the exchange rate closer to what the market would demand. At the same time, the United States can't survive without China's heavy investment in U.S. government bonds (in total, roughly $500 billion in 2008). In this sense, the relationship between the superpowers bears some remarkable similarities to the interaction between the United States, Europe, and Japan—a mixture of economic rivalry and competition over global status, amid a generally nonviolent strategic backdrop—what Joseph Nye and Robert Keohane called "complex interdependence" (Keohane & Nye 2001).

THE BALANCE OF POWER TRIANGLE

As we mentioned, the balance of power theory assumes that major powers, in the pursuit of increased security and influence, will combine forces with other nations that share the same enemies. These alliances will shift frequently over time as different nations develop greater capacity to wage war and thereby become a new threat. Overall, no single country will rise above the rest, and every major power's essential identity will be preserved (or at least the basic number of major players will remain stable).

Does this pattern of behavior hold true in our case? First, we will discuss the nature of a three-way balance of power, usually referred to as tripolarity. Four alliance patterns are possible in a tripolar system, as illustrated in Figure 3.1: (1) a very

MÉNAGE À TROIS

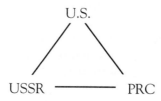

Example: Gorbachev Era

UNIT VETO

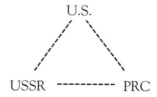

Example: 1962

MARRIAGE

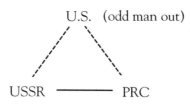

Example: 1950s

ROMANTIC TRIANGLE

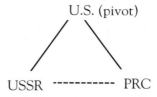

Example: 1972 (Nixon in China,
Nixon in Moscow)

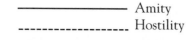

——————————— Amity
------------------ Hostility

Figure 3.1 The tripolar system's possible configurations
Source: Adapted from Lowell Dittmer, "The Strategic Triangle: A Critical Review." In J. Kim Ilpong, ed.,
The Strategic Triangle (New York: McGraw-Hill, 1987).

cordial "ménage à trois," in which all major powers cooperate with one another;
(2) the "unit veto" system, in which none of the players cooperates; (3) the interme-
diate stages of a "marriage," in which one player ("odd man out") is positioned
against the other two; and (4) the "romantic triangle," in which one player ("pivot")
has good relations with each of the others, which are antagonistic to each other
(Dittmer 1987).

Figure 3.1 also gives examples of the possible alliances in a tripolar system. The
"marriage" and "romantic triangle" arrangements have numerous examples and
deserve more attention. Segal and the contributors to his volume (1982) generally

credit China with best understanding the nature of the triangle and with taking the most active role in changing its nature over time. After all, it was China that attempted to mend fences with the Eisenhower administration and ultimately invited Nixon to Beijing. And it was China that severed relations with the Soviets against Moscow's wishes.

The United States demonstrated some diplomatic sophistication beginning in the mid-1960s, particularly during the Nixon administration, when it abandoned twenty years of ideological principles in favor of an improved strategic position by warming up to China and working with the Soviets (perhaps trusting them both too much). One can hardly imagine two more unlikely individuals to meet with Chinese leaders in Beijing than Richard Nixon and Ronald Reagan, both passionate Cold Warriors from the outset!

Under Gorbachev, the Soviet Union maneuvered itself into something close to a pivot position when it continued to work closely with the Chinese during the Tienanmen Square period as U.S.–Chinese relations cooled significantly. This move represented a departure for the Soviets, who tended to view the "China Factor" with some contempt—particularly in the presplit days when the Chinese were viewed as mere pupils.

CONCLUSION: STILL A TRIANGLE?

By the 1960s, all superpowers were clearly cognizant of the tripolar dynamics in which they were enmeshed and made some effort to jockey for the best position—namely, the pivot role. Barring diplomatic success, each player at least attempted to avoid being locked in the least desirable position—"odd man out." For example, one can attribute China's eagerness to open diplomatic relations with the United States in the late 1960s to Beijing's perception of significantly improved U.S.–Soviet relations and the fear of being "left out"—even if its actions resulted in giving extraordinary influence to the United States. Likewise, Gorbachev knew that combining his good relations with the United States with improved ties to China could ultimately put him in the pivot position, although this scenario never materialized.

Today, the relationship between the three is beginning to resemble a more normal, nonviolent rivalry, where the likelihood of war between any of the three is increasingly unlikely. This is not to say that military posturing is irrelevant. All three states are working to upgrade their strategic military capability. But overall, rivalry is expressed more in terms of trade, diplomatic status, regional influence, and so forth. Russia continues to reach out to its neighbors and resists the expansion of NATO, albeit in subdued ways. China, for its part, is beginning to form economic pacts with countries in the region (*New York Times*, November 30, 2004, A5). This said, neither is attempting to forge new military alliances or deploy troops overseas—although this describes the policy of the United States, which in recent years must be seen as the most aggressive and expansionist of the three.

QUESTIONS TO CONSIDER

1. What does the future hold for this great power triangle? With the demise of the Soviet Union and the end of East–West antagonism in the European theater, is China the ultimate "odd man out" from here on? Or will the United States now play that role as China and Russia strive to balance power?

2. To what extent were forces other than balancing power significant in determining alignment choices by the superpowers? Did ideology make a difference? What about perceptions?

3. To what extent were the needs of humanity served by the tripolar relationship? Were people on the planet safer? More free? Better fed? What does this tell us about politics and morality?

KEY FIGURES
SINO–SOVIET–AMERICAN RELATIONS

Josef Stalin   Soviet Communist Party leader, 1928–1953. He introduced collectivization and industrialization policies in tune with his view of socialism. Stalin allied with Nazi Germany at the beginning of World War II, then with the Allies after Hitler's attack on Russia in 1942. After the war, his actions in Eastern Europe and elsewhere contributed to the emergence of the Cold War.

Mao Zedong   Leader of the Chinese Communist Party and the Chinese Revolution in 1949. He led China from 1949 to 1976, taking it through various phases of development and crisis.

Harry Truman   U.S. President, 1945–1953. He presided over the outbreak of the Cold War. His "Truman Doctrine," defending pro-U.S. and democratic regimes with force, shaped U.S. policy toward the Soviet Union and China for many years.

Nikita Khrushchev   Leader of the Soviet Communist Party, 1953–1964. He undertook a number of economic and political reforms that liberalized life in Russia to some extent while also challenging the West.

John F. Kennedy   U.S. President, 1961–1963. He dealt with repeated Soviet challenges to U.S. power in Cuba, Berlin, Vietnam, and elsewhere. He helped inaugurate détente after the Cuban Missile Crisis.

Richard Nixon   U.S. President, 1969–1974. Although an ardent anti-Communist, as a member of the House of Representatives and Vice President, he adopted a pragmatic, strategic approach while in office. He is credited with consolidating détente and establishing relations with China.

Leonid Brezhnev   Soviet Communist Party leader, 1964–1982. He enjoyed a businesslike relationship with Richard Nixon, although the Soviet Union's relations with China soured during his rule.

(continued)

(*continued*)

Mikhail Gorbachev   Soviet Premier, 1985–1991. He undertook radical political and economic reforms that resulted in the introduction of a pro-Western democratic government in Moscow, the democratization of Eastern Europe, the end of the Cold War, and the collapse of the Soviet Union.

Deng Hsiao Ping   Leader of the People's Republic of China (PRC) beginning in 1976 with the death of Mao. While maintaining strong Communist Party control over China, he introduced market reforms that helped accelerate the country's development and opening to the rest of the world.

Jimmy Carter   U.S. President, 1977–1981. He formally recognized the PRC as the only government of China and signed the SALT II arms control treaty with the Soviet Union. The Soviet invasion of Afghanistan in 1979 prompted him to impose sanctions on Russia and increase U.S. military spending.

Henry Kissinger   Senior U.S. foreign policymaker under Presidents Nixon and Ford, serving as National Security Adviser and Secretary of State. His realist approach to international affairs guided a pragmatic, unsentimental U.S. foreign policy that improved relations with both the Soviet Union and China.

Ronald Reagan   U.S. President, 1981–1989. A well-known anti-Communist, Reagan imbued his first term with anti-Russian and anti-Chinese rhetoric, expanded the military, and eschewed arms control. During his second term, he presided over a more conciliatory approach that contributed to major arms control agreements with Moscow, the collapse of the Berlin Wall, and the end of the Cold War.

Hu Jintao   President of China beginning in 2002. He was elevated to the Politburo in 1993 by his mentor, Deng Hsiao Ping, presumably because he held reformist credentials, although this has not always been clear to observers.

CHRONOLOGY
SINO–SOVIET–AMERICAN RELATIONS

1945
At the close of the Second World War, Russia, the United States, and China are victorious allies.

1945–1947
The Soviet Union conspires with local Communists in Eastern Europe to install sympathetic regimes across the region.

1947
In response to threats from Communist rebels against pro-U.S. forces in Greece and Turkey, Harry Truman announces his plans to provide direct military and economic assistance. This new policy is dubbed the "Truman Doctrine."

1948
West Berlin is cut off from the rest of Germany by a road and rail blockade. Over 18 months, the United States supplies the city by air.

1949
The Soviet Union successfully tests an atomic bomb. Mao Zedong's People's Liberation Army takes power in Beijing as the Nationalist government begins its exile in Taiwan. NATO is formed. The Warsaw Pact is formed shortly thereafter.

1950
North Korea, with Soviet encouragement, invades South Korea in hopes of unifying the country under communism. China later joins the fight on the side of the North Koreans.

1953
The Korean War armistice ends the fighting without resolving the conflict.

1954
The PRC shells the Taiwanese islands of Quemoy and Matsu. The United States threatens nuclear retaliation. The incident is repeated in 1958.

1956
Soviet military forces invade Budapest and replace the West-leaning government of Hungary.

1959
Sputnik, the first human-made satellite, is launched by the Russians, prompting a decades-long "space race."

1961
The East German government erects a concrete wall around West Berlin to prevent East Germans from emigrating.

1962
Cuba allows the deployment of Russian nuclear weapons, prompting a U.S. blockade of the island. The weapons are withdrawn after tensions come close to the breaking point. Mao Zedong repudiates the Soviet version of socialism.

1963
A U.S.–Soviet "hotline" is installed to prevent lapses in communication during a crisis.

1964
The Tonkin Gulf Resolution inaugurates a period of significant U.S. military involvement in Southeast Asia. China tests an atomic bomb.

1968
The Soviet Union deploys troops to Prague to suppress reformist movements in Czechoslovakia.

1968–1969
China and Russia engage in sporadic border clashes.

(continued)

(*continued*)

1969
SALT I is signed by the United States and Russia, signaling the beginning of détente.

1971
Nixon visits China.

1979
The United States and Soviet Union sign SALT II. The United States formally recognizes the PRC. The Soviet Union invades Afghanistan.

1981
Ronald Reagan assumes office. He refers to the Soviet Union as an "evil empire" and begins a dramatic increase in military spending.

1983
Reagan unveils the military's Strategic Defense Initiative, dubbed "Star Wars" by the press.

1985
Mikhail Gorbachev becomes Chairman of the Communist Party of the Soviet Union and almost immediately begins a series of economic and political reforms at home and in Eastern Europe. Russia announces a unilateral moratorium on nuclear testing.

1987
The United States and Russia sign the Intermediate-Range Nuclear Forces Treaty, the first nuclear arms reduction treaty.

1989
Gorbachev signals to Eastern European governments that political reforms are acceptable. In rapid succession, after the dismantling of the Berlin Wall in November, each socialist government in Eastern Europe falls amid protests and street demonstrations. The Warsaw Pact is dissolved.

1990
A coup attempt in Moscow is thwarted by Russian President Boris Yeltsin, and Mikhail Gorbachev is reinstalled as his ally. They negotiate the dismantling of the Soviet Union into its fifteen republics. The Soviet flag is lowered on December 25, 1990.

1991
The United States and Soviet Union are allies in the Persian Gulf War.

2002
Russia joins NATO as a junior member.

2003
The United States and the United Kingdom invade Iraq. Russia, China, France, and Germany object, bringing these countries closer together.

REFERENCES

Allison, Graham. *Essence of Decision: Explaining the Cuban Missile Crisis*, 2nd ed. (New York: Addison Wesley Longman, 1999).

"At CSCE Summit, Yeltsin Warns of 'Cold Peace.'" *Current Digest of the Post-Soviet Press* 46 #49 (January 4, 1995): 8–9.

Camilleri, Joseph. *Chinese Foreign Policy: The Maoist Era and Its Aftermath* (Seattle: University of Washington Press, 1980).

Chai, Winberg. *The Foreign Relations of the People's Republic of China* (New York: Putnam's Sons, 1972).

China Daily. "WTO Performance called 'outstanding.'" New York, November 17, 2004, p. 11.

Dittmer, Lowell. "The Strategic Triangle: A Critical Review" in J. Kim Ilpong, ed., *The Strategic Triangle* (New York: MacGraw-Hill, 1987): 17–33.

"Eastern Cheers, Russian Jeers, American Silence." *Bulletin of the Atomic Scientists* (January/February 1997): 5–7.

Gaddis, John Lewis, and Terry L. Diebel, eds. *Containing the Soviet Union* (New York: Pergamon-Brassey's, 1987).

Higgins, Trumbull. *The Perfect Failure: Kennedy, Eisenhower and the CIA at the Bay of Pigs* (New York: Norton, 1987).

Keohane, Robert O., and Joseph Nye, Jr. *Power and Interdependence*, 3rd ed (New York: Longman, 2001).

Kissinger, Henry. *White House Years* (Boston: Little, Brown, 1979).

McCormick, James M., ed. *A Reader in American Foreign Policy* (Itasca, IL: Peacock, 1986).

Nathan, James A., and James K. Oliver. *United States Foreign Policy and World Order*, 4th ed. (Glenview, IL: Scott, Foresman, 1989).

New York Times, November 30, 2004, A5.

New York Times, December 6, 2004, special Business Day issue.

Rourke, John T. *Making Foreign Policy: United States, Soviet Union, China* (Pacific Grove, CA: Brooks/Cole, 1990).

Segal, Gerald, ed. *The China Factor: Peking and the Superpowers* (New York: Holmes & Meier, 1982).

Spanier, John. *American Foreign Policy Since World War II*, 11th ed. (Washington, DC: Congressional Quarterly Press, 1988).

Stoessinger, John G. *Nations in Darkness: China, Russia, and America*, 5th ed. (New York: McGraw-Hill, 1990).

Ulam, Adam B. *The Rivals: America and Russia Since World War II* (New York: Viking, 1971).

Waltz, Kenneth. *Theory of International Politics* (Reading, MA: Addison-Wesley, 1979).

Yahuda, Michael. "China and the Great Power Triangle." In Segal, ed., *The China Factor* 26–41.

4

■ ■ ■

The National
Interest: 9/11

INTRODUCTION

"National interest" is an incredibly elastic concept—capable of stretching to encompass any potential foreign threats for which an overzealous internationalist wants to prepare. It can also shrink to cover only life-threatening dangers on your doorstep. Because of the concept's malleability, we could easily dismiss it as a mere rhetorical flourish. Beneath the rhetoric, however, lies a fundamental question of what really matters in American foreign policy. Drawing the line between vital interests and peripheral preoccupations is the great question of our time.

Historically, national interest has come to include more and more issues. In the early days of the nation-state, it was possible to say that the national interest was nothing more than the monarch's interests: "I am the state," Louis XIV once declared to no one's objection. As states came to be based on popular sovereignty, however, the interests of the citizenry as a whole had to be taken into account. The happiness of the people—which included economic vitality, agricultural prosperity, a sense of confidence and security, and so forth—became the principal end of national policy. It even extended to the security of citizens living outside the territory of the state. Most powerful states have been quick to intervene—often militarily—when their citizens come under attack overseas (see Chapter 10). The most powerful ones even try to anticipate potential threats, taking steps to mitigate them in advance, perhaps by creating a "buffer zone" of friendly governments along the border or by moving troops overseas to facilitate quick deployment at great distances.

Americans have not always accepted the U.S. role as leader of the free world. Prior to the entry of the United States into World War I, for example, most opinion makers in the country agreed that the United States should remain aloof from European troubles. After the war, U.S. membership in the League of Nations and the establishment of a standing army were rejected by Congress. Meanwhile, the White

House and State Department had grown attached to American leadership and repeatedly advanced its necessity. At the heart of this debate was the question of whether American idealism—its quest for peace and justice—should push the country into a leadership role in world affairs (exporting idealism, as it were) or whether it should avoid all "entangling alliances" (to use George Washington's phrase). This debate was ultimately resolved with the Japanese attack on Pearl Harbor.

The period from 1947 to 1991, although dangerous, had the virtue of providing American policymakers with a relatively stable international system. It was easy to think of the world in terms of the Soviet bloc and the Western bloc, and the dominant issues involved preventing nuclear war. The debate was primarily between "doves" and "hawks" (See Chapter 12 on Vietnam). With the end of the Cold War and the attacks on September 11, 2001, this debate became far more complex. The various proposals fall into three general categories: the national interest approach, the "hegemonic imperative" school, and the "multilateralist" position.

The national interest position, often espoused by politicians seeking the votes of unemployed steel or textile workers, aims at defining national interest in narrow terms. As put by Charles Krauthammer, "[T]he internationalist consensus is under renewed assault. The assault this time comes not only from the usual pockets of post-Vietnam liberal isolationism (e.g., the churches) but from a resurgence of 1930s-style conservative isolationism" (Krauthammer 1990/1991, 23). Alan Tonelson argued that George H. W. Bush administration's attachment to Cold War activism was misguided, and it neglected the simple fact that U.S. power must be founded on a strong domestic society and economy. "The contrast between American victories in the Cold War and the Gulf War, and growing domestic social and economic decay shows that the traditional benchmarks for evaluating United States foreign policy are sorely inadequate" (Tonelson 1992, 145). William Pfaff argued that, as the world system becomes more complex and unpredictable, U.S. capability will be based as much on inner strength and resistance to instability abroad as on the ability to project power beyond the country's borders (Pfaff 1990/1991). Most national interest authors emphasize the need for the United States to withdraw from nonessential international obligations. They urge a renewed emphasis on programs that directly benefit the United States, although they do not dismiss all international activities. "An interest-based foreign policy would tend to rule out economic initiatives deemed necessary for the international system's health if those initiatives wound up siphoning more wealth out of this country than they brought in" (Tonelson 1991, 38).

Such analysts see no further need for U.S. involvement in the North Atlantic Treaty Organization given the dissolution of the Warsaw Pact, as well as U.S. maintenance of military bases across the world, and call for a large-scale withdrawal of troops. Furthermore, they question the merits of an overwhelming nuclear missile deterrent in the face of the collapse and democratization of the United States' principal nuclear adversary, the Soviet Union, and call for unilateral disarmament (Krasner 1989). After the gruesome deaths of U.S. marines in Somalia, Senator Jesse Helms of the Senate Foreign Relations Committee blocked U.S. participation in other United Nations (UN) missions (Sterling-Folker 1998, 287). Congressional leaders also blocked the payment of UN dues until the United States nearly lost its voting rights (Tessitore & Woolfson 1999, 300).

Some national interest advocates emphasize the need for reducing oil dependency and import dependency generally, whereas others focus on the need to control foreign investment flows into the country to preserve U.S. control of critical resources, industries, and even symbolic entities, such as Rockefeller Plaza and the Seattle Mariners. Protectionism, investment controls, export promotion, and maintenance of an undervalued currency are among the international economic policies consistent with this approach.

Analysts who accept the national interest approach emphasize the primacy of American sovereignty; however, liberals and conservatives disagree on what in America needs fixing. Liberal neoisolationists stress repairing urban decay, alleviating poverty, fighting racism, and rebuilding schools. Neoconservatives, in contrast, seek reductions in government regulations and handouts to the poor and a reversal of the decline of "family values." Conservatives dismiss liberal isolationism as merely a ploy "to spend the maximum amount of money on social programs at home and the minimum abroad" (Kristol 1990, 20).

Many feel that the United States is still, both by duty and by right, the leader of the free world. With the collapse of the Soviet Union, we no longer need to worry about an overwhelming threat to our security. But with that collapse go much of the order and stability of the international system and the risk of new, unforeseen dangers (Gaddis 1987; 1991). Many like-minded authors argue that the United States has the capability to lead and lacks only the will. Joseph Nye has argued that in terms of what we can afford as a nation, we are far too tight-fisted in dealing with global problems (Nye 1990). Richard Cooper argued before Congress that the United States must not shrink from global responsibilities for fear of what it will cost (U.S. Congress 1990). Former Secretary of State Alexander Haig echoed the sentiment, pointing out that it is up to the executive to promote a domestic consensus about the need for American leadership abroad and then to act on that consensus (Haig 1991).

There is a further sense from many authors that the United States has the right not only to lead but also to act unilaterally. Although they pay some lip service to multilateral institutions, they imply that the United States has the best ideas, the strongest institutions, and the natural gifts required to create world order. Charles Krauthammer pointed out: "American preeminence is based on the fact that it is the only country with the military, diplomatic, political and economic assets to be a decisive player in any conflict in whatever part of the world it chooses to involve itself" (Krauthammer 1990/1991, 24). Coupled with this assumption of preeminence comes a disdain for the cumbersome mechanisms of the UN and the assumption that the UN will never have effective enforcement powers. This tone has been criticized as "triumphalism."

In their exuberance, some have gone so far as to declare the end of international conflict. With the end of the Cold War, so the thinking goes, we are at the conclusion of the grand struggle between liberalism and authoritarianism—the "end of history" itself (Fukuyama 1989). Given this situation, we may find ourselves well and truly in an age without the threat of global war. Naturally, some have steered clear of such dramatic predictions and contented themselves with pointing out the unique nature of America's position in the world, with a call for continued leadership and international engagement (Huntington 1989).

The most extreme version of the presumption of American global leadership emerged in the 1980s from the Project for a New American Century led by William Kristol, a student of Leo Strauss. He was joined by Richard Perle, Paul Wolfowitz, Dick Cheney, and others who would feature prominently in the administration of George W. Bush (see below). Harking back to the words of Teddy Roosevelt, these writers emphasized the need for American "greatness." The United States should lead—not necessarily to make the country safer or the world better, but for the sake of leadership itself. As put by Anne Norton, "It is not threats that should incite war, but opportunity" (Norton 2004, 191). Rather than advocating cautious gradualism and prudence, this group called for quick, decisive blows that would establish American preeminence. It entails:

> . . . enthusiasm for innovation, for intervention, for utopias. Nothing can wait, everything must be done now. No one need be consulted, for local custom and established preferences must fall before the rational force of liberal (yes, liberal) values. Liberal values require not the consent of the governed, but the force of arms. (Norton 2004, 191)

We will see that this attitude has colored the Bush administration's bold initiatives in security affairs.

More subtle are the debates among would-be supporters of U.S. hegemony concerning the goals of U.S. leadership. On the one hand, some feel that U.S. internationalism should be firmly rooted in American idealism and that the nation should devote its energies to supporting and sustaining democracy and human rights. For example, candidate Bill Clinton argued for, among other things, sanctions against China for its repression of students in 1989; support for Somalis, Kurds, and Bosnians fighting against authoritarian enemies; and admission of Haitian refugees into the United States on humanitarian grounds (see also DLC 1991). On the other hand, many feel that the United States need not be a crusader. Its international engagement should be based on a sort of expanded self-interest, they argue. A stable world order is good for America because it minimizes surprises, allows for methodical planning, and usually results in economic prosperity. The object of U.S. foreign policy should be to discourage instability by supporting the status quo, particularly where existing regimes are already pro-United States. Krauthammer and others stress that the great enemy is no longer an organized opposition but rather disorder itself. They emphasize the need to contain this "chaotic sphere" in international relations by controlling the spread of weapons, intervening in civil wars before they spread, maintaining existing troop deployments in an effort to respond more rapidly to crises, and otherwise taking on the burden of enforcing international law—unilaterally if necessary (Krauthammer 1990/1991; Gaddis 1991). Nowhere in this discussion, however, is there any mention of U.S. compliance with international law if such compliance undermines U.S. interests.

Finally, an alterative form of internationalism, one that emphasized collaboration over leadership and unilateralism, emerged after the collapse of the Soviet Union.

So-called multilateralists are skeptical of the argument that the United States has either the capability or the prerogative to lead the world. Foremost among their concerns is the fact that the world is no longer bipolar and will never be unipolar. At best, the world is tripolar, with Germany, Japan, and the United States at three opposite poles (Tarnoff 1990). With the end of the Cold War, raw military might has become largely obsolete. We live in an age of economics. As pointed out by Fred Bergsten, "The central task in shaping a new American foreign policy is to set priorities and select central themes. Those choices must derive from America's national interests, which have shifted sharply in the direction of economics" (Bergsten 1992, 4).

The economic issue has led many to urge a collaborative U.S. policy based on close cooperation among the United States, Japan, and Europe (via Germany) (U.S. Congress 1990). The tripartite arrangement will go the farthest to promote open markets, liberal monetary policy, and free investment activities (Tarnoff 1990). Analysts emphasize the need to work through multilateral institutions, such as General Agreement on Tariffs and Trade (GATT) and the International Monetary Fund (IMF), and to create yet more stronger rules and enforcement mechanisms to preserve open markets (Aho & Stokes 1990/1991). They assume that a failure to continue expanding free trade will quickly lead to a rapid retreat into protectionism.

This urge to "go multilateral" stems not only from an acceptance of the U.S. decline into parity (or at least the rise of Europe and Japan), but also from a hope that security concerns will continue to remain back-burner issues in the future. Some have pointed out that democracies do not go to war with each other, concluding like the "endists" that the threat of global conflict is virtually over (Jervis 1992). War has become less likely because of the nature of states, and it has become less profitable and therefore less attractive to rational actors interested in maximizing gains over losses (Kaysen 1991). The implication of these developments is that we have reached a point when collective security may finally be a feasible method for dealing with all international conflict—a solution that would eliminate the need for American unilateralism. Russett and Sutterlin feel that now is the time to give the UN the authority and capability to intervene actively in conflict situations not only to "keep" the peace but also to "make" it. The success of the UN in the Persian Gulf War:

> . . . can enhance the United Nations' ability not just to restore the status quo as it existed prior to a breach of the peace, but also to change the parameters of the global order to something more favorable than existed under the prior status quo. In this it may even go beyond the vision of the U.N. founders. (Russett & Sutterlin 1991, 82)

In the Clinton administration, the Secretary of State Madeleine Albright and the Vice President Al Gore were noted for their enthusiasm for the multilateral approach. Their propensity to urge an assertive U.S. leadership role, including a military one, has been described as "assertive multilateralism" (Sterling-Folker 1998, 284). A draft presidential directive—PRD-13—called for a broader and more dynamic UN role, including a standing UN army and a willingness to place U.S. troops under UN command. Though no longer U.S. policy as early as 1994, this position was assailed by Republican critics and remained an issue into the 1996 presidential campaign.

SEPTEMBER 11 AND THE GREAT DEBATE

It was against this backdrop that the attacks on the World Trade Center occurred. We will now review the events immediately prior to and after that dreadful day to see to what extent the visions of the world shaped American policymakers' preparations and responses. We will see that the events galvanized the Bush administration's hegemonic imperative perspective and put those advocating the other two approaches on the defensive. (The account is excerpted from the 9/11 Commission Report.)

The Drumbeat Begins

In the spring of 2001, the level of reporting on terrorist threats and planned attacks increased dramatically to its highest level since the millennium alert. At the end of March, the intelligence community disseminated a terrorist threat advisory, indicating a heightened threat of Sunni extremist terrorist attacks against U.S. facilities, personnel, and other interests.

On March 23, in connection with discussions about possibly reopening Pennsylvania Avenue in front of the White House, Clarke warned National Security Advisor Condoleezza Rice that domestic or foreign terrorists might use a truck bomb—their "weapon of choice"—on Pennsylvania Avenue. That would result, he said, in the destruction of the West Wing and parts of the residence. He also told her that he thought there were terrorist cells within the United States, including al Qaeda.

In response to these threats, the FBI sent a message to all its field offices on April 13, summarizing reporting to date. It asked the offices to task all resources, including human sources and electronic databases, for any information pertaining to "current operational activities relating to Sunni extremism." It did not suggest that there was a domestic threat.

On April 20, a briefing to top officials reported "Bin Laden planning multiple operations." When the deputies discussed al Qaeda policy on April 30, they began with a briefing on the threat.

In May 2001, the drumbeat of reporting grew louder, with reports to top officials that "Bin Laden public profile may presage attack" and "Bin Laden network's plans advancing." In early May, a walk-in to the Federal Bureau of Investigation (FBI) claimed there was a plan to launch attacks on London, Boston, and New York. Attorney General John Ashcroft was briefed by the Central Intelligence Agency (CIA) on May 15 regarding al Qaeda generally and the current threat reporting specifically. The next day brought a report that a phone call to a U.S. embassy had warned that bin Laden supporters were planning an attack in the United States using "high explosives." On May 17, based on the previous day's report, the first item on the Counter-Intelligence Security Group's (CSG)'s agenda was "UBL: Operation Planned in U.S." The anonymous caller's tip could not be corroborated.

Late May brought reports of a possible hostage plot against Americans abroad to force the release of prisoners, including Sheikh Omar Abdel Rahman, the "Blind Sheikh," who was serving a life sentence for his role in the 1993 plot to blow up sites in New York City. The reporting noted that operatives might opt to hijack an aircraft or storm a U.S. embassy. This report led to a Federal Aviation Administration (FAA) information circular to airlines noting the potential for "an airline hijacking to free terrorists incarcerated in the United States." Other reporting mentioned that Abu Zubaydah was planning an attack, possibly against Israel, and expected to carry out several more if things went well. On May 24 alone, counterterrorism officials grappled with reports alleging plots in Yemen and Italy, as well as a report about a cell in Canada that an anonymous caller had claimed might be planning an attack against the United States.

Reports similar to many of these were made available to President Bush in morning intelligence briefings with Director of Central Intelligence (DCI) Tenet, usually attended by Vice President Dick Cheney and National Security Advisor Rice. Although these briefings discussed general threats to attack America and American interests, the specific threats mentioned in these briefings were all overseas.

On May 29, Clarke suggested that Rice ask DCI Tenet what more the United States could do to stop Abu Zubaydah from launching "a series of major terrorist attacks," probably on Israeli targets, but possibly on U.S. facilities. Clarke wrote to Rice and her deputy, Stephen Hadley, "When these attacks occur, as they likely will, we will wonder what more we could have done to stop them." In May, CIA Counterterrorist Center (CTC) Chief Cofer Black told Rice that the current threat level was a 7 on a scale of 1 to 10, as compared to an 8 during the millennium.

High Probability of Near-Term "Spectacular" Attacks

Threat reports surged in June and July, reaching an even higher peak of urgency. The summer threats seemed to be focused on Saudi Arabia, Israel, Bahrain, Kuwait, Yemen, and possibly Rome, but the danger could be anywhere—including a possible attack on the G-8 summit in Genoa. A June 12 CIA report passing along biographical background information on several terrorists mentioned, in commenting on Khalid Skeikh Mohammed, that he was recruiting people to travel to the United States to meet with colleagues already there so that they might conduct terrorist attacks on bin Laden's behalf. On June 22, the CIA notified all its station chiefs about intelligence suggesting a possible al Qaeda suicide attack on a U.S. target over the next few days. DCI Tenet asked that all U.S. ambassadors be briefed.

That same day, the State Department notified all embassies of the terrorist threat and updated its worldwide public warning. In June, the State Department initiated the Visa Express program in Saudi Arabia as a security measure in order to keep long lines of foreigners away from vulnerable embassy spaces. The program permitted visa applications to be made through travel agencies, instead of directly at the embassy or consulate.

A terrorist threat advisory distributed in late June indicated a high probability of near-term "spectacular" terrorist attacks resulting in numerous casualties. Other reports' titles warned, "Bin Laden Attacks May be Imminent" and "Bin Laden and Associates Making Near-Term Threats." The latter reported multiple attacks planned over the coming days, including a "severe blow" against U.S. and Israeli "interests" during the next two weeks.

On June 21, near the height of the threat reporting, U.S. Central Command raised the force protection condition level for troops in six countries to the highest possible level, Delta. The U.S. Fifth Fleet moved out of its port in Bahrain, and a U.S. Marine Corps exercise in Jordan was halted. U.S. embassies in the Persian Gulf conducted an emergency security review, and the embassy in Yemen was closed. The CSG had foreign response teams, known as FESTs, ready to move on four hours' notice and kept up the terrorism alert posture on a "rolling 24 hour basis."

On June 25, Clarke warned Rice and Hadley that six separate intelligence reports showed al Qaeda personnel warning of a pending attack. An Arabic television station reported bin Laden's pleasure with al Qaeda leaders who were saying that the next weeks "will witness important surprises" and that the U.S. and Israeli interests will be targeted. Al Qaeda also released a new recruitment and fund-raising tape. Clarke wrote that this was all too sophisticated to be merely a psychological operation to keep the United States on edge, and the CIA agreed. The intelligence reporting consistently described the upcoming attacks as occurring on a calamitous level, indicating that they would cause the world to be in turmoil and that they would consist of multiple—but not necessarily simultaneous—attacks.

On June 28, Clarke wrote to Rice that the pattern of al Qaeda activity indicating attack planning over the past six weeks "had reached a crescendo." "A series of new reports continue to convince me and analysts at State, CIA, DIA [Defense Intelligence Agency], and NSA that a major terrorist attack or series of attacks is likely in July," he noted. One al Qaeda intelligence report warned that something "very, very, very, very" big was about to happen, and most of bin Laden's network was reportedly anticipating the attack. In late June, the CIA ordered all of its station chiefs to share information on al Qaeda with their host governments and to push for immediate disruption of cells.

The headline of a June 30 brief to top officials was stark: "Bin Laden Planning High-Profile Attacks." The report stated that bin Laden operatives expected near-term attacks to have dramatic consequences of catastrophic proportions. That same day, Saudi Arabia declared its highest level of terror alert. Despite evidence of delays possibly caused by heightened U.S. security, the planning for attacks was continuing.

On July 2, the FBI Counterterrorism Division sent a message to federal agencies and state and local law enforcement agencies summarizing information regarding threats from bin Laden. It warned that there was an increased volume of threat reporting, indicating a potential for attacks against U.S. targets abroad from groups "aligned with or sympathetic to Osama bin Laden." Despite the general warnings, the message further stated, "The FBI has no information indicating a credible threat of terrorist attack in the United States." However, it went on to emphasize that the possibility of attack in the United States could not be discounted. It also noted that the July 4 holiday might heighten the threats. The report asked recipients to "exercise extreme vigilance" and "report suspicious activities" to the FBI. It did not suggest specific actions that they should take to prevent attacks.

Disruption operations against al Qaeda–affiliated cells were launched, involving twenty countries. Several terrorist operatives were detained by foreign governments, possibly disrupting operations in the Gulf and Italy and perhaps averting attacks against two or three U.S. embassies. Clarke and others told us of a particular concern about the possible attacks on the Fourth of July. After it passed uneventfully, the CSG decided to maintain the alert.

The CSG arranged for the CIA to brief intelligence and security officials from several domestic agencies. On July 5, representatives from the Immigration and Naturalization Service (INS), the FAA, the Coast Guard, the Secret Service, Customs, the CIA, and the FBI met with Clarke to discuss the current threat. Attendees report that they were told not to disseminate the threat information they received at the meeting. They interpreted this direction to mean that although they could brief their superiors, they could not send out advisories to the field. A National Security Council (NSC) official recalls a somewhat different emphasis, saying that attendees were asked to take the information back to their home agencies and "do what you can" with it, subject to classification and distribution restrictions. A representative from the INS asked for a summary of the information that she could share with field offices. She never received one.

That same day, the CIA briefed Attorney General Ashcroft on the al Qaeda threat, warning that a significant terrorist attack was imminent. Ashcroft was told that preparations for multiple attacks were in late stages or already complete and that little additional warning could be expected. The briefing addressed only threats outside the United States.

The next day, the CIA representative told the CSG that al Qaeda members believed the upcoming attack would be "spectacular," qualitatively different from anything they had done to date.

Apparently as a result of the July 5 meeting with Clarke, the interagency committee on federal building security was tasked to examine security measures. This committee met on July 9, when thirty-seven officials from twenty-seven agencies and organizations were briefed on the "current threat level" in the United States. They were told that not only the threat reports from abroad but also the recent convictions in the East Africa bombings trial, the conviction of Ahmed Ressam, and the just-returned Khobar Towers indictments reinforced the need to "exercise extreme vigilance." Attendees were expected to determine whether their respective agencies needed enhanced security measures.

In mid-July, reporting started to indicate that bin Laden's plans had been delayed, maybe for as long as two months, but not abandoned. On July 23, the lead item for CSG discussion was still the al Qaeda threat, and it included a mention of suspected terrorist travel to the United States.

On July 31, an FAA circular appeared alerting the aviation community to "reports of possible near-term terrorist operations . . . particularly on the Arabian Peninsula and/or Israel." It stated that the FAA had no credible evidence of specific plans to attack U.S. civil aviation, though it noted that some of the "currently active" terrorist groups were known to "plan and train for hijackings" and were able to build and conceal sophisticated explosive devices in luggage and consumer products.

Tenet told us that in his world "the system was blinking red." By late July, Tenet said, it could not "get any worse." Not everyone was convinced. Some asked whether all these threats might just be deception. On June 30, the SEIB contained an article titled "Bin Laden Threats Are Real." Yet Hadley told Tenet in July that bin Laden was trying to study U.S. reactions. Tenet replied that he had already addressed the Defense Department's questions on this point; the reporting was convincing. To give a sense of his anxiety at the time, one senior official in the Counterterrorist Center told (administration officials) that he and a colleague were considering resigning in order to go public with their concern.

Government Response to the Threats—pp. 263–265

National Security Advisor Rice told us that the CSG was the "nerve center" for running the crisis, although other senior officials were involved over the course of the summer. In addition to his daily meetings with President Bush, and weekly meetings to go over other issues with Rice, Tenet was speaking regularly with Secretary of State Colin Powell and Secretary of Defense Donald Rumsfeld. The foreign policy principals routinely talked on the telephone every day on a variety of topics.

Hadley told (administration officials) that before 9/11, he and Rice did not feel they had the job of coordinating domestic agencies. They felt that Clarke and the CSG (part of the NSC) were the NSC's bridge between foreign and domestic threats.

There was a clear disparity in the levels of response to foreign versus domestic threats. Numerous actions were taken overseas to disrupt possible attacks—enlisting foreign partners to upset terrorist plans, closing embassies, moving military assets out of the way of possible harm. Far less was done domestically—in part, surely, because to the extent that specifics did exist, they pertained to threats overseas. As noted earlier, a threat against the embassy in Yemen quickly resulted in its closing. Possible domestic threats were more vague. When reports did not specify where the attacks were to take place, officials presumed that they would again be overseas, though they did not rule out a target in the United States. Each of the FBI threat advisories made this point.

Clarke mentioned to National Security Advisor Rice at least twice that al Qaeda sleeper cells were likely in the United States. In January 2001, Clarke forwarded a strategy paper to Rice warning that al Qaeda had a presence in the United States. He noted that two key al Qaeda members in the Jordanian cell involved in the millennium plot were naturalized U.S. citizens and that one jihadist suspected in the East Africa bombings had "informed the FBI that an extensive network of al Qaeda 'sleeper agents' currently exists in the US." He added that Ressam's abortive December 1999 attack revealed al Qaeda supporters in the United States. His analysis, however, was based not on new threat reporting but on past experience.

The September 11 attacks fell into the void between the foreign and domestic threats. The foreign intelligence agencies were watching overseas, alert to foreign threats to U.S. interests there. The domestic agencies were waiting for evidence of a domestic threat from sleeper cells within the United States. No one was looking for a foreign threat to domestic targets. The threat that was coming was not from sleeper cells. It was foreign—but from foreigners who had infiltrated into the United States.

A second cause of this disparity in response is that domestic agencies did not know what to do, and no one gave them direction. Cressy told us that the CSG did not tell the agencies how to respond to the threats. He noted that the agencies that were operating overseas did not need direction on how to respond; they had experience with such threats and had a "playbook." In contrast, the domestic agencies did not have a game plan. Neither the NSC (including the CSG) nor anyone else instructed them to create one.

This lack of direction was evident in the July 5 meeting with representatives from the domestic agencies. The briefing focused on overseas threats. The domestic agencies were not questioned about how they planned to address the threat and were not told what was expected of them. Indeed, as noted earlier, they were specifically told that they could not issue advisories based on the briefing. The domestic agencies' limited response indicates that they did not perceive a call to action.

Clarke reflected a different perspective in an e-mail to Rice on September 15, 2001. He summarized the steps taken by the CSG to alert domestic agencies to the possibility of an attack in the United States. Clarke concluded that domestic agencies, including the FAA, knew that the CSG believed a major al Qaeda attack was coming and could be in the United States.

Although the FAA had authority to issue security directives mandating new security procedures, none of the few that were released during the summer of 2001 increased security at checkpoints or onboard aircraft. The presentation mentioned the possibility of suicide hijackings but said that "fortunately, we have no indication that any group is currently thinking in that direction." The FAA conducted twenty-seven special security briefings for specific air carriers between May 1 and September 11, 2001. Two of these briefings discussed the hijacking threat overseas. None discussed the possibility of suicide hijackings or the use of aircraft as weapons. No new security measures were instituted.

Rice told us she understood that the FBI had tasked its fifty-six U.S. field offices to increase surveillance of suspected terrorist plots. An NSC staff document at the time describes such a tasking as having occurred in late June, but does not indicate whether it was generated by the NSC or the FBI. Other than the previously described April 13 communication sent to all FBI field offices, however, the FBI could not find any record of having received such a directive. The document asking field offices to gather information on Sunni extremism did not mention any possible threat within the United States and what the FBI's directives should contain and did not review what had been issued earlier.

Acting FBI Director Pickard told us that in addition to his July 19 conference call, he mentioned the heightened terrorist threat to individual calls with the special agents in charge of field offices during their annual performance review discussions. In speaking with agents around the country, we found little evidence that any such concerns had reached FBI personnel beyond the New York Field Office.

The head of counterterrorism at the FBI, Dale Watson, said he had many discussions about possible attacks with Cofer Black at the CIA. They had expected an attack on July 4. Watson said he felt deeply that something was going to happen. But he told us the threat information was "nebulous." He wished he had known more. He wished he had had "500 analysts looking at Osama bin Laden threat information instead of two."

Attorney General Ashcroft was briefed by the CIA in May and by Pickard in early July about the danger. Pickard said he met with Ashcroft once a week in late

June, through July, and twice in August. There is a dispute regarding Ashcroft's interest in Pickard's briefings about the terrorist threat situation. Pickard told us that after two such briefings, Ashcroft told him he did not want to hear about the threats anymore. Ashcroft denies Pickard's charge. Pickard says he continued to present terrorism information during further briefings that summer, but nothing further on the "chatter" the U.S. government was receiving.

The attorney general told us that he asked Pickard whether there was intelligence about attacks in the United States and that Pickard said no. Pickard said he replied that he could not assure Ashcroft that there would be no attacks in the United States, although the reports of threats were related to overseas targets. Ashcroft said that he therefore assumed the FBI was doing what it needed to do. He acknowledged that, in retrospect, this was a dangerous assumption. He did not ask the FBI what it was doing in response to the threats and did not task it to take any specific action. He also did not direct the INS, then still part of the Department of Justice, to take any specific action.

In sum, the domestic agencies never mobilized in response to the threat. They did not have direction and did not have a plan to institute. The borders were not hardened. Transportation systems were not fortified. Electronic surveillance was not targeted against a domestic threat. State and local law enforcement were not marshaled to augment the FBI's efforts. The public was not warned.

Phoenix Memo—pp. 272–277

In July 2001, an FBI agent in the Phoenix field office sent a memo to the FBI headquarters and to two agents on international terrorism squads in the New York Field Office, advising of the "possibility of a coordinated effort by Osama bin Laden" to send students to the United States to attend civil aviation schools. The agent based his theory on the "inordinate number of individuals of investigative interest" attending such schools in Arizona.

The agent made four recommendations to FBI headquarters: compile a list of civil aviation schools, establish liaison with those schools, discuss his theories about bin Laden with the intelligence community, and seek authority to obtain visa information on persons applying to flight schools. His recommendations were not acted on. His memo was forwarded to one field office. Managers of the Osama bin Laden unit and the Radical Fundamentalist unit at FBI headquarters were addressees, but they did not even see the memo until after September 11. No managers at the headquarters saw the memo before September 11, and the New York Field Office took no action.

Zacarias Moussaoui

On August 15, 2001, the Minneapolis FBI Field Office initiated an intelligence investigation on Zacarias Moussaoui. He had entered the United States in February 2001 and had begun flight lessons at Airman Flight School in Norman, Oklahoma. He resumed his training at the Pan Am International Flight Academy in Eagan, Minnesota, starting on August 13. He had none of the usual qualifications for flight training on Pan Am's Boeing 747 flight simulators. He said he did not intend to become a commercial pilot but wanted the training as an "ego boosting thing." Moussaoui stood out because, with little knowledge of flying, he wanted to learn how to "take off and land" a Boeing 747.

The agent in Minneapolis quickly learned that Moussaoui possessed jihadist beliefs. Moreover, Moussaoui had $32,000 in a bank account but did not provide a plausible explanation for this sum of money. He had traveled to Pakistan but became agitated when asked if he had traveled to nearby countries while in Pakistan (Pakistan was the customary route to the training camps in Afghanistan). He planned to receive martial arts training and intended to purchase a global positioning receiver. The agent also noted that Moussaoui became extremely agitated whenever he was questioned regarding his religious beliefs. The agent concluded that Moussaoui was "an Islamic extremist preparing for some future act in furtherance of radical fundamentalist goals." He also believed that Moussaoui's plan was related to his flight training.

There was substantial disagreement between Minneapolis agents and the FBI headquarters regarding what Moussaoui was planning to do. In one conversation between a Minneapolis supervisor and a headquarters agent, the latter complained that Minneapolis's Foreign Intelligence Surveillance Act (FISA) request was couched in a manner intended to get people "spun up." The supervisor replied that was precisely his intent. He said he was "trying to keep someone from taking a plane and crashing into the World Trade Center." The headquarters agent replied that this was not going to happen and that they did not know whether Moussaoui was a terrorist.

There is no evidence that either FBI Acting Director Pickard or Assistant Director for Counterterrorism Dale Watson was briefed on the Moussaoui case prior to 9/11. Michael Rolince, the FBI assistant director heading the Bureau's International Terrorism Operations Section (ITOS), recalled being told about Moussaoui in two passing hallway conversations, but only in the context that he might be receiving telephone calls from Minneapolis complaining about how headquarters was handling the matter. He never received such a call. Although the acting special agent in charge of Minneapolis called the ITOS supervisors to discuss the Moussaoui case on August 27, he declined to go up the chain of command at FBI headquarters and call Rolince.

On August 23, DCI Tenet was briefed about the Moussaoui case in a briefing titled "Islamic Extremist Learns to Fly." Tenet was also told that Moussaoui wanted to learn to fly a 747, paid for his training in cash, was interested to learn the doors do not open in flight, and wanted to fly a simulated flight from London to New York. He was told that the FBI had arrested Moussaoui because of a visa overstay and that the CIA was working on the case with the FBI. Tenet told us that no connection to al Qaeda was apparent to him at the time. Seeing it as an FBI case, he did not discuss the matter with anyone at the White House or the FBI. No connection was made between Moussaoui's presence in the United States and the threat reporting during the summer of 2001.

[It is worth noting that Moussaoui was charged with conspiracy to commit terrorism, use weapons of mass destruction, and aircraft piracy, among other things. He was the only individual to be tried in the United States in connection with the events of 9/11. After lengthy delays over evidence, the formal trial took place in early 2006, resulting in a conviction and a life sentence without parole. Throughout the trial he behaved erratically—confessing and then retracting his confession, for example—and refused to cooperate with court-appointed counsel. Ultimately, the jury decided that his decision to withhold key information from authorities contributed to the success of the 9/11 attacks. At the same time, they generally believed that he was not a central figure and therefore did not deserve to be executed (*New York Times*, May 4, 2006, A1, A28).]

Time Runs Out

As Tenet told us, "the system was blinking red" during the summer of 2001. Officials were alerted across the world. Many were doing everything they possibly could to respond to the threats.

Yet no one working on these late leads in the summer of 2001 connected the case in his or her inbox to the threat reports agitating senior officials and being briefed to the President. Thus these individual cases did not become national priorities. As the CIA supervisor "John" told us, no one looked at the bigger picture; no analytic work foresaw the lightning that could connect the thundercloud to the ground.

On September 11, four aircrafts were hijacked. Two were flown into the World Trade Center towers, resulting in their collapse and the deaths of nearly 3,000 individuals. Another was flown into the Pentagon, killing hundreds, and the fourth was forced into the ground in rural Pennsylvania when the passengers revolted.

CONCLUSION: AFTERMATH AND DEBATE

The disasters that took place on September 11, 2001, prompted a strong and virtually unanimous response from policymakers and legislators on both sides of the aisle. The war against terror became the new, defining focus of U.S. foreign policy, playing much the same role as anticommunism during the Cold War (*Chicago Tribune*, September 6, 2002). The United States was determined to lead the fight, without direction from the rest of the world (although U.S. officials were careful to obtain UN approval first). Operation Enduring Freedom in Afghanistan was very much an American operation, as was the establishment of the Karzai government after the defeat of the Taliban.

The George W. Bush administration began to formulate what has been dubbed the "Bush Doctrine." Simply put, it means that, particularly where terrorist threats are concerned, the United States should not wait until the attacks occur to retaliate, but rather seek out plotters and strike preemptively. This philosophy underpins the decision to attack Iraq in advance of its attacking U.S. interests directly. Presumably, this action would be taken not by seeking international approval through the UN, but as part of America's role as global hegemon. As put by the Director of Policy Planning in the State Department, Richard Haass:

> We're not looking to turn international relations in 2002 into the Wild West. We understand that restraint and rules still need to be the norm. But there may well be a place for exceptions. You have to ask yourself whether rules and norms which have grown up over hundreds of years in one context are adequate to changing circumstances. (*Chicago Tribune*, September 4, 2002)

Prior to the September 11, 2001, terror attacks, senior members of the Bush administration had called for a more "muscular" foreign policy involving preemptive strikes against America's threats. Paul Wolfowitz, while serving in the first Bush administration, spearheaded the drafting of the Defense Planning Guidance, calling for preemptive strikes against potential enemies as opposed to the mere containment of threats. He was joined by Richard Perle and other "Vulcans" who favored an activist role for the United States in reshaping the world. As explained by Daalder and Lindsay:

> This group argued that the United States should actively deploy its overwhelming military, economic, and political might to remake the world in its image—and that doing so would serve the interests of other countries as well as the United States. They were less worried about the dangers of nation-building and more willing to commit the nation's resources not just to toppling tyrants, but also to creating democracies in their wake. (Daalder & Lindsay 2003, 47)

In September 2002, President Bush released the annual National Security Strategy. In it, he promoted a vision of American leadership that is expansive and dramatic. In order to reshape the balance of power in the world so as to "favor human freedom," the United States must be willing to confront those who would acquire weapons of mass destruction for radical purposes. "[A]s a matter of common sense and self-defense, America will act against such emerging threats before they are fully formed. . . . [W]e will not hesitate to act alone, if necessary, to exercise our right of self-defense by acting preemptively" (Daalder & Lindsay 2003, 123). As he put it more directly in a speech to the West Point graduating class in June 2002, "[W]e must take the battle to the enemy, and confront the worst threats before they emerge. In the world we have entered, the only path to safety is the path of action" (Prestowitz 2003, 22).

The strategy has broad support in American society, which helps explain why the invasion of Iraq was very popular. Even with the failure to find the weapons of mass destruction (a key rationale for the invasion) and the difficulties in suppressing the insurrection, public support was strong through 2003 and was still evenly split through 2006.

It was not until the summer of 2002, when Bush administration officials leaked plans to invade Iraq and replace Saddam Hussein, that some voices of dissent and concern were raised. Perhaps most troubling to Bush was the opposition of loyal Republicans who served in the Senate and had previously supported his father. James Baker opined that a military strike, although well intentioned, was ill advised without a UN resolution to back it up (Baker 2002). Senior Democrats have gone on record against the proposal. Even after the war's successful outcome in April 2003, some questions arose regarding whether ignoring international law was necessary.

Thus a new debate has begun, focused on the limits of the Bush Doctrine of unilateral, preemptive strikes. It seems to be having some effect, as in September 2002, the White House indicated some willingness to consider a debate in Congress and at the UN prior to launching an attack. It may be useful to dust off the pages of the Great Debates of the past as the United States attempts to find its way through a post–September 11 world.

The invasion of Iraq, discussed in detail in Chapter 8, provides a laboratory to test the validity of these various approaches. National interest advocates were split on the issue, since they disagreed on whether Iraq posed a clear and present danger to the U.S. homeland. Once it was clear that there were no stockpiles of weapons of mass destruction, they concluded that the effort was a waste of precious resources that would have been better spent protecting U.S. territory and moving against al Qaeda targets. Needless to say, advocates of the hegemonic imperative were the authors of the policy, although some have been surprised at how difficult the operation has proved to be. Troop levels and budget expenditures have been far higher than anticipated. The insurgents, once dismissed as "dead-enders" by the Secretary of Defense Donald Rumsfeld, have become the focus of concerted military operations. And multilateralists are resisting the urge to say "I told you so." Secretary of State Colin Powell, an unlikely multilateralist, resigned his position with few regrets, other than his inability to stop Vice President Dick Cheney and the other "Vulcans" from their ill-advised purposes (Woodward 2004, 129).

QUESTIONS TO CONSIDER

1. What is the relationship between world events and foreign policy theories? To what extent do the former shape the latter?

2. How were the various theories expressed by the two presidential candidates? Where does Barack Obama fall? And John McCain?

3. How can you judge which approach is best? Is it primarily a matter of unquestioned values, or should the effectiveness of the approach be a factor?

KEY FIGURES
9/11

George H.W. Bush   U.S. President, 1989–1993. He involved the UN in U.S. policy more deeply than had past U.S. Presidents.

Bill Clinton   U.S. President, 1993–2001. He maintained the multilateralist policies of George Bush.

James Baker III   U.S. Secretary of State, 1989–1993. He cautioned George W. Bush against a unilateral, preemptive strike against Iraq.

George W. Bush   U.S. President, 2001–2009. He generally promoted a unilateralist approach.

Colin Powell   U.S. Secretary of State, 2001–2005. He warned George W. Bush of the risks involved in unilateral military operations.

Donald Rumsfeld   U.S. Secretary of Defense, 2001–2006. He promoted and directed the Iraq invasion.

(continued)

(continued)

Paul Wolfowitz U.S. Deputy Secretary of Defense, 2001–2005. He helped author the Defense Planning Guidance in 1992 under the first President Bush, calling for preemptive strikes against potential enemies, as opposed to mere containment of threats.

Richard (Dick) Cheney U.S. Vice President, 2001–2009. He consistently advocated preemptive strikes.

Charles Krauthammer Syndicated columnist. He is known as a supporter of the "hegemonic imperative."

Ross Perot Businessman, frequent presidential candidate, and supporter of the "national interest" approach.

Patrick Buchanan Journalist, frequent presidential candidate, and supporter of the "national interest" approach.

Jesse Helms U.S. Senator from North Carolina, 1972–2003, and Chairman of the Senate Foreign Relations Committee. He often opposed multilateralism.

George Tenet Director of Central Intelligence, 1997–2004.

Osama bin Laden Leader of the al Qaeda terror network.

John Ashcroft Attorney General, 2001–2005.

Richard Clarke National Security Council (NSC) counterterrorism coordinator, 1997–2001.

Stephen Hadley Deputy National Security Advisor, 2001–2005.

Condoleezza Rice National Security Advisor, 2001–2005.

Zacarias Moussaoui Frenchman convicted in connection with the 9/11 plot.

Colin Powell Secretary of State, 2001–2005.

Abu Zubaydah Alias for Zein al Abideen Mohaned Hussein—Palestinian al Qaeda operative.

Mohammed Atta Egyptian who led the 9/11 plot; he hijacked American Airlines flight 11.

Thomas Pickard Acting FBI Director, June 25–September 4, 2001.

CHRONOLOGY
9/11

1989
November   The Berlin Wall falls.

1991
December   The Soviet Union is dismembered.

2001
April 20   Richard Clarke gives a briefing to top officials, reporting that "Bin Laden [is] planning multiple operations."

June 30   Multiple sources indicate that bin Laden is planning a "spectacular" attack, although most indications point to overseas targets.

July   The "Phoenix memo" is transmitted to FBI headquarters warning of Middle Eastern men taking flight training.

August 23   The CIA is briefed on the case of Zacarias Moussaoui, who has been taking flight training in Minnesota.

September 11, 2001

6:00am   Mohammed Atta and Abdul Aziz al Omari begin the attack by boarding a flight from Portland, Maine, to Boston, Massachusetts.

7:40am   All the hijackers have made their way on board American Airlines flight 11 in Boston. Others are boarding United Airlines flights 175 and 93 and American Airlines flight 77 in Boston, Newark, and Dulles, respectively.

8:14am   American flight 11 is hijacked. By 9:28, all four flights will have been hijacked by the al Qaeda terrorists.

8:25am   The FAA first learns of the hijacking of American flight 11. It alerts the military at 8:38 and jets are scrambled by 8:46.

8:46:40am   AA11 strikes the north tower of the World Trade Center. It will be followed at 9:03:11 by flight UA175 striking the south tower.

8:54am   AA77 is hijacked and flown toward the Pentagon, which it will strike at 9:37:46.

9:25am   The FAA center at Dulles International Airport orders a nationwide ground stop.

9:57am   Roughly 30 minutes after it is hijacked, the passengers on board UA93 revolt. The plane crashes in a wood near Shanksville, Pennsylvania, at 10:03:11.

REFERENCES

Aho, Michael, and Bruce Stokes. "The Year the World Economy Turned." *Foreign Affairs* 70 #1 (1990/1991): 160–178.

Baker, James. "The Right Way to Change a Regime." *New York Times*, August 25, 2002.

Bergsten, Fred. "The Primacy of Economics." *Foreign Policy* 87 (Summer 1992): 3–24.

Chicago Tribune, September 4, 2002.

Chicago Tribune, September 6, 2002.

Daalder, Ivo, and James Lindsay. *America Unbound: The Bush Revolution in Foreign Policy* (Washington, D.C.: Brookings Institution Press, 2003).

Democratic Leadership Council (DLC). *The New American Choice: Opportunity, Responsibility, Community.* Resolutions Adopted at the DLC Convention, Cleveland, Ohio, 1991.

Fukuyama, Francis. "The End of History?" *National Interest* 16 (Summer 1989): 3–18.

Gaddis, John Lewis. *The Long Peace: Inquiries into the History of the Cold War* (New York: Oxford University Press, 1987).

Gaddis, John Lewis. "Toward the Post–Cold War World." *Foreign Affairs* 70 #2 (Spring 1991): 102–122.

Haig, Alexander. "The Challenges to American Leadership." In Schmergel, Greg, ed., *U.S. Foreign Policy in the 1990s* (New York: Palgrave, 1991): 34–46.

Huntington, Samuel. "No Exit: The Errors of Endism." *National Interest* 17 (Fall 1989): 3–11.

Jervis, Robert. "The Future of World Politics: Will It Resemble the Past?" In Sean Lynn-Jones and Steven E. Miller, eds., *America's Strategy in a Changing World* (Cambridge: MIT Press, 1992): 3–37.

Kaysen, Carl. "Is War Obsolete? A Review Essay." In Sean Lynn-Jones and Steven E. Miller, eds., *The Cold War and After: Prospects for Peace* (Cambridge: MIT Press, 1991): 81–103.

Krasner, Stephen. "Realist Praxis: Neo-isolationism and Structural Change." *Journal of International Affairs* 43 #1 (1989): 143–160.

Krauthammer, Charles. "The Unipolar Moment." *Foreign Affairs* 70 #1 (1990/1991): 23–33.

Kristol, Irving. "Defining Our National Interest." *National Interest* (Fall 1990): 16–25.

Norton, Anne. *Leo Strauss and the Politics of American Empire* (New Haven: Yale University Press, 2004).

Nye, Joseph. *Bound to Lead: The Changing Nature of American Power* (New York: Basic Books, 1990).

Pfaff, William. "Redefining World Power." *Foreign Affairs* 70 #1 (1990/1991): 34–48.

Prestowitz, Clyde. *Rogue Nation: American Unilateralism and the Failure of Good Intentions* (New York: Basic Books, 2003).

Russett, Bruce, and James Sutterlin. "The U.N. in a New World Order." *Foreign Affairs* 70 #2 (Spring 1991): 69–83.

Sterling-Folker, Jennifer. "Between a Rock and a Hard Place: Assertive Multilateralism and Post–Cold War U.S. Foreign Policy Making." In James Scott, ed., *After the End: Making U.S. Foreign Policy in the Post–Cold War World* (Durham, NC: Duke University Press, 1998): 277–304.

Tarnoff, Peter. "America's New Special Relationships." *Foreign Affairs* 69 #3 (Summer 1990): 67–80.

Tessitore, John, and Susan Woolfson, eds. *A Global Agenda: Issues Before the 54th General Assembly of the United Nations* (Lanham, MD: Rowman and Littlefield, 1999).

Tonelson, Alan. "Prudence or Inertia? The Bush Administration's Foreign Policy." *Current History* 91 #564 (April 1992): 145–150.

Tonelson, Alan. "What Is the National Interest?" *The Atlantic Monthly* (July 1991): 35–52.

U.S. Congress, House. *U.S. Power in a Changing World.* Special Report 28-802 prepared for the Committee on Foreign Affairs, 101st Congress, 2nd Session, 1990.

Woodward, Robert. *Plan of Attack* (New York: Simon & Schuster, 2004).

5

■ ■ ■

Rationality: The Cuban Missile Crisis

INTRODUCTION

When making a decision, we typically know in advance what we want. We consider the facts at hand, come up with a few alternative courses of action, imagine what might happen if we pick each one, and then choose the alternative that gets us what we wanted in the first place. This is the epitome of what is meant by rationality. Any other method is not purely rational, although the result is not necessarily wrong or bad. We sometimes make choices based on habit or tradition, or we feel driven by our emotions. Our analysis of the situation and consideration of alternatives may be cursory. Anyone who has ever worked on a committee knows that groups rarely make decisions based on a careful calculation of costs and benefits—they typically go for the least common denominator. And this tells us nothing about putting the decision into practice.

Scholars have learned that if they assume rationality on the part of the people they study, it is possible to predict how different decision makers will address similar situations, which in turn allows us to anticipate numerous events. The field of game theory attempts to explain how rational actors interact with one another. When an actor faces a decision the outcome of which depends on what another actor decides, it is often possible to design a matrix that shows the range of outcomes. You can select the alternative that each actor will choose based on these outcomes and the goals each actor brings. For example, where two players face the option of cooperating or not cooperating, but where cooperating opens up the possibility of losing something of considerable value, one can predict that the actors will likely shun that option (this helps to explain everything from an international arms race to marital infidelity).

With respect to the Cuban Missile Crisis, we see two sets of actors. On the one hand, we have the "game" of superpower relations, where each country plays a game of "chicken" with the other. On the other hand, we have the interactions between domestic decision makers within each country (presidents, advisors, generals, and so forth). As we explore the story of the Cuban Missile Crisis, consider whether the various players are behaving "rationally"—that is, identifying goals, exploring options, selecting the "best" option, and seeing it fully implemented.

RATIONALITY AND THE CUBAN MISSILE CRISIS

Almost as soon as it was resolved, the October 1962 Cuban Missile Crisis became the object of scholarly attention. It was one moment, suspended in time, when the earth's survival hung in the balance. President John F. Kennedy himself is reported to have estimated that the chances of a nuclear war were "between one out of three and even" (Allison 1999, 1). Fidel Castro felt the odds were twenty to one that a U.S. invasion of Cuba was virtually inevitable, and he urged Nikita Khrushchev to launch a full-scale nuclear strike in retaliation. Given the extreme danger and risk of the situation on the one hand and its successful conclusion on the other hand, this episode in world history has become a popular case study of conflict management and crisis decision making. Because of the ease of hearing from actual participants in the crisis, particularly since the end of the Cold War, and the voluminous documentary evidence available to scholars (including secret tapes of White House meetings), analysts have considerable details to study.

We will focus on what the Cuban Missile Crisis teaches us about how policy is developed and implemented in a crisis. A crisis, as defined by Charles Hermann (1969), is a problem that combines the elements of surprise, salience, and urgency. In other words, the problem erupts with little warning, directly threatens a high-priority value, and must be resolved quickly to avoid negative consequences. From another point of view, a crisis is "coercive diplomacy" used by an adversary to blackmail or intimidate a nation into submission without the direct use of force (Craig & George 1990). Avoidance of bloodshed is the primary concern in such situations, even though the risk of war is usually extremely high.

Hermann assumes that in a crisis situation, decisions are made at the top levels in a bewildering "pressure cooker" environment. Issues of lesser importance are set aside, all energy is put into gathering facts and alternatives, and stress levels are high. Conditions are ideal for intensive and creative problem solving as the combined energy and talent of some of the most able men and women in the country are brought to bear on a single issue. Of course, the reverse can also happen when decisions based on few facts must be made quickly by people with a great deal to lose. The actual outcomes depend on many factors, including the personalities, perceptions, and decision-making styles of the key participants, the degree of contingency planning that preceded the crisis, and the organization of the decision-making unit itself. To the extent that information is made available, options and objectives are clearly and creatively articulated, and the implications of various choices are thoroughly understood, the likelihood of a sound decision increases.

Before determining whether the decisions made during the Cuban Missile Crisis meet our ideal standard, we will review the history of the event.

THE CUBAN MISSILE CRISIS

Precursors

In 1960, John F. Kennedy ran for president on a platform of narrowing the "missile gap" between the Soviet Union and the United States. Upon reaching office, he was surprised to learn that, according to the Central Intelligence Agency (CIA), the missile gap was larger than he expected—but it was in America's favor. Soviet leaders were acutely aware of the U.S. advantage in number, quality, and deployment of nuclear missiles, however, and were considering options to achieve a balance.

In 1959, Fidel Castro became the leader of Cuba and, in 1961, declared himself unabashedly Marxist, to the dismay of American defense planners. His presence in the hemisphere represented a "bridgehead of Sino–Soviet imperialism and a base for Communist agitation" (Ferrell 1985, 362). U.S. agents made several attempts on Castro's life in these early years, and in 1961, the United States helped orchestrate a failed amphibious invasion of Cuba aimed at overthrowing the regime. Conservatives in Congress accused Kennedy of being "soft on Communism."

These events, combined with a disastrous U.S.–Soviet Union summit meeting in June 1962 that gave Khrushchev the impression that Kennedy was a political lightweight, set the stage for the Soviet decision to deploy nuclear missiles in Cuba in May 1962 (Fursenko & Naftali 1997, 179). By deploying missiles, Khrushchev hoped to achieve a nuclear balance, protect Cuba from U.S. invasion, and keep Castro in the Soviet camp (rather than defecting to the more radical China). He wanted to deploy several medium-range missiles, along with defensive antiaircraft batteries, between May and November 1962 without revealing his plans to the United States. Once the installations were in place, Khrushchev hoped the United States would feel obliged to accept this change in strategic balance (Gartoff 1989, 23; Trachtenberg 1985, 163).

U.S. officials suspected Soviet intentions and tried to get information through both open and secret channels. Each time they met with firm denials. It was not until October 15, 1962, that the United States had proof of Soviet activities: photographs of Soviet nuclear installations in Cuba taken by an American U-2 spy plane. The Cuban Missile Crisis had begun.

The Crisis Erupts

Early the next morning, Kennedy was presented with the information from the photographs by his national security advisor, McGeorge Bundy, who stressed the seriousness of the situation: The Soviets now had the capability to attack more than half of the United States, including Washington, D.C., with only a few minutes' warning. The president was astonished by the report. As put by Robert Kennedy, the president's brother and U.S. Attorney General, "[T]he dominant feeling was one of shocked incredulity" (Kennedy 1969, 27). President Kennedy determined during that first meeting that some forceful response was incumbent upon the administration, although not all agreed. (Secretary of Defense Robert McNamara wondered aloud whether this discovery constituted, in and of itself, a mortal danger.) Nonetheless, given the political climate at home and worldwide, Kennedy determined that this situation qualified as a crisis.

By that evening, a group that came to be known as the ExComm (Executive Committee of the National Security Council—even though it included individuals who did not belong to the council) was organized by the president and was generating options for responding to the news. Potential actions included blockade or quarantine, surgical air strike followed by invasion, diplomatic overtures and negotiation, talks with Castro, and leaving things alone (Sorenson 1965, 735). Although everyone acknowledged that air strikes followed by invasion were the only means of being sure the missiles were removed, most did not want to pursue that option as a first alternative. The diplomatic option was ruled out as too timid and passive. Ultimately, the air strike/invasion option and the blockade option were deemed the only viable responses, and the blockade was considered far weaker under the circumstances.

For nearly a week, the ExComm deliberated to develop a final operational plan that could win unanimous approval. As time went on, the air strike option was set aside for two principal reasons. First, if done without warning, an air strike would be seen by the rest of the world as a "Pearl Harbor in reverse" (as put by John McCone, the director of the CIA; Fursenko & Naftali 1997, 226) or as an unprovoked attack against an unprepared enemy. Second, the air strike option was never guaranteed success by military planners, in part because no air strike is ever guaranteed and because the missiles were considered "moveable targets" and therefore able to be relocated without warning. The blockade, in its favor, was a less "final" solution. The United States could rather easily escalate its response if a blockade failed. Also, a blockade was considered a fairly forceful reaction—an act of war according to international law. It might be enough to force the Russians to back down and negotiate a settlement. A blockade could not, in itself, remove the missiles, however. And the ExComm had to consider what to do if the Russians attempted to run the blockade. The crisis might simply be relocated rather than solved.

By Friday evening, October 20, President Kennedy had made the decision to impose a blockade, citing the advantage of giving Khrushchev more time to consider the implications of the situation (Sorenson 1965, 691). Kennedy readily acknowledged that "there isn't a good solution . . . but this one seems less objectionable" (National Archives 1988, 7). The decision was made formal on October 22, when Kennedy spoke to the nation in a televised address. He announced the existence of the missiles, his intent to see them removed, and the approach he intended to use to do that. He made sure to keep his options open. He underlined the gravity of the problem for both American and Soviet audiences:

> My fellow citizens: let no one doubt that this is a difficult and dangerous effort on which we have set out. No one can foresee precisely what course it will take or what costs or casualties will be incurred. . . . The path we have chosen for the present is

full of hazards, as all paths are—but it is the one most consistent with our character and courage as a nation. (National Archives 1988, 10)

The Blockade Aftermath

Over the next four days, the situation worsened. Khrushchev, alarmed to learn that the Americans had discovered his missiles, was relieved when he learned of the block-ade. He considered the blockade the policy of a weak leader, and he intended to take advantage of it. He ordered the Cuban installations accelerated and instructed ships carrying nuclear equipment to move quickly to beat the blockade. Only at the last minute, once the blockade was in place, were other Russian ships ordered to halt (prompting Secretary of State Dean Rusk to make the famous remark: "We're eyeball to eyeball and I think the other fellow just blinked!"). At the same time, Khrushchev moved to ensure his direct control over the nuclear missiles that were operational to prevent an accidental launch (fearing Castro's impulsiveness).

Meanwhile, the United States began a diplomatic assault against Russia in the Organization of American States (OAS) and the United Nations (UN) Security Council, where virtually every nation approved the U.S. response and demanded a withdrawal of Soviet missiles (Blight 1990, 17). Robert Kennedy undertook back-channel negotiations through Georgi Bolshakov as well as front-door meetings with Anatoly Dobrynin, the Soviet Union's envoy in Washington, both to determine Russian thinking and to communicate American resolve (Fursenko & Naftali 1997, 249–252). Perhaps most important, the Kennedy administration mobilized active-duty and reserve personnel and moved a half-million troops with accompanying equipment into the south Florida area. It sent every possible signal that an invasion force was prepared to act at any moment. (This helps explain Castro's alarm.)

Khrushchev also used a variety of channels to communicate his intentions. He communicated through an American businessman in Moscow, through journalists, and through KGB agents in Washington. Ultimately, a letter was delivered through Alexander Fomin (a code name for Aleksandr Feklisov) to John Scali, a reporter with ties to the Kennedy administration. The initial proposal involved removal of the mis-siles by the Soviet Union in exchange for a promise to respect Cuban sovereignty by the United States. While the ExComm was formulating a response to this mes-sage, it received a second message via Radio Moscow adding the caveat that Jupiter missiles—American medium-range missiles based in Turkey—also be removed.

The administration did not know what to believe after receiving conflicting proposals at almost the same time. If they had known that Fomin was acting on his own initiative, the confusion would have been even greater (Garthoff 1989, 80). Add to this the downing of an American U-2 over Cuba at the same time (October 27, 1962), and it was frankly impossible to know what was taking place. (The downing was not even authorized by Moscow; Garthoff 1989, 91.) For that matter, the United States was guilty of sending mixed signals of its own. It had ordered the con-stant over-flight of the Arctic region by bombers with nuclear weapons, and one of them strayed into Soviet airspace at about this time. In fact, Khrushchev was very personally involved in the formulation of proposals, and the second proposal to remove missiles from Turkey came when he considered an invasion of Cuba less likely (Garthoff 1989, 82).

Negotiating the Resolution

The ExComm made two decisions on Saturday, October 27. The first was to make final preparations for an invasion of Cuba to begin on Monday (Blight 1990, 18), and the second was to draft a formal response accepting the conditions detailed in Khrushchev's first proposal. This latter move was suggested by Soviet expert Llewellyn Thompson and was nicknamed the "Trollope Ploy." Thompson also exerted considerable energy to convince a downhearted President Kennedy to implement the plan. In addition to drafting a message to be sent to Khrushchev, Kennedy dispatched his brother Robert to present the American position as well as to offer a "sweetener": secret removal of the Jupiter missiles over a five-month period.

On October 28, Khrushchev's response accepting these terms was received at the White House. The Cuban Missile Crisis was at an end. By November 19, much to Castro's chagrin, the missiles had been dismantled and removed.

ANALYSIS OF THE DECISION TO BLOCKADE CUBA

Although several critical decisions were made at various points prior to and during the crisis, two are easiest for American audiences to study: (1) Kennedy's decision to reveal the existence of the missiles and impose a blockade, and (2) Kennedy's decision to accept the terms of the first Khrushchev letter and ignore the second message. To determine whether these two decisions by Kennedy were "rational," we should consider his goals, assess the quality of the search for options and their respective outcomes, and check whether the final choice promised to achieve his original goals. To the extent that the decision-making process comes close to this ideal model, we can say that it was rational (Allison 1999, 33).

The decision to impose a blockade was reached after roughly four days of intensive deliberations in the White House. Within twelve hours of learning about the missiles, Kennedy had assembled a collection of individuals chosen for their authority over certain key areas of foreign policy and their subject-matter expertise. He called in the secretaries of state and defense, the director of the CIA, the national security advisor, and the joint chiefs of staff (chaired by Maxwell Taylor). Douglas Dillon, secretary of the treasury; Theodore Sorenson, presidential counsel; Pierre Salinger, press secretary; and Robert Kennedy were also included, though more for their relationships to President Kennedy than for their policy roles. Six other men from the State and Defense Departments were brought in for their expertise, and Lyndon Johnson, the vice president, was permitted to join the group. The ExComm met regularly, sometimes for ten hours at a time (not all members met all the time). The group had no obvious seniority system, although Robert McNamara and Robert Kennedy informally led the discussions.

The ExComm structure has been praised as a nearly ideal form for crisis decision making, in that the individuals were present, as Sorenson later put it, "on our own, representing the president and not individual departments" (Sorenson 1965, 679). Furthermore, as the days wore on, the group met without the president, divided into smaller caucuses, and otherwise ignored traditional rank and protocol as they deliberated. Robert Kennedy commented, "It was a tremendously advantageous procedure that does not frequently occur within the executive branch of the government, where rank is often so important" (Kennedy 1969, 46). Specifically, the arrangement minimized the tendency for peer pressure to lead group members to take a more hard-line approach than would normally be the case ("groupthink"; see Janis 1972). It also worked against any bureaucratic struggle over turf.

The first decision required was to determine whether the placement of missiles in Cuba was indeed a threat to national security. In fact, that question did not even come up until the evening of October 16, and then at the instigation of McGeorge Bundy—not the president. McNamara made it clear that he did not consider the new missiles a threat. The joint chiefs unanimously disagreed ("White House" 1985, 184). Kennedy dismissed McNamara's assessment, although he did not necessarily agree with the joint chiefs either. He was more concerned about conservatives in Congress who, he felt, would likely have him impeached if he ignored the missiles.

Once the problem was identified, the process of clarifying the goals and options began, though not necessarily in that order. Early on, Kennedy determined, with general approval, that the missiles must be removed, but that the use of force should be a last resort. Kennedy weighed not only U.S. security concerns, but also the response of the American public and North Atlantic Treaty Organization (NATO) allies. The Europeans, he surmised, would not be especially alarmed at the presence of Soviet missiles in Cuba because they lived every day with the prospect of a Soviet attack from the Ukraine and eastern Russia. Kennedy kept in mind that a trade-off of Cuban missiles for Jupiter missiles would seem eminently reasonable to U.S. allies ("October 27, 1962" 1987/1988, 58). As the crisis evolved, avoiding global nuclear war was likely the highest priority on Kennedy's mind and shaped his willingness to ignore Soviet provocations.

McNamara was the first to clearly articulate three options for dealing with the crisis: (1) a "diplomatic" option involving public declarations, consultations with allies, UN resolutions, and other gestures aimed at condemning and publicizing the Soviet move; (2) a "middle course" of aggressive surveillance and interdiction (read: blockade) of new weapons bound for Cuba; and (3) a "military" option with several variants ranging from air strikes on narrowly selected targets (missile launchers and installations) to a broad-ranging series of attacks on all Cuban military facilities followed by an amphibious invasion ("White House" 1985, 182). Other ideas were mentioned, including taking retaliatory measures, doing nothing at all, and somehow persuading Castro to expel the weapons (Sorenson 1965, 682). Beyond these general categories of action, the ExComm questioned the specific implementation of each approach at length. Should an air strike be preceded by a public ultimatum, or should it be a surprise? Should diplomatic initiatives include a specific ultimatum and a deadline for withdrawal? Should an exchange of missiles in Turkey (which President Kennedy had once ordered removed) be offered up front to persuade the Soviets to settle the problem quickly? Should the nuclear arsenal be put on alert and forces mobilized? What contingencies should be made for a likely Soviet move in Berlin?

By the evening of October 16, the choices seemed to have been whittled down to two: blockade and diplomacy versus air strikes and invasion. When the president seemed to be leaning toward an air strike, McNamara essentially halted the discussion: "I think tonight we ought to put down on paper the alternative plans and probable, possible consequences thereof in a way that State and Defense could agree on, even if we disagree and put in both views. . . . [T]he consequences of these actions have not been thought through clearly" ("White House" 1985, 189). His suggestion was accepted, and the group split into two committees, each drafting the pros and cons of different options. Heavy emphasis was placed on extrapolating the outcomes and implications of each action, including the variations of the actions. Exactly how will oncoming ships be treated at the blockade perimeter? What about submarines? Will the OAS, NATO, and UN support the United States? Should classified information regarding the missiles be divulged? How and where will the Soviets respond to air strikes? Will Berlin be affected? (It is interesting that the joint chiefs initially anticipated that there would be no Soviet response to a U.S. air strike—a scenario Kennedy rejected.) Note this emotional exchange about the implications of an air strike between Undersecretary of State George Ball and McGeorge Bundy:

Ball: *This [surprise attack scenario] just frightens the hell out of me as to what's going beyond. . . .*
Bundy: *. . . What goes beyond what?*
Ball: *What happens beyond that. You go in there with a surprise attack. You put out all the missiles. This isn't the end. This is the beginning . . . ("White House" 1985, 194)*

This process of deliberation, development of options, extrapolation of possible outcomes, and assessment of risks, reactions, and secondary options proceeded for three full days before a decision was made. At one point, the ExComm actually organized a sort of "moot court," assigning certain members to be advocates for particular policy options while others "cross-examined" them to identify weaknesses. The blockade ended up as the most attractive option. It at least had a chance of resolving the crisis, and at minimal cost. Deputy Secretary of Defense Roswell Gilpatrick explained, "Essentially, Mr. President, this is a choice between limited action and unlimited action, and most of us think that it's better to start with limited action" (Sorenson 1965, 693–695).

In reconsidering this decision-making ordeal, we see that the participants self-consciously and painstakingly went out of their way to be rational. Although the initial decision to declare the problem a crisis may have been rather poorly thought out, the decision to impose a blockade resulted from a very systematic, impartial, and thorough process. An alternative point of view is that President Kennedy manipulated the process from behind the scenes, and some evidence indicates that Robert Kennedy played the role of president-in-absentia. Also, one can ask whether the consideration of only a half-dozen alternatives to a situation that threatened the future of humankind was adequate. Herbert Simon and James March argue that in the best of all worlds, the most we can expect of organizational decision making is "satisficing": selecting the first option that satisfies the key elements of a solution, even though other options might have met a wider range of objectives (March & Simon 1958).

RESPONSE TO THE SOVIET OFFERS

Several days of rancorous debate in the UN Security Council and a number of close calls on the high seas east of Cuba preceded the exchange between the U.S. and Soviet governments of what seemed to be genuine offers at settlement. Three messages in particular arrived at the White House on Friday, October 26, and Saturday, October 27. Adding information about the downing of the U-2 on Saturday morning, one could say that four messages were delivered. The ExComm had to decide which of these conflicting messages to take seriously.

The most significant message delivered on Friday was a lengthy, disjointed letter from Khrushchev about the risks of nuclear war. He compared the crisis to a knot that he and Kennedy were pulling tighter and tighter each day. Unless they reversed their course, the only way to undo the knot would be to cut it. Buried in this message was the "germ of a reasonable settlement: inasmuch as his missiles were there only to defend Cuba against invasion, he would withdraw the missiles under UN inspection if the U.S. agreed not to invade" (Sorenson 1965, 712). At roughly the same time this message was received and translated, Alexander Fomin was communicating a similar proposal to John Scali on his own authority, although later reports indicate that Fomin thought Scali was the one who put forward the proposal (Fursenko & Naftali 1997, 265). Combined, the two messages offered a way out of the crisis.

On Saturday morning, the Soviet news agency TASS announced that the Soviet Union would be willing to withdraw its missiles from Cuba if the United States dismantled its missiles in Turkey. Although the message was sent publicly over the airwaves, Khrushchev did not intend to put any particular pressure on the United States; the channel was chosen simply to accelerate communication of the message (Fursenko & Naftali 1997, 276). Nevertheless, Khrushchev was well aware that this proposal was more demanding than the earlier one. It was simply a gamble on his part, though one based in part on informal talks between Robert Kennedy and Dobrynin. The effect of the second message was despondency at the White House. The growing sense of alarm and urgency was based in part on the mistaken notion that the Cuban weapons were not yet operational but soon would be. The White House feared that local Cuban commanders might take it upon themselves to order a launch without Moscow's approval.

The transcript of the ExComm meetings make it clear that President Kennedy was deeply shaken by Khrushchev's second letter:

> . . . We're going to be in an unsupportable position on this matter if this [the trade] becomes his proposal. In the first place, we last year tried to get the missiles out of [Turkey] because they're not militarily useful. . . . Number 2, . . . to any man at the

United Nations or any other rational man this will look like a very fair trade. . . . I think you're going to find it very difficult to explain why we are going to take hostile military action in Cuba against these sites—what we've been thinking about. The thing that he's saying is, "If you'll get yours out of Turkey, we'll get ours out of Cuba." I think we've got a very tough one here. ("October 27, 1962" 1987/1988, 366–367)

The president's advisors, arguing against the trade-off, pointed out that it would be undercutting a NATO ally and might undermine the entire alliance. This debate engendered a search for alternatives, although the pressure of time seems to have constricted the number of options considered. McNamara and others pushed for an immediate cessation of work on the missile sites and some form of warning and implicit threat to the Soviets to remove the missiles within forty-eight hours. From that point, it seems to have been assumed that air strikes would have to begin by Tuesday at the latest.

As the ExComm prepared a reply to the messages, the option of simply ignoring the second message was raised. The following pivotal exchange occurred between Llewellyn Thompson and President Kennedy:

JFK: . . . *[W]e're going to have to take our weapons out of Turkey. I don't think there's any doubt he's not going to retreat now that he's made that public, Tommy—he's not going to take them out of Cuba if we.* . . .

Thompson: *I don't agree, Mr. President. I think there's still a chance that we can get this line going [i.e., ignore the second letter].*

JFK: *He'll back down?*

Thompson: *The important thing to Khrushchev, it seems to me, is to be able to say, "I saved Cuba—I stopped an invasion."* . . . *("October 27, 1962" 1987/88, 59)*

Some in the administration surmised that the second letter might have been written by the alleged "hawks" in Khrushchev's Politburo and that ignoring it might effectively elevate Khrushchev's status in his own government. We now know that this was merely wishful thinking and Khrushchev was, in fact, in firm control of the government at this time.

At any rate, the ExComm decided to issue a response that simply did not mention the Turkish missiles. At the same time, secret communications relayed in a meeting between Robert Kennedy and Dobrynin indicated a willingness by the United States to remove the Jupiter missiles at a later time. The ExComm continued to make detailed preparations for an air strike/invasion policy. The starting time for the attack was given as Thursday at the latest. The decision to ignore the U-2 downing was another U.S. effort to postpone the military option as long as possible.

The delay proved felicitous because Khrushchev's response arrived on Sunday morning. Was Khrushchev's cooperation the result of U.S. prudence, or were Kennedy administration officials simply lucky? In retrospect, much hinged on some communications that no one at the White House was aware of. A KGB agent who worked as a bartender at the National Press Club overheard a number of conversations between American journalists, including speculation by Warren Rogers that a U.S. invasion of Cuba was imminent. This information was communicated to Moscow along with reports of hospitals in Florida being warned to prepare for casualties and other rather disconnected observations that convinced Khrushchev on Friday that war was imminent (Allison 1999, 350). Although he had changed his mind in the interim, the downing of the U-2, unauthorized as it was, further alarmed Khrushchev and prompted him to accept the American response. He doubtless feared that the situation was spiraling out of control. Two recent revelations support this view. One is that Castro had actively encouraged the local Soviet commander to launch the missiles against the United States without seeking prior authorization from Moscow. The other is that on October 27, the commander of a Soviet submarine armed with nuclear weapons was seconds away from firing a nuclear-tipped torpedo at an American sub destroyer in retaliation for dropping depth charges when he was persuaded by his senior officers to desist (*Chicago Tribune* 2002). Khrushchev may have felt it was only a matter of time until a nuclear accident would force Washington's hand.

CONCLUSION: RATIONALITY TESTED

Thus, although the White House was operating on largely false assumptions and the messages that seem to have mattered most to Moscow were not the ones the administration deliberately sent, the outcome was a peaceful one. We should continue to ask whether the decision-making process was rational, however. Clearly, the White House believed that no action that could be seen as "final" ought to be taken if at all possible. This stalling ultimately proved to be the most prudent deliberate move. This policy was as much the result of Kennedy's frazzled emotional condition and fear of commitment, however, and could easily be considered "nonrational." Robert McNamara, in his popular 2003 documentary "The Fog of War," had a more succinct explanation: "It was luck that prevented nuclear war! . . . Rational individuals came *that close* to the total destruction of their societies."

Much of the Kennedy administration's decision-making process was based on flawed intelligence and therefore faulty assessments of Soviet behavior and intentions. This stemmed in part from the organizational structures and processes in place at the time. In addition, once decisions were made, they were often not carried out according to plan. The implementing agencies frequently filtered the instructions from the White House through their own standard operating procedures and institutional cultures.

As it happens, the most significant actions that the administration took involved the substantial preparations for war that were telegraphed to Moscow on a daily basis. In retrospect, it was perhaps this state of readiness that made the deepest impression on the Soviet leadership and prompted them to take the other messages coming from Washington seriously. Warnings, blockades, speeches at the UN, and so forth, carried a powerful punch when placed against the backdrop of hundreds of thousands of Marines and soldiers gathering in Florida.

Interestingly enough, the Cuban Missile Crisis signaled the beginning of a long and winding process of superpower détente. Having faced a nuclear exchange, both Moscow and Washington took steps over the next few years to prevent such a crisis from recurring. The "hotline" was installed in 1963 to allow the heads of each government to communicate at any time. Major arms control agreements and military safeguards were negotiated during both Lyndon Johnson's and Richard Nixon's administrations between 1963 and 1972. Thus although the world can fault the superpowers for bringing it to the brink of annihilation, we can take comfort from the fact that important lessons were learned and acted upon.

QUESTIONS TO CONSIDER

1. To what extent were decision makers during the Cuban Missile Crisis motivated by habit, prejudice, emotion, or other non-rational impulses? Would other people in the same situation have reached the same decisions?

2. To what extent did group dynamics and social pressures influence the ExComm's decision making? Would these individuals have reached the same decisions alone?

3. How did the Kennedy administration's decision making differ from that of other cases discussed in the text? What about the Roosevelt administration's response to Pearl Harbor? What about the Bush administration's reaction to the 9/11 attacks or its planning in 2003 before its attack on Iraq?

KEY FIGURES
THE CUBAN MISSILE CRISIS

John F. Kennedy   U.S. President, 1961–1963. It was his responsibility to set U.S. policy with respect to detection and removal of Soviet missiles in Cuba in 1962.

Nikita Khrushchev   Soviet Premier, 1953–1964. He led the Soviet Union to both deploy and withdraw nuclear missiles in and from Cuba.

Fidel Castro   Leader of the Cuban government since 1959. He sought Soviet protection after the failed Bay of Pigs invasion.

John Scali   American newsman. He was used for back-channel negotiations with Aleksandr Feklisov.

Aleksandr Feklisov (Fomin)   Soviet KGB operative based in Washington, D.C.

Anatoly Dobrynin   Soviet Ambassador to the United States, 1962–1986.

Selected Members of ExComm

Robert F. Kennedy   Attorney-General of the United States, 1961–1964. As the brother of President Kennedy, he always had influence in shaping national policy in many areas. He conducted the meetings of the Executive Committee.

Dean Rusk   U.S. Secretary of State, 1961–1963.

George Ball   Undersecretary of State, 1961–1966.

John McCone   Director of Central Intelligence Agency, 1961–1965.

McGeorge Bundy   National Security Advisor, 1961–1966.

Robert McNamara   U.S. Secretary of Defense, 1961–1968. He discounted the threat presented by the Russian missiles.

Llewellyn Thompson   Ambassador-at-Large, 1962–1966. Former U.S. Ambassador to the Soviet Union, he was the only Russia expert on ExComm.

CHRONOLOGY
THE CUBAN MISSILE CRISIS

1959
Fidel Castro takes power in Cuba at the head of a Communist revolution.

1960
John F. Kennedy is elected to be the youngest president in U.S. history.

1961
The Kennedy administration withdraws support for Cuban exiles who suffer defeat at the Bay of Pigs. Castro demands additional military support from the Soviet Union to defend against future U.S. attacks.

1962
June   Soviet Premier Nikita Khrushchev comes away from his summit meeting with Kennedy unimpressed.

September   The Soviet Union begins deploying nuclear missiles in Cuba.

October 15   American U-2 aircraft detect Soviet activity in Cuba.

October 16–20   ExComm deliberates, ultimately recommending a blockade first and an invasion second.

October 22   Kennedy announces his plan to the nation by televised address.

October 23   Kennedy orders the blockade against Cuba. Later that day, Adlai Stevenson presents photos of the Cuban sites to the UN Security Council.

(continued)

(continued)

October 24   Russian vessels turn away from the blockade, prompting Dean Rusk's "eyeball to eyeball" comment.

October 26   A conciliatory message is sent by Khrushchev, followed shortly thereafter by a more intransigent demand for the withdrawal of U.S. missiles from Turkey.

October 27   The "Trollope Ploy" is formulated in response to two conflicting Russian messages. The conciliatory message is treated as a genuine compromise and largely accepted.

October 28   Khrushchev agrees to withdraw the missiles from Cuba. Kennedy secretly agrees to withdraw U.S. missiles from Turkey.

November 19   Removal of Soviet missiles from Cuba is complete.

REFERENCES

Allison, Graham. *Essence of Decision: Explaining the Cuban Missile Crisis*, 2nd ed. (New York: Addison Wesley Longman, 1999).

Blight, James G. *The Shattered Crystal Ball: Fear and Learning in the Cuban Missile Crisis* (Savage, MD: Rowman and Littlefield, 1990).

Chicago Tribune, October 14, 2002, p. 3.

Craig, Gordon, and Alexander George. *Force and Statecraft* (New York: Oxford University Press, 1990).

Ferrell, Robert, ed. *The Twentieth Century: An Almanac* (New York: World Almanac, 1985).

Fursenko, Aleksandr, and Timothy Naftali. *"One Hell of a Gamble": Khrushchev, Castro and Kennedy, 1958–1964* (New York: W. W. Norton, 1997).

Garthoff, Raymond. *Reflections on the Cuban Missile Crisis*, rev. ed. (Washington, DC: Brookings Institute, 1989).

Hermann, Charles. "International Crisis a Situational Variable." In James Rosenau, ed., *International Politics and Foreign Policy* (New York: Free Press, 1969): 113–137.

Janis, Irving. *Victims of Groupthink* (Boston: Houghton Mifflin, 1972).

Kennedy, Robert. *Thirteen Days: A Memoir of the Cuban Missile Crisis* (New York: W. W. Norton, 1969).

March, James, and Herbert Simon. *Organizations* (New York: Wiley and Sons, 1958).

National Archives. *The Cuban Missile Crisis: President Kennedy's Address to the Nation, October 22, 1962* (Washington, DC: U.S. Government Printing Office, 1988).

"October 27, 1962: Transcripts of the Meetings of the ExComm." *International Security* 12 #3 (Winter 1987/1988): 30–92.

Sorenson, Theodore. *Kennedy* (New York: Harper & Row, 1965).

Trachtenberg, Mark. "The Influence of Nuclear Weapons in the Cuban Missile Crisis." *International Security* 10 #1 (Summer 1985): 135–163.

"White House Tapes and Minutes of the Cuban Missile Crisis." *International Security* 10 #1 (Summer 1985): 171–203.

2

International Security

6

■ ■ ■

Nationalism: The Russian–Chechen Conflict

INTRODUCTION

The nation is an essential building block of international society. A nation is a group of people who are more or less united around a common language, culture, religion, race, ethnicity, or some other identifying factor. It is almost entirely subjective, and the only way to determine whether a nation exists is to interview its members—other methods will probably fail. Nationalism is a political movement wherein members of a nation seek to express their identity by forming a separate political unit—a state. Chauvinism and xenophobia are the dark sides of nationalism—a feeling that one's nation is not only unique and special, but inherently superior to others, with the implication that other nations are either irrelevant or threatening. Self-determination is the legal concept that allows all nations the right to establish a state of their own—at least in principle.

As we consider the troubles in Chechnya—a territory within the Russian Federation—it is useful to imagine a hypothetical. Suppose the United States was made up of only 75% white English speakers. Suppose further that each of the various Native American tribes that inhabited the present territory of the United States back when the Pilgrims landed on Plymouth rock still retained their original powers, along with territory, representatives in the Congress, and so forth. Imagine that they also retained their old rivalries and mutual suspicions, such that periodic wars broke out in various segments of the country. Imagine the slaves that were liberated by the Civil War had all migrated to, say, the Rocky Mountains and now represented a powerful faction in the Congress. Also imagine that each of these actors retained their own languages, cultures, social structures, and so forth. Finally, imagine that the central government in Washington was being pressed to grant each of these groups full autonomy within a loose confederation and that federal troops were being attacked all around the country.

This bizarre-sounding scenario is not too far from the reality of Russian politics today. As a result of hundreds of years of conquest and dismemberment, the Russian Federation is a nation in name only. Even after the break up of the Soviet Union which spawned fifteen new states, the question of governing a multiethnic state remains. In Russia, there are at least forty-eight distinct ethnic groups, most of which have their own language, culture, religious traditions, social structures, and historical identities that make them as distinct from (and sometimes hostile to) each other as they are from the Russian majority. Note that our ignorance of their ethnic identity in no way diminishes its importance to those who possess it.

"CIVILIZATION" AS AN INTERNATIONAL RELATIONS CONCEPT

With the fall of the Berlin Wall in 1989 and the collapse of the Soviet Union in 1991, the Cold War came to an end. This prompted a number of international relations scholars to ask whether some new overarching conflict would replace the Cold War as the defining struggle of our time. Samuel Huntington provided an interesting answer in the concept of a "clash of civilizations" (Huntington 1996). To Huntington, a civilization is more than a nation—it encompasses many nations and usually spans a continent. It refers to a grouping of people around core beliefs about how the world works and how mankind relates to it. It usually involves attitudes about the nature of God, man's capacity for independent action, the basic place of man in society, and so forth. It touches on questions of individualism versus communitarianism, the scientific method versus faith-based knowledge, freedom versus structure, and so forth. Huntington identified seven such "civilizations": Western, Latin, African, Confucian, Hindu, Slavic, and Islamic.

These civilizations are by their nature in competition and conflict with each other, and the differences are irreconcilable. Whereas distance and lack of technology prevented these groups from interacting, they are now in almost constant contact. Where two civilizations abut each other, Huntington predicts the conflicts will be particularly intractable. This is apparent in Palestine, Bosnia, Kashmir, Afghanistan, and other areas. The concept has also been used to explain Islamic terrorism in the West. It is clear that Osama bin Laden sees his role as a vanguard in the struggle between Islam and the West. He has used such terminology in explaining the September 11 attacks (CFR 2004).

Although it may seem that the Islamic civilization has "bloody borders" (as once put by Huntington 1999), it is also clear that the concept of "civilization" raises as many questions as it answers. Why, for example, have most wars involved members of the same civilization? And why did so few of these types of conflict manifest themselves during the Cold War? Why can countries from different civilizations have long-standing warm relations? Those who challenge the "civilization" concept point out that Western culture has shown remarkable "portability" in the sense that the principles of the Enlightenment have been embraced by almost every society in the world. Francis Fukuyama has argued that Western culture is destined to expand globally by virtue of its vitality and inherent appeal (Fukuyama 1992). Bruce Russett and those who emphasize globalization as a means toward international cooperation point out that democracy, that most Western of institutions, has appeared in every region of the world (although it has admittedly had better success in some areas than others; Russett 1993). Still others stress the difficulties in spelling out exactly what is meant by "culture" and then applying that definition to the real world. The fact is that most societies embody several competing cultures—note that even in the United States there are "culture wars" that pit secularism against traditional religion. And once you've found a civilization, there is no guarantee it will stay put—culture is dynamic and ever-changing.

This said, the case of Chechnya seems to become more clear once we factor in cultural elements. Huntington himself has argued that Chechnya is an archetypal case of a clash of civilizations since we find a Slavic society trying to control a Muslim one. He therefore predicts that there is unlikely to be a negotiated settlement of this dispute any time soon.

A THUMBNAIL SKETCH OF THE CHECHEN PEOPLE

The roughly one million Chechens (a name assigned by Russian invaders—they call themselves Nokhchii; Dunlop 1998, x) have their roots in the Caucasus Mountains since the Stone Age (see Map 6.1). For centuries they lived here in relative isolation, organized in clans (teips) somewhat like the Scots. They nurtured a warrior

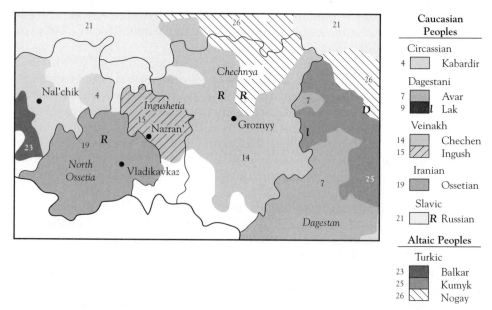

Map 6.1 Ethnolinguistic groups in the Caucasus region

culture dominated by men who encouraged family loyalty, although they also organized quasi-democratic structures similar to the Iroquois Nation encountered by
American colonists 300 years ago. Each teip enjoyed equal status, and no single
leader dominated—except during military crises. Their military tactics involved
small raiding bands and careful use of the topography of the region—which they
naturally knew far better than any invaders (Dunlop 1998, 20).

It was not until the Middle Ages that the Chechen people became subject to a
more powerful external actor: Islam. The religion spread to the Caucasus beginning
around 600 A.D., but affected each national community differently. Those in Dagestan to the east developed a more orthodox and militant form of Islam, whereas the
Chechens embraced a more mystical and magical style based on the teachings of
itinerant Sufis (Fowkes 1998, 10). Thus although Islam played an important role in
the thoughts and emotions of the Chechens, it did little to unite them to the people
of the surrounding area.

HISTORY OF CHECHNYA'S CONFLICT
WITH RUSSIA SINCE 1990

Russia was an unwelcome intruder to the Caucasus in the 16th century when Ivan
the Terrible first launched probing attacks in the hope of easily expanding his empire.
It was Peter the Great, however, who invaded in the early 1700s and established
Russian dominance for good. The region was annexed in 1722, although it would take
Catherine the Great's efforts to subdue the region in the 1760s (Dunlop 1998, x).

Russia's intervention prompted a violent backlash by the Chechens who
rallied behind Sheik Mansur. He led on the basis of religion and proved more
successful as a preacher than a military commander. After holding off the Russians
for six years, he was defeated in 1791. The new Russian ruler, Viceroy Aleksei
Yermolov, ruled with an iron fist, deporting, killing, and terrorizing opponents. In
spite of this, the Chechen resistance persisted. The period 1817–1864 has been
described as the Chechen War. Sheik Shamil, himself from Dagestan, obtained
the support of the Chechens in his struggle against Russian imperialism. As a religious figure, he was able to appeal to Islam to mobilize large numbers of Chechens
who were able to defeat the Russians in a number of pitched battles. His legacy has
been mythologized and serves as a potent symbol of Chechen independence even
today (Lieven 1998, 304). His life ended violently, however, as Russians hunted
him down and, after killing him, expelled roughly 100,000 Chechens from the
area. As many as 75,000 of these refugees later died in disease-infested camps. It
has been estimated that Russians killed roughly half of the Chechen population
over a period of one hundred years (Dunlop 1998, 20).

Chechens gradually migrated back to their homeland beginning in the 1860s
and proved to be a useful ally to the Boshevik revolutionaries in 1917. It did not
take long before Chechen demands for autonomy ended the alliance, however. By
1925, the Communists in Moscow had launched a pacification program reminiscent
of czarist tactics. Once their power was established, the Russians attempted to
remove key elements of Chechen culture, including the language (as well as Arabic

script) and the religion. The army was called in once again to quell a rebellion in 1929 (Dunlop 1998, 59).

Rebellions occurred in 1939 and 1942. Frustrated by the distraction this caused to the war effort, Russians acted in 1944 with what can best be described as genocide. Roughly 400,000 Chechens were forcibly removed and relocated to central Asia. Many died in transit and as many as 150,000 died in the camps (Fleming 1998). Meanwhile, Ukrainians and Russians were brought in to take over the homes and farms of those who had been expelled. They proceeded to change the place names, local histories, and everything that connected the Chechens to the area. After two hundred years, the Russians had finally subdued the Chechens. Or so it seemed.

With Stalin's death in 1954, the Chechens were permitted to gradually return to the region. They were not, however, permitted to occupy their homes and farms, but instead had to settle for apartments in the cities where they were often a minority. Mikhail Gorbachev, however, was the first Soviet leader to show the Chechens the respect they craved. After his ascension in 1985, he received delegates from the region who requested greater autonomy. Although they were granted additional rights and status, they were denied the thing they most sought: status as a union republic. As a mere autonomous republic, Chechnya had only limited autonomy from Moscow. More important is the fact that, once the Soviet Union collapsed, it was only the union republics that were granted full independence. Chechnya was not so lucky.

THE FIRST CHECHEN WAR: 1990–1996

Chechen leaders, beginning in November 1990, began to assert their own independence from Moscow. Duko Zavgayev, the Russian-appointed ethnic Chechen who presided over the area's Communist Party hierarchy, approved the formation of the National Congress of the Chechen People (OKChN) in hopes of appeasing nationalist elements. General Dzhokar Dudayev, a Russian general, was elected its chairman. For the next nine months, Chechen leaders jockeyed for position in the fast-moving political environment. By August 1991, demonstrators demanded the removal of Communist Party leadership in favor of the OKChN committee. They prevailed on September 6, when Zavgayev resigned and turned power over to the committee under the leadership of Hussein Akhmadov and General Dudayev. On September 15, the party structure dissolved itself and was replaced with a pro-Moscow Provisional Supreme Council (VVS). Dudayev's forces announced the dissolution of the council three weeks later and went on to win parliamentary elections on October 27th. On November 2, 1991, the National Congress formally declared independence from Russia.

Boris Yeltsin, the new president of the Russian Federation, responded to the declaration by imposing martial law on the region (although this decision was reversed by the Russian Parliament). The military attempted to impose order by disarming Chechen fighters, but more often than not, it was Russian soldiers who surrendered their weapons to the Chechens. Some estimate that Chechens collected almost 25,000 automatic rifles during 1992 (Lieven 1998, 64). The Russian troops were eventually withdrawn in June.

While Chechnya positioned itself against Moscow, it did little to secure the support of its neighbors. Ingushetia to the west, with which it shared many cultural traits, was disappointed in Grozny's lack of support for its territorial claims on neighboring Ossetia. This led the Ingush to side with Russia in the coming conflict. The regime in Grozny also alienated would-be allies in Georgia to the south by providing asylum to rebels who were fighting the regime in Tbilisi. Some support flowed from Chechen expatriates living overseas, but to a large extent, the Chechens were isolated against Russia (Lieven 1998, 97).

Throughout the 1992–1994 period, Dudayev fought off numerous contenders, relying increasingly on nationalist appeals and a confrontational foreign policy to secure public support. He also became increasingly dependent on the mafia and other gangster elements as his capacity to impose order throughout the region ebbed. Would-be challengers were as often as not divided against each other, which meant Dudayev could maintain control over the central government for the time being (Lieven 1998, 68). Ruslan Khasbutalov, for example, emerged in mid-1994 in the hope of overthrowing the regime, but when promised Russian support failed to materialize, he was defeated. Still other militant factions followed military leaders Aslan Maskhadov and Shamil Basayev.

As conditions in Chechnya deteriorated and guerrilla groups organized increasingly successful raids into Russian territory, the Yeltsin government made preparations to launch an all-out attack on Grozny—the first of several ill-fated military ventures. Yeltsin attempted to coordinate offensive operations with Dudayev's rivals, only to have repeated assaults go awry. On one occasion, opposition forces took their cue from Moscow and launched an assault on Dudayev's forces, only to pull back when Russian air support failed to come (Siren & Fowkes 1998, 110). Having failed to work closely with local militants, Yeltsin decided to launch a full assault using mechanized Russian divisions. Quick and easy victory was expected.

Beginning in early December 1994, Yeltsin attempted to coordinate a leaflet-drop on Chechnya to warn all parties to lay down their weapons. On December 11, Russians began bombing selected targets in the hope of stirring up a rebellion against Dudayev. The combination of these two actions had the reverse effect. All Chechen groups drew closer together, which prompted the spontaneous mobilization of hundreds of fighters in the mountains and left Russia facing a united, armed Chechen population for the first time since the 1940s. On December 18, 1994, Russian troops moved into northern Chechnya and on into Grozny with roughly 100,000 troops and 200 tanks.

The tanks met with determined resistance—the first of many instances when Chechen fighters would take advantage of their mobility, familiarity with Grozny streets, and canny tactics. The roughly 6,000 Chechen fighters in Grozny (of which only 3,000 were active at any one time) had only a few hundred well-trained fighters, but they had considerable supplies of weapons, often taken from Russian soldiers. Their weapon of choice was the antitank grenade launcher. Marksmen positioned themselves in the upper stories of apartment buildings and waited for the Russian tank columns to proceed single-file down narrow streets. A single shot at the first and last tanks in the column would immobilize the entire unit. The rest could be destroyed by less proficient fighters (Knezys & Sedlickas 1999, 19). In December, the Chechens were able to turn back the Russian army within two days. The Russians withdrew to the northern sections of Chechnya in January 1995. Conditions in Grozny continued to deteriorate, however, as refugees streamed out of the city, leaving behind the sick and elderly in squalor and fear. Russians reoccupied Grozny in late January after a period of sustained bombardment. The Chechens regained control of key buildings in June. Once it was clear that the fighting was stalemated, a cease-fire was agreed to in October. When fighting resumed in 1996, the Chechens were mostly on the defensive. In April, Dudayev was killed in a Russian rocket attack.

Under the direction of Shamil Basayev, Chechen fighters launched a counter-offensive in August 1996. Russians were targeted and pinned down in remarkably effective strikes. Eventually, the Russians were relieved, but not before it was made clear to Boris Yeltsin that a military victory was impossible. By the end of 1996, the Russian army had fully withdrawn from Chechnya.

THE SECOND CHECHEN WAR: 1997–2000

For nearly two years, Chechnya and Russia had an uneasy and often violent peace. With Russian troops gone, Chechnya held presidential elections that were won by one of the heroes of the war—former chief of staff Aslan Maskhadov. He attempted to carve out a more productive relationship with Moscow while pressing for independence at every opportunity. He and Yeltsin signed a formal peace agreement on May 13, 1997, described at the time with great optimism as the end of centuries of conflict.

From 1997 to 1999, order broke down in Chechnya. Militants carried out a string of terrorist attacks in Russia and Dagestan, culminating in the assassination of Russian General Gennadi Shipgun and the bombing of a Russian apartment building. Leaders in Russia were under pressure to put an end to the attacks and by the fall of 1999 were making plans to reinsert the military into northern Chechnya (Gordon 2000). Vladimir Putin (newly appointed prime minister and soon-to-be president) put his reputation as a hard-liner on the line.

On August 8, 1999, Russian helicopter gun ships attacked Chechen militants who had infiltrated into Dagestan. As the fighting intensified, Russians attacked other areas in Chechnya and quickly occupied the northern half of the country. On October 3, Russians bombed Grozny in preparation for a land assault involving 100,000 troops. By November, Grozny had fallen into Russian hands and organized resistance had come to an end.

THE HISTORY SINCE 2000

Putin installed moderate Islamic legal scholar Akhmad Kadyrov to govern the province until elections could be held. Other Chechen leaders such as Aslan Maskhadov and Shamil Basayev were driven underground and began to adopt a more extremist philosophy. The influence of foreign Islamic terror networks increased once the Russian dominance was consolidated (Bowers, Derrick, & Olimov 2004).

The hopelessness of the situation for some Chechen separatists contributed to their adoption of suicide bombing as a weapon (Hilsum 2004). As early as mid-2000, just a few months after the Russian invasion, suicide bombers struck Russian troops in and around Grozny. The number and audacity of the attacks increased gradually until roughly fifty Chechen rebels, including a dozen women (so called "black widows" sworn to avenge the deaths of their husbands and brothers killed by Russian troops), seized a crowded Moscow theater in October 2002. Russian forces, frustrated by an extended stand-off, used a nerve agent to paralyze the attackers and their hostages (roughly 800 theatergoers and theater personnel). The dosage was incorrectly measured, however, and in addition to killing the hostage-takers, 129 of the hostages were also killed.

Vladimir Putin is determined to end Chechen resistance and has rejected any calls for a negotiated settlement. He described the Chechen rebels as lawless Islamic terrorists and his war in Chechnya as a front line in the battle against al Qaeda. What is perhaps ironic about his characterization is that, although probably not true in 1999 when the war broke out, it seems to be increasingly accurate. Foreign governments questioned the validity of this portrayal, but are generally muted in their criticisms of what have been widely described as draconian measures (Baev 2004, 343). President George Bush applauded Russian support in the war against al Qaeda after the September 11 attacks, whereas Europeans applauded Putin's opposition to Bush's war in Iraq in 2003. The result was considerable room for maneuver in his antirebel policy.

Putin sought to give legitimacy to the counterinsurgency measures by holding a series of elections in 2003 and again in 2004. In early 2003, the government in Moscow and the appointees in Grozny collaborated to draw up a new constitution. The result, however, was criticized by human rights activists as regressive in that it granted the region less autonomy than other parts of the Federation and required the use of the Russian language in official business (CRS 2004, 202). Tens of thousands of Russian troops were allowed to participate in the vote on the grounds that they were on permanent deployment. The elections themselves were only loosely monitored because of the precarious security situation (one of the reasons for international skepticism about their fairness), and the outcome was not widely respected. The reports of 96% approval for the constitution was too high to command respect (CRS 2004, 202). In October, Akhmad Kadyrov was elected with 81% of the vote, although important opposition candidates were either disqualified or induced to withdraw.

The measures did not, however, stem the violence. Chechen militants became increasingly violent against each other, the Russian military, and the Kadyrov regime. Kadyrov himself stopped counting the number of assassination attempts against him. In August 2003, two Russian commercial aircraft were downed within hours of each other, resulting in ninety deaths. Then in May 2004, Kadyrov himself was felled in a bombing that took a dozen of his staff and other bystanders. Finally, in September 2004, Chechens took hostage 1,000 children, parents, and teachers in a school in Beslan in southern Russia. After three days, as ambulance workers came to extract the bodies of twenty victims of early violence, a melee ensued. Children and others ran for their lives as the hostage-takers opened fire. Russian forces returned fire, killing most of the rebels. The final death toll was well over 200, many of them children.

Given the violence on both sides, the prospects for a peaceful solution are remote. The Russian occupation seems to be coinciding with an increased role for Islamic militants in the region—something one author calls "Palestinization" (Khatchadourian 2003). Moderates are either killed or marginalized while extremists are locked in a battle of ideology, religion, and revenge. An estimated 100,000 Chechens and 25,000 Russians have died since 1994, while more than 250,000 Chechens are refugees. At least 3,000 have been buried in fifty mass graves around the region. Thus far, no one has demonstrated the capacity to exercise authority in the area with any approximating civil rights or rule of law. As put by Nabi Abdullaev, "the Chechen conflict is not so much about who will govern Chechnya. It is about whether Chechnya will be governed at all" (2004, 333). Russia continues to pin its hopes on various leaders it has put forward and managed to get elected, but their status is weak among Chechens. Memorial, the Russian human rights group, has called for a negotiated settlement leading to Chechen independence. Although this may be the only solution to the ongoing terrorism, it is doubtful that it will give the Chechen people peace and justice.

In August 2008, violence flared up between Russia and its southern neighbor Georgia. Russian peacekeepers were positioned in South Ossetia and Abkhazia after a cease-fire agreement in 1992 and as an expression of support to the local inhabitants who were granted Russian passports. After clashes between Georgian and South Ossetian forces, both Georgia and Russia mobilized forces (*New York Times*, September 16, 2008, A1). Georgia shelled Russian installations in the region, prompting a full-scale military response that culminated in Georgian forces being repulsed from South Ossetia and Abkhazia and Russians occupying key points within Georgia. Both sides, according to Human Rights Watch, committed large-scale violence against civilians, and estimates of total casualties are in the low thousands (HRW 2008). After a peace agreement brokered by French President Nicolas Sarkozy, Russian forces withdrew back to previous positions in October.

CONCLUSION: NATIONALISM OR SOVEREIGNTY?

It seems clear that the Chechens harbor aspirations of self-government, but it is also clear that they do not speak with a single voice regarding when and how this will happen. Many if not most rebels invoke Chechen nationalism for what appear to be self-serving reasons and are inclined to take up arms even against the general wishes of ordinary citizens. Chechen public opinion is not routinely measured, given the instability of the situation and the dangers of speaking out against Russian rule, so we don't really know how many want independence and how intensely they want it. The Russian government is not especially interested in learning Chechen opinion but is content to declare all Chechen separatists an enemy of the state deserving of imprisonment or death. And so to a certain extent, there is no way to know the nature of Chechen nationalism or the extent to which it is causing the violence we have studied.

This is not unusual where civil war is concerned. As we see in the Bosnian and Serb case (Chapter 10), unscrupulous and self-aggrandizing leaders have routinely manipulated national symbols and stirred up historic grievances and resentments in order to rally troops in the hope of rising to power. Some of the world's worst violence has been perpetrated by such individuals. Even in India (Chapter 15), nationalist leaders represented only part of the country they were trying to liberate, and they held on to power in large part by letting them govern themselves in a federal system. Nearly all newly independent countries have had to deal with minorities that did not necessarily want the country that was handed to them—even when it was done with the best of intentions, let alone when it wasn't.

QUESTIONS TO CONSIDER

1. Where else in the world are there unresolved nationalist impulses? Why is this such a common occurrence?

2. Which factors take precedence: Religion? Ethnicity? Historical grievances? Competition between elites?

3. Is the rebellion in Chechnya primarily a nationalist movement or an extension of global Islamic terrorism?

KEY FIGURES
THE RUSSIAN–CHECHEN CONFLICT

Aslambek Aslakhanov   Chechen member of the Russian Duma and rival to Kadurov. Offered a senior job by Putin to take him out of the running.

Shamil Basayev   Chechen rebel leader, described as a threat to the U.S. by Department of State. Not to be confused with the 19th-century militant of the same name.

Gen. Dzhokar Dudayev   Elected President of Chechnya by the National Congress of Chechen Peoples in 1991. Declared the independence of the oblast.

Yegor Gaidar   Opposition leader in mid-1990s, leader of Russia's Choice party.

Pavel Grachev   Minister of Defense.

Akhmad Kadyrov   Administrator of Chechnya prior to elections in 2003. A moderate Muslim legal expert, he opposed Russian occupation during the first Chechen War, but became a favorite of Vladimir Putin when he condemned Shamil Basayev's efforts at creating an Islamic state. He governed the area after the second Russian invasion, was elected President in 2003 and assassinated in 2004.

Khattab   Chechen rebel who tried to form alliances with al Qaeda.

Aslan Maskhadov   Chechen rebel leader, successor to Gen. Dudayev in 1996.

(continued)

(*continued*)

Vladimir Putin Russian President, 1999–2008.

Dmitrij Medvedev Russian President, 2008–present.

Salman Raduyev Chechen rebel leader.

Mikhail Saakashvili Georgian President

Sergei Shakhrai Deputy P.M. and a Cossack (ethnic rival of the Chechens) assigned to head up negotiations on Chechnya's future status.

Boris Yeltsin President of the Russian Federation, 1991–1999.

Nicolas Sarkozy French President

CHRONOLOGY
THE RUSSIAN–CHECHEN CONFLICT

1722
Peter the Great annexes Chechnya.

1791
Sheik Mansur is defeated after holding out against Russian troops for six years.

1817–1864
The Chechen War. Russians consolidate control over the region.

1922
The Soviet Union moves to consolidate control in Chechnya and the Caucasus.

1944
Soviet leaders in Moscow empty the region of Chechens, evacuating 400,000 to Central Asia.

1950s
Chechens are gradually permitted to return to Chechnya.

1985
Chechens appeal for union republic status. They are denied.

1991
Gen. Dzhokar Dudayev is elected President of Chechnya by the National Congress of Chechen Peoples as the group declares the region's independence. Boris Yeltsin becomes President of the new Russian Federation after the dismemberment of the Soviet Union. Chechnya is not granted its independence, unlike the fifteen former Soviet Republics.

1992

Yeltsin assigns Sergei Shakhrai, the Deputy Prime Minister and a Cossack (ethnic rival of the Chechens) to head up negotiations on Chechnya's future status.

Georgian government signs agreement with South Ossetian rebels allowing Russian peacekeepers into the region.

1993

Shakhrai forms the government of Umar Avturkhanov to replace that of Dudayev. Russia provides the new regime with weapons.

1994

Moscow–Grozny talks break down.

November   Yeltsin and the Security Council order an outright invasion of Chechnya by Russian troops. Russian Air Force begins attacks on Grozny. Roughly 100,000 die during the first Chechen war. Russian troops storm Grozny.

1996

April   Gen. Dudavey is killed by Russian troops and is replaced by Aslan Maskhadov, who retakes the capital Grozny.

August   Alexander Lebed is dispatched by Yeltsin to negotiate a peace, leading to a postponement of a decision on Chechnya's final status until 2001.

1997

February   Aslan Maskhadov is elected president of Chechnya. What follows is a period of lawlessness dominated by a struggle between the warlords, organized in the Majlis-ul Shura (People's Council) and dominated by Shamil Basayez, and Maskhadov's government.

1999

September   Shamil Basayev launches attacks on apartment buildings in Moscow and elsewhere.

October   Russia invades Chechnya a second time.

December   Premier Vladimir Putin is elevated to the presidency by Yeltsin upon the latter's resignation. He is elected to the position in March.

2000

February   Russian forces control all of Chechnya. Akhmad Kadyrov is installed as interim leader.

June   First suicide bombing by Chechen rebels in Grozny kills two Russian special police.

July   Multiple suicide attacks kills scores of Russians in coordinated, synchronized attacks.

2002

October   Moscow theater attack involving "black widows"—Chechen suicide bombers who are survivors (widows, daughters, sisters) of Chechen terrorists who have been killed by Russian forces. Many carry slogans written in Arabic. The assault by Russian security forces includes a gas attack that kills all the hostage takers and 129 of the 800 hostages.

December   Suicide bomber kills 70 in Chechnya.

(continued)

(*continued*)

2003

July   "Black widow" kills herself and 15 others in a suicide bombing at a rock concert in Moscow. A total of 200 were killed in twenty suicide bombings across Russia in 2003.

March 23   Referendum in on Russian-drawn constitution for Chechnya—widely criticized as premature and manipulative. About 25,000 "permanently based" troops joined in the voting. Turnout was high and the proposals were approved by 96%.

August   Two Russian civilian aircraft are downed by Chechen rebels, resulting in ninety deaths.

September   Kadyrov forces seize opposition media prior to the presidential elections.

October 5   Presidential elections held in Chechnya. Akhmad Kadyrov, an Islamic law expert and Putin protege, wins in tainted vote.

2004

May 9   Akhmad Kadyrov is assassinated in a bombing that took more than a dozen lives.

June   Maskhadov leads a raid into Ingushetia, killing dozens of policemen.

August   Presidential elections held in Chechnya. Alu Alkhanov wins election in which his principal rival is removed from the ballot on a "technicality."

September   Chechen rebels seize a large elementary school in Beslan in southern Russia and take 1,000 students and teachers hostage. As rescue workers retrieve twenty bodies, an explosion erupts, causing children to run away in a panic. As the hostage-takers proceed to gun down the fleeing children, Russian security forces open fire. Twenty of the hostage-takers are killed (although perhaps that many escape) and more than 200 hostages die.

October   Alu Alkhanov becomes president with Russian support.

2005

March   Separatist Chechen leader Aslan Maskhadov is reported killed by Russian authorities.

November   Russian-backed parties win local elections in tainted vote.

2006

South Ossetians hold a referendum on independence from Georgia. The result is overwhelmingly favorable.

2008

August 7   Georgian forces shell a Russian outpost in south Ossetia as Russian peacekeepers in South Ossetia and Abkhazia invade parts of Georgia. Thousands are killed in indiscriminate attacks on civilians by both sides.

October   Russians complete their withdrawal from Georgia to South Ossetia after an agreement brokered by French President Nicolas Sarkozy.

References

Abdullaev, Nabi. "Chechnya Ten Years Later." *Current History* (October 2004): 332–336.

Baev, Pavel K. "Instrumentalizing Counterterrorism for Regime Consolidation in Putin's Russia." *Studies in Conflict & Terrorism* 27 (2004): 337–352.

Bowers, Stephen R., Ashley Ann Derrick, and Mousafar Abdulvakkosovich Olimov. "Suicide Terrorism in the Former USSR." *The Journal of Social, Political and Economic Studies* 29 #3 (Fall 2004): 261–279.

Congressional Research Service (CRS). "Analysis of the Conflict: Elections and Pacification Efforts." *International Debates* (October 2004): 201–205.

Council on Foreign Relations (CFR). "Causes of 9/11: A Clash of Civilizations?" 2004. Available at http://www.cfrterrorism.org/clash.html.

Dunlop, John B. *Russia Confront Chechnya: Roots of a Separatist Conflict.* (Cambridge: Cambridge University Press, 2004).

Fleming, William. "The Deportation of the Chechen and Ingush Peoples: A Critical Examination." In Fowkes, Ben, ed. *Russia and Chechnya: The Permanent Crisis* (London: Macmillan Press, 1998): 65–86.

Fowkes, Ben, ed. *Russia and Chechnya: The Permanent Crisis* (London: Macmillan Press, 1998).

Fukuyama, Francis. *The End of History and the Last Man* (New York: Free Press, 1992).

Gordon, Michael. "A Look at How the Kremlin Slid into the Chechen War." *New York Times,* February 1, 2000.

Hilsum, Lindsey. "The Conflict the West Always Ignores." *New Statesman* 133 #4672 (January 26, 2004).

Hodgson, Quentin. "Is the Russian Bear Learning? An Operational and Tactical Analysis of the Second Chechen War, 1999–2002." *Journal of Strategic Studies* 26 #2 (2003): 64–91.

Human Rights Watch (HRW). "Georgia: International Groups Should Send Missions Investigate Violations and Protect Civilians."August 17, 2008. Available at http://www.hrw.org/english/docs/2008/08/17/georgi19633.htm. Accesssed on October, 13, 2008.

Huntington, Samuel. *The Clash of Civilizations and the Remaking of World Order* (Norman: Oklahoma University Press, 1996).

Huntington, Samuel. "A Local Front of a Global War." *New York Times,* December 16, 1999: A31.

Khatchadourian, Raffi. "The Curse of the Caucasus," *Nation* Vol. 277 #16 (November 17, 2003): 31–36.

Knezys, Stasys, and Romanas Sedlickas. *The War in Chechnya* (College Station: Texas A&M University Press, 1999).

Lieven, Anatol. *Chechnya: Tombstone of Russian Power* (New Haven: Yale University Press, 1998).

New York Times, "Georgia Offers Fresh Evidence on War's Start." September 16, 2008, A1.

Russett, Bruce. *Grasping the Democratic: Principles for a Post–Cold War World* (Princeton: Princeton University Press, 1993).

Siren, Pontus, and Ben Fowkes. "An Outline Chronology of the Recent Conflict in Chechnya." In Fowkes, Ben, ed. *Russia and Chechnya: The Permanent Crisis* (London: Macmillan Press, 1998): 170–182.

7

...

Collective Goods: The Kyoto Protocol

INTRODUCTION

As a result of increasing human activity and economic growth, a growing number of issues cross national boundaries. Refugees, ocean pollution, space exploration, pandemics, ozone depletion, and global warming are but a few examples. These problems, although the product of specific actions in specific states in most cases, affect much of the planet. Once in place, they are not easily solved by just one or two countries, but require collective action from numerous players.

A "pure" collective good is one that does not belong to any one player, nor could it. Once in place, it cannot be withheld from any one player, but is available to all (in practice, very few things fit this description, but many come close). This is not to say that a collective good is free, however. Typically, collective goods require considerable sacrifice and expense, and the story of the creation of collective goods comes down to the fight over who will pay for it. A simple example would be how a group of four roommates divides up the bill for a pizza. One simple solution would be to split the bill equally. But suppose one person goes to pick up the pizza and feels that his time and gas are worth something—and makes the argument that his share of the bill should be lower. What if one person is carbo-loading for a marathon and plans to eat more than one-fourth of the pie— should he pay more? What if one person is short of cash that day—can he pay less and work it off by doing everyone's dishes? Perhaps you've had this experience. Because we're dealing with roommates, where no one has ultimate authority, the solution will probably be negotiated (unless one is a weight-lifter and simply knocks a few heads to get his way).

This situation emerges in international affairs when sovereign states have problems that are inherently trans-boundary in nature. Sometimes, governments agree on the need for a collective good, such as rules to govern chlorofluorocarbon (CFC) emissions to prevent depletion of the ozone layer (which protects living things on earth from some of the sun's harmful ultraviolet rays). Acknowledging the need for a collective good is merely the first step, however. Questions may arise regarding the source of the CFCs, for example, and states may insist that those who have caused the most damage historically should be expected to pay the most for the repair now. If these states are willing to make the contribution, then all will be well—but such is often not the case. It is more likely that, unless some actors emerge as leaders who are willing to shoulder the bulk of the costs of the collective good, no solution will emerge (Olson 1965). A widely held belief is that the creation of a collective good requires a single player able and willing to absorb most of the costs of its creation and maintenance. Such an actor is called a *hegemon* (Kindelberger 1986).

Once the collective good is in place, how does one maintain it? Because it isn't possible to deny the good to anyone, one cannot simply "charge admission" (although, as mentioned earlier, this idea rarely holds in practice, and so states are, in fact, charged admission). Suppose governments agree to strict guidelines on CFC emissions, for example, and a few states are willing to make deep cuts. What if other countries decide to renege on their commitments and revert back to CFC production? The benefits of the program will probably still occur, and the "free riders" will enjoy the same benefits as the burden carriers. Only if a major player refuses to go along is the collective good jeopardized (such an actor is called a "spoiler"). The incentive to cheat is clearly high. But if there are enough free riders, problems could arise. If nothing else, those carrying the burden will grow to resent their sacrifice and the unfairness of the arrangement. There will probably need to be some penalties for noncompliance, but these may be difficult to design and enforce given the inability to deny benefits to cheaters.

The story of the creation of the rules on global-warming gases is illustrative of the problems inherent in collective goods.

GLOBAL WARMING

As we all know from the tremendous precautions taken by astronauts to protect themselves against the cold of space, the earth would become a frigid wasteland without a capacity to trap solar energy as it bounces off its surface (see Figure 7.1). Misnamed the "greenhouse effect" (actual greenhouses operate on a different principle of physics), this is accomplished by the thin layer of atmosphere that covers the globe. A few substances, including carbon dioxide and methane, are able to absorb and trap ultraviolet rays from the sun and thereby assist in preventing heat from escaping into space (Sparber & O'Rourke 1998, 2).

Another well-known fact is that the planet's average surface temperature has gone through rather dramatic swings over its long history. Most recently, it was nearly ten degrees cooler during the great Ice Age that resulted in the spread of Northern Hemisphere glaciers well south of the current Canada–U.S. border.

Two more facts are known as well. First, since the Industrial Revolution at the end of the 18th century, humanity—especially the peoples of the West—has been

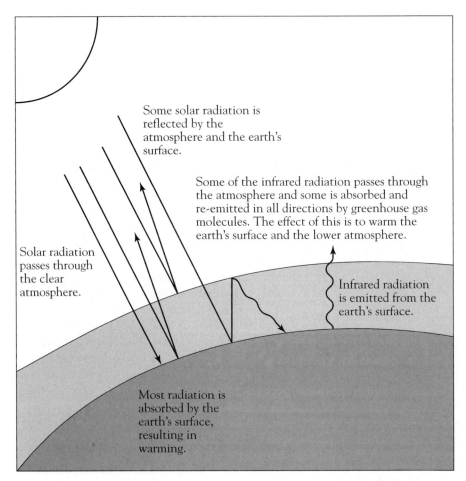

Figure 7.1 Solar radiation

burning fossil fuels at a tremendous rate, in contrast to the entirety of human experience to that point. Second, earth's surface temperature has been moving inexorably higher over the past hundred years.

Noting these facts, observers—both scientists and amateurs—began expressing concern in the early 1980s over the possibility that human activity was intensifying the greenhouse effect to the point that the earth was experiencing human-induced global warming. As put by Breidenich and her coauthors:

> Most scientists believe that anthropogenic [human-generated] emissions of greenhouse gases increase the heat-absorbing capacity of the atmosphere and will result in a corresponding increase in the global average temperature. This warning is predicted to have various global impacts, including the melting of the polar ice

caps; rising sea levels; increased intensity and frequency of storms; changes in amounts and timing of precipitation; changes in ocean currents; and an enlarged range for tropical diseases such as malaria, cholera and dengue fever. (Breidenich et al. 1998, 316)

Conservative estimates indicate that the planet may continue warming at the rate of three or four degrees per century unless some intervention occurs to reverse the trend. Although this may not sound like much, it is useful to recall that during the Ice Age, the earth's temperature was a mere seven degrees cooler than today on average. One group of environmental organizations has created a web site (Global Warming: Early Warning Signs, www.climatehotmap.org) that maps specific, local events (updated regularly) that are harbingers of global warming around the planet.

Among the specific alerts: The polar ice caps are beginning to melt and break up. A piece of the Antarctic ice shelf the size of Rhode Island (1,260 square miles) broke off and floated out to sea in March 2002. Scientists attribute this and other breakups of Antarctic ice to a nearly five-degree (Fahrenheit) warming of the area since 1945. Watery patches have appeared in the Arctic where the ice has not melted in the past. The area covered by sea ice has declined by roughly 6% since 1980. Glaciers in the Himalayas have shrunk dramatically (close to 100 feet per year), leading some to predict the loss of all central and eastern glaciers by 2035. In Spain, half of the glaciers present in 1980 are now gone. Partly as a result of ice melting, sea levels are rising at three times the normal rate, resulting in increased flooding in low-lying areas from Bangladesh to the Chesapeake Bay. Mangrove forests in Bermuda's coasts are dying off due to rising sea water levels.

In addition, global weather patterns are likely to change significantly. For example, the temperate zones of the planet will shift northward, resulting in longer growing seasons in Scandinavia and Canada and more tropical climates in China and Missouri. For countries that are already tropical, the resulting changes in rainfall could lead to desertification of some areas. Ocean temperatures will rise, contributing to intensification of tropical storm and hurricane activity, along with unusual phenomena such as El Niño. To illustrate, high temperatures in Great Britain are increasingly rising above sixty-eight degrees Fahrenheit (more than twenty-five days per year in the 1990s versus fewer than five days per year in the 1770s). Severe heat waves were common in 1998 and 1999, resulting in hundreds of fatalities in cities such as Chicago. Changes in Indonesia's temperatures have contributed to a spreading of malaria into higher elevations (Telesetsky 1999).

These changes will, in turn, bring about important socioeconomic changes, including a redistribution of the world's agricultural centers and increased food scarcity in some areas, both of which will contribute to large-scale movements of populations in search of food security. This migration could contribute to shifts in global power distributions and an increase in local conflicts. It is probably enough to offer this list of potential problems (and a few opportunities).

Global warming remains an extremely controversial issue. One reason is the continuing disagreement among scientists about it. Although an overwhelming majority of climatologists are on record stating that human activity is contributing to global warming, a small minority rejects this conclusion as premature. The existence of the merest dispute has been seized upon by politicians and firms that are predisposed to resist the standard remedies for global warming. The George W. Bush administration, for example, explained its resistance to cuts in carbon dioxide emissions in terms of continuing doubts among scientists. According to Lindsay, "uncertainty also explains why global warming has not yet emerged as a burning issue in the United States. . . . Few Americans list global warming as a top environmental concern . . . and by a two-to-one margin they say it will not pose a serious threat during their lifetime" (Lindsay 2001, 27).

CREATING RULES ON GLOBAL WARMING GASES

Global warming is controversial largely because of the types of solutions that exist. When it comes to reducing the biggest culprit—carbon dioxide—what is required is a reduction in the burning of fossil fuels and an increase in carbon-absorbing forests. At this point, however, considerable resistance emerges in seeking alternatives to fossil fuels. Two important factors are coal-burning power plants and the internal combustion engine. They are the predominant contributors to the 30% increase in carbon dioxide concentrations in the atmosphere since 1750 (Telesetsky 1999, 781). Dramatic changes would require auto manufacturers, utility companies, highway contractors, and most mining companies to either drastically curtail production or undertake considerable research to develop new products. Some, including former Vice President Al Gore, have suggested that nothing less than the replacement of the internal combustion engine will be enough to begin to solve the problem (Gore 1993).

Although these emissions occur mostly in the developed West, the developing South is industrializing at a rapid rate and is expected to emit a large share of global-warming gases (the name for all gases that contribute to the phenomenon, including carbon dioxide and methane). In addition, developing countries are guilty of removing one of the key natural defenses against carbon dioxide concentrations by cutting large portions of the planet's forests. Young trees are especially effective recyclers of carbon dioxide because they absorb it through their leaves and convert it to oxygen. Deforestation has cost the earth a large fraction of its forests in recent years, and relatively little of it has grown back. The forests are being eliminated in part to provide farmland to the growing populations of the developing world, which also increases demand for fossil fuels. The problem is thus exacerbated doubly.

Getting to Kyoto

In the late 1980s, governments around the world began debating whether and how the problem of global warming could be tackled. In 1988, a panel of scientists and government officials proposed reducing carbon dioxide levels by 20% by 2005 as a starting point (Barrett 1998). That same year, the UN General Assembly invited the UN Environmental Programme and the World Meteorological Organization to form the Intergovernmental Panel on Climate Change—a collection of 2,000 climatologists from more than 100 countries—to study the facts regarding global warming. They reported in 1990 that human-induced emissions were, in fact, contributing to the earth's gradual warming.

The issue was placed on the agenda of the UN Conference on the Environment and Development, scheduled for June 1992 in Rio de Janeiro, Brazil. The meetings were intended to be a dramatic, high-level event where the world's leaders would address and develop answers for a wide range of environmental problems, from desertification to ocean pollution. What emerged from the meetings was a series of broad agreements—mostly on principles—and a laundry list of policy goals. Buried in the mix was the UN Framework Convention on Climate Change (FCCC) that called upon sponsoring states to keep emissions of global-warming gases to 1990 levels to prevent acceleration of temperature increases in the years to come. But little more was spelled out at that time, and the signatories agreed to meet again to hammer out the details in the form of a "protocol" of legally binding measures (Breidenich et al. 1998, 318).

As put by Lindsay:

> Global warming poses a collective goods dilemma. Countries know that pursuing virtuous global warming policies makes little sense if no one else follows suit. Any individual reduction on their part will be swamped by emissions from others. Indeed, going first could be economically lethal . . . Fairness issues exacerbate the collective goods problem. (Lindsay 2001, 27)

Four groups of states emerged early on, and most of the negotiations involved trade-offs between them. First and foremost was the European bloc, led by Germany and France, which called for the deepest cuts in emissions. These countries were driven by both ideological and practical considerations. On the one hand, pollution in Europe had prompted the emergence of a strong and active environmental movement that considered global warming a "clear and present danger," the substance of which was beyond debate (Gelbspan 2002). These states also were in a position to explore alternatives to fossil fuels by virtue of the fact that most countries were concerned about their dependence on foreign oil and had already begun efforts to wean themselves off it. France had begun a massive nuclear power program in the 1960s and had significantly reduced its reliance on coal-burning plants, for example. It also introduced numerous energy-saving initiatives and fuel taxes to encourage efficiency. By 2000, per capita energy use in Europe was half that of the United States—a fact that has bred deep resentment of the United States' efforts to give itself exceptions from the Kyoto Protocol (Mathews 2001). The European states were consistently the most forceful advocates for deep cuts and strong legal commitments.

The second group consisted of mature, developed economies that, for a variety of reasons, were not yet ready to make the deep cuts Europe proposed. This group, labeled "industrialized laggards" by European analysts, consisted of Canada, Japan, and Australia, and was led by the United States (Oberthur & Ott 1999, 17). The U.S. position remained consistently skeptical throughout the 1990s. Even at Rio de Janeiro, the George H. W. Bush administration refused to endorse the full array of agreements reached, preferring to adopt a "wait-and-see" approach. The Clinton administration, prodded by Vice President Gore, warmly welcomed the Rio agreements on principle, although it found its hands were tied when it came to making specific, legal commitments. Members of the U.S. Senate, in particular, expressed their deep concern with any treaty that might result in economic stagnation or unemployment. They also opposed any agreement that would treat developing countries more leniently than Western countries. In 1997, the Senate unanimously passed a resolution prohibiting the White House from signing any global warming agreement that did not remedy these issues (Barrett 1998, 22).

The nations in this group worked to minimize mandatory cuts in emissions. Australia managed to negotiate an increase for itself, for example. The United States sought permission for moderate reductions in emissions by offsetting them with increases in the size of its carbon dioxide–absorbing forests ("carbon sinks"). This group also promoted various emissions-trading schemes that would allow high polluters to reduce their exposure by exchanging credits with low-polluting countries in a variety of ways.

The third group was the Eastern European states in economic transition. Although they were known to be very heavy polluters, their difficult economic transitions created a pollution windfall. High failure rates for their heavy industries meant that many smokestacks were idled, and pollution levels plummeted even as unemployment lines swelled.

Finally, the developing countries sought special protections during the negotiation of the Kyoto Protocol. They argued that, given their dependence on industrialization for economic growth, it was unfair to ask them to set aside poverty-alleviating development for the sake of the environment. Besides, they pointed out, global warming was almost entirely the fault of Western industrialization in the past—hence the need for Western states to carry the bulk of the cost of emissions controls. They pointed out that, on a per capita basis, developing countries produced very little pollution (for example, China emits one tenth of the carbon dioxide emitted by the United States per capita—Oberthur & Ott 1999, 21). Oil-exporting countries pleaded for rules that would not jeopardize their export levels, lest they collapse economically and politically. Only the small island states in the developing world felt strongly that global warming should be halted (given their special vulnerability to rising ocean levels).

Pollution Trading at Kyoto

One of the first steps undertaken at Kyoto was the establishment of an emissions baseline against which future rules would be measured. This goal was achieved with relative ease, because it is possible to measure carbon dioxide emissions with considerable precision and thereby estimate the total volume of global-warming gases coming from each country. The negotiators developed a table that listed the total amount of emissions and each country's share (see Table 7.1). Special attention was given to the so-called Annex I countries that were responsible for the overwhelming majority of pollution—namely, the industrialized West.

Table 7.1   1990 Emissions Baseline for Kyoto Protocol Signatories

	Total CO_2 Emissions for 1990 (thousands of gigagrams)	Share of Annex I Country Totals
United States	4,957	36.00
European Union	3,289	24.05
France	367	2.68
Germany	1,014	7.24
Italy	429	3.14
United Kingdom	577	4.22
Australia	289	2.11
Canada	463	3.38
Japan	1,155	8.45
Economies in Transition	3,364	24.60
Russia	2,389	17.47
Poland*	415	3.03

*Poland and a few other economies in transition were allowed to utilize 1988 or 1989 levels as the baseline (slightly higher than 1990).
Source: UN Framework Convention on Climate Change, www.unfccc.int.

Once the baselines were established, the pollution trading began in earnest. Almost every participant in the Kyoto negotiations entered the discussion with the goal of minimizing costly reforms. Even the Europeans sought ways to permit some European Union members to have small reductions, or even increases, in carbon dioxide emissions. The three principal ways of reducing the emissions reduction targets were to (1) plead "special circumstances," (2) exchange emissions with lower-polluting countries, and (3) devise offsetting mechanisms involving improvements to the environment. The first strategy was taken up by many developing countries and most of the U.S.-led bloc. Australia was perhaps the most successful, negotiating for itself the right to increase its carbon dioxide emissions to 8% above its 1990 baseline (see Table 7.2).

The second strategy was also promoted by the U.S. delegation against the resistance of the Europeans. The Americans argued that, because the goal of the Kyoto meeting was reduction of global levels of global-warming gas levels, so long as one country's increase was offset by another country's decrease, the total objective could be met. They proposed to create a "market for emissions," whereby countries would be allowed to convert some of their emissions into a "budget" that they could sell to countries that were well ahead of global emissions averages. In particular, the United States was interested in taking advantage of the collapse of East European emissions resulting from economic depression and deindustrialization, which created "hot air" opportunities (Barrett 1998). At the end of the day, this arrangement was approved by the signatories, although it was not enough to

Table 7.2   Kyoto Targets for 2002–2012, Relative to 1990 Base Year*

United States	93%
European Union	92%
France	92%
Germany	92%
Italy	92%
United Kingdom	92%
Australia	108%
Canada	94%
Japan	94%
Economies in Transition	103%
Russia	100%
Poland*	108%

*Poland and a few other economies in transition were allowed to utilize 1988 or 1989 levels as the baseline (slightly higher than 1990).
Source: UN Framework Convention on Climate Change, www.unfccc.int.

satisfy the U.S. negotiators. Even the Europeans negotiated a special arrangement whereby their emissions were counted as a whole. As a consequence, Germany and France's deep emissions cuts would allow increases in emissions in Spain and Greece ("joint implementation").

The third strategy was promoted by the United States and some developing countries. The U.S. delegation pressed especially hard for a more generous treatment of so-called carbon sinks. Given the carbon-absorbing character of forests, and given the United States' commitment to reforestation, the government believed it should get credit for reductions in emissions as a result of forest absorption (Barrett 2001). Some have estimated that approval of this strategy could allow the United States to cut in half the reductions it must make against the 1990 baseline (Telesetsky 1999, 805).

Developing countries pressed for arrangements that, like the World Bank's Global Environmental Facility, would give developed countries credit for helping a developing country lower its global-warming gas emissions. Special projects and initiatives under the so-called Clean Development Mechanism would be graded according to the degree of emissions reduction they produced, and the donor country would have its emissions for the year cut by a similar amount (Coghlan 2002, 168–171). This tactic is intended to use market incentives to cause states to do good (Breidenich et al. 1998, 325).

As these provisions were negotiated and (mostly) adopted at Kyoto, more general issues were debated as well. The United States pressed for a more flexible deadline for reducing emissions than the drop-dead deadline proposed by the Europeans. Ultimately, compromise was reached on the establishment of a five-year period rather than a single date for achievement of the targets. The average emissions per year for the period 2008–2012 would be the ultimate test of compliance with Kyoto—meaning that the final day of reckoning would not come until 2012. So long as targets were reached, on average, during this period, countries would be considered compliant. Further, the United States insisted on lax enforcement mechanisms with respect to noncompliance. Other than regular reporting to the FCCC Secretariat, no specific set of enforcement mechanisms was created, although the parties to the Kyoto have agreed to consider this question in the future (Breidenich et al. 1998, 330). With the United States' ultimate rejection of the treaty, it is possible that the Europeans will insist on tougher enforcement measures (Gelbspan 2002).

As a way to prevent adoption of a meaningless treaty, the negotiators agreed that it would not come into force until it was ratified by at least fifty-five states responsible for at least 55% of the world's global warming gasses. This meant that almost all of the world's major polluters would have to come on board before the Kyoto Protocol would take legal effect.

IMPASSE AT THE HAGUE

The Kyoto meetings ended in passage of the Kyoto Protocol, signed by the United States, European states, and more than 100 other participants, albeit not without the dramatic and personal intervention of Al Gore, the Japanese prime minster, and other high-ranking diplomats. The meetings also benefited from the able chairmanship of Raul Estrada of Argentina, who had led previous FCCC meetings and knew the participants well (Reiner 2001, 38).

The meetings were declared a victory by environmentalists, but it was a hollow victory at best. The agreement, after all, faced almost unanimous Senate opposition and left many contentious issues unresolved. As put by Reiner, "The Kyoto Protocol, prepared in December 1997, had masked irreconcilable differences among participants by papering over many fundamental disagreements among and within the negotiating parties" (Reiner 2001, 36).

History was not working in favor of resolving global warming. Most countries, including the United States, continued to expand carbon dioxide emissions during the 1990s. In the United States, the proliferation of sport-utility vehicles, which emit up to five times more global-warming gases than their passenger-car counterparts, made achieving reductions difficult. Even in the Netherlands, where the government implemented tough emission-reducing policies, emission levels did not fall. Those countries that had reduced emissions had done so largely because of reasons beyond their control. Germany benefited from the collapse of heavy industry in the East after reunification, and the United Kingdom was able to reach its targets by using its newly discovered North Sea oil to convert coal-burning power plants to less-polluting oil-burning ones (Reiner 2001, 37).

The signatories gathered again at The Hague in November 2000 with the goal of eliminating ambiguities and "agreements in principle" left over from Kyoto.

Because little had changed in the U.S. position and the Senate's attitude, there was little expectation of success. The practicalities of the negotiations were also hampered by the U.S. presidential election and its notorious "Florida fiasco" that kept Al Gore and other Clinton administration officials away from the meetings at critical times. The apparent opposition of candidate George W. Bush did nothing to improve the mood at the meetings.

Even as American negotiators felt compelled to be cautious, newly elected Green politicians in the German (and French) delegations felt emboldened to press for deeper concessions, including cutting back the emissions-trading schemes. The result was an agreement to disagree. Although the United States did not block approval of the agreements by other states, it refused to endorse the result. As put by the chief U.S. negotiator at The Hague:

> [European countries] ignored environmental and economic realities, insisting on provisions that would shackle the very tools that offer us the best hope of achieving our ambitious target at an affordable cost. . . . Some seem to have forgotten that [emissions trading] is a fundamental feature of the Kyoto Protocol—accepted by all parties as a legitimate means of meeting our targets. . . . Some of our negotiating partners also chose to ignore physical realities of our climate system, depriving parties of another important [tool] by refusing them credit for carbon [sinks]. . . . And finally, they ignored the political reality that nations can only negotiate abroad what they believe they can ratify at home. (Frank E. Loy, Department of State press release, November 25, 2000, in AJIL 2001, 648)

Decisions on outstanding issues were postponed until meetings to be held in Bonn and Marrakech over the next year.

THE CURRENT SITUATION

The new Bush administration, which was led by two former oil men, had an ideological and political antipathy toward the Kyoto Protocol. It mistrusted the scientific basis for the sacrifices being required of the United States, was strongly wedded to market schemes that would permit the country to reduce its exposure, and was antagonistic toward any enforcement mechanisms that would punish noncompliance. This said, candidate Bush had promised to shrink the role of coal-burning power plants in the United States during his tenure, but was forced to backpedal shortly upon taking office under pressure from utility companies.

Seeing no way to accommodate both the demands of the European and developing countries and the interests of conservatives and industry in the United States, the Bush administration formally rejected the Kyoto Protocol in March 2001. Environmental Protection Agency chief Christine Todd Whitman was charged with making the announcement that the Kyoto treaty was "dead" as far as the United States was concerned.

Nevertheless, the United States sent representatives to the Bonn and Marrakech meetings later in the year and even succeeded in winning considerable concessions from chastened Europeans eager to bring the United States back into the process. Negotiators in Bonn agreed to most of the U.S. demands regarding carbon sinks and emissions trading, for example (AJIL 2001, 649). The United States also watched from the sidelines as the negotiators reached final agreement on the provisions of the Kyoto Protocol in Marrakech in November 2001.

The last position of the Bush administration was that it would not interfere with efforts by other countries to implement the Kyoto Protocol and would work toward reducing what it calls "greenhouse gas intensity"—emissions per unit of economic activity (total emissions divided by GDP). The target of 18% reduction by 2011 will result, admittedly, in an overall increase in emissions (AJIL 2002, 487). And with each new scientific report confirming the scientific evidence that global warming is induced by human activity, the Bush administration's skepticism about the urgency of the problem grew increasingly anachronistic. Even Bush's own climate change experts finally gave their support to this scientific conclusion (CCSP 2006).

Meanwhile, countries have ratified the Kyoto Protocol. The FCCC maintains a running tally of ratifications by a number of countries and the proportion of total emissions they represent (see web site, www.unfccc.int). At the 2002 Johannesburg Summit on Sustainable Development, the governments of Russia and Canada announced that they were moving ahead with ratification, meaning that the 55% target would be exceeded. The Kyoto Protocol officially came into effect in February 2005. As of May 2006, that chart showed 163 ratifications by countries that, together, were responsible for 61.6% of global emissions of greenhouse gases.

The Russian and Canadian ratifications present the United States with an odd situation. As with the cases of the International Criminal Court, the Convention on the Rights of the Child, and the Landmine Ban, new international rules and institutions are being created without direct U.S. involvement (Stiles 2004). In fact, many American firms wonder why they do not have the opportunity to participate in emissions trading and other schemes like the Europeans and Japanese. As far as whether this means the problem of global warming is now under control, we should recall that it was a watered-down version of Kyoto that was adopted, and that even the original Kyoto Protocol was not particularly robust. The treaty provides numerous exceptions, exemptions, and exclusions that may well make it a less-than-effective tool for solving the original problem.

CONCLUSION: THE CHALLENGE OF PROVIDING COLLECTIVE GOODS

The Kyoto Protocol to the UN Framework Convention on Climate Change became international law in 2002, in spite of U.S. opposition. This case helps to demonstrate several important aspects of collective goods that might come as a bit of a surprise. First, this process calls into question the widely held assumption that a "hegemon" is needed to create a collective good (Kindelberger 1986). U.S. leadership was clearly beside the point after a critical mass of countries had reached agreement on

Kyoto. Furthermore, even if all the signatories work hard to implement the agreement (an unlikely scenario given the temptation to cheat), little change in global warming trends will probably occur. So long as Americans continue to produce more than one third of the world's total global-warming gas emissions, other states' efforts may be negligible. Ultimately, the collective good of maintaining (or lowering) the earth's temperature will likely not be achieved in spite of the treaty.

Second, the story of the Kyoto Protocol illustrates the way in which economics and international law intersect. The schemes to trade emissions, in particular, were clever ways of using the market to achieve socially beneficial results. Although innovative, the schemes were seen by some as merely a shell game that would ultimately allow heavy polluters to delay needed reforms.

Finally, the Kyoto Protocol story illustrates the difficulty of achieving agreements on economic sacrifices in the face of even slightly ambiguous science. In contrast to the Montreal Protocol, which brought about strict, binding limits on CFC emissions in the face of unanimous scientific agreement on their deleterious effects on the ozone layer, the Kyoto Protocol failed in part because a few scientists were unwilling to endorse the majority view concerning global warming (Lindsay 2001). From another perspective, this case shows how science can be manipulated by self-interested politicians and industrialists (one is reminded of how cigarette manufacturers misrepresented scientific findings on the links between smoking and cancer).

QUESTIONS TO CONSIDER

1. Can financial incentives be used to induce reductions in carbon dioxide emissions? If so, how?

2. To what extent do ethical values govern the decision to pollute?

3. On the basis of what principles should the cost of pollution abatement be distributed?

KEY FIGURES
THE KYOTO PROTOCOL

Bill Clinton   U.S. President, 1993–2001. He supported the basic framework of the Kyoto Protocol, although his administration sought ways to give the United States separate rules.

George W. Bush   U.S. President, 2001–2009. His administration rejected the Kyoto Protocol.

Al Gore   U.S. Vice President, 1993–2001. The author of *Earth in the Balance*; he was a strong supporter of stricter pollution controls.

John Prescott   British Deputy Prime Minister, 1997–2007. As the country's senior environmental policy official, he was instrumental in pressing for the Kyoto Protocol's conclusion.

Mikhail Kasyanov Russian Federation Prime Minister. He announced the country's plans to ratify the Kyoto Protocol in 2002.

Raul Estrada Chairman of the FCCC meetings leading to the Kyoto Protocol.

Timothy Wirth Under U.S. Secretary of State for Global Affairs, 1993–1997. He was the principal U.S. negotiator at the Kyoto meetings.

CHRONOLOGY
THE KYOTO PROTOCOL

1988
The Intergovernmental Panel on Climate Change (IPCC) is formed by UN Environmental Programme and the World Meteorological Organization. Officials in Toronto recommend a reduction of carbon dioxide emissions by 20% by 2005.

1990
IPCC issues a report declaring its certainty that human activity is resulting in pollutants that will intensify the greenhouse effect. The panel predicts that the earth's temperature will increase by one degree Celsius by 2025.

1992
The UN Conference on the Environment and Development is held in Rio de Janeiro. It results in the Framework Convention on Climate Change (FCCC), among other agreements.

1995
Signatories to the FCCC meet in Berlin to outline specific targets on emissions.

1997
Signatories agree to the broad outlines of emissions targets in Kyoto, Japan. The United States dissents.

2000
Efforts to accommodate American and Australian objections to the Kyoto draft agreement fail at a meeting of signatories in The Hague.

2001
George W. Bush withdraws U.S. endorsement of the Kyoto Protocol and goes back on a campaign promise to reduce reliance on coal-burning power plants. After important break-throughs in Bonn in June, participants in the November Marrakesh meetings finalize the provisions of the Kyoto Protocol without U.S. support.

2002
Russia and Canada ratify the Kyoto Protocol to the FCCC, bringing the treaty into effect officially on February 16, 2005.

2007
Australia ratifies the Kyoto Protocol.

REFERENCES

American Journal of International Law. "U.S. Rejection of Kyoto Protocol Process." *American Journal of International Law* 95 #3 (July 2001): 647–650.

American Journal of International Law. "Bush Administration Proposal for Reducing Greenhouse Gases." *American Journal of International Law* 96 #2 (April 2002): 487–488.

Barrett, Scott. "Political Economy of the Kyoto Protocol." *Oxford Review of Economic Policy* 14 #4 (Winter 1998): 20–43.

Breidenich, Clare, Daniel Magraw, Anne Rowley, and James W. Rubin. "The Kyoto Protocol to the United Nations Framework Convention on Climate Change." *American Journal of International Law* 92 #2 (April 1998): 315–331.

Climate Change Science Program (CCSP). "Report Reconciles Atmospheric Temperature Trends." Press release. May 2, 2006.

Coghlan, Matthew. "Prospects and Pitfalls of the Kyoto Protocol to the United Nations Framework Convention on Climate Change." *Melbourne Journal of International Law* #1 (May 2002): 165–184.

Gelbspan, Ross. "Beyond Kyoto Lite: The Bush Administration's Absence from the Global-Warming Talks Could Actually Lead Other Nations to Pursue a Bolder Approach." *The American Prospect* (February 25, 2002): 26–29.

Gore, Al. *Earth in the Balance: Ecology and the Human Spirit* (New York: Plume, 1993).

Kindelberger, Charles. *The World in Depression, 1929–1939* (Berkeley: University of California Press, 1986).

Lean, Geoffrey. "Russia and Canada Shock Summit with Plans to Ratify Kyoto Treaty." *New Zealand Herald*, April 9, 2002.

Lindsay, James M. "Global Warming Heats Up: Uncertainties, Both Scientific and Political, Lie Ahead." *Brookings Review* 19 #4 (Fall 2001): 26–30.

Mathews, Jessica T. "Estranged Partners." *Foreign Policy Magazine* (November/December 2001): 48–53.

Oberthur, Sebastian, and Hermann E. Ott. *The Kyoto Protocol: International Climate Policy for the 21st Century* (Berlin: Springer, 1999).

Olson, Mancur. *The Logic of Collective Action* (Cambridge, MA: Harvard University Press, 1965).

Reiner, David. "Climate Impasse: How the Hague Negotiation Failed." *Environment* 43 #2 (March 2001): 36–43.

Sparber, Peter, and Peter E. O'Rourke. "Understanding the Kyoto Protocol." *Briefly: Perspectives on Legislation, Regulation, and Litigation* 2 #4 (April 1998).

Stiles, Kendall. "Theories of Non-hegemonic Cooperation." Paper presented at the annual meetings of the American Political Science Association, Chicago, September 2–5, 2004.

Telesetsky, Anastasia. "The Kyoto Protocol." *Ecology Law Quarterly* 26 #4 (November 1999): 797–814.

8

■ ■■ ■

Military Power: The Persian Gulf Wars I and II

INTRODUCTION: POWER

Why do countries with larger militaries so often lose wars? Military resources are certainly vital to a nation's power. As pointed out by Rothgeb, they provide (1) the impression of power (which may be enough in and of itself to bring about compliance with your wishes), (2) expanded vehicles for influencing others (tactical air strikes, naval blockades, invasions, and so forth), and (3) resistance to others' efforts at influencing your own policies (anti-aircraft weapons and anti-missile defense, for example) (Rothgeb 1993, 192).

This is not to say that military capability is sufficient to guarantee success. Success also depends in large part on whether resources match circumstances. Consider, for example, the simple fact that in 1990, the U.S. military lacked camouflage uniforms suitable for a desert environment (they were jungle green). In the 1930s, Russia attacked Finland wearing drab grey coats that were easy to spot against a snow-white background. More importantly, when the fight is over peoples' hearts and minds—persuading them to abandon Islamic fundamentalist violence, for example—it is entirely possible that having the capability to kill the enemy will only serve to inflame opposition. Having the capacity to bomb industrial targets may make very little difference when fighting a less developed country, as the United States discovered during the Vietnam War.

Success also depends on the deployment of forces at particular places and times. Certainly the deployment of massive numbers of men (roughly one million over a one-month period), warships, and amphibious landing craft and various support ships (nearly 7,000) were essential to the successful invasion at Normandy in June 1944.

Likewise, as we will see, having a substantial U.S. fleet in the Persian Gulf (to the east of Kuwait) manned by thousands of Marines prevented the Iraqi regime from concentrating its forces on the border with Saudi Arabia during the first Gulf War, making it easier for General Norman Schwarzkopf to attack from the west. But much also depends on command, control, communication, and intelligence ("C3I" in military vernacular). American offensives in Iraq during the two wars under review focused heavily on "decapitation": removing the ability of commanders to communicate with troops in the field and orchestrate movements. American forces also aimed at "blinding" the enemy by eliminating its electronic surveillance capacity by knocking out radar installations, for example.

Finally, success also depends a great deal on the training and morale of the individual soldiers, sailors, and pilots. Larger armies have often lost wars when troops have simply been unable or unwilling to fight. During the first World War, Russian soldiers deserted en masse in protest over the Tsarist regime that was ultimately overthrown in 1917. During the Vietnam War, troop morale was unusually low, and drug use and insubordination among the infantry were serious problems for American commanders. Moving from a drafted army to an all-volunteer force in the 1970s dramatically improved troop morale for the United States, although those gains have been reduced as tours in Iraq have been extended from 12 to 15 months with shorter home leaves in recent years. Some have called this a "back-door draft" (White 2004).

As you read about these wars, consider the role that military capacity and ability played in shaping the outcomes. To what extent did the United States have the right tools and strategies for each conflict? What was done well and what was done poorly? How might the outcomes have been different if different approaches had been taken? And how do these lessons apply to how the United States should deal with its enemies in the future?

THE FIRST PERSIAN GULF WAR

On August 2, 1990, the Iraqi army, fourth largest in the world, led by more than 4,000 tanks, poured across the Kuwaiti border to overrun a nation roughly the size of Connecticut. One might ask, given the ultimate outcome, why did Saddam Hussein do it? To answer this question, one must understand both the circumstances of the invasion and the character of the Iraqi regime and its leader. A longtime member of the Baathist political movement, Saddam Hussein began his career as a torturer for the short-lived Baathist regime that governed Iraq from 1958 to 1963. Upon its return to power in 1968, the party rewarded Hussein's loyalty and energy with the position of deputy chairman of the Revolutionary Command Council, where he set about ensuring that the party would never again be victimized by factional infighting as it had in 1963. Within a few years, he emerged as the de facto leader of the state and, with the wealth he derived from oil after the 1973 price hike, covered himself with riches and power. He assumed the presidency in 1979 and immediately purged the upper ranks of the party, often carrying out the executions personally and with great publicity (Miller & Mylroie 1990, 45).

The legacy of Hussein's rule is well known. Several villages populated by ethnic Kurds in the northern regions of Iraq were attacked with chemical weapons during the 1980s on the grounds that they sought a separate statehood. The Shia Muslim majority of Iraq (as opposed to the minority Sunni to which Hussein belonged) was a frequent target of Saddam's internal attacks because of their support for the radical Ayatollah Khomeini in neighboring Iran. His relations with Kuwait, Syria, and Saudi Arabia were also tense.

Kuwait had a reputation for arrogance borne of its record-breaking wealth. Many Arabs resented the Kuwaiti practice of hiring other Arabs for the most menial jobs they were not willing to do themselves and then denying the workers any political or civil rights. It was widely believed that Kuwaitis were siphoning oil from the Rumaila oil field in Iraqi territory (*New York Times*, September 3, 1990, A7). And Kuwait, to whom Iraq owed billions, regularly exceeded its OPEC-imposed production quota to reap unfair profits at OPEC's expense.

In the months leading up to the invasion, the U.S. position was mixed—a problem that dogged George H.W. Bush during his 1992 presidential reelection campaign. U.S. envoy to Iraq, April Glaspie, was accused of telling Saddam Hussein in June that territorial disputes between Arab neighbors were strictly a regional matter, hinting that the United States would stand on the sidelines. Although this has been denied (*New York Times*, March 21, 1991, A17), rumors persisted through 1992. According to a CIA official, the United States knew as early as January 1990 that Iraq was prepared to attack Kuwait (*New York Times*, September 25, 1991, A18). It was not until Iraq spoke openly in July 1990 of military action against both Kuwait and the United Arab Emirates that the United States signaled its willingness to intervene by deploying combat ships to the Gulf (*New York Times*, July 25, 1990, A1).

The Diplomatic Phase: August 2, 1990–January 16, 1991

Within a week of the invasion of Kuwait, Iraqi forces began to amass on the Saudi Arabian border to the south. In order to deter an Iraqi attack on the enormous Saudi oil fields, the United States sought and obtained permission to deploy the 82nd Airborne Division along the border. With this "trip-wire" force in place, the United States began to expand its size in order to withstand an assault in case Iraq decided to attack after all. At the same time, President George Bush sought the support of other countries, focusing especially on powerful European allies and Arab countries most directly threatened by Iraq in the hope of pressuring Saddam Hussein to withdraw from Kuwait.

The UN Security Council was active in the days and weeks after the invasion, passing a dozen resolutions that included issuing a sweeping condemnations of the Iraqi "breach of the peace," demanding a restoration of the situation to pre–August 1, 1990 conditions (Resolution 660), and setting up extensive economic and diplomatic sanctions in the hope they would force Iraq to leave Kuwait (Resolution 661). These sanctions were to be enforced by the U.S.-led coalition through sea power (Resolution 665). Ultimately, in a dramatic show of unity, the foreign ministers of the Security Council members approved Resolution 678 on November 29, 1990, which authorized nations to enforce all preceding sanctions "by all necessary means"—a clear signal that military intervention had the UN's blessing. Resolution 678 was in a sense a sign of the failure of diplomatic efforts by James Baker of the United States, Tariq Aziz of Iraq, and Eduard Shevardnadze of the Soviet Union to reach a settlement on the Kuwaiti problem.

Until late October, American and European diplomats held out hope that some compromise could be reached between Iraq and Kuwait that would avert the need for further war. Economic sanctions were imposed throughout the period. According to Tucker, "those sanctions were almost completely successful in stopping Iraqi oil exports, and Iraqi imports were reduced by 90%. These economic sanctions were unprecedented in modern history" in their severity (Tucker & Hendrickson 1992, 101). By late August, the Western powers, Japan, and the Soviet Union were essentially speaking with one voice. By the end of September, 250,000 troops from this combined force were deployed in Saudi Arabia.

The Soviets, unwilling to join the coalition itself, were especially active in seeking a compromise between the parties in the crisis. Up to the day before the beginning of the ground offensive, Soviet emissaries were pressing for a deal that would prevent war to no avail. "Although the American-led coalition had the capability to do as it threatened, the Iraqi government apparently believed that it possessed the military muscle needed to neutralize any moves by the coalition. Thus Iraq largely ignored the American threats made in the fall of 1990 and the winter of 1991" (Rothgeb 1993, 101).

American demands, which were more modest in the early weeks of the crisis, became more and more inflexible as the U.S. military presence grew. Bob Woodward of the *Washington Post* has argued that the decision to rely entirely on military force was made as early as late October and that all diplomatic moves from that point were largely posturing and rhetoric (Woodward 1991). Others have argued that, given White House priorities, the military option was far preferable to either maintaining the sanctions or withdrawing (Mintz 1993).

On November 6, a few days after the midterm election, George Bush announced his decision to double U.S. troop strength in the Gulf, from roughly 250,000 to more than 500,000—half of America's active-duty combat forces. The decision to rely on military solutions, as fate would have it, soon revealed itself to be irreversible—and perhaps this was the intention of the president. Thus it was, with a UN-imposed deadline of January 15, 1991, for Iraqi compliance with all UN resolutions, that the region was poised for war.

The Air War Phase: January 17–February 23, 1991

Those who watched the events unfold on television will long remember the beginning of the air war on Baghdad early in the morning of January 17 (3:00am local time). President Bush appeared on television to declare the beginning of the attack as well as its purpose, making frequent references to the U.S. invasion on D-Day 1944: "The liberation of Kuwait has begun."

The tactic in the air war was fairly simple: destroy all targets that could conceivably support the Iraqi war effort. As a result, not only such things as radar installations, military airfields, and bunkers, but also electrical power plants, highways, water treatment facilities, and commercial airports were on the list of targets. Within less than a week of bombing, Baghdad had no water or electricity (*New York Times*, January 20, 1991, A1). Early attacks were carried out primarily by Tomahawk cruise missiles and Stealth fighters, which were launched from ships offshore and could hug the ground and pass below radar. Although Iraq eventually responded with anti-aircraft artillery, the defense of Baghdad was anemic at best, and after the first few hours, Iraqi air defenses were essentially "blind" (*New York Times*, January 17, 1991, A1).

Iraq responded the next day with Scud missile attacks on Israel, a move aimed at widening the war and undermining Arab support for the United States. In an unprecedented show of restraint, Israel refrained from retaliating against Iraqi targets. U.S. bombers attempted to destroy Iraqi Scud launchers with only partial success. The A-10 "Warthog" was now brought in for its slow, low-level flying abilities, and the operations moved toward destroying the Republican Guard and other ground troops in Kuwait (*New York Times*, January 20, 1991, A1). At home, the war began to take on a surrealistic feeling. Emphasis on technical details of missile targeting led some to describe this as the "Nintendo War" (Florman 1991). Daily reports of targets destroyed and images from cameras mounted on missile nose cones seemed like so many graphics from a video game (see Map 8.1). Estimates of Iraqi civilian casualties vary, but the general consensus is that 7,000 were killed as a direct result of the bombing (Hooglund 1991, 4). Troop losses during this phase of the war seem to have numbered around 75,000. The condition of Iraqi soldiers captured and of refugees coming into Jordan gave visible evidence of widespread disease and malnutrition in the Iraqi capital and on the front lines.

The Ground War Phase: February 24–February 28, 1991

In the middle of February, new deadlines were set, new ultimata laid down, and new battle plans set in motion. On February 24 (4:00am local time), U.S.-led troops and tanks stormed southern Iraq and Kuwait in a dramatic sweep from the west through miles of barren desert (see Map 8.1). In what was dubbed the "Hail Mary" operation—an allusion to a last-ditch pass by a football quarterback into a crowd of receivers in the end zone—U.S. General Norman Schwarzkopf ordered the deployment of troops originally massed on the Kuwaiti border to positions stretching 150 miles westward along the Saudi–Iraq border. Marine forces were kept in the waters off Kuwait City, thus forcing the Iraqis to maintain a strong presence and leave their rear relatively unguarded. U.S. and British divisions stormed into the desert, performing a pivoting maneuver at and around Kuwait, thereby completely isolating Iraqi troops stationed in the area. The tank battle that ensued was extremely lopsided, in that only American tanks were equipped with targeting systems that allowed them to fire while moving at full speed and through dust and smoke. "We're meeting the enemy, and we're not having any trouble destroying him," said the military spokesman on Tuesday after thirty-six hours of fighting (*New York Times*, February 26, 1991, A1).

Within forty-eight hours, nearly all of southern Iraq and most of Kuwait were in coalition hands, and Iraqi soldiers were surrendering by the battalion. Tens of

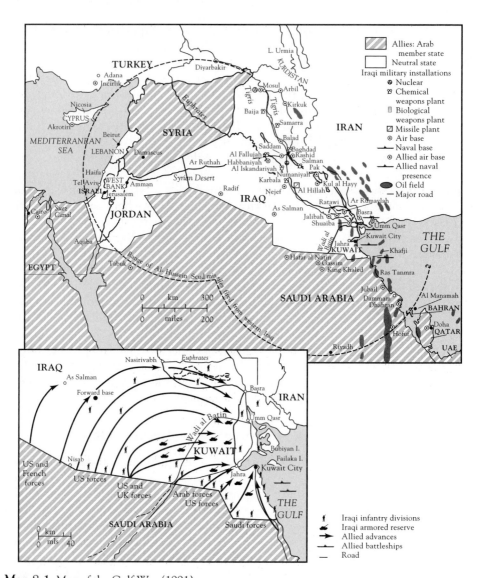

Map 8.1 Map of the Gulf War (1991)
Source: Michael Dockrill, *Atlas of the Twentieth Century World History* (New York: Harper/Perennial, 1991), 114–115

thousands of fleeing Iraqi troops lined the road leading northward out of Kuwait City, many of them with Kuwaiti hostages. Coalition jets targeted the troops as if they were still part of the fighting.

After 100 hours of fighting on the ground and the expulsion of Iraqi forces from Kuwait, President Bush officially announced a cessation of hostilities on February 28, 1991.

THE INTER-WAR PERIOD: MARCH 1991–MARCH 2003

A wide range of problems fell to the coalition governments with the end of the war. Saddam Hussein's forces destroyed oil tanks and set 500 oil wells on fire, leading to an oil spill of some 6 million barrels (Canby 1991, 2). Iraqi forces moved to suppress uprisings in Kurdistan and in Shia-dominated cities in the south. Finally, the question of Iraqi weapons and general compliance with UN resolutions dealing with war reparations and boundary guarantees are yet to be finally resolved. The environmental catastrophe after the Gulf War served to destroy not only the region's wildlife but also the Kuwaiti regime's credibility. Countless delays, largely the result of bureaucratic incompetence in Kuwait, prevented the speedy extinguishing of fires at the 500 wells. It took a total of fifteen months to finally put out all the fires—but at least five months of this time were largely wasted. The regime has struggled with the question of restoring its stature ever since, the most recent development being the formation of a strong anti-monarchy movement in the parliament, a move that may be throttled by a regime still unsure of its tolerance for dissent.

U.S. troops left the region by May, although the humanitarian crisis in northern Iraq after the displacement of thousands of Kurds reached epidemic proportions shortly after the end of the war. Some 300,000 Kurds were killed by Iraqi troops, both before and after the war, through systematic razing of Kurdish villages. Ultimately, to protect and provide for these people, a zone of Iraq north of the 36th parallel (roughly 20,000 square miles) was declared a sanctuary by the UN and patrolled by peacekeeping forces (*New York Times*, May 19, 1991, A8). To the south, Shia Moslems rebelled against Hussein and were suppressed, not only immediately after the war but throughout 1991. Not until the summer of 1992 did the UN act to impose a no-fly zone over the southern regions of Iraq (south of the 32nd parallel). This had the effect of eliminating the more wanton aspects of Iraqi reprisals, and it also led to a more permanent role for U.S. pilots charged with enforcing the rule.

The destruction of Iraqi weapons precipitated several violent and nearly disastrous encounters between Iraqi officials and UN inspectors throughout 1992. Given the task of destroying all Iraqi "weapons of mass destruction" by the Security Council, the UN inspectors went into Iraqi nuclear weapons laboratories and other extremely sensitive sites (*New York Times*, July 25, 1991, A1). UN inspectors were toyed with as early as 1992 and as recently as 1998. In retaliation for obstructing weapons inspections in 1998, the United States and United Kingdom launched punitive air strikes in December. This prompted the Hussein regime to ban inspectors all together. News reports indicated that Hussein had secretly managed to obtain the necessary materials to assemble three nuclear warheads in spite of it all (Tessitore & Woolfson 1999, 49).

By the late 1990s, the coalition that had organized the Gulf War counteroffensive had splintered. Russia and China were joined by France in their efforts to end the economic sanctions against Iraq, which had already cost the country tens of billions in lost oil revenues and were increasingly linked to deteriorating health and nutrition levels among Iraqi children. A growing number of nonprofit organizations began to mobilize against the sanctions, including the Iraq Action Coalition, which posted a web site and began a petition drive in the United States. Ramsey Clark, former U.S. attorney general, founded the International Action Center and joined UNICEF and the UN's Food and Agriculture Organization to deplore the effects of sanctions on children (Clark 1998). As of mid-2000, the stalemate between the pro-sanctions and anti-sanctions forces seemed unbreakable.

ENTER THE VULCANS

Shortly after the election of George W. Bush in November 2000, the president-elect was given an international affairs orientation. In it, neoconservative idealists such as Richard Perle, Paul Wolfowitz, and Vice President-elect Dick Cheney explained their vision of a democratic Middle East, anchored by a post-Saddam Iraq. Although other senior Bush administration officials, including Secretary of State Colin Powell and National Security Advisor Condoleezza Rice, were more cautious, the message was clear: Saddam should have been removed back in 1991. For them, the question was not whether the United States would remove him, but when and how. Paul Wolfowitz urged a more aggressive U.S. foreign policy across the board, introducing a serious discussion of "preemption"—the launching of military strikes to discomfit America's enemies (PBS 2004).

The terror attacks on September 11, 2001, prompted serious deliberations in the White House about retaliation. All agreed that strikes against Afghanistan were called for, but that an attack on Iraq should be postponed, at least until the Afghan situation was settled (Woodward 2004, 25). That said, senior members of the administration continued to argue that Saddam Hussein had links to al Qaeda and thereby to the 9/11 attacks, although the only evidence was the alleged presence in Baghdad of a shadowy figure: Abu Musab al-Zarqawi. It was a link that Colin Powell was never willing to assert. This said, the impression left by U.S. policymakers in the run-up to the war was so strong that on election day 2004, the vast majority of those voting for Bush believed Saddam had been involved in the September 11 attacks (Pew/CFR 2002).

As the war in Afghanistan began to wind down in late 2001, the president's attention turned to Iraq. On December 28th, General Tommy Franks, Commander of the Central Command, laid out several scenarios for removing the Saddam Hussein regime (Woodward 2004, 53–60). The message was clear: Saddam posed a serious and immediate threat to the United States, and the United States could take him out—even if acting alone—with acceptable casualties. The administration began preparing the public for an extension of the war against terror in the January 2002 State of the Union address by declaring that al Qaeda was only part of the problem. Iraq, Iran, and North Korea made up the "axis of evil" bent on threatening the United States and its allies around the world. In April, Bush announced on British television that he had decided that Saddam must go. "The worst thing that could happen would be to allow a nation like Iraq, run by Saddam Hussein, to develop weapons of mass destruction, and then team them up with terrorist organizations so they can blackmail the world. I'm not going to let this happen" (Woodward 2004, 120).

By July 2002, Bush administration war planning was becoming clear to the outside world (*New York Times,* July 29, A1). Secretary of Defense Donald Rumsfeld strongly favored a highly mobile, high-tech force with a small number of troops (roughly 200,000) that would quickly strike from Kuwait, leapfrogging towns along the Euphrates on its way to Baghdad. Planning had moved beyond the hypothetical stage.

It was at this point that Colin Powell intervened. He spoke with President Bush about the dangers of occupying a country. "You are going to be the proud owner of 25 million people. You will own all their hopes, aspirations and problems. You'll own it all" (Woodward 2004, 150). This was privately called the "Pottery Barn rule"—you break it, you own it. Powell pressed the president to wait until he had worked to bring together a coalition worthy of the name as well as a UN Security Resolution that explicitly authorized the use of force. His intervention, while largely unwelcome, was successful. Bush spoke in harsh terms to the UN in September 2002, making clear his exasperation with Saddam's obstructionism and his concern about the threat he posed to the world. At roughly the same time, the White House published the National Security Strategy laying out the "Bush Doctrine" of preemptive strikes against threats to the country, a policy strongly favored by neoconservatives but condemned by international legal experts as reckless (Boyle 2004, 149; Tiefer 2004, 189). The White House also succeeded in October in persuading Congress to pass a resolution authorizing the use of force against Iraq (by a vote of 77–23 in the Senate).

The Security Council passed a strongly worded resolution a few weeks later, prompting the Iraq regime to once again permit weapons inspectors on site. The action, however, created more confusion, as the Iraqi government received mixed reviews from weapons inspectors under the director of Hans Blix. The ambiguities of the situation were enough for some Security Council members to argue that war should be postponed as long as possible. It also did not help the debate that France and Russia stood to make substantial gains from the survival of Saddam's regime by way of oil contracts that had been negotiated years earlier. Donald Rumsfeld did little for his part to mend relations by dismissing France and Germany as "old Europe" in contrast to such new NATO members as Poland and Hungary, which had adopted a more pro-U.S. position (Purdum 2003, 67).

After months of posturing by Security Council members, Colin Powell gave them a detailed presentation, reminiscent of the Adlai Stevenson presentation during the Cuban Missile Crisis. In this case, however, France, Russia, China, and Germany were unpersuaded on the need to end sanctions and launch a military strike. The February speech included satellite photos, tapes of intercepted telephone conversations, and even a simulated vial of anthrax to make the point that Saddam had weapons of mass destruction in spite of eleven years of sanctions. The implication was obvious: sanctions do not work and therefore force is necessary. Another implication was clear: you're either with us or against us. Bush's policy was not aimed at compromise or accommodation of criticisms. There was more political benefit to be gained by clearly identifying adversaries (Allman 2004, 209).

France and Russia announced their intention to use their veto to block any new resolution, however, and so the issue was taken off the agenda. The United States would have to settle for the support of Britain, Spain, Australia, Poland, and a handful of other countries in its war in Iraq.

THE WAR IN IRAQ

In a meeting on March 19, 2003, Bush's "war cabinet" (Rumsfeld, Powell, Cheney, Tenet, Rice, and General Franks) approved the plan of attack that had emerged from more than a year's planning. On March 20, U.S. aircraft launched what it called a "shock and awe" air campaign designed to disrupt and demoralize the Iraqi high command. The next day, an invasion force of 183,000, supported by another 150,000 in the region, moved northward from Kuwait (a northern front was not possible because Turkey had refused to participate) and quickly seized ground (see Map 8.2). The southern city of Basra was surrounded and then taken by British forces early on while American troops moved up the Euphrates River.

Resistance was lighter than expected, although the Republican Guard did not surrender as hoped. Militias, formed prior to the invasion, launched attacks against the thinly stretched lines of troops (Hersh 2004, 258).

In spite of a few setbacks, the coalition forces moved into Baghdad itself in early April, and on April 9, American troops were pulling down a statue of Saddam Hussein in the heart of the city. The Iraqi army had "melted away." On May 1, in spite of warnings against chest-thumping, George W. Bush celebrated the "end of major hostilities" by flying a jet onto the deck of the aircraft carrier USS Abraham Lincoln off the coast of San Diego, California. His stirring speech, replete with references to D-Day and other heroic moments, was delivered under a massive banner declaring "Mission Accomplished."

Paul Bremer was appointed Administrator of the Coalition Provisional Authority (CPA) on May 6, taking the place of General Jay Garner as the civilian leader,

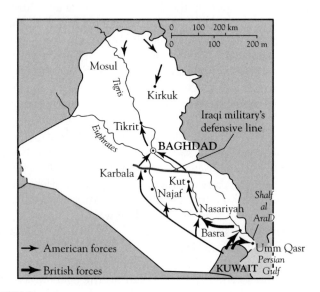

Map 8.2 The 2003 Invasion
Source: Compiled from various *Washington Post* maps.

answerable to Donald Rumsfeld. He quickly established a command center in one of Saddam's principal palaces in downtown Baghdad, surrounding the area with a security perimeter known as the "Green Zone," where coalition forces and CPA staff could operate without fear of attack. Other parts of Baghdad and Iraq were designated "yellow" and "red" zones—the latter being off-limits to all but heavily protected troops. Although most of the country has been safe, several insurgent groups emerged over the course of the occupation, leading to intense battles for control in places like Fallujah and Sadr City—a neighborhood of Baghdad dominated by Moqtada al-Sadr, a radical Shia cleric with aspirations of national power. Casualties of coalition forces continued to rise throughout 2003, with more killed in December than in March or April (see Figure 8.1).

As time went on, the red zones increased in size and number, until by early 2004, whole cities were off-limits to U.S. troops. Coalition troops carried out organized attacks in Najaf, Fallujah, and Sadr City during 2004, killing thousands of insurgents. In Sadr City, the stand-off between Moqtada al-Sadr's forces and the coalition was ultimately settled through the intervention of Grand Ayatollah Ali al-Sistani, who brokered a cease-fire and the withdrawal of Sadr's militia from holy sites. In early 2004, in addition to suicide bombings (which killed more than 700 in the first half of 2004 alone), roadside bombs, mortar and grenade attacks, and open battles, insurgents began to resort to kidnappings of foreigners. By the end of September, 140 foreigners had been kidnapped and paraded before the world press, many of them later beheaded. The actions served to undermine the coalition as some of the smaller contributors began to withdraw their forces. The end result was

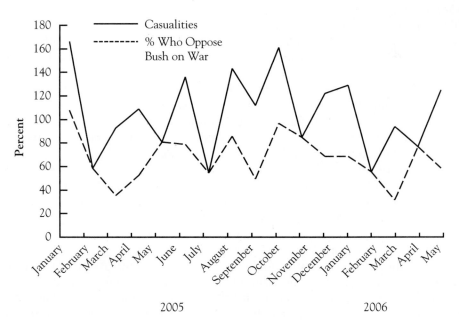

Figure 8.1 Trends in the war—casualties and public support

a continued strong military presence of roughly 150,000—a level far higher than had initially been planned by Bush administration. The announcement in February that intelligence on weapons of mass destruction was almost entirely flawed shook the American public's confidence in the abilities of the Bush administration (some critics referred to WMDs as "weapons of mass delusion"; Allman 2004, 309). With more than 130 deaths in April and the discovery of torture being committed by U.S. troops in prisons such as that at Abu Ghraib (apparently with the tacit approval of senior commanders and Washington officials), talk of "quagmire" became increasingly common in the United States (Thomas 2004). A solid majority (58%) opposed the administration's handling of the war, although this figure would decline by the end of the year (and did not prevent President Bush's reelection in November).

News on the war was not entirely negative, however. The UN Security Council, thanks in part to an increased willingness on the part of the Bush administration to moderate its language, showed itself willing to accept the CPA's legitimacy in Iraq and offered its help in preparing for elections in January 2005. On June 28, sovereignty was formally (if not practically) transferred to a new Iraqi regime under Prime Minister Iyad Allawi, a moderate Shia who has proved capable of generating support from Iraqis and Americans alike. Saddam's capture in December 2003 no doubt went far to reassure Iraqis that his regime would not reemerge. Likewise, the removal of insurgent bases in cities such as Fallujah in late 2004 was a major tactical victory. And while some soldiers were responsible for abuse and torture, others, including Lt. Gen. David Petraeus, were successful in implementing "hearts and minds" programs that enhanced the reputation of the American military (Nordland 2004). He was placed in charge of the "surge" of troops in 2007, which involved the addition of 20,000 new American troops and a new counterinsurgency strategy. By February 2009, newly-inaugurated President Barack Obama reached agreement with military commanders and the Iraqi government on the removal of nearly all American forces by mid-2010.

The surge was controversial (most members of Congress opposed it) not only because it would likely cost more American lives but also because the Iraqi government was failing to meet most of the performance targets the White House and Congress had given it. As the number of troops increased, operations in Baghdad and elsewhere intensified. American casualties peaked in May at 131—the deadliest month of the war. By April 2008, U.S. casualties had reached 4,000. But insurgents were removed from many neighborhoods, which created a breathing space that allowed Iraqis to return to normal. A year later, casualties were down and security had improved to the point that most observers considered the surge a success.

On the political side, although more political parties began participating in elections, there was still considerable tension between regions and between religious sects. Resolution of the issue of oil revenue distribution had yet to be resolved, as was the case on all but a handful of the benchmarks. Nouri al-Maliki, the Prime Minister who assumed office in May 2006, maintained the confidence of the American government but was not successful in bringing Sunnis into government as had been hoped. Nonetheless, both he and President Bush began in June 2008 to openly discuss plans to withdraw the bulk of American troops over a 16-month timetable, something the American President tentatively supported in August.

CONCLUSION: THE LIMITS OF MILITARY POWER

What do the two Gulf Wars tell us about the nature of power, as understood in terms of both capability and influence? Much depends on one's assessment of the extent of coalition victory. Clearly the immediate aims of dislodging Iraq from Kuwait and Saddam from Baghdad were achieved, although only by resort to force. In spite of Iraq's almost complete dependence on oil exports, the sanctions did not have the effect of changing the government's policy in Kuwait or inducing Saddam to step down (although no one will ever know whether they might have eventually worked).

On the other hand, the formation of the coalition in the first Gulf War was a remarkable victory, especially given obvious tensions between Security Council members manifested in the second Iraq war. Saddam learned that defiance is less useful than strategic ambiguity (Cooper, Higgott, & Nossal 1991). The coalition also enjoyed a degree of political legitimacy that is rare thanks to the approval of UN bodies throughout the operation (Russett 1994), something that was obviously lacking in the case of the 2003 invasion.

Dissenting voices have pointed out that the war failed to dislodge the Iraqi regime or protect its political opponents (Byman 2000), which in turn motivated many senior Bush officials to call for a preemptive strike in 2003 to finish the job. But the failure to locate weapons of mass destruction or clearly link Saddam to 9/11 has led many to conclude that the end of the first war was perhaps more successful than had been originally thought.

At any rate, the continuing insurgency in Iraq—albeit at lower levels—demonstrates that military superiority alone does not guarantee that an invader will win the "hearts and minds" of the people. The U.S. military has learned that much more important is a political settlement to the problems and the establishment of local authority and governing capacity.

QUESTIONS TO CONSIDER

1. Was military forced used effectively in 1991 or 2003? How might it have been used differently?

2. To what extent was resorting to military force a sign a weakness or strength?

3. Did the Gulf Wars achieve the political objectives of the two Bush administrations? Why or why not?

KEY FIGURES
THE PERSIAN GULF WAR

Saddam Hussein   Iraqi President, 1979–2003. His armies invaded Kuwait on August 2, 1990.

George H.W. Bush   U.S. President, 1989–1993. He organized the coalition that liberated Kuwait on February 28, 1991.

George W. Bush   U.S. President, 2001–2009. He ordered the invasion and occupation of Iraq in 2003.

Boutros Boutros-Ghali   UN Secretary-General, 1992–1996. He served as a mediator between the Security Council and Iraqi officials.

Kofi Annan   UN Secretary-General, 1997–2007. He expressed opposition to the invasion plans and later described them as illegal.

General Norman Schwarzkopf   U.S. Commander, Central Command, at the time of the Gulf War. He led the military offensive to retake Kuwait.

Tariq Aziz   Iraqi Foreign Minister during the Gulf War. He acted as Saddam Hussein's representative at the UN.

Eduard Shevardnadze   Soviet Foreign Minister during the Gulf War. He pressed for a diplomatic settlement.

Mikhail Gorbachev   Soviet Communist Party Chairman, 1985–1991.

General Tommy Franks   U.S. Commander, Central Command at the time of the Iraq invasion.

Colin Powell   U.S. Secretary of State, 2001–2005. He warned George W. Bush of the risks involved in occupying Iraq after the invasion, but spoke on behalf of the administration to the UN Security Council.

Donald Rumsfeld   U.S. Secretary of Defense, 2001–2006. He promoted and directed the Iraq invasion.

Paul Wolfowitz   U.S. Deputy Secretary of Defense, 2001–2005. He was among the first to advocate the removal of Saddam Hussein by force.

Dick Cheney   U.S. Vice President, 2001–2009. He consistently advocated the forceful removal of Saddam Hussein.

George Tenet   Director of Central Intelligence, 1997–2004. He argued that although not airtight, the evidence that Saddam Hussein had weapons of mass destruction in 2003 was strong.

Tony Blair   United Kingdom Prime Minister, 1997–2007. He has consistently been George W. Bush's strongest supporter in the war in Iraq.

Moqtada al-Sadr   Nephew of Baqir al-Sadr, slain Shia leader, and leader of a mass uprising in Sadr City in Baghdad.

Abu Musab al-Zarqawi   Palestinian linked to al Qaeda who is alleged to have operated in Baghdad in 2002. His organization was responsible for kidnappings and beheadings of foreigners in 2004.

Iyad Allawi   Prime Minister of Iraq after the transfer of sovereignty on June 28, 2004. A secular-minded Shia Muslim, he enjoyed considerable support from the Iraqi populace while maintaining the confidence of the U.S. authorities.

Grand Ayatollah Ali al-Sistani   Senior Shia cleric who emerged as a moderate peacemaker able to command the respect of nearly the entire Shia community in Iraq.

Nouri al-Maliki   Prime Minster of Iraq, beginning October 2006.

General David Petraeus   Commander of multinational forces in Iraq from 2007 to 2008, where he commanded the "surge." He was later promoted to commander of Central Command.

CHRONOLOGY
THE PERSIAN GULF WAR

1932
Great Britain draws the boundaries between Iraq and Kuwait as part of its dismantling of the Ottoman Empire.

1961
Kuwait is granted its independence over Iraq's protests.

1979
Saddam Hussein becomes President of Iraq.

1980
The Iran–Iraq War begins with Iraq's invasion of Iran in retaliation for its destabilization efforts in southern Iraq.

1988
The Iran–Iraq War ends.

1990
July   The Iraqi government challenges Kuwaiti policies and sovereignty.

August 2   Iraqi forces attack and defeat Kuwaiti defenses.

August 5   U.S. forces are deployed to Saudi Arabia.

November 6   President George H.W. Bush announces a large increase in troop strength.

November 29   The UN Security Council sets a deadline for Iraqi withdrawal from Kuwait.

1991
January 17   Coalition forces launch air strikes against Iraqi forces in and around Kuwait.

(continued)

(*continued*)

January 20   Coalition forces achieve air superiority.

January 26   Iraqi forces begin releasing Kuwaiti oil into the Persian Gulf.

February 23   Coalition forces launch a ground strike against Iraqi forces.

February 28   Iraqi forces surrender.

May   U.S. troops are withdrawn from Kuwait. Kurds rebel against Saddam Hussein's regime. A "no-fly" zone is created in northern Iraq to discourage Iraqi attacks against rebels.

1992
A "no-fly" zone is created in southern Iraq. UN weapons inspectors are rebuffed in Baghdad. Paul Wolfowitz directs drafting of Defense Planning Guidance, calling for preemptive strikes against potential enemies, as opposed to mere containment of threats.

1998
The United Kingdom and the United States launch air strikes against Iraqi weapons installations. Iraq bars UN weapons inspectors.

2002
The U.S. proposes an invasion of Iraq to overthrow Saddam Hussein's regime. The White House consistently argues that Iraq is rebuilding a stockpile of weapons of mass destruction and had ties to al Qaeda and the September 11 terror attacks.

September 17   President Bush releases the National Security Strategy, which clarifies the new "Bush Doctrine" of preemptive strikes.

October 11   The U.S. Senate, by a vote of 77–23, approves a resolution granting President Bush the authority to use force to disarm Saddam Hussein.

2003
February 5   Colin Powell makes the case that Iraq has weapons of mass destruction before the UN Security Council. France and Russia are unmoved and continue to oppose a new resolution.

March 19   Cabinet members approve the plan of attack.

March 20   Air campaign begins, described as "shock and awe." The 1st Marine Division enters Iraqi territory the next day and quickly advances toward Baghdad.

April 9   A statue of Saddam Hussein is toppled in downtown Baghdad, symbolizing the end of his government. Hussein himself would eventually be found in a spider hole on December 13. The collapse of Hussein's regime leads to large-scale looting of government facilities.

May 1   George W. Bush lands a jet on the deck of the USS Abraham Lincoln to celebrate "mission accomplished." U.S. casualties number 138.

July 22   Uday and Qusay, Saddam's sons, are killed in a shootout in Mosul.

August   More than 110 are killed in two truck bombs in Baghdad and Najaf.

October   David Kay, the U.S. weapons inspector, issues the first of several reports indicating that no weapons of mass destruction had been found in Iraq. In January 2004, he acknowledges an intelligence failure.

May   After uprisings in Najaf and Fallujah, a truce is announced. Sadr City in Baghdad continues to see unrest directed by Moqtada al-Sadr.

2004
June 28   Sovereignty is formally transferred to Iraqi nations, with Iyad Allawi as leader of the new government.

September   American casualties in Iraq pass the 1,000 mark.

November   American forces attack Fallujah to break the back of the Iraqi insurgency. Insurgents are routed in house-to-house combat, but Abu Musab al-Zarqawi escapes.

2005
January 30   Elections for the Transitional National Assembly bring roughly eight million voters to the polls and hand victory to the Shia United Iraqi Alliance.

April   Kurdish leader Jalal Talibani is named president and Shia leader Ibrahim Jaafari becomes the prime minister.

August   A draft constitution is produced by the assembly without Sunni support. It is later approved overwhelmingly in a referendum.

December 15   Iraqis vote for a permanent government. The Shia United Iraqi Alliance wins a plurality, but must wait until May 2006 before it can negotiate formation of a coalition government led by Jawad al-Maliki.

2006
May 20   Nouri al-Maliki is installed as the new Prime Minster of Iraq.

2007
January 10   President Bush announces the "surge" involving an increase by 20,000 in American troop levels in the hope of regaining control of Baghdad and other areas. Counterinsurgency operations increase in the Spring.

May   One hundred thirty-one Americans are killed—the highest levels since 2004. Casualties drop dramatically thereafter, but 2007 is the deadliest year, with 852 deaths.

2008
April   Total American deaths pass 4,000. Violence in Iraq reaches low enough levels that most observers declare the surge a relative success. Benchmarks for the Iraqi government go largely unmet, however.

August   President Bush and Prime Minster al-Maliki tentatively agree on a gradual drawdown of U.S. troops.

REFERENCES

Allman, T. D. *Rogue State: America at War with the World* (New York: Nation Books, 2004).

Boyle, Francis A. *Destroying World Order: U.S. Imperialism in the Middle East Before and After September 11* (Atlanta: Clarity Press, 2004).

Byman, Daniel. "After the Storm: U.S. Policy Toward Iraq Since 1991." *Political Science Quarterly* 115 #4 (Winter 2000): 493–520.

Canby, Thomas Y. "After the Storm." *National Geographic* (August 1991): 2–35.

Clark, Ramsey, ed. *The Children Are Dying: Reports by the UN Food and Agriculture Organization* (New York: International Action Center, 1998).

Cooper, Andrew, Richard Higgott, and Kim Nossal. "Bound to Follow? Leadership and Followership in the Gulf Conflict." *PSQ* 106 (1991): 391–410.

Florman, Samuel. "Engineers and the Nintendo War." *Technology Review* 94 #5 (July 1991): 62.

Hooglund, Eric. "The Other Face of War." *Middle East Report* (July–August 1991): 3–13.

Hersh, Seymour. *Chain of Command: The Road from 9/11 to Abu Ghraib.* (New York: HarperCollins Publishers, 2004).

Miller, Judith, and Laurie Mylroie. *Saddam Hussein and the Crisis in the Gulf.* (New York: Random House, 1990).

Mintz, Alex. "The Decision to Attack Iraq." *Journal of Conflict Resolution* 37 #4 (December 1993): 595–619.

New York Times, July 25, 1990, A1.

New York Times, September 3, 1990, A7.

New York Times, March 21, 1991, A17.

New York Times, September 25, 1991.

Nordland, Rod. "Iraq's Repairman." *Newsweek* July 5, 2004, pp. 22–30.

PBS. "Frontline: The War Behind Closed Doors—Chronology." Available at http://www.pbs.org/wgbh/pages/frontline/shows/iraq/etc/cron.html.

Pew/Council on Foreign Relations. "Americans Thinking About Iraq, But Focused on the Economy." October 2003. Available at http://www.people-press.org/report/162/americans-thinking-about-iraq-but-focused-on-the-economy.

Purdum, Todd S. *A Time of Our Choosing: America's War in Iraq* (New York: Times Books, 2003).

Rothgeb, John G., Jr. *Defining Power: Influence and Force in the Contemporary International System* (New York: St. Martin's Press, 1993).

Russett, Bruce. "The Gulf War as Empowering the United Nations." In John O'Loughlin, Tom Mayer, Edward Greenberg, eds. *War and Its Consequences: Lessons from the Persian Gulf War.* (New York: HarperCollins Publishers, 1994): 185–197.

Tessitore, John, and Susan Woolfson, eds. *A Global Agenda: Issues Before the 54th General Assembly of the United Nations* (Lanham, MD: Rowman and Littlefield, 1999).

Tiefer, Charles. *Veering Right: How the Bush Administration Subverts the Law for Conservative Causes.* (Berkeley: University of California Press, 2004).

Thomas, Evan. "The Vietnam Question" *Newsweek*, April 19, 2004, pp. 28–35.

Tucker, Robert W., and David C. Hendrickson. *The Imperial Temptation: The New World Order and America's Purpose* (New York: Council on Foreign Relations, 1992).

White, Josh, "Soldiers Facing Extended Tours." *Washington Post*, June 3, 2004, p. A01.

Woodward, Robert. *The Commanders* (New York: Simon & Schuster, 1991).

Woodward, Robert. *Plan of Attack* (New York: Simon & Schuster, 2004).

9

■ ■ ■

Terrorism: Al Qaeda

INTRODUCTION

Before September 11, 2001, international terrorism was mostly an abstraction for many Americans—something the Israelis and British were forced to deal with, but not us. As long as we stayed home and minded our own business, we would be safe from international threats. After September 11, this illusion was shattered. Terrorism quickly became one of the country's top priorities. In the months after the September 11 attacks, as pointed out by President George W. Bush in his January 2002 State of the Union address, tens of billions of dollars of new spending were approved for homeland security, a vast international anti-terror coalition was formed and new international laws adopted, and a war was fought and won in Afghanistan, resulting in the capture of thousands of al Qaeda operatives and the displacement of an entire regime (Bush 2002; *Christian Science Monitor* September 9, 2002, 1).

Defining terrorism seems easy when one considers such brazen acts of devastation. In practice, however, it is not always easy to categorize groups and actions neatly. Consider the following alternative definitions of terrorism:

> The unlawful use of force against persons or property to intimidate or coerce a government, the civilian population, or any segment thereof, in furtherance of political or social objectives. . . .
>
> Premeditated, politically motivated violence perpetrated against noncombatant targets by sub-national groups or clandestine agents. . . .
>
> The unlawful use or threat of violence against persons or property to further political or social objectives. It is generally intended to intimidate or coerce a government, individuals or groups or to modify their behavior or policies. . . . (Beres 1995, 3–4)

These definitions share several elements: (1) Terrorism involves violence—sometimes against civilian targets. (2) Terrorism has a political objective. (3) The terrorist expects that the political objective can be achieved by sowing fear. In most cases, terrorism is the act of an organized and politically motivated group that is expressing its profound dissatisfaction with the order of things, whether it be the occupation of territory by a foreign power, rule of a country by a racial minority, despotic government by a dictatorial regime, or something else.

Note that terrorism differs markedly from two other violent phenomena found in international life: international crime and warfare. International crime is conducted primarily for the purpose of accumulating wealth, and violence and political machinations are a means to that end. On the other hand, even where terrorists engage in garden-variety criminal activities, such as theft and drug-running, these actions are pursued to finance their political acts and agenda. Warfare involves state actors interacting with each other, and their actions are governed by codes of conduct and international law. Combatants must wear uniforms, refrain from targeting civilians, feed and protect prisoners, and so forth. The objective in war is to incapacitate the enemy, which is primarily a physical rather than a psychological goal (Tucker 1997, 67).

Terrorists share a great deal with guerrillas, who are usually better financed and organized but use many of the same tactics and have many of the same goals. Terrorists and guerrillas typically are both weaker than the governments they challenge and must therefore resort to hit-and-run attacks and other low-intensity tactics (bombings, assassinations, sabotage). Guerrillas differ in that they are always territorially based and are usually focused on seizing power to govern some land mass. Thus the Peruvian Shining Path, the Tamil Tigers, and the Euskadi Ta Askatasuna (ETA) are interested in replacing existing governments in their homelands with their own members in Peru, Sri Lanka, and Spain, respectively. Their grievances are typically concrete and even understandable within the context of the state system and the goal of self-determination. Most countries in the world formed when some local group or nation sought to achieve independence from an alien government, and in almost all cases, violence was part of the strategy. Many guerrillas who were successful have gone on to lead their countries as statesmen. Many of the prime ministers of Israel, for example, were guerrillas in their youth, as were Mao Zedong, Fidel Castro, and Nelson Mandela. One could even argue that George Washington was a guerrilla (he was portrayed as such by the British during the Revolutionary War).

Terrorists may also have concrete political goals, including replacing a government or controlling territory, but, as we have learned, this is not the only motivation. Terrorist organizations may have a broad set of goals that transcend controlling a particular state or region, and their membership may be drawn from many different nations. Their targets may include numerous states or nonstate actors across the globe, making them a genuine transnational threat.

Of the transnational terrorist organizations in the world, al Qaeda stands out and is therefore the focus of our study here. Al Qaeda is unusual in many respects, however, as we will make clear.

ISLAMIC FUNDAMENTALISM

It is impossible to understand al Qaeda without knowing something of Islamic extremism. At its core, Islam is a conservative, family-centered, monotheistic faith that shares a great deal with Judeo-Christian religious tradition (Muslims generally feel a kinship with such "people of the book" and share a lineage to Abraham). Founded in the seventh century by the Prophet Mohammed (the story of his miraculous calling resembles in many ways the experiences of Moses and the Apostle Peter), Islam expanded quickly through the Middle East through both conversion and conquest. In its early days, its teachings on government and human rights were extremely progressive, since they encouraged democratic institutions, civil rights for women, and the empowerment of ordinary people (in contrast to the feudal and caste-based system of the day; al-Turabi 1987).

After the death of the Prophet and his immediate successors (the Caliphs), Islam experienced considerable splintering and decline. Today there is no single leader of the Muslim world (the *ummah*). Rather, numerous Islamic scholars (*ulama*), like theology professors or rabbinical scholars, spend their energies interpreting the Islamic holy writ (the *Qur'an,* giving revelations from the angel Gabriel to Mohammed, and the *Hadith,* stories and statements of Mohammed) and statements of earlier scholars.

A major schism occurred shortly after the death of the Prophet Mohammed and gave rise to two major Islamic movements: the Sunni and the Shia. From time to time, Islamic spiritualists (Sufi) and martyrs develop followings and become the source of other new schools and societies. The varieties of "Islams" are so diverse that what is permitted in some quarters is forbidden in others, sometimes leading to deadly arguments. Note, for example, the fact that every Muslim nation in the world (with the exception of the secular government of Saddam Hussein in Iraq) unequivocally condemned the September 11 attacks and hundreds of ulama went on record to declare terrorism to be an un-Islamic act (Schafer 2002, 18). This background is mentioned to make it clear that Islam is a varied and complex religious movement that defies easy generalization. One should add to this the fact that many Islamic traditions have adopted and incorporated social traditions from particular regions that existed long before Islam appeared. In Bangladesh, for example, Muslims continue to recognize Hindu castes in their day-to-day practice. The status and treatment of women varies dramatically across different Muslim communities, in part due to local traditions.

Among these myriad branches and sects, a few have developed relatively recently to challenge the mainstream. In the mid-1700s, in the wake of the European and Ottoman imperial conquests of North Africa and the Middle East, a few began to challenge the prevailing Muslim orthodoxy. They argued that Muslims had become lax and confused, having embraced too much of their Western invaders' ways and/or perverting the ways of the Prophet. They took it upon themselves to cleanse the society through teaching, organizing, and, in a few cases, violence. Muhammad Ibn Abdul Wahhab, for example, preached a puritanical form of Islam that he thought was practiced by Muslims at the time of the Prophet (Davidson 1998, 50). In 1744, he formed an alliance with the patriarch of the Saud family to defeat what they considered polytheistic heresy among other Muslims. The alliance succeeded for a time in conquering the Arabian peninsula and reclaiming the holy cities of Mecca and Medina, only to be driven out by the Ottomans (based in Turkey). The House of Saud reclaimed the territory over time, and by 1932, it was able to establish an Islamic monarchy that ruled using the Qur'an as its legal reference (*shariah* law). Osama bin Laden is a self-professed Wahhabi (Wright 2001, 264).

In Egypt, where Western influence was pervasive, Hasan al-Banna emerged as a teacher and activist. He organized the Society of Muslim Brothers in 1928 to urge fellow Muslims to return to the pure tenets of the faith. He aspired to restore not only the moral and social organization but also political structures of the earliest period of Islam. The movement proved extremely popular and received support from secular politicians, such as Gamal Abdel Nasser and Anwar Sadat, who took power in the 1950s. It attracted a following among Muslims who were radicalized by the creation of the state of Israel, although al-Banna was not especially militant himself. The Society he founded provided health care, education, and other services (even a Scouting program for youth) that were aimed at inculcating a respect for basic Muslim values.

The Society also had a secret military organization that engaged in assassination, leading to the murder of al-Banna by Egyptian authorities in 1949 (Davidson 1998, 26). His successor also failed to restrain the violent tendencies of the Brotherhood, and during the 1960s, the organization was repressed. From the 1970s, it grew in strength and served as an inspiration to so-called fundamentalist ("fanatically puritanical" might be a better term), anti-Western movements across the region. These sects included the Gam'a Islamiya (Islamic Group), led by the "Blind Sheikh," Omar Abdul Rahman, who later collaborated with Osama bin Laden (Davidson 1998, 101; O'Ballance 1997, 19).

In 1978, Iran's Ayatollah Ruhollah Khomeini, a Shiite as well as a teacher and activist, led a popular uprising against the corrupt ruler Shah Reza Pahlavi. From his position at the helm of Iran, he was able to propagandize revolutionary Islamic fundamentalism by setting up Iran as a model, as well as provide shelter and direct support to revolutionary movements in the region and beyond (O'Ballance 1997). His regime was particularly instrumental in building Hezbollah (Party of God) in Lebanon in the early 1980s as a service organization with a strong military wing whose aim is the elimination of the state of Israel (Davidson 1998, 169).

OSAMA BIN LADEN AND THE FOUNDING OF AL QAEDA

It was in this context that Osama bin Laden came of age. One of the many children of a successful Saudi businessman, bin Laden studied engineering and Islamic law (his personal fortune has been conservatively estimated at $30 million; Gunaratna 2002, 19). In 1979, the Soviet Union invaded Afghanistan to establish a Communist regime on its southern border. Bin Laden was impressed by the strength of the resistance mounted by local Afghans, who came to be known as mujahaddin. He, along with Abdullah Azzam, began organizing various projects to bring relief supplies and war materiel to the mujahaddin in Afghanistan. In 1984, they organized the MAK (Afghan Service Bureau). They were part of a growing Arab presence in Afghanistan where, eventually, Islamic militants gathered from around the world (Huband 1998, 2). In the process of fighting together, these militants became increasingly radicalized as they saw the results of their struggle against the Soviet forces. When the Soviets withdrew in 1989, the mujahaddin, and bin Laden in particular, took full credit for their defeat (Wright 2001, 250). Furthermore, they took credit for the eventual collapse of the Soviet Union itself (bin Laden took personal offense at the West claiming credit for what was an Islamic victory; Gunaratna 2002, 22).

Hoping to capitalize on the energy of the Afghan movement, bin Laden and Azzam joined with Muhammed Atef and others to found al Qaeda (the Base) in 1988 as a mechanism for keeping militants in contact with each other, coordinating their actions against anti-Islamic forces, and providing training and supplies for this purpose. By 1989, several militants had been sworn in as the first cadre of al Qaeda fighters (Gunaratna 2002, 23). They established their headquarters in Peshawar, Pakistan, with the help of the ISI (CIA-equivalent) of Pakistan.

Azzam's views of the organization were somewhat more moderate than those of bin Laden, who had started training guerrillas as early as 1986. In 1989, Azzam was murdered by Egyptian radicals who later became leaders of al Qaeda (Gunaratna believes bin Laden conspired with Ayman Mohammed Rabi' al-Zawahiri in the attack; Gunaratna 2002, 25). After 1989, the movement became more intransigent and active.

Three other important developments stimulated the growth and orientation of al Qaeda. In August 1990, U.S. troops were deployed in northern Saudi Arabia at the invitation of the Saud royal family to defend the area from the Iraqi forces that had just invaded Kuwait. After the defeat of Iraq, the American troops remained. Bin Laden believed that the willingness of the Saud family to allow infidels into Saudi Arabia—the home of the two holiest sites of Islam (Mecca and Medina)—was a betrayal of the Prophet and an abdication of their sacred duty to protect the shrines. He labeled them as apostates and called for their destruction (Wright 2001, 265).

In 1991, the Saudi regime expelled bin Laden for sedition, but the Sudanese government soon welcomed him and roughly 500 militants (Wright 2001, 251). After moving the headquarters of al Qaeda to Khartoum, bin Laden took advantage of the government's hospitality to build several prosperous businesses and sign lucrative contracts, thereby significantly increasing the organization's assets and cash flow. In 1996, however, the Sudanese asked bin Laden to leave under considerable pressure from the United States and other Western states. By this time, the Taliban had seized power in Afghanistan and offered him safe haven.

While in Afghanistan, bin Laden's stature and power rose considerably. He developed a close relationship with Mullah Mohammed Omar and became highly influential in the regime. It was bin Laden who encouraged the Taliban to destroy giant Buddha statues in Bamiyan, to international outcry (Gunaratna 2002, 43, 62). Al Qaeda provided 2,000 militants (055 Brigade) to help the Taliban fight the Northern Alliance during the late 1990s, earning the respect and gratitude of the regime. It was from here that bin Laden issued three fatawa proclaiming it the duty of all Muslims to destroy the Saudi regime and to kill Americans, and Jews, and any Westerners who were blocking the establishment of puritanical Islam (these can be found in the appendix of Alexander and Swetnam 2001). It was also from Afghanistan that al Qaeda launched its most notorious attacks, against two U.S. embassies in Africa in 1998, against the USS *Cole* in 2000, and against the World

Trade Center and Pentagon in 2001. These attacks, along with other minor strikes, killed a total of 3,300 individuals and injured more than 6,000.

The last attack, on September 11, 2001, began the most recent change in al Qaeda's fortunes. It prompted a massive retaliation by the United States and other states, including a global crack-down on al Qaeda's militants, finances, and sponsors, culminating in the defeat of the Taliban regime and the death and capture of thousands of militants in October and November of 2001.

DESCRIBING AL QAEDA

It is useful at this point to focus on the goals, structure, and financing of al Qaeda, so as to better illustrate the character of a major terrorist organization. It is important to underscore that al Qaeda is unique in several respects. To begin, it is uniquely transnational in structure and scope, including cells and operations in more than fifty countries with militants and financial backers in dozens of countries. It is also uniquely vitriolic in its orientation, surpassing even the militancy of other Islamic organizations (for example, the Saudi fundamentalist Advice and Reformation Committee announced that bin Laden's 1996 fatwa was merely a personal statement; Huband 1998, 115). It has been described as an "apocalyptic" organization, whose goal is primarily destruction and chaos in an attempt to usher in a new world, putting it on a par with Nazism (Herf 2002).

Al Qaeda's Goals

Bin Laden is a Wahhabi, taking an extremely puritanical approach to Islam. Only the Taliban embodied this view in its everyday practices, which included strict enforcement of dietary, moral, and other codes found in Islam. The Taliban, for example, viewed the place of women in society as extremely subordinate and inferior. Women were banned from schools and the business world and were not allowed to receive medical care from male doctors (since there were no female doctors, the implication was clear; Wright 2001, 264). Its absolutist view meant that not only infidels from other faiths, but also modern regimes that tolerated Western culture, were viewed as threats. Thus it is easy to understand why Anwar Sadat and Hosni Mubarak of Egypt were targeted by al Qaeda allies for assassination (the attempt was successful in the case of President Sadat). Likewise, attacks on Saudi leaders are consistent with this view.

The religious leaders of al Qaeda, especially Ayman Mohammed Rabi' al-Zawahiri, spend considerable energy working to legitimize their version of Islam to the world. This is done through religious instruction to the militants as well as through public pronouncements. The fatwa is used heavily as a religiously sanctioned call for action by all Muslims. Not only do al Qaeda clerics issue these from time to time, but in recent years, bin Laden himself has been taking on the trappings of priesthood, naming himself "Sheik" and issuing fatawa (plural of fatwa) on his own authority (Wright 2001, 255). He has always endeavored to maintain a strict lifestyle so as to inspire piety and self-discipline in the ranks. Interestingly, bin Laden is one of the first Islamic militants to embrace terrorists of the Shiite school of Islam, in spite of the considerable hostility that has dominated Sunni–Shiite relations over the years. As a result, he has developed ties with both Iran and Lebanon's Ebola, much to the consternation of Western intelligence and defense agencies (Gunaratna 2002; see also Chapter 4).

In "Join the Caravan," bin Laden urges all Muslims to take up the cause of jihad (struggle) against Jews and Christians (Zionists and crusaders) as an individual obligation (Gunaratna 2002, 87). Why join the jihad? (1) So that nonbelievers do not dominate; (2) because of the scarcity of manpower; (3) fear of hellfire; (4) fulfilling the duty of jihad and responding to the call of Allah; (5) following in the footsteps of pious predecessors; (6) establishing a solid foundation as a base for Islam; (7) protecting those who are oppressed in the land; (8) seeking martyrdom (Gunaratna 2002, 88).

A special problem for al Qaeda (and all Islamic militants) is the fact that the Qur'an and the Prophet's teachings specifically outlaw suicide and violence against innocents (particularly women and children). With respect to the ban on suicide, clerics have emphasized that the struggle requires the sacrifice of all things, including life itself. Those who take that ultimate step are assured "martyr" status and eternal bliss in heaven (there is even mention of women). Thus it is not suicide at all, in a religious sense. With respect to killing innocents, they have argued that the end justifies the means, however. Because the goal is the eradication of opposition to Islam (defending the faith is one meaning of jihad, a central tenet of Islam), and because opposition includes whole nations of people, everyone is to some degree culpable. Although women and children are not appropriate targets in and of themselves, they may be killed incidentally, according to al Qaeda's clerics (Gunaratna 2002, 76).

This religious underpinning explains why some have argued that the best weapon against al Qaeda may be a religious one. If moderate clerics, for example, can convince the puritanical fanatics that they are interpreting the holy writ incorrectly, they can undermine recruitment efforts (Miles 2002). Likewise, because the struggle is ideological and cultural, Western actors must convey the desirability of liberal democratic principles and the market (Berman 2001).

To help clarify the relative uniqueness of al Qaeda, consider other terrorist organizations, such as the Palestine Liberation Organization (PLO), the Provisional Irish Republican Army (IRA), and ETA. Each has carried out hundreds of killings of both military personnel and civilians through shootings and bombings in order to alter the policies of states. But each is territorially based. And each has been willing to engage in negotiations with the target state.

Consider the story of ETA, for example. Formed in the 1950s by Basque separatists in Spain and France, ETA fought against the repression of Basque identity and culture by Spanish dictator Francisco Franco, who targeted Basques in part because they had fought against him during the Spanish Civil War prior to World War II. In the early years, their demand for an independent Basque homeland and their limited acts of violence in the 1950s and 1960s were not entirely repudiated by the rest of the world, and France apparently provided sanctuary to ETA militants (Martinez-Herrera 2002, 11). Many in Spain's pro-democracy community secretly applauded ETA's assassination of Franco's heir-apparent in 1973. ETA has also enjoyed the support of roughly one in six residents of the Basque region—particularly from those who identified themselves as ethnically Basque—and its various allied political parties have consistently received enough votes to win seats in the local parliament and mayorships (Martinez-Herrera 2002, 6). After Franco died in 1975, ETA stepped up its attacks, killing nearly 100 each year in the late-1970s, even as the new leader, King Juan Carlos, instituted constitutional rule and agreed to considerable autonomy for the Basque region (Woodworth 2001, 6). ETA argued (with considerable support from Basque parties) that the constitutional reforms were mere window-dressing and that Basque rights were still limited and Spanish police were still brutal (points that were supported by outside investigators; AI 2002).

But in the late-1990s, the mood shifted. An increasing number of Basques were split on the issue of independence and thousands rallied to call for a peaceful settlement of the dispute with Spain. ETA's support dwindled to 5% in the region, and the government of Spain estimated its full-time military force at just thirty (BBC 2006). On March 22, 2006, ETA announced a permanent cease-fire and a willingness to support constitutional means to secure Basque independence. A similar pattern was followed by the IRA and PLO, although the situation in Palestine is far more volatile (see Chapter 1 on the Camp David Accords).

Al Qaeda's Organization

Al Qaeda differs from most terrorist organizations in that it is not territorially based, but rather has a consciously global presence (Table 9.1). Its essential elements consist of a governing council (*shura majlis*) that includes roughly one dozen bin Laden loyalists who help staff four policy committees (military, religious, financial, and public relations). These bodies behave in ways that resemble a philanthropic foundation by issuing overall purposes and guidelines, reviewing proposals for terrorist actions, and approving, funding, and sometimes organizing those actions. The proposals usually come from individual terrorist cells and regional offices.

Roughly 5,000 militants make up the rank-and-file of al Qaeda. They work in small, largely disconnected cells (called *anqud*—grape cluster) made up of between two and fifteen individuals. The cells are relatively autonomous in their operations and are expected to be self-sustaining financially to a large extent (many cells rely on credit card fraud and theft). They are only vaguely aware of what other cells are planning and can organize their own operations with al Qaeda's blessing. Abu Zubaydah was responsible for coordinating their performance until his capture in March 2002 in Pakistan. The 055 Brigade, formed in Afghanistan, is organized along more traditional military lines and was the group encountered by coalition forces fighting in that country in October and November 2001.

Election to al Qaeda is a very high honor for an Islamic militant. Al Qaeda officials generally select only one of every ten men who pass through their training camps. They are looking for "young Muslim men who are pure, believing and fighting for the cause of Allah" (Gunaratna 2002, 72). The key factors seem to be absolute loyalty and the willingness to sacrifice everything, including one's life, in

Table 9.1   Al Qaeda's Global Network

Countries with Islamic Militant Organizations Linked to al Qaeda	Countries with al Qaeda Terrorist Cells (Working Alone)	Countries with Sources of al Qaeda Funding	Countries Where al Qaeda Attacks Have Occurred
Yemen	United States	United Kingdom	Yemen
Egypt	United Kingdom	Germany	Somalia
Algeria	Germany	Saudi Arabia	Egypt
Malaysia	France	United Arab Emirates	Saudi Arabia
Chechnya (Russia)	Netherlands	Sudan	United States
Somalia	Belgium	Sweden	Philippines
Philippines	Canada	Denmark	Indonesia
Lebanon	Spain	Norway	Spain
Iran		Algeria	
Tajikistan		Germany	
Uganda		United States	
Indonesia		Philippines	
China		Pakistan	
Eritrea			
Bosnia			
United Kingdom			
Palestine			
Uzbekistan			
Kashmir (India)			
Sudan*			
Pakistan*			
Afghanistan*			

*Former al Qaeda headquarters.
Sources: Gunaratna 2002; Alexander and Swetnam 2002.

the cause. In addition, al Qaeda fighters must be among the most highly skilled of those trained in the camps.

Terrorist attacks are generally carefully planned and executed, although they are not always successful. An attack was attempted against the USS *Sullivan*, but failed when the boat loaded with explosives sank (it was overloaded). Likewise, assassination attempts against Hosni Mubarak, Bill Clinton, and Fidel Ramos (then president of the Philippines) were foiled for various reasons. Numerous terrorist attacks have also been detected and prevented, including a series of attacks planned on New York City landmarks (such as the UN and Holland Tunnel) in 1999. Detecting and linking attacks to al Qaeda is especially difficult because, unlike most terrorist organizations, the group rarely claims responsibility. In fact, it goes to great lengths to sow doubt about its role in the attacks, in part to add to the organization's mystique.

In the case of the September 11 attacks, planning began in the spring of 2000 under the direction of Mohammed Atta. Twenty militants were selected from several different cells, organized into four five-man teams, and allowed to secret themselves into the United States on student visas or across the Canadian border. This activity was followed by training at several flight schools around the country, the purchase of one-way business-class tickets, and other preparations.

Training covers the gamut of information that would-be terrorists might need to know, including religious indoctrination. A ten-volume (later eleven) "encyclopedia" of terrorism was written and published by al Qaeda in the mid-1990s (discovered by American intelligence agencies in 1999). It explains how to build explosives, how to use various weapons, how to organize paramilitary attacks, and how to build weapons of mass destruction. (Bin Laden is believed to have purchased some fissile materials in his quest for an atomic weapon. He may already have the capability to launch an attack with a "dirty" bomb that would scatter radioactive material [Gunaratna 2002, 70].) The encyclopedia also provides training on how militants should blend into the host society, even if it means violating Islamic lifestyle codes (Gunaratna 2002, 70).

The geographic spread of al Qaeda is remarkable. Although its headquarters has moved between Pakistan, Sudan, and Afghanistan, its cells can be found in more than fifty countries. The countries with the largest number of militants are Algeria (where al Qaeda supports the Islamic Salvation Front), Egypt (where it has ties with the Muslim Brotherhood), and Yemen (where the USS Cole was attacked). There are still militants scattered across Pakistan, the Middle East, and Central Asia (al Qaeda left Bosnia in 1995 to the relief of local militants, who considered them too brutal). Al Qaeda has close ties with Islamic militants in Chechnya, Tajikistan, Iran, Pakistan, Palestine, Lebanon, western China, the Philippines, Saudi Arabia, and, increasingly, in Southeast Asia and Africa—notably Indonesia, Malaysia, Uganda, and Somalia, where al Qaeda–trained militants killed eighteen American soldiers in 1992 (Gunaratna 2002, Ch. 3 and 4). Interestingly, Iraq and Libya are not known to have supported al Qaeda, although they have supported other terrorist organizations.

More troubling to Western audiences is the fact that al Qaeda has active cells and regional nodes in the United Kingdom, France, Germany, the United States, and other developed states. Ramsi Yousef and Sheikh Omar Abdul Rahman, who were loosely linked to al Qaeda, were based in a Brooklyn community center when they orchestrated the first World Trade Center bombing. In September and October 2002, the U.S. Justice Department arrested several individuals living in Buffalo, Portland, and Detroit on charges of conspiring with al Qaeda. Previously, cells had been identified in Washington, D.C., Chicago, New Jersey, and elsewhere in the United States. London has long been a principal hub of al Qaeda planning and financing, as are France and Germany, which has four known cells (Gunaratna 2001, 111–131). The subway and bus bombings in London in July 2005 were reportedly carried out by Islamic militants with sympathies—but not direct ties—to al Qaeda.

The cells and regional offices maintain frequent contact by means of the most modern communications channels. In the past, they have used cellular telephones, satellite phones, encrypted e-mails, and secret web sites to maintain contact with their worldwide membership. This fact enabled the FBI to eavesdrop on communication between al Qaeda headquarters and militants, thereby enabling agents to anticipate and break up several planned attacks in the late 1990s. In response, al Qaeda has switched to more traditional (and slower) methods of face-to-face communication. Given the lack of infiltrators, spies, and defectors, this trend may mean that future al Qaeda operations will be more difficult to detect.

Of considerable urgency to the United States is the high level of activity of al Qaeda–affiliated operatives under the leadership of Abu Musab al-Zarqawi in Iraq, who have been apparently responsible for the deaths of dozens of Americans and thousands of Iraqis (especially Shiites) since 2003. He is alleged to have masterminded the Madrid train bombings (see below), as well as several spectacular attacks on mosques and kidnappings. In October, he formally linked his organization to al Qaeda's. That said, his status is mysterious. Some have claimed that he died in 2004, others that he was captured and then released by the United States in 2005. Still others claim that his activities are in fact quite limited (some believe bin Laden "fired" him) and that it is the United States that has amplified his role through astute propaganda (Ricks 2006). He was confirmed killed by an American air strike in July 2006.

Al Qaeda's Finances

Al Qaeda has a reputation for being very well financed, thanks to Osama bin Laden's fortune. However, it is estimated that the entire operation of al Qaeda costs only about $40 million per year and that bin Laden's fortune plays almost no part in its day-to-day funding. On the one hand, al Qaeda operations are generally very inexpensive. The September 11 attacks, the organization's most expensive by far, cost only $500,000 by most estimates. Local cells are expected to take care of their own finances to a large extent (the attackers in the first World Trade Center bombing had to get the deposit back on the truck that exploded to pay for their airfare home!). On the other hand, bin Laden has made several shrewd business decisions that have allowed al Qaeda to prosper from excellent returns on the investments. While in Sudan, in particular, he began several enterprises, including a bank, a large farming operation, a tannery, and a construction company, and he signed contracts to build a major highway and several buildings for the Sudanese government (Wright 2001, 251).

Al Qaeda also receives much of its funding from Islamic clerics and wealthy Muslim sympathizers in the Middle East. Saudi Arabia, for example, has uncovered a donation of $50 million from a group of fundamentalist clerics in 1999. Khalid bin Mahfouz, a wealthy Saudi banker, has transferred funds and facilitated other transactions over the years. The Dubai Islamic Bank in the United Arab Emirates has also been directly implicated (Alexander & Swetnam 2001, 29). Numerous nonprofit organizations, as well as banks, have been identified by law enforcement authorities in dozens of countries as front operations through which millions are transferred to al Qaeda. In reality, many of those who have handled al Qaeda funds were unaware of it because the monies typically pass through several legitimate businesses or organizations on their journey between source and destination (Wright 2001, 252).

In more recent years, al Qaeda has been forced to become more creative and resourceful, as much of its funding has been cut off by Western governments. Those who carried out the Madrid bombings (see below) were partly financed by the sale of hashish (*Los Angeles Times* May 23, 2004, A1). It reportedly flowed through Morocco and on to Madrid and other European capitals. Dramatic increases in the sale of opium in Afghanistan, in spite of the government's efforts, could in turn provide resources for al Qaeda bases located near the poppy fields.

AL QAEDA AFTER SEPTEMBER 11

As of September 10th, 2001, bin Laden felt extremely sure of himself, it would seem. He had brought about the defeat and collapse of the Soviet Union in a mere five years. He had expelled the Americans from Somalia with a single attack. He had survived a full-scale cruise missile attack after the Africa attacks. He was beginning to feel powerful in the extreme. He had reached the conclusion that the United States was weak, tentative, and easily intimidated. He expected to remove them from Saudi Arabia in the future. It seems reasonable, given this view of his own importance, that bin Laden believed the September 11 attacks might bring down American democracy and capitalism once and for all.

The purpose of terrorism is outlined in terrorist manuals:

> [T]hey build a reserve of fighters by preparing and training new members for future tasks; they serve as a form of necessary punishment, mocking the regime's admiration among the population; they remove the personalities that stand in the way of the Islamic *da'wa* (call); they publicize issues; they help to reject compliance and submission to the regime and its practices; they provide legitimacy to the Islamist groups; they spread fear and terror through the regime's ranks; and they attract new members to the organization. (Gunaratna 2002, 75)

To this we could add that terrorism is also intended to provoke repression and over-reaction on the part of the target government, as this response breeds resentment, which in turns swells the ranks of militants. The abuses committed by American troops at Abu Ghraib and (allegedly) in Guantánamo Bay, Cuba, have become effective rallying cries for al Qaeda operatives and Iraqi militants across the Middle East. Recruitment has become so easy that several militant groups—including al Qaeda—have created application forms to facilitate processing (Darling 2004). They have been found in Baghdad, Fallujah, Tehran, and elsewhere.

It is unlikely, therefore, that the Bush administration surprised bin Laden with the forceful response provided by the United States, its allies, and the UN. In a matter of hours after the September 11 attacks, the UN General Assembly, the UN Security Council, and NATO had voted unanimously to approve war against al Qaeda. Thousands of Western troops were deployed to support the tens of thousands of Northern Alliance forces. Within a few weeks, in spite of stiff opposition, they broke through and seized control of Kabul and Kandahar, taking hundreds of prisoners.

In addition, the international community agreed to impose harsh penalties against al Qaeda, Afghanistan, and any private or public organizations affiliated with the terrorist group. To illustrate the degree of international commitment to the war against al Qaeda, even Cuba, which has had extremely poor relations with American governments over the years, agreed to help the United States by capturing and returning any prisoners who might escape from the various detention centers in Guantánamo Bay on Cuba's eastern coast. Al Qaeda's repudiation among Middle Eastern governments has been unequivocal and unanimous (with the exception of kind words from Iraq). In Pakistan, President Pervez Musharraf has purged Islamic fundamentalists from ISA and other government agencies, although the government has yet to establish clear control over the pro–al Qaeda regions in the north. The fight against Islamic militancy has become a defining feature of the post–September 11 international system, to the point that it has evolved into, to a large extent, the new "cold war." Al Qaeda attacks in Madrid, Spain, in March 2004 (on the anniversary of the U.S.–U.K. invasion of Iraq) resulted in nearly 200 deaths and thousands of casualties. The goal seems to have been to influence the upcoming elections in Spain—and perhaps they did, in that the anti-war opposition party was swept to power and Spain began plans to withdraw its troop from Iraq (*Los Angeles Times* March 12, 2004, A1).

Al Qaeda's position at this point is far weaker than before the World Trade Center attacks. It has lost in the neighborhood of 1,000 militants in Afghanistan, Pakistan, the Philippines, and elsewhere. Tens of millions in assets have been frozen. The organization has no headquarters and many of its most closely guarded secrets are now in the hands of Western governments. Although Osama bin Laden is still alive as of this writing (March 2009)—He continues to issue messages from time to time from undisclosed locations), many of his top lieutenants have been killed or captured, including Ahmed Khalfan Ghailani, who was captured in Pakistan and provided a wealth of intelligence information to interrogators (*Los Angeles Times* August 16, 2004, A1). However, this is not to say that al Qaeda has been defeated.

The organization has proved to be quite resilient in the past, having survived expulsion from two states during the 1990s. Given the cell structure of the organization, it is able to reconstitute itself rather quickly. Bin Laden has also made arrangements for his succession (although the loss of his second-in-command, Abu Zubaydah, in March 2002 was a serious blow (Gunaratna 2002, 228). Thus there is reason to believe that the organization will continue to carry out attacks against Western targets. Attacks against a French tanker near Yemen and against American military personnel training in Kuwait and the Philippines, along with a massive attack against foreigners in Indonesia in the fall of 2002, signaled a renewed capacity to commit acts of terror (*Chicago Tribune* October 15, 2002, 1).

In at least one area, the situation may be to al Qaeda's advantage. The destruction of the World Trade Center was greeted with celebration in many circles in the Arab world. It established al Qaeda as the most daring and single-minded challenger to the Western world. This sort of recognition will likely enhance the organization's recruitment efforts, because it adds to the prestige of those who share al Qaeda's goals. It is also likely that as governments move against al Qaeda militants and fundamentalist organizations, they will overreact and provoke a backlash that will further bolster the organization's recruitment. It is intriguing to note that groups allied to the organization endorsed U.S. presidential candidate John McCain in 2008 (*Washington Post* October 22, 2008, A13)—perhaps because it hoped for a continuation of the military approach and the enhanced recruiting this provided? Or perhaps this was merely some bravado by terrorists who sensed that their days are numbered. After all, the general consensus is that the "surge" in Iraq is working and that an increasing number of Iraqis have turned against the foreign militants who have made their lives more dangerous (see Chapter 8).

CONCLUSION: THE LESSONS OF THE WAR ON TERROR

What does the al Qaeda story teach us about terrorism generally? First and foremost, it is wrong to think that terrorists are always unorganized, unfocused, or undisciplined. The al Qaeda example illustrates that they can be highly focused (even though the goals may border on the irrational), highly organized, and extremely disciplined (to the point of fanaticism). The degree of focus eliminates any possibility of self-doubt—a prerequisite of fanaticism. As a consequence, there may be no possibility of reasoning or negotiating with its members. This contrasts sharply with most terrorist organizations, which have at least a few reasonable objectives and generally seek only greater political power. Al Qaeda's quest to rid the Arab and Muslim world of Western influence is a political nonstarter, leaving no room for compromise.

Second, al Qaeda demonstrates that terrorist groups with disparate objectives can find common cause and collaborate with one another. This is not the first time this has happened: During the 1970s, the Irish Republican Army, the Basque ETA, and other radical groups worked together. Never before has a global structure like al Qaeda's existed, however. Its defeat will, therefore, require a global response.

Al Qaeda demonstrates the destructive potential of terrorist organizations and raises the stakes. Although more people have been the victims of terrorist attacks over the history of the conflicts in Palestine, Northern Ireland, Kashmir, and other areas, never before has a terrorist organization carried out a single, massive attack that killed thousands in an instant. Potential victims must now take the terrorist threat as seriously as if they were defending against a state-sponsored military attack. Unfortunately, terrorists do not play by the same rules as states: They do not reside in one country, they do not wear uniforms, they do not march in columns and ranks, and they do not comply with the Geneva Conventions. Thus states may be faced with dilemmas with regard to appropriate and effective tactics and strategies. A military solution will likely go only so far, but a criminal approach may give the terrorists too many opportunities for escape.

This said, it would be prudent for Western states to consider seriously what types of actions might exacerbate the situation. Repression or over-reaction, for example, might increase recruitment, whereas half-measures might leave the organization too strong. The invasion of Iraq in March 2003 has been paradoxical in that it is fairly clear now that the purported ties between Saddam Hussein and al Qaeda, trumpeted by the Bush administration prior to the attack, were minimal. On the other hand, the presence of American troops in Baghdad has served as a magnet for insurgents and terrorist guerrillas who have flooded into the country across ill-guarded borders. All of this was predicted in advance (Lemann 2002).

Perhaps the most profound implication of al Qaeda's actions is the loss of the sense of security felt by most Americans before September 11. Although the nation has perfected the art of denial, the gnawing realization persists in the back of people's minds that there is nowhere to hide. Such is life in the 21st century.

QUESTIONS TO CONSIDER

1. Are there other terrorist groups that make use of other systems of religious teachings to justify their violence?

2. How much should the West curtail its civil liberties in its struggle against al Qaeda?

3. How do al Qaeda's structure and operation compare with those of other transnational organizations, such as nongovernmental organizations (NGOs) or multinational firms?

KEY FIGURES
GLOBAL TERRORISM AND AL QAEDA

Hassan al-Banna   1906–1949. He was the founder of the Society of Muslim Brothers in Egypt, a precursor to the Muslim Brotherhood that provided support to Osama bin Laden's al Qaeda in the 1990s.

Ayatollah Ruhollah Khomeini   1902–1989. He was the leader of the Iranian Revolution in 1978 that placed a revolutionary Shiite regime in power.

Sheikh Omar Abdul Rahman   Leader of the Gama Islamiya (Islamic Group) in Egypt. With support from al Qaeda, his group carried out the first World Trade Center attack in 1993.

Osama bin Laden   Born in 1957. Heir to a business fortune and Afghan mujahaddin, he was co-founder of Afghan Service Bureau (MAK) in 1984 and al Qaeda in 1988. His organization claimed responsibility for the attacks on the U.S. embassies in Tanzania and Kenya on August 7, 1998, and on the USS Cole in 2000. He has also been blamed for the September 11 attacks in the United States.

Hassan al-Turabi   Islamic leader of Sudan since seizing power in 1989. He provided safe haven to al Qaeda from 1991 to 1996 and has carried out a bloody civil war against Christian and animist separatists in the south.

Ayman Mohammed Rabi' al-Zawahiri   Egyptian Islamic cleric who emerged as the dominant religious authority of al Qaeda after the assassination of Abdullah Azzam in 1989.

Abu Musab al-Zarqawi   Islamic militant of Jordanian descent, active in Iraq, formally allied to al Qaeda since October 2004.

(continued)

(*continued*)

Muhammad Ibn Abdul Wahhab   Eighteenth-century Islamic cleric who developed a puritanical interpretation of Islam that became the foundation of the Saudi regime in Arabia.

Sheikh Dr. Abdullah Azzam   1941–1989. A Muslim *ulama*, he was active in the Jordanian Muslim Brotherhood and founded the Afghan Service Bureau (MAK) with Osama bin Laden in 1984.

Mullah Mohammed Omar   Spiritual leader of the Taliban regime in Afghanistan. He worked closely with Osama bin Laden to impose an autocratic, puritanical rule on the country.

CHRONOLOGY
GLOBAL TERRORISM AND AL QAEDA

1744
Muhammad Ibn Abdul Wahhab joins forces with the future House of Saud, bringing a puritanical form of Islam to a position of power.

1916
The Sykes-Picot agreement between France and Great Britain consolidates European control over the Middle East, to the dismay of Arab leaders.

1928
Hassan al-Banna founds the Society of Muslim Brothers in Egypt.

1932
The House of Saud establishes control over the Arabian peninsula and rules following the dictates of Wahhabism.

1942
The Society of Muslim Brothers forms a militant "secret apparatus."

1949
Al-Banna is assassinated by the Egyptian government after violent attacks by his followers.

1964
Ayatollah Khomeini is expelled from Iran for sedition.

1979
The Soviet Union invades Afghanistan, sparking a guerrilla war. Ayatollah Khomeini seizes power in a popular uprising and begins to support fundamentalist Islamic militants in the region.

1983
Sharia law is imposed in Sudan.

1984
Osama bin Laden and Abdullah Azzam found the Afghan Service Bureau (MAK) to provide support to the Afghan mujahaddin. They later create training camps for local and Arab guerrillas.

1988
Bin Laden, Azzam, Mohammed Atef, and Abu Ubaidah al Banshiri found al Qaeda as a base of support to mujahaddin in Afghanistan and elsewhere. They join fundamentalist militant organizations in Egypt and Sudan to found the International Islamic Front for Jihad Against the Jews and Crusaders.

1989
Taking credit for expelling the Soviet forces from Afghanistan, bin Laden returns to Saudi Arabia, where he opposes the Saud family.

1990
U.S. troops are deployed to protect Saudi Arabia from Iraq, prompting bin Laden to declare the House of Saud to be "apostates" of Islam.

1991
Bin Laden is expelled from Saudi Arabia and moves the headquarters of al Qaeda from Peshawar, Pakistan, to Khartoum, Sudan, where he develops a close and profitable relationship with the ruling National Islamic Front.

1992
The first al Qaeda attack occurs. It is a largely unsuccessful attempt to kill American troops en route to Somalia by way of Yemen. In Algeria, the government, fearing gains by the fundamentalist Islamic Salvation Front, cancels elections. The country plunges into violence.

1993
The first World Trade Center attack occurs in February under the direction of Ramsi Yousef and Sheikh Omar Abdul Rahman. Attacks against American soldiers in Somalia are carried out by al Qaeda–trained militants.

1994
Saudi Arabia revokes bin Laden's citizenship.

1995
Al Qaeda attacks Americans based in Saudi Arabia.

1996
Al Qaeda issues the first of three fatawa declaring jihad against Americans, the House of Saud, and Westerners generally.

1998
On August 7, two truck bombs explode at the U.S. embassies in Kenya and Tanzania, killing 234 and injuring nearly 5,000.

1999
Governments in the West and Middle East begin a systematic crack-down on al Qaeda militants. Osama bin Laden is placed on the FBI's "Ten Most Wanted" list. Some anti-Taliban Afghan clerics issue a fatwa against bin Laden, authorizing his assassination. Reports emerge that bin Laden suffers from kidney and liver disease.

2000
October 5   Suicide bombers attack the *USS Cole* in Yemen, killing seventeen sailors.

(*continued*)

(*continued*)

December   The UN Security Council passes Resolution 1333, imposing sanctions on the Taliban pending bin Laden's extradition.

2001

September 11   Four aircraft are highjacked by teams of suicide bombers. Three are flown into the World Trade Center and the Pentagon. One aircraft is recaptured by passengers and crashes in western Pennsylvania (it is believed its destination was the Capitol in Washington, D.C.). Nearly 3,000 people are killed. The next day, the UN Security Council approves a resolution authorizing "all necessary means" to neutralize the terrorists responsible.

October–November   Northern Alliance fighters, with ground and air support from the United States, remove the Taliban from power in Afghanistan, killing hundreds of Taliban and al Qaeda fighters and taking hundreds more captive. Many, including possibly bin Laden, flee to Pakistan and other locations.

2002

March   Abu Zubaydah, al Qaeda's second-in-command, is arrested in Pakistan.

October   Al Qaeda is linked to an attack against a French oil tanker in Yemen and the killing of American military personnel in Kuwait and the Philippines. A major attack in Indonesia kills more than 180. The U.S. Congress authorizes President Bush to employ force against Iraq, which is linked to international terrorism by the administration.

2003

March   The United States and Britain attack Iraq. Among the reasons given is a link between Saddam Hussein's regime and the September 11 attacks, a claim that is later discredited.

2004

March   Ten bombs detonate on crowded commuter trains in Madrid, Spain, killing nearly 200. Al Qaeda is found responsible, although not until the voters in Spain turn out the sitting government in part over its support for the war in Iraq.

July   Ahmed Khalfan Ghailani, a top al Qaeda operative, is captured and interrogated in Pakistan.

September   In Russia, hundreds die in an attack on a school orchestrated by Chechen guerillas with al Qaeda ties.

2005

July   A series of attacks on public transportation in London kills more than fifty. Islamic militants claim responsibility, although their ties with al Qaeda are unlikely.

2006

January   Osama bin Laden offers a cryptic truce to the West. He later recants.

References

Alexander, Yonah, and Michael S. Swetnam. *Usama bin Laden's al Qaida: Profile of a Terrorist Network* (Ardsley, NY: Transnational Pubs, 2001).

Al-Turabi, Hasan. "Principles of Governance, Freedom and Responsibility in Islam." *American Journal of Islamic Social Science* 4 #1 (1987): 1–11.

Amnesty International (AI). "Amnesty International Report 2002 – Spain." 2002. Accessed on May 8, 2006 at: http://web.amnesty.org/web/ar2002.nsf/eur/spain!Open.

BBC. "Who are ETA?" published on-line on March 22, 2006. Accessed May 8, 2006 at: http://news.bbc.co.uk/cbbcnews/hi/newsid_3500000/newsid_3501500/3501554.stm.

Beres, Rene Louis. "The Meaning of Terrorism: Jurisprudential and Definitional Clarifications." *Vanderbilt Journal of Transnational Law* 28 (March 1995): 239–256.

Berman, Paul. "Terror and Liberalism." *American Prospect* 12 #18 (October 22, 2001): 18–27.

Bush, George. "The President's State of the Union Address." Washington, D.C., January 29, 2002.

Chicago Tribune, October 15, 2002, 1.

Christian Science Monitor, September 9, 2002, 1.

Darling, Dan. "Want an al Qaeda Job? Apply Now – With References, Please." *The American Enterprise* 15 #6 (September 2004): 1.

Davidson, Lawrence. *Islamic Fundamentalism* (Westport, CT: Greenwood Press, 1998).

Gunaratna, Rohan. *Inside Al Qaeda: Global Network of Terror* (New York: Columbia University Press, 2002).

Herf, Jeffrey. "What Is Old and What Is New in the Terrorism of Islamic Fundamentalism?" *Partisan Review* 69 #1 (Winter 2002): 25–33.

Huband, Mark. *Warriors of the Prophet: The Struggle for Islam* (Boulder, CO: Westview Press, 1998).

Lemann, Nicholas. "The War on What?" *The New Yorker* (September 16, 2002): 36–44.

Los Angeles Times, August 16, 2004, A1.

Martinez-Herrera, Enric. "Nationalist Extremism and Outcomes of State Policies in the Basque Country, 1979–2001." *International Journal on Multicultueral Societies* 4 #1 (January 2001): 1–22.

Miles, Jack. "Theology and the Clash of Civilizations." *Cross Currents* 51 #4 (Winter 2002): 451–460.

O'Ballance, Edgar. *Islamic Fundamentalist Terrorism, 1979–95: The Iranian Connection* (New York: NYU Press, 1997).

Ricks, Thomas. "Military Plays Up Role of Zarqawi." *Washington Post* April 10, 2005, A01.

Schafer, David. "Islam and Terrorism: A Humanist View." *The Humanist* 62 #3 (May–June 2002): 16–21.

Tucker, David. *Skirmishes at the Edge of Empire: The United States and International Terrorism* (Westport, CT: Praeger, 1997).

Woodworth, Paddy. "Why Do They Kill?" *World Policy Journal* 18 #1 (Spring 2001): 1–12.

Wright, Robin. *Sacred Rage: The Wrath of Militant Islam* (New York: Touchstone Book, 2001).

10

■■■

Intervention: Bosnia

INTRODUCTION

As Americans consider their foreign policy choices in the post–Cold War era, a key question is whether the United States should play the role of global policeman. Should American troops be used to alter the domestic affairs of foreign nations? On the surface the obvious answer seems to be no, but in many instances in the past, the answer has been a resounding yes. Whether justified in terms of humanitarianism, enforcement of international law, or some strategic imperative, the United States has been rather quick to deploy its troops.

To better understand this interventionist tendency, we will look carefully at three very different cases drawn from the past thirty-five years. Before doing so, however, we will review various theories of intervention. The most obvious reason for U.S. intervention is strategic: The United States intervenes when its global interests are jeopardized (Deibel & Gaddis 1987). Given the way a great power strives for stability and preservation of the status quo, the temptation to intervene where the system is unstable can be irresistible. Some 2,500 years ago, when the small island of Melos petitioned Athens for respect of its neutrality, Athens refused, stating that it simply could not tolerate such an implicit challenge to its status as the dominant regional power. "The strong do what they can and the weak do what they must," was Athens's blunt reply.

Though not a particularly noble reason for intervention, its advocates often point to the need to preserve the balance of power and prevent enemies from encroaching on the American sphere of influence. The Monroe Doctrine of the early 19th century cautioned would-be imperialists in Europe from snatching colonial prizes in the Western Hemisphere. The Roosevelt Corollary to that warning had the military teeth to back it up and coincided with American intervention in Cuba, Nicaragua, Guatemala, Panama, Mexico, and across Latin America shortly after the turn of the century. Since World War II, various senior diplomats have justified U.S. intervention as simply preserving the status quo. George Ball, a former under secretary of state, pointed out that it is up to great powers—in this case, the

United States—to enforce international standards of peace and stability, unilaterally if necessary (Barnet 1968, 258).

Another key factor cited by many analysts to justify intervention is the desire to spread liberal values and (during the Cold War) block the encroachment of Communist ideology. Certainly the idealism of the Woodrow Wilson, Franklin Delano Roosevelt, and Harry Truman administrations, as well as the intense anti-Communist passions displayed by Secretary of State John Foster Dulles under Eisenhower, demonstrate that democracy, freedom, and the free market were all key preoccupations of U.S. policymakers. Wilson drew up his "Fourteen Points" during World War I to map out a way to make the world "safe for democracy." As he put it when trying to persuade Congress to declare war on Germany in 1917:

> We have no selfish ends to serve. We desire no conquest, no dominion. We seek no indemnities for ourselves, no material compensation for the sacrifices we shall freely make. We are but one of the champions of the right of mankind. (Wilson 1990, 15)

When Harry Truman challenged Congress in 1947 to fund the incipient Cold War offensive, he declared: "I believe that it must be the policy of the United States to support free peoples who are resisting attempted subjugation by armed minorities or by outside pressures." Presidents Lyndon Johnson, Ronald Reagan, and George W. Bush added their own doctrines, with the result that the United States gradually expanded the scope of unilateral intervention it considers justified.

Insurrections in the Third World were not unusual during the Cold War years, but only a few warranted U.S. intervention. It was those situations that combined evidence of Communist meddling with a threat to an existing U.S. alliance where intervention was most likely.

Related to this is the notion that the United States has an obligation to alleviate acute suffering around the world. Although more limited in its application, "humanitarian intervention" has become more important since the end of the Cold War. This stems in part from the increasing number of states that have "imploded" (where the central government has ceased to function effectively)—sometimes as a result of the loss of support from one of the superpowers—or where civil war has broken out. The doctrine declares that where innocent civilians are suffering extreme abuse—especially genocide—the world in general and the United States in particular have a "responsibility to protect" (ICISS 2001). As put by Bill Clinton in an address to American peacekeeping troops in Macedonia:

> But never forget, if we can do this here, and if we can then say to the people of the world, whether you live in Africa, or Central Europe, or any other place, if somebody comes after innocent civilians and tries to kill them en masse because of their race, their ethnic background or their religion, and it's within our power to stop it, we will stop it. (White House OPS 1999)

It is important to point out that humanitarian intervention often looks very different from other forms of intervention, in that U.S. troops are deployed on a more limited scale and with more strict "rules of engagement" (don't fire until fired upon, don't seek out the enemy, minimize civilian casualties and physical damage). They also perform more acts of community service, such as working to build schools, providing medical treatment to civilians, and helping to train the local police force. In some cases, there is no clear "enemy," except perhaps lawless bands of marauding criminals.

A final factor that has contributed to the U.S. decision to intervene is economic interest. Marxist interpretations of U.S. intervention have long stressed the role of major capitalist actors in the shaping of U.S. foreign policy. Harry Magdoff has probably gone as far as any Marxist to explain the dynamic. He argues that, although one may not find capitalists dictating policy to their political counterparts, the two groups have an unusual harmony of interest. American foreign investments bring large profits and extraordinary monopoly control for both business and government. American firms can control access to key raw materials, such as oil, which in turn are essential to the military—hence collusion between major capitalists and the Pentagon. These sorts of factors lead to a tendency for the state to intervene aggressively when foreign economic interests are threatened—which, as it turns out, usually involves attacking anti-capitalist Third World rebels (Magdoff 1969).

For years, Yugoslavia was at the center of major power struggles for control over southern Europe. The Ottomans, Hungarians, and Austrians each took a turn at Balkan domination. Sarajevo entered the history books as the spot where World War I began. Much of the post–World War I settlement at Versailles was inspired by an international desire to provide justice and peace to the Balkans. The breakup of the Yugoslav Federation during the 1990s illustrated the limits of anarchy in some ways, even as it revealed the failures of international law. As civil war was transformed into international conflict with the secession and recognition of an increasing number of the country's republics, an ever-growing international military presence attempted to restore peace. At the same time, the international community used the Yugoslav experience to reinstate the principle of war crimes guilt, thus paving the way for the establishment of the first permanent International Criminal Court.

The atrocities of the wars in the former Yugoslavia have been embedded in the international consciousness thanks to the work of war crimes prosecutors, journalists, and government- and UN-sponsored fact-finding missions. We have heard stories of summary executions of civilians, mutilations of enemy soldiers, concentration camps, and the use of rape as a weapon of war. These wars also included aerial bombardment of residential zones, economic sanctions, and diplomatic isolation imposed by Western forces, each painfully damaging in its own way.

HISTORY TO 1918

To a certain extent, the history of ethnic relations in Yugoslavia has followed a common pattern: increasingly mobilized linguistic and religious communities are overwhelmed by a foreign invader; the communities either collaborate or resist; the invader becomes increasingly unable to maintain control of the fringe territory; a new invader unseats the previous power, which gives the local community the opportunity to develop a new political arrangement (*Economist*, August 23, 1992, 36). In the process, differences among the communities become exaggerated and rivalries based on the different experiences emerge.

The earliest Balkan peoples arrived near the dawn of man and were organized at the family, clan, or tribe level. It was not until the early Middle Ages that nations became a force to be reckoned with. Bulgaria reached its zenith during the 10th century, Croatia dominated in the 11th century, and Bosnia and Serbia were each independent kingdoms of some note in the 14th century. Although these moments of glory may seem quaint episodes from the modern perspective, they became embedded in the concept of "rightful heritage" that continues today: "In the nineteenth century the national leaders, looking back on this period, tended to consider the maximum extension of their medieval kingdoms as the natural historical boundaries for their nations" (Jelavich 1983 1, 27).

By the 15th century, the Balkans were the battleground of empires, much like Poland to the north. Contact with numerous powerful empires left its imprint on Balkan society and spirit (see Map 10.1). In each region, the population represented a fusion of original inhabitants with subsequent invaders, an amalgamation achieved through military conquest by a stronger group, the absorption of one people by another owing to the weight of numbers, or the acceptance of another language because of the cultural attraction offered by a more advanced civilization (Jelavich 1983 1, 27).

By 1500, the Muslims had established firm control over the leaders of the Balkan peoples, forcing them to embrace Islam and submit to the "Porte," as the central government was called. The Ottoman hold continued through the 17th century, when Russian and Hapsburg (a central European dynasty embracing a wide variety of nationalities) armies seized and controlled fringe territories. In other cases, such as Serbia, local Muslim strongmen emerged, exercising considerable independence without sanction from the Porte. In Croatia, the Hapsburgs, though dominant, permitted the surviving Catholic elites to exercise considerable discretion and power over the domain. Orthodox Serbs remained considerably organized, thanks largely to geography and the tenacity of the Orthodox hierarchy.

During the second half of the 18th century, war raged across the region, particularly in Bosnia and Serbia, where local Serbs rebelled against despotic Muslim leaders with the Porte endorsement. By 1806, the Serbs, successful on the battlefield and far from the Porte's power, established an independent kingdom (Jelavich 1983, 1, 196).

Croats repeatedly sought greater autonomy and status within the Hapsburg empire, demanding control of newly acquired territories to the south and east. Croat nationalism began to emerge by 1830. They resented Hapsburg attempts to "divide and rule" by offering some benefits to a few without extending them to the people at large (Cohen 1992, 369). The unrest boiled over into full-fledged rebellion in 1848, and again in 1871. Croatia was granted additional powers, but not independence (Jelavich 1983, 1, 206).

The conflict was exacerbated by the active involvement of Russia, the Hapsburgs, and other continental powers that were eager to bring stability and their presence to a volatile, strategic region. The Treaty of San Stafano (1877) provided for an independent Serbia and Montenegro as well as a huge Bulgaria under Russian occupation. The Congress of Berlin in 1878 was called by the other European powers to adjust this Russian power play and settled on a much smaller Bulgaria and Bosnia-Herzegovina's inclusion in the Hapsburg Empire (Jelavich 1983, 1, 358). The problem of Macedonia was finessed by simply leaving it under Ottoman control—the

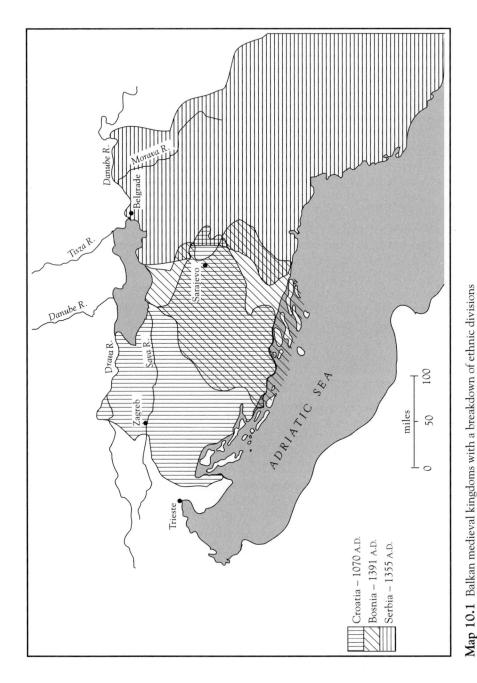

Map 10.1 Balkan medieval kingdoms with a breakdown of ethnic divisions

Source: Adapted from Barbara Jelavich, *History of the Balkans: 18th and 19th Centuries* (New York: Cambridge University Press, 1983). Reprinted with the permission of Cambridge University Press.

Croatia – 1070 A.D.
Bosnia – 1391 A.D.
Serbia – 1355 A.D.

ADRIATIC SEA

miles

0   50   100

Danube R.
Morava R.
Belgrade
Tisza R.
Danube R.
Sarajevo
Drava R.
Sava R.
Zagreb
Trieste

last major bastion of Muslim power. Increasingly, Balkan peoples understood that they could achieve more by joining together, but the years of conquest and division had left profound animosities. Serbs considered Bosnia and Macedonia their rightful heritage, based largely on medieval and ethnic considerations. Croats felt largely the same way about Bosnia. The Muslim population of Bosnia was never considered "authentic" by Serbs or Croats, coming as it did as a product of Ottoman imperialism (Djilas & Mousavizadeh 1992, 26). Not only were these antagonisms ethnically based, but it soon became clear that concrete balance-of-power considerations made suspicion and apprehension rational attitudes. None of the Balkan states had the capacity to ensure its own safety, and any alliance between neighbors could tip the balance against a lone state. Hence competing experiences combined with outside powers, perceptions of national heritage, religion, language, and security concerns to prevent a lasting bond among the nations (Armour 1992, 11).

In 1908 the traditional leadership in the Ottoman Empire was overthrown by the "Young Turk" revolt. These young colonels were determined to bring a sense of national unity to all the empire's colonies. The Balkan states saw the move as a concrete threat to their hard-earned independence and for the first time organized a strong alliance. The alliance was so confident that in 1912 it launched an attack against Turkish forces and succeeded in pushing them virtually off the continent. Ironically, it was as a result of the alliance's success that the most tragic episode of Balkan relations began. The question of territorial compensation aroused intense disagreement, because each nation felt its military victories had earned it more spoils of war than it was slated to receive.

The first World War was sparked by a gunman in Sarajevo, a member of a Serbian nationalist group, who shot the Austrian Archduke Ferdinand in July 1914. Austria declared war on Serbia, Serbia allied with Russia, Russia declared war on Austria, Austria allied with Germany, and so on. Four years and 16 million deaths later, the war ended.

As the defeated Hapsburg and Ottoman Empires were dismantled, many new nation-states were formed. Even before the war ended, Croats and Slovenes were organizing a united Yugoslavia. A Yugoslav Committee was formed, which then prepared a draft constitution providing for Serbian participation. When the proposal was forwarded to the Serbian monarchy, it was accepted almost immediately. "Thus the organization of the Yugoslav state was primarily the work of national committees, and the initiative came from the Hapsburg South Slavs" (Jelavich 1983, 2, 147). The proposal had to be validated in London, where the territory was formally mapped. On December 1, 1918, the Kingdom of the Serbs, Croats, and Slovenes was officially proclaimed (Cohen 1992, 369).

1918 TO 1980

The first attempt at Yugoslav federation failed after ten years, when the largely nationality-based parliament demanded more autonomy for the various regions than the central government in Belgrade was willing to concede (see Map 10.2). Serbs in

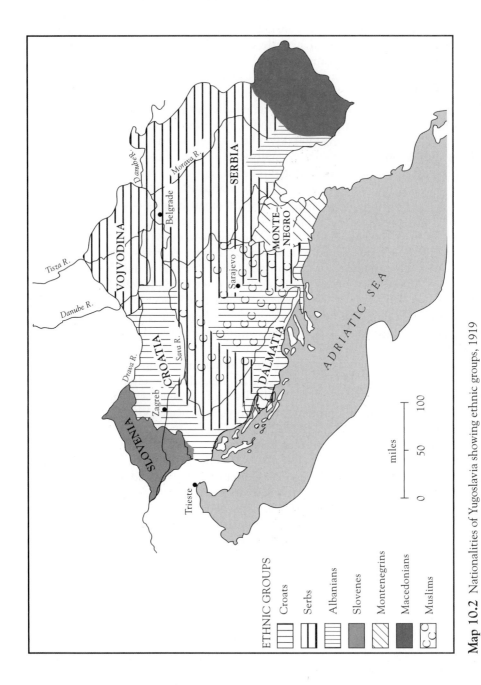

Map 10.2 Nationalities of Yugoslavia showing ethnic groups, 1919

Source: Barbara Jelavich, *History of the Balkans: 18th and 19th Centuries; 20th Century* (New York: Cambridge University Press, 1983), vols. 1 and 2. Reprinted with the permission of Cambridge University Press.

ETHNIC GROUPS

Croats

Serbs

Albanians

Slovenes

Montenegrins

Macedonians

Muslims

Belgrade hoped to instill a sense of national unity, but these efforts merely exacerbated tensions (Cohen 1992, 370). "The basic problem of the state was that, despite the hopes of some intellectuals and political leaders before 1914, a Yugoslav nationality did not come into existence" (Jelavich 1983 2, 151).

Questions of language use, representation in the government, and self-rule became extremely intense in the late 1920s. In 1929, after violent demonstrations in Zagreb, King Alexander dismantled the parliamentary institutions and imposed a form of dictatorship on the country. He was assassinated in 1934, and his successor brought back some of the democratic structures, only to see his country overwhelmed by German Nazi forces in 1941.

The wartime experience of Yugoslavia has been suggested as a cause of the present antagonism. One reason is that the Catholic Croatian region was treated very differently than the Orthodox Serbian areas. Croatia was granted independence and membership in Axis-led international organizations. This diplomatic status and newfound autonomy, after years of failed attempts, was greeted warmly by many Croats. The Catholic hierarchy gave firm instructions to the clergy to serve the new rulers. In the words of the Zagreb archbishop: "These are events . . . which fulfill the long dreamed of and desired ideal of our people. . . . Respond readily to my call to join in the noble task of working for the safety and well-being of the Independent State of Croatia" (MacLean 1957, 88). The Ustase movement, a fascist Croatian group based in Italy, undertook a systematic and egregious rule of terror. Serbs who resided in Croatia were the primary targets, and they "suffered greatly at the hands of the Croatian fascists" (Cohen 1992, 371). According to the current Bosnian Serb leader, some 700,000 Serbs were killed from 1941 to 1945 at Croatian Catholic and Muslim hands, prompting him to vow, "We will never again be history's fools" (Karadzic 1992, 50).

Meanwhile, Josip Broz-Tito, leader of the outlawed Communist Party, organized a highly effective resistance movement in the mountains around Serbia and Bosnia. Many peasants with weapons were ready to take to the mountains, as their forefathers had done so many times before.

By the end of the war, tensions were extremely high among the various groups. Partisans regularly rounded up and shot Croatian fascists. One incident reveals the depth of animosity:

> As the Ustase were being led off to execution, a peasant woman rushed into the middle of them and began scratching and hitting at them, screaming all the time. The Partisans had difficulty pulling her off them. Then the shots rang out and she again rushed forward, this time among the corpses, dancing in the blood. "A-ah!" she gasped, dripping with sweat and blood. It seemed the Ustase had slaughtered all her sons. (MacLean 1957, 156)

Fearful of such reprisals, one particularly large group of Ustase surrendered to the British in the closing days of the war, only to be sent back to the partisans. Reports indicate that between 40,000 and 100,000 of them were killed within days (Jelavich 1983, 2, 272).

Tito organized a government among the partisans, although a royal government-in-exile in London had the support of the United States and Great Britain. To consolidate his political support in Yugoslavia, Tito declared Macedonia, previously a province of Serbia, a full-fledged republic in the future Yugoslavia, a status that did, and still does, profoundly disturb Greece to the south and Bulgaria to the east. Tito received Soviet support and recognition and moved early after the war to join the emerging Soviet bloc as a socialist state. An ill-fated Soviet Union–inspired attempt at a Balkan federation failed by 1948, which contributed in part to the eventual separation of Yugoslavia and the Soviet Union.

Tito embarked on a unique and solitary path toward socialism based on decentralized worker organizations, tolerance of nationalities, and intense socialist propaganda campaigns (Jelavich 1983, 2, 388). He hoped that socialist solidarity and idealism, combined with dynamic economic growth and prosperity, would lead to a pan-Yugoslav nationalism. But throughout all of Yugoslav history, ethnic tensions remained high. As put by Jelavich:

> With the loosening of the central bonds, more authority was transferred to the capitals of the republics, the majority of which had been, and still were, strongholds of fervent nationalist sentiments. When disputes arose over economic or political questions, the local leaders tended to dust off the old flags and symbols and return with enthusiasm to the battles of the past. . . . (Jelavich 1983, 2, 388)

Tito and his government felt compelled in 1971 and again in 1981 to use force to suppress first Croatian and later Kosovo Albanian demands for greater autonomy and more national rights. Through it all, Tito continued to appeal to the people's socialist solidarity to overcome these political disputes. In the final analysis, however, Marxism failed as an integrative force in Yugoslavia (Braun 1983, 37). Tito died in 1980 without a clear successor. As would be seen in the 1990s, with the removal of the communist state, "all that remained was the nation, and the ideology of nationalism" (Hayden 1992, 43).

AFTER TITO

The decade of the 1980s brought economic hardship and lack of central leadership in Yugoslavia, which together fostered nationalist demands in Croatia. The League of Yugoslav Communists failed to maintain cohesion, even though after forty years many party officials, military commanders, and government agents were firmly entrenched in the federal bureaucracy (Cohen 1992, 370). By 1987, Slobodan Milosevic emerged as the sole Serbian leader, resentful that Croatians and others had encroached on federal authority:

> Through his brash articulation of Serbia's political discontent, and particularly his populist mobilization of Serbian ethnic consciousness at mass rallies—sometimes referred to as "street democracy"—Milosevic challenged the oligarchic Titoist style of managing the "national question" and also provoked a sharp nationalist backlash from Yugoslavia's other republics and ethnic groups. (Cohen 1992, 371)

The winds of democracy swept through Yugoslavia in the tumultuous fall of 1989. Between April and December 1990, each republic held elections. In Slovenia, Croatia, Bosnia, and Macedonia, new democratic parties were elected, while former Communists were returned to power in Serbia, Montenegro, and Vojvodina.

Although the elections of 1990 were an impressive exercise in regime transition, the results left the country even more politically fragmented than it had been during the last days of Communist rule. Thus, whether born-again Communists or non-Communists, both the newly elected political authorities and the bulk of the opposition forces in all regions of Yugoslavia were committed to programs of regional and ethnic nationalism that seriously challenged the power of the federal system. (Cohen 1992, 371)

Milosevic, after an undemocratic election, spearheaded efforts to preserve the federation with Serbia at the center and found considerable support among the federal power elite. He proposed a "modern federation," which would preserve the size of the military and the dominance of the Communist Party. In the meantime, he supported efforts by Serbs who resided outside of Serbia to exercise self-determination while maintaining their potential rights to citizenship in Serbia proper.

The question of ethnic rights for minorities came to a head later in 1990, when the Croatian assembly approved a constitution that failed to specifically mention protection of the rights of Serbs living in Croatia. This move was repeated across the nation. As put by Hayden:

The solution found in the various Yugoslav republics was the creation of systems of a constitutional and legal structure that guarantees privileges to the members of one nation over those of any other residents in a particular state. (Hayden 1992, 41)

Serbians living in Krajina, a Croatian city where Serbs are in the majority, began demonstrating against Croatian authority and seized control of government bureaus and facilities. In early 1991, the Croatian government moved to suppress the unrest.

WARFARE IN SLOVENIA AND CROATIA

During the first part of 1991, Slovenia and Croatia moved toward outright independence, and the legitimacy of the shared federal presidency was challenged throughout the country. In March, when the Croatian delegate was scheduled to take his seat at the head of the table, the Serbian delegation protested his ascension and in May vetoed it altogether (*New York Times*, May 16, 1991, A1).

Although attempts were made to preserve the federal structure, irreconcilable demands and fast action toward independence and diplomatic recognition in Slovenia and Croatia frustrated the efforts (*New York Times,* June 7, 1991, A5). Meanwhile, U.S. Secretary of State James Baker urged national leaders to preserve the federation, a statement that the military apparently interpreted as "a green light for military intervention should secession occur" (Cohen 1992, 373). When the Croatian and Slovene parliaments approved independence resolutions on June 26, 1991, the George H. W. Bush administration announced its "regret" for such "unilateral action" and warned of a "dangerous situation" (*New York Times,* June 27, 1991, A1). On June 28, Yugoslav army tanks battled Slovene troops that had taken control of border posts. Slovenia defeated the incursion and held firm to independence in spite of several offers for increased autonomy in the old federation. When Yugoslav troops began to make new inroads, European Community (EC) officials offered to mediate the dispute. By early July, EC mediators managed to identify the terms of a settlement, but when a cease-fire was accepted in August, it became clear that many soldiers in the field had no loyalty to the Belgrade government, prompting the EC mediators to declare that the Yugoslav army units were "out of control" (*New York Times,* August 30, 1991, A3).

In Croatia, violence first erupted in Zagreb and then quickly spread across the region inhabited by Serbs. Early on, the tactics used by both sides strayed far from traditional rules of war. Serb fighters used Croatian civilians as human shields when attacking Croatian outposts, forcing the defenders to shoot at relatives (*New York Times,* July 31, 1991, A1). On the other side, Serbian soldiers with Croatian relatives agonized over orders to shoot (*New York Times,* October 1, 1991, A1). The Yugoslav defense minister, Veljko Kadijevic, negotiated several cease-fires with the Croats during these months, only to be dismissed by an impatient Milosevic.

By the end of the initial phase of hostilities in March, some 10,000 were dead and 500,000 were homeless. The fighting intensified in the fall and continued through most of 1992. Vukovar was described as a "wasteland" in November after eighty-six days of shelling and aerial bombardment (*New York Times,* November 21, 1992, A1). By December, the military actions lost most of their strategic content and took on the form of vendettas. Reports of unconfirmed atrocities became commonplace by early 1992.

The international community was ill prepared to intervene in this situation, coming as it did during the collapse of the Soviet Union and the general restructuring of international institutions and practices. The EC wanted desperately for this situation to be resolved without military intervention, even of peacekeepers, and the EC lost several diplomats in the skies of Croatia in their efforts to mediate a peaceful settlement. NATO forces were unable to intervene because the treaty prohibited the use of the forces outside the member countries' collective borders. The Council for Security and Cooperation in Europe was untested and required unanimity in its decision making, and the UN was happy to let regional organizations take the first crack before intervening (Cohen 1992, 373). It was not until September that the Security Council began to issue a series of resolutions condemning Serbian and Yugoslav army support of Serbian militiamen in Croatia.

At any rate, the Western response was tepid at best. In spite of Germany's insistence, the EC did not officially extend diplomatic recognition to Croatia until January 1992 (nearly one month after Germany), and the United States waited until the spring. These delays hampered attempts to treat the problem as an inter-national, rather than civil, conflict. Some have argued that this inaction helped bring on the war (Mastnak 1992, 11).

Over several months beginning in November, the UN Security Council deliber-ated a proposal to send a group of peacekeeping forces to monitor a future cease-fire in Croatia. This force, originally pegged at 10,000, was ultimately increased to 14,000 and was deployed strategically not only in the Serb-inhabited zones of Croatia ("pink zones") but also in Belgrade and Sarajevo. Wanting to assure himself that the UN troops would not be in serious danger, the new secretary general, Boutros Boutros-Ghali, waited until a cease-fire held for several days. This did not happen until March, following Croatian, Serb, and eventually Serb Croatian support (although in the case of Serbs living in Croatia, supporters of the peacekeeping operation had to force out an intransigent leadership; *New York Times*, February 22, 1992, A1). The troop arrival on March 16 marked the end of civil war in Croatia for the time being. Unrest erupted again in early 1993 but was contained.

WARFARE IN BOSNIA

No sooner had peacekeepers arrived in Croatia than a full-scale war broke out in Bosnia-Herzegovina, which so dominated international affairs that the Croatian struggle paled in comparison. The war generated 2 million refugees and 140,000 dead or missing (11,000 died in Sarajevo alone). The scale of atrocities approached World War II proportions, introducing a new concept in international discourse: "ethnic cleansing." Bosnian leaders declared their independence from the rest of Yugoslavia in October 1991, and a referendum was scheduled for early March 1992. Ethnic Serbs, who make up roughly one third of the Bosnian population, protested the formation of an independent state where they would be outnumbered by their erstwhile enemies, and they boycotted the vote. On March 1, 1992, the country overwhelmingly approved independence. Within a month, Serb irregulars were fighting in the streets of Bosnia with the support of the local leader, Radovan Karadzic. After firing on pro-independence demonstrators, Serb sharpshooters were forced to flee the country, and a large guerrilla force formed in the mountains sur-rounding Sarajevo and beyond. Serbian leaders in Bosnia received considerable sup-port from the Serbian government, which by late April had declared itself, along with Montenegro, Vojvodina, and a reluctant Kosovo, a new Yugoslav federation.

The international community acted swiftly to grant recognition to Bosnia and within one month had moved to include it in the community of nations, although some feared that this speed was as unwise as the delays had been vis-à-vis Croatia (Cohen 1992, 374). Discussion of deploying peacekeepers began almost immedi-ately, but Boutros-Ghali slowed things down by pointing out that the level of vio-lence in Bosnia posed a grave danger to any future deployment. He also rejected a call from Bosnian Muslim President Alija Itzebegovic for an "intervention force" on the grounds that it would require "many tens of thousands" of troops in a very dangerous situation (*UN Chronicle*, September 1992, 8). In May, Boutros-Ghali withdrew most of the UN observers from Sarajevo, although he ultimately approved Cyrus Vance's recommendation to increase the force already there from 10,000 to 14,000.

The scale of destruction in Bosnia far exceeded that in Croatia. The artillery barrage against Sarajevo continued virtually uninterrupted for the next year, sometimes with as many as 3,000 shells falling on the city in a single day. Serbs moved quickly to gain control of Bosnian territory, and by summer, with only one third of the population, Serbs controlled nearly three fourths of the territory, cutting off access to several towns and villages populated by Muslims in the eastern region of the country. The refugee population grew at the rate of 30,000 per day in the early months of the war.

After some hesitation to take sides (particularly on the part of Russia—a historic Serbian ally), the UN Security Council began in May 1992 to condemn not just the war and its associated atrocities but specifically Serbia and the Serbs of Bosnia. The United States and EC nations imposed economic and diplomatic sanctions against Serbia and Montenegro in April, expanding them in May, and the French, British, and American representatives on the Security Council raised questions about Yugoslavia's continued membership in the UN (in September that membership was revoked, in spite of serious legal questions; "Current Development" 1992, 832). On May 30, the Security Council placed blame for the violence squarely on Serbia and called for sanctions on the basis of Chapter VII of the UN Charter (*New York Times*, May 31, 1992, A1).

The focus of UN efforts in Bosnia was to provide humanitarian assistance to the besieged Muslims in Sarajevo and other towns and villages that were cut off from food and fuel supplies. The Sarajevo airport, overrun by Serb gunmen, was eventually opened thanks to Security Council intervention and diplomatic activity, including a personal visit by François Mitterand, president of France (*New York Times*, June 29, 1992, A1). The Serbs continued to block access to more remote villages on the grounds that even humanitarian assistance had a concrete military impact, which prompted the Security Council to pass a resolution in late June allowing military escorts for humanitarian aid convoys. When this failed, the Security Council approved the use of "all necessary means"—a phrase taken from the Gulf War—to ensure that aid reached its destination (*Economist,* August 15, 1992, 37–38). Although the UN avoided direct confrontation, in March 1993 the rather innovative tactic of air drops delivered significant amounts of food. Perhaps the most heroic figure in the war was General Phillippe Morillon, commander of UN forces in eastern Bosnia, who made saving Srebreniza his personal quest. Entering the Muslim enclave despite shelling and inadequate food, he defied the Serbian troops to attack the helpless city. Even this effort largely failed, however, because many Muslims were eager to abandon the city (against Bosnian Muslim military leaders' hopes), and the secretary general was growing weary of Morillon's grandstanding (*New York Times*, April 8, 1993, A5).

Eventually, the UN became actively involved in evacuating Muslims from such cities as Srebreniza. UN intervention raised disturbing questions about its complicity with Serbian "ethnic cleansing," a practice that involved deliberate depopulation of Muslim-dominated regions. Ethnic cleansing involved not only simple removal of persons by the thousands but also mass executions and even large-scale rape to alter the gene pool of those who remained behind (*New York Times*, May 22, 1992, A1). The Serbs were soundly condemned by the Security Council, the General Assembly, and the Human Rights Commission. Reports of not only ethnic cleansing but also death camps prompted charges of "war crimes" and the approval in September of the creation of a war crimes tribunal along the lines of the Nuremberg Trials (see Chapter 18). In a conference held in London in August, Acting Secretary of State Lawrence Eagleburger warned Serb delegates:

> [W]e should, here at this conference, place squarely before the people of Serbia the choice they must make between joining a democratic and prosperous Europe or join-ing their leaders in the opprobrium, isolation, and defeat which will be theirs if they continue on their present march of folly. (U.S. State Department, September 1992, 1)

It was not just one group that was guilty of atrocities, however; other develop-ments took place during the first months of the war. To begin, Croats and Muslims were guilty of atrocities and ethnic cleansing as well. For example, in early June, Bosnian Muslims and Croats who lived in Bosnia were reported to have rounded up whole villages and killed the inhabitants. Radovan Karadzic, the Bosnian Serbs' leader, was convinced that Muslims were working for years to dominate the country through means of population control:

> The Bosnian Muslims want, ultimately, to dominate, relying on a very high birthrate. They even wanted to move some Turks from Germany to Bosnia to help build their Islamic society. Since such a strategy of domination would be at the expense of Bosnian Serbs, we have resisted it by protecting our own villages. . . . We have not been fighting to gain territory. We have been fighting for the principle that there will be three autonomous communities in Bosnia-Herzegovina in order that no one of the three dominates the other. . . . We are fighting to protect our-selves from becoming vulnerable to the same kind of genocide that coalition waged upon us in World War II when 700,000 Serbs were killed. Today, Serbs would be 60% of the population of Bosnia if this genocide had not been committed. We will never again be history's fools. (Karadzic 1992, 50)

In addition, numerous Serbs opposed violence. In late May, tens of thousands demonstrated in the streets of Belgrade against Slobodan Milosevic and called for his resignation. In the village of Gorazde, an ethnically mixed community, Serb residents were angry with Karadzic's policy of ethnic cleansing. When asked about his remarks that Serbs and Muslims are inherently hostile, they responded: "Remarks like that are simply stupid. . . . Serbs and Muslims have lived in the same valleys, used the same roads, worked in the same places, and intermarried throughout history. Now Karadzic wants to tear us apart" (*New York Times*, March 9, 1993, A5).

Serbian parliamentary leader Milan Panic, a longtime resident of the United States, pressed for a liberal solution to the Yugoslav problem and even ran a strong campaign for president until his defeat and eventual ouster in the fall. He portrayed the situation this way:

> I look at all this a little like a family feud. One family happens to be mine, the Serbs. They happen to live across the river in Bosnia. But they are my family, they are Serbs. To ask Serbs from one side of the river not to help Serbs on the other side is not fair. . . . Now I'm not saying send the army. But we need to help each other, to protect each other. (Panic 1992, 49)

The struggle in Yugoslavia was far from simple because it involved the mutually exclusive goals of territorial integrity and self-determination for a multiethnic state (Woodward 1992, 54). When past experience is overlaid on such a Gordian knot, it is no surprise that there are enough virtue and blame for all.

Peace negotiations under American and European auspices began in earnest in early 1993 with the so-called Vance–Owen plan (named after its diplomatic creators), which would have divided the country into ten more or less ethnically homogeneous areas. Negotiators representing the Muslim and Serb governments expressed strong interest in the plan, but it was ultimately rejected by the Yugoslav parliament in Belgrade under the leadership of Milosevic. Gradually, plans that focused on dividing the country along lines of actual military occupation seemed more realistic and became the foundation for the Dayton Accords.

In 1995, Serb forces stepped up their offensive in spite of NATO threats of retaliation. They overran two safe havens, Srebreniza and Zepa, in the summer and continued shelling Sarajevo. Negotiations for a peace settlement began in earnest in August, shortly before a mortar attack on Sarajevo cost the lives of nearly forty Muslims who were waiting in line at a market on August 28. Two days later, NATO followed through on its threat of aerial bombardment and maintained the shelling until September 14, at which time the tentative agreement to begin full-scale negotiations solidified (the bombing probably did not help move forward the peace process and ran the risk of backfiring; Malanczuk 1997, 414).

Beginning in late September, an extended, secret negotiation took place at Wright-Patterson Air Force Base near Dayton, Ohio. Alija Itzebegovic, Slobodan Milosevic, and Franjo Tudjman signed the agreement with U.S. Secretary of State Warren Christopher on November 21, 1995, signaling both an end to the fighting and the division of Bosnia into two quasi-states: the Serbian Republic centered in Pale and a Muslim-Croat Federation centered in Sarajevo. Although Bosnia is still formally a unified country and the Sarajevo regime is represented in the United Nations, in fact the country has been divided ethnically—one of the goals of the ethnic cleansers.

The Dayton Accords have been implemented primarily by NATO troops from France, the United Kingdom, and the United States, who divided the country into areas of supervision, much like Germany after World War II. The force of roughly 40,000 has encountered periodic resistance and has been criticized for failure to aggressively pursue those accused of war crimes, but in all it has performed as well as expected in preserving stability in the region.

WARFARE IN KOSOVO

Ironically, the structure of the Dayton Accords inadvertently sowed the seeds of a new conflict in the Balkans, this time in Kosovo (Judah 2000, 125). Kosovo, formerly an autonomous republic inside Serbia, is inhabited primarily by ethnic Albanians who have fairly strong ties with the nation of Albania to the south (see Map 10.3). A Serb minority complained of abuse by Albanians in the late 1980s, and in response the Belgrade government rescinded the region's autonomy. Over several years, opposition groups began to coalesce in Kosovo, most aiming for at least a restoration of home rule if not independence, although they differed on the means to be employed to achieve either goal. Ibrahim Rugova, the Kosovar president elected in 1992, consistently favored a peaceful, negotiated settlement, whereas the Kosovo Liberation Army (KLA) took a more radical approach. After the Dayton Accords, Rugova and many Kosovars realized that a peaceful approach would never attract the attention of Western diplomats and was therefore doomed.

Beginning in 1997, KLA attacks against Serb military and police installations in Kosovo prompted retaliatory actions that began a tit-for-tat cycle of escalating violence. It is unclear to what extent the KLA was hoping for Serb reprisals, but it is easy to imagine that a lesson from the Bosnian experience was that Serb atrocities

Map 10.3 Yugoslavia after the Dayton Accords
Source: Viktor Meier, *Yugoslavia: A History of Its Demise* (New York: Routledge, 1999). Reproduced by permission of Taylor & Francis Books UK.

were likely to ultimately prompt NATO intervention (which was Kosovo's only real hope for independence; Ignatieff 2000, 28).

Western diplomats were slow to focus attention on Kosovo. In the meantime, the collapse of the Albanian government of Sali Berisha in 1997 created an opportunity for KLA fighters to consolidate their strongholds in Albania near the Kosovo border and to increase their stockpile of small arms (Judah 2000, 128). By 1998, sporadic violence was the norm in Kosovo. The United States ultimately dispatched Richard Holbrooke, the master diplomat who spearheaded the Dayton Accords, to forge a truce between the factions. In October, Milosevic, under threat of NATO aerial bombardment, agreed to pull back his police and military forces and allow international observers to monitor human rights conditions in Kosovo (*Economist*, October 17, 1998, 53). In January, however, a Serb reprisal that left forty-five ethnic Albanians dead brought an end to the deal. Western diplomats brought Milosevic to Rambouillet, near Paris, to force a peace treaty between Serbs and Albanian Kosovars, again under threat of bombing. The agreement called for NATO deployments in and around Kosovo and the withdrawal of Serb forces, while preserving the fig leaf of Serb sovereignty over the region. Ultimately, Milosevic considered this too great a violation of his country's independence and decided to take his chances on surviving a bombing campaign. As put by Judah, "He was going to risk the bombs and go for broke" (Judah 2000, 227). Milosevic was counting on the collapse of NATO resolve in the face of CNN reports of child victims and such. He also counted on Russian support in the corridors of power.

On March 22, 1999, NATO began a bombing campaign that intensified as it went on for 78 days. While the bombs fell, Serb police forced Albanians out of Kosovo in the hope of more easily exposing the remaining KLA fighters (Ignatieff 2000, 41). Nearly one million refugees flooded Albania, Macedonia (which was already protected by a UN force), and Bosnia (where Milosevic hoped war would break out again). The bombardment did little to protect the KLA, however, and Serbs regained control of numerous towns and roads. The Serbs were unable to completely dislodge the guerrillas, and the diplomatic collapse did not take place as Milosevic had predicted.

All his calculations had failed. NATO had not split, he was unable to spark new wars in Macedonia and Bosnia and, in the end, the Russians had proved unwilling or unable to help him (Judah 2000, 279).

On June 10, 1999, following Milosevic's agreement to Western demands, the NATO bombardment was called off and NATO troops from neighboring Bosnia began to take up positions around the Kosovar capital with UN Security Council approval.

WAR CRIMES TRIBUNAL

In the background of the Yugoslav situation beginning in 1993 was the prospect that those responsible for atrocities would wind up on the docket in the Hague. The International Criminal Tribunal for the former Yugoslavia (ICTY), though starting slow, began to issue indictments for war criminals in 1994 and started its first trial in mid-1995. The first conviction was handed down for Dusko Tadic two years later. Gradually, during 1998 and 1999, an increasing number of those indicted (more than sixty, including leaders of the Pale and Belgrade governments) either surrendered or were captured and arrested by NATO forces in and around Bosnia. The pace of the trials and convictions picked up, and as of mid-2000, ten had been convicted and nearly forty were in custody awaiting imminent trial.

Critics point out that NATO forces have been slow to go after those indicted, often leaving them alone even when they know their whereabouts. Even more serious are charges of complicity by the Belgrade government in providing asylum to many of those indicted. The indictments against Milosevic in May 1999 meant that he was a prisoner in his own country (the decision to issue the indictment was prompted in part by a fear on the part of Chief Prosecutor Louise Arbour that Milosevic would flee to Belarus or some other safe haven).

With the fall of the Milosevic regime in 2000, the new president, Vojislav Kostunica, was pressured by the West to transfer him to the Hague Tribunal. Under threat of aid being cut off, Kostunica relented and, in defiance of Serbian nationalists, surrendered Milosevic to the ICTY. The Tribunal finally had its star suspect in custody. The trial itself began amid chaotic media attention on February 12, 2002, after a flurry of confusing and disjointed statements by Milosevic, who refused to recognize the authority of the trial. His plea of "not guilty" was entered on his behalf by the Tribunal. The charges against him include genocide, murder, extermination, torture, plunder, and cruel treatment of civilians, stemming from Serbia's actions in Croatia, Bosnia, and Kosovo. After months of meandering and often confusing and inflammatory testimony, at a point when it seemed to some that trial might never end, Milosevic was found dead in his cell on March 12, 2006. Reaction to his death was naturally mixed, with one man on the street in Vrajne, Serbia, commenting "He was a big Serb. Maybe he made a few mistakes. . . ." On the other hand, Richard Dicker of Human Rights Watch lamented that his death was "a terrible setback first and foremost for the victims of horrific crimes in the former Yugoslavia, and because it deprives the tribunal of a chance to render a verdict on his true role" (*New York Times*, March 12, 2006). At the same time, many feel justice was done—at least in a cosmic sense.

CONCLUSION: WHITHER YUGOSLAVIA?

Have the great powers of the late 20th century done any better at bringing peace and justice to the Balkans, or have they simply manipulated local conflicts for strategic ends? Although NATO intervention halted the bloodletting in Bosnia and no doubt helped prevent the spread of warfare during the Kosovo crisis, the conflict has always been on Western (specifically U.S.) terms. This has often meant delayed and minimal intervention. The Bosnia conflict, after all, cost nearly 250,000 lives before NATO became directly involved. Even the UN admits that the international community failed in its effort to protect the citizens of

Srebreniza and other safe havens (United Nations 1999). Likewise, intervention in Kosovo did little in the short run to protect ethnic Albanians but created instead an opportunity for Serb aggression. Conversely, Western intervention has sometimes been precipitous for strategic reasons, as with Germany's sudden recognition of Slovenian and Croatian independence without regard for the security implications. Even more uncharitably, one could interpret the entire Western initiative in the Balkans as an attempt to both shore up and extend NATO influence in southern Europe (Gervasi 1998, 20). Certainly an important loser in all of this strategic jockeying has been Russia.

Since 2003, the Kostunica government has adopted a less conciliatory attitude toward the West. Nationalism appears to be resurgent, and the government has resisted Western pressure to cooperate. The United States imposed economic sanctions in April 2004 over the government's refusal to extradite a number of ICTY indictees. Ratko Mladic, for example, is reported to be living in Serbia, although local leaders deny this (*Los Angeles Times*, August 1, 2004, A14). The country has also experienced a number of profound disturbances. In 2003, the Serbian prime minister, reformer, and unifying figure Zoran Djindjic was assassinated, and in March 2004, new violence erupted in Kosovo, resulting in more than thirty deaths (*The Times of London*, March 19, 2004, A11). Throughout this period there has been no progress on negotiations over the status of Kosovo. And finally, in May 2006, Montenegrins voted to secede from Serbia—completing the countries dissolution.

The Western initiative has nevertheless been somewhat measured and constrained compared with past great power machinations. The decision to act through the UN to a considerable degree validates the norm of multilateralism. Likewise, the decision to establish a war crimes tribunal was intended to make clear that more than strategic considerations were at stake. As put simply by Senator Joseph Biden, "I think we did the right thing in our seventy-eight day air campaign, and we succeeded. The war against Milosevic was of great consequence" (Biden 1999).

QUESTIONS TO CONSIDER

1. How does one judge the merits of a nation's demand for self-determination? At what point does such a demand become the concern of the international community? What criteria do the international community use to grant or deny the demand?

2. To what extent should justice take precedence over stability and peace? To what extent do the needs of ethnic communities justify the use of force to alter the political status quo?

3. What force ought to be used by the international community to remedy injustices? How much voice should the great powers have in deciding and implementing these choices? Should, for example, the international community send troops to stop genocide in the Sudan?

KEY FIGURES
YUGOSLAVIA'S DISMEMBERMENT

Slobodan Milosevic   President of Serbia, 1987–2000. He is generally considered responsible for the wars that took place in the Yugoslavian region during the 1990s. He died while on trial for war crimes at the Hague.

Josip Broz Tito   President of Yugoslavia, 1946–1980.

Vojislav Kostunica   President of Serbia, 2000–2008. He won elections and international support, leading to Milosevic's resignation.

Radovan Karadzic   Local leader of the Bosnian Serbs. Currently in hiding as an indicted war criminal.

Louise Arbour   Chief Prosecutor of the ICTY. She pursued Milosevic's arrest and prosecution.

Bill Clinton   U.S. President, 1993–2001. He deployed U.S. troops to Bosnia under NATO.

Richard Holbrooke   U.S. diplomat who spearheaded the Dayton Accords.

Alija Itzebegovic   Leader of the Bosnian Muslims.

Franjo Tudjman   President of Croatia, 1990–1999.

Warren Christopher   U.S. Secretary of State, 1993–1997.

Boutros Boutros-Ghali   UN Secretary General, 1991–1996. He questioned Western interest in Yugoslavia in contrast to its neglect of Rwanda.

George H. W. Bush   U.S. President, 1989–1993. He supported UN operations in Bosnia.

CHRONOLOGY
YUGOSLAVIA'S DISMEMBERMENT

1444
The Ottoman Empire defeats the Serbs at the battle of Varna.

1806
Serbians establish an independent kingdom. The Ottomans later reassert a degree of control.

1848
Croatia takes Austria's side in the rebellion against Hungary.

1871
A Croatian rebellion against Austria is unsuccessful.

1877
The Treaty of San Stefano establishes an independent Serbia and Montenegro.

(continued)

(*continued*)

1878
European powers revise the largely Russian San Stefano Treaty, leaving Serbia under Austrian rule.

1912
Balkan forces expel the Ottomans from the region, precipitating a two-year struggle for territory in the region.

1914
Austrian Archduke Ferdinand is assassinated in Sarajevo by a Serbian nationalist, sparking the outbreak of World War I.

1918
The Kingdom of the Serbs, Croats, and Slovenes is proclaimed after the end of World War I.

1929
A dictatorship is imposed in response to ethnic unrest.

1941
The Nazis conquer the Balkans. Croat fascists (Ustase) join forces with them.

1946
Tito is elected leader of the newly proclaimed Yugoslav Socialist Republic under Soviet sponsorship.

1971
Tito suppresses a Croatian uprising.

1980
Tito dies, leaving a leadership void. Eventually, a rotating presidency is established that shares power among the various republics.

1981
The central government suppresses an Albanian uprising.

1990
Bosnia, Slovenia, Croatia, and Macedonia declare independence and hold elections.

1991
Violence erupts as Serbian forces clash with Croatians. The war continues until 1992.

1992
Violence erupts in Bosnia between Serbs and Croat/Muslim forces. The war lasts until the Dayton Accords are signed in 1995.

1993
The International Criminal Tribunal for the former Yugoslavia founded.

1995
Serbs overrun Srebreniza, a UN-declared safe haven. NATO forces attack Serb artillery in Sarajevo.

November 21   The Dayton Accords are signed, ending the war and leaving Bosnia divided into Serb and Muslim sectors with NATO acting as a buffer.

1997
Kosovo Liberation Army forces attack Serb outposts. Serbia attacks.

1999
NATO bombs Serb installations to protect Kosovars. Serbia withdraws.

2000
Elections in September yield a victory for Milosevic's opponent, Kostunica. Street protests prompt Milosevic to resign.

2001
Milosevic is extradited to the ICTY.

2002
Milosevic's trial begins.

2003
Moderate Serb Prime Minister Zoran Djindjic is assassinated.

2004
Violence erupts in Kosovo. United States imposes economic sanctions as punishment for failure to surrender ICTY indictees.

2006
Slobodan Milosevic dies in his cell in the Hague on March 12.

REFERENCES

Armour, Ian. "Nationalism vs. Yugoslavia." *History Today* 42 (October 1992): 11–13.

Barnet, Richard J. *Intervention and Revolution: The United States in the Third World* (New York: New American Library, 1968).

Biden, Joseph. "Bosnia and Kosovo: Lessons for U.S. Policy." Director's Forum, Woodrow Wilson International Center for Scholars, July 22, 1999.

Braun, Aurel. *Small-State Security in the Balkans* (Totowa, NJ: Barnes & Noble Books, 1983).

Cohen, Leonard J. "The Disintegration of Yugoslavia." *Current History* 91 #568 (November 1992): 369–375.

"Current Development—UN Membership of the 'New' Yugoslavia." *American Journal of International Law* 86 #4 (October 1992): 830–833.

Djilas, Aleska, and Nader Mousavizadeh. "The Nation That Wasn't." *New Republic* (September 21, 1992): 25–31.

The Economist (August 15, 1992): 37–38.

The Economist (August 23, 1992): 36.

The Economist (October 17, 1998): 53.

Gervasi, Sean. "Why Is NATO in Yugoslavia?" in Sara Flounders, ed., *NATO in the Balkans: Voices of Opposition* (New York: International Action Center, 1998): 20–46.

Hayden, Robert. "Yugoslavia: Where Self-determination Meets Ethnic Cleansing." *New Perspectives Quarterly* 9 #4 (Fall 1992): 41–46.

ICISS (International Commission on Intervention and State Sovereignty). *The Responsibility to Protect*. Ottawa: International Development Research Center, 2001. Available online at: www.dfait-maeci.gc.ca/iciss-ciise/pdf/Commission-Report.pdf.

Ignatieff, Michael. *Virtual War: Kosovo and Beyond* (New York: Metropolitan Books, 2000).

Jelavich, Barbara. *History of the Balkans: Vol. 1: 18th & 19th Centuries; Vol. 2: 20th Century* (New York: Cambridge University Press, 1983).

Judah, Tim. *Kosovo: War and Revenge* (New Haven, CT: Yale University Press, 2000).

Karadzic, Radovan. "Salvation Is a Serbian State—Interview." *New Perspectives Quarterly* 9 #4 (Fall 1992): 50–51.

Los Angeles Times, August 1, 2004, A14.

MacLean, Fitzroy. *The Heretic: The Life and Times of Josip Broz Tito* (New York: Harper, 1957).

Malanczuk, Peter. *Akehurst's Modern Introduction to International Law*, 7th ed. (New York: Routledge, 1997).

Mastnak, Tomas. "Is the Nation-State Really Obsolete?" *Times Literary Supplement*, August 7, 1992, 11.

Meier, Viktor. *Yugoslavia: A History of Its Demise* (New York: Routledge, 1999).

New York Times, May 16, 1991, A1.

New York Times, June 7, 1991, A5.

New York Times, June 27, 1991, A1.

New York Times, July 31, 1991, A1.

New York Times, August 30, 1991, A3.

New York Times, October 1, 1991, A1.

New York Times, February 22, 1992, A1.

New York Times, May 22, 1992, A1.

New York Times, May 31, 1992, A1.

New York Times, June 29, 1992, A1.

New York Times, November 21, 1992, A1.

New York Times, March 9, 1993, A5.

New York Times, April 8, 1993, A5.

New York Times, March 12, 2006, A1.

Panic, Milan. "The Future Is Forgetting—Interview." *New Perspectives Quarterly* 9 #4 (Fall 1992): 47–50.

Stavrianos, L. S. *The Balkans: 1815–1914* (New York: Holt, Rinehart & Winston, 1963).

The Times of London, March 19, 2004, A11.

UN Chronicle (September 1992): 8.

United Nations. "Kosovo: Recovering from Ravage." *UN Chronicle* #4 (December 1999): 54–55.

U.S. State Department Dispatch Supplement, September 1992, 1.

Wachtel, Andrew Baruch. *Making a Nation, Breaking a Nation: Literature and Cultural Politics in Yugoslavia* (Stanford, CA: Stanford University Press, 1998).

Wilson, Woodrow. "The World Must Be Made Safe for Democracy." In John Vasquez, ed., *Classics of International Relations*, 2nd ed. (Englewood Cliffs, NJ: Prentice Hall, 1990), 12–15.

White House, Office of the Press Secretary. "Remarks by the President to the KFOR Troops" (Skopje, Macedonia), June 22, 1999.

Woodward, Susan. "The Yugoslav Wars." *Brookings Review* 10 #4 (Fall 1992): 54.

Yugoslavia (Stanford, CA: Stanford University Press, 1998).

11

■ ■ ■

Intelligence: Pearl Harbor

INTRODUCTION

Intelligence is a word pregnant with intrigue and mystery. In fact, intelligence, as used in government circles, simply means the gathering and analysis of information on foreign policy problems. The vast majority of intelligence is gathered and analyzed the same way research papers are written—by informed observers using public documents. It is common knowledge in Washington, D.C., that the *New York Times* routinely provides better information about unfolding events than the Central Intelligence Agency (whose job is to know what is going on). Some more unusual sources of intelligence include spying, electronic surveillance, and satellite reconnaissance. As technology has advanced, the significance of electronic information gathering has increased, typically at the expense of traditional spying.

Today, analysts rely increasingly on electronic intelligence, including telephone intercepts (both cellular and ground-based), e-mail and Internet traffic monitoring, and other electronic communications. The National Security Agency, along with the CIA and various defense and diplomatic intelligence-gathering organizations, monitors and catalogs millions of conversations and e-mails each day in dozens of languages. Such intercepts have allowed U.S. federal agencies to discover various terrorist plots in advance. However, the flow of information is often overwhelming and takes days—even weeks—to translate and interpret. Such delays may have prevented the U.S. government from identifying pre-September 11, 2001, communications that could have prompted a heightened state of alert. Many intelligence experts complain that electronic intelligence is supplanting human intelligence as the principal source of information, even though it is relatively easy for an organized threat to come together without relying on communications that could be monitored.

The case of Pearl Harbor shows what can happen when officials rely too heavily on one particular type of information—in this case, the ability to crack diplomatic messages between officials in Tokyo and Japan's representatives in Washington. The Pearl Harbor story also tells us something about how intelligence is organized. Because of their separate sources of information, the Army and the Navy were expected to share information—but often they did not. A similar observation was noted in the investigations after September 11, when it was discovered that the Immigration and Naturalization Service had files on several of the terrorists, the NSA had some intercepted conversations, and other agencies had additional bits of information that, if placed side-by-side, might have led an analyst to infer that an attack was imminent.

PROLOGUE

In the pre-dawn hours of Sunday, December 7, 1941, a Japanese task force under the command of Vice Admiral Chuichi Nagumo bore down upon Oahu. His formidable armada centered around six aircraft carriers. Upon reaching a point some 220 miles north of the island, they launched two successive waves totaling 350 aircraft—forty torpedo bombers, seventy-eight fighter aircraft, 103 high-level bombers, and 129 dive bombers. Their targets were the ships of Admiral Husband E. Kimmel's U.S. Pacific Fleet at moorings in Pearl Harbor. Before a single shot had been fired, Commander Mitsuo Fuchida, leader of the air strike, knew that the Japanese had achieved total surprise, and so advised the flagship, Akagi, by the code word Tora! Tora! Tora! (Tiger! Tiger! Tiger!). At 0750, Fuchida signaled for the general attack. Approximately four hours later, his aircraft, the last to leave the scene, touched down on Akagi's flight deck. He and his men left behind a devastating sight. They had sunk, capsized, or damaged in varying degrees a total of eighteen warships— eight battleships, three light cruisers, three destroyers, and four auxiliary craft. The U.S. Navy's air arm had lost eighty-seven aircraft of all types. The Japanese had also destroyed seventy-seven aircraft of the Army's Hawaiian Air Force. An additional 128 aircraft had been damaged. Worst of all, 2,403 personnel of the Army, Navy, and Marine Corps, and civilians, had been killed, were listed as missing, or died later of wounds. Those wounded but not killed totaled 1,178. (Prange 1986, xxxi–xxxii)

The overwhelming reaction to the events at Pearl Harbor was shock and anger— shock that the United States could be so unprepared for such an attack and anger at those responsible, principally Imperial Japan. The unity and resolve that Pearl Harbor instilled in the American people carried them through four years of bloody conflict across the globe. Shortly before the war ended, however, probing questions arose concerning who in the U.S. government was responsible for the obvious lapses that made Pearl Harbor possible, if not likely. Before we turn to these issues, a brief overview of the antecedents to the attack on Pearl Harbor is essential (see Chronology).

PEARL HARBOR: THE CONTROVERSY

As early as 1944, with World War II nearly over, isolationists and Republicans in Congress and elsewhere began to question openly the origins of American involvement in the war. Roosevelt himself was mistrusted by many Americans who took his affable, confident demeanor to be a mask for an otherwise unscrupulous character. Roosevelt's desire to enter the war in support of Britain was well known, and his critics surmised that he had twisted and perhaps even precipitated events in such a way that the American people would ultimately come around to his side. To the cynic, Pearl Harbor was not only avoidable, but also contrived.

During the 1940 election campaign, Roosevelt promised to keep the country out of the war then raging in Europe and Asia. At the same time, he confided to his close advisors that he wished to quickly bring the American people around to supporting his quasi-alliance with Britain after the election. In October 1940, he told Admiral James Richardson, commander of the Pacific Fleet (before being replaced by Admiral Husband Kimmel in January 1941), that he expected war to start with a Japanese "error" (Theobald 1954, 192). According to Bailey:

> Franklin Roosevelt repeatedly deceived the American people during the period before Pearl Harbor . . . He was like the physician who must tell the patient lies for the patient's own good. . . . The country was overwhelmingly non-interventionist to the very day of Pearl Harbor, and an overt attempt to lead the people into war would have resulted in certain failure and an almost certain ousting of Roosevelt in 1940, with a consequent defeat of his ultimate aims. (Bailey 1948, 11–13, in Chamberlin 1965, 3)

Roosevelt quickly abandoned his campaign promises after his third electoral victory. Even before his inauguration, Roosevelt responded to British pleas for military aid by pushing through Congress the lend-lease program, waiving the provisions of the Neutrality Act. Roosevelt secured congressional support in part by promising that the United States would not be pulled into war, although at the same time his closest advisor Harry Hopkins was secretly assuring Churchill that the country would stick with him come what may (Chamberlin 1965, 5). Roosevelt implemented lend-lease with enthusiasm—not only allowing the provision of weapons on credit, but also protecting the delivery convoys to Britain with warships. This policy led to attacks on U.S. vessels in the Atlantic in the fall and Roosevelt's order to retaliate and ultimately to shoot "enemy" ships on sight in October. As early as May, Roosevelt exaggerated the German threat, warning that the U.S. coasts were vulnerable to invasion in an effort to heighten public fears. The Atlantic Charter, signed in August, so fully committed the United States to cooperate with Britain that it amounted to an alliance.

Some have interpreted Roosevelt's actions as deliberately provocative to the Japanese to the point of recklessness. The negotiations with Japan during 1941 involved little of the give-and-take typically associated with diplomacy. Japan, on its side, sought U.S. approval (or at least tolerance) of its conquest and annexation of much of China, with the possibility of U.S. support for a complete occupation of the country. For its part, the United States wanted to see Japan's exit from China (and later Indochina) as well as its abrogation of the Tripartite Pact—an alliance signed with Germany and Italy in September 1940. The United States also sought assurances that Japan would no longer threaten the Philippines, a U.S. stronghold, and British and Dutch colonies in the South Pacific and Southeast Asia (these included Burma, Singapore, Malaya, Indonesia, Papua New Guinea, and Australia). Virtually every Japanese and U.S. proposal focused on these mutually exclusive demands. What made American policy threatening, according to Roosevelt's critics, was the economic embargo on Japan, imposed gradually beginning with the refusal to renew a rather bland trade agreement in 1939 and culminating in the much more damaging July 26, 1941, sanctions that cut off vital oil exports (Theobald 1954, 193). These actions, according to revisionist critics, forced the Japanese to take the offensive in Asia in search of alternative sources of fuel and raw materials.

As the negotiations dragged on through 1941, the Japanese repeatedly urged American negotiators to open trade again, offering various, if minor, concessions on China. During the fall, Japanese Ambassador Admiral Kichisaburo Nomura and special envoy Saburo Kurusu, after a number of unsuccessful talks, proposed a summit meeting between Roosevelt and Japanese Premier Prince Fumimaro Konoye. The preconditions imposed by the United States were unacceptable to Japan, however, and the meeting never took place. Revisionist historian Charles Beard asked: "Did the Japanese proposal offer an opportunity to effect a settlement in the Pacific and were the decisions [U.S. officials] made in relation to it actually 'looking' in the direction of peace?" (Beard 1965, 51). Both diplomatic intercepts and the Ambassador to Japan Joseph Grew indicated that the Japanese were sincere and should be heeded. Grew advocated "constructive conciliation" and warned that failure to work with the Konoye government might lead to its downfall (Rauch 1965, 58).

The talks stalemated in spite of repeated attempts by the Japanese to keep them going. Even after the Konoye administration was replaced by the militaristic government of General Hideki Tojo, Tokyo put forward at least two more proposals for a temporary arrangement that would secure U.S. recognition of Japan's position in China and a removal of the economic sanctions in exchange for assurances of no further Japanese conquests or attacks in the Pacific. Secretary of State Cordell Hull dismissed these proposals perfunctorily and in his final message of November 26, largely perceived as an ultimatum shrouded in veiled threats, left only the weakest hint of further concessions (Trefousse 1982, 35).

Not only did this diplomatic intransigence indicate a willingness (if not eagerness) to go to war over China and Southeast Asia, but the military deployments of 1941 seem to have been calculated to invite a surprise attack—the sort of attack Roosevelt had already indicated would be necessary to turn the American people around. In late 1940, Roosevelt ordered the Pacific Fleet to be docked in Pearl Harbor rather than in California to serve as a deterrent. Admiral Richardson opposed this plan on the grounds that it would leave the fleet too exposed, and he lost his job for his protests. Admiral Kimmel was more willing to support this forward basing despite the increased vulnerability it involved, and he was given the command. Then, in the spring of 1941, Roosevelt ordered a sizable portion of the Pacific Fleet reassigned to duty in the Atlantic to fight German submarines. This decision left the outpost even less defended than before. According to Theobald: "The retention of the Fleet in Hawaii, especially after its reduction in strength in

March 1941, could serve only one purpose, an invitation to a surprise Japanese attack" (Theobald 1954,195).

In the days preceding the attack on Pearl Harbor, Washington officials failed to convey to officers in the field all they knew about the seriousness of diplomatic tensions with Japan. This lapse, though excused by Roosevelt's supporters, is consistent with the reckless policy of a war-bent Roosevelt. Intelligence reports indicating that November 30 was the deadline for diplomatic settlement set by Japan were not clearly conveyed to Hawaiian commanders, nor were the signs of December 3–7 showing that the Japanese were in the final stages of breaking diplomatic relations and declaring war. Instead, the news was either kept in Washington or transmitted through the slowest of means, almost as if to ensure that the island would be unprepared for an attack (Theobald 1954, 197). Some have even hinted that Roosevelt knew the silent fleet was en route to Pearl before the fact (Coox 1990, 121).

In fact, the conspiracy theory seems to assume that Roosevelt had far more information and control over events than is logically conceivable. As pointed out by Morison:

> Even if one can believe that the late President of the United States was capable of so horrible a gambit, a little reflection would indicate that he could not possibly have carried it off. He would have needed the connivance of Secretaries Hull, [Republicans] Stimson and Knox, Generals Marshall, Gerow . . . Admiral Stark, and many of their subordinates, too—all loyal and honorable men who would never have lent themselves to such monstrous deception. (S. Morison 1965, 94)

Not only would such a conspiracy have required the involvement of even the lowly radar men in Oahu who mistook the Japanese invasion force for a group of B-17s returning from California, but it would have required all these individuals to knowingly put at risk the largest concentration of military power in the Pacific— hardly the sort of behavior possible from those who would be expected to fight the war in the ensuing months and years (Kahn 1991/1992, 149). Unless one goes so far as to opine that Roosevelt wanted us not only to be in the war but to lose it as well.

Likewise, the point that the United States actually provoked a war with Japan through diplomatic confrontation is overblown. Although several diplomatic cables indicated a certain sincerity on the part of the Japanese negotiators, the overwhelming majority of their instructions were bellicose. As put by Feis:

> Leaving Konoye to go on with his talks with the United States, the Army and Navy threw themselves at once into the plans for action [in August 1941]. The Operations Section of the Army began to get ready to capture Malaya, Java, Borneo, the Bismark Archipelago, the Indies, and the Philippines; it was to be ready by the end of October. The Navy finished its war games. These included the surprise attack on Pearl Harbor and the American fleet there. At the end of the games the two general staffs conferred on the result and found it satisfactory. By the end of September these steps towards war—if diplomacy should fail—were well under way . . . If Konoye was ready and able—as Grew thought—to give Roosevelt trustworthy and satisfactory promises of a new sort, he does not tell of them in his

"Memoirs." Nor has any other record available to me disclosed them. He was a prisoner, willing or unwilling, of the terms precisely prescribed in conferences over which he presided. . . . It is unlikely that he could have got around them or that he would have in some desperate act discarded them. The whole of his political career speaks to the contrary. (Feis 1965, 3941)

Once the Japanese war plans were in place, the country made ridiculous demands on Washington, tantamount to U.S. surrender in the Pacific (Rauch 1965, 62). War, to the Japanese planners, was the expected outcome. It is no surprise, therefore, that talks were allowed to fail; even the negotiators themselves were kept in the dark about these war plans, lest it diminish their appearance of sincerity (Levite 1987, 52). If there was a conspiracy for war, it could be found more easily in the Imperial Conference than in Roosevelt's inner circle.

To a certain extent, the Roosevelt and Truman administrations fueled the popularity of conspiracy theories of Pearl Harbor in that the initial investigations so alarmed senior officials that they attempted to shift the blame to subordinates: "The administration created scapegoats who then attracted the attention of those who wished to discredit Roosevelt and his supporters" (Melosi 1977, 162). The eventual dismissal of Admiral Kimmel and Hawaiian sector army commander General Walter Short created deep resentment among those who felt they had been left in the dark. Successive investigations in Hawaii, the White House, and Congress did little to clear up the confusion. Looking elsewhere for an explanation of the lapse that made Pearl Harbor possible, one can cite a large number of instances of organizational failure and poor judgment on the part of both senior and midlevel officials. Perhaps the most direct comment in this regard is made at the conclusion of Wohlstetter's major work on the subject:

> The fact of surprise at Pearl Harbor has never been persuasively explained by accusing the participants, individually or in groups, of conspiracy or negligence or stupidity. What these examples illustrate is rather the very human tendency to pay attention to the signals that support current expectations about enemy behavior. If no one is listening for signals of an attack against a highly improbable target, then it is very difficult for the signals to be heard. (Wohlstetter 1962, 392)

In 1941, particularly after the January warning of a potential attack on Pearl Harbor turned out to be a false alarm, American military planners were preparing for a possible surprise attack in the South Pacific. Roosevelt was well aware of Japanese tendencies for dramatic gestures and had made sure that American commanders in the Philippines and around Indochina were alerted to the possibility of attack. This was the logical place for a Japanese attack because a victory there would not only damage American capabilities, but more than likely bring territorial gains as well. Military planners in Washington doubted the Japanese ability to cross the Pacific and attack Hawaii—something Secretary of War Stimson later acknowledged publicly (E. Morison 1965, 70). Based on the tendency to look to Asia rather than Hawaii, war warnings emphasized the former region. Even the last war warning delivered on November 27 by the navy mentioned only "the Philippines, Thai or

Kra peninsula, or possibly Borneo" as likely targets of Japanese aggression (Trefousse 1982, 173). As put by Prange:

> The human inclination to believe what one wants to believe, to see what one wants to see, no doubt played a part in the Pearl Harbor drama . . . This lack of genuine, gut-level belief [in the threat of Japanese attack], as opposed to a cool, academic setting forth of theoretical possibilities, was the fundamental cause of the United States being caught flat-footed on December 7, 1941. All other sins of omission and commission were its sons and daughters. (Prange 1986, 525, 529)

Thus many signals pointing to Hawaii were either dismissed or ignored (we will say more about this later). More importantly, many critical developments were simply never conveyed to the commanders stationed at Pearl Harbor. In an angry article written after the war, Admiral Kimmel listed the bits of information that were in the hands of Washington planners and intelligence officials but were never transmitted to him: (1) details of intercepted diplomatic cables proving the deterioration of negotiations—especially Japan's rejection of Hull's ten-point note received on December 6 and 7; (2) information on Japan's strong efforts to secure detailed information on the facilities and ships at Pearl Harbor; and (3) specific deadlines announced by the Japanese, including the 1:00 PM Washington time deadline (7:00 AM Hawaii time) on December 7 when relations were severed. As he put it: "I cannot understand now—I have never understood—I may never understand—why I was deprived of the information available in the Navy Department in Washington on Saturday night and Sunday morning" (Kimmel 1965, 77). About the failure to transmit this information, Trefousse commented:

> Why this information was never forwarded to Pearl Harbor is a more serious question. If anybody should have known about Japanese interest in the anchorage of the Pacific Fleet, it was obviously Admiral Kimmel. Yet he neither received the messages nor any summary of them—a good example of the poor dissemination of intelligence information at the time. (Trefousse 1982, 47)

Washington planners were reluctant to communicate too much of the information drawn from the decoded signals in order to minimize security leaks. If the Japanese suspected that their codes had been broken, they would have immediately changed them. Furthermore, because intelligence was gathered separately by the army and the navy, inter-service rivalry led to some delays in sharing crucial information (Clausen 1992). In addition, some communications were given higher priority for decoding based on assumptions about Japanese behavior. Thus the flood of cables from Tokyo to the Japanese embassy was handled expeditiously, whereas the trickle of messages from the Hawaiian consulate was almost ignored, even though it was the channel through which the detailed schemas of the Pearl Harbor facilities were being transmitted (Levite 1987, 53). Finally, Washington commanders feared that sending too much information might devalue the importance of each item and lead to complacency. This was a special concern with war warnings, which were sent with some regularity from January to December 1941 (Trefousse 1982, 71).

The ability to transmit vital information was further hampered by an apparent lack of anxiety in some circles in the Washington bureaucracy, culminating in the absence of several key individuals—not to mention whole departments—over the weekend of December 6 and 7. Secretary Stimson was unavailable, and his Chief of Staff George Marshall was riding horses on Sunday morning in Washington (while it was still night-time in Hawaii). They were not available to respond vigorously to the 1:00 PM deadline. Admiral Harold Stark, chief of naval operations, did not take the warning very seriously. As a result, the only response to the direct threat was sent to Hawaii at 12:18 PM, Washington time, and was not received until after the bombs had started falling (Trefousse 1982, 69).

On November 27, two crucial messages were transmitted to commanders in Hawaii. They were the army's and the navy's war warnings, which called upon all American forces in the Pacific to go on extreme alert, as can be seen in the army's version:

> Negotiations with Japan appear to be terminated to all practical purposes with only the barest possibilities that the Japanese Government might come back and offer to continue. Japanese future action unpredictable but hostile action possible at any moment. If hostilities cannot, repeat cannot, be avoided, the United States desires that Japan commit the first overt act. This policy should not, repeat not, be construed as restricting you to a course of action that might jeopardize your defense. Prior to hostile Japanese action you are directed to undertake such reconnaissance and other measures as you deem necessary but these measures should be carried out so as not, repeat not, to alarm civil population or disclose intent. (Trefousse 1982, 174)

Although the warning seems unambiguous in retrospect, General Short and Admiral Kimmel complained later that the messages were confusing. They seemed to indicate that alertness should be heightened, but it should be done almost secretly so as not alarm the locals. This was clearly not possible if by defensive measures the Washington commanders envisioned deployment of the fleet in the high seas. As a consequence, Kimmel and Short did little to change their ordinary routine over the next week. General Leonard Gerow, who received Short's rather bland response to the warning, failed to understand that he had not grasped the seriousness of the situation, and so the matter was dropped (E. Morison 1965, 70).

The importance of this failure of leadership and judgment is debatable. At no time did Washington officials have any hard evidence that Japan intended to attack Pearl Harbor on December 7 (Levite 1987, 71). Prange explained the Japanese preparations:

> We have seen how meticulously the Japanese perfected their planning; how diligently they trained their pilots and bombardiers; how they modified weapons to achieve maximum damage; how persistently they dredged up and utilized information about the U.S. Pacific Fleet. They balked at no hazard, ready to risk a wild leap to achieve their immediate ends. (Prange 1981, 736)

A useful analogy might be that a homeowner would take seriously a rumor of burglars in the neighborhood but dismiss reports of terrorists driving tanks!

A point rarely made about war preparedness at Pearl Harbor is that the fleet may have been in even greater danger had it been alerted and deployed. After all, within ten minutes of the attack, all the navy's shipboard anti-aircraft guns were manned and firing, but with little effect (Clausen 1992, 9). Had the fleet been at sea, it still would have been outgunned and even more vulnerable to attack. Pearl Harbor provided the benefit of a shallow berth. Though not eliminating the risk of aerial torpedo attack, as the local commanders learned with chagrin, it did allow salvage of almost all the ships that were hit and even sunk, not to mention the rescue of the crews (Wallin 1968, 283). The most serious lapse was in the air force, which left its planes wingtip to wingtip at every airfield on the island. Had American planes been airborne (in itself a departure from procedure), the Japanese planes might have been sighted and engaged sooner. At any rate, given the overwhelming military might brought to bear on the area by a committed Japanese force, Pearl Harbor was destined to be a bloodbath, warning or no.

The classic question remains: How much did Washington know and when did it know it? This query refers to the intelligence capabilities of the U.S. government in 1941. Resources that are common today, such as spy satellites, electronic eavesdropping devices, night-vision goggles, and aerial reconnaissance, were either not available or of limited utility due to the primitive nature of the devices. Aerial reconnaissance, though used during World War II, was of little value to a remote outpost such as Pearl Harbor, given the range and altitude capabilities of existing aircraft. Even radar, which was available, was a novelty that even its operators did not understand. Given these technological constraints, the means available for gathering intelligence on the Japanese consisted of only (1) public sources (newspapers, tourists), (2) diplomatic communications (ambassadors' analyses), (3) espionage (human intelligence), and (4) signals intelligence (intercepting coded radio messages).

By 1940, public sources of information from Japan were severely limited due to heavy censorship imposed by the government. Although reporters generally had a good idea of what was going on, they could not print it. What was worse, at the turn of the decade, many of the most seasoned analysts were reassigned and replaced with far more inexperienced staff (Levite 1987, 46). With the economic sanctions imposed in July 1941, the many American traders, seamen, and investors who had previously kept in touch with Japan turned their attention elsewhere and were no longer available as a public intelligence source.

Ambassador Joseph Grew exerted considerable energies not only to acquire information on the Japanese government's intentions, but also to convey his impressions and analysis to the secretary of state. He was the one who predicted the collapse of the Konoye administration and shared the Pearl Harbor attack rumor nearly a year before its occurrence. Unfortunately, because of his tendency to speculate without hard evidence, the Washington team discounted his opinions in favor of what they saw as the most important "hard intelligence": signals intercepts. That the government did not rely on espionage, as would be expected, is explained this way:

> In sharp contrast to Great Britain, Germany, Japan, and the Soviet Union, which were investing, at the time, a lot of resources in espionage, the United States deliberately refrained from engaging in this type of intelligence activity due to moral, political, and budgetary considerations. (Levite 1987, 50)

The key element of U.S. intelligence on Japan came through the extensive message decoding operation known as MAGIC. Through it, the army, under the direction of the Signals Intelligence Section, was able to intercept and translate almost all Japanese diplomatic cables to the United States and Hawaii from 1937 to 1941 (except for an eighteen-month period in 1939–1940 when a newly introduced code had to be broken). In fact, the U.S. decoding efficiency was so high that American diplomats and senior officials often had copies of the cables before the Japanese delegates themselves. Clearly, U.S. negotiators benefited greatly by knowing precisely how much latitude the Japanese delegates were permitted by their home office. Americans also could follow the changing tone of the messages to gauge the increasing likelihood of war (Kahn 1991/1992, 143).

Important interceptions obtained via MAGIC included the following: the announcement that the Imperial Conference had approved a strategy of aggression in the South Pacific in July 1941; a conciliatory message wedged between numerous belligerent ones on November 15, 1941; a self-imposed Japanese deadline of November 22 (later extended to November 29) for a settlement with the United States, after which "things are automatically going to happen"; instructions to embassies to destroy documents and codes on December 3; the fourteen-part message rejecting Cordell Hull's ten-point note on December 6–7; and the December 7 announcement that relations would be severed at 1:00 pm, Washington time (Trefousse 1982, 48). In addition, military planners in Washington were vaguely aware of messages to Japanese spies in Hawaii, also intercepted and interpreted through MAGIC. A controversial message over Tokyo radio known as the "winds execute" signal was detected by army intelligence on December 4 but never conveyed to Hawaiian commanders. This signal was a coded announcement that relations with the United States were being severed.

Although some have complained that these diplomatic communications were not relayed quickly enough to the commanders in Hawaii, the truth is they did not provide a consistent and coherent picture of Japanese plans in and of themselves. According to Wohlstetter, this was because of the overabundance of "noise":

> In short, we failed to anticipate Pearl Harbor not for want of the relevant materials, but because of a plethora of irrelevant ones. Much of the appearance of wanton neglect that emerged in various investigations of the disaster resulted from the unconscious suppression of vast congeries of signs pointing in every direction except Pearl Harbor. (Wohlstetter 1962, 388)

Because the diplomatic corps was not privy to the details of war plans, even this exhaustive source was not adequate. For its part, navy intelligence was working on breaking the military codes. But due to lack of staff, most of whom were working in the Signal Corps (collecting communications) rather than cryptography, the navy was unable to crack the essential military codes and was forced to rely on mere traffic patterns to keep track of the Japanese fleet's deployment. By simply monitoring which ships were in radio communication at different times, it was possible to locate them with some precision. At various times, some ships went silent, but typically only when they were close to the mainland and captains could receive instructions by hand.

As of December 1941, the bulk of the Japanese fleet was detected moving south toward Indochina and Indonesia—with the exception of one large carrier group, which could not be located due to radio silence (Kahn 1991/1992, 145). Intelligence analysts naturally assumed a repetition of the previous pattern and did not bother to alert Hawaii about this "lost fleet" (something that particularly annoyed Hawaiian commanders after the fact). In fact, the fleet was bound for Hawaii with lengthy and detailed orders that earlier had been hand-delivered in Japan. Thus the fleet was able to maintain radio silence in spite of their distance. This situation also made diplomatic intervention to stop the fleet impossible without revealing its location and thereby causing a major incident.

The last line of intelligence gathering—on site in Hawaii—also proved inadequate. Navy radar operators on Oahu spotted a large blip on their screens early on the morning of December 7 indicating a large group of aircraft some 135 miles offshore. They were puzzled and a bit suspicious of this signal and called in to their base for clarification, only to be told that the blip was probably a group of army B-17s coming from the coast and to "forget it." No one bothered to check with the army to confirm the planes' estimated time of arrival. The radar operators, having already worked a half-hour past quitting time, then shut off the machines and left (Trefousse 1982, 77).

To answer the question of how much the "U.S. government" knew is not the same as determining how much different individuals within the government were aware of. As we mentioned, intelligence details were shared grudgingly between the army and the navy, and the difficulty in processing the flood of signals forced the cryptography staff into a sort of intelligence triage, passing along only those messages they considered most vital. Many errors of judgment and cooperation were therefore made, although it is difficult to place blame on any one person.

Wohlstetter maintains that never before had the United States collected so much information on a potential belligerent, implying that the government did have the capacity, by pooling all of these facts and figures, to predict that an attack on Pearl Harbor on December 7 was likely (Wohlstetter 1962, 382). Kahn and Levite take exception to this conclusion by arguing that even if all the information had been centralized, the resulting picture would still have been ambiguous and confusing (Kahn 1991/1992; Levite 1987). As put by Levite:

The United States was indeed poorly equipped, organized, and deployed to collect information regarding Japan's intentions and capabilities in general, and their preparations for attack on Pearl Harbor in particular. In fact, the overall picture is one in which the United States not only lacked systematic coverage of the Japanese military, but its sources were actually drying up in the period immediately preceding the Pearl Harbor attack . . . It would seem that under the collection conditions prevailing prior to the Pearl Harbor attack, it would have taken an incredible stroke of luck for the United States to obtain concrete advance warning of Japan's intention to launch the attack. (Levite 1987, 60)

CONCLUSION: THE LESSONS OF PEARL HARBOR

Because one cannot assume that intelligence gathering will ever yield the "smoking gun" proving an adversary's intent, the lesson of Pearl Harbor is not primarily to increase intelligence gathering efforts. These will always be inadequate in some way. Instead, there are two principal lessons of Pearl Harbor. First, intelligence, once gathered, should be centralized, to allow analysts with a global perspective to assess the meaning of the material, and then disseminated as rapidly and widely throughout the government as security permits. Second, decision makers should think creatively about an adversary's possible tactics and strategies. Rather than assume a particular chain of events is inevitable, they should assume it is merely likely and consider other less probable scenarios.

QUESTIONS TO CONSIDER

1. To what extent has the U.S. government attempted to remedy the organization and attitudinal problems revealed by the Pearl Harbor disaster? Could such a disaster happen again?

2. Who or what is most to "blame" for Pearl Harbor? Roosevelt? Inter-service rivalry? Tojo? Inept radar operators? Admiral Kimmel and General Short? Inadequate technology?

3. To what extent did the Pearl Harbor experience influence American military strategy in the postwar era? How has it affected nuclear strategy, for example?

KEY FIGURES
PEARL HARBOR

Franklin Roosevelt   U.S. President, 1933–1945. He embraced a more internationalist role for the United States in world affairs and supported Britain during the early months of World War II. He reacted swiftly to Japan's attack on Pearl Harbor and presided over the country's war efforts until his death a few days before Germany's surrender.

General Hideki Tojo Japanese Premier, 1941–1944. The dominant militarist in the Tokyo government, he is broadly considered the mastermind of Japan's aggression in the 1930s and 1940s. He was later executed as a war criminal.

Admiral Husband Kimmel Commander of the U.S. Pacific Fleet, stationed at Pearl Harbor in 1941. He, along with Army General Short, was blamed for inadequate preparation for the Japanese attack.

General Walter Short Commander of the Hawaiian Sector of the U.S. Army. His unwillingness to work with Admiral Kimmel was cited as a cause for the military's lack of preparedness for the Pearl Harbor attack.

Cordell Hull   U.S. Secretary of State, 1933–1944. He spearheaded Roosevelt's international-ist policy and was awarded the 1945 Nobel Peace Prize.

Prince Fumimaro Konoye Japanese Premier, 1937–1939 and 1940–1941. He was known for his attempts to block the political rise of the military.

Admiral Kichisaburo Nomura Japanese Ambassador to the United States in 1941.

CHRONOLOGY
PEARL HARBOR

1931
Japan attacks Manchuria. U.S. Secretary of War Henry Stimson succeeds in pressing a policy of non-recognition by the United States.

1933
Japan leaves the League of Nations under protest after imposition of sanctions.

1937
Japan launches war on China.

1935–1939
The United States passes the Neutrality Acts.

1939
July   The United States cancels its bilateral trade agreement with Japan.

September   Germany attacks Poland; France and Britain declare war—World War II begins.

November   Neutrality Act of 1939 commits the United States to sell arms to belligerents on a cash-and-carry basis.

1940
June   France falls to Germany.

(continued)

(*continued*)

September   Congress enacts the draft by one vote. Germany, Italy, and Japan sign the Tripartite Pact, pledging mutual support in the event any of the three is attacked.

December   U.S. President Franklin Roosevelt receives an urgent request for lend-lease aid from British Prime Minister Winston Churchill in violation of the 1939 Neutrality Act.

1941

January   Congress approves the lend-lease after Roosevelt's reiteration of formal neutrality. Pearl Harbor is placed on high alert after rumors of a Japanese attack.

March   U.S. Secretary of State Cordell Hull and Japanese Ambassador Kichisaburo Nomura negotiate in Washington over continued Japanese conquests in China and Japan's adherence to the Tripartite Pact.

July   The Japanese Imperial Conference endorses policy of military conquest in the Pacific.

July 24   Japan moves into Indochina after pressuring the pro-Nazi Vichy government in France to relinquish its colonial holdings.

July 26   The U.S. government freezes Japanese assets and takes control of trade. Some argue that cutting off Japan from American oil and markets forced it to go to war.

August 6   Japan offers concessions on China issue in exchange for an end to the U.S. freeze on assets—the United States rejects the offer. Japan begins plans for an attack on Pearl Harbor. They are ready by late October.

August 9–14   Roosevelt and Churchill meet in Newfoundland and issue the Atlantic Charter, which includes U.S. support for the British and Chinese fight against Japan in the Pacific and rejection of Japanese domination of Manchuria.

August 17   The United States warns Japan of a possible American resort to force to implement the Atlantic Charter.

August–September   Japanese Prime Minister Fumimaro Konoye meets with Churchill.

September–October   U.S. destroyers are attacked in the Atlantic. Roosevelt adopts a shoot-on-sight policy against German U-boats.

September 6   Konoye offers the proposal for the summit with Roosevelt. U.S. Ambassador to Japan Joseph Grew warns that the Konoye government may fall if the United States rejects the offer.

October 2   The United States rejects Konoye's proposals and defers the summit meeting. Negotiations show no further progress from this point on.

October 16   Hideki Tojo, leader of the Japanese War Party, becomes prime minister when the moderate Konoye cabinet falls.

November 3   Ambassador Grew warns that the Japanese may be planning a secret attack and urges conciliation in Washington. Army Chief of Staff George Marshall and Harold Stark, chief of naval operations, recommend to Roosevelt that all support short of war with Japan should be given to China, but reiterate that Germany is the "most dangerous enemy." Roosevelt approves the proposal. The United States rejects the Japanese Imperial Conference's "Proposal A." Cordell Hull warns in an earlier Cabinet meeting that Japan may be planning a secret attack.

November 17   By a thin margin, Congress passes amendments to the Neutrality Act to allow convoy escorts into war zones. Special Japanese envoy Saburo Kurusu joins Nomura in Washington to begin negotiations (with a secret Japanese deadline of November 30).

November 20   The United States receives Japanese "Proposal B." It again demands an end to Japanese actions in the Pacific and China.

November 22–26   Hull weighs and rejects "modus vivendi" based on Proposal 5 in a ten-point note offering new proposals. Meanwhile, a Japanese carrier force leaves Japan for Hawaii under radio silence.

November 27–29   The United States Army and Navy send secret war alerts to Pacific bases. Japanese cabinet secretly rejects the U.S. proposals, although this response will not be conveyed until December 7.

December 1   The order to commence the Pearl Harbor attack given to carrier groups: "Climb Mount Nitaka." The Japanese destroy codes in their embassy and move troops south from Indochina. Roosevelt sends an urgent message of peace to Emperor Hirohito.

December 2   Roosevelt receives part of the Japanese rejection of the November 26 offer through code breaking; Roosevelt interprets it as a sign that war is imminent.

December 5–6   The Japanese destroy codes in their embassy and move troops south from Indochina.

December 6   Roosevelt sends an urgent message of peace to emperor Hirohito. Roosevelt receives part of the Japanese instructions to their ambassador in the United States to deliver a declaration of war to Roosevelt by 1:00PM, Washington time.

December 7   Cryptographers in Washington intercept Japanese instructions to their ambassador in the United States to deliver a declaration of war to Roosevelt by 1:00PM, Washington time. The message is not conveyed to Pearl Harbor prior to attack. Washington learns of the Pearl Harbor attack at 7:55AM, Hawaii time, but a Japanese legate fails to convey the declaration of war until after the attack has already started.

December 8   Roosevelt delivers his "Day of Infamy" speech, after which Congress unanimously approves a declaration of war on Japan. Germany and Italy declare war on the United States within a week.

REFERENCES

Bailey, Thomas A. *The Man in the Street* (New York: Macmillan, 1948).

Beard, Charles A. "Appearance and Realities" in Waller, ed., *Pearl Harbor: Roosevelt and the Coming of the War* (Boston: Heath, 1965): 48–56.

Chamberlin, William Henry. "Roosevelt Maneuvers America into War" in Waller, ed., *Pearl Harbor: Roosevelt and the Coming of the War* (Boston: Heath, 1965): 1–13.

Clausen, Henry, with Bruce Lee. *Pearl Harbor: Final Judgement* (New York: Crown Publishers, 1992).

Coox, Alvin D. "Repulsing the Pearl Harbor Revisionists: The State of Present Literature on the Debacle" in Hilary Conroy and Harry Way, eds., *Pearl Harbor Reexamined: Prologue to the Pacific War* (Honolulu: University of Hawaii Press, 1990): 119–126.

Feis, Herbert. "The Road to Pearl Harbor" in Waller, ed., *Pearl Harbor: Roosevelt and the Coming of the War* (Boston: Heath, 1965): 3147.

Kahn, David. "The Intelligence Failure of Pearl Harbor." *Foreign Affairs* 70 #5 (Winter 1991/1992): 138–152.

Kimmel, Husband. "Admiral Kimmel's Story" in Waller, ed., *Pearl Harbor: Roosevelt and the Coming of the War* (Boston: Heath, 1965): 72–79.

Levite, Ariel. *Intelligence and Strategic Surprises* (New York: Columbia University Press, 1987).

Melosi, Martin V. *The Shadow of Pearl Harbor: Political Controversy over the Surprise Attack, 1941–1946* (College Station: Texas A&M University Press, 1977).

Morison, Elting E. "An Unanswerable Question" in Waller, ed., *Pearl Harbor: Roosevelt and the Coming of the War* (Boston: Heath, 1965): 68–72.

Morison, Samuel E. "Who Was Responsible?" in Waller, ed., *Pearl Harbor: Roosevelt and the Coming of the War* (Boston: Heath, 1965): 94–98.

Prange, Gordon W. *At Dawn We Slept: The Untold Story of Pearl Harbor* (New York: McGraw-Hill, 1981).

Prange, Gordon W., with Donald M. Goldstein and Katherine V. Dillon. *Pearl Harbor: The Verdict of History* (New York: McGraw-Hill, 1986).

Rauch, Basil. "Principle in International Policy" in Waller, ed., *Pearl Harbor: Roosevelt and the Coming of the War* (Boston: Heath, 1965): 57–68.

Theobald, Robert A. *The Final Secret of Pearl Harbor: The Washington Contribution to the Japanese Attack* (New York: Devin-Adair, 1954).

Trefousse, Hans. *Pearl Harbor: The Continuing Controversy* (Malabar, FL: Krieger Pub, 1982).

Waller, George, ed. *Pearl Harbor: Roosevelt and the Coming of the War* (Boston: Heath, 1965).

Wallin, Homer Norman. *Pearl Harbor: Why, How, Fleet Salvage, and Final Appraisal* (Washington, DC: Naval History Division, 1968).

Wohlstetter, Roberta. *Pearl Harbor: Warning and Decision* (Stanford, CA: Stanford University Press, 1962).

PART

3

...

International Cooperation

12

. . .

Democratic Peace Theory: Vietnam Homefront

INTRODUCTION

Until several major powers became democratic, public opinion was important only to the extent that soldiers were willing to fight and citizens were willing to pay taxes without excessive pressure from the state. By 1900, it was clear that publics matter. War in a democracy is a hazardous endeavor for any politician seeking reelection. Although a democratic nation united in battle is an awesome force, democracies are uniquely prone to discouragement when wartime sacrifices seem to outweigh promised benefits. Politicians have been forced to break off an unpopular fight to save their political skins. This is especially true where the public was led to believe that the war would be easy and quick.

Furthermore, democracies are ill-equipped to start wars. Although most executives have some discretion about deploying troops, it is difficult to ramp up to a major invasion without showing your cards. Legislatures must approve increased military budgets, approve a draft, and possibly make the formal declaration of war (although this last step has become obsolete). As a result, it is virtually impossible for democracies to launch a surprise attack.

In spite of domestic politics and institutional impediments to starting wars, democratic governments have in fact engaged in numerous wars—but not with each other. This is the starting point of the "democratic peace theory," a relatively recent set of observations that aims to explain why democratic governments rarely go to war with each other. Looking back over the last 200 years, scholars have identified only a handful of cases where two governments with the rudiments of democracy went to war. Two of those—the American Revolution and the War of 1812—were essentially the same operation, which could just as easily be classified as a civil war. The rarity of this type of event goes far beyond randomness and therefore warrants explanation.

Some of the pattern could be a historical fluke. After all, during the 20th century, it just so happened that the world's democratic states were allies during the two World Wars and the Cold War. It would be reckless for allies to allow disputes between them spill over into warfare. Not that this is unheard of. After all, Greece and Turkey fought over Cyprus during the 1960s and 1970s. But it is worth noting that no shots have been fired between them since both governments adopted democratic regimes.

Some have argued that the link is primarily economic (Friedman 2007, 580–604). The idea is that democratic governments routinely adopt open-trade policies that result in their being economically interdependent. Governments, the theory goes, do not start wars against their customers and depositors. But World War I was begun by countries that were more deeply enmeshed in each other than any other group of countries up to that point (perhaps ever). In fact, most wars take place between neighbors over territorial control, with economic interests often figuring prominently (France and Germany went to war three times between 1870 and 1939 over control of the Rhine River Valley and its rich ore deposits).

Still others argue that it is mostly a question of respect for rules and peaceful dispute settlement (Doyle 1983). Democracies sign treaties, create and join international organizations, and go to court with each other far more often than their autocratic counterparts. But this does not necessarily mean they comply with the rules any better. The United States covertly supported the Contras in Nicaragua in the 1980s as they attempted to overthrow the Communist government there. It was charged with violating the rules of sovereignty and lost in a case before the International Court of Justice. The United States denied any wrongdoing throughout the ordeal. But overall, it would seem that international law is primarily a democratic thing, as is an overall respect for law and non-violent dispute settlement.

The jury is still out on the whys and wherefores of the democratic peace theory. In this case, we will focus on the question of domestic support for warfare. In light of declining support for the Iraq War, it is worth examining whether this reflects a pattern. Even today, Americans continue to experience a sense of deep personal ambivalence with regard to Vietnam. Could we have won the war? Was our cause just? Who was to blame for our failure? These doubts and questions were at the root of the public opposition to the war, which in turn contributed to the fall of two presidents and a dramatic change in our foreign policy priorities. As put by former Secretary of Defense George Ball:

> We have never recovered from the anger and divisiveness of the latter 1960s, and I find increasing evidence of the baleful mark left by our Vietnam experience on almost all aspects of American life. . . . (Ball 1982, 467)

To better understand both how public opinion was formed during the war and how this opinion may or may not have affected policy, we will briefly review the key events of the Vietnam War itself. U.S. involvement in Vietnam's civil war dates back at least to World War II and began in earnest in 1954, when the French colonists withdrew from Vietnam after their defeat at Dien Bien Phu. Ho Chi Minh, leader of the Vietcong Communist guerrillas since 1941, became the leader of the provisional North Vietnamese government in Hanoi, while a succession of largely unpopular governments emerged in Saigon with U.S. support. The rest of the story can be told most quickly with the simple chronology.

PUBLIC OPINION AND VIETNAM

The American public generally favors presidents who deal decisively with foreign policy crises, even when their efforts fail. In the case of Vietnam, public support was not only strong, but also sustained until 1968. After the Tet Offensive, the domestic consensus on the rightness of the U.S. war effort in Vietnam underwent a palpable shift, which directly affected the way the White House fought the war. To better understand this shift, we need to look at the chain of events that preceded and followed it.

TONKIN GULF AND RALLY 'ROUND THE FLAG

The Kennedy administration came to office with a call to sacrifice in the fight against communism. Kennedy referred to a "New Frontier" of progress and leadership. In the aftermath of the Sputnik shock, the "missile gap" scare, the fall of Cuba to communism, and other deeply troubling events, the country seemed to be on a war footing. Although Kennedy met with a setback in the failed invasion of Cuba at the Bay of Pigs, he captured the country's imagination with his firm stand against Moscow over the Cuban missiles (Kattenburg 1980, 210). Thus for reasons of national pride and compassion for the citizens of "captive nations," as well as out of simple fear, the American public was favorably disposed in the early 1960s to undertake a crusade on distant shores (Levy 1991, 16). Although Vietnam had not yet entered the public consciousness, Kennedy and Vice President Lyndon Johnson could feel assured of the public's latent support.

After Kennedy's assassination in November 1963, Johnson came to power in the White House. His attitude was far less patient than that of Kennedy, who had tolerated the overthrow of South Vietnam's leader Ngo Dinh Diem after refusing to support the unpopular president. Johnson was more eager to score victories on the battlefield, where the Communist Vietcong insurgents, funded and supplied by North Vietnam, were making significant progress. Looking for a popular rationale for deploying more troops to the region, Johnson seized upon an incident in the Gulf of Tonkin. Two U.S. patrol boats had exchanged fire with North Vietnamese warships near the coast, prompting an outcry from the White House that was echoed on Capitol Hill. Johnson asked Senator William Fulbright to shepherd a resolution giving Johnson broad powers to retaliate immediately and in the future.

The Tonkin Gulf Resolution was passed on August 7, 1964, by a vote of eighty-eight to two. As pointed out by Herring:

> From a domestic political standpoint, Johnson's handling of the Tonkin Gulf incident was masterly. His firm but restrained response to the alleged North Vietnamese attacks won broad popular support, his rating in the Louis Harris poll skyrocketed from 42% to 72% overnight. He effectively neutralized [hawkish Republican presidential hopeful Barry] Goldwater on Vietnam, a fact which contributed to his overwhelming electoral victory in November. (Herring 1986, 122)

Kattenburg explained, however, that this support was largely naïve, because the American public did not fully understand the nature of the war that was underway.

> [T]he American people wanted to believe [the New Frontier rhetoric], and believe they did. When the number of U.S. military men increased from under 1,000 to about 15,000 in Vietnam in a little over six months, few people realized that the New Frontier had in effect started the process of extending U.S. borders to those of Indochina with Thailand. (Kattenburg 1980, 209)

Lyndon Johnson won an overwhelming victory against Goldwater in 1964, campaigning as the peace candidate (a position he reversed shortly after the election; Kattenburg 1980, 251). Support for the war was at 65% by late 1965, and with news of the bombing campaigns, public opinion was supportive (Mueller 1973, 119). This "spike" in public support is an illustration of the "rally 'round the flag" phenomenon, whereby large segments of the public express support for the president's policies in any crisis situation, regardless of the substance of the policies. Leslie Gelb argued that in spite of the emergence in 1965 of an anti-war movement, "the widespread belief that South Vietnam should not be lost to communism generated and sustained that war" (Gelb 1976, 103). Nevertheless, letters opposing the bombing campaign poured into Capitol Hill offices after the announcement (Herring 1986, 133). Overall, the signals sent by the public in the early stages of the war were contradictory and confusing. Political leaders could and did read into them what they wanted.

GROWING SKEPTICISM

During 1966 and 1967, Johnson's policy of escalation was in full swing. By the end of 1967, nearly half a million troops were deployed and nearly 10,000 had fallen in combat. Sustained bombing of the North, coupled with CIA covert operations, supported the Marines in the field. Vietnam was very much on the minds of Americans, to the point that it was viewed as the single most significant issue of the day by 1967. However, as the fight wore on, three different groups of Americans began to question the rightness of the war.

The first to defect was a group of already disenchanted individuals who later came to form the core of the anti-war movement across college campuses. We will say more about the peace movement later, but by 1965, it largely consisted of pacifists, leftists, and radicals, but also included a growing number of house-wives, moderate academics, and various celebrities. By mid-1965, anti-war groups could muster crowds of 15,000 and more (Levy 1991, 126). In November 1965, a major march in Washington, D.C., which hoped to appear respectable by includ-ing major mainstream figures, nonetheless deteriorated into a circus of sorts. It was not until the Fulbright hearings of early 1966 that dignified opposition could be articulated.

Of much greater significance to Johnson than anti-war demonstrations was the defection of several high-level policy advisors and members of Congress, who had previously supported the policy of escalation. Senator Fulbright began hearings on the war in the spring of 1966 with Senate Majority Leader Mike Mansfield's tacit support (Herring 1986, 172). At the hearings, the Senate Foreign Relations Committee questioned senior officials as well as prominent outsiders to the adminis-tration to make the point that the war had no clear objective or plan of action. In August 1967, Secretary of Defense Robert McNamara gave the committee much ammunition by stating that the intensive bombing campaign in the North not only was failing to achieve its objective of halting the supply of material to the South, but likely would never succeed.

A group of senior unofficial advisors to Johnson, including such respected fig-ures as former Secretary of State Dean Acheson, advised him privately in mid-1967 and publicly thereafter that the war could not be won and that he should look for a way out. The newly appointed Secretary of Defense Clark Clifford consistently encouraged Johnson to begin troop withdrawals and a general pro-gram of "Vietnamization"—turning over the prosecution of the war to local South Vietnamese forces (Karnow 1983, 559–562).

Most of these defections were by individuals who were firmly committed to U.S. leadership in the fight against communism. It wasn't that they opposed the New Frontier; they simply felt that Vietnam, with its largely illegitimate govern-ment, ill-defined battle fronts, and ambiguous context, ought not be the test case (Gelb 1976, 111).

Overall, as documented by Holsti and Rosenau (1984), elite opinion in the United States shifted dramatically against the war. Table 12.1 shows that 38% of the elites in the country began by favoring the war and ended by opposing it; only 16% consistently supported the war effort. If one adds the "ambivalent supporters," whose enthusiasm for the war clearly waned, to the "critics," "converted critics," and "ambivalent critics," then three fourths of the elites in the country were either crit-ical or tending to be more critical of the war at its end than at its outset (Holsti & Rosenau 1984, 33). This kind of pressure from individuals who tended to play an active role in politics was overwhelming for Johnson.

The third group that became disenchanted with the war was the "general" public—that poorly organized mass of opinion that pollsters constantly seek to mea-sure and plot. Although the nature of public opinion prior to 1968 was uncertain, it seems that the U.S. public's perception changed slowly after 1965 from an initial and fairly general understanding that external aggression was being resisted by the South Vietnamese, to a largely unexpressed image of Vietnamese, both southern and

Table 12.1   Classification of Attitudes on Vietnam

When the war first became an issue:	Toward the end of U.S. involvement			
	I tended to favor a complete military victory.	I tended to feel in between these two.	Not sure	I tended to favor a complete withdrawal.
I tended to favor a complete military victory.	SUPPORTERS (n = 363, 15.9%)	AMBIVALENT SUPPORT-ERS (n = 346, 15.2%)		CONVERTED CRITICS (n = 867, 380.0%)
I tended to feel in between these two.	CONVERTED SUPPORTERS (n = 128, 15.6%)	AMBIVALENTS (n=128, 5.6%)		
Not sure		AMBIVALENT CRITICS (n = 63, 2.8%)		CRITICS (n = 378, 16.6%)
I tended to favor a complete withdrawal.				

Source: Ole Holsti and James Rosenau, *American Leadership in World Affairs* (Boston: Allen & Unwin, 1984).

northern, resisting the imposition by U.S. means of a type of U.S.-made order upon Vietnam (Kattenburg 1980, 244).

The press played some role in all of this. As early as 1963, it was reporting on the confusing nature of the war. Stanley Karnow criticized the corrupt regime of the Diem family in the mainstream magazine *Saturday Evening Post* (Levy 1991, 52), and visual reports from televised news media brought home the brutal and ugly nature of this conflict. The question of a "credibility gap" between official military projections and the reality of televised reports became the focal point of the debate on the war by 1968. Ultimately, the Tet Offensive tipped the balance ever so slightly against the war (see Figure 12.1 on public opinion).

TET SHOCK AND JOHNSON'S "RESIGNATION"

During the January 1968 lunar new year celebrations (called Tet) in Vietnam, the Vietcong and North Vietnamese Army (NVA) took advantage of a general lull in the fighting to launch an all-out offensive on every conceivable target in South Vietnam. The "Tet Offensive" brought Vietcong and NVA troops as far south as Saigon, outside the U.S. embassy complex there. Cities, airfields, and fuel depots were all targeted by the most visible and dramatic military operation of the war.

All of this was covered in painful detail and was exaggerated to melodrama by the American media (Levy 1991, 145). Although the military engagement was clearly won by U.S.-led troops, the psychological effect of the event was to shock the American public into a realization that this war was far from over. Walter Cronkite, "the most trusted person in America," said on February 27, 1968, after an

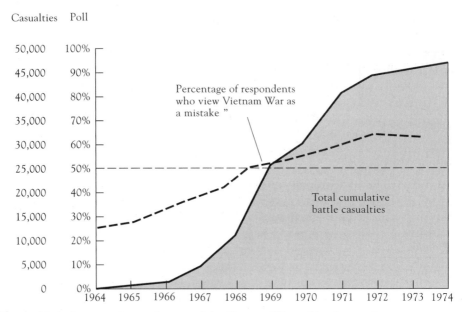

Figure 12.1 Americans' attitudes toward the Vietnam War and battle casualties
Sources: Various issues of Gallup Poll annual editions.

analysis of Tet, that it seemed "more certain than ever that the bloody experience of Vietnam is to end in a stalemate" (Karnow 1983, 547). Shortly thereafter, Martin Luther King, Jr., declared his opposition to the war. A majority of Americans for the first time agreed that U.S. involvement in Vietnam was "a mistake," although there was no consensus on how the country should extricate itself from the conflict (roughly half of those who opposed current policy felt the United States should escalate the war to finish the job, and roughly half felt troops should simply withdraw; Karnow 1983, 546). By 1968, the U.S. public seemed to agree that preserving South Vietnam was not vital to U.S. national interest (Kattenburg 1980, 244).

On the political front, the Tet Offensive coincided with the beginning of the 1968 presidential campaign. Although Johnson was assumed to be the party's nominee, he had failed to file as a candidate in time for the New Hampshire primary in March. A relatively unknown senator named Eugene McCarthy, running on an anti-war platform, inundated the state with an army of clean-cut college students and managed to secure just 300 votes less than write-in candidate Johnson in what was seen as the political upset of the decade. Certainly, all those who voted for McCarthy were not doves (three of five, in fact, believed the United States should escalate the effort in Vietnam; Kearns 1976, 354), but the event galvanized opposition to Johnson within the Democratic Party. Within a week, Senator Robert Kennedy had announced his candidacy for the presidency and declared his opposition to the war as the key issue of the race (Karnow 1983, 559). As put by Roche:

> The defection of Robert Kennedy was a decisive event in the anti-war saga. At last the anti-war forces had a senior, legitimate political figure who could not be written off as a Hanoi stooge or some species of eccentric. (Roche 1976, 131)

Lyndon Johnson had suddenly become what he feared most—the "war candidate." Furthermore, his visceral antipathy toward Robert Kennedy knew no bounds. He was haunted by Kennedy in his dreams (Kearns 1976, 264). Johnson immediately set out to draft a full-blown peace proposal, to be announced before the next round of primary elections in April. Finally, on March 31, Johnson announced a halt to the bombing of North Vietnam, a beginning of troop withdrawals, and his own decision not to run for reelection. The Tet Offensive, though failing to topple the South Vietnamese government, succeeded in felling a U.S. president.

During this stage, Johnson clearly was heavily influenced by public opinion. As stated by advisor William Bundy:

> My own impression—for what it is worth—is that the thrust of professional civilian advice would probably have been toward the most limited possible force increases, but that the change in bombing policy was greatly influenced—particularly in Secretary Clifford's actions and recommendations—by a sense of the progressively eroding domestic political support that was so dramatically evident to us all during the month of March. (Schandler 1977, 329)

The combination of elite and mass opinion (as expressed most concretely in New Hampshire) had a significant impact on the president's decision. What is less clear is the impact, if any, that the by-now large anti-war/peace movement was having.

THE PEACE MOVEMENT

The anti-war demonstrations of the 1960s and 1970s were among the most dramatic outpouring of public sentiment on a foreign policy issue in U.S. history. Roughly half a million people gathered in Washington, D.C. for the Vietnam Moratorium in October 1969. During the student protests after the Kent State/Cambodia incidents, 450 college campuses across the country were closed (Levy 1991, 155–159). In fact, the peace movement was strong among veterans of the war and even soldiers in Vietnam. Desertions rose to some 500,000 over the course of the war, and toward its end, many officers were reluctant to assign dangerous missions because of numerous incidents of "fragging" (assassination by another soldier) (Kattenburg 1980, 284). Estimates are that nearly 10 million of the 27 million draft-eligible men deserted, fled to another country, or obtained legal deferments to avoid service.

In general terms, the resistance of the youth of the country to the war effort went far to debilitate its prosecution but did not in and of itself alter government policy. In fact, Herring concludes:

> Anti-war protests did not turn the American people against the war, as some critics have argued. . . . Public opinion polls make abundantly clear, moreover, that a majority of Americans found the anti-war movement, particularly its radical and "hippie" elements, more obnoxious than the war itself. In a perverse sort of way, the protest may even have strengthened support for a war that was not in itself popular. (Herring 1986, 173)

According to Gelb:

> Passionate opposition and intellectual arguments, in the end, counted for very little and changed few minds. The argument that finally prevailed at the end of the Johnson Administration was the weight of dead Americans. (Gelb 1976, 112)

The anti-war movement was never centralized. It consisted of a wide variety of interests organized primarily at the local level at certain major universities and cities. The San Francisco Bay area, with the University of California at Berkeley as the focal point, was early on a key hub of the movement. Some of the important organizations associated with the anti-war movement were the Students for a Democratic Society (which later spawned a small terrorist group known as the Weathermen), the National Mobilization Committee to End the War, the Vietnam Moratorium Committee, and the National Peace Action Coalition. The principal elements of the movement were pacifist, radical, and anarchist in the early stages. Even the early leaders disagreed over methods and aims. It seems in retrospect that the only thing they shared was a disgust with the war. This problem would come back to haunt the more moderate elements of the movement in later years because it became apparent that anti-war activists were successful only to the extent that they focused exclusively on Vietnam (Levy 1991, 48). For example, when an effort was made to organize a massive anti-war demonstration in front of the Pentagon in October 1967, many were content to sing folk songs and sign petitions, whereas others in the group physically assaulted the military police (Levy 1991, 136).

This split became especially pronounced during the 1968 election campaign, when a large number of activists joined forces with Eugene McCarthy and Robert Kennedy to work for gradual change. In the meantime, anarchists and radicals, who called for an overthrow of the political system itself through civil disobedience and even violence, became more active (Brown 1976, 122). The contrast was vividly displayed during the tumultuous 1968 Democratic convention in Chicago.

On the floor of the convention, for those delegates whose credentials were approved—the fight, though acrimonious—was relatively formal. For the better part of a day, the convention delegates debated inclusion of an anti-war plank in the party platform, which was quickly countered by a plank supporting administration policy. When the vote was finally tallied, it demonstrated a profound split: 1,568 in favor and 1,041 against the pro-administration policy (Levy 1991, 149).

Outside the convention hall, a large number of anti-war protesters assembled to confront, before a live television audience, the aggressive Chicago police force. As put by Shils:

> Hippies, pacifists, socialists, propagandists for a North Vietnamese and Vietcong victory came together and challenged the Chicago police. The provocation was deliberate and successful. The police responded as they were desired to respond, and the television services showed the entire country what the establishment was like— heavy-handed, monstrous, brutal, and incompetent. (Shils 1976, 57)

In a famous moment, the crowd, recognizing the cameras were rolling, began chanting "The whole world is watching!" Viewers at home were generally repelled by both sides of this confrontation, and it generated little sympathy for the anti-war movement.

The Nixon administration continued the policy of rapid troop withdrawal begun by Johnson in April 1968, and the peace movement lost some momentum. The urgency of changing government policy dissipated, and the movement returned to its more radical roots as moderates lost interest. The revelations in April 1970 that the administration had escalated the war by launching large-scale bombing raids in Cambodia and Laos, however, stirred a new enthusiasm for protest. Almost no campus was pro-war by this time (Shils 1976, 56). Unrest broke out, most notably at Kent State University, where National Guardsmen, under the direction of Governor James Rhodes, fired into an unruly crowd with live bullets, killing four students. The outrage that followed the incident paralyzed the educational system of the country. For the first time, the public's sympathy was with the demonstrators (Kattenburg 1980, 278).

Did the peace movement change policy? Lyndon Johnson never appreciated the message that the activists conveyed, and he always felt unable to communicate with them. They did not seem to understand the feelings of self-sacrifice, devotion to country, and dread of communism that were so important to Johnson's generation. Likewise, Johnson feared the freedom, tolerance, and moral outrage spoken of by the students and activists.

Even leaders of the anti-war movement recognized that they achieved few of their goals regarding changing public policy (although this may be a function of unrealistic expectations).

THE NIXON ERA AND CONGRESSIONAL REASSERTION

Richard Nixon at one point claimed to have a "secret plan" to end the war in Vietnam. Just as Johnson had misled the public in the 1964 election, Nixon's claims were deceptive. The only plan was to escalate the violence while pursuing confidential contacts with the North Vietnamese (Levy 1991, 152). In fact, Nixon ended up dropping even more bombs on Indochina than Johnson had (Roche 1976, 135).

The reality that the war was not ending soon prompted an intensification of general opposition to the war. "Lou Harris observed that 'a literal race' was on between successive Nixon announcements of further troop withdrawals and a grow-ing public appetite for faster and faster removal of troops from Vietnam" (Levy 1991, 161). Twenty-six percent of respondents thought that troop withdrawals were progressing too slowly in late 1969. In May 1971, that figure was up to 45%, and in November 1971, it reached 53%. This increase in opposition paralleled the growth in cumulative casualty figures and mounting financial costs of the war. The mid-1971 publication of the Pentagon Papers, a collection of classified documents related to prosecuting the war, revealed a pattern of deception and secret escalation on the part of successive administrations (*New York Times* 1971, xi). The Cambodia revelations and the My Lai massacre of Vietnamese civilians by Lieutenant William Calley's unit all combined to create a new public consensus—this time in favor of rapid withdrawal regardless of the implications for South Vietnamese sovereignty (Kattenburg 1980, 258).

Nixon's general plan of "peace with honor" finally came to fruition shortly after the 1972 election with the Paris Agreement of January 1973. By then the public felt no remorse over the "loss" of Vietnam—only relief at the end of the conflict. When Saigon fell in mid-1975, President Gerald Ford did nothing to prevent it.

Congress had grown increasingly restive, adopting a variety of tactics to limit presidential prerogative. After the Fulbright hearings in 1966–1967, several other committees followed suit—taking testimony from witnesses, traveling to Vietnam on fact-finding missions, and ultimately issuing anti-war resolutions aimed at cur-tailing the length and scope of the war. The Tonkin Gulf Resolution was repealed in late 1971, although an effort to prevent further military operations pending a formal declaration of war was defeated. After a string of resolutions calling for withdrawal by a given deadline, Congress passed a bill banning all further military operations in Vietnam in 1973 (after the troops had already been withdrawn). In an effort to pre-vent future unilateral executive military interventions, Congress passed the War Powers Act over President Nixon's veto. The net result of congressional reassertion was a collapse of much of the power that had accreted to the White House over the period after World War II. The question of presidential war powers is still one of the most hotly debated constitutional issues of our time (note the Senate debate on the Gulf War in 1991).

CONCLUSION: DID DEMOCRACY BRING PEACE?

The experience of Vietnam can teach several lessons to those wondering about the role of democratic institutions and public opinion in war time. One conclusion that can be drawn is that democratic regimes are perfectly capable of entering into war—even wars that are widely considered ill-advised and even unjust. Democratic institu-tions in the United States are not strong enough to rein in a determined Executive, nor can they always do so where the public is favorably disposed for war.

First, the public and legislatures are a disadvantage when it comes to informa-tion and analysis. The Executive can claim that a crisis exists without actually proving it, and the public and their elected representatives are loath to disagree.

Doing so runs the obvious risk of being wrong and winding up supporting the nation's enemies. Especially where the enemy is a regime that is autocratic and corrupt and which cannot be trusted to provide good information, the safer strategy is to simply go along with the President's assessment. Of course, if the enemy were another democratic regime, complete with uncensored newspapers and a parliament that debates publicly, it would naturally be harder for a President to misrepresent its intentions. In that sense, the democratic peace theory is probably on to something.

On the other hand, as more and more information became available to prove that the military strategy being used was not working, the public and politicians became increasingly frustrated and increasingly bold in expressing their disapproval. Ultimately this opposition became impossible for the President to ignore, and he began a policy of phased withdrawal. So even where the enemy is not another democracy, the democratic peace theory correctly anticipated a tendency for democracies to have a harder time fighting any type of war.

Did the Vietnam experience shape subsequent wars? The "Vietnam Syndrome" is the term used to describe the reluctance of American presidents and the American people to commit troops to foreign theatres. Note for example that the U.S. took no action when Communists took over in Cambodia and slaughtered hundreds of thousands of people. Ultimately it was Vietnam that intervened militarily to overthrow the genocidal regime (Power 2002). The United States was also quick to withdraw troops from Beirut, Lebanon, when they were attacked by a car bomber. It was not until the first Persian Gulf War (Chapter 8) that the United States committed tens of thousands of ground troops to battle. And the strategy used in this case—decapitation—was specifically designed to be quick and relatively low-cost. There was no interest in a drawn-out war of attrition.

Although there are naturally many differences between Iraq and Vietnam, talk of the Vietnam Syndrome has intensified, and many wonder whether the United States will be able to extricate its troops from what appears to be an increasingly difficult situation (Greenberg 2004). Two thirds of Americans opposed President Bush's handling of the war and three fourths considered the costs to have outweighed the benefits as of May 2006 (Polling Report 2006). As of this writing (October 2008), American battle deaths are close to 4,500. It seems clear that the American people are demonstrating once again that they are not interested in long-term wars where the outcomes and purposes are uncertain (Solomon 2005). The implications for policymakers are increasingly obvious.

The democratic peace theory is generally confirmed by the evidence of the Vietnam War, although not all of its elements were tested. You should ask whether a better test is the recent confrontation between Russia and Georgia (see Chapter 6), where two government that were both democratically elected engaged in full-scale, if short-lived, armed violence between regular troops.

QUESTIONS TO CONSIDER

1. What role did democratic institutions play in starting and ending the war in Vietnam?

2. To what extent did Nixon and Johnson misjudge fundamental American attitudes? What are the apparent limits to patriotism in the United States?

3. What are the lessons of Vietnam in terms of the role of public opinion? How do they relate to the Bush administration's handling of the war in Iraq?

KEY FIGURES
VIETNAM HOMEFRONT

John F. Kennedy   U.S. President, 1961–1963. He supported expanding U.S. military assistance to South Vietnam, although he became disillusioned with its government.

Lyndon Johnson   Vice President, 1961–1963, and U.S. President, 1963–1969. He presided over the dramatic increase in U.S. military involvement in Vietnam, based in part on the Tonkin Gulf Resolution he persuaded Congress to pass. He eventually chose not to run for reelection in 1968 because of public opposition to his Vietnam policies.

Richard Nixon   U.S. President, 1969–1974. He completed the American withdrawal from Vietnam and negotiated, with Henry Kissinger, the Paris Peace Accords. He also directed a series of massive bombing campaigns in Vietnam and Cambodia.

Henry Kissinger   Senior advisor to Presidents Nixon and Gerald Ford as National Security Advisor and Secretary of State. He promoted a pragmatic approach to Vietnam that included both escalation and withdrawal.

Robert McNamara   U.S. Secretary of Defense, 1963–1968. An early supporter of military intervention in Vietnam, he later testified before Senator Fulbright's committee that the effort was failing.

Dean Acheson   U.S. Secretary of State, 1949–1953. He offered objections to the war beginning in 1967.

Clark Clifford   U.S. Secretary of Defense, 1968–1969. He encouraged President Johnson to withdraw troops from Vietnam.

Ho Chi Minh   Leader of the Vietnamese Communist Party, he governed North Vietnam from 1949 to 1969.

Nguyen Van Thieu   South Vietnamese President, 1967–1975.

Ngo Dinh Diem   Leader of South Vietnam from 1955 until his overthrow in 1963.

William Fulbright   U.S. Senator from Arkansas. He helped pass President Johnson's Tonkin Gulf Resolution in 1964 and later conducted hearings critical of Johnson's conduct of the Vietnam War.

Barry Goldwater   Unsuccessful U.S. presidential candidate in 1964. He believed Lyndon Johnson was not going far enough to support South Vietnam.

Hubert Humphrey   U.S. Vice President, 1963–1969. He was an unsuccessful presidential candidate in 1968.

William Westmoreland   Commander of U.S. forces in South Vietnam, 1964–1968.

Eugene McCarthy   Unsuccessful U.S. presidential candidate in 1968. He opposed U.S. involvement in Vietnam.

Robert F. Kennedy   Former U.S. Attorney General and candidate for president in 1968. He opposed the war and was assassinated in 1968.

George McGovern   Unsuccessful U.S. presidential candidate in 1972. He opposed U.S. involvement in Vietnam.

Daniel Ellsberg   Defense Department official who resigned and then released the Pentagon Papers to the *New York Times* in 1971.

Abby Hoffman   Anti-war activist.

Tom Hayden   Anti-war activist.

Walter Cronkite   Eminent news anchor. He came out against the war in Vietnam in 1968.

Martin Luther King, Jr.   Eminent civil rights leader. He came out against the war in Vietnam in 1968.

CHRONOLOGY
VIETNAM HOMEFRONT

1955
January   U.S. military advisors begin training the South Vietnamese army.

July   The Soviet Union and China begin providing aid to North Vietnam.

October   Ngo Dinh Diem becomes president.

1956
Diem begins a crackdown on Communist sympathizers (Vietminh).

1957
May   Diem and Eisenhower meet in Washington, D.C.

October   The North Vietnamese government helps organize a guerrilla army (Vietcong) in South Vietnam.

1959
May   The Ho Chi Minh Trail, running through Laos and Cambodia from Hanoi into South Vietnam, becomes an operational supply route for material for the Vietcong.

July   The first Americans die in Vietnam fighting.

(continued)

(*continued*)

1960

April   Universal military conscription is imposed in North Vietnam.

November   An unsuccessful coup attempt against Diem occurs amid growing protests over the regime in South Vietnam.

December   Civil war erupts in Laos, with Soviets supplying the rebels.

1961

May   The Geneva Conference on Laos leads to the creation of a neutral government.

Lyndon Johnson returns from a visit to South Vietnam with a recommendation for more aid to the Diem regime.

October   Maxwell Taylor and Walt Rostow recommend covert military aid after a visit with Diem, but Kennedy opts for more financial support.

1962

February   The United States organizes formal military support in South Vietnam and increases the number of advisors there from 700 to 12,000.

1963

January   The Vietcong score victories in battles with the South Vietnamese army; army unrest increases in the South.

May–June   Some Buddhist demonstrators are shot and others commit suicide by self-immolation.

August   The United States urges Diem to change his repressive policies and warns of a coup attempt.

November   General Duong Van Minh overthrows Diem in coup; Diem is assassinated.

December   U.S. advisors in South Vietnam number 15,000; U.S. aid in 1963 equals $500 million.

1964

January   General Nguyen Khanh seizes power in Saigon.

June   Robert McNamara and Dean Rusk encourage more support; the U.S. military plans a bombing raid against North Vietnam.

August   The Tonkin Gulf incident, involving purported North Vietnamese attacks on U.S. intelligence ships off the coast, leads to passage of the Tonkin Gulf Resolution, giving Lyndon Johnson significant powers to respond.

Autumn   Johnson rejects retaliatory bombing after Viet Cong raids against U.S. installations.

1965

February   Operations Flaming Dart and Rolling Thunder begin systematic bombing of North Vietnam.

General Khanh is removed by Phan Huy Quat in Saigon.

March   The first Marines land at Da Nang airfield.

June   Nguyan Cao Ky becomes the new prime minister, with Nguyan Van Thieu as South Vietnam's president.

July   In light of the defeats for the South Vietnamese army, Johnson authorizes the deployment of forty-four more battalions.

December   Johnson suspends the bombing campaign over Christmas to induce the North Vietnamese to negotiate.

U.S. troop strength reaches 200,000.

1966
January   Bombing of North Vietnam resumes.

Spring   The battles of Hue and Da Nang give the South Vietnam–U.S. forces major victories.

December   U.S. troop strength reaches 400,000.

1967
Spring   Johnson secretly corresponds with North Vietnamese officials on peace options; the North Vietnamese demand a halt to bombing prior to beginning negotiations.

August   McNamara testifies before Congress that the bombing campaign is ineffective.

October   A massive anti-war protest takes place at the Pentagon.

November   General William Westmoreland exudes confidence during a trip in the United States.

December   U.S. troop strength reaches 500,000.

1968
January   The Tet Offensive—involving Vietcong and North Vietnamese attacks on South Vietnamese cities—is repulsed, but demonstrates the strength of the North Vietnamese forces to a surprised American audience.

March   Johnson decides to halt the war escalation and announces he will not run for re-election.

April   Paris peace talks begin between the United States and North Vietnam.

July   The Democratic convention in Chicago is the scene of anti-war demonstrations.

October   Johnson halts the bombing.

December   Troop strength peaks at roughly 540,000.

1969
January   South Vietnam is included in the Paris peace talks.

March   President Richard Nixon begins secret bombing of Cambodia.

June   Thieu and Nixon announce the withdrawal of 25,000 U.S. troops under the rubric of "Vietnamization."

October   A massive anti-war demonstration takes place in Washington.

(*continued*)

(*continued*)

November   The My Lai massacre is revealed.

December   U.S. troop strength is down to 480,000.

1970
April   Nixon reveals the covert attacks against Cambodia.

May   Four students are killed in an anti-war protest at Kent State University.

Autumn   Nixon explores the possibility of simultaneous withdrawal with the North Vietnamese.

December   Troop strength is down to 280,000.

1971
March   Lieutenant William Calley is convicted of murder in connection with the My Lai massacre.

June   The Pentagon Papers are published, leading to an investigation of Daniel Ellsberg.

December   Troop strength is down to 140,000.

1972
January   Nixon reveals the secret talks between Kissinger and North Vietnamese officials (dating back to February 1970).

March   The North Vietnamese army attacks across the frontier.

April   Nixon approves the bombing of Hanoi.

August   Paris negotiations continue in spite of South Vietnamese resistance.

October   The United States and North Vietnam reach an accord; Thieu opposes it.

December   After the collapse of talks, the bombing raids resume.

1973
January   The peace accords are signed in Paris.

March   The last U.S. troops leave South Vietnam.

August   Congress forces the Nixon administration to halt the bombing of Cambodia.

November   Over Nixon's veto, Congress passes the War Powers Act.

1974
January   War is initiated again.

1975
January   The final North Vietnamese push begins.

March   Hue falls.

April   Saigon falls; South Vietnam ceases to exist.

*Karnow (1983, 670–686) provides the best chronology available.

REFERENCES

Ball, George. *The Past Has Another Pattern* (New York: W. W. Norton, 1982).

Brown, Sam. "The Defeat of the Antiwar Movement" in Anthony Lake, ed., *The Vietnam Legacy: The War, American Society and the Future of American Foreign Policy* (New York: New York University Press, 1976): 120–127.

Doyle, Michael. "Kant, Liberal Legacies, and Foreign Affairs, Part I," *Philosophy and Public Affairs* 12 #3 (Summer 1983): 205–235.

Friedman, Thomas. *The World is Flat: A Brief History of the Twenty-First Century* (New York: Picador, 2007).

Gelb, Leslie. "Dissenting on Consensus" in Anthony Lake, ed., *The Vietnam Legacy: The War, American Society and the Future of American Foreign Policy* (New York: New York University Press, 1976): 102–119.

Greenberg, David. "Why Vietnam Haunts the Debate Over Iraq." Available at: hnn.us/articles/4778.html.

Herring, George C. *America's Longest War: The United States and Vietnam, 1950–1975*, 2nd ed. (Philadelphia: Temple University Press, 1986).

Holsti, Ole R., and James N. Rosenau. *American Leadership in World Affairs: Vietnam and the Breakdown of Consensus* (Boston: Allen & Unwin, 1984).

Karnow, Stanley. *Vietnam: A History* (New York: Viking Press, 1983).

Kattenburg, Paul. *The Vietnam Trauma in American Foreign Policy, 1945–1975* (New Brunswick, NJ: Transaction Books, 1980).

Kearns, Doris. *Lyndon Johnson and the American Dream* (New York: New American Library, 1976).

Lake, Anthony, ed. *The Vietnam Legacy: The War, American Society and the Future of American Foreign Policy* (New York: New York University Press, 1976).

Levy, David W. *The Debate Over Vietnam* (Baltimore: Johns Hopkins University Press, 1991).

Mueller, John. *War, Presidents, and Public Opinion* (New York: John Wiley & Sons, 1973).

New York Times. The Pentagon Papers (New York: New York Times Co., 1971).

Polling Report. "ABC News/Washington Post Poll. May 11–15, 2006." Available at: www.pollingreport.com.

Power, Samantha. *A Problem from Hell: America and the Age of Genocide*. (New York: Basic Books, 2002).

Roche, John P. "The Impact of Dissent on Foreign Policy: Past and Future" in Anthony Lake, ed., *The Vietnam Legacy: The War, American Society and the Future of American Foreign Policy* (New York: New York University Press, 1976): 128–138.

Schandler, Herbert Y. *The Unmaking of a President: Lyndon Johnson and Vietnam* (Princeton, NJ: Princeton University Press, 1977).

Shils, Edward. "American Society and the War in Indochina" in Anthony Lake, ed., *The Vietnam Legacy* (New York: New York University Press, 1976): 40–65.

Solomon, Norman. "Beyond the Vietnam Syndrome." Anti-War.Com. Available at: http://www.antiwar.com/solomon/?articleid=7252, accessed on May 19, 2006.

13

■ ■ ■

Human Security: The HIV/AIDS Pandemics

INTRODUCTION

"Security" has traditionally referred to a state's capacity to protect its own citizens and territory from attacks or other threats. We also understand that "economic security" includes protection from cheap foreign imports, excessive foreign borrowing, foreign ownership of key domestic resources, and so forth. Neither approach, however, pays enough attention to individuals, according to advocates of the "human security" approach. As explained on the Human Security Gateway:

> "Human security focuses on the protection of individuals, rather than defending the physical and political integrity of states from external military threats—the traditional goal of national security. Ideally, national security and human security should be mutually reinforcing, but in the last 100 years far more people have died as a direct or indirect consequence of the actions of their own governments or rebel forces in civil wars than have been killed by invading foreign armies. Acting in the name of national security, governments can pose profound threats to human security." (Human Security Gateway 2008)

This approach is particularly prized by human rights activists and Western governments, all of whom worry that, in the quest for more conventional forms of security, governments—particularly those in the developing world—run roughshod over the needs of individuals. They deplore, for example, the abuse of individuals in the Democratic Republic of Congo over the past five years where civil war has been exacerbated by governments in the region that support and harbor combatants, some of whom have been accused of genocide. Ordinary people found themselves without access to basic services such as clean water and basic health care, as well as being exposed to cholera, dysentery, malaria, and AIDS. As many as 1,000 people have died each day of various causes directly related to the conflict since its inception (International Crisis Group 2008).

The United Nations created a special Commission on Human Security to clarify the international communities key concerns and responsibilities. Specifically, the Commission concluded that the top ten priorities ought to be:

1. Protecting people in violent conflict
2. Protecting people from the proliferation of arms
3. Supporting the security of people on the move
4. Establishing human security transition funds for post-conflict situations
5. Encouraging fair trade and markets to benefit the extreme poor
6. Working to provide minimum living standards everywhere
7. According higher priority to ensuring universal access to basic health care
8. Developing an efficient and equitable global system for patent rights
9. Empowering all people with universal basic education
10. Clarifying the need for a global human identity while respecting the freedom of individuals to have diverse identities and affiliations. (Commission on Human Security 2003)

Item number seven is of special interest to us in this chapter. As we see in the Congo, diseases spread more rapidly where institutions have degraded. This is particularly true where pre-conflict conditions were already poor. Finally, where the disease itself is resistant to normal treatments, we might witness a "pandemic."

HISTORY OF RECENT PANDEMICS

Epidemics are nothing new—in fact, they are among the oldest things in human existence. They have contributed to the decimation of whole civilizations in the past. The bubonic plague (also known as the Black Death) is thought to have killed roughly half of Europe's population in the mid-1300s. Diseases brought by Columbus and other explorers to the New World wiped out as many as ninety million people, eradicating entire races (more than 90% of the population of Hispaniola—modern Haiti and Dominican Republic—were killed by smallpox) (Pratt 1999, 178). The influenza epidemic of 1918 killed roughly twenty million—far more than died in World War I (Gostin 2004, 565). Smallpox killed roughly 50 million in the 1700s and has been blamed for 300 million in the 20th century. Total deaths from HIV/AIDS have been estimated at twenty million worldwide (with 70% of these in Africa).

Thanks to breakthroughs in scientific research by Pasteur, Jenner, and others, vaccines and therapies have been identified for many of the world's worst diseases. In addition, medical training, sanitation, communication, and transportation have dramatically improved in almost every corner of the planet, which has made this knowledge more accessible. In theory at least, one might think that pandemics should be controllable. But other factors seem to undermine many of these advances.

In terms of immediate causes, illnesses are spreading due to urbanization and urban sprawl, which puts people in closer contact with diseased animals and with each other. Unsafe practices on the part of individuals—especially with respect to sanitation, food preparation, sexual practices, and seeking medical attention and vaccines—have allowed diseases to spread much faster than otherwise. But these immediate causes are explained by broader trends that include poverty and ignorance, which make expensive treatments inaccessible, undermine education efforts with respect to safe practices, and limit what services states can provide. Poor nutrition undermines the immune system, making all more vulnerable to infection. Civil unrest and warfare invariably impede access to health care and undermine safe practices. Social discrimination may cause parts of the population to be exploited and thus become vulnerable to the spread of disease—particularly in the case of rape or prostitution. Finally, the entire global system may be at fault at some level. The capitalist market pushes firms to pursue more lucrative drugs (such as cold remedies or cures for indigestion) over vaccines for Third World diseases (such as malaria). Powerful states may see no reason to spend tax monies on tropical diseases that do not affect them directly and prefer instead to invest in national defense (Spectar 2001). And technical innovations and lowered trade barriers make it far easier for people and products to move rapidly over international boundaries, making it nearly impossible for anyone to be entirely safe.

Consider the recent SARS (Severe Acute Respiratory Syndrome) epidemic. It was first diagnosed in Guangdong province in southeastern China in November 2002. By May 2003, the number of cases increased from a handful to more than 7,000 and climbing. Within the first six months of the disease's appearance, more than 500 people had died in ten countries; cases of infection appeared in more than thirty countries, from Hong Kong to Sweden, and from Kuwait to Brazil (WHO 2003). The problem caused a political crisis in China, where government officials who concealed the extent of the outbreak were fired and public confidence in the regime fell.

Given the urgency of these epidemics, governments have become increasingly involved in finding solutions—but in so doing, they must interact with scientists, activists, pharmaceutical firms, and health care workers on a daily basis. Consider the eradication of smallpox—one of the singular achievements of the 20th century. As deaths from smallpox climbed to the hundreds of millions, governments were eager to devote state funds to the problem. But politicians could do nothing more than encourage scientists and take their advice. Ultimately, governments applied the insights of Edward Jenner, whose study of cowpox had led to a rudimentary vaccine in the 1790s, to buy up vast quantities of the improved vaccines. They engaged the help of doctors and nurses, school principals and teachers, and even neighborhood leaders to disseminate the vaccine as widely as possible. By the 1930s, smallpox had been contained in most industrialized countries. In 1948, the World Health Organization was created by governments and staffed by doctors and researchers. Smallpox was naturally one of its greatest concerns. But it was as yet impossible to produce the vaccine in enough areas to bring the perishable product to the people. But in the 1950s, as a result of research in private firms, as well as universities and government-funded clinics, the vaccine was freeze-dried and could then be transported around the world.

With this new product in hand, WHO staff members, supported by physician associations and major governments, were able to overcome the skepticism of several states (including the Soviet Union) and reached agreement in 1967 to eradicate smallpox by 1977. Governments provided funding, access, and encouragement as thousands of experts fanned out across the world. Reaching urban areas and coastal regions was easy. The drama of smallpox eradication came in the efforts to travel into the hinterland of poor countries, where "roads had to be cut through jungle by hand, rivers bridged, and floodwaters crossed by boat" (Pratt 1999, 184). Stories are told of Western and local physicians performing outreach, wading through snake-infested waters to get the vaccines to remote villages, and thousands of local health officers being trained to use the simple, two-pronged needle that injected just the right amount of vaccine—sometimes more than 1,000 times a day. By 1977, the last case of natural smallpox was identified (and cured) in Somalia.

In the remainder of the chapter, we will review the international effort to combat HIV/AIDS, with special emphasis on the role of Non-Governmental Organizations (NGOs) and nonstate actors. We will consider general patterns in the spread of HIV/AIDS since the 1980s and the contrasting responses of medical experts and government policymakers. In particular, we will consider the priorities and philosophical orientations of each and ask whether these can be reconciled.

HIV/AIDS

The Human Immunodeficiency Virus, which results in the Acquired Immunodeficiency Syndrome, has infected roughly thirty-five million people and will soon reach a death toll of twenty million, making it the most deadly disease in the history of humanity, surpassing both the 1918 influenza and the bubonic plague of the Middle Ages (Spectar 2001, 254). AIDS patients are dying at the rate of roughly three million per year. Roughly three fourths of those infected are in Sub-Saharan Africa (see Figure 13.1). Only about one of six affected reside in developed countries, where infection rates peaked in the mid-1990s and survival rates have increased dramatically, thanks in large part to costly anti-retroviral drugs. At this point, it is clear that HIV/AIDS is primarily a developing phenomenon, especially since India and China are likely to be its next major targets.

Manifestations of the disease were first noted in America in the late 1970s, and in Africa in 1983, although the virus has been discovered in frozen blood samples dating back to the late-1950s (Okigbo et al. 2002, 619). The virus has mutated and now manifests itself in about at least ten different strains as well as several recombinations, each of which is responsive and resistant to different treatments. The disease is transmitted primarily by certain body fluids—mostly blood and semen—and early educational programs in the West focused on safe sexual practices—particularly in the male homosexual community—and the use of clean needles by intravenous drug users. Government agencies and hospitals also monitored and cleaned up the blood

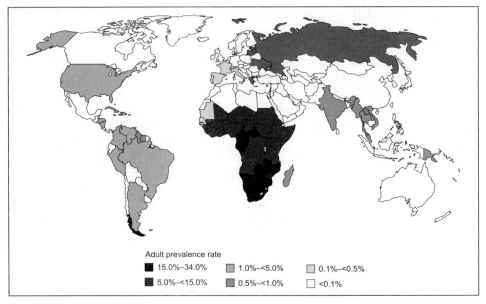

Figure 13.1 A Global View of HIV Infection—2005
Source: UNAIDS 2006, 14.

supply. Sex workers were also monitored more closely and given treatment to prevent the spread by heterosexual sex.

In Africa, however, HIV/AIDS has spread primarily via heterosexual intercourse and transmission to children during pregnancy by infected mothers. This stems from a combination of poverty, illiteracy, unsafe sexual practices, and social mores (Okigbo 2002). The infection rate in adults in some Sub-Saharan African cities is well over half, although there are indications that in some countries the infection rate may have peaked in the mid-2000s—although the total number of infections continues to rise, albeit at a somewhat slower pace (UNAIDS 2006, 11). Pregnant women still have rising rates of infection in southern Africa, rising from 20% to 30% in South Africa from 1997 to 2004, for example. Meanwhile in the rest of Africa, infection rates among pregnant women are declining slightly (from 14% in 1997 to 7% in 2004 in Kenya, for example).

As a result of the high number of young adults contracting AIDS, Africa has experienced dramatic social and economic dislocations. Agricultural output fell by 50% from 1995 to 2000 in Zimbabwe as a result of the deaths of thousands of farmers (Spectar 2001, 261). Industrial output in other countries in the region has fallen as a result of "absenteeism, lower productivity, higher overtime costs, higher levels of health/treatment spending, more outlays for death benefits, additional staff recruitment and training expenses" (Spectar 2001, 261). It is estimated that economic growth on the continent will decline by more than 1% each year for two decades as a result of HIV/AIDS. Furthermore, the large number of children left orphaned is placing significant burdens on the survivors, some of whom have been forced to bring up to ten children into their homes.

Of particular concern has been the relatively recent emergence of HIV/AIDS in Asia where, although the rate of infection is still quite low, given the enormous population size and density, it is feared that the absolute number of infections could eclipse other regions. Here the virus appears to be spreading primarily in the sex worker and IV drug–using populations with the result that urban areas have been hit the hardest—although there are early indications that it is spreading to rural areas as well (UNAIDS 2006, 25). In New Delhi, for example, the infection rate among drug users rose from 5% in 2000 to 14% in 2003. The infection rate among all adults in central Bangladesh rose from 1.5% in 1999 to 5% in 2004 and in Karachi, Pakistan, it rose from almost nothing in 2003 to 22% in 2004.

Such is the state of affairs with respect to the HIV/AIDS pandemic. The picture is still dismal, although there is evidence that new infections may soon begin to decline. Of course, even if there were no new infections beginning today, the burden of treating (and burying) those already infected will be crippling for many countries.

THE INTERNATIONAL RESPONSE TO HIV/AIDS

International actors can be classified in many ways, and a relatively simple typology distinguishes three types. Government agencies are distinguished by their accountability to political leaders. They are typically fully-funded from tax revenues and are staffed by employees whose careers will be entirely within government. There are also international organizations that are similarly structured, with professional staffs that are paid by governments via the institution. The next category is NGOs, described earlier. Their key characteristic is their private, non-profit status. They may spend their time on scholarly research, advocacy, public outreach, or public service provision—or some combination of these. Universities are a sub-set of NGOs. Finally, there are private agencies that operate for profit—corporations.

But the fact is that these different categories of institutions are often more similar than not. They almost all have divisions or bureaus where experts can carry out studies in a quasi-academic environment. Most corporations have extensive research and development units, some of which are essentially left alone to think (IBM is famous for having created such an office). Governments have set up similar think-tanks within larger departments. Governments have also funded research institutes that are essentially left alone. And finally, private researchers and independent NGOs routinely receive government funding. Thus one particular individual scientist might find herself working at a private university on a government grant that produces a discovery that a private corporation brings to market. It is difficult in such situations to say exactly where government ends and the private sphere begins.

The international community has mounted a relatively aggressive campaign to halt HIV/AIDS, combining scientific research supported by government funding with aid-sponsored outreach and educational programs. In each facet, non-state actors have played the key role. After all, were it not for physicians and researchers, the AIDS epidemic would merely be a mysterious string of deaths and illness without a name or a source. Likewise, governments are not equipped to cure diseases or provide therapies on their own, but must rely on experts.

To begin, the diagnosis of the virus was carried out by private researchers, some of whom had no direct connection to governments or international organizations. David Serwadda, a pulmonary specialist working in Uganda, was the first to identify HIV in Africa in 1983 (Okigbo et al. 2002, 619). Governments and international organizations still depend on ordinary physicians and technicians to identify cases. In Africa, one of the most important gateways is the nurses at the pre-natal clinics where pregnant mothers are screened, often for the first time. The search for a cure is primarily a private endeavor, carried out by researchers at universities, laboratories such as the Pasteur Institute in France and the Centers for Disease Control and Prevention in Atlanta, and at pharmaceutical firms such as GlaxoSmithKline, where the anti-retroviral "cocktail" is being mass-produced.

The story of AZT illustrates the blending of public, private, and non-profit agencies. AZT, formally known as zidovudine, was first developed by Jerome Horwitz in 1964 under a grant from the American National Institutes of Health. Although it did not work well on cancer as originally hoped, the drug was later refined in the mid-1980s by Samuel Broder, Hiroaki Mitsuya, and Robert Yarchoan (all of the National Cancer Institute), who worked with Janet Rideout and others at Burroghs Wellcome Company—now known as GlaxoSmithKline. They obtained a patent in 1986 and the Food and Drug Administration approved it for general use in 1987 (Wikipedia 2006). Thus we can see the involvement of all three players.

At the international level, the organization that has taken "point" is the World Health Organization (WHO). This international organization is a hybrid, in that, since its founding, it has brought together both diplomats and physicians to deal with international health. Based in Geneva, Switzerland, the organization has a universal membership of states and a professional staff of physicians and medical researchers. The staff carries out policy discussions and makes recommendations to the representatives of states, who then approve or reject them and set the funding levels. The staff also interfaces with the local medical professionals and relevant government health agencies through face-to-face contact and expert consultations.

WHO also links with numerous NGOs through an established consultation system. A total of 182 NGOs have formal relations with the WHO as of January 2006. It is the focal point for reporting by hundreds of institutes and individual researchers in cases of epidemic outbreaks and carries out ongoing consultations to improve reporting and cataloging the data (WHO 2000). Some of these networks are disease-specific, such as FluNet, which links laboratories in eighty-nine countries. Others are supported by WHO but run by governments, such as the Global Public Health Intelligence Network in Canada. At any rate, WHO works to communicate new information to local practitioners through its web site and weekly newsletters, as well as through large-scale conferences (a conference in 2000 brought together representatives of more than fifty private research institutes, as well as numerous government agencies and state-run laboratories; WHO 2000). The WHO also uses its financial resources to purchase HIV-related medications and therapies (WHO 2006).

WHO was instrumental in creating UNAIDS—a collaborative endeavor created in 1994 by various UN organizations to pool resources and talent and coordinate anti-AIDS programs. WHO is the lead agency in the collaborative, which includes the High Commissioner for Refugees, UNICEF, the World Food Program, the United Nations Development Program, the UN Population Fund, the UN Office on Drugs and Crime, the International Labor Organization, UNESCO, and the World Bank. The HIV/AIDS phenomenon has so many dimensions, it seemed reasonable to attack the problem from different angles. UNICEF naturally focuses on women and children—especially pregnant women, whom it tries to educate and support. The World Bank, as a relatively well-endowed development bank, has been a principal funding agency, having provided roughly two billion dollars to other international and local agencies.

ALTERNATIVE STRATEGIES

HIV/AIDS has always been controversial. When it was first identified in the United States, it was found primarily in the male homosexual community and among intravenous drug users. This brought considerable ambivalence in the public at large, as many saw the illness as divorced from their own lives. Social conservatives even went so far as to dismiss the disease as self-inflicted (or perhaps divinely inflicted) and therefore unworthy of investigation with tax-payer dollars. Even today, many governments, including the Bush administration, emphasize the moral dimension of HIV/AIDS. The United States insisted that a major UN statement in 2001 list abstinence and fidelity in marriage be first in the list of preventive measures that should be taken (DeYoung 2001, 72).

We will consider the views of several groups in turn, beginning with the U.S. government to provide a reference point. We will then turn to the human rights approach, followed by the North–South approach. The challenges faced by NGOs that advocate the latter two approaches helps illustrate the limits to NGO influence.

U.S. Government

The Centers for Disease Control (CDC) has been the lead agency on the issue, which has allowed the political elites to skirt the question of blame. By focusing on the technical dimensions of the illness, the scientists at the CDC have been able to present their findings dispassionately with minimal resistance. On the other hand, when it has come to taking positions in international fora, the United States has been more ambivalent. The Clinton administration addressed the AIDS crisis in part as a trade issue, since many governments and NGOs were demanding exemptions to the patent for AZT. AZT could be manufactured for well under a dollar a dose, but was sold for over six dollars due to GlaxoSmithKline's exclusive rights to the drug. Clinton was concerned about the implications of abandoning intellectual property rights for American firms and therefore supported the firm's position (Fidler 2004, 120).

The Bush administration, for its part, also supported the patent issue. In addition, it was more unwilling to spend much on international AIDS programs. It provided only one billion dollars to the Global Fund for AIDS in 2001 and 2002 combined—far below the level that could be expected of the country that produces nearly one quarter of world economic output. As put by Paul Zeitz, director of the Global AIDS Alliance, "It's outrageous that the president gives such short shrift to the Global Fund. It is the best hope yet for the fight against AIDS; yet the president has let the Fund down" (Lobe 2003). But in early 2003, the Bush administration announced plans to donate $15 billion for UNAIDS over five years (2004–2008) in concentrated effort on the Sub-Saharan African and Caribbean nations most affected.

Part of the motivation for this increase came not from humanitarian concerns but rather from fears that political instability could result from the effects of the disease. The 2002 National Security Strategy document argued that AIDS was threatening the administration's goals of fighting terrorism in Africa. In particular, AIDS threatens the administration's goals of promoting stable democracy and liberal economic and political values generally (Fidler 2004, 126). As explained by Secretary of State Colin Powell: "AIDS is not just a humanitarian or health issue. It not only kills. It also destroys communities. It decimates countries. It destabilizes regions. It can consume continents. No war on the face of the earth is more destructive than the AIDS pandemic" (Spectar 2003, 538).

Both governments were concerned about the security implications of AIDS, and in 2000, the United States helped orchestrate a special session of the UN Security Council to focus on AIDS as a security issue, for example. This was the first time the Security Council addressed a public health issue, since its mandate is to deal with violent crises and threats to security. In the resulting resolution, member-states acknowledged several particularly dangerous aspects of AIDS:

> The Security Council,
>
> *Deeply concerned* by the extent of the HIV/AIDS pandemic worldwide, and by the severity of the crisis in Africa in particular, . . .
>
> *Recognizing* that the spread of HIV/AIDS can have a uniquely devastating impact on all sectors and levels of society, . . .
>
> *Further recognizing* that the HIV/AIDS pandemic is also exacerbated by conditions of violence and instability, which increase the risk of exposure to the disease through large movements of people, widespread uncertainty over conditions, and reduced access to medical care,
>
> *Stressing* that the HIV/AIDS pandemic, if unchecked, may pose a risk to stability and security, . . .
>
> *Expresses* keen interest in additional discussion among relevant United Nations bodies, Member States, industry and other relevant organizations to make progress, *inter alia*, on the question of access to treatment and care, and on prevention. (UNSC Resolution 1308 2000)

This statement was further expanded in 2001 at an international UN conference held in New York to discuss HIV/AIDS. The meetings resembled the UNCED gathering in that nearly all states sent very senior representatives, including heads of state and government, and were joined by thousands of NGO representatives and international organization spokesmen. The result, much like at UNCED, was a broad statement of principles (the Declaration of Commitment on HIV/AIDS) and a more specific and measurable Action Guide. Although none of these are treaties and have no legally binding effect (meaning that it is not likely any country will be sanctioned for failing to achieve the goals), the high visibility and priority given to the topic seemed to have finally lifted HIV/AIDS to the forefront of the many international issues states are actively addressing. Among other things, states committed to increase funding to developing countries struggling with AIDS to between seven and ten billion per year by 2005, starting with a major fundraising campaign in 2002. The conferees also agreed to support the work of the UNAIDS joint task force, both financially and politically.

Human Rights Advocates

Moral issues continue to influence national positions. The Vatican, for example, repeatedly opposes references to condom use in international statements, and Islamic countries block specific references to male homosexual intercourse and sex with prostitutes because these are contrary to Sharia law (DeYoung 2001, 73). This has prompted many human rights activists to advocate a different emphasis: the right to health. As explained by Fidler,

> Although human rights treaties have long recognized infectious disease control as a legitimate reason for restricting enjoyment of civil and political rights, the relationship between public health and these rights was not prominent until after WHO's creation. Various responses to HIV/AIDS, including quarantine and isolation, and widespread stigma and discrimination against people living with HIV or AIDS, brought renewed public health attention to civil and political rights. . . . Human rights advocates argued that access to [anti-retroviral] treatments formed part of the right to health under international law. The global HIV/AIDS campaign embodied the inter-dependence and indivisibility of civil and political, economic, and cultural rights claimed in international human rights discourse. (Fidler 2004, 113)

Amnesty International has issued the following demands to government to achieve a human rights–centered approach:

1. Fulfill the international commitment to the right to health.
2. Remove funding conditions that inhibit the prevention of HIV/AIDS.
3. Ensure equal access to treatment.
4. Ensure equal access to information.
5. Guarantee sexual and reproductive rights.
6. Safeguard women's rights and stop violence against women.
7. Ensure participation of people living with HIV/AIDS.
8. Share equally the benefits of scientific progress.
9. Affirm the right to privacy and confidentiality.
10. Ensure monitoring and evaluation for human rights and evidence-based solutions. (AI 2006)

This approach, which has been prompted not only by human rights activists such as the organization ACT UP, but also by most in the scientific community (narrowly defined), has advantages and disadvantages, which might explain some governments' resistance to it. For one, it urges states to provide resources and remedies, not just out of humanitarian concern, but as a matter of legal obligation. The implication is that when states refuse to provide these resources, or refuse to participate in international coordination efforts (which happens routinely—especially with respect to reporting obligations), they can be held accountable as law-breakers rather than merely chided as misers. Naturally, no government wants its actions to be obligatory in this sense—they want freedom of operation. That said, the approach also constrains states in their selection of strategies. As pointed out in the Fidler quote, they must respect basic human rights in every respect of their strategies, taking care not to discriminate on the basis of sexual orientation or gender, ensuring the empowerment of women in societies where they are routinely abused, and setting aside some patent and copyright protections in the name of health. Again, states see difficulties in some of these demands and therefore resist them.

NGOs have consistently pressed this agenda in multiple arenas. Of particular interest is their engagement with the international institutions. NGOs have provided hard facts, policy recommendations, and specific encouragement to the WHO and leaders of UNAIDS over the years. This takes place informally through face-to-face (or e-mail-to-e-mail) contact, through speech-making and literature distribution at international conferences (the 2001 meeting referred to earlier was attended by thousand of AIDS activists and experts), and by inclusion on various blue-ribbon commissions and working groups. As technical experts, NGOs are uniquely qualified to generate, disseminate, and interpret scientific data. As mentioned earlier, it would be impossible for more government agencies to address the topic without this material. Therefore, they have been remarkably successful in pressing their particular approach to the issue.

NGOs have been assisted by the endorsement of numerous governments as well. Consider the issue of patents. Many governments—especially Brazil and South Africa—have been making the case for patent exemptions with the support of these NGOs. African governments hope to turn the crisis into a genuinely transnational issue that Western governments will be forced to reckon with. In particular, they have demanded access to medicines that have been on the market in the West for years—such as AZT and its successors. The drug companies naturally balk at the notion of giving away drugs that cost them hundreds of millions to design and produce. The African governments are therefore asking Western governments to buy up the drug, or at least remove their patent protections so cheaper generic versions can be produced. Part of the reason for South Africa's position was the pressure exerted upon by local activists in the Treatment Action Campaign, which was able to shame the government (beginning in 1998) into acknowledging its failure to secure anti-retroviral drugs—especially for pregnant women (TAC 2006).

Brazil, for example, launched a nationwide initiative to produce AZT and other drug therapies locally and distribute them free of charge in 2000. In the first three years of the program, the government spent nearly a half-billion dollars to provide drugs to all of Brazil's 85,000 AIDS patients, with the result that AIDS mortality dropped by half in São Paulo alone. Even more important, the state saved almost the same amount as it spent on avoided hospitalizations and other expenses (MAP Symposium 2002, 8). When the patent expired in 2005, the issue became moot.

North–South Perspective

This brings up the last issue that has been taken up by various NGOs—again with the support of multiple states. That is the approach that views the AIDS issue primarily as an element in the North–South debate. During the 1960s and 1970s, newly independent states in the developing world argued that their poverty was not so much the product of their own failings but rather the result of an unjust international system. In particular, they pointed out, the free market had a tendency to punish societies that were already poor and technologically backward and that there was little they could do to reverse the situation. Western powers discriminated against developing countries in trade, investment, and finance and tended to be miserly when it came to foreign aid—showing clear preferences to assist only those states that were strategically important.

Although this language has generally subsided as more and more developing countries adopt pro-Western free-trade policies, the AIDS issue helped bring it back. It has been combined with general skepticism about globalization and the benefits of free-trade programs promoted by Western governments. The argument is that the West has invested huge amounts of money to suppress AIDS at home, but has largely ignored the problem in the developing world. This is reflected in foreign aid flows, drug patent rules, and overall attitudes of indifference. As put by Peter Piot, director of the UNAIDS program: "The world stood by while AIDS overwhelmed sub-Saharan Africa." And Stephen Lewis, UN Special Envoy on AIDS in Africa stated:

> How can this be happening, in the year 2003, when we can find over $200 billion to fight a war on terrorism, but we can't find the money to prevent children from living in terror? And when we can't find the money to provide the antiretroviral treatment for all of those who need such treatment in Africa? This double standard is the grotesque obscenity of the modern world. (Fidler 2004, 107)

Critics of Western policy point out that it was not until the 1990s that they took the problem seriously. In the United States, a CIA-sponsored study that predicted dramatic increases in AIDS-related deaths (accurately, as it happened) was met with indifference by senior U.S. officials in 1990 (Spectar 2001, 273). Once the AIDS crisis peaked in the West, aid to Africa began to slump—a trend that was exacerbated by the end of the Cold War when Africa's strategic importance dropped. AIDS-related WHO spending fell from $130 million to $20 million during the first half of the 1990s, while UNICEF spending dropped from $45 to $20 million. Although the West was willing to spend close to $200 billion to remedy the

Y2K computer glitch (which wound up not being a problem), it is unwilling to spend the same to provide anti-retroviral drugs to all the world's AIDS patients (Spectar 2001, 275).

For those who take this approach, the remedy to the problem must involve a dramatic shift in structures and goals. This is similar to the arguments made by other anti-globalization activists who have protested at World Bank meetings and economic summit meetings. Although it is difficult to get a clear sense of what the outcome of such dramatic reforms would be, the short-term goal is a dramatic increase in foreign aid aimed at providing drugs and other treatments to those most in need.

CONCLUSION: ACHIEVING HUMAN SECURITY

Pandemics are a global concern in that they are often impervious to national boundaries. Furthermore, the disease itself is often highly resistant to medical intervention, even when coordinated by powerful governments. When it is the lack of effective government that is responsible to the rise of the pandemic in the first place, the chances of success are greatly diminished.

In the case of HIV/AIDS, the international community in all its manifestations has increasingly taken responsibility for addressing the crisis. As we have seen, private foundations, non-profit medical organizations, international organizations, and private individuals have joined with governments in the West and in Africa to find solutions. At the same time, it is also clear that some of the activity has been mostly rhetorical.

As we see in Chapter 2 on the League of Nations, anarchy is a powerful force in international affairs, typically swamping humanitarian impulses. This raises questions about whether the international state system is compatible with the goal of enhancing human security. The thought has prompted utopians, from Karl Marx to John Lennon, to imagine a stateless world or a world with a single government. Whether this is worth pursuing and how it might be accomplished is a much broader question than can be addressed in a chapter such as this.

QUESTIONS TO CONSIDER

1. To what extent have states embraced the notion that health care is a basic right—part of "human security"?

2. What evidence is there that pandemics can damage a country's security? What about the other way around?

3. To what extent can non-state actors solve the problem of human security where states are unwilling to do so?

CHRONOLOGY
THE HIV/AIDS PANDEMICS

1918
Twenty million die from influenza.

1948
World Health Organization is founded.

1959
First suspected case of AIDS in Africa—identified in 1998.

1967
WHO launches smallpox eradication program.

1977
Smallpox is eradicated.

1981
HIV virus is first identified.

1987
AZT approved for general use by the U.S. Food and Drug Administration.

1990
CIA briefs White House on AIDS pandemic. It was largely ignored.

1994
UNAIDS program is founded.

2000
Brazil begins producing and distributing generic AZT in defiance of patent laws.

At U.S. urging, UN Security Council Resolution 1308 declaring AIDS a major security threat is adopted.

2001
UN General Assembly approves the Declaration of Commitment on HIV/AIDS.

2003
George W. Bush announces $15 billion, five-year initiative on AIDS in Africa.

2005
AZT patent expires.

REFERENCES

Amnesty International (AI). Action on HIV/AIDS and Human Rights, May 2006. Available at: www.ai.org.

Commission on Human Security. "Report of the Commission on Human Security." May 1, 2003. Available at http://www.humansecurity-chs.org/finalreport/Outlines/outline.html. Accessed on October 11, 2008.

DeYoung, Karen. "Between the Lines: Immune to Reality," *Foreign Policy* 126 (Sept–Oct 2001): 72–73.

Fidler, David. "Fighting the Axis of Illness: HIV/AIDS, Human Rights, and U.S. Foreign Policy," *The Harvard Environmental Law Review* 17 (Spring 2004): 99–136.

Gostin, Lawrence. "Pandemic Influenza: Public Health Preparedness for the Next Global Health Emergency," *Journal of Law, Medicine and Ethics* 32 (Winter 2004): 565–572.

Human Security Gateway. "What is Human Security?" Available at http://www.humansecurity gateway.info/. Accessed on October 11, 2008.

International Crisis Group. "Democratic Republic of Congo. Available at http://www.crisisgroup. org/home/index.cfm?id=1174&l=1. Accessed on October 11, 2008.

Lobe, Jim. "World Community Gives Bush AIDS Pledge Mixed Reception." Inter Press Service, January 29, 2003.

MAP Symposium. "The Status and Trends of the HIV/AIDS in the World." Durban, Monitoring the AIDS Pandemic (MAP) Network Symposium, July 5–7, 2002.

Okigbo, Charles, Carol A. Okigbo, William B. Hall, Jr., and Dhyana Ziegler. "The HIV/AIDS Epidemic in African American Communities: Lessons from UNAIDS and Africa," *Journal of Black Studies* 32 #6 (July 2002): 615–653.

Pratt, David. "Lessons for Implementation from the World's Most Successful Programme: The Global Eradication of Smallpox," *Journal of Curriculum Studies* 31 #2 (1999): 177–194.

Spectar, J. M. "The Hybrid Horseman of the Apocalypse: The Global AIDS Pandemic and the North–South Fracas," *The Georgia Journal of International and Comparative Law* 29 (Winter 2001): 253–299.

Spectar, J. M. "The Olde Order Crumbleth: HIV-Pestilence as a Security Issue and New Thinking about Core Concepts in International Affairs," *Indiana International and Comparative Law Review* 13 (2003): 481–542.

TAC. Overview of the Treatment Action Campaign. Available at: http://www.tac.org.za/community/about. Accessed on July 6, 2006.

UNAIDS. *2006 Report on the Global AIDS Epidemic* (New York: UN, 2006).

WHO. *Global Outbreak Alert and Response: Report of a WHO Meeting*, April 26–28, 2000, Geneva, Switzerland.

WHO. "Cumulative Number of Reported Probable Cases of SARS." 2003. Available at: www.who.int/csr/sarscountry/2003_05_08/en/.

WHO. WHO's involvement in UNAIDS. Available at: www.unaids.org/en/Cosponsors/who/default.asp. Accessed on July 3, 2006.

Wikipedia. Zidovudine. Wikipedia, the free encyclopedia. Available at: www.en.wikipedia.org/wiki/AZT. Accessed on July 4, 2006.

14

...

Economic Interdependence: North–South Trade

INTRODUCTION

Ever since Marco Polo returned from China with exotic products and stories of still more, the modern world economy has become increasingly networked. Thanks to ocean-going vessels, national highways, trains, trucks, and airplanes, goods, people, services, and ideas moved across international boundaries with increasing ease and speed. The advent of the internet, as Thomas Friedman has argued, has made the world so small that it is "flat" (Friedman 2007). With the click of a mouse, a young man in a small village west of Hafizabad in northeastern Pakistan can read Barack Obama's response to the latest anti-American video from Osama bin Laden (which is also available online) and post a comment on his blog to add to the discussion. Then he can order a new flash drive from a company in Taiwan and get it delivered within a week. All of this just before he hops on an overcrowded bus, chatting to his brother on the Motorola Razor he picked up from a local vendor, to the Crescent Bahuman Ltd. garment factory to make some more Levi Strauss blue jeans for export to a Wal-Mart in Ames, Iowa (Levi-Strauss 2008).

Most countries rely heavily on foreigners to produce the goods, grow the food, mine the ore, develop the software, or write the stories they want. And most countries rely on others buying these things from them. Likewise, few countries can survive without a great deal of foreign investment, loans, currency, and securities. Oil is produced by a handful of countries but is essential to the economic survival of almost all. And on it goes.

All of this describes a phenomenon known as interdependence. Simply put, interdependence refers to "mutual dependence" between countries. This can involve the

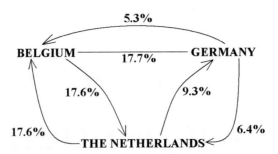

Figure 14.1 Share of Exports Flowing between Germany, Belgium, and the Netherlands, 2007
Source: CIA Factbook. Available at https://www.cia.gov/library/publications/the-world-factbook/geos/be.
html#Econ. Accessed on October 4, 2008.

low levels of trade, as we might find between two developing countries on different continents, or deep mutual dependence, as we find between Belgium, Germany, and the Netherlands (see Figure 14.1). Not only do they trade heavily with each other, but they also depend on exports for much of their overall nation income. Germany's exports are equal to 29% of its total national earnings, for example. The figures for the Netherlands and Belgium are 37% and 45%, respectively (Econstats 2008).

Scholars and policymakers are particularly interested in cases where countries are closely intertwined economically. Optimists point out that such ties often bind countries into long-lasting friendships—or at least an awkward stalemate. The "democratic peace theory" argues that democratic countries that do a great deal of business with each other are far less likely to go to war (Russett & O'Neal 2001). Skeptics point out that in World Wars I and II we saw countries with very close trade ties and high levels of lending and investment nearly destroy each other (at least this shows that trade levels are less important than shared governmental systems). All agree that, as pointed out in Chapter 20, increased interdependence can create an unstable economic system as disturbances in one area can sweep across the globe and unhinge economies 10,000 kilometers away.

Still others note that increased interdependence is usually not balanced, with the result that some countries are far more vulnerable than others. It is to this issue we now turn as we endeavor to understand how developing countries responded to becoming integrated into the world economy in the second half of the 20th century.

BASIC CONCEPTS

Before discussing the developing world's approach to interdependence in general and trade in particular, a few terms warrant definition:

Free trade is the conduct of trade without interference by government. Products and services and investments move according to market forces of supply and demand rather than as a result of government manipulation. It is reasonable to say that this condition has never existed in reality, but it is an important abstract ideal.

Tariffs are taxes imposed by governments on imports, usually to protect local industries, whether "infant" or "sunset." Infant industries are usually small, inefficient companies that are trying out new technologies and cannot compete head-to-head against more mature and sophisticated foreign firms and therefore seek (and often get) governments to impose tariffs. The same is often true of companies that have been around for a few generations and cannot afford to upgrade their machinery or must pay a large number of retirees. These "sunset" industries—such as steel mills in Pennsylvania or automobile makers in Great Britain—often feel overwhelmed by younger, more nimble companies in Asia and seek tariffs against their goods. Other ways governments may interfere with market forces include quotas—or numerical ceilings on particular imports, and subsidies, which involve direct payments to firms to allow them to lower prices while still making normal profits.

Governments also work with each other to either promote or interfere with market forces. *Liberalization*—meaning a lowering of barriers to trade—has often been achieved through careful mutual negotiation involving reciprocity or balanced give-and-take. Sometimes this is done by a few countries in a particular region to produce a regional trade agreement. It has also been done on a global level based on the principle of non-discrimination, meaning that trade openness should be made available to all states that wish to join the compact. Furthermore, every country should extend any trade access it has given to another member of a trade compact to all the other members of the same compact. This is particularly important where the agreement is meant to be global, as is the case with the General Agreement on Tariffs and Trade (GATT). This is known as "most-favored nation" status. On the other hand, most regional trade agreements involve some level of "preference"—meaning that access to markets is given to some countries but not all. In still other cases, governments negotiate among themselves a mostly illiberal arrangement known as managed trade, meaning that governments manipulate the supply and demand of goods and services by bargaining and negotiating, with the result that a government may force its own firms to export fewer items than they might be able to sell without restraint.

With this vocabulary established, let us consider the problems of poor countries in the world economy.

CONDITIONS AFTER WORLD WAR II

Few poor countries were independent and even fewer were influential when several dozen states gathered at Bretton Woods, New Hampshire, in July 1944 to forge institutions that would—it was hoped—usher in an era of economic liberalization that would prevent the economic collapse that contributed to the rise of autocracy in Europe during the 1930s. Conditions in Europe after World War II were desperate, and even the World Bank—now thought of as the world's quintessential development agency—was designed primarily to rebuild the continent. The concerns of developing nations were simply not on the minds of negotiators (Finlayson & Zacher 1981, 581). The key trade institution that emerged from these talks—the

International Trade Organization—was ultimately suspended and replaced by the GATT, although both were founded on the principles of reciprocity and non-discrimination. The vision was of a liberal economic order in which all states would reduce barriers to all forms of trade in order to allow market forces to reward and punish producers and not governments.

But almost immediately, developed nations altered the bargain and gave themselves important exemptions for political purposes. The United States secured an exemption to continue its considerable farm subsidies enacted during the Great Depression, while the United Kingdom received permission to continue to grant special trade concessions to their former colonies that were now members of the Commonwealth. Developed countries also made a special series of arrangements to allow them to protect textiles—a sunset industry—from more competitive imports from the developing world (Strange & Newton 2004, 238).

Furthermore, many of the benefits of membership in the GATT were of little significance to developing countries. They had few tariffs and so could not participate in the grand tariff-cutting negotiations that characterized the early years of GATT whereby government reduced the most significant barriers to trade through mutual liberalization (Harvard 1968, 1807). Because agriculture was largely removed from the negotiations, and because the vast majority of developing countries depended on agricultural exports, GATT offered little hope to them.

Developing countries began to mobilize in the late-1950s to express their frustrations with GATT. This prompted the membership to organize special committees that were tasked with measuring and critiquing trade policies that impeded developing country exports. The result was a series of pledges by developed countries to do better, but that did not impress the audience of poor countries who in turn developed a "Program of Action" in 1961 to articulate their demands more precisely (Wells 1969, 68–69). These included permission to raise tariffs to protect infant industries, preferential arrangements with certain developed countries without retribution, and reduction of agricultural subsidies by developed countries. Some developed countries—Great Britain in particular—were sympathetic to developing countries' demands, but not enough of them could make enough progress to prevent them from taking their case to the United Nations General Assembly.

THE CREATION OF UNCTAD AND THE NIEO

The General Assembly was a far more hospitable forum than GATT, as every country enjoyed membership there and could demand equal time at the microphone. Furthermore, the large number of newly independent countries—almost all of which were poor—gave that category of country a solid majority, enabling them to control the agenda and pass resolutions to their liking. It was a time of diplomatic confrontation between poor and rich countries, and the Soviet bloc was eager to join in on the side of the developing world (Wells 1969, 73). The conflict was laced with ideological competition, with industrialized countries advocating free market orthodoxy, and developing and Socialist countries advocating a version of what came to be known as "dependency" theory.

The principal argument of the South, a general term for the emerging developing country coalition, was that the global trading system was inherently unfair—not just because some governments in the North (shorthand for industrialized Western countries) were deviating from GATT rules as noted earlier, but also because even when trade was open and free, developing countries came out the worse for it. Argentine economist Raúl Prébisch noted that when countries sell goods that are labor-intensive (agricultural products, minerals, textiles, and so forth), they cannot expect to come out ahead if they in turn purchase capital-intensive goods (machines, consumer electronics, automobiles, etc.). The "terms of trade" will result over time in the country running trade deficits that will have to be financed through borrowing from wealthy countries. Ultimately, they will buy expensive imports with foreign money and be unable to earn enough hard currency from their exports to make up the difference. Even where a country begins to industrialize, it will find its infant industries overwhelmed by foreign competition in a free market. Trade, it was argued, would not alleviate poverty—it might even exacerbate it (Hilary 2004, 38). This, along with other "stylized facts," as put by American economist Anne Kreuger (1997, 4), was persuasive to many governments in the South and explains their general skepticism of GATT norms (Krasner 1985, 113).

Furthermore, developing countries in the early-1960s had far more similarities than differences. It is important to remember that it would be many years before Arab oil would dominate the world economy and even longer before East Asian countries would compete head to head with industrialized countries on high-end electronics. At this point, even the more advanced developing countries were heavily reliant on agricultural trade, generally uncompetitive in industrial goods, and dependent on foreign aid and markets. It was therefore relatively easy for them to speak with one voice. And dependency theory gave them a script that was powerful and somewhat effective (Krasner 1985, 114).

The General Assembly approved a special conference on the issue of trade and development to be held in 1964. The UN Conference on Trade and Development (UNCTAD) provided a forum "open to all states belonging to the United Nations . . . [and] imposes no contractual obligations [unlike GATT]. In addition, it provides a forum devoted exclusively to studying and advocating methods of resolving problems of development through aid as well as trade." (Harvard 1968, 1811–1812). As a result, many developing countries joined UNCTAD, and they quickly became the dominant voice in the organization.

UNCTAD suffered from several institutional weaknesses, however, the most important being its inability to require members to enact any particular policies. It could only make recommendations and carry out research. The organization also had a critical political weakness: because the demands coming out of UNCTAD mostly involved weak and poor countries attempting to persuade wealthy and powerful countries to make sacrifices on their behalf, they were largely doomed from the outset. The only thing that worked in the South's favor was a desire on the part of the North to ultimately make GATT universal. The developed countries therefore worked to keep developing countries in GATT. The best way to do this was concede some of their demands. But to a large extent, UNCTAD was counterproductive because of its more ideological and confrontational approach. Even the research produced by UNCTAD experts was heavily discounted by Western governments because it was considered biased in favor of poor countries (Doyle 1983, 443).

GATT attempted to reform itself in order to keep developing countries involved in its approach. Specifically, the members instituted Part IV of the General Agreement, which allowed developing countries to legally expect preferential treatment in tariff negotiations, specifically, that developed countries should not expect developing countries to lower their trade barriers to the same extent when negotiating trade-offs. Failure on the part of developed countries to comply with this new rule could give rise to "joint action," meaning a more public and general debate on the country's failures. Presumably, this extra negative attention would spur the wealthy country to action. The provision also created a Committee on Trade and Development where member-states would gather to address specifically how the international trading system could be made more hospitable to poor countries (Harvard 1968, 1810; Wells 1969, 66; Finlayson & Zacher 1981, 582–583).

Many developed countries were sincerely committed to this new norm, although it did not go far enough from the developing country point of view. In 1968, however, an important breakthrough was achieved when the United States accepted the "Generalized System of Preferences" (GSP) that developing countries had proposed in 1964 at the first UNCTAD meetings. The concept was fairly simple: all the developing countries would be exempted from GATT's Article I principle of "most favored nation" treatment. In so doing, they would be treated by the developed world in the same way as the former British colonies were treated by the United Kingdom. They would be entitled to maintain protections on their own markets, while at the same time, developed countries would grant them easier access to their own markets. The argument was that infant industries and inefficient farms in the Third World could not be expected to compete head-to-head with products from the North, and so these countries should be allowed to discriminate without penalty (Whalley 1990, 1320). The United States only agreed to the plan if the concessions were temporary, dealt only with developed country tariffs (as opposed to agricultural subsidies, for example), and were provided to all developing countries. Later on, in the late 1970s, the GSP was made permanent through the "Enabling Clause," although a provision was included that reduced special protections once a country reached a certain level of development, or "graduated" (Story 1982, 770). For example, The United States and European Union decided that Singapore, Taiwan, Hong Kong, and South Korea had graduated from the GSP in the late 1990s and withdrew special concessions (Hong Kong 1997). Naturally, developing countries resist this loss of benefits, but seem to have little leverage to prevent it.

Developing countries, while heartened by the North's concessions in the 1960s, found them generally disappointing, once again. They noted that some of the highly touted GATT reforms had important loopholes that allowed developed countries to maintain high tariffs and non-tariff barriers. For example, since the GSP was limited to tariffs, and was implemented only partially, and since strict "rules of origin" were imposed by developed countries that excluded many products that had ingredients and parts made in the developing world (but that were labeled "made in Japan" or "made in France"), it is estimated that the GSP resulted in only a 2% increase of exports from the South to the North (Whalley 1990, 1321; Grimwold 2004, 14). Likewise, the Part IV amendment covered only manufactured goods rather than agricultural products or other primary products, and so the benefits were limited to a few "newly industrializing" countries (NICs) like Brazil and Taiwan. It also did not cover all manufactured goods, since textiles and clothing—two of the South's most competitive industries—were covered under other deals (Grimwade 2004, 13–16). In the early 1970s, the West also experienced a severe economic downturn that resulted in dramatic changes in currency values and high, albeit temporary, increases in tariffs and non-tariff barriers. Concessions previously made to developing countries were among the first to be reversed. Their earlier promise to freeze new tariffs was broken (Fiallo 1984, 243).

Ultimately, it was becoming clear that although they were growing (by close to 5% a year on average), developing countries were not keeping up with either the developed countries or their own growing populations (UNCTAD 1984, 285). They felt as though they were swimming against the current—which meant that the ultimate aim should be to change the direction of the current, a task easier said than done.

It was mostly a case of too little, too late. By now the developing countries had formed the Group of 77, a coalition of (at the founding) seventy-seven developing countries that acted in concert at the UN in general and UNCTAD in particular. Further, in late 1973, the Arab members of the Organization of the Petroleum Exporting Countries (OPEC), having previously gained control over many foreign oil installations through "nationalization" (the government-mandated purchase of foreign assets), instituted a politically motivated embargo on oil sales. The result was a dramatic increase in the world price of oil and the transfer of billions of dollars from the North to the Middle East. OPEC members became some of the wealthiest countries in the world almost overnight, and the rest of the world understood for the first time the power that the developing world could exert on the world economy. Feeling their new power, developing countries were less concerned about reforming the GATT and aimed at reforming the entire global system (Krasner 1985, 114). This culminated in the proclamation in 1974 at a special session of the UN General Assembly of a "Program of Action on the Establishment of a New International Economic Order." (UNCTAD 1984, 289). The move was meant to be nothing short of revolutionary. As put by Julius Nyerere, President of Tanzania:

> Our coming together in the Group of 77 has the purpose of enabling us to deal on terms of greater equality with an existing Center of Power. Ours is basically a unity of opposition. And it is a unity of nationalisms . . . The unity of the entire Third World is necessary for the achievement of fundamental change in the present world economic arrangements . . . the object is to complete the liberation of the Third World countries from external domination. That is the basic meaning of the New International Economic Order. And unity is our instrument—our only instrument—of liberation. (Iida 1988, 375)

The NIEO, as the program came to be known, called for a wide range of changes to the world economy—most of which would involve changes in developed country policies. Among the most controversial demands are:

- Increases in foreign aid to the level of 0.7% of Gross National Product by all developed countries.
- Further reductions in not only tariffs but also non-tariff barriers by developed countries on products from the South.
- Special international arrangements to shore up commodity prices—especially agricultural prices—involving a large pool of funds to repurchase surpluses in boom years and sell them back in lean years.
- New sources of low-interest lending through the International Monetary Fund or some other international organization.
- New mechanisms to transfer technology from the North to the South without payments of royalties and other patent protections.
- An enhanced food aid regime.

Although the program gave lip service to the free market, it is clear that developing countries at the time were deeply suspicious of open-trading systems and far preferred a "managed" system whereby they could achieve some measure of predictability and security—even if this resulted in slower overall growth (Krasner 1985, 115). Most developing countries by this point had altered their domestic economic policies to implement the import substitution industrialization, meaning that they were providing considerable government funds to particular sectors and industries and protecting them from foreign competition in order to help them establish themselves. Whether on the basis of populist or socialist philosophies, the result was that many governments had adopted a version of central planning to carry out their development strategy (see India in Chapter 15). Brazil, Argentina, Mexico and other NICs were racking up very impressive growth rates in the process, setting an example for the rest of the developing world. A new international economic age seemed to have dawned. Little did they know that the Third World's power had already reached its zenith.

THE COLLAPSE OF THE G-77 AND NIEO

The first indication that the Third World's power had already reached its peak was during the Tokyo Round of GATT trade negotiations that ended in 1979. Although they succeeded in locking in some of the preferential treatment they secured earlier, the United States was able to include the graduation provision mentioned earlier. Also, they were unable to persuade developed countries to weaken their safeguard protections that allowed them to temporarily block a surge of new imports from developing countries. As put by the Yugoslav delegate: "You can hardly say the Third World got any additional benefits from these talks . . . In general the poorer countries are just where we were six years ago" (Story 1982, 770). Almost all developing countries boycotted the signing ceremony in protest. Only a handful ultimately agreed to it.

The developing world was experiencing a number of changes in the late 1970s. To begin with, import-substitution industrialization was reaching the end of its useful life. As we will see in the case of India (Chapter 15), once the domestic market is saturated with lower-quality, locally produced goods, it is very difficult for firms to continue to expand. They must find new markets to grow, but their products cannot compete with foreign-made goods. Meanwhile, governments must continue to show their support for the firms or else they will lose the political support of their owners and employees. They resorted to borrowing (rather than increasing taxes and caus-ing outrage) from foreign banks that were flush with OPEC dollars (oil exporters deposited much of their earnings in Western banks immediately after the embargo). But many of the loans were provided on a short-term basis at market rates and came due at roughly the same time as oil prices took another bounce in 1979. Argentina, Poland, and a number of other NICs were caught in a very weak position and soon found they could not keep up their payments. When the oil prices dropped again in 1982, the remaining oil exporting NICs were hit with the same financial crisis. In August, a full-blown Third World debt crisis sapped the power out of the Group of 77 and put it in the hands of the developed world.

Western powers, including specifically the United States, Great Britain, Germany, and the International Monetary Fund, presented the developing world with a new pro-gram that came to be known as the Washington Consensus. In brief, it called on nations to abandon import-substitution industrialization, adopt strict fiscal policies to balance their government budgets, accept foreign investment and goods, and promote exports to earn foreign currency.

The developing world was fractured by the ordeal, with some debtor nations agreeing to the IMF's terms, OPEC countries enjoying their wealth (and sharing some of it), still other countries—mostly in East Asia—enjoying new opportunities since they had implemented liberal policies already, and the poorest countries (known as "least developed countries") being left largely on their own (Narlikar 2003). Each group of countries had different interests and capacities, but generally found they had little in common with each other (Doyle 1983, 431).

What emerged instead was a clustering of groups around particular issues such as agriculture, intellectual properties, safeguards, foreign aid, and investment policies. In the remainder of this chapter, we will focus especially on agriculture, because this affects most developing countries and has been an increasingly bitter issue of debate with developed countries.

AGRICULTURE IN URUGUAY AND BEYOND

At the end of the 1970s, low-income developing countries earned almost two fifths of their export income from farm goods, whereas NICs earned just less than a third (World Bank 1984, 22). Yet the United States and Europe continued to place high barriers against Third World food imports. By the mid-1980s, the amount of subsidy given to most food growers in the West (including Japan) was well over a third of the total farm earnings. Rice was subsidized to the tune of 80% of farm receipts, and in Japan, imports of all rice were banned outright. Sugar, milk, wheat and most grains received subsidies averaging over half of the total farm receipts (FAO 2003).

In spite of this, commodities from the developing world were still competitive with these heavily subsidized products, and so most developed countries also imposed significant tariffs. Even after developed countries made efforts to cut tariffs during the 1990s, the average of tariff peaks on many commodities were well over 100%, meaning that the price of many commodity imports were twice what they might normally be. Only a few countries that were members of certain regional preference groups, such as the British Commonwealth or the European-sponsored Lomé Convention, benefited from significantly reduced tariffs. The result was that during the 1980s and 1990s, although the growth of agricultural trade worldwide was a healthy 3.5% per year, the volume of Third World exports grew less than 2% each year between 1979 and 1992 (FAO 2003). The least developed countries actually saw their revenues from agricultural exports decline from a little over $5 billion to under $4 billion, or a drop of more than 2.5% per year. This group became net food importers after 1987 and now imports roughly twice as much as they sell (see Figure 14.2).

As if these problems were not enough, developed countries have further moved to block efforts by developing countries to become more sophisticated agricultural producers by impeding sales of processed foods. A phenomenon known as "tariff escalation" has become increasingly significant since the early 1980s, in spite of efforts to remedy

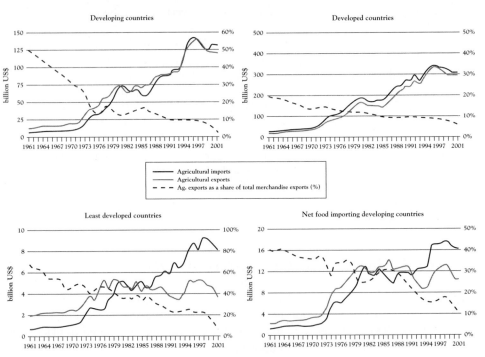

Figure 14.2 Trends in Agricultural Trade, 1961–2001
Source: FAO 2003.

this. For example, even after years of tariff reductions, as of the end of the 1990s, the European Union placed a 21.1% tariff on chocolate, although cocoa beans could enter duty-free. In Canada, the tariff on chocolate was 59%—again cocoa beans were duty-free. In Canada, raw sugar had an 8.5% tariff, whereas refined sugar was taxed at the rate of 107%, or more than twice the value. In Japan, raw sugar had a 225% duty but refined sugar had a 328% tariff. In Europe, the same figures were 135% and 161%, respectively (FAO 2003). Because of these and other government policies, the price of sugar in the EU in the late 1990s was ten times higher than the prevailing world price. The developed world's governments were spending more than half the total value of the sugar trade ($11.6 billion) on subsidies and other price supports ($6.35 billion) to protect domestic sugar producers. This amounted to a massive transfer of money from sugar consumers in the West to a small number of struggling sugar growers and processors both through higher prices and through higher tax levels. Taken together, developed countries spend about $300 billion each year on agriculture support, or a bit less than the combined national incomes of all fifty-six Sub-Saharan African countries (including South Africa)—home to 670 million people (Rice 2003, 258).

It is perhaps easy to understand why developing countries were focused on changing international rules governing agricultural trade. One could make the argument that the rules that have developed over the years represent one of the great injustices in the modern era.

Mobilization against European and American price supports began in earnest in the mid-1980s after an agricultural crisis that saw a drop in production by half between the mid-1970s and 1982. Yet, the European Communities (predecessor to the EU) enjoyed surpluses in sugar, wheat, and other commodities. The United States retaliated with increased subsidies of its own in what came to be known as the "subsidy war." It became clear not only to the developing world but also to governments in such industrialized nations as Canada and Australia that no one would be able to compete. And so in 1986 the Cairns Group of Fair Trading Nations was organized—named after a city in Australia where preliminary meetings were held. The Cairns Group consisted of Australia, Argentina, Brazil, New Zealand, and Uruguay and was later joined by Chile, Canada, Colombia, Fiji, Hungary, Indonesia, Malaysia, the Philippines, and Thailand (Narlikar 2003, 130). These countries were strong agricultural exporters but did not engage in high levels of subsidization and therefore had the most to lose from the current world order. They proposed a freeze on new price supports and a gradual reduction over time as part of the upcoming Uruguay Round negotiations. Although the United States tentatively supported the proposal, the European countries—particularly France—were opposed.

But the Cairns Group had several resources at its disposal that made resistance risky. To begin, they had market leverage, providing about 20% of the world's cereals and other commodities—far more on average than the EC, United States, or Japan. Further, they were an important market for goods from the subsidizing countries, buying roughly 10% of Japan and Europe's goods and 30% of America's exports (Narlikar 2003, 139).

Second, because the group's membership came from all over the world and included representatives of most of the major country groupings, it had credibility with most of the world—also known as "legitimacy." Latin America was represented by five important countries, the developed world had three members, Asia and the Pacific were represented—even Eastern Europe and by implication the Communist bloc were represented (recall that the Cold War had not yet ended when the Cairns Group was formed). Add to this the United States' support for the general aims of the Group, and it is clear that one could not simply dismiss it.

Finally, the Group was careful to support each of its demands with the type of statistical analysis that was difficult for the EC to refute (Narlikar 2003, 142). Of course, the fact that so much money was being spent on so few at such harm to so many allowed them to make their case without fanfare or hyperbole. After all, the Cairns Group members were simply advocating a return to first principles: reciprocity, non-discrimination, and most-favored nation treatment. After all, the various regional trade agreements and agricultural subsidies were created as exceptions to GATT law.

That said, from time to time the Latin American members of the group would engage in diplomatic theatrics by walking out of conferences or loudly condemning small concessions, which helped galvanize the other members and increase global support.

In the end, the Cairns Group helped to broker the Blair House Accords between the United States and EU in late 1992, although in the end, the agreement fell far short of what the group had sought and led to animosities among its members (Narlikar 2003, 143). The parties agreed among themselves to a gradual phase-out of about one fifth of their tariffs on certain agricultural goods over six years, using the high water mark of 1991–1992 tariff levels—a small victory at best.

A further achievement with mixed implications was the acceptance of subsidies in principle, albeit at lower levels. Subsidies were placed in three "boxes": green (those that were permissible), amber (those that should be reduced), and red (those that were prohibited). In the amber box were placed any subsidies that clearly distorted trade, although 5% supports were still permissible (Williams 2004, 14). The Cairns Group opposed the amber box and called for the elimination of all subsidies that distort trade flows. Poorer countries in Asia and Africa argued along similar lines, but also called for an exemption for developing countries that would allow them to maintain trade-distorting subsidies of their own. The final result was a 36% reduction of export subsidies across the developed world and a shift from quotas to tariffs in anticipation of later tariff cuts (Grimwade 2004, 19).

These mixed results were further diminished, as implied earlier, by the failure on the part of developed countries to actually implement the agreements. Tariffs were calculated from quotas in dishonest ways, inflating the distorting effects of the earlier quotas. To explain, because quotas raise prices in predictable ways by reducing supply (assuming a constant demand), it is fairly easy to calculate exactly how much those prices were raised, convert that to a percentage, and thereby determine the tariff equivalent of a quota. But the specific mathematical calculations were not closely supervised by the GATT, and so European and American governments sometimes exaggerated the price increases their quotas had caused, then used that higher figure in setting a new tariff rate. The result was therefore more protectionism rather than less. The Americans gained an extra 44% price hike, while the Europeans gained 61% in the process (Grimwade 2004, 21). When it came time to cut tariffs, because the treaty called for average cuts across several goods, these countries further manipulated the system by cutting their lowest tariffs by the highest percentages, and their highest tariffs by the lowest percentages, thereby achieving a high average tariff rate reduction. As explained by Grimwade: "For example, if there are four products, three of which have a 10% tariff and one a 100% tariff, a country could cut the three lower tariffs to 5% and leave the 100% tariff unchanged, giving an average tariff reduction of 37.5% [(50 + 50 + 50 + 0 over four = 150/4 = 37.5%)], which is more than is required under the Agreement" (2004, 21).

With respect to subsidies, developed country governments simply shifted reduced subsidies in the amber box in order to increase subsidies in the green box, with the result that overall agricultural subsidies actually increased from 1990 to 1997 from 31% to 40% of farm receipts—all the while staying within the rules of the Agreement (Grimwade 2004, 21).

What becomes clear is that most developed countries are not sincerely interested in reducing price supports and increasing imports where agricultural goods are concerned. Developing countries still push for real change, but the result has been stalemate. The stalemate on agriculture explains much of the overall stalemate at the current Doha Round of GATT negotiations (Williams 2004).

CONCLUSION: INTERDEPENDENCE OR DEPENDENCE?

The story of the developing world's approach to international trade demonstrates that economic interdependence is intensely political and likely always will be. In particular, as more and more governments become democratic, leaders and citizens will demand protection from the vicissitudes of international trade—especially if the country suffers from low levels of development and technological sophistication. As household incomes in Africa continue to stagnate and sometimes decline while incomes grow exponentially in the West, as well as in India and China of late, it becomes clear that the world economy does indeed play favorites. Although many governments in the Third World have been guilty of degrading their economies with short-sighted policies, it is also clear that the benefits of free trade are being denied to them by the very governments that have promoted trade liberalization since the Bretton Woods conference. As a result, blame for the plight of the world's poor farmers can be spread widely.

QUESTIONS TO CONSIDER

1. Are developing countries justified in seeking special concessions from developed countries? How would this relate to their foreign debt, for example?

2. To what extent does their unity affect developing countries' influence? How does this relate to OPEC's ability to control oil prices?

3. How does economic liberalism shape developed country policies on trade with the developing world? Do other principles take precedence over free trade? What about the proposal at the World Trade Organization to take into account the rights of workers in establishing trade rules?

CHRONOLOGY
NORTH–SOUTH TRADE

1944
July   The Bretton Woods conference produces agreements on the creation of a new international trade institution.

1961
Disappointed with developed country initiatives in their behalf, developing countries draw up a Program of Action.

1964
UNCTAD is formed.

1965
GATT's Part IV provisions come into effect.

1968
Generalized System of Preferences is incorporated into the GATT.

1971
The United States adopts protectionist measures to combat a trade deficit.

1973
OPEC countries impose an oil embargo on the West and raise oil prices.

1974
Developing countries at the UN promulgate the New International Economic Order.

1979
Tokyo Round of the GATT is completed. Developing countries are dissatisfied.

Oil prices skyrocket after the collapse of the Iranian government.

1982
Blair House agreement defuses tensions between the United States and the European Union over agricultural subsidies. Developing countries complain that the concessions are too small.

Debt crisis erupts, effectively ending the NIEO agenda.

1995
World Trade Organization is formed.

1999
Seattle ministerial meeting is disrupted by protests on the outside and disagreements over agricultural, environmental, and human rights issues on the inside.

2001
GATT begins the Doha Round of trade negotiations. By 2003 they are effectively stalled.

REFERENCES

Doyle, Michael W. "Review: Stalemate in the North–South Debate: Strategies and the New International Economic Order," *World Politics* 35 #3 (April 1983): 426–464.

Econstats. "Econstats: Global Economic Data." Available at http://www.econstats.com/home. htm. Accessed on October 6, 2008.

Food and Agriculture Organization (FAO). "FAO Support to the WTO Negotiations," (2003). Available at http://www.fao.org/docrep/005/Y4852E/y4852e02.htm. Accessed on October 2, 2008.

Fiallo, Fabio R. "The Negotiations Strategy of Developing Countries in the Field of Trade Liberalization," in Pradip K. Ghosh, ed. *International Trade and Third World Development* (Westport, CT: Greenwood Press, 1984): 240–249.

Finlayson Jock A. and Mark W. Zacher. "The GATT and the Regulation of Trade Barriers: Regime Dynamics and Functions," *International Organization* 35 #1 (Autumn 1981): 561–602.

Friedman, Thomas. *The World Is Flat 3.0: A Brief History of the Twenty-first Century.* (New York: Picador, 2007).

Grimwade, Nigel. "The GATT, the Doha Round and Developing Countries," in Homi Katrak and Roger Strange, eds. *The WTO and Developing Countries.* (New York: Palgrave Macmillan, 2004): 11–37.

Harvard Law Review. "Free Trade and Preferential Tariffs: The Evolution of International Trade Regulation in GATT and UNCTAD," *Harvard Law Review* 81 #8 (June 1968): 1806–1817.

Hilary, John. "Trade Liberalization, Poverty and the WTO: Assessing the Realities," in Homi Katrak and Roger Strange, eds. *The WTO and Developing Countries.* (New York: Palgrave Macmillan, 2004): 38–62.

Hong Kong. "Graduation of Hong Kong from the EU's Generalized System of Preferences." Commercial Information Circular # 170/97, Ref. CR EIC 230/20/1 XIX. November 20, 1997. Available at http://www.tid.gov.hk/english/aboutus/tradecircular/cic/eu/1997/ci17097.html. Accessed on October 6, 2008.

Iida, Keisuke. "Third World Solidarity: The Group of 77 in the UN General Assembly," *International Organization* 42 #2 (Spring 1988): 375–395.

Krasner, Stephen. *Structural Conflict: The Third World against Global Liberalism.* (Berkeley: University of California Press, 1985).

Kreuger, Anne O. "Trade Policy and Economic Development: How We Learn," *American Economic Review* 87 #1 (March 1997): 1–22.

Levi Strauss. Levi Strauss and Company Supplier List, April 2008. Available at www.levistrauss.com/downloads/factorylist.pdf. Accessed on October 4, 2008.

Milner, Chris. "Constraints to Export Development in the Developing Countries," in Homi Katrak and Roger Strange, eds. *The WTO and Developing Countries* (New York: Palgrave Macmillan, 2004): 213–232.

Narlikar, Amrita. *International Trade and Developing Countries: Bargaining coalitions in the GATT & WTO.* (London: Routledge, 2003).

Russett, Bruce M. and John O'Neal. *Triangulating Peace: Democracy, Interdependence, and International Organizations.* (New York: W.W. Norton, 2001).

Story, Dale. "Trade Politics in the Third World: A Case Study of the Mexican GATT Decision," *International Organization* 36 #4 (Autumn 1982): 767–794.

Strange, Roger and Jim Newton. "From Rags to Riches? China, the WTO and World Trade in Textiles and Clothing," in Homi Katrak and Roger Strange, eds. *The WTO and Developing Countries*. (New York: Palgrave Macmillan, 2004): 233–256.

UNCTAD. "Policy Issues in the Fields of Trade, Finance and Money and Their Relationship to Structural Changes at the Global Level," in Pradip K. Ghosh, ed. *International Trade and Third World Development*. (Westport, CT: Greenwood Press, 1984): 278–299.

Wells, Sidney. "The Developing Countries GATT and UNCTAD," *International Affairs* 45 #1 (January 1969): 64–79.

Whalley, John. "Non-Discriminatory Discrimination: Special and Differential Treatment Under the GATT for Developing Countries," *The Economic Journal* 100 #103 (December 1990): 1318–1328.

Williams, Marc. "The World Trade Organization and the Developing World: Convergent and Divergent Interests," Paper presented at the annual meetings of the International Studies Association, March 17–20, 2004, Montreal, Quebec.

15

. . .

Decolonization and Development: India Rising

INTRODUCTION

The story of almost every developing country in the world today is a story of breaking free from a mother country (decolonization) and learning to expand their economic and social capacity (development). Doing so involves struggles against many foes, both internal and external. Not only must a national liberation movement decide how to confront a foreign power endowed with considerable resources, but it must also convince local citizens to join in and figure out what to do with those who do not. But achieving independence for some countries has proven to be the easy part. The next step involves organizing a state, establishing proper roles for the government, and finding ways to obtain and channel resources to the best targets.

Decolonization began almost as soon as the first empires were established. In some ways, the collapse of the Roman Empire could be seen as the emergence of numerous new political entities. Generally we focus on modern imperialism–specifically the period of global conquest that began in the late 18th century and involved the establishment of European control over Africa, Asia, and Oceania. It was these regions that, beginning in the late 1940s, were able to take advantage of the relative decline in European power after World War II to negotiate or fight their way to sovereignty for their new nation. This was done in almost every conceivable way and with broad range of outcomes. For example, as we will see, Indians were largely able to pressure the British to withdraw by means of a series of large-scale strikes, peaceful protests, and civil disobedience—known collectively as "non-violent resistance." On the other extreme, Algerians fought house to house for six years against determined French resistance, resulting in almost a half million casualties on both sides.

In most cases, leaders of newly elected or appointed indigenous governments negotiated their independence over a period of time, then peacefully stood side-by-side with representatives of the colonial power as European flags were lowered and local flags were raised. These new states quickly joined the United Nations as fully independent, sovereign states. During the 1960s, more than forty new states became members, raising the organization's total membership from eighty-two to 126 (UN 2008). Some did not achieve complete independence right away or they retained special ties to the mother country. Canada, for example, achieved home rule in 1867 but was not fully sovereign until 1982. It still maintains its membership in the British Commonwealth—an economic and political organization designed to give former British colonies special privileges. Palau, administered by the United States for thirty years under UN auspices, became independent in 1978 and is now governed under a "compact of free association" with the United States, giving the United States responsibility for its national defense.

As was mentioned, achieving independence and becoming a member of the UN was the easy part for some countries. Some slipped into economic and political chaos almost as soon as their new flags were raised. Belgian Congo was granted independence precipitously in 1960 in the face of an increasingly violent independence movement. Only the thinnest veneer of government was in place as the Belgians left. Congolese soldiers rose up against the few Belgian officers who had remained behind to help create an indigenous army. This prompted a Belgian re-intervention, Belgian support for a rival government in the south, and a year-long civil war followed by UN peacekeeping. Stability did not come until Mobutu Sese Seko—one of the world's most corrupt and ruthless dictators—seized power in 1965 (Callaghy 1984).

Other newly independent countries experienced precipitous economic collapses requiring emergency assistance from abroad—often from the former colonial ruler. Within two years of its independence from Pakistan, Bangladesh experienced a catastrophic famine, for example. But most enjoyed positive, if not sustainable, growth. Far more common was the emergence of dependent economic relations with the outside world, based on heavy reliance on a few export markets, foreign capital, and foreign technology.

To address this problem of dependency, and to establish themselves as the central authority in the new state, governments across the developing world adopted state-centered economic strategies. The problem they faced was deciding what the goal should be. For some states it was merely economic independence. For others it was overall economic growth, as measured by the gross national product divided by the total population. Still others imagined an end point where all the citizens of the country would have their basic needs met and be productive members of the economy. These advocated the use of UN Development Program's "human development index" to measure development. "The HDI measures the overall achievements of a country in three basic dimensions of human development—longevity and health, education and knowledge, and a decent standard of living" (Dutt 2006, 120). A few have even gone so far as to define development as the "self-actualization" of all of their people—the achievement of a deeper and more meaningful sense of self and fulfillment. As envisioned by Amartya Sen, this is nothing less than genuine personal and societal freedom (Sen 1999; Dutt 2006, 157).

Regardless of their ultimate aim, almost every newly independent country's government opted for increased economic independence and self-reliance. They expanded the size of the public sector, hiring large fractions of the citizenry into government jobs. They restricted foreign imports and foreign investment as a matter of national policy and directed considerable money into local industry, often nationalizing foreign assets. One of the more extreme examples of this is the Saudi Arabian government's decision in 1973 to buy controlling interest in Aramco, an American-owned oil company that had been operating in the country since the 1930s. Control of oil exports has generated untold wealth and power for the House of Saud. Fidel Castro seized control of American and other foreign assets in Cuba without compensation in the 1960s after his successful Communist revolution. Most governments, such as Mexico, found a middle ground by permitting foreign firms to operate on condition of increased local ownership and management, as well as a requirement to keep more profits in the country.

During the 1980s, a major financial crisis prompted most developing countries to pursue public loans from Western government and the International Monetary Fund. These actors had always been skeptical of the nationalist approaches to development and instead advocated a more classically liberal approach of limited government and increased free trade and investment. They used their new leverage to push governments into a variety of policies, including selling off state-owned firms (privatization), reducing public spending—especially of programs designed to prop up inefficient companies, lowering barriers to foreign goods and capital, and lowering the values of their currencies so they more correctly reflect the strength of the national economy. The result has been a dramatic increase in foreign investment in the developing world, although not necessarily a dramatic increase in economic growth or public welfare. In many cases this is due to financial mismanagement and even corruption. But some advocates of the new approach, such as Joseph Stiglitz, formerly of the World Bank, have even questioned whether it will ever work, even if implemented correctly (Stiglitz 2003).

The experience of India will help us better understand the dilemmas nations face as they strive for independence from a colonial master only to find they must now struggle to define their economic future.

INDIA BEFORE INDEPENDENCE

Indian civilization is more than 8,000 years old and has been conquered and occupied by a dozen foreign nations. As a result, Indian civilization is an amalgam of much of human civilization with a result that is nonetheless unique and distinctive (Bose & Jalal 2004, 16). Every major religion is represented, as are many of the world's races and cultural traditions. Key influences, however, are those of the Aryans in 1500 BC, who introduced Hinduism and the caste system; the Mughals in the 1500s and 1600s, who brought Islam and strong central government; and the British in the 1700s, who brought parliamentary government and the English language, among other things. Taken together, India is uniquely positioned to interface with the modern world economy (Dutt 2006, 13). This does not mean, however, that it has always done so

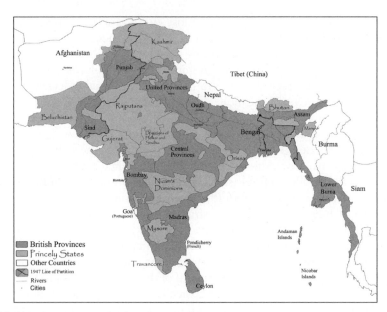

Figure 15.1 India During and After the British Raj
Source: http://upload.wikimedia.org/wikipedia/commons/e/e6/British_india.png

successfully. India has found that interacting with the outside world can be extremely painful and has therefore displayed considerable ambivalence.

Although they established democratic institutions, built a nationwide network of railroads, and introduced modern technology to India, the British, who had arrived in the early 1600s and established control over most of the sub-continent of South Asia by 1800, were a mixed blessing at best. They began as traders and businessmen under the East India Company, one of the world's first multinational corporations. As their control increased, spreading from east to west, the British Crown directed their activities more and more directly until 1858 when India was annexed as a colony after the suppression of an uprising of Indian soldiers against their British commanders (see Figure 15.1). The British took over large tracts of land to cultivate cash crops for export: indigo, cotton, jute, and opium. These cash crops generated few benefits to Indian farmers (Dutt 2006, 129). In addition, the British promoted the importation of English textiles into India under a free trade policy. Because local cottage industry in textiles could not compete with the very efficient mills in Birmingham, many Indians lost their livelihoods (Dutt 2006, 131).

By the 20th century, British colonial officials had spread throughout the sub-continent, governing mostly indirectly through a network of English-speaking Indian civil servants. India had become essential to the British Empire, both politically and economically, as the trade surplus between Britain and India helped compensate for trade deficits with the rest of the world. Likewise, during both World War I and II, the British depended on Indian soldiers to fight (Bose & Jalal 2004, 102).

On the other hand, with these military sacrifices added to an increasingly depressed economy, conditions of local Indians were difficult—except for a brief period during World War I when the British were too distracted to maintain full control over the region. The experience of life without the British presence made their full return in the 1920s deeply resented. Beginning in 1921 under the leadership of Mohandas Gandhi and Jawaharlal Nehru, a non-violent campaign to push them out once and for all took hold (Dutt 2006, 132).

Gandhi's campaign, applying "satyagraha" (soul-force), was dramatic and ambitious. It consisted of unifying the Indian people through active recruitment at the local level into the Congress Party, followed by a series of boycotts, demonstrations, strikes, and other forms of civil disobedience aimed at exposing the violence inherent in the system (Sharma 1999, 67). The task was made more difficult by the lack of unifying cultural identity among Indians and the resistance of British colonial officers. Muslims in particular sought to protect themselves from what they thought would be a future nation dominated by nationalistic Hindus, whereas most of those living in rural areas did not speak Hindi or English and had little concept of what a unified country would do for them. Still others were attached to traditional monarchies that hoped to become fully independent of everyone.

Ultimately, the various efforts to expand Indian influence in the central and local government failed to appease those calling for independence, and so in 1942, the British formally began the process of preparing India for the British departure. The fact that the ultimate removal of colonial rule was generally peaceful (at least so far as Indian–British relations were concerned) meant that existing political and economic institutions could carry over from one regime to the next with a minimum of disruption—something many newly independent countries did not enjoy. Further, it is interesting to note that because the British allowed Indians to participate in governance in a variety of parliamentary bodies, and many of India's elite were trained in the finest British universities, Indians were able to manage and even reform these institutions with little difficulty (Sharma 1999, 71). In addition, Nehru and Gandhi both endeavored to ensure that the new government would be secular, meaning that no one religion would have a position of privilege. The state would not support a particular religion, it would not make religious affiliation a condition of appointment, it would allow members of all faiths to be free to practice and proselyte, and so forth. Conscious efforts were made to provide each religious group a sense of engagement with the new government. That the country has held together for this long is a testament to the effectiveness of these early nation-building initiatives (see Figure 15.2).

This said, Nehru was unable to persuade a large percentage of Muslims to stay in the country, and so at the same time as India was brought into the world, the state of Pakistan, including both modern Pakistan and Bangladesh, was also born. Shortly after independence, thousands died in the border violence between Muslims fleeing India and Hindus fleeing Pakistan. A full-scale war continued for two years. In Kashmir, a Hindu king agreed to join the state of India in spite of his kingdom being inhabited mostly by Muslims. Pakistan has claimed a right to govern the territory, with tensions flaring into full-scale war in 1965 and 1971. Pakistan has supported an ongoing rebellion against Indian forces in Kashmir since 1989.

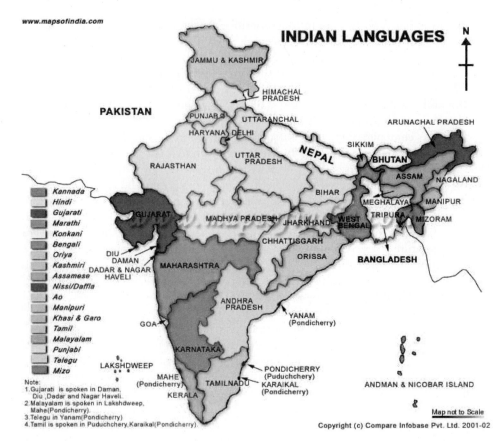

www.mapsofindia.com

Figure 15.2 Indian Linguistic Diversity

INDIA UNDER NEHRU

Gandhi never held political office as a matter of choice. Rather, Nehru was India's first Prime Minister in 1947 at the head of the Congress Party (see Table 15.1). By this point the Party had no governing program or ideology, but was by far the most inclusive and popular and was able to take credit for the country's independence. Nehru's goals were three-fold at the outset: (1) draft a constitution and secure public approval for it; (2) in the process, ensure that all Indians would feel included in a secular state; and (3) dramatically increase economic growth with an eye to reducing poverty. His concern was to create a new state that would enjoy both political and economic stability—the goal of virtually all governments of new states.

The Constitution was approved in 1949, just two years after independence, and established a federal government with considerable powers reserved to the central government, as well as a bicameral legislature and independent judiciary including a constitutional court to resolve disputes over interpretation of the new document.

Table 15.1   Prime Ministers of India

Leader	Period	Party
Jawaharlal Nehru	1947–1964	Congress
Lal Bahadur Shastri	1964–1966	Congress
Indira Gandhi	1966–1977	Congress
Morarji Desai	1977–1979	Janata
Charan Singh	1979–1980	Janata
Indira Gandhi	1980–1984	Congress
Rajiv Gandhi	1984–1989	Congress
V.P. Singh	1989–1990	Janata Dal
Chandra Shekhar	1990–1991	Janata Dal
P.V. Narasimha Rao	1991–1996	Congress
A.B. Vajpayee	1996	BJP
H.D. Deve Gowda	1996–1997	Janata Dal
I.K. Gujral	1997–1998	Janata Dal
A.B. Vajpayee	1998–2004	BJP
Manmohan Singh	2004+	Congress

Full terms are shaded.

English was adopted as the official language of the country on the grounds that doing so did not privilege any of the local or native languages. It was also spoken by the country's educated elite who were leading the country.

The document itself provided important freedoms to the Indian people, including equal rights, freedom from exploitation, freedom of religion, freedom of culture and education, and a ban on "untouchability." This last item meant that members of the lowest caste who were shunned and relegated to the most degrading jobs could have access to all government services and posts and could not be discriminated against by private actors (Dutt 2006, 54). Note that this does not mean that Indians have lived by these norms, particularly in their relations with each other. But it does mean that Nehru's inclusive, secular conception of the state prevailed in 1949 and continues to heavily influence Indian politics today.

On the economic front, Nehru initially hoped to expand India's economy far beyond the British legacy and lift the millions of India's rural workers out of poverty. The effort would be Herculean in scope since poverty was endemic, industry anemic, and agriculture distorted by years of British rule and exploitation. Roughly two fifths of Indians lived below the poverty line, meaning that they were at risk of serious disease or hunger. They were victims of famine repeatedly and had few prospects of a better life. The vast majority of rural dweller had either no land or such small tracts that they could not feed themselves from it. Three fifths of those living in the countryside owned 6% of the arable land in 1947. Their situation was reinforced by lack of education, lack of social status (many were untouchable), lack of access to power, and lack of access to credit (Sharma 1999, 157).

The aim of India's planners in the 1950s was to increase the investment rate, which in turn required increasing savings and improving the investment climate (Bhagwati 1998, 27). The state would fill the gaps. In 1948, the Industrial Policy Resolution passed by the legislature established the legal framework for a mixed economy in which private firms would coexist with state-owned corporations. The state would have exclusive powers over "schedule A" industries, including munitions and armaments, atomic energy, iron and steel, heavy machinery, mining, machine tools, coal, transportation (except automobile and truck), telecommunications, and electrical power. Private firms could support state plans in "schedule B" industries, such as chemicals, drugs, fertilizers, rubber, and so forth. The rest were left to private industry (schedule C) (Dutt 2006, 105). New firms had to be licensed, and there was a limit to the total number of licenses. This continued until 1970.

The resources and supports provided to these major industrial sectors were considerable, although they went to only relatively few firms and factories. The Tata Group was a special beneficiary, enabling the well-established firm to become dominant in the Indian economy. But these resources were not always put to the most efficient use. Expensive, modern equipment was imported at great cost, but was not always used productively, leading to a net loss to the economy. The lack of competition from foreign firms—not to mention would-be local start-ups—made the firms less nimble and innovative. The key problem, however, was the lack of consumers with enough money to buy all the goods. Once the government decided to emphasize self-reliance over international trade, the firms could not sell off their inventories and prices dropped. In addition, they could not expand fast enough to provide jobs for India's ever-growing population. As a result, India's economy grew by a mere 3% a year during the 1950s (Sharma 1999, 80).

Some question whether this pro-growth strategy was wise, given the poverty rate. In response, senior economist Jagdish Bhagwati commented:

> I have often reminded the critics of Indian strategy, who attack it from the perspective of poverty which is juxtaposed against growth, that it is incorrect to think that the Indian planners got it wrong by going for growth rather than attacking poverty: they confuse means with ends. In fact, the phrase 'minimum income' and the aim of providing it to India's poor were very much part of the lexicon and at the heart of our thinking and analysis when I worked in the Indian Planning commission in the early 1960s. (Bhagwati 1998, 25)

Although efforts were made to redistribute land from those with land to those without it, they generally failed. Wealthy elites were able to challenge the efforts in court, and in some cases were able to clarify their property rights, which in turn allowed them to evict families that had squatted on the land for generations. Efforts to place a ceiling on the size of one family's lands were circumvented by clever title manipulations. Even where the state dispossessed certain land owners, they were able to reap windfall profits from the sale to the government, and the lands were often retained by the state rather than redistributed (Sharma 1999, 110–118). Even the development assistance provided to poor villages was largely diverted. So decades later, the same percentage of Indians were still living below the poverty line in 1980 as in 1950 (World Bank 2003, i).

INDIA UNDER INDIRA

Nehru died in 1964 having helped create and establish a new nation, complete with a constitution and a functioning economy and society. Upon his death, his daughter Indira Gandhi (no relation to Mohandas) was shortly acknowledged as the leader of the Congress Party, and in 1966 she assumed the mantle of the Prime Minster's office, a position she would hold for sixteen years.

Her political stature was uncertain until she decided to side with the left-leaning elements in the Party and push a more populist, interventionist economic strategy with the intent of strengthening the central government and increasing India's self-reliance (Hardgrave & Kochanek 1993, 362). Socialism was enshrined in the Constitution, banks were nationalized, as were the coal industry, insurance companies, and many textile firms. Perhaps most significant, the government moved to restrict foreign investment through the Foreign Exchange Regulation Act in the name of India's economic and political autonomy. By the mid-1970s, India had the most heavily regulated economy outside the Soviet bloc (Hardgrave & Kochanek 1993, 363).

The result was substantial political success for Gandhi. She won resounding victories at the polls in 1971 and 1972, aided in part by a dramatic military victory over Pakistan in December 1971.

The other side of her development program was agricultural modernization. The result has been called the "Green Revolution," and it enabled India as a country to become self-sufficient in food. The basic premise that guided the policy was that land tenure and ownership issues would need to wait until after new technologies and techniques were used to increase yields. The state provided low-cost fertilizers, high-yield seeds, and chemical pesticides (including some, like DDT, that had been banned in the West). The results were spectacular. Within twenty years, the yield per planted acre increased by 50%, particularly in rice and wheat production (Sharma 1999, 138–143).

Although the total output of grains has increased dramatically, this has not meant that the poor are eating better. On the contrary, the proportion of Indians who are living below the poverty line and eating less than 2,000 calories a day (40%) was still the same in 1990 as it was in 1950 (Sharma 1999, 29). This stems from the fact that although the technologies of the Green Revolution were made widely available in the 1960s, only a few were able to make use of them. Doing so required access to those in power, an understanding of global markets, technological sophistication, and a minimum amount of land. The result was that a new class of farmers emerged during the Green Revolution: the capitalist. Neither the traditional aristocracy nor the landless tenant farmers or day laborers took advantage of the opportunity—the former by choice and the latter by default. But the more inventive large land owners were able to fully implement the new programs and reaped remarkable rewards, moving from production for the local market to selling for export. These wealthy farmers went on to become a potent political force, providing considerable support for anti-Congress political parties such as Janata.

At the same time, the macroeconomic reforms were causing their own sort of damage. Foreign investors and creditors responded unfavorably to the programs, and domestic corruption increased dramatically as business people sought ways to get through the expanding red tape. Inflation was increasing and shortages were common. Add to this the threat Indira Gandhi posed to state-level governments and elites and it is easier to understand why both the poor and the rich across the country engaged in widespread protests during 1974 (Chadda 2000, 43). The final crisis came when a high-level court ruled that Gandhi had violated election laws in her 1971 campaign and that her victory was therefore invalid. Her choice was to resign or suspend the Constitution (Kulke & Rothermund 1986, 324). She opted for the latter.

From 1975 to 1977, Indira Gandhi governed directly without resort to legislative approval and managed to restore order in the streets. But none of this improved her standing with the people of India. She opted to cancel the required 1976 elections and instead imprisoned a number of her most determined political opponents. She gave more powers to her son Sanjay, who rose to become her most trusted advisor during this period. She also imposed a ban on strikes and other strong economic measures that helped bring prices down. But civil liberties were seriously infringed upon and opposition to her government remained high. She decided to hold elections in 1977, miscalculating that conditions in the country and her standing with the public had improved enough to win. She also waited until a few weeks before the vote to release her political opponents (Kulke & Rothermund 1986, 325). She lost the election anyway and in 1977 the opposition Janata coalition took power—the first non-Congress government since India's independence.

Janata only governed for three years before being replaced by Congress once again. Janata liberalized Indian economic policy, continuing policies that Indira had begun a few years earlier. In the agricultural sector, it removed state controls over agriculture, cutting taxes on grains, cutting tariffs on fertilizer imports, and so forth (Sharma 1999, 203). In the macroeconomic realm, fewer changes were made. Many of the licenses, investment restrictions, and trade protections remained.

The Janata government was inherently fragile, having been an assemblage of regional and state-level parties and elites—mostly a coalition of necessity to block another Gandhi term. Once they came to power, their ideological and personal differences became clear and prevented them from governing for an extended period (Chadda 2000, 45). Even though they tried to establish control over state governments, the effort was in vain, and in 1980 Congress again controlled the national legislature and many state governments. Congress would remain in control even after the death of Indira Gandhi (by assassination) in 1984 and the assumption of her post by Rajiv Gandhi.

INDIAN ECONOMIC LIBERALIZATION

Rajiv Gandhi shared a tendency for centralizing power with his mother, and although the Congress Party leadership was reluctant to turn over the party to him, once they had done so, the transition was final. By 1989, his reputation for arrogance and aloofness, combined with the unequal effects of his economic liberalization policies, resulted in Congress once again being turned out for a time by a Janata coalition. In 1991, while campaigning to return his party to power, he was assassinated.

In 1985, Rajiv played a pivotal role in the seventh five-year plan (1985–1990), which aimed to "improve productivity, absorb modern technology and promote fuller utilization of capacity. To provide larger scope to the private sector . . ." (Dutt 2006, 110). Janata was committed to maintaining some of these reforms.

But it was the arrival in power of P.V. Narasimha Rao in 1991 as the new and relatively untested leader of the Congress Party that things began to change dramatically. He appointed as his Finance Minster the economist Manmohan Singh, who had written the proverbial textbook on liberal economic growth. He left a successful academic career to work his way up the Finance Ministry in India and as a result understood not only the theory but the practice and politics of economic policy. He also had extensive contacts in the international financial community, which would come in handy as India faced one of its worst balance of payments crises during his tenure.

In 1991, a convergence of events gave Singh the opportunity of a lifetime to dramatically alter India's economic policy. The new team of Congress leaders was sincerely committed to liberalization. They had witnessed the unprecedented growth of Asian states such as South Korea and Taiwan and believed that fears of neo-imperialist cooptation—something that drove the policy of self-reliance in the past—were overblown. On the contrary, they had concluded that India's policy of producing domestically what could be more cheaply obtained from abroad had led to increased poverty and high levels of both inefficiency and corruption. They concluded that only by competing on the world stage could the country achieve high levels of economic growth and ultimately be seen as a major power by the rest of the world. They hoped this could be done without sacrificing the goals of poverty alleviation and equitable income distribution (Dutt 2006, 112). Second, India faced a balance of payments crisis that threatened to completely deplete its financial reserves. Its imports so far outstripped its exports that the nation as a whole lacked the resources—especially internationally respected "hard" currency (viz. dollars, yen, marks)—to pay the difference and was forced to go to the International Monetary Fund (IMF) to obtain a loan. Fortunately, India had not waited until the crisis was a catastrophe, and so it was able to negotiate a fairly generous deal (Stiles 1991). Nonetheless, the IMF required India to undertake dramatic economic reforms as a condition of receiving the funds. India agreed, in part because doing so gave Singh and other politicians greater leverage with critics back in India. They could always say that the more painful measures were "forced" upon them by the IMF and that the country had no choice but to carry them out (Bhagwati 1998, 35–36).

As described by two of Singh's strongest supporters:

Manmohan Singh set about the task with the zeal of a reformer. Wide ranging tax reforms were fitted into a scheme of fiscal stabilization, and there was some action on the expenditure front as well. Containment of defence expenditures, cuts in fertilizer subsidies and slow and systematic efforts to reduce the interest burden on the budget were some of the more significant achievements. (Ahluwalia & Little 1998, 4)

With respect to the specifics of the reform measures, F.M. Singh said in August 27, 1991:

> The thrust will be to increase the efficiency and international competitiveness of industrial production and to utilize foreign investment and technology to a much greater degree than in the past, to improve the performance and rationalize the scope of the public sector, and to reform and modernize the financial sector so that it can more efficiently serve the needs of the economy. (Datt & Sundharam 2001, 231, cited in Dutt 2006, 111)

Foreigners were permitted to own up to 51% of industries (later increased to 74%) in certain high-priority areas such as high-tech industries or production that required large-scale investment to be successful. "Sick" firms were allowed to go bankrupt, even if they were state-owned. State-owned firms that were productive were given more freedom (Dutt 2006, 106). Licensing was no longer applied to a number of industries beginning in 1991—automobiles, appliances, leather and skins—and gradually expanded to cover most economic activity.

The results were nothing short of astonishing. The country's gross national product increased at an annual rate of 6.5% during the plan's period, exceeding the ambitious targets set by Singh and Rao (Dutt 2006, 112). Exports expanded by 75% between 1990 and 1995, and imports rose by only half, causing the trade deficit to shrink significantly (Srinivasan 1998, 211), with the result that the country's hard currency reserves rose to a solid $80 billion in 2002 (World Bank 2003, 19). The poverty rate fell from roughly 45% during the 1980s to 36% during the 1990s, and 29% in the year 2000 (World Bank 2003, 1). Prices of most manufactured goods fell dramatically and personal consumption increased (Dutt 2006, 107). What was perhaps most remarkable about the reforms is that, unlike in Russia or Eastern Europe, they were introduced a bit at a time; the pacing was neither too slow nor too fast and were therefore absorbed more readily by the affected groups (Bhagwati 1998).

Employment expanded—especially in the service sector, which grew from roughly $1 billion in 1991 to nearly $10 billion in 2001. The IT sector alone grew from 7.5% of the national economy to 10.5% during the same period (World Bank 2003, 5). Cell phones were introduced for the first time in India in 1994. By 1996, there were one million of them in the hands of Indian consumers. In general, thanks to their many outstanding universities, command of English, cosmopolitanism, and eagerness to prove themselves, Indians are among the most savvy high-tech entrepreneurs and are more than willing to embrace new technology when it is affordable (Friedman 2005).

This is not to say that India's reforms have benefited the whole country or everyone in it. Incomes vary widely across regions and social classes. Foreign investment and technology have primarily been attracted to a few big cities, such as Mumbai (formerly Bombay) and the surrounding area, New Delhi, Chennai (formerly Madras), and Bangalore (Dutt 2006, 107). Predominantly rural states have also benefited less as agricultural growth has not kept pace with the technology sectors. Agricultural output rose only by 1.7% between 1997 and 2001, and its share of the national wealth declined from 28% in 1993 to 23% in 2001 (World Bank 2003, 113). The growth the farming sector has seen can be largely attributed to continued government subsidies for fertilizers and pesticides, neither of which can continue indefinitely. On the contrary, much of India's arable land—perhaps as much as half—has been seriously degraded as a result of the overuse of chemicals and is at risk of losing its productivity (World Bank 2003, 74). Although poverty rates have fallen as measured by the government, 44% of Indians still live on less than one dollar a day, in part because land holding patterns are still remarkably similar to those in 1950 (World Bank 2003, 83).

A key problem stems from India's service provision, especially at the local level. Although state spending increased by roughly 10% a year during the last half of the 1990s, this has not translated into more services being provided to Indians on the whole. Any increases in spending on public services have been swallowed up by rising wages rather than expanded or improved coverage. The problem is profound, as noted by a World Bank study in 2003 that reported a lack of primary health care workers around the country. Not that they haven't been hired or trained. But in most Indian states, absenteeism hovers around 50%, ranging from only 35% in Orissa state to 58% in Bihar (World Bank 2003, 41). In other words, in a typical health clinic with ten nurses slated to be on duty at any given time, patients seeking care will only find five actually present. In part because the government is not focused on achieving particular social outcomes, such problems as high population growth rates continue (see Figure 15.3).

In spite of this, conditions have been improving for many Indian poor as literacy rates have increased, infant mortality declined, and sanitation and access to clean water have improved since the 1980s. But India still lags far behind such countries as China, Brazil, and even Pakistan (World Bank 2003, 132).

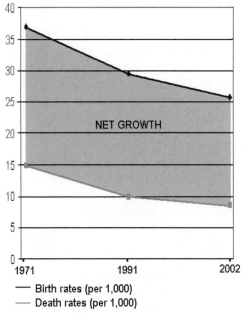

Figure 15.3 Relative changes in Indian birth and death rates, 1971–2002
Source: Dutt 2006, 100.

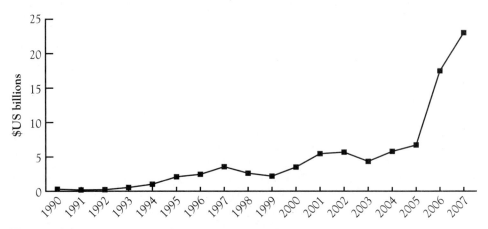

Figure 15.4 Inflows of Foreign Direct Investment to India, 1990–2007
Source: World Bank.

At the macroeconomic level, there are also concerns that India has not yet gone far enough. Its tariff rates are still far higher than comparable Asian nations—twice those of China, for example. And private investment is showing signs of slipping, with rates falling from 10% in the 1980s to 7% in the early 2000s (World Bank 2003, 5).

CONCLUSION: INDIA TODAY

India today is a study in contradictions. The author recently visited a village west of Coimbatore—a bustling city with all sorts of modern amenities, including several universities, a large train station, a busy airport, and a bustling shopping district. The village and its roughly 600 residents are, however, a throwback to feudalism, where a landlord controls almost all the surrounding fields, which sharecropper farmers cultivate. The caste system—including untouchability—is alive and well (an untouchable caste woman explains that although she is not permitted to enter the temple, she doesn't mind standing outside since the gods will pass by her on their way in). The state provides only rudimentary services (water is turned on at a public tap for only a few hours a day). Only about 10% of the village has basic sanitation, and the ditches and roadways serve as the community's toilets. Yet several of the village's residents are working on their college degrees (there are several new technical colleges within five miles), and an internet café just a mile down the road is always busy. And Mumbai, with its high-tech firms and "Bollywood" film studios, are just a cheap two-hour flight away. It is very difficult to generalize about a country where such contradictions exist in a single village.

What is perhaps most remarkable is that India since 1991 has entered a phase of remarkable stability and predictability in its economic policies—this in spite of the fact that power has changed hands a number of times. The BJP, a Hindu nationalist conservative party, came to power in 1998 under A.B. Vajpayee after a period of unstable Janata rule. Although it adopted a more conservative cultural program and fell into the same in-fighting as Janata, the party was able to stay in power until 2004, during which it further reduced the role of the state in the economy. In 2004, under the leadership of Sonia Gandhi, Rajiv's widow, Congress won again. However, as an Italian-born former Catholic, Sonia decided not to assume the Prime Minster's post for fear of public reaction to a foreign leader, but instead offered it to Manmohan Singh, the original architect of the 1991 reforms. Needless to say, he remains committed to liberalization.

Perhaps the most intriguing feature of modern India is not the country's nuclear weapons or endemic poverty, but the phenomenon known as "outsourcing." Outsourcing involves the transfer by a company of activities formerly done in-house to a contractor that can do it more cheaply and efficiently. Although the outsourcing of manufacturing activities has been going on for decades (no doubt the reader is wearing foreign-made clothing with an American label!), outsourcing services is a relatively new phenomenon (See Figure 15.4). It began in India in 1994 when American Express moved much of its day-to-day account processing to Bangalore (Dutt 2006, 146). Since then, roughly half a million jobs have been relocated from Western countries to India in a search for lower costs—especially wages—and similar if not higher performance (Greene 2006, 12). Call centers, help lines, accounting activities, and even legal consulting have flourished as Indians create and staff companies that enjoy easy access to Western customers thanks to high-speed internet connections, VoIP technology, and compatible computer software programs (Friedman 2005). Some estimate that ultimately as many as one sixth of all banking and insurance jobs will move from the West to India (around two million) (Dutt 2006, 147).

Although this would seem to be a tremendous boon for India, the fact is that the sector is still only able to employ a small fraction of the technology graduates coming out of India's many universities, and the trend has almost no effect on the rural poor, except to increase the gap between haves and have-nots. But just because an industry's growth doesn't benefit everyone is no reason to stifle or disparage it. It simply raises another issue for Indians to consider as they struggle to define what independence and development mean for their country.

QUESTIONS TO CONSIDER

1. What lessons can we learn from the Indian case about the proper role of government in national development?

2. Has the definition of development changed over the course of India's history? If so, how has this affected development policy?

3. To what extent has the past impinged upon the present as successive Indian governments' attempts at policy reform?

KEY FIGURES
INDIA RISING

Mohandas (Mahatma) Gandhi Principal activist and organizer for India's non-violent independence movement.

Jawaharlal Nehru First Prime Minister of India.

Indira Gandhi Daughter of Nehru, Prime Minister of India.

Rajiv Gandhi Son of Indira, Prime Minister of India.

P.V. Narasimha Rao Prime Minister of India during the 1990s. He introduced the liberal reforms that are still in place.

A.B. Vajpayee Prime Minister of India as leader of the BJP.

Sonia Gandhi Widow of Rajiv, leader of the Congress Party.

Manmohan Singh Architect of India's economic reforms during the 1990s as Finance Minister. Prime Minister of India beginning in 2004.

CHRONOLOGY
INDIA RISING

1858
India comes under direct rule of the British crown.

1885
Indian National Congress founded to lobby for new relations with Great Britain.

1920–1922
Mohandas Gandhi launches anti-British civil disobedience campaign.

1942–1943
Congress launches "Quit India" movement.

1947
British rule comes to an end as India and Pakistan gain their independence.

1947–1948
Hundreds of thousands die in widespread communal bloodshed after partition.

1948
War with Pakistan over disputed territory of Kashmir.

1964
Death of Prime Minister Jawaharlal Nehru.

1966
Nehru's daughter Indira Gandhi becomes prime minister.

1971

Third war with Pakistan over creation of Bangladesh, formerly East Pakistan.

1975

Indira Gandhi declares state of emergency after being found guilty of electoral malpractice.

1975–1977

Nearly 1,000 political opponents imprisoned.

1977

Indira Gandhi's Congress Party loses general elections.

1980

Indira Gandhi returns to power.

1984

Indira Gandhi is assassinated, after which her son, Rajiv, becomes prime minister.

1989

Falling public support leads to Congress defeat in general election.

1991

Rajiv Gandhi is assassinated by suicide bomber sympathetic to Sri Lanka's Tamil Tigers.

1991

Economic reform program is begun by Prime Minister P.V. Narasimha Rao and Finance Minister Manmohan Singh.

1996

Congress suffers worst ever electoral defeat at the hands of the BJP.

1998

BJP forms coalition government under Prime Minister Atal Behari Vajpayee.

2004

May   Surprise victory for Congress Party in general elections. Manmohan Singh is sworn in as prime minister.

2006

February   India's largest-ever rural jobs scheme is launched, aimed at lifting around 60 million families out of poverty.

2007

May   Government announces its strongest economic growth figures for 20 years—9.4% in the year to March.

REFERENCES

Ahluwalia, Isher Judge and I.M.D. Little, eds. *India's Economic Reforms and Development: Essays for Manmohan Singh* (Delhi: Oxford University Press, 1998).

Ahluwalia, Isher Judge and I.M.D. Little. "Introduction" in Isher Judge Ahluwalia and I.M.D. Little, eds. *India's Economic Reforms and Development: Essays for Manmohan Singh* (Delhi: Oxford University Press, 1998): 1–20.

Baghwati, Jagdish. "The Design of Indian Development" in Isher Judge Ahluwalia and I.M.D. Little, eds. *India's Economic Reforms and Development: Essays for Manmohan Singh* (Delhi: Oxford University Press, 1998): 23–47.

Baxter, Craig, Yogendra K. Malik, Charles H. Kennedy, and Robert C. Oberst. *Government and Politics in South Asia*, 5th ed. (Boulder: Westview Press, 2002).

Bose, Sugata and Ayesha Jalal. *Modern South Asia: History, Culture, Political Economy* (New York: Routledge, 1997).

Callaghy, Thomas. *The State-Society Struggle: Zaire in Comparative Perspective* (New York: Columbia University Press, 1984).

Chadda, Maya. *Building Democracy in South Asia: India, Nepal, Pakistan* (Boulder: Lynne Reinner Publishers, 2000).

Datt, R. and K.P.M. Sundharam. *Indian Economy* (New Delhi: S. Chand & co, 2001).

Dutt, Sagarika. *India in a Globalized World*. (Manchester: Manchester University Press, 2006).

Friedman, Thomas, *The World Is Flat: A Brief History of the Twenty-First Century* (New York: Farrar, Straus and Giroux, 2005).

Greene, William. "Growth in Services Outsourcing to India: Propellant or Drain on the US Economy?" Office of Economics Working Paper, US International Trade Commission, January 2006.

Hardgrave, Robert L., Jr. and Stanley A. Kochanek. *India: Government and Politics in a Developing Nation*, 5th ed. (New York: Harcourt, Brace & Jovanovich, 1993).

Kulke, Hermann and Dietmar Rothermund. *A History of India* (New York: Dorset Press, 1986).

Sen, Amartya Kumar. *Development as Freedom* (New York: Oxford University Press, 1999).

Sharms, Shalendra D. *Development and Democracy in India* (Boulder: Lynne Reinner Publishers, 1999).

Srinivasan, T.N. "India's Export Performance: a comparative analysis," in Isher Judge Ahluwalia and I.M.D. Little, eds., *India's Economic Reforms and Development: Essays for Manmohan Singh* (Delhi: Oxford University Press, 1998): 197–228.

Stiglitz, Joseph. *Globalization and Its Discontents* (New York: W.W. Norton, 2003).

Stiles, Kendall. *Negotiating Debt: The IMF's Lending Process* (Boulder: Westview Press, 1991).

Tendulkar, Suresh D. "Indian Economic Policy Reforms and Poverty: An Assessment," in Isher Judge Ahluwalia and I.M.D. Little, eds., *India's Economic Reforms and Development: Essays for Manmohan Singh* (Delhi: Oxford University Press, 1998): 280–309.

United Nations. "Growth in United Nations membership, 1945-present". Available at http://www.un.org/members/growth.shtml. Accessed on September 10, 2008.

United States Government—Central Intelligence Agency. CIA Factbook: Palau. Available at https://www.cia.gov/library/publications/the-world-factbook/geos/ps.html. Accessed on September 10, 2008.

World Bank. *India: Sustaining Reform, Reducing Poverty*. (New York: Oxford University Press, 2003).

16

■ ■ ■

Globalization:
Sweatshops and
Outsourcing

INTRODUCTION

Globalization

In the summer of 1996, Sydney Schanberg related the following account in a *Life* magazine story:

> As I traveled [in Pakistan], I witnessed conditions more appalling than [the last]—children as young as six bought from their parents for as little as $15, sold and resold like furniture, branded, beaten, blinded as punishment for wanting to go home, rendered speechless by the trauma of their enslavement. One 12-year-old Pakistani, Kramat, who had been making bricks since he was sold by his achingly poor father six years ago, his teeth now rotting, his hair tinged with red streaks, a sign of malnutrition, said morosely: "I cannot go anywhere. I am a prisoner." (Schanberg & Dorigny 1996, 39)

Also in 1996, Charles Kernaghan of the National Labor Committee, a watchdog group that monitors corporate labor practices, testified before a congressional committee that many American apparel companies knowingly used suppliers in developing countries that practiced indentured servitude, used child labor, and repressed and failed to pay their workers (Kernaghan 1999). One such company manufactured the Kathie Lee clothing line, which was sold nationwide by Walmart (in 1995 it earned $9 million for the line's namesake, talk show host Kathie Lee Gifford). When it was revealed that the Kathie Lee clothing company subcontracted to factories that employed girls as young as thirteen to work for thirty-one cents per hour for fifteen-hour shifts, Gifford was indignant. As the reports were confirmed to her through company sources, she pledged to improve working conditions and offered to open up all of the company's factories to independent inspection (Press 1996, 6). Finally, the American public took notice of an international problem that linked Walmart shoppers with children in developing countries more directly than anyone had ever understood before.

Thus began the full-blown campaign known as the anti-sweatshop movement. Many students became activists in the United Students Against Sweatshops campaign and succeeded in persuading their colleges to stop using sweatshops to manufacture their apparel. Beyond understanding that children are being made to work in horrible conditions, however, few really understand the sources of this situation and the implications of the efforts to stop it.

During the 2004 presidential campaign, Senator John Kerry railed against "Benedict Arnold CEOs" who plotted to take jobs away from Americans and hand them to Indians and Chinese on the other side of the world (Mankiw & Swagel 2006, 11). Although this "outsourcing" had similarities to the type of corporate decisions that led to sweatshops, it had a distinctly middle-class dimension. Hundreds of thousands of layoffs had occurred in the technology and service sectors during the 1990s and 2000s, with many of those jobs being picked up by Indian and Chinese firms where highly trained technicians and engineers could do the same work for a small fraction of the cost of their American counterparts (Ghausi 2002; Kasbekar 1999). Some have predicted that by 2015, roughly 3.3 million jobs will be lost (Drezner 2004). Anyone who has spoken to a tech support person from India has experienced this white-collar outsourcing.

In this case, we will explore the phenomenon known as the "global factory" (Rothstein & Blim 1992), which is an important aspect of globalization (Mittelman 2000). Today, the production of manufactured goods as well as services is dispersed throughout the world and thereby links corporate units, warehouses, middlemen, workers, and consumers across many nations as never before in the history of capitalist production. In addition, corporations extend their brand names and products into every corner of the world in the hope of establishing new markets for their goods. Although the notion of an international division of labor is nothing new (the concept dates back to the 18th century), what is different now is the degree to which the linkages are dense and close, leading to a transformation of social structures around the world (Gill 1995, 76). This idea helps to explain everything from sweatshops in Indonesia, to downsizing in Seattle, to merger mania in New York, to the emergence of a global culture and the withering away of differences between states and nations.

The global factory arose from modern innovations such as the assembly line process, faster communication and transportation—particularly the Internet where high-tech jobs are concerned—and the opening of national markets through the World Trade Organization. What is unique about this new structure, however, is how ancient, traditional social arrangements interact with the Western capitalist system. What might have been a tolerable situation, such as the work of young daughters on a family farm, becomes exploitative and dangerous when transferred to a garment factory or a plantation. The contrast between these situations and the lofty language of workers' rights articulated by Western investors, middlemen, and consumers makes the situation all the more bizarre.

It is obvious that everyone on the planet is increasingly linked and that what happens in one spot on the globe almost invariably affects others on the opposite side.

This adage applies not only to global production but also to international finance, travel, and even politics. Just as globalization has brought everyone closer together, so has it created considerable tension. An imbalanced currency in Thailand exposes financial weaknesses in Brazil. A sick cow in England causes panic in Spain. A mosquito carrying a disease that originated in Egypt bites and kills an old man in Chicago.

In the most extreme example, the World Trade Center and Pentagon bombers claimed they were aiming to cripple the United States economically and psychologically as part of their fight against Western culture (however hypocritical or cynical the claim). Ironically, they took advantage of globalization to carry out the attack. The funding came from Osama bin Laden, who inherited considerable sums from his family's international construction businesses. The terrorists were generally successful for their own part and some had spent their formative years studying in Western colleges, thanks to modern travel and liberal immigration policies. That they would select modern aircraft as their weapon, rather than, say, a crude homemade bomb, adds to the paradox. One could argue that globalization contributed to providing both the ends and the means of the attack.

As we consider sweatshops and outsourcing, we will find numerous interpretations of the effects of globalization. Given its controversial character, the material is presented here almost as a debate, with the reader being left to do most of the interpretation.

THE SWEATSHOP PHENOMENON

Sweatshops are nothing new. Workers—especially women—have been required to labor in cramped, dangerous conditions since the Industrial Revolution in the 1750s. In the 18th century, the French government actually created sweatshops as a way of rescuing destitute women and children from a life on the street (DiCaprio 1999, 519). The sweatshop was commonly instituted in the textile industry by garment manufacturers in Great Britain and the United States who felt squeezed by middlemen and suppliers demanding ever-lower manufacturing costs in spite of high clothing costs. The difference was "sweated" out of labor through low wages and a form of indentured servitude, which were easier to arrange with children and women, who were particularly vulnerable in the workplace.

Sweatshops became a target of labor and humanitarian activists by the early 1900s, spurred in the United States by a series of catastrophes (including fires) in which hundreds of workers lost their lives in the early part of the 20th century. Gradually, worker safety regulations, child labor laws, and legislation that protected workers' rights to organize were passed by federal and state agencies. By the 1940s, sweatshops were thought to be a thing of the past.

In the 1980s, however, sweatshop garment factories were discovered in New York and Los Angeles, giving rise to another outcry. Sweatshops and debt bondage (where a loan is provided to cover a working fee that is paid off over a period of time, during which the worker is forced to stay on) were particularly prevalent in the textile industry and in agriculture, where new downward price pressures were becoming particularly intense, in part because of the international market forces mentioned earlier. During 1981–1984, the federal government successfully prosecuted twenty cases of slavery (*U.S. News &*

World Report January 16, 1984, 68). Sweatshops in Queens were hidden behind store-fronts to prevent detection by the 800 federal work inspectors (down from more than 1,000 in the 1970s). During the 1990s, the trend continued, to the point that, by 1993, as many as half of all women's garments were made by factories that violated minimum wage and other labor laws (*U.S. News & World Report* November 22, 1993, 48).

Overseas, an estimated 200 million children under age 14 (the lowest legal working age in any country) work full-time (although for many, working a mere forty hours per week would be a relief). The problem is particularly acute in South Asia. It is estimated that in Pakistan, 11 million children work six days per week for nine or ten hours per day (Schanberg & Dorigny 1996). Their employers are in vio-lation of international labor codes drafted by the International Labour Organization, including the Minimum Age Convention of 1973 and conventions against forced and bonded labor (*UN Chronicle* 1986).

Sweatshops do not operate in a vacuum, to be sure. Although many market to local and regional outlets, others are linked to well-known Western brands. Some of the most famous offenders were Nike, Reebok, the Gap, Mattel, and Disney. The White House quickly became involved in setting up a national task force to investi-gate and regulate the issue. In August 1996, eight apparel firms, a half-dozen human rights organizations, and several trade union representatives were organized into the Apparel Industry Partnership with the aim of establishing a workplace code of conduct (Appelbaum & Dreier 1999, 77). In spite of pressure by the Labor Department and activists, the result was a relatively weak set of standards guaranteeing only that corpo-rations will work to abide by local labor standards in whatever country they operate. Since then, the activists (joined by a few companies) have come up with the Social Accountability 8000 code, a laundry list of basic workplace standards that grant firms SA8000 certification and the right to affix a "no sweat" label to their products. Avon and Toys 'R' Us expressed an early interest in certification (Spar 1998, 9).

A number of U.S. legislators have taken up the sweatshop issue as well. Donald Pease (D-Ohio) and Tom Harkin (D-Iowa) introduced bills to ban the importation of products manufactured by child labor during the George Bush administration (Senser 1994, 13). It was in part because of threats of harsher regulations that the voluntary codes of conduct were agreed upon.

THE OUTSOURCING PHENOMENON

For most Americans, the question of sweatshops is a relatively distant and abstract one, involving poor children in Asia producing goods that cost less in American stores. Only those working in the manufacturing sector, a gradually shrinking population, were directly affected. This changed when the advent of high-speed Internet connections, coupled with better education levels, legal structures, and growth in the Third World made the exportation of certain high-tech activities feasible and profitable. Many activities in today's economy require neither face-to-face interaction nor the shipment of heavy goods. A telephone line is all that is needed to set up a tech support office, telemarketing agency, or even business consulting service. Add an Internet connection and it is possible to transmit a bank's depositor data, manuscripts in need of copy-editing, and so forth. One can even find firms overseas that diagnose x-rays and CAT scans overnight in Bangalore, India—just in time for a 7am surgery in New York (Leonhardt 2006).

The result has been the loss of many jobs held by people with advanced degrees and high salaries. Although analysts disagree on the scale of the phenomenon, a widely cited estimate point to an average of roughly 200,000 white collar jobs lost to Indian and other firms as a result of outsourcing in the United States (Drezner 2004). As we will see below, firms have found that they only recoup a fraction of the wage differential between Third World and American workers, often encounter great diffi-culties in managing information flows, and sometimes encounter such high levels of consumer complaint that they reconsider the arrangement (Weidenbaum 2005). The lack of highly skilled workers is pushing wages up in the technology sector in India, sometimes at the rate of 15% per year (Schieber 2004). Not that outsourcing is entirely problematic. Some have estimated that the U.S. economy gains twelve to fourteen cents for every dollar it spends on overseas outsourcing (Drezner 2004). In some cases, firms have been able to hire more workers in the United States with the savings it gains from outsourcing. Overall, the benefits are diffused across the national economy in the form of cost and price savings (Mankiw 2004).

COMPETING PERSPECTIVES

Globalization is a concept that has generated more "heat" than "light." Although the meaning and significance of globalization are still unclear, people have devel-oped strong and contrary positions on its worth. Much of the debate on globaliza-tion (and, by implications, on sweatshops) focuses on the values, philosophies, and personal backgrounds of the debaters.

Robert Gilpin identifies three principal points of view on globalization: the free market perspective, the populist (or nationalist) perspective, and the communitarian perspective. Free market advocates ascribe to globalization the power to bring in "an era of unprecedented prosperity as more and more nations participate in the global econ-omy, and as financial and technology flows from developed to less developed countries lead to equalization of wealth and development around the world" (Gilpin 2000, 297). Populists, such as Ross Perot and Patrick Buchanan, "blame globalization for most of the social, economic and political ills afflicting the United States and other industrial societies" (Gilpin 2000, 297). They accuse globalization of weakening the indepen-dence and inherent vitality of the economies and societies of the major powers. Com-munitarians, in contrast, criticize globalization on the grounds that it foists "a brutal capitalist tyranny, imperialist exploitation and environmental degradation upon the peoples of the world. They fear a world dominated by huge multinational corporations that will remove all obstacles limiting economic growth . . ." (Gilpin 2000, 298).

We will separate out two facets of the free market perspective: the overall growth of the global economy and the economic development in the Third World per se. Many worry that attacks against sweatshops may ultimately undermine growth in developing countries—which is a very different argument than saying that the search for ever-lower wages will help the global economy as a whole. Also, we will separate out the structural Marxist approach from the humanitarian view under the umbrella of the communitarian perspective. The first focus is on the arguments against sweatshops and outsourcing made by labor unions.

Labor Perspective

Perhaps the most familiar commentary on globalization in the United States comes from the defenders of working-class people. The trade union movement and other populist organizations have built a strong case against free trade and global investment. They point to the tendency since the early 1970s for the wealthy to get an ever-increasing share of national wealth relative to the working class and middle class. For example, in early 2000, the Economic Policy Institute and the Center of Budget and Policy Priorities reported that during the 1990s, the average income of the wealthiest one fifth of Americans grew by 15%, whereas the income of the middle class grew by only 2% and that of the poorest one fifth stayed the same. In 1999, household income for the wealthiest one fifth of the population was ten times greater than the income for the poorest one fifth (AFL-CIO 2000). By 2003, after two years of recession, average household incomes had fallen by $1,500 per year and poverty had increased steadily since 2000 (U.S. Census Bureau 2004). One fifth of all jobs in the United States provide wages that are too low to support a family of four above poverty, let alone provide insurance or other benefits (AFL-CIO 2004).

Even some economists have acknowledged that worker insecurity increased during the 1990s during the era of "downsizing." Aaronson and Sullivan analyzed trends in employment longevity and noted that the number of workers who choose to stay with a company for more than ten years has dropped substantially over the last twenty years. In the mid-1980s, the average man aged 45 to 54 had been at his place of employment thirteen years. By 1995, that figure had dropped to less than ten years (Aaronson & Sullivan 1998, 21). The overall rate of "displacement" (all forms of involuntary change of workplace) doubled between 1988 and 1995 for workers with five years of tenure on the job. This trend in turn contributed to much higher levels of anxiety about job security during the 1990s and may have contributed to relatively low wage increases throughout the decade. As put by Labor Secretary Robert Reich, "Wages are stuck because people are afraid to ask for a raise. They are afraid they may lose their job" (Reich 1997, in Aaronson & Sullivan 1998, 17). This whole problem is attributed to globalization, where wage competition has spread internationally. Once the recession began to spread in 2000 and 2001, pressure to keep low-wage jobs intensified for labor, but so did pressure to find new sources of cheap labor in order to lower prices still further. The result was the dramatic expansion of outsourcing to new types of activity, including service sector jobs such as tech support and customer service, which was increasingly performed by middle-class Indians in Mumbai and Bangalore. Even the most sanguine economists acknowledge that trade causes localized pain in any national economy in the form of job losses (Mankiw 2006).

Wage competition is most intense for low-skilled work, according to this perspective (Freeman 1995). People who work in a company that manufactures textiles or footwear in the United States and receive wages of, say, ten dollars per hour (including benefits) are directly threatened by overseas workers who are willing to do the same job for ten cents per hour and no benefits. Nike CEO Phil Knight, while still a business school student, made plans to build an entire company based on outsourcing manufacturing to low-wage countries, making none of the product in the United States or other countries where the consumers were located. He was not alone. More and more firms relocated relatively low-tech industrial production to developing countries after 1975. During the 1980s, hundreds of U.S. firms moved to Mexico to establish "maquiladoras"—manufacturing plants located just across the border that could use cheap Mexican labor, pay lower corporate taxes, and be freed from American health, safety, and environmental regulations, while retaining easy access to the U.S. market. During the 1990s, even more companies relocated to China for the same reasons, except that strict anti-union laws and an authoritarian government made Chinese workers even more placid than those in Mexico. Anecdotal evidence points to a direct zero-sum relationship between the relocation of these jobs and higher unemployment among unskilled workers in the United States (Korten 1995, 229–237).

For labor unions, then, the sweatshop issue primarily involves protecting American jobs and wages in the face of the globalization of the assembly line. The alliance that has formed between student activists and trade unionists is seen by many as a healthy and even exciting new type of activism. It closes the rift that goes back to the Vietnam War, when trade union leaders condemned anti-war protesters (Appelbaum & Dreier 1999, 77). Others fear that unions may be manipulating students to support protectionist measures that may ultimately hurt overseas workers (Olson 2000).

Global Free Market Perspective

It can be said that liberals (in the 18th-century sense of the term) invented globalization. They have consistently been skeptical of the prominence attached to the state by populists and instead have imagined and designed an international structure that minimizes territorial and political boundaries. Their vision of the world is the Internet, where countries simply do not matter anymore (Hudson 1999). Liberals first thrilled at what they called "interdependence" in the 1970s, and they were among the first to identify "globalization" (Ruggie 1995). Although some liberals fear such a world order might grow out of control, most believe it is government interference in the marketplace of goods and ideas that has brought misery to humanity.

Bryan and Ferrell wrote that when the spread of multinational corporate investment and the lowering of trade and investment barriers through the World Trade Organization open up global markets, the potential exists for creative and entrepreneurial activity to flourish worldwide (Bryan & Ferrell 1996). Economists point to the dramatic increase in average incomes worldwide as a direct result of fewer economic barriers, lower transportation costs, and new technologies. Micklethwait and Wooldridge point out that globalization simply has not contributed to a dramatic rise in overall incomes but has done so by creating new jobs, contrary to the forecasts of populists. The North American Free Trade Agreement, which populists expected to eliminate U.S. jobs, has instead generated 14 million new job openings since 1994 (Micklethwait & Wooldridge 2000, 109). Their biggest fear is that trade unions may hijack globalization for narrow, short-sighted reasons: "[T]he goal of eradicating child labor is a noble one, but when it has been linked to trade, it has nearly always been for protectionist reasons and has often had disastrous consequences for those it has tried to help" (Micklethwait & Wooldridge 2000, 113). If wages seem to decline, the cause is primarily a mismanaged economic transition from local to global production (Richardson 1995).

Some analysts stress that wage differentials are not as serious a concern as labor defenders claim because they are directly related to productivity. As Golub points out, if one takes into account the cost of output per worker-hour, then wages are virtually the same worldwide (Golub 1999, 22). In the Philippines, for example, although wages are roughly one tenth the wages of American workers, worker productivity is even less, with the result that work done in the Philippines is actually 8% more expensive than work done in the United States. Similar figures apply to Malaysia and India (although the same is not true in Mexico and South Korea, where relative productivity outpaces relative wages; Golub 1999, 23). When the relative purchasing power of these low wages is factored in, the developing country, workers are actually better off than their Western counterparts because they can buy far more per unit of output (i.e., a Bangladeshi who is paid fifty cents to produce one shirt each hour can buy more local goods at the end of a ten-hour day with five dollars than can her counterpart in New York who is paid five dollars to produce ten shirts per hour and thereby earns fifty dollars).

Sweatshops, though deplored in principle, are accepted as part of the process of globalization, as is outsourcing. As put by Greg Mankiw, one-time chairman of George Bush's Council of Economic Advisors, "When we talk about outsourcing, outsourcing is just a new way of going international trade. . . . Outsourcing is the latest manifestation of the gains from trade that economists have talked about at least since Adam Smith" (Mankiw 2006, 8). Corporations have pointed out that consumers benefit tremendously when producers take advantage of wage differentials, and this pressure from consumers forces producers to seek ever-lower wage rates. In the 1980s, Levi Strauss tried to keep its production in the United States and maintain high relative wage rates in developing country factories, but it could not sustain those practices. It had to close fifty-eight U.S. plants and lay off more than 10,000 workers to stay competitive (Korten 1995, 233). As put by Reebok's Indonesia representative: "Cutting costs is part of our business" (Brecher & Costello 1994, 20). "Costs of running a factory are about 16 percent more if you comply with the new labor laws" in China, according to one exporter. Because customers don't seem to care much about the treatment of workers, compliance guarantees you will lose sales (*South China Morning Post* October 27, 2003, 2). All these problems are blamed on pressures to get prices ever lower in a Walmart-dominated retail environment. In the high-tech sphere, products must now hit the market quickly as they will likely be eclipsed by some new innovation within eight months (Ghausi 2002).

Developmental Perspective

Still other liberals question whether Western criticism of sweatshops misses the point that those in sweatshops are, after all, working. In countries where unemployment is higher than 50% and low-paying farm labor accounts for most of the jobs, many see employment in factories as the way out of perpetual poverty. Consider, for example, that in 1990 a typical Chinese farmer earned $1,130 per year, whereas an unskilled Chinese factory worker made roughly $2,000 and a skilled factory worker earned $5,800. During a recent visit to Bangladesh, the author met dozens of adult men with children to raise who earned only enough for one or two servings of rice per day (less than ten cents) working as hired farm help in depressed villages. In comparison, the young women who eagerly went to the garment factory each morning in the city and earned two dollars per day were in the upper middle class.

From this point of view, the anti-sweatshop campaign and the anti-outsourcing backlash are seen with skepticism in Third World capitals. Molly Ivins has argued that they actually made development more difficult for many of these countries, although it may help those who are already working in the factories (Ivins & Smith 1999). Particularly when linked to trade unions, the sweatshop movement seems to be aimed at curtailing exports of garments and other basic manufactured goods, which could lead to severe depression in many countries. Already most developing countries are working hard to improve the climate for international business, and they are finding it difficult to keep the factories that have relocated there. International capital always has other opportunities to reduce wages by relocating to another developing country (in Bangladesh, wages are kept low to prevent companies from moving to China, for example). Even worse, the alternative to sweatshop jobs going to developing countries is the possibility that the manufacturing process will simply be mechanized, thereby eliminating the jobs entirely (Kristof 2002). The flow of contracts to Indian firms will likely create four million new well-paying jobs and contribute directly to the lifting of the nation out of poverty in a generation (Mehta 2005).

Structural Marxist Perspective

In response to the developmental perspective, numerous scholars have developed a structural analysis of the world economy based loosely on the work of Marx, Lenin, Fernand Braudel, and Immanuel Wallerstein. This structural Marxist perspective argues that the development that occurs as a result of globalization is not the sort of development any country should want. Rather, it is better understood as taking a subordinate place in the global economy, where countries must surrender control over their national destinies to provide the raw material of capitalist production. As early as the 1700s, economists began to note that capitalist production tended to concentrate relatively high-tech activities in advanced, industrialized nations, whereas low-tech activities were sloughed off to remote, inhospitable regions (Mittelman 2000, 54). Later, Lenin pointed out that not only was high-tech manufacturing concentrated in the powerful countries, but so were banking and corporate decision making, which led to a global structure that transcended traditional imperialism in search of both raw materials and labor and new consumer markets. Gradually, more and more regions were brought into this "world economy," such that national boundaries became increasingly insignificant in the pursuit of efficiency and profit (Wallerstein 1991; Korten 1995, 239). As put by Ernst Mandel, "Capital by its very nature tolerates no geographical limit to its expansion" (Mandel 1975, 310).

It was on these Marxist ideas that the concepts of the global factory and the global assembly line were based in more recent years (Gereffi 1994).

In this context, sweatshops are viewed as merely part of the inexorable expansion of capital production on a global scale. A product moves in steps from raw material to finished good, going from factory to factory in a "commodity chain" in which profits gradually increase as one gets closer to the point of final sale. Sweatshops are driven to a large extent by pressures from brand-name companies seeking lower production costs. They put pressure directly on international traders and overseas buyers and indirectly on the factories themselves. As put by Gereffi:

> The main job of the core company in buyer-driven commodity chains is to manage these production and trade networks and make sure all the pieces of the business come together as an integrated whole. Profits in buyer-driven chains thus derive not from scale economies and technological advances as in producer-driven chains, but rather from unique combinations of high-value research, design, sales, marketing, and financial services that allow the buyers and branded merchandisers to act as strategic brokers. . . . (Gereffi 1994, 99)

Factory managers constantly complain of being required to reduce costs so as to maintain contracts with foreign companies. They are in an extremely vulnerable position because the company can change suppliers with the stroke of a pen.

In spite of these relatively new mechanisms of exploitation, structural Marxists see very little new in the contemporary debate about globalization (Germain 2000). Although this might give some hope that we need not fear that some horrific new problem has emerged, it also offers a pessimistic prediction that there is no reason to expect anything to change much, no matter how many well-intentioned campaigns are mounted. Although anti-slavery campaigns in the 1800s ended the more blatant forms of slavery in the West, these activities simply shifted to the Third World. And although it may be possible to end formal slavery, child labor, and indentured servitude in time, there is no reason, based on this perspective, to expect that conditions will markedly improve for the workers of the world. By implication, the only solution is global revolution.

Humanitarian Perspective

Those who are squeamish about a violent overthrow of the global capitalist system focus instead on piecemeal reform and attempts to improve the living conditions of those most injured by global capitalism. The effort at humanitarian reform is as old as capitalism itself. Although it does not repudiate such age-old institutions as wage labor, private ownership of land, the assembly line, or outsourcing, it strives to create minimum standards of human treatment. National labor standards, as mentioned earlier, have been set up since the turn of the 20th century, although their enforcement has often been spotty.

In the post–World War II era, the International Labour Organization became a forum for countries to institute new standards of conduct in their treatment of wage labor. Slavery, indentured servitude, child labor, and other practices were banned, and countries were urged to establish minimum worker safety standards, reasonable wages, vacation and overtime practices, and so forth. These treaties were endorsed by almost every country, although compliance was not consistent. Although most developed countries already complied with these rules when they were established, few developing countries did. Even socialist countries (which were touted as a "worker's paradise") did not allow such basic worker freedoms as the right of workers to independently organize and strike.

When the sweatshop issue emerged in the 1980s and exploded in the 1990s, the treatment of most workers violated principles enshrined in treaties that not only had been accepted as a worthwhile aspiration but had also been explicitly accepted by the countries in question and had become the law of the land. Thus the sweatshop campaign can be seen as an effort to enforce international standards rather than set new ones. It may be unrealistic to expect that the movement can accomplish much more than this.

In this respect, the sweatshop campaign is having a measurable impact. Global corporations such as Nike and Reebok are often little more than a brand name, as we have seen. As a result, their image and reputation are all-important. In addition to joining the Apparel Industry Partnership and endorsing the Social Accountability 8000 code of conduct, many textile firms have hired independent auditors to carry out on-site inspections of garment factories overseas. Some have allowed human rights activists to tour factories, although they have generally done so under close corporate supervision (UNITE! 2000). Some apparel manufacturers have even engaged in political protests of their own, as evidenced by the nearly industry-wide boycott of Myanmar's military dictatorship. Some clothing businesses are finding it easier to take principled positions now that the entire industry is under scrutiny (Spar 1998). Still others are fighting back, arguing that poor countries are better off with sweatshops than nothing (Sowell 2002). They criticize the "self-righteous" campaigners who protest WTO meetings (as they did again in Cancun in 2002) for making life more difficult for the poor.

CONCLUSION: GLOBALIZATION

How do these issues relate to the broader question of globalization? It is clear that the anti-sweatshop campaign and outsourcing skepticism have brought to the attention of Western audiences the links between disparate social groups across the planet. It is hard not to think of Pakistani child workers when purchasing a soccer ball in Memphis, or of young Malaysian factory workers when buying a pair of pants in London. But recognizing the links and even understanding them is not the same as understanding whether they are good or bad or how to change them. Globalization can be seen as merely a fact of human existence. It may be up to us to determine what values are jeopardized by it.

QUESTIONS TO CONSIDER

1. How strong is the corporate claim that sweatshops and the job losses from outsourcing are a necessary evil brought about by consumer demand and a tough competitive environment? What contrary evidence can be brought to bear?

2. To what extent are sweatshops and outsourcing merely the extension of the global spread of laissez-faire capitalism? Is it possible to solve the problem in one factory or corporation without changing the global system?

3. What are the dangers of the anti-sweatshop campaign and outsourcing skepticism? What are the alternatives for achieving the same objective of improving living conditions for workers in developing countries?

REFERENCES

Aaronson, Daniel, and Daniel Sullivan. "The Decline of Job Security in the 1990s: Displacement, Anxiety, and Their Effect on Wage Growth." *Economic Perspectives* 22 #1 (1998): 17–43.

AFL-CIO. "Income Equality Nosedives: The Rich vs. Everyone Else." Available at: www.aflcio.org/articles/gap/index.html. Accessed on January 18, 2000.

Appelbaum, Richard, and Peter Dreier. "The Campus Anti-Sweatshop Movement." *The American Prospect* (September 1999): 71–83.

Brecher, Jeremy, and Tim Costello. *Global Village or Global Pillage: Economic Reconstruction from the Bottom Up* (Boston: South End Press, 1994).

Bryan, Lowell, and Diana Ferrell. *Market Unbound: Unleashing Global Capitalism* (New York: John Wiley & Sons, 1996).

DiCaprio, Lisa. "Women Workers, State-Sponsored Work, and the Right to Subsistence During the French Revolution." *Journal of Modern History* 71 #3 (September 1999): 519–545.

Drezner, Daniel. "The Outsourcing Bogeyman." *Foreign Affairs* (May/June 2004): 22–34

Freeman, Richard. "Are Your Wages Set in Beijing?" *Journal of Economic Perspectives* 9 #3 (Summer 1995): 15–32.

Gereffi, Gary. "The Organization of Buyer-Driven Chains: How U.S. Retailers Shape Overseas Production Networks." In Gary Gereffi and Miguel Korzeniewicz, eds., *Commodity Chains and Global Capitalism* (Westport, CT: Greenwood Press, 1994).

Germain, Randall, ed. *Globalization and Its Critics: Perspectives from Political Economy* (New York: St. Martin's Press, 2000).

Ghausi, Nadjya. "Trends in Outsourced Manufacturing—Reduced Risk and Maintaining Flexibility when Moving to an Outsourced Model." *Assembly Automation* 22 #1 (2002): 21–26.

Gill, Stephen. "Theorizing the Interregnum: The Double Movement and Global Politics in the 1990s." In Bjorn Hettne, ed., *International Political Economy: Understanding Global Disorder* (Halifax, NS, Canada: Fernwood Publishing, 1995): 65–99.

Gilpin, Robert. *The Challenge of Global Capitalism: The World Economy in the 21st Century* (Princeton, NJ: Princeton University Press, 2000).

Golub, Stephen. *Labor Costs and International Trade* (Washington, DC: AEI Press, 1999).

Hudson, Yaeger, ed. *Globalism and the Obsolescence of the State* (Lewiston, NY: Edwin Mellon Press, 1999).

Ivins, Molly, and Fred Smith. "Opposing Views on Sweatshops." *Insight on the News* 15 #44 (November 29, 1999): 40–47.

Kasbekar, Vijay. "I.T. Outsourcing: India Leads." *Asian Review of Business and Technology* October 1, 1999, 1.

Kernaghan, Charles. "Sweatshop Blues: Companies Love Misery." *Dollars & Sense* 222 (March–April 1999): 18–22.

Korten, David. *When Corporations Rule the World* (New York: Kumarian Press, 1995).

Kristof, Nicholas, "Let Them Sweat." *New York Times* June 25, 2002.

Leonhardt, David. "Political Clout in the Age of Outsourcing." *New York Times* April 19, 2006.

Mandel, Ernst. *Late Capitalism* (London: NLB, 1975).

Mankiw, N. Gregory. "Outsourcing Redux." Unpublished op. ed. Available at www.gregmankiw.blogspot.com/2006/05/outsourcing-redux.html. Accessed on May 7, 2006.

Mankiw, N. Gregory, and Phillip Swagel. "The Politics and Economics of Offshore Outsourcing." Unpublished manuscript. March 2004.

Mehta, Neil Singhvi. "Future of Outsourcing: India Is Seeing Giant Strides in Practices." *Advocate* February 22, 2005, 19.

Micklethwait, John, and Adrian Wooldridge. *A Future Perfect: The Essentials of Globalization* (New York: Crown Business, 2000).

Mittelman, James. *The Globalization Syndrome: Transformation and Resistance* (Princeton, NJ: Princeton University Press, 2000).

Olson, Walter. "Look for the Kiwi Label." *Reason* 32 #3 (July 2000): 52–57.

Press, Eyal. "Kathie Lee's Slip." *The Nation* 262 #24 (July 17, 1996): 6–8.

Reich, Robert. *Locked in the Cabinet* (New York: Alfred Knopf, 1997).

Richardson, J. David. "Income Inequality and Trade: How to Think, What to Conclude." *Journal of Economic Perspectives* 9 #3 (Summer 1995): 33–55.

Rothstein, Frances Abrahamer, and Michael Blim, eds. *Anthropology and the Global Factory: Studies of the New Industrialization in the Late Twentieth Century* (New York: Bergin & Garvey, 1992).

Ruggie, John Gerard. "At Home Abroad, Abroad at Home: International Liberalization and Domestic Stability in the New World Economy." *Millennium* 24 #3 (1995): 3–27.

Schanberg, Sydney, and Marie Dorigny. "Six Cents an Hour." *Life* 19 #7 (June 1996): 38–47.

Scheiber, Noam. "As a Center for Outsourcing, India Could Be Losing Its Edge." *New York Times* May 9, 2004, C3.

Senser, Robert. "Danger! Children at Work." *Commonweal* 121 #14 (August 19, 1994): 12–15.

South China Morning Post October 27, 2003, 2.

Sowell, Thomas. "Truth About Third World 'Exploitation'." *Human Events* 58 #36 (September 2002): 21.

Spar, Debora. "The Spotlight on the Bottom Line: How Multinationals Export Human Rights." *Foreign Affairs* 77 #2 (March–April 1998): 7–13.

UN Chronicle. "50 to 200 Million Children Under 15 Are in World's Work Force, ILO Says." *UN Chronicle* 23 (November 1986): 116.

UNITE! "Sweatshops Behind the Swoosh," April 25, 2000 report. Available at www.uniteunion.org/pressbox/nike-report.html.

U.S. Census Bureau, "Income, Poverty, and Health Insurance coverage in the United States: 2003," by Carmen DeNavas-Walt, Bernadette D. Proctor and Robert J. Mills (Washington, D.C.: General Printing Office, 2004).

U. S. News & World Report January 16, 1984, 68.

U. S. News & World Report November 22, 1993, 48.

Wallerstein, Immanuel. *Geopolitics and Geoculture: Essays on the Changing World-System* (New York: Cambridge, 1991).

Weidenbaum, Murray. "Outsourcing: Pros and Cons." *Business Horizons* (July/August 2005): 311.

17

...

Economic Regionalism: Europe Uniting

INTRODUCTION

A global order based on respect for law and tolerance of differences seems beyond our grasp, but many hope that spheres of peace can be established at the regional level. A region is whatever its members choose; it typically involves contiguous territory, common culture, and interdependent economies and societies. Although regional organizations have tended to fall flat (the Organization of African Unity is a case in point), there are indications that in Europe and perhaps elsewhere, regionalism is healthy and offers a real opportunity for improving people's living conditions. Economic integration is one type of regionalism, involving reduced obstacles to trade, investment, and migration. Political integration leads to some form of federal or unitary state. The United States represents political integration well, and the European Union illustrates what is meant by economic integration.

Regional economic organizations can generally be categorized in terms of their objectives and methods. The least painful or controversial steps typically involve standardization of industrial or technical designs, such as agreeing on the gauge of railroads. This makes it somewhat easier to market goods beyond a company's local customer base. More difficult and painful are efforts to increase regional trade directly through mutual reductions in tariffs and quotas (a free trade zone). These efforts are often combined with the establishment of a common regional tariff to be placed on imports from outside the region (customs union). The tariff serves as an inducement to help soften the blow of opening domestic markets to goods from other regional players—at least goods from outside the region will still be more expensive for a time. The next most difficult level of integration involves removal of non-tariff barriers that interfere with the flow of goods and services. For example, one country in the region may have an especially high corporate tax rate, which means products from that state are necessarily more expensive. Harmonization involves making as many government policies as possible uniform across the region so that no business or consumer is penalized. Tax rates, banking interest rates, retirement benefits, teaching certification requirements, and so forth must be made as uniform as possible.

The most difficult—and therefore rare—is outright federalization of a region, whereby the entire area is brought under a single political authority. Although some allowances may be made for local autonomy, major national policies would fall under a single jurisdiction. This would include economic, social, legal, and security policies traditionally managed at the local level. Federalization has taken place in only a few instances, such as the formation of the United States in the 1780s and of Germany in the 1870s, although some believe Europe is now pointed in this direction.

Plans for European unity began out of disgust with war and carnage—not World War II, but the Thirty Years' War. After the end of the devastating war in 1648, French royal advisor de Sully developed a "Grand Design" for European unity based on religious tolerance. Though stillborn, de Sully's proposal was the first of a string of concepts calling for European unity. After the nearly successful attempt of Louis XIV to secure French domination over Europe in the early 1700s, William Penn and the Quakers in Britain, along with the Abbe de Saint-Pierre in France, developed complex and elaborate schemes for a form of collective security for Europe (Heater 1992, 54, 58). During the nineteenth century, while idealists continued to work on a global organization, which culminated in the League of Nations, the great powers experimented for a time with the Concert of Europe—an informal arrangement among the dominant European powers to keep minor conflicts in check through collaborative intervention.

The period of planning and scheming for Europe demonstrated a tension between the goals of preserving sovereignty and creating genuine supranational institutions that could coordinate state action. To a large extent, this tension has yet to be resolved.

THE EMERGENCE OF THE COMMON MARKET: 1945–1957

The Common Market originated from both external and internal forces. The post–World War II environment was utter devastation and called for urgent and dramatic steps. In addition, the growing and clear threat of Soviet Communist encroachment on Western European democracy prompted an acceleration of reconstruction and stabilization efforts. Administrative efficiency and capital utilization required a regional rather than a national approach. The result was American enthusiasm for the Marshall Plan and the regional cooperation it entailed.

In Europe, the disastrous experience with fascism and German expansionism led many to adopt a "never again" attitude. Plans were developed to solidify democratic regimes, punish fascists, and channel German war-making capacity into a broader European network. Germans sought a means to legitimize their new democratic state and put Nazism behind them. These factors, combined with the strength of Christian Democratic parties across Europe, along with their pro-Europe policies, paved the way for Jean Monnet and Paul-Henri Spaak to have great influence.

In 1948, European leaders organized a conference at the Hague, in the Netherlands, where the European Movement was founded to act as a sort of continental lobbying group to press for more integration and unity. Winston Churchill promoted European unity in a series of speeches in the late 1940s, and he served as president of the Hague conference. Here again, a conflict emerged between the "federalists"—mainly the French and Germans—who envisioned a powerful European federal government, and the "unionists," who sought merely ad hoc agreements to deal with particular problems piecemeal (Gerbet 1987, 39).

A series of events in 1948–1950 brought the conflict between federalist and unionist conceptions of Europe to a head. Europe suffered an extreme economic and social crisis after the disastrous harvest of 1948. Soviet expansion in Eastern Europe seemed relentless and foreboding. The rise of Communist parties in France, Italy, and other Western European states seemed to mirror the threat to the East. The United States thus had reason to intervene in dramatic fashion to rescue Europe from what appeared an inevitable World War III, fought this time over German industry. Jean Monnet wrote of his feelings at the time:

> [I recall] the anxiety that weighed on Europe five years after the war: the fear that if we did nothing we should soon face war again. Germany would not be its instigator this time, but its prize. So Germany must cease to be a potential prize, and instead become a link. At that moment, only France could take the initiative. What could be done to link France and Germany . . . ? (Monnet 1979, 289)

The Marshall Plan (formally known as the European Recovery Program) was an essential stopgap measure for the United States to provide necessary capital and materials for European reconstruction; the Bretton Woods institutions (World Bank and International Monetary Fund [IMF]) had proved inadequate to the task. In conjunction with the Marshall Plan, the Organization for European Economic Cooperation (OEEC) was quickly founded in 1948 to give Europeans a role in distributing the resources that flowed from the United States. The OEEC did not have authority to force nations to coordinate their plans, but "thanks to the part played by the Secretariat, the member states became used to cooperating and comparing their economic policies" (Gerbet 1987, 36).

The OEEC was not the first regional organization devoted to economic coordination in Europe. In fact, the Benelux countries (Belgium, the Netherlands, and Luxembourg) had already gone far to create a common market and customs union among themselves. Beginning in 1922, Belgium and Luxembourg pledged to eliminate tariff barriers with each other (thus creating a common market) and to coordinate their trade policies toward the rest of the world (thus creating a customs union). They also promoted the free movement of labor and capital, thereby increasing labor migration and foreign investment. When the Netherlands joined in 1947, the group became a genuinely multilateral arrangement, complete with regional institutional structures and governing authority. This Benelux arrangement served as a model for what was later to become the European Economic Community (Hurwitz 1987, 11).

The economic cooperation forged in the 1940s coincided with efforts at military and political cooperation, although the two efforts soon diverged. Northern Europe organized a peacetime military alliance shortly after the war, culminating in the Brussels Treaty Organization in 1948, to which the United States was almost immediately invited. The North Atlantic Treaty Organization (NATO), founded in 1949, pledged mutual assistance in the event of an attack against any member and grew to include Germany, Italy, and European countries both to the north and to the south. NATO also provided significant American military support for Europe, including hundreds of thousands of U.S. troops and substantial stockpiles of nuclear weapons. Efforts to forge a truly European military pact failed in the 1950s, which may have led to greater attention to the economic sphere.

Economics and politics were never separate as far as European integration was concerned. An important illustration is the emergence of the European Coal and Steel Community (ECSC). By 1950, German industry was on the road to rapid recovery. In fact, Germany was consuming so much coal and coke from the Ruhr valley near the Rhine that France and other Europeans were experiencing shortages. Jean Monnet, the leader of France's industrial plan, saw this crisis as an opportunity to introduce the plans for integration he had developed as early as 1941. As he saw it, integrating German coal and French iron ore production would solve not only France's immediate shortage problem, but a much wider problem as well:

> All successive attempts to keep Germany in check, mainly at French instigation, had come to nothing, because they had been based on the rights of conquest and temporary superiority—notions from the past which happily were no longer taken for granted. But if the problem of sovereignty were approached with no desire to dominate or take revenge—if on the contrary the victors and the vanquished agreed to exercise joint sovereignty over part of their joint resources—then, a solid link would be forged between them, the way would be wide open for further collective action, and a great example would be given to the other nations of Europe. (Monnet 1979, 293)

Thus the ECSC was a way both to keep Germany's military capacity in check and to support French economic goals. As put by Robert Schuman, the French premier who formally proposed Monnet's concept, "The community of production, which will in this manner be created, will clearly show that any war between France and Germany becomes not only unthinkable but in actual fact impossible" (Hurwitz 1987, 20).

The ECSC was created in 1951 with the signing of the Treaty of Paris on April 18 by France, Germany, Italy, and the Benelux countries. It provided for a High Authority, an international panel with powers to organize production levels, map out distribution, and promote equity across the member states. Article 9 of the treaty specified that "in the performance of these duties, [the High Authority] shall neither seek nor take instructions from any Government or any body. . . . Each member state undertakes to respect this supranational character" (Heater 1992, 162). The federalists carried the day insofar as the ECSC is concerned. The treaty also provided for a parliament made up of delegations from member countries based on population, a council with advisory powers where each state had one vote, and a court to review actions of states relative to the High Authority's decisions.

The ECSC quickly demonstrated its effectiveness and provided the impetus for the creation of yet more regional institutions. Monnet was instrumental in establishing

Euratom—a European organization to facilitate cooperative development of nuclear technology.

Efforts by France and Great Britain to exert influence overseas in the mid-1950s failed. Both countries then sought refuge in a regional home where their influence could be strong. The British emphasized their Atlantic ties to the United States, whereas the French looked to Europe.

The Soviet intervention in Hungary convinced Europeans that the time had come to create what unity they could, a decision given form at a conference in Messina, Italy, in 1955 (Kusters 1987, 81). Although the French government fell in solidly behind the integration plans (partly out of fear that other Europeans would proceed without France), the British distanced themselves from what they considered a continental question.

Paul-Henri Spaak was the principal author of the 1957 Treaty of Rome, the formal agreement that created the Common Market (officially called the European Economic Community—EEC). He had served as the first head of the OEEC in 1948 and head of the Council of Europe in 1949 and was known as "Mr. Europe" (Heater 1992, 165). Spaak supported the ECSC but was eager for greater integration. He became chair of the team charged at the 1955 Messina conference with drafting a treaty for a customs union and common market. The EEC was constituted with the objective of promoting

> throughout the Community a harmonious development of economic activities, a continuous and balanced expansion, an increased stability, an accelerated raising of the standard of living and closer relations between its member states (Article 2).

Countries joined the EEC for a variety of reasons. Germany saw membership as a vehicle for international acceptance, a way to regain its sovereignty—an ironic goal, because other Europeans saw it as a way to lose theirs! (Urwin & Paterson 1990, 188). France hoped to use the EEC to dominate European politics diplomatically and to placate the strong political pressure of French farmers. Italy hoped the EEC could provide economic and diplomatic rehabilitation as well as development funding for its southern half. The Benelux countries were eager to lower continental trade barriers, which they felt discriminated against their own, more efficient industries. As time went on, these different motivations created interesting and often complex political alliances and antagonisms.

THE EEC AT WORK: 1957–1973

The first task of the EEC was to promote free trade within the community. This goal was to be achieved through the creation of a common market in which barriers to trade are dropped, a customs union through which each country's trade with other nations is uniform, free movement of labor and capital, and harmonization of social policy. The formation of a common market took less time than expected (Williams 1991, 51). As early as 1968, all internal tariffs on industrial products were eliminated—almost two years ahead of schedule (Wistrich 1990, 33).

The ease with which the common market was created was due largely to non-diplomatic factors. The 1960s saw extraordinary growth in Europe. Average annual growth rates for the EEC-Six ranged from 4.4% for West Germany to 5.7% for France. It was relatively easy for the EEC-Six to lower trade barriers without fear of unemployment rising from more intense competition. If a firm was not competitive in one sector, another opportunity soon presented itself. Not only did the economies of the EEC-Six grow during this period, but trade was also diverted from non-EEC to intra-EEC partners. In 1958, EEC countries imported only 29% of all goods from the other EEC-Six; by 1972, that figure had risen to 52% (Williams 1991, 33).

The other principal activity of the EEC during the 1960s was to establish the Common Agricultural Program (CAP). Considered a crucial element of the Treaty of Rome (Article 38) by France, the CAP provided for a common market and customs union in all foodstuffs, price guarantees, and structural reforms. In addition, the CAP aimed at ensuring "a fair standard of living for the agricultural community." Although such an approach seems excessive by today's standards, Marsh points out that in the 1950s, Europe was a net food importer and had recently imposed food rationing. Farmers were able to argue that the only way to ensure that Europe would have sufficient food was by producing it at home. Success in agriculture was considered essential for national security (Marsh 1989, 148).

The key element in this equation was price guarantees, which placated the highly politicized and powerful farm lobbies in France, Italy, and Germany. Although several options existed, the EEC-Six decided in 1962 to proceed with a price support mechanism involving the purchase by the community of surplus production to be stored until it could be sold without lowering the price. To appease German farmers, the price levels agreed upon were the high, heavily subsidized German prices. This decision made the CAP far and away the most significant EEC expense. The Council of Ministers had hoped at the time that the high price supports would be temporary, that the common market would force inefficient producers out of business. This was not the case. Instead, the price supports became a permanent element in the EEC (Taylor 1983, 237). As pointed out by Lodge, the CAP is neither capitalist nor effective, but it has become such a vital ingredient in the political and even physical landscape of Europe that any attempt at reform risks consequences that could easily outweigh the benefits (Lodge 1990, 212). It is interesting that revisions to the Treaty of Rome in the late 1980s included significant downsizing of the CAP and experimentation with alternative policies to maintain prices.

With de Gaulle out of office in 1969, the EEC proceeded with the accession of Great Britain, Denmark, Ireland, and Norway (where the proposal was rejected in a referendum). Given Britain's heavy reliance on imports of food from New Zealand and Australia and the relatively small size of its agricultural sector, it was disadvantaged by the EEC's emphasis on the CAP. Differences of opinion were left largely unresolved, and the accession was completed in 1973. This "first enlargement" came amid optimism for the future of the EEC. A 1972 summit meeting that included three "members in waiting" committed the community to deeper integration, including "completion of the internal market, common tariffs, a common currency, and a central bank" (Williams 1991, 50). Few anticipated the trying years that were soon to come.

THE EUROPEAN COMMUNITY UNDER STRESS: 1973–1985

The quadrupling of the price of oil in 1973 had devastating effects on European economies. A decade of stagflation set in, and Britain's economic life was in constant jeopardy. The linchpin of stable currencies was gone, and demands by the Organization of Petroleum Exporting Countries (OPEC) for oil importers to end their support of Israel went far to undermine the political unity that contributed to economic cooperation. France and Germany abandoned Israel, whereas the Netherlands endured the oil embargo. The British pound collapsed in the mid-1970s, and labor unrest in France and Italy derailed those countries' economic growth. Germany struggled with terrorism, and Ireland and Italy pleaded for additional development financing from the EEC. None of the Europeans knew how to respond to the growing trade threat from Japan and the Far East. As put by British Prime Minister Edward Heath:

> After the oil crisis of 1973–1974 the Community lost its momentum and, what was worse, lost the philosophy of Jean Monnet: that the Community exists to find common solutions to common problems. (Williams 1991, 50)

Amid this unraveling came a crisis of identity over Britain's role in the community. As a major industrial power, the United Kingdom expected to play a leading role in the EEC, but it had been "absent at the creation" and therefore was forced to deal with a set of rules and procedures that were not of its making. The most significant contention was about the budget. Britain continually found itself in conflict with the Franco–German "axis" during the 1970s (Urwin & Paterson 1990, 187).

Before going too far, we will discuss the EEC budget. Originally, the budget was simply based on a national quota calculated loosely in terms of gross national product (GNP) and renegotiated each year by the members. In 1970, this system was replaced with the "own resources" concept: The EEC would claim certain revenues on the grounds that they belonged by right to Europe as a whole. For a variety of reasons, Great Britain in the late 1970s was consistently sending Brussels some $3 billion more than it was getting back; at the same time, France was netting some $800 billion (Taylor 1983, 238).

The inequity of the situation was exacerbated by Britain's political ambivalence about European federalism generally. In 1979, Margaret Thatcher was elected prime minister on an anti-EEC platform. Her government exaggerated the United Kingdom's disadvantage by focusing on absolute rather than per capita revenues. Considering the EEC process seriously flawed and even illegitimate, the Thatcher government took an aggressive position that alienated the other EEC members. She told the EEC members bluntly, "I want my money back."

In 1982, Britain began to press the EEC for some form of financial relief. It demanded a rebate of 1.5 billion European Currency Units (ECU) to be paid by CAP beneficiaries (France and Italy in particular). When agreement was slow in coming, it threatened to use its veto to block further action by the community. Great Britain came close to precipitating a profound split in the community by 1984. Helmut Kohl of Germany left a meeting in protest. In essence, Germany called Britain's bluff. This is not to say that the United Kingdom failed. On the contrary, the EEC provided a 1 billion ECU rebate in 1984 and promised additional rebates of roughly two thirds of the difference between Britain's tax-generated payments to the EEC and its receipts from Brussels (Urwin & Paterson 1990, 193). However, as part of this arrangement, Germany was permitted to increase substantially its share of EEC expenses—and power.

Apart from the budgetary and philosophical tensions in the community, a serious problem arose from the growing disparity of development among the members of the EU. Moving from the EEC-Six to the EC-Nine had not been particularly painful, in and of itself, except for the budget question described earlier. However, the additions of Greece in 1981 and of Spain and Portugal in 1986 created unexpected stress.

Greece was permitted to enter the EEC prematurely, EEC officials today acknowledge. Greek industry is still not competitive with that in the rest of Europe. Greek agriculture is far too tropical and labor-intensive to survive full integration (for example, the average size of a Greek farm is only one fifth that of a Luxembourg farm). The Greek government in power in the early 1980s proved to be one of the few pro-EC governments that the Greek people would elect. Successive Greek regimes have challenged the membership decision (Williams 1991, 65).

Spain and Portugal applied for membership in 1977 and were admitted in 1986, despite serious reservations. Spain's size and the three Mediterranean countries' poverty placed heavy burdens on the rest of Europe. Spain and Portugal hoped their accession would guarantee newfound democracy and preserve their strong links to Europe. The EEC nations feared the imbalance of prices, wages, and wealth between Spain and Portugal and the rest of the community. The accession was permitted only with seven- to ten-year transitional provisions in fishing, semitropical foods, external industrial tariffs, and budget obligations (Williams 1991, 69). Efforts to rectify the discrepancies have come primarily through regional development programs administered by the European Regional Development Fund (ERDF). Never more than 10% of the total EEC budget, the funds funneled through the ERDF were aimed primarily at rural Mediterranean regions (not countries), although a program set in place in the mid-1980s provided funds for certain depressed industrial areas (Williams 1991, 130).

The last significant policy issue tackled during the 1970s was monetary reform. The notion of a European Monetary System (EMS) had been discussed early after the Treaty of Rome was signed, but it did not take shape until the collapse of the dollar-centered Bretton Woods system in 1971 forced Europeans to take more responsibility for their own monetary stability. The Werner Report calling for fixed exchange rates that would fluctuate in parallel was implemented in 1971. This system proved untenable after the oil crisis, however. Because inflationary pressures hit different countries unequally, and because each nation decided to adopt a different monetary strategy to deal with the crisis, currency values began to separate dramatically. Maintaining fixed exchange rates required intervention by the governments (for example, buying and selling currency, increasing interest rates), so in 1978 the "snake" system, as it was called, was abandoned in favor of the EMS, known as the "snake in the tunnel" approach (Wistrich 1990, 35).

The EMS allowed European currencies to fluctuate freely in relation to one another within a 4.5% band around the Deutsche Mark. Governments accepted the responsibility to unilaterally adopt policies that would either raise or lower the value of their currencies relative to the Mark whenever they approached the limits of this range. The agreement was actually drawn up and signed by the central bankers of the EEC and was to be implemented by them rather than by political leaders. The bankers agreed not only to conservative monetary principles but also to consultation, coordination, and convergence of money policy. The members also agreed to the creation of a new accounting unit, the ECU, a forerunner of today's euro.

The Exchange Rate Mechanism (ERM) was also included in the EMS. It provided for warnings to be issued to the banks of countries whose currencies fell outside a narrower 3.5% band around the Deutsche Mark, although strong currencies used heavily in the European banking system were permitted a slightly wider range of tolerance. The effect was to impose particularly strict discipline on smaller countries (Lehment 1983, 187).

The end of this period of relative turmoil came with an epiphany—a deep recognition that the EEC was at a crossroads. The community could either continue the unionist approach advanced by Thatcher or adopt the federalist approach, which was embraced by Germany, France, and the Netherlands.

RENEWAL: 1986–2006

European countries were in position to respond to the dramatic changes that took place on the world stage in the late 1980s and early 1990s because they were undergoing far-reaching changes of their own. Beginning as early as 1984, EEC leaders launched a series of dramatic reforms of their institutions. Specifically, they strengthened the free trade regime of Europe, undertook initiatives into new economic and social policy arenas, added new members, and began to coordinate and strengthen community-wide security and foreign policy positions.

Single European Act

In 1984, the European Parliament approved a draft treaty of European union that committed countries to eventually merge their foreign and defense policies. By 1985, talk had begun to shift to the need for genuine unification of economic policies across the EEC, and committees were formed to study the question of a single market. British official Lord Cockfield developed a plan of action with a list of 282 directives to be adopted by the end of 1992 (Goldstein 1991–1992, 130). At the December 1985 Luxembourg summit, the Single European Act (SEA) was approved; it was ratified in 1986. The treaty represented a major modification of the Treaty of Rome and called for implementation of the "four freedoms":

1. Free movement of goods. This involved dismantling the many non-tariff barriers that were not specifically listed in the Treaty of Rome and were still impeding trade in the community, including the establishment of a minimum sales tax (value added tax [VAT]) rate with numerous exclusions.
2. A free market in services. This included banking, insurance, transportation, airlines, telecommunications, and so on.

3. Free movement of people—in other words, unrestricted immigration within the community.
4. A free market in capital—specifically, a pledge to eliminate government intervention in currency exchange and the eventual establishment of a common currency (the Delors Plan gave this movement its impetus; see the next section).

Beyond the important symbolism of the SEA, the concrete changes were substantial. By the end of 1992, virtually all government-made barriers to trade were eliminated, and efforts were set in motion to create united markets in fields that had none. For example, trucks may now travel across the EU without stopping at border crossings. This, in and of itself, cuts costs and improves efficiency substantially. Banking is liberalized to the point that any stable European bank can establish subsidiaries anywhere in the EU. Commercial insurance is liberalized, and plans are under way to do the same in the airline industry. By the end of 1992, some 95% of the SEA proposals had been implemented.

At the institutional level, although the SEA modifies the Treaty of Rome, it does so by simply changing the powers of existing bodies. The European Parliament is given greater voice in such matters as admitting new members (Lodge 1990, 216). The commission is strengthened and its scope of operation is broadened, which increases the likelihood that Europe-wide policies will be developed. Perhaps most important, the prospects for further progress have been strengthened by the adoption of majority rule on the Council of Ministers, thus eliminating the debilitating use of the veto (Pinder 1986, 73).

The Euro

In 1988, the European Council (or summit meeting) commissioned the new president of the European Commission, Jacques Delors, to devise a plan for monetary and currency union. In 1989, the Delors Plan was accepted. It called for a three-phase process to begin with the establishment of a European System of Central Banks (ESCB) centered on a European Central Bank and each of the twelve nations' central banks—to be governed with little political interference. This network would be the vehicle through which the European Commission and Council of Ministers would set monetary and currency policy, including the gradual harmonization of fiscal policy (government spending and taxation), currency valuation (exchange rates), monetary policy (interest rates, money supply), and bank powers (political independence of central bank leaders). After the nations of Europe completed this transition phase and satisfied the requirements of prudent monetary policy (defined flexibly by the Council of Ministers and European Council), the members of the community pledged to abandon their own currencies and central bank controls and hand over monetary policy to a single European entity (Habermeier & Ungerer 1992, 27–29).

Beginning in 1989, via the Delors Plan, European leaders moved toward establishing a single regional currency. Two key ingredients to such a venture are harmonizing and strengthening domestic fiscal and monetary policies and establishing and accepting powerful new central organs capable of setting regional monetary policy. In both cases, governments are required to adopt major changes to their way of running their national economies, which runs counter to prevailing ideology and political strategy. Many Europeans resisted EEC encroachment on monetary policy, including especially Margaret Thatcher, whose conservative colleagues voted her out in early 1992 over her opposition to deeper integration. Likewise, more radical regimes objected to the need to subordinate their own developmental and redistributive policies to the demands of Brussels bureaucrats. The collapse of the value of the British pound and the Italian lira in 1992 provoked considerable debate in the United Kingdom and Italy, leading to a withdrawal from European monetary plans in the former and a redoubled effort to implement fiscal discipline in the latter (Gilpin 2001, 37–38).

Although politicians had considerable trepidation and hesitation, the euro was introduced in 1998 (as part of the Maastricht Treaty discussed later) and began to appear not only in government-to-government transactions but also in the prices of ordinary products sold in stores across Europe. After suffering an initial dip on the international exchange markets, the euro stabilized at a level slightly higher than the U.S. dollar and continues to gain credibility. On January 1, 2002, national currencies were officially eliminated and the euro became legal tender Europe-wide. Although there have been some complaints that merchants concealed price hikes in the currency conversion to euros, most Europeans welcomed the stability and strength of the new currency—even in Germany.

Not all EU members have joined the euro scheme, with the United Kingdom being a notable holdout. The main reason is the difficulties involved in meeting fiscal and monetary policy constraints. In the early 1990s, a serious recession gripped the region, and very few countries were able to reach the target of keeping budgetary deficits to less than 3% of GDP. But by the late 1990s, the situation had changed substantially. From a high of 5.5% in 1993, overall budget deficits relative to GDP had fallen to less than 1% for Europe as a whole. Several countries even projected budget surpluses for the year 2000 (EC 2000, 5).

Maastricht Treaty

With the end of the Cold War in 1989 and the reunification of Germany in 1990, Europe faced a very different political context. As put by *The Economist*, "This is the decade the European Community was invented for" (Colchester 1992, S1). Amid the turmoil of political upheaval, Germany and France pressed for the rapid and full adoption of the spirit of Monnet and Spaak: European union. Rather than wait for a united Germany to assert its own identity, both Helmut Kohl and François Mitterand moved to incorporate it into the EEC network and subordinate German expansion to European imperatives. The withdrawal of Margaret Thatcher from British political life accelerated the process. These forces, along with the growing threat from Japan and questions about the future American role in Europe, were key to the pell-mell pace of the negotiation of the Maastricht agreements in December 1991. The Maastricht agreement was finalized in relative secrecy, but with the strong support of the negotiators. Once the treaty was signed, it required the ratification of each member state before it went into force. In June 1992, the Danish electorate rejected the treaty by a slim margin; in September 1992, the French approved it by an equally slim margin. Leaders became concerned that they had failed to communicate the advantages of the EU clearly enough to their electorates. Ultimately, the Danes took another vote and approved the treaty, as did other European nations by large margins. The British Parliament finally approved the action without resort to a formal referendum. On January 1, 1994, the Maastricht Treaty went into effect.

The first element of the Maastricht Treaty was the strengthening of the EU-led integration itself, to be accomplished by 2000. The EU's authority was extended into such areas as education, health policy, consumer protection, law enforcement, immigration, and even culture. The Council of Ministers now act on the basis of a qualified majority vote (taking into account the size of the countries in tabulating their vote, but eliminating the veto altogether), but it must obtain the European Parliament's approval on many questions. The commission, though somewhat weaker in relation to the council, retains the initiative as the only organ authorized to propose new programs. The principle of "subsidiarity" limits the EU's authority to those programs where collective action is clearly preferable to national unilateralism—but the specific parameters of this concept have to be determined in the pro-integration European Court of Justice.

In practice, the commission continues to exert considerable authority over EU policy. An important episode illustrates the limits of council and governmental authority. In the late 1980s, the practice of feeding cows meat and bone meal was outlawed in Great Britain when it was discovered that cows were contracting bovine spongiform encephalopathy, better known as "mad cow disease." The epidemic ultimately affected more than 175,000 cows during the 1990s. In 1990, several European countries imposed unilateral bans on British beef. Under pressure from the commission, these countries lifted the ban a few weeks later. In 1995, however, Stephen Churchill died of Creutzfeldt-Jakob disease, which was linked in a March 1996 study by the British health ministry to mad cow disease. Within days of the announcement, the commission issued a ban on the importation of all British beef products (Decision 94/239/EC of March 27, 1996). To protest the action, which it considered overly drastic and hasty, the UK government decided to use its political and institutional clout to obstruct other actions by the commission in other areas of EU policy. A month later, the United Kingdom agreed to end its virtual boycott of EU activities in exchange for a pledge by the commission to gradually lift the ban. In fact, the ban remained in effect for nearly three years. The United Kingdom tried to persuade the European Parliament to pass a motion of censure against the commission, which would have resulted in its dissolution, but failed.

EU Enlargement

After a lengthy application process that ended in each country conducting a national referendum, Sweden, Finland, and Austria were admitted into the EU in January 1995. Norway and Switzerland, though approved for admission, opted against it in the face of popular opposition.

The accession of these three nations proceeded without major difficulty and prompted European leaders to press for further enlargement by reaching out to long-time applicants Turkey, Malta, and Cyprus as well as the Central European nations of Slovenia, Hungary, Poland, and the Czech Republic. The EU members laid out more precise membership criteria in 1993, which now include (1) stable democracy and protection of fundamental human rights, (2) a functioning market economy, and (3) the ability to "take on the obligations of membership" (EC 2000).

The EU's experience with democratization has become a model for the world. Many scholars have noted that the EU has just the right combination of sticks and carrots to induce would-be members to strengthen democratic institutions quickly (Hafner-Burton 2005). The EU was directly involved in Greek politics when it suspended its Association Agreement (intended as a sort of "probationary membership" after the military's overthrow of the government in 1967). The economic pain Greece suffered appears to have contributed directly to the restoration of democracy in 1973 (Pevehouse 2002, 524). In 1989, the EU set aside funds for Eastern European countries that were interested in eventual EU membership but that would have to first go through considerable economic and political reforms. The so-called PHARE program targeted ten Eastern European countries. In an internal performance evaluation, analysts concluded that the program was particularly instrumental in helping states draft new legislation in the area of justice and home affairs (primarily by nurturing pro–civil-rights community organizations). The general conclusion was that these new states would not have been capable of carrying out most of the projects due to a lack of funds and expertise (EU 2003). Not only does the EU provide inducements, but it is quite willing to bar membership to states that have not yet consolidated the democratic transition, as the leaders of Slovakia and Turkey have learned (Smith 2003, 135).

In the French city of Nice in late 2000, EU members agreed to extend membership to ten Eastern European countries, pending approval by the citizens of each EU member-state. In October 2002, after a second attempt, the citizens of Ireland approved the plan—the last country to do so. This resulted in memberships in 2004 for Hungary, Poland, the Czech Republic, Slovenia, Slovakia, Estonia, Latvia, and Lithuania, as well as Malta and Cyprus. Membership for Cyprus was complicated by the division of the island between Turkish and Greek government structures. Last-minute efforts to resolve the dispute in order to allow inclusion of the entire island came to naught, and so only the Greek-controlled areas were formally incorporated (see Map 17.1). Membership for Turkey continues to run up against Greek opposition and a checkered human rights and economic record for the Ankara government, although Turkey is working hard to improve its laws and image (*Los Angeles Times* August 3, 2002, A7).

European Constitution

The question that will doubtless dominate EU news over the next few years is the adoption of a draft constitution. After negotiating for roughly a year, members of a constitutional convention put forward a draft document for member states to approve. This was done in June 2004, at which point the constitution is being passed along to each of the twenty-five member-states for their ratification. Should any state fail to ratify (either because the legislature rejects or a referendum fails), then the constitution will remain a proposal. What would most likely happen is the "no" countries would be given a chance to try again, as was the case for the Maastricht agreement.

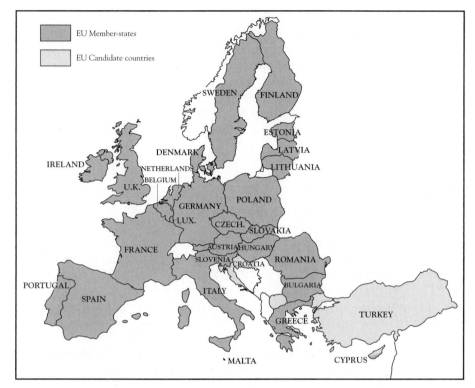

EU Member-states

EU Candidate countries

SWEDEN   FINLAND

ESTONIA

LATVIA

DENMARK   LITHUANIA

IRELAND   NETHERLANDS

BELGIUM

U.K.

GERMANY   POLAND

LUX.

CZECH.   SLOVAKIA

AUSTRIA   HUNGARY

FRANCE

SLOVENIA   CROATIA   ROMANIA

PORTUGAL   ITALY   BULGARIA

SPAIN

GREECE   TURKEY

MALTA   CYPRUS

Map 17.1 European Union Membership

The constitution is an intriguing document since on the surface it appears to constitute little more than institutional housecleaning, although many believe it is in fact a revolutionary step. The principal goal of the framers was to streamline and clarify the structures of the EU, bringing all the various bodies under a single government. But the Commission, Council, and Parliament of Europe would all remain—essentially unchanged. A new post of Foreign Minister would be created, along with the post of EU President—but the functions these two would fill are already being performed by existing actors (EC 2004). Unlike Maastricht, then, the EU does not seem to extend the powers of EU institutions in any dramatic way (Federal Union 2004).

This said, the constitution provides for a new Charter of Fundamental Rights, analogous to the American Bill of Rights or the European Convention on Human Rights. Although the list of rights is not especially controversial in itself, it is the fact that the European Court of Justice would be expected to enforce them that worries some. Opponents of the proposal see the constitution as "federalism by stealth" in that it appears to give a veto to the EU over a broader range of policies than before. Euro-skeptics in Britain, for example, argue that such an agreement could mean that Britain will be forced to adopt the euro, accept the European

Court of Justice as a court of final appeal for all British legal questions, and essentially result in loss of British sovereignty (EUFAQ 2004). Every EU member must ratify the Convention before it can take effect. In mid-2005, the voters in France and the Netherlands soundly defeated it, prompting several states to cancel their own votes. The European Council, fearful that further votes could doom the Convention, opted to set aside the timetable and instead begin renegotiating the treaty. A new, somewhat weaker treaty was approved in Lisbon in 2007, but after it was rejected by Irish voters in June 2008, efforts to begin new negotiations were abandoned.

Security Cooperation

European governments have long been heavily involved in European security arrangements, although the arrangements have tended to be disconnected and relatively weak. The Western European Union, though still on the books, is nothing like the "non-North American NATO" it was originally envisioned to be. Efforts to reinvigorate it through Title V of the Maastricht Treaty have faltered. The European actions of failing to take a unified position on Bosnia in the early 1990s and allowing the United States to take the lead in Kosovo a few years later have led many to believe that much work is necessary on European security initiatives.

The EU provides for a High Representative for the Common Foreign and Security Policy of the Union, who will help form a consensus on foreign policy positions, but as yet, this representative has not become a significant voice. The EU has also established an intelligence and policy planning unit. In 1997, the European Council signed the Treaty of Amsterdam, which is designed to give more weight and urgency to common union policies, in the hope that states will choose to "constructively abstain" rather than block union policies (EC 2000). There are currently plans in place for a new rapid-reaction force, but this effort probably will not progress very far until Turkey drops its opposition. Europeans are more likely to continue to support and strengthen the Organization for Security and Cooperation in Europe, which has played a key role in enhancing democracy and peace in southern Europe (Department of State 1995).

CONCLUSION: REGIONALISM AND EUROPE

There is no question that the European Union is the most dramatic, far-reaching, and successful example of regional integration today. In the 1970s, skeptics predicted the withering away of the EEC in the face of French and British sovereign demands. Today, however, most international scholars see the EU as a new standard for international cooperation. This result has been achieved in spite of a difficult decade that dealt with the reintegration of East Germany, high unemployment, and austerity in the quest for admission to the euro system.

Serious obstacles must be overcome before the experiment can be declared a success. Europe does not yet speak with one voice on all matters of security, and the United States has a heavy presence in European military matters through NATO. The Constitution has been blocked by several states, with the result that it may never be implemented. And in Italy and other states, anti-EU and anti-immigrant parties are performing increasingly well at the polls. Even in Eastern Europe, democracy seems not to be spreading as hoped. Romania, Bulgaria, Belarus, and Ukraine may even be backsliding toward authoritarianism. Nevertheless, the European states do coordinate their foreign policies on everything from trade to the environment. At the World Trade Organization, the United Nations, and other international organizations, to hear one European country's positions is generally to hear all their positions.

QUESTIONS TO CONSIDER

1. What key factors are reviving European integration? Are these forces relatively constant, or will they wax and wane?

2. Who wants European unity? The masses? The "Eurocrats"? The politicians? What does each expect to get from European unity?

3. Why is it so difficult to move from negative integration to positive integration to political unity? Will these obstacles persist in the future?

KEY FIGURES
EUROPE UNITING

Jean Monnet   Deputy-general, League of Nations, 1919–1923; President and founder, ECSC, 1952–1955.

Jacques Delors   President, European Commission, 1985–1995. He spearheaded the Single European Act and the creation of the euro.

Paul-Henri Spaak   Prime Minister of Belgium at various times between 1938 and 1949. He led the European coordination of Marshall Plan aid and served as Secretary General of NATO, 1957–1961. He is known affectionately as the "Father of Europe."

Margaret Thatcher   British Prime Minister, 1979–1990. She worked against a number of EEC programs and proposals during her tenure.

Robert Schuman   French Foreign Minister, 1948–1952. He crafted the ECSC with Jean Monnet.

Helmut Kohl   Chancellor of Germany, 1982–1998. He promoted deeper European integration.

CHRONOLOGY
EUROPE UNITING

1922
Belgium, Luxembourg, and the Netherlands agree to form a free trade zone.

1948
The European Movement is founded in the Netherlands. The Marshall Plan is promulgated and the OEEC, predecessor to the OECD and EEC, is founded.

1949
The Council of Europe is formed.

1954
The ECSC is formed to regulate steel production.

1957
The Treaty of Rome is signed, creating the European Economic Community.

1962
The Common Agricultural Program is instituted to support farm prices.

1963
Charles de Gaulle of France blocks British membership to the EEC.

1971
The Luxembourg Compromise provides a veto to each member-state on certain issues.

1973
Great Britain, Denmark, and Ireland join the EEC in the first "enlargement."

1978
The EMS replaces previous currency stabilization schemes.

1981
Greece is admitted to the EEC.

1982
British Prime Minister Margaret Thatcher demands changes in regional funding arrangements.

1985
The Single European Act is approved.

1986
Spain and France are admitted to the ECC.

1989
The Delors Plan for a regional monetary union is approved.

1990
European states impose restrictions on British beef amid fears of "mad cow" disease.

1991
The Maastricht Treaty is approved, pending ratification by each EEC member.

1992

Almost all of the trade barriers outlined in 1985 (as part of the SEA) are removed. A currency crisis in the United Kingdom and Italy leads to the dismantling of the European Monetary System.

1994

The Maastricht Treaty comes into effect, resulting in the creation of the European Union.

1995

Sweden, Finland, and Austria are admitted to the EU.

2000

Fifteen European Union member-states agree in Nice, France, to admit twelve new members, pending approval by citizens of all fifteen states.

2002

The euro is adopted region-wide as national currencies are eliminated. Ireland becomes the last country to ratify the Nice Agreement, paving the way for the admission of most Eastern European states by 2005.

2004

Ten new countries are added to the EU, bringing the total to twenty-five. The new members are the Czech Republic, Estonia, Hungary, Latvia, Lithuania, Poland, Slovakia, Slovenia, Cyprus, and Malta. The European Constitution is approved at a diplomatic conference and approved by sixteen countries before voters in France and the Netherlands rejected it in 2005.

2007

European diplomats approve a new constitution in the Treaty of Lisbon, but it is rejected by Irish voters in 2008.

REFERENCES

Colchester, Nico. "The European Community—A Survey." *The Economist* (July 11, 1992): S1–S30.

Department of State. "Fact Sheets: NATO, Partnership for Peace, OSCE, and NATO Enlargement." U.S. Department of State Dispatch, June 5, 1995.

European Commission (EX). "Public Finances in EMU—2000: Report of the Directorate General for Economic and Financial Affairs." May 24, 2000.

European Commission (EC). "Summary of the Agreement on the Constitutional Treaty." A provisional document of the European Commission. June 28, 2004. Available at www.efah.org/pdfcount.php?fln=constitution_eu_5.pdf.

European Union FAQ. "What is the EU Constitution?" Working paper of the European Union FAQ. Available at http://www.eurofaq.freeuk.com/eurofaq1b.html. Accessed on October 10, 2004.

European Union (EC). *Phare ex post evaluation of country support implemented from 1997–1998 to 2000–2001: Consolidated summary report* (Brussels: EU, 2003).

Federal Union. "What is the Draft European Constitution?" Working paper of the Federal Union, 2004. Available at http://www.federalunion.org.uk/europe/constitutioncampaign1.shtml.

Gerbet, Pierre. "The Origins: Early Attempts and the Emergence of the Six (1945–52)." In Pryce, ed., *The Dynamics of European Union* (New York: Croom Helm, 1987): 35–48.

Gilpin, Robert. *International Economic Stuff!!!* (Princeton, NJ: Princeton University Press, 2001).

Goldstein, Walter. "EC: Euro-stalling." *Foreign Policy* 85 (Winter 1991–1992): 129–147.

Habermeier, Karl, and Horst Ungerer. "A Single Currency for the European Community." *Finance and Development* (September 1992): 26–29.

Hafner-Burton, Emelie M. "Trading Human Rights: How Preferential Trade Agreements Influence Government Repression." *International Organization* 59 #3 (Summer 2005): 593–629.

Heater, Derek. *The Idea of European Unity* (New York: St. Martin's Press, 1992).

Hurwitz, Leon. *The European Community and the Management of International Cooperation* (New York: Greenwood Press, 1987).

Hurwitz, Leon, ed. *The Harmonization of European Public Policy: Regional Responses to Transnational Challenges* (Westport, CT: Greenwood Press, 1983).

Kusters, Hanns Jurgen. "The Treaties of Rome (1955–57)." In Roy Pryce, ed., *The Dynamics of European Union* (London: Croom Helm, 1987): 78–104.

Los Angeles Times August 3, 2002, A7

Lehment, Harmen. "The European Monetary System." In Leon Hurwitz, ed., *The Harmonization of European Public Policy* (Westport, CT: Greenwood Press, 1987): 183–196.

Lodge, Juliet. "European Community Decision-Making: Toward the Single European Market." In D.W. Urwin and W.E. Paterson, eds., *Politics in Western Europe Today* (London: Longman, 1990): 206–226.

Lodge, Juliet, ed. *The European Community and the Challenge of the Future* (New York: St. Martin's Press, 1989).

Lodge, Juliet, ed. *European Union: The European Community in Search of a Future* (New York: St. Martin's Press, 1986).

Marsh, John. "The Common Agricultural Policy." In Juliet Lodge, ed., *The European Community and the Challenge of the Future* (New York: St. Martin's Press, 1989):148–166.

Monnet, Jean. *Memoirs* (New York: Doubleday, 1979).

Pevehouse, Jon. "Democracy from the Outside-In? International Organizations and Democratization." *International Organization* 56 #3 (Summer 2002): 515–549.

Pinder, John. "Economic Union and the Draft Treaty." In Juliet Lodge, ed., *European Union* (New York: St. Martin's Press, 1989): 70–87.

Pryce, Roy, ed. *The Dynamics of European Union* (New York: Croom Helm, 1987).

Smith, Karen E. *European Union Foreign Policy in a Changing World* (London: Polity, 2003).

Spruyt, Hendrick. *The Sovereign State and Its Competitors* (Princeton, NJ: Princeton University Press, 1996).

Taylor, Paul. *The Limits of European Integration* (New York: Columbia University Press, 1983).

Tilly, Charles. *Coercion, Capital, and European States, 1990–1992* (London: Blackwell, 1992).

Urwin, Derek, and William Paterson, eds. *Politics in Western Europe Today: Perspectives, Policies and Problems Since 1980* (New York: Longman, 1990).

Williams, Allan M. *The European Community: The Contradictions of Integration* (Cambridge: Blackwell, 1991).

Wistrich, Ernest. *After 1992: The United States of Europe* (New York: Routledge, 1990).

World Bank. *World Development Report* (New York: Oxford University Press, 1999).

18

■ ■ ■

International Law: The Nuremberg Trials

INTRODUCTION

International law is a collection of principles, rules, and procedures designed to govern international affairs—particularly relations among nation-states. It is derived from a wide variety of sources: treaties, conventions, protocols, traditions, scholarly writings, customs, habits, and so on. Although international law aims at creating the sort of order in international society that exists in domestic society, it lacks a crucial element: centralized enforcement. Because there is no world government, international law can be applied only by the consent of members of the international community. Historically, international citizens have been reluctant to take the risks required to enforce international law militarily, so wars come and go as always. An important exception to this rule was the disposition of Nazi war criminals in 1945.

States dominate the character and implementation of international law. To a large extent, it is a system of rules under which actors other than states (e.g., firms, international organizations, individuals, minority groups) have little voice or standing. For example, the premier international tribunal—the International Court of Justice—restricts its contentious proceedings to states. Only if a government chooses to promote the cause of some other actor may that figure's case be heard (this has happened very rarely). Thus crimes by and against private individuals have almost always been prosecuted in national, not international, courts.

Where the behavior of individual soldiers and officers in combat is concerned, states have been careful to prevent even national courts from exercising jurisdiction. Military justice permits officers of a nation's defense force to judge individual soldiers and sailors, granting them limited rights to defend themselves. The Hague and

Geneva Conventions create international standards of conduct in wartime, but provide no automatic enforcement by way of an international tribunal. Governments have resisted creating such a permanent arrangement, as was seen recently in the United States' objections to its service men and women being brought before the newly formed International Criminal Court.

How should the world community respond to the systematic slaughter of six million Jews, some two million Soviet prisoners of war, thousands of handicapped persons, and still more Gypsies, Poles, and other ethnics? How do civilized nations respond to one regime's ruthless plan for global domination? How does one punish behavior that was never before imagined?

These questions faced American, British, French, and Soviet military and diplomatic leaders in the waning months of World War II and ultimately led to the war crimes trials at Nuremberg. Looking back, we can ask: On what basis were the leaders of a nation judged as criminals? Were these charges and the ensuing judgments justified? Have these actions and decisions set any precedent for the bloody acts of scores of other countries in dozens of other wars since that time? Are we a more civilized world after the Nuremberg Trials?

ORGANIZING THE TRIALS

Early on, the behavior of Hitler's Germany in World War II was described as criminal. Statements by Roosevelt, Churchill, and later Stalin condemned the aggressive acts of a ruthless dictator, the mistreatment of prisoners of war, and the systematic slaughter of millions (although the full extent of the atrocities did not become clear until concentration camps were liberated and documents examined). Clearly, this was no gentleman's war, and the objectives of the Allied forces quickly escalated far beyond a simple return to the status quo. Nothing less than the eradication of Nazi institutions and ideology would suffice to avenge the atrocities and restore world order.

In this context, it is understandable that radical measures were conceived regarding the planned treatment of the leaders of the Nazi regime after the war. Churchill and much of the British government favored the summary execution of Nazi leaders upon their capture by Allied troops. Henry Morgenthau, the U.S. secretary of the treasury, strongly advocated the execution of Nazi leaders, the deportation of former SS officers, and the total deindustrialization of Germany. He even contemplated arresting the children of senior German officials in an effort to purge the society of all real and potential Nazi influence (Smith 1981, 40). Soviet leaders advocated a purge of all senior and mid-level Nazis (roughly 50,000 in all).

When Henry Stimson, the powerful U.S. secretary of war, began to promote the notion of a public legal proceeding, some individuals in Washington began planning for such an event. From the start, the idea of a trial was highly controversial because it necessitated breaking new diplomatic, military, and legal ground. Which laws had the Nazis broken? Which individuals were truly responsible? Who should gather documents and on what basis? What forum should be used for this trial? How could the procedure be anything other than a "high-class lynching"?

In late 1944, Stimson used a proposal developed by a mid-level officer, Murray Bernays, to flesh out his idea and gather support from other cabinet officers. He found the road very hard; even the Joint Chiefs of Staff were skeptical of his proposal. Once the controversial questions were raised, the proposal was nearly dropped. "After six weeks in which the plan had repeatedly been examined, debated, and revised, only to be challenged once more, not a single government department had formally approved it" (Smith 1981,112).

As was common in wartime planning, policy decisions were swept along by events on the battlefield. In January 1945, reports from Belgium described the slaughter of eighty American prisoners of war by Nazi guards apparently acting under specific orders. The act so directly violated the 1924 Geneva Convention on the treatment of POWs that Roosevelt was prompted to formally endorse the idea of a war crimes trial. By March, American officials were speaking in favor of a wide-reaching war crimes trial and ultimately managed to persuade and cajole British and Russian "diplomats" to accept their viewpoint.

The key sticking points until the finalization of the plan in June were the notion of a German conspiracy to commit aggressive war and the prosecution of organizations themselves. Both were new ideas to the Europeans because conspiracy trials are uniquely American inventions. The definition of "aggressive war" not only was weak at the time but continues to elude the United Nations to this day. Finally, proving the guilt of an entire organization was never attempted at even the domestic level, and serious questions were raised about whether it was possible or appropriate. After all, not all members of an organization have equal culpability if the organization becomes involved in crimes. And only individuals can be accused of crimes, not social institutions. These questions were ultimately left unresolved, and it would be up to the judges at Nuremberg to determine the merits of the charges separately. Perhaps most important, the actions of the victorious Allies were never held up for judgment. Allied leaders knew that the fire-bombing of Dresden and the atomic annihilation of Hiroshima and Nagasaki would not stand up very well to objective legal analysis (Taylor 1993).

The organization of the trial was based on the four-member alliance that had defeated Germany. American, British, Soviet, and French judges were named, along with an alternate for each one. They heard all the documentary, film, and oral testimony about the crimes of twenty-two men chosen for their prominence, breadth of experience in different aspects of the Nazi regime, and direct participation in war crimes. Prosecutors from each country gathered documents, interrogated witnesses and defendants, and undertook cross-examination. Each defendant was allowed a German defense attorney of his choosing, and all materials were made available in German and English, with the hearings simultaneously translated into English, French, German, and Russian (a first for IBM).

The defendants in the Nuremberg Trials were all notorious in their own right, although as would become clear during the proceedings, they differed dramatically in their degree of participation and control over the commission of atrocities and war crimes. Hermann Goering and Rudolf Hess were perhaps the closest to Adolf Hitler himself, although Goering's influence had waned and Hess was profoundly schizophrenic. Other prominent organizers of Nazi rule gathered at Nuremberg included

Ernst Kaltenbrunner (SS), Hans Frank (governor-general of Poland), Arthur Seyss-Inquart (Anschluss organizer), Alfred Rosenberg (theoretician/East Europe commander), Julius Streicher (prominent anti-Semite), Baldur von Schirach (Hitler Youth leader), Konstantin von Neurath (member of the "secret cabinet"), Albert Speer (production/ labor organizer), Fritz Saukel (labor), and Hans Fritzsche (propagandist). In addition, leaders of the military (Admiral Karl Doenitz, Admiral Erich Raeder, General Alfred Jodl, Field Marshall Wilhelm Keitel), the economy (Walter Funk, Hjalmar Schacht), and the formal government (Franz von Papen) were assembled.

Each defendant was charged with one or more of the following counts: (1) conspiracy to commit aggressive war, (2) crimes against peace, (3) war crimes (traditional), or (4) crimes against humanity (see Smith 1977, Chap. 1). Count 3, traditional war crimes, was the easiest to establish because clear treaty provisions already existed. The Hague Convention of 1907 and the Geneva Convention of 1924 clearly prohibit the harsh treatment of prisoners of war, the use of chemical and bacteriological weapons, and deliberate attacks on defenseless noncombatants. Of the eighteen men charged with traditional war crimes, only two (Hess and Fritzsche) were acquitted. The German high command, the Nazi Party organization, and other supporting organizations had left behind an unambiguous paper trail detailing the planning and perpetration of abuses of rules of war as codified in the treaties. German leaders often went to great lengths to conceal their actions by burning the bodies of their victims and inventing gross lies to explain away deaths, "acutely aware that the world would hold the Wehrmacht (German military) responsible for such outrages and killings," as put by a senior aide to Jodl (Conot 1983, 189). Even as they attempted to hide the facts of these atrocities, however, they carefully preserved a record on film and on paper.

The other counts raised serious problems of ex post facto prosecution. As put in the final judgment at Nuremberg: "It was urged on behalf of the defendants that a fundamental principle of all law—international and domestic—is that there can be no punishment of crime without a preexisting law . . ." (Falk et al. 1971, 97).

To be sure, the notion of a crime against humanity, though intuitively appealing, had never been mentioned or discussed prior to Nuremberg. The concept was put forward originally by the Soviet judge, General I. T. Nikitchenko, as a way to punish the Nazis for the Holocaust. In light of the doctrine of sovereign immunity, which allows a government to treat its own citizens in any way it pleases, there was no traditional international law against Germans killing Jewish Germans. "Crimes against humanity" was a device to make such prosecution possible. Given the fact that such a law did not exist in 1939, the defense charged that new laws were being invented and applied retroactively to their clients.

To meet this objection, lawyers for the prosecution argued that even though the law had not been codified on paper, there existed in 1939 an international moral consensus against genocide (the deliberate slaughter of a race of people). As put by Robert Jackson, the American prosecutor:

> It is true, of course, that we have no judicial precedent for [these charges]. But International Law is more than a scholarly collection of abstract and immutable principles. It is an outgrowth of treaties and agreements between nations and of accepted customs . . . The real complaining party at your bar is Civilization. (Falk et al. 1971, 84, 87)

Sir Hartley Shawcross, the British prosecutor, expressed the idea more directly:

The rights of humanitarian intervention on behalf of the rights of man, trampled upon by a state in a manner shocking the sense of mankind, has long been considered to form part of the recognized law of nations . . . If murder, rapine, and robbery are indictable under the ordinary municipal laws of our countries, shall those who differ from the common criminal only by the extent and systematic nature of their offenses escape accusation? (Conot 1983, 180)

The judges at Nuremberg determined during the trial that Nazi atrocities were so far beyond what could be considered civilized behavior, even in time of war, that they upheld the charge of "crime against humanity." Documents indicating the desperate speed with which extermination camps carried out the "Final Solution" to exterminate all European Jews clearly pointed to a complete abandonment of any pretense at humanity in the waning years of the war.

The crime of conspiring to commit aggressive war involved at least four different legal problems:

It was submitted that ex post facto punishment is abhorrent to the law of all civilized nations, that no sovereign power had made aggressive war a crime at the time the alleged criminal acts were committed, that no statute had defined aggressive war, that no penalty had been fixed for its commission, and no court had been created to try and punish offenders. (Falk et al. 1971, 97)

The Kellogg-Briand Pact of 1928 was a lofty pledge by the world's major powers never to resort to war. The signatories (which included Germany) declared "in the names of their respective peoples that they condemn recourse to war for the solution of international controversies, and renounce it as an instrument of national policy in their relations with one another" (Falk 1971, 46). The judges at Nuremberg determined that this treaty by itself was sufficient to show that international law prohibited the initiation of war (although very narrow provisions existed in which preemptive war was permissible). Through the course of their deliberations, the judges settled on the fact that Germany planned its attacks far in advance, that the Nazis attacked neutral nations, and that they did so without regard for international law. Hitler himself offered the most telling comment when he said, with regard to his plan to attack France via neutral Belgium and Holland, "Breach of the neutrality of Holland and Belgium is meaningless. No one will question it when we have won" (Conot 1983, 191).

The existence of a conspiracy was all-important to the Americans. Collusion and organized crime were not considered separate offenses in Europe, so the French judges in particular had great difficulty with this concept, as well as with the notion of charging whole organizations with crimes. As it happened, however, the charge of conspiracy could be proven thanks to the meticulous record-keeping of the Third Reich. At several meetings, with attendance recorded, Hitler, Goering, and others explained plans to annex first Austria and then Czechoslovakia and later to invade Poland. Plans to breach the Moscow Pact and attack the Soviet Union in 1941 were clearly articulated at a number of secret gatherings, along with the program to exterminate all Jews in Europe (the "Final Solution"). The guilt of an individual defendant could have easily been determined by his presence at such meetings, but the judges showed leniency if the defendant later acted to delay or scale back the implementation of the plans.

The question of whether the Nuremberg Tribunal had the authority to prosecute heads of state for war crimes was—and still is—a tricky legal problem. After all, the court derived its authority from the military occupation forces and was not directly connected to the United Nations or the International Court of Justice. To a large extent, it could be said that such a trial was merely a complicated way for victorious nations to seal their success. On the other hand, the Allies' position of power permitted them to treat their prisoners with far more harshness than they actually used. Under the circumstances, the Allies that organized the trial felt they were offering the accused far more respect, compassion, and fairness than they deserved. The alternatives of a "show trial," summary executions, and a wide-scale purge were rejected on the grounds that none of these gave the criminals any opportunity to defend themselves. The process would have appeared entirely political and idiosyncratic. (The Russians made it clear they looked forward to executing any apparent war criminal who fell into their hands, whereas the French favored greater leniency.) As put by Robert Jackson:

> If these men are the first war leaders of a defeated nation to be prosecuted in the name of the law, they are also the first to be given a chance to plead for their own lives in the name of the law. Realistically, the Charter of this Tribunal, which gives them a hearing, is also the source of their only hope . . . Despite the fact that public opinion already condemns their acts, we agree that here they must be given a presumption of innocence, and we accept the burden of proving criminal acts and the responsibility of these defendants for their commission. (Falk et al. 1971, 82)

It is clear, in retrospect, that although one might quibble about the impartiality of a tribunal of victors judging the actions of a vanquished government, and although one might ask whether the full array of legal protections accorded under any given country's legal system was offered to the Nuremberg defendants, the accused did receive relatively fair treatment. The judges were clearly disposed to give each defendant the benefit of the doubt and often ruled against the prosecution's requests—particularly in granting defendants' rights of reply. During the trial, each defendant was permitted not only to have a defense of his own choosing but also to call witnesses (the vast majority of witnesses were German themselves—and often senior aides to the defendants during the war), review documents, and speak on his own behalf at several junctures. It was possible to appeal sentences (although none of these efforts was successful). Whatever bias emerged during the trial tended to be in favor of social status—the judges showed a marked penchant to give intellectuals and professionals leniency—rather than political views. As put in a *New York Times* editorial written at the conclusion of the trial, "In short, the international tribunal had meted out what it was supposed to mete out—stern and exact justice, but justice, not vengeance" (Conot 1983, 435).

COURTROOM DRAMA

The trial itself was largely tedious and disorganized, involving primarily a rambling discussion of documents (many were read out loud in their entirety) and enumeration of countless minor incidents, obscure characters, and secret meetings. During the final weeks of the trial, as the warm and humid Bavarian sun beat down on the poorly insulated courtroom, the judges themselves had great difficulty staying awake! In contrast, graphic films of concentration camp victims, angry confrontations between prosecutors and defendants during cross-examination, and the coldly frank discussion of mutilation, crematoriums, and experiments on human specimens could not help but hold the attention of the international audience.

The trial opened on November 20, 1945, after eight months of gathering documents, interrogating defendants and witnesses, and registering the charges. The judges of the tribunal were Francis Biddle and John Parker of the United States, Lord Geoffrey Lawrence and Norman Birkett of the United Kingdom, I.T. Nikitchenko and A.F. Volchov of the Soviet Union, and Donnedieu de Vabres and Robert Falco of France. The dominant voices on the tribunal were Birkett and Nikitchenko, who were involved in drafting the charter of the court. De Vabres spoke consistently for leniency in sentencing, and Lawrence did much to promote orderliness and efficiency during the proceedings.

The first three months of the trial presented a detailed account of the crimes committed by the defendants and the broader Nazi regime. The prosecution used some 5,000 different documents, which had been translated from German, to show the planning and execution of the Nazi leadership's goal of world domination, starting with the subversion of the Weimar Republic in 1931 and the famous Reichstag fire, which propelled the Nazis into full control of a police state (an event that was later proven to be the fault of Goering himself). The establishment of a system of state-sponsored terrorism, the placing of the economy on a war footing, and the beginnings of abuses against Jews came next.

From then on, the narrative became somewhat haphazard as prosecutors took advantage of the availability of witnesses when convenient. They attempted to prove that a wide array of German institutions and agencies were implicated in the atrocities. For example, the Reichsbank (central bank of Germany) laundered the considerable amount of jewelry, watches, and even gold teeth through its official accounts during the heyday of Jewish exterminations after 1942. The Hitler Youth organization was so effective in shaping the next generation that Hitler was known to tell regime opponents that he cared little for their complaints because he already "had" their children. The army's blind obedience made the invasion of Germany's neutral neighbors possible, and Gestapo and SS repression prevented internal uprisings. Even the industrial system was intertwined with atrocities as millions of POWs and Jews were put to work in weapons-making factories and other programs. Evidence was laid out in painful detail through testimony, documentary films, and written records.

By mid-March of 1946, the defense had its turn to present its case. As put by Conot:

> Since in the minds of the defense as well as of the prosecution, there was little doubt that the essence of the Nazi regime's criminality had been proved, the one task of the individual accused in attempting to show his innocence or mitigate his guilt was to disassociate himself from the group, to demonstrate that he had not participated in the alleged "common plan" and had not been involved in violations of international law or crimes against humanity. (Conot 1983, 330)

Nearly all the defendants took the stand during the trial, which gave rise to the most interesting and dramatic moments. Goering was first. After he articulated his basic position that he was in fact heavily involved in all of the Third Reich's highest bodies, he went on to explain that, according to international law, his actions were not criminal. In a heated cross-examination by Jackson, Goering pointed out that bombing campaigns by the Luftwaffe, which were categorized as part of his war crimes, were no worse than Allied attacks on Dresden and other German cities and that most charges against him were ex post facto. Jackson was disarmed by Goering's able self-defense (Conot 1983, 338). Even Jackson's sympathetic biographer acknowledged that Goering had the upper hand (Gerhart 1958, 394). The judges permitted Goering considerable latitude to give speeches while explaining his answers, according to observers. Although this infuriated Jackson, it did not especially help Goering either, and Jackson was able to argue a strong case on the major charges. Goering was found guilty on all four counts and sentenced to death. He avoided the noose only by taking a cyanide capsule before his execution.

Few defendants had the arrogance of Goering. Some were apologetic and remorseful, but most waffled about their prominence and responsibility. Keitel admitted his guilt from the stand: "I cannot make white out of black." Schirach and Frank also admitted complicity, with the latter exclaiming, "A thousand years will pass and still this guilt of Germany will not have been erased!" In his final statement, Saukel said, "In all humility and reverence, I bow before the victims and the fallen of all nations, and before the misfortune and suffering of my own people, with whom I alone must measure my fate." Many Nuremberg defendants excused their behavior on the grounds that they were either ignorant of the regime's worst offenses or not senior enough to have set policy, or else they were simply "doing their job." Jodl, the stern military man, said, "As for the ethical code of my action, I must say that it was obedience." Rosenberg weakly rationalized his participation in the Holocaust by pointing out that the Jewish Talmud itself says Gentiles are inferior, and therefore it is no crime to treat Jews as inferiors. The capacity for Nazi self-justification was so great that it has prompted numerous psychological studies of complicity in institutionalized violence. (Note the famous Milgram experiments in which college students willingly administered apparently lethal levels of electric shock to their peers because a scientist in a lab coat told them to do so.)

For many defendants, the documentary evidence was overwhelming, establishing attendance at key meetings and certain knowledge and authorization of atrocities.

Where documents were not enough, the prosecution was usually able to bring German eyewitnesses to testify against their former superiors. Ribbentrop's secretary, Margaret Blank, inadvertently gave the prosecution vital evidence of his close ties to Hitler, even though she had been called as a defense witness! The commander at Auschwitz testified that Kaltenbrunner, contrary to his own testimony, was fully aware of the large-scale gassing at the extermination camp.

In general terms, the prosecution was assisted by the relatively weak performance of the defense attorneys. The judges' efforts to give the defendants leeway in answering questions and in utilizing and translating documents made the task of the prosecution difficult nonetheless. The general consensus on the part of most observers—German and Allied—was that the trial gave all parties ample opportunity to present their cases in the best possible light. Jackson offered in summation: "Of one thing we may be sure, the future will never have to ask, with misgiving, what the Nazis could have said in their favor. The fact is that the testimony of the defendants has removed any doubt of their guilt" (Conot 1983, 469).

THE JUDGMENT

The eight justices met during most of September 1946, immediately after the conclusion of the trial, and quickly handed down sixteen convictions. For example, the justices were unanimous in their decisions on the guilt of Goering, Ribbentrop, Kaltenbrunner, and Streicher and debated only briefly the convictions of Keitel, Jodl, Rosenberg, Frank, Frick, Saukel, and Seyss-Inquart. On the grounds that these individuals played an active and direct role in the planning and execution of Nazi war crimes, each was sentenced to be hanged.

Regarding the other defendants, the judges debated vigorously. Three were sentenced to life in prison: Hess, Funk, and Raeder. Because Funk and Raeder were judged to be outside the inner circle of Hitler advisors and Hess was clearly only marginally competent, they received lighter sentences. The moderate sentences of Doenitz (ten years), Speer (twenty years), Neurath (fifteen years), and Schirach (twenty years) were based not so much on guilt on specific charges but rather on extenuating circumstances and compromises among the judges. Bradley Smith argues that the personal background of the defendants had much to do with their sentences, because professional types were consistently treated more kindly than the uneducated ruffians in the group (Smith 1977, 305).

Three defendants were acquitted largely due to a fluke of rules. Early on, the judges determined that unless a defendant was convicted by a clear majority (three countries against one), that individual should be acquitted. Out of a total of seventy-four individual charges, there were twenty-two acquittals—a surprisingly high failure rate, considering that the defendants had been carefully selected for their obvious culpability. In the case of von Papen, the Russians called for the death penalty, as they had throughout the proceedings for nearly all the defendants, and the French called for a light sentence on principle. The British and American judges were unconvinced by the evidence and called for acquittal. Thus, although the French and Russian judges disagreed about the penalty, their agreement on the need for conviction led to Papen's acquittal by producing a 2-2 stalemate. After considerable discussion, the judges decided to go back to the previous convictions of Fritzsche and Schacht and acquit because of the remarkable similarities in the cases of all three men.

The charges against certain Nazi and German organizations were upheld. Rather than urging the prosecution of any member of these groups, however, the judges instructed future prosecutors to ascertain on a case-by-case basis the individual culpability of each member. The result was a cumbersome and ultimately short-lived legal process that resulted in only a few hundred prison sentences over the next two years. The urgency of the Cold War pushed World War II business to the back burner everywhere but in Israel, where World War II war crimes trials continue to this day.

On October 16, 1945, the defendants sentenced to death were hanged outside the courtroom (with the exceptions of Goering and Bormann, who had already died). Their bodies were later cremated and their ashes scattered near Munich. Thus the birthplace of Nazism became its grave.

IMPLICATIONS OF THE NUREMBERG TRIALS

The Nuremberg Trials offer a significant and rich example of international law in all of its aspects: as a general body of values and principles, as a set of codified treaties, and as a feature of domestic law. Also, in these trials we see both the development and application of international law—a rare opportunity. Finally, the Nuremberg Trials offer a legacy that is very much alive today, as illustrated by George Bush's call for the prosecution of Saddam Hussein on war crimes charges in 1991.

A crucial problem becomes clear when we consider the Nuremberg Trials—that is, the dilemma of applying law that is not yet codified in treaty form. German defendants and later critics have argued that the law applied at Nuremberg was ex post facto, especially insofar as crimes against peace and humanity are concerned. Linking the concept of aggressive war with the unenforceable Kellogg-Briand Pact created further difficulties. Nothing in existing international law (as of 1939) expressly forbade a head of state from launching any sort of war under penalty of death. On the contrary, given the heritage of colonialism with all its bloody dimensions, the many minor and major wars fought throughout the 19th and early 20th centuries, and the escalation in weaponry and tactics, it could easily have been inferred that the type of war Germany contemplated was perfectly legal according to existing legal codes and customs.

So why was the effort made to prosecute the Nazi leadership? As Jackson and others put it, the nations that held the power at the time agreed to establish a new standard for international behavior. They could do that most quickly by establishing a judicial precedent at Nuremberg—in spite of the absence of formally codified laws (see Harris 1954, 491). International law was viewed as a sort of global common law—an ad hoc collection of rules and judgments that are handed down to future generations for their own interpretation. Although this view is certainly convenient, the general trend since World War II has been to codify explicit declarations—worded generally—as a precursor to more specific and binding treaties. Thus the Universal Declaration on Human Rights of 1949 has served as a backdrop for the more recent Declaration on the Rights of the Child, which in turn will permit more forceful agreements on child labor laws and health standards. Perhaps the most significant result of the Nuremberg proceedings was not the convictions themselves, but the articulation of general principles.

Since the trials, several new treaties have been drafted that articulate specific crimes related to the Nazi actions. The Geneva Convention was updated in 1949 to cover a wider array of acts against prisoners of war and noncombatants. The United Nations established in 1950 the International Law Commission, which has as its mission the codification of existing rules and principles. An important first step was the drafting of the Genocide Convention in 1949, which prohibits any attempt to destroy a "national, ethical, racial or religious group" and clearly makes all individuals involved in such crimes responsible and punishable "whether they are constitutionally responsible rulers, public officials or private individuals" (Articles II and IV) (see Woetzel 1960).

The so-called Nuremberg Principles were accepted by the United Nations in 1950 and offer legal justification for the actions of the tribunal. For example, Principles I and II state:

> Any person who commits an act which constitutes a crime under international law is responsible therefore and liable to punishment. The fact that internal law does not impose a penalty for an act which constitutes a crime under international law does not relieve the person who committed the act from responsibility under international law.

This notion of personal responsibility has also been written into domestic laws, including the Constitution (Basic Law) of Germany and the field manuals of the U.S. Army. The principles further specify that all accused persons have a right to a fair trial and list specific crimes that warrant prosecution: crimes against peace, war crimes, and crimes against humanity. These terms were applied in the Tokyo War Crimes Trials and the Adolf Eichmann trial of 1961. They also became the touchstone for a growing number of war crimes tribunals in the 1990s.

In 1993, the UN Security Council established the first international war crimes tribunal not related to World War II to investigate and prosecute charges of genocide in Bosnia. The next year, the council set up a panel to deal with the atrocities in Rwanda. There is some discussion about doing the same in Cambodia to prosecute those responsible for the genocide in the 1970s (Tessitore & Woolfson 1999, 279). In each case, the appointment of judges, the treatment of defendants, and the list of crimes were drawn almost directly from the Nuremberg experience. A major difference is that the laws utilized at Nuremberg have now been codified in the

Nuremberg Principles, the Genocide Convention, the International Covenant on Civil and Political Rights, and other treaties that deal with the rights of minorities, refugees, women, and children. The scope of the charges is now broader and includes such crimes as the use of rape as a weapon of war. Furthermore, these laws have been incorporated into the constitutions of most countries. No one can claim ignorance of these fundamental standards of conduct.

The Yugoslav and Rwandan war crimes tribunals have functioned continuously since their founding, although they have not met with unqualified success. The Rwandan court was plagued with inefficiencies and other flaws, and it did not hand down its first conviction until 1999. Nevertheless, the judges on the court succeeded in establishing the guilt of a prominent local official in Rwanda on the charge that failure to use his authority to stop the massacres was tantamount to participation. In the Yugoslav court, the number of indicted individuals continues to rise, along with the status of the defendants. In mid-1999, the leader of the Yugoslav Republic, Slobodan Milosevic, was indicted, which made him a prisoner in his own country. In 2000, after a contested election, Milosevic resigned from office in favor of the opposition candidate, Vojislav Kostunica. The next year, he was arrested by the new government on corruption charges and ultimately turned over to the Hague tribunal (under considerable pressure from Western governments). His war crime trial began in February 2002 and continued until his death in captivity.

Perhaps the greatest honor paid to the Nuremberg prosecutors was the decision taken by more than 100 nations on June 17, 1999, to approve the Rome Statute for an International Criminal Court by a vote of 120-7, with twenty-one abstentions, after nearly ten years of negotiation. The scope of the new court will be almost the same as that of the Nuremberg Tribunal. Eighteen judges will render decisions based on a formal trial. The court officially opened for business in July 2002, although the United States has opted out. As put by Tina Rosenberg, "Such a court would be a fitting heir to the tribunals, which, after fifty years, still represent what chief U.S. prosecutor at Nuremberg, Robert Jackson, called 'one of the most significant tributes that Power has ever paid to Reason' " (Rosenberg 1995, 691). In mid-2004, the ICC officially began its work by opening investigations into genocide in the Democratic Republic of the Congo and Uganda.

CONCLUSIONS: INTERNATIONAL LAW AND JUSTICE

To what extent have the Nuremberg Principles and new treaties affected the actual conduct of international affairs and the conduct of war in particular? A complete answer is impossible here. The press usually begins the debate by considering acts committed during wartime. During the Vietnam War, it became clear by the late 1960s that atrocities were being committed both deliberately and inadvertently as a result of U.S. military operations. The "carpet bombing" missions of hundreds of 8-52 bombers saturating large sections of North Vietnam with heavy bomb payloads resulted in thousands of civilian casualties. Several U.S. officers were accused of and formally charged with violations of military law as a result of large-scale attacks on unarmed civilians.

The villages of My Lai and Son My were attacked by American forces at the height of the Vietnam War. Villagers were rounded up and shot in a particularly brutal way by American servicemen under orders to maximize their "body count" of Vietnamese casualties. It is clear from the testimony delivered at the court-martials of those involved, including Lt. William Calley, that many prisoners of war were killed and many villages razed to increase body count statistics, and these actions were tolerated and even implicitly encouraged by commanders. Calley seems to have played the role of scapegoat for a system that was fundamentally corrupt (Falk et al. 1971, 226). The same cannot be said of those convicted of prisoner abuse in Iraq (at Abu Ghraib prison), where there is tangible evidence (in the form of damning photos) that soldiers went far beyond the Geneva Convention restrictions as they stripped prisoners, applied electroshocks, forced them to adopt degrading positions and intimidated them with guard dogs (*New York Times* 25 August 2004, A14).

Perhaps more serious, war criminals who win wars are unlikely to be charged, let alone prosecuted. Not only will the victors still have the protection of their government, but they will also have a hand in deciding the parameters of war crimes themselves. The Russians during the Nuremberg Trials were careful to prevent the judgment from encompassing their own misdeeds during the war. As the saying goes, "If the traitors are victorious, none dare call it treachery."

Terrorism is a quasi-military action against primarily civilian targets. Although the acts of terrorists are not explicitly covered by existing international law, they are clearly violations of the domestic law in places where they occur. The Reagan administration prosecuted terrorists through domestic U.S. courts if they had been involved in attacks on American citizens. In some cases, bringing the terrorists into custody has involved some reactive military and diplomatic maneuvers, such as the recent case involving the United States, the United Kingdom, and Libya over the release of individuals held in Libya and wanted for the downing of Pan Am flight 103 over Lockerbie, Scotland, in 1988. The suspects were ultimately released, a trial conducted, and convictions were handed down against two Libyan operatives. The trial marked the beginning of a concerted effort by the Muammar Khadafi regime in Tripoli to improve its relations with the West—a strategy that has worked well and has been seen as a model of how to rehabilitate a pariah state.

Overall, the Nuremberg Trials served many important purposes, although they clearly fell short of the ambitious goal to prevent future war crimes. Without the trials, much of the information we now have about the Holocaust would have remained unorganized. Without the trials, German leaders likely would have been shot summarily and treated very differently depending on which country had captured them. The trials prevented the martyrdom of Nazi leaders, as well as a popular uprising against the occupation forces. They went far in helping Germany establish firm anti-Nazi laws and a constitutional government. The elevation of what were perhaps subconscious moral principles to the level of international law has also served an important moral purpose, if not becoming a cure-all for the world's evils. As put by Harris, "It has become a test of faith that the victors now live by the rules of law they used to condemn and punish the leaders of Hitler's Germany" (Harris 1954, 560).

QUESTIONS TO CONSIDER

1. Were the Nuremberg Trials really a legal undertaking or merely window dressing for what was essentially the spoils of victory? How can such trials be governed purely by law?

2. To what extent is the Nuremberg experience a precedent? In law? In morality? In social interaction? How could the Nuremberg Principles be applied in Yugoslavia? In Somalia? In Chicago?

3. How effective were the Nuremberg Trials in ending fascism and genocide?

KEY FIGURES
THE NUREMBERG TRIALS

Hermann Göring (Goering)   Founder of the Gestapo (secret police) and second ranking Nazi after Hitler (although he plotted his overthrow in the waning months of World War 11). He was the most prominent defendant at Nuremberg.

Rudolf Hess   Deputy Führer (third most powerful leader) in the Nazi regime and senior defendant at Nuremberg. He flew to England in 1941 in a bizarre attempt to negotiate peace. He was held captive until the Nuremberg trials.

Ernst Kaltenbrunner   Leader of the Nazi elite military branch and a defendant at Nuremberg.

Arthur Seyss-Inquart   Leader of the Austrian Anschluss and a defendant at Nuremberg.

Albert Speer   Organizer of industrial production under Hitler and a defendant at Nuremberg.

Fritz Sauke   Organizer of concentration camp labor under Hitler and a defendant at Nuremberg.

John Jackson   U.S. Supreme Court Justice, who served as chief prosecutor at Nuremberg.

Francis Biddle   Senior American judge of the Nuremberg tribunal.

Lord Geoffrey Lawrence   British judge of the Nuremberg tribunal.

I. T. Nikitchenko   Russian judge of the Nuremberg tribunal.

Donnedieu de Vabres   French judge of the Nuremberg tribunal.

Adolf Eichmann   Nazi war criminal convicted in Israel.

Slobodan Milosevic   Leader of Serbia and defendant at the Yugoslav War Crimes.

CHRONOLOGY
THE NUREMBERG TRIALS

1907
The Hague Convention on legitimate military tactics is signed.

1919
The League of Nations Covenant is signed. It provides for prohibitions against aggression.

1924
The Geneva Convention on treatment of prisoners of war (POWs) is signed.

1925
The Kellogg-Briand Pact outlawing aggressive war is signed.

1933
Hitler's Nazis burn the Reichstag building to create panic and secure emergency powers.

1935
The Nuremberg Race Laws against Jews are decreed, removing German citizenship.

1938
Germany invades Austria, declaring "anschluss" (unification) of the two countries. Anti-Semitic laws are extended.

1939
Germany attacks Poland, starting World War II.

1942–1945
Nazis kill roughly six million Jews, Slavs, and others in the Holocaust.

1944
Murray Bernays of the U.S. State Department proposes a war crimes tribunal after the war.

1945
January   Eighty American POWs are murdered by Nazi guards, prompting Franklin Roosevelt to endorse a war crime trial in principle.

May 8   Germany capitulates. Subsequently, Nuremberg defendants are arrested by American, British, and Russian troops.

November 20   The Nuremberg Trials open. Prosecution begins its case.

1946
March   The defense stage of trial begins.

September   Judges deliberate and render verdicts.

October 16   Defendants sentenced to death are hanged.

(*continued*)

(*continued*)

1994

The International Criminal Tribunal for the former Yugoslavia (ICTY), established in 1993 by the UN Security Council, begins hearing cases in the first international war crimes tribunal since Nuremberg and Tokyo. A War Crimes Tribunal for Rwanda is founded by the UN Security Council subsequent to the genocide that took place there in that year.

2002

International Criminal Court begins operation. Slobodan Milosevic appears before the ICTY. He is the first former head of state to be formally tried before an international war crimes tribunal.

WEBSITES

Detailed Nuremberg Sites Run by Universities and NGOS:

www.yale.edu/lawweb/avalon/imt/imt.htm,

www.ess.uwe.ac.uk/genocide/wwwzres.htm,

www.holocaust.history.org/works/imt/0l/htm.cOOl.htm

Nuremberg Higher Superior Court: www.justiz.bayern.de/olgn/imte-more.htm

REFERENCES

Conot, Robert E. *Justice at Nuremberg* (New York: Harper & Row, 1983).

Falk, Richard, Gabriel Kolko, and Robert Jay Lifton, eds. *Crimes of War: A Legal, Political-Documentary, and Psychological Inquiry into the Responsibility of Leaders, Citizens, and Soldiers for Criminal Acts in Wars* (New York: Random House, 1971).

Gerhart, Eugene C. *America's Advocate: Robert H. Jackson* (New York: Bobbs-Merrill, 1958).

Harris, Whitney R. *Tyranny on Trial: The Evidence at Nuremberg* (Dallas: Southern Methodist University, 1954).

Rosenberg, Tina. "From Nuremberg to Bosnia." *The Nation* 260 #19 (May 15, 1995): 688–691.

Smith, Bradley F. *Reaching Judgment at Nuremberg* (New York: Basic Books, 1977).

Smith, Bradley F. *The Road to Nuremberg* (New York: Basic Books, 1981).

Taylor, Telford. *The Anatomy of the Nuremberg Trials* (New York: Little, Brown, 1993).

Tessitore, John, and Susan Woolfson, eds. *A Global Agenda: Issues Before the 54th General Assembly of the United Nations* (Lanham, MD: Rowman & Littlefield, 1999).

Woetzel, Robert K. *The Nuremberg Trials in International Law* (New York: Praeger, 1960).

19

■ ■ ■

Human Rights: Apartheid in South Africa

INTRODUCTION

Human Rights

"Inalienable rights," a notion fundamental to the American system, means that people enjoy certain privileges simply by virtue of being human, and no government has the right to take those privileges away. Where the rights originated matters little; "inalienable" means that they came before governments were ever established. When we speak of "human rights" in international affairs, we are generally referring to those inalienable rights. They include not only the familiar freedom of speech, freedom from slavery and discrimination, and the right to participate in public life, but also rights with unique importance on the global level: self-determination, prohibition against genocide, and the right to peace. Over time, a consensus has developed on these and still other economic and social rights, such that countries that routinely and wantonly violate them are frequently the object of international censure.

This consensus has been expressed in the form of several important documents, the most celebrated of which is the Universal Declaration of Human Rights. This statement (not a binding law) was drafted shortly after World War II by representatives of more than fifty countries under the leadership of Eleanor Roosevelt, Franklin Roosevelt's widow. In it, governments agree that such fundamental civil rights as freedom of speech, thought, and assembly are paramount and that no government should restrict them without a strong public purpose. The document also declares that democracy and all its ancillary characteristics (elections, a free press, due process in the courtroom, and so forth) are the ideal form of government.

317

The document further urges states to attend to the economic, social, and physical needs of their citizens, and it declares that all people have a right to such things as an education, housing, food, and employment.

Over the years, the rights enumerated in the Universal Declaration have been expanded upon and made more binding, such that today governments have gone so far as to intervene militarily to overthrow regimes that have repeatedly violated fundamental human rights in egregious ways (see Chapter 10). At the very least, many governments that have violated basic human rights have been subjected to diplomatic and economic penalties and sanctions. South Africans understand this relationship better than most.

> Either the white man dominates or the black man takes over. I say that the non-European will not accept leadership—if he has a choice. The only way the Europeans can maintain supremacy is by domination. . . . And the only way they can maintain domination is by withholding the vote from the non-Europeans. (Dr. Daniel F. Malan, South African Prime Minister, 1948–1954)
>
> We, the people of South Africa, declare for all our country and the world to know that South Africa belongs to all who live in it, black and white, and that no government can justly claim authority unless it is based on the will of all the people . . . that only a democratic state based on the will of all the people can secure their birthright without distinction of colour, race, sex or belief. . . . (Freedom Charter of the African National Congress, 1955)

These two quotes present the essence of the struggle in South Africa. Unlike the civil rights movement in the United States, South Africa pitted a minority in power against an overwhelming but largely powerless majority. That minority controlled most of the wealth, schools, businesses, and property of the country against the will of the majority. Moreover, that minority became more and more determined, during the middle part of this century, to maintain not only its power but also its exclusive right to citizenship in an ever more narrowly defined state.

Many misconceptions exist about the nature of apartheid, the policy of separation of the races in South Africa. Furthermore, there is much ignorance about the origins and basis for this national policy. Although the history that follows is extremely brief, we hope it will shed some light on this vital and burning issue of international politics.

ORIGINS OF SOUTH AFRICA: 1652–1910

Beginning in the days of Magellan, the Cape of Good Hope was recognized as a useful way station for travelers between Europe and India. The Dutch first decided in 1652 to establish a permanent claim and settlement under the leadership of Jan van Riebeeck. He almost immediately set about establishing a viable farming colony populated by "freeburghers" (pioneer farmers), which extended into the neighboring territory. Native black tribes opposed this encroachment, which prompted van

Riebeeck to assert white superiority by force. Within fifty years, black slaves from other African territories were imported to expand the farming capacity of the colony. "Thus he persuaded the company to take the four decisions that shaped South Africa: to found the colony, to settle freeburghers, to establish superiority over the local tribes and to import slaves" (Lapping 1986, 4).

By the end of the 18th century, the Dutch were unable to control overseas territories because they were under attack by Napoleon's France. The British first protected and then purchased the Cape Colony in 1815, dispatching a colonial administration to govern the settlement. They introduced "pass laws" for the first time, which obliged the nomadic African Khoikhoi to carry a written "pass" proving their association with a particular Dutch settler. The British presence was resented from the start by the now-independent Dutch settlers, or Boers ("farmers"). In 1815, while carrying out an arrest order against several Boers, a British detachment was attacked. The offending Boers were arrested and later hanged at Slachter's Nek—an event that served as a symbol of British authoritarianism (Lapping 1986, 10).

British officialdom became ever more ubiquitous as English-speaking missionaries attempted to establish schools for both Afrikaner (descendants of Dutch settlers) and black children. Ultimately, the Boers decided that they could no longer tolerate the imposition of British culture and power, and they embarked on one of the great migrations of people in history: the Great Trek. In 1837, some 6,000 Afrikaners began moving both eastward along the coast and some 800 miles northward into largely unpopulated wilderness to found a new homeland for themselves. The principal concentrations were in the area south of the current city of Johannesburg in the Orange Free State and along the coast near modern-day Durban in Natal province. By 1854, some 10,000 Afrikaners and an equal number of colored and black servants had migrated from Cape Colony toward what would become the heart of South Africa.

White South African propaganda maintains that the Boers arrived in an unpopulated territory where blacks later migrated (in part drawn by the prosperity of the whites) (Republic of South Africa 1973, 10). In fact, not only does ample archaeological evidence reveal a substantial African presence before the Great Trek, but the Zulu nation under Shaka Zulu had already advanced far into the same territory and engaged in several bloody skirmishes with the advancing Boers. The most famous skirmish involved trekker Piet Retief who, after being tricked by a Zulu interpreter, was cornered along with his pioneers by several thousand Zulu warriors on December 15, 1838. By virtue of their position against a mountain pass, the Boers were able to protect their rear and face the Zulus with overwhelming firepower. Although 3,000 Zulus were killed, not a single Boer perished. Many Afrikaners attribute the Boers' success to a covenant with God entered into the day before, offering Afrikaner devotion and piety in exchange for victory (Lapping 1986, 16). (They also promised to build a church, which was later converted to a stable.)

The Boers eked out a living during the first years after their trek, but in 1867, mineral discoveries began to rapidly alter the character of their nation. Rapid population growth after the discovery of diamonds in Kimberly, in the western Orange Free State, overwhelmed the underequipped British authorities, who quickly moved en masse to administer the territory. Famous explorers, financiers, and speculators from across the empire converged on the area and made easy fortunes. Cecil Rhodes became one of the richest men in the world by purchasing numerous apparently dry wells from impatient excavators—the holes actually contained billions of dollars worth of diamonds.

Within ten years, the British government, with Afrikaner urging, established race-based laws to govern the ownership of diamond mines. As put by Brown: "The momentous step in the development of apartheid occurred in 1867 when diamonds were discovered along the Orange and Vaal rivers. . . . [I]n 1875 the right to own and operate a diamond concession was permitted only to whites" (Brown 1981, 59). From 1875 on, the blacks of South Africa were effectively excluded from profiting from the most promising opportunity to come to the African continent until the oil strikes in Libya. Instead, they were relegated to the status of mere laborers. The same was true for gold mining after it started around Johannesburg in 1880.

A radical interpretation does not seem out of place:

Whenever superior races settle on lands where lower races can be profitably used for manual labour in agriculture, mining and domestic work, the latter do not tend to die out, but to form a servile class. This is the case, not only in tropical countries where white men cannot form real colonies, working and rearing families with safety and efficiency, and where hard manual work, if done at all, must be done by "coloured men," but even in countries where white men can settle, as in part of South Africa and of the southern portion of the United States. (Hobson 1965, 258, in Magubane 1979, 8)

As further explained by Magubane:

South Africa is not a plural society; it is a society with a dual labor market: a primary (white) market of relatively secure, well-paid jobs, and a secondary (black) market of insecure, filthy, low-paid jobs. African workers are confined to a marginal, yet indispensable, role by fraud, violence, and a system of institutionalized racism that protects "the white masters of the world." (Magubane 1979, 17)

As the end of the century neared, the struggle for control of gold and diamonds in the heart of South Africa continued to intensify. Although the British were able to establish clear control in the Kimberly area, Afrikaners held out in the Orange Free State and farther to the north in the Transvaal, where the plucky Boer Paul Kruger retained control in 1899 after three abortive British seizures. In 1899, a new British governor, Alfred Milner, embarked on a systematic, all-out effort to dislodge the independent Afrikaners from the Transvaal and elsewhere in the north by deploying a large British army into the region. The Boer War that ensued lasted nearly three years and caused tens of thousands of casualties. In particular, the British introduced "concentration camps" by capturing thousands of women and children and interring them in tent cities across the region, where disease and malnutrition took some 26,000 civilian lives. In the countryside, the British practiced a "scorched earth" policy to deprive the Boer guerrillas of finding sustenance from the land (Lapping 1986, 31).

After the Boers finally surrendered in 1902, the British moved to consolidate their gains by inviting more British settlers into the country and establishing a united federal state with the consent of the Afrikaners in the Transvaal and the Orange Free State (a form of expansive home rule tantamount to independence was offered as an inducement). A new generation of Afrikaner politicians, led by Jan Smuts and Louis Botha, embraced the British offers. In 1910, the Union of South Africa was proclaimed a part of the British Empire.

ESTABLISHMENT AND CONSOLIDATION OF APARTHEID: 1910–1965

Part of the deal made with the Afrikaners involved British concessions on social policy. A series of race-related laws guaranteeing Afrikaner superiority was implemented in the 1910s. Before discussing the details of these and other laws, we will look at the philosophy and social norms that undergird apartheid.

The Afrikaners held that their presence in South Africa was more than merely a coincidence of human migration—rather it was the product of divine intervention on behalf of the white race. Dr. Daniel Malan, prime minister in 1948–1954 and former Dutch Reformed Church minister, declared:

> We hold this nationhood as our due, for it was given us by the architect of the universe. His aim was the formation of a new nation. The last hundred years have witnessed a miracle behind which must lie a divine plan. Afrikanerdom is not the work of men but the creation of God. . . . Not because we Afrikaners are tremendously good people, but because God, the Disposer of the lot of the nations, has a future task for our People. (Lapping 1986, 66)

Malan "made the attempt with as ambitious—or ridiculous—a claim as any politician has ever made: that God's destiny for the Afrikaner people, the reason he had chosen them, punished them, saved them, was to preserve the white race" (Lapping 1986, 71).

Shortly after the consolidation of the republic, the Transvaal and Orange Free State enacted a number of restrictive racial policies. In particular, new pass laws forced blacks, "coloreds" (blacks originally imported from other parts of Africa), and a growing Indian immigrant population to carry identification cards at all times. Failure to produce the pass when confronted by a police officer typically resulted in incarceration. Controls on physical movement were combined with continued restrictions on property ownership, and severe limitations on nonwhite suffrage prompted protests and petitions by certain educated blacks, four of whom formed the African National Congress (ANC) in 1912. These Africans asked little more than a retention of certain rights they had been granted prior to 1910 as British subjects. They failed to get a hearing with the king in 1913 under the leadership of Sol Plaatje. In the meantime, the Native Lands Act was passed in London, thereby creating a system of reservations for blacks—some 7.3% of South Africa's poorest land was designated for the more than 60% of the population that was black. Rather than alienate the newly pacified Afrikaners, the monarchy and Parliament in London refused to reverse the policy.

An important parallel development occurred in the Indian community, where Mohandas Gandhi, the advocate of nonviolent resistance and future leader of India, organized a series of demonstrations against pass laws and property restrictions. Although for a time he was successful in securing a softening of pass law enforcement, the effort was fairly short-lived (Lapping 1986, 49).

In the 1920s and 1930s, relations among Africans, Afrikaners, and the English deteriorated. Black worker strikes in 1918, born of frustration with the failure of the ANC accommodation, led to massive arrests. Meanwhile, the Afrikaner workers protested and struck over the limited promotions some black mine workers received (some whites were passed over by British managers), and in 1922 Prime Minister Jan Smuts ordered troops to quell the disturbance. Some 200 Afrikaner miners were killed in the ensuing action. The event led to an electoral victory for pro-Afrikaner militants in 1924, which in turn led to strengthened white worker rights and eventual removal of the limited black electoral franchise by 1936.

Black workers began to adopt an increasingly militant style in the 1940s. By 1944, Anton Lembede had organized the Youth League, loosely affiliated with the ANC, and began training what would become the next generation of ANC leadership: Nelson Mandela, Walter Sisulu, and Oliver Tambo (Lapping 1986, 82). They adopted a more consciously pro-black, anticapitalist philosophy and urged violence and widespread action against the white government.

Conservative Afrikaner politicians latched onto the misery of the Depression with its attendant anti-British and anti-Jew fearfulness and the symbolism surrounding the centennial of the Great Trek to catapult themselves into power in the 1948 elections—the first to produce an all-Afrikaner cabinet. The importance of the 1948 election cannot be exaggerated. At the same time the United States was working to desegregate the military, schools, and all public facilities, the Afrikaner government in South Africa embarked on a program to introduce and intensify racial separation. In 1950, Prime Minister Malan appointed Dr. Hendrik F. Verwoerd minister of native affairs. Verwoerd, in this position and later as prime minister until his assassination in 1966, was the single most important architect of apartheid (Lapping 1986, 106).

Verwoerd's legislative strategy took a systematic approach to separating the races. The Population Registration Act set out to classify every resident of South Africa by race. It then "empowered the government to mark off areas for residence, occupation and trade by the different races and then to move each race into its own area, by force if necessary" (Lapping 1986, 105). This basic classification was refined and clarified over the years, although as recently as 1985, nearly 800 people had their racial classifications legally changed. The Prohibition of Mixed Marriages Act ensured racial purity in mainstream family relations, whereas the Immorality Amendment Act of 1957 outlawed any intercourse whatever between individuals of different races.

Verwoerd was famous for his promotion of the status and symbolic powers of black tribal leaders across South Africa. He promoted himself as the great "Bantu" (Native African) chief of chiefs and joined the tribal leaders in elaborate ceremonies reaffirming their legitimacy as rulers of black nations. The South African government began to emphasize differences among the various black tribes:

> In a nutshell, the inescapable feature of the South African situation is that South Africa is a country of many nations: Four million whites of European origin, four million Xhosa, four million Zulu, two million Tswana, two million Sotho and so on. Each group is a minority—there is in fact no single majority group. (Republic of South Africa 1973, 29)

Verwoerd hoped to accomplish the dual goal of undermining black solidarity and creating a vast network of black supporters of the white Pretoria regime. In this context, the Bantu Authorities Act of 1951 designated specific homelands for each of ten major African tribes that resided in South Africa (see Map 19.1). Regardless of where members of these various tribes happened to be living at the time, the

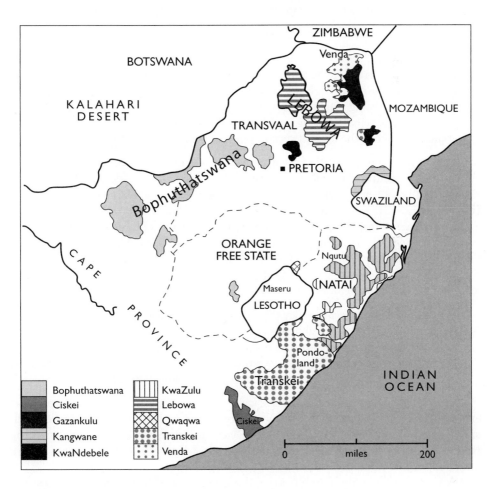

Map 19.1 The Homelands

government expected that they would migrate to their areas and away from white cities. In these territories, the black leaders were permitted control of certain governmental functions (subsidized often to the tune of 75% of their budgets by Pretoria), and "tribal citizens" could exercise their right to vote. South African citizenship was denied, however. In the late 1960s, a few of these homelands were granted independence by the Pretoria government (Transkei in 1976, Bophuthatswana in 1977, Venda in 1979, and Ciskei in 1981), although this move did little to change their government other than reinforce the separate legal status of homelands residents. As put by one of Verwoerd's successors in a speech before Parliament:

> If our policy is taken to its logical conclusion as far as the black people are concerned, there will not be one black man with South African citizenship. . . . Every black man in South Africa will eventually be accommodated in some independent new state in this honourable way and there will no longer be a moral obligation on this parliament to accommodate these people politically. (Omond 1985, 102)

In this context, Verwoerd argued that education was to be strictly controlled and segregated:

> Native education should be controlled in such a way that it should be in accord with the policy of the state. . . . If the native in South Africa today in any kind of school in existence is being taught to expect that he will live his adult life under a policy of equal rights, he is making a big mistake. . . . There is no place for him in the European community above the level of certain forms of labor. (Omond 1985, 80)

Lemon has pointed out that South Africa is one of the only countries where the educational system for a majority of its citizens is specifically designed to restrict, rather than create opportunities by limiting them to a homeland-specific training (Lemon 1987, 52). This policy was later extended to the university level.

In general terms, living conditions for blacks were deplorable, so the government had to adopt very aggressive measures to force as many Africans as possible to relocate to their respective homelands. Over a five-year period, many thousands of blacks were moved out of white neighborhoods. The elderly and infirm were specifically targeted for removal. As put by one of Verwoerd's successors in 1967:

> It is accepted government policy that the Bantu are only temporarily resident in the European areas of the Republic for as long as they offer their labour there. As soon as they become, for one reason or another, no longer fit to work or superfluous in the labour market, they are expected to return to their country of origin or the territory of the national unit where they fit ethnically. (Lapping 1986, 154)

By 1980, roughly half of black Africans were residing in the Bantustans—the end result of thirty years of government effort (Lemon 1987, 199). Estimates indicated that as many as 3.5 million people were relocated in connection with the Native Lands Act during the 1980s, with another 1.8 million being vulnerable to future expulsion (Omond 1985, 114).

A variety of laws, including restricted property rights, intensified pass laws, and the Separate Amenities Act of 1953, which prohibited multiracial use of public facilities, were passed and enforced with great vigor.

These actions created a large migrant worker population in South Africa. The mere relocation of workers did little to spur the relocation of the workplace. In 1970, some 1 million blacks were forced to migrate to work. That figure had increased to 1.4 million by 1982 (Lemon 1987, 199). Such an imposed lifestyle wreaked havoc on the black family:

> From the standpoint of the homelands and their people, the economic and social disadvantages of the migrant labour system are overwhelming. Socially, the break-up of family life and impediments to normal sexual relationships affect some of the most basic human needs . . . illegitimacy, bigamy, prostitution, homosexuality, drunkenness, violence and the breakdown of parental authority [are] direct effects of the system, whilst venereal disease, tuberculosis, malnutrition and beriberi are some of the indirect results of the lifestyle of migrant laborers. Men are degraded by a system which deprives them of a family role, whilst women are left behind feeling lonely and helpless, anxiously waiting for letters and money from their husbands. (Lemon 1987, 200)

Not all blacks accepted the new order. The ANC attracted an increasingly diverse assortment of followers—coloreds, Indians, Communists, academics—with a leadership under growing pressure to radicalize the movement. Albert Luthuli, ANC leader in the 1950s, was cautious about radical demands and worked to keep the ANC legal and able to work with the government. In 1952, the ANC initiated what was expected to be a series of peaceful demonstrations and civil disobedience gestures as part of this moderate approach. The campaign degenerated into a series of melees between police and passersby untrained in nonviolent techniques. The government cracked down on ANC leaders, restricting their travel to their own neighborhoods. Although the ANC consequently lost stature with the government, its membership grew from a mere 7,000 to some 100,000 (Lapping 1986, 119).

In 1955, the organization held a momentous Congress of the People to protest apartheid laws and draft a plan of action. The Freedom Charter was the result of the Congress's desire for a democratic, multiracial South Africa. In addition to civil rights, the Freedom Charter called for land reform, labor rights, and redistribution of wealth to "the people as a whole." It represented the most radical and united statement by blacks in South Africa's history and became a rallying cry for all opponents of apartheid.

The South African government, dismayed at the apparent power of the ANC as an alternative political order, responded ferociously. The leaders of the ANC were declared traitors to the state and were imprisoned. As a direct consequence, the world's attention was drawn even more sharply to the plight of blacks in South Africa. A lengthy and bitter trial ensued under the glaring eye of international public opinion. The government's prosecutor bungled the charges of treason and Communist sympathies, instead creating ideal opportunities for the ANC leaders to make their own case publicly, clearly, and eloquently. Nelson Mandela presented himself as the indignant lawyer and future leader of the ANC with this scathing attack on the legitimacy of the proceedings:

> Firstly, I challenge it because I fear that I will not be given a fair and proper trial. Secondly, I consider myself neither legally nor morally bound to obey laws made by a parliament in which I have no representation. In a political trial such as this one,

which involves a clash of the aspirations of the African people and those of whites, the country's courts, as presently constituted, cannot be impartial and fair. In such cases, whites are interested parties. To have a white judicial officer presiding, however high his esteem, and however strong his sense of fairness and justice, is to make whites judges in their own case. . . . The white man makes all the laws, he drags us before his courts and accuses us, and he sits in judgment over us.... I feel oppressed by the atmosphere of white domination that lurks all around in this courtroom. Somehow this atmosphere calls to mind the inhuman injustices caused to my people outside this courtroom by this same white domination. (Mandela 1990, 134)

In the end, all of the accused were acquitted, primarily because of prosecutorial incompetence.

Having failed to achieve its goal through the use of laws then on the books, the government, now under Verwoerd himself, adopted new laws. The ANC was included among outlaw organizations under the 1960 Unlawful Organization Act. By 1963, such prominent ANC leaders as Walter Sisulu, Nelson Mandela, Robert Sobukwe, and Oliver Tambo were imprisoned or forced into exile.

The 1960 Sharpeville Massacre was a case of police impatience. The Pan-African Congress, a black organization with more radical objectives than the ANC, organized a demonstration of 5,000 people in what was thought to be a model township. However, unemployment, dissatisfaction with the pass laws, and forced migration had created intense hostility with the white government. The marchers surrounded a police station, where they waited for most of the day. Then a scuffle broke out, the crowd surged forward, and the police began shooting into the throng. Nearly 100 blacks were killed—most of them in the back—in the ensuing chaos. Luthuli called for a day of work stoppage and peaceful protest, which the government in turn repressed by arresting 18,000 strikers across the country. New laws permitted the government to detain suspects indefinitely with a judge's approval and to detain for interrogation anyone the police wanted. The Public Safety Act allowed the government to declare a state of emergency and thereby suspend most of the few remaining civil rights in specific areas for limited but renewable periods of time (Omond 1985, 158). By 1963, South Africa was reviled in international circles as the worst human rights violator on the planet.

STALEMATE: 1965–1988

The period from 1965 to 1988 can be described as a stalemate between a galvanized but largely leaderless black community and an increasingly ambivalent white government unable to maintain both social domination and economic prosperity. The inflexible apartheid of the Verwoerd era was inherently unstable. Although it protected the white population from association with blacks, it deprived the nation of its most important asset: black labor and intellect. At best, black Africans were learning to manipulate the system for their own ends—hardly the basis for legitimate government (Lambley 1980, 125). Even more serious was the impact of increasingly strict international economic and diplomatic sanctions on the vitality of the South African economy. These objective conditions would ultimately force the white government to reverse most of apartheid's structures during the 1980s and begin the process of democratizing the country in the 1990s.

A leaderless black community drifted for much of the 1960s, when new philosophies and organizational structures began to emerge. Steve Biko, a black medical student in Natal province, worked to form an all-black student group known as the South African Student Organization in 1968. Steve Biko put it eloquently:

> Black Consciousness is an attitude of mind and a way of life. . . . Its essence is the realization by the black man of the need to rally together with his brothers around the cause of their oppression—the blackness of their skin—and to operate as a group to rid themselves of the shackles that bind them to perpetual servitude. It is based on a self-examination which has ultimately led them to believe that by seeking to run away from themselves and emulate the white man, they are insulting the intelligence of whoever created them black. This philosophy of Black Consciousness therefore expresses group pride and the determination of the black to rise and attain the envisaged self. . . . (Fatton 1986, 78)

In the context of the spread of this Black Consciousness movement, black students across South Africa protested their forced education in Afrikaans in the 1970s. In Soweto, an overcrowded township near Johannesburg where many black intellectuals resided, feelings were particularly strong and spilled over into large demonstrations. In June 1976, protests swelled to tens of thousands. On one occasion, the police fired into the crowd, which then went on a rampage through neighboring black and white areas for several days. In the end, nearly 600 black protesters were killed and some 3,000 were wounded. The police incarcerated and beat numerous individuals, not the least of whom was Steve Biko himself, who died after police beatings.

Government repression intensified even as leaders of the Nationalist Party, which ruled South Africa for most of the century, began to reconsider the long-term viability of apartheid. Executions of blacks increased from roughly fifty each year in the mid-1970s to 125 per year in 1977–1980 (Omond 1985, 144). Outdoor meetings were banned selectively at first and then outright in 1983. Declarations of states of emergency became more common, and travel restrictions intensified.

On the other hand, the new prime minister, P. W. Botha, began to seriously consider relaxing apartheid laws as early as 1979 in the face of growing opposition in the South African business community. Business leaders pointed out that the economy would thrive best if the work force—largely black—was stable and content and if blacks could become affluent enough to provide a market for goods made in South Africa (St. Jorre 1986, 63). Foreign firms operating in compliance with the voluntary pro–civil rights standard known as the "Sullivan principles" were proving that a policy of racial equality in the workplace could increase both productivity and profitability.

In the early 1980s, several regulations were passed that loosened some of the more "purely irritating" aspects of apartheid, including the laws against interracial marriage. The number of blacks admitted to white universities increased, restrictions on black job advancement relaxed, and pass laws became more permissive (Omond 1985, 47, 85). In 1984, a new constitution provided for the election of two new non-white assemblies. Reverend Allan Boesak of the newly formed United Democratic Front (UDF), a loose coalition of moderate anti-apartheid organizations, warned prospective Indian voters in 1983:

> Working within the system for whatever reason contaminates you. It wears down your defenses. It whets your appetite for power. . . . And what you call "compromise" for the sake of politics is in fact selling out your principles, your ideals and the future of your children. . . . (Lapping 1986, 171)

Other moves toward relaxation of apartheid did little to satisfy blacks. The ANC continued to grow in popularity and strength, subsuming the Black Consciousness movement in 1984 and attracting the endorsement of even the UDF moderates (Brewer 1986, 274).

In Sharpeville in 1984, black residents protested proposed rent and bus fare increases by targeting black administrators in the area. Violence spread rapidly as many collaborators were subjected to the "necklace" (a tire, doused in gasoline, placed around the victim's neck and set on fire). Unable to control the unrest, the government declared a state of emergency (particularly around Port Elizabeth) in July 1985 (Lemon 1987, 339). Eight thousand people were arrested in the first year and more than 750 killed by police and army forces. The army quickly gained a reputation for brutality by beating and electrocuting detainees on their way to prison. Children were specifically targeted during this period—many of them shot in the back while fleeing the soldiers. Children incarcerated under the state of emergency were, like their adult counterparts, subjected to torture, beating, terror, and often death (Lawyers 1986, 6–8). Efforts to have children receive medical treatment at hospitals were frustrated by the police practice of arresting any injured patients—thus many died without treatment after being shot during a demonstration. Likewise, attempts by physicians to reveal the extent of prison violence were halted by official cover-ups. The state of emergency was extended several times until it began to be lifted piecemeal in 1989 and 1990. Thirty more antiapartheid groups were banned, including the UDF, and some 50,000 individuals were detained from 1985 to 1988.

White South Africans were divided to the breaking point over the pace and direction of reform. Racist Afrikaners broke with the National Party to form the Conservative Party, which soon became the major opposition in Parliament and activated a latent vigilante organization—the Afrikaner Resistance Movement. Conservative Party leader Andries Treurnicht defiantly declared:

> People who think that Mr. Botha's "crossing of the Rubicon" and his abdication of white government mean the end of the Afrikaner and broader white nationalism are making a big mistake. We will not allow the Oppenheimers and American pressure groups to create a potpourri of people or to establish a nonracial economic empire upon the ruins of a white Christian culture and civilization.

A people is only conquered when it has destroyed its own spirit. We are not prepared to consider national suicide . . . no one will silence the awakening white nation. The battle for the return of our political self-determination has only just begun. (Treurnicht 1986, 100)

Liberal white politicians increasingly joined antiapartheid parties—particularly after the state of emergency began in 1985. This culminated in the formation of the National Democratic movement in 1987. Botha's political support was thus threatened from both the left and the right until in 1989 he felt compelled to resign his post.

International sanctions intensified during the mid-1980s, including disinvestment by numerous foreign firms operating in the country. By the end of the decade, some $12 billion in foreign investment had been withdrawn or sold to local investors (in soft local currency that was of no use in repaying mounting foreign debts). International banks, bending to pressure from institutional depositors and shareholders and universities, city governments, and pensions, began to impose conditions of political reform on debt rescheduling. By 1989, the net effect of these sanctions was that the South African economy, according to local independent estimates, was 15 percent smaller than it should have otherwise been.

To express their dismay in 1985, 91 South African business leaders took out an ad in the country's largest newspaper, calling for "the granting of full South African citizenship to all our people." Still others met with Walter Sisulu, leader-in-exile of the banned ANC, at his headquarters in Zambia to discuss dismantling apartheid (Mann 1988, 81).

DISMANTLING APARTHEID: 1989–1994

After Botha's resignation in 1989, the new government of F.W. de Klerk moved aggressively to dismantle the most disturbing and fundamental aspects of apartheid, in spite of growing white violence and continuing black violence.

Between 1989 and 1991, the legislative keystones of apartheid were removed one by one: the Group Areas Act, the Separate Amenities Act, the Population Registration Act, and various provisions barring peaceful political assembly and organization. The state of emergency was lifted throughout much of the country (although continuing unrest may well have justified retaining the provision in certain areas), and police powers were circumscribed. Perhaps most dramatic of all, Nelson Mandela was released from prison in February 1990, shortly after Walter Sisulu was released and less than a year before Oliver Tambo, president of the ANC, returned to South Africa after a thirty-year exile.

As put by Payne:

By removing most of apartheid's legal underpinnings by June 1991, with the notable exception of black voting rights, South Africa had made a major and largely unanticipated first step toward creating a relatively egalitarian and non-racial society. The overwhelming white support in the March 1992 referendum for de Klerk's reforms underscored the commitment to change. Dismantling the more intractable social and economic components of a legal system of racial domination into which all South Africans had been socialized for almost half a century was clearly a more Herculean endeavor. Nonetheless, the vast majority of South Africans had embraced a hopeful but uncertain future. (Payne 1992, 149)

The political processes at work in South Africa centered on the Convention for a Democratic South Africa (CODESA), a constitutional convention that brought together nearly all black and most white parties and the homelands governments. Although some parties rejected the legitimacy of the exercise, it had the full backing of the government, the Inkatha Party, and the ANC. A referendum of white voters in February 1992 revealed that an overwhelming majority supported the CODESA efforts to establish a fully democratic government in South Africa. The result went far to marginalize white conservatives, who felt compelled to join the process. The funerals of Afrikaner nationalist Andries Treurnicht and black Communist leader Chris Hani in April 1993 were a study in contrasts, with tens of thousands mourning Hani and only a few hundred turning out for Treurnicht.

Events in September and October of 1993 dramatically changed the prospects for a peaceful transition to democracy for South Africa. The CODESA process reached its conclusion with the drafting of a federal-style constitution, which was expected to be ratified by the white-controlled Parliament. Prior to that, a "super-cabinet" consisting of representatives from each party involved in the CODESA had been proposed, accepted by Parliament, and organized to control the National Party's cabinet during the transition (*New York Times* September 24, 1993, A1). The "transitional executive council" (TEC) had the power to override de Klerk's government to assure fairness in the national elections set for April 27, 1994. These remarkable steps forward resulted in an end to the sweeping economic and diplomatic boycotts imposed on South Africa by the United Nations, the Organization for African Unity, the Commonwealth, and the European Community, not to mention the United States. Loans and investments were expected to flow freely into South Africa to take advantage of the end of sanctions (*Christian Science Monitor* 1993). As recognition for their achievement, Nelson Mandela and Frederick de Klerk were awarded the Nobel Peace Prize in mid-October.

These historic achievements were not just the beginning of South Africa's healing, but also marked an intensified and broader conflict. The ANC–Inkatha rivalry intensified as black-on-black violence resulted in an average of ten deaths each day. A short-lived show of solidarity by Mandela and Buthelezi collapsed into mutual recriminations as Buthelezi pulled his Inkatha Freedom Party out of CODESA. He demanded virtual autonomy for the KwaZulu region he governed—something Mandela was unwilling to grant. Blacks in Buthelezi's native Natal province were split in their support of the ANC and Inkatha, and many saw Buthelezi's efforts as a last-ditch attempt to retain some degree of power.

In April 1994, black, white, and colored South Africans voted in what was universally described as a peaceful, fair, and open election. The ANC won 63% of the vote. On May 10, 1994, Nelson Mandela was sworn in as South Africa's president.

POSTAPARTHEID SOUTH AFRICA

The inauguration ceremony of Nelson Mandela was a mixture of pomp and party. He declared:

> We enter into a covenant that we shall build a society in which all South Africans, both black and white, will be able to walk tall, without any fear in their hearts, assured of their inalienable right to human dignity—a rainbow nation at peace with itself and the world. . . . Never, never, never again shall it be that this beautiful land will again experience the oppression of one by another. . . . (Sparks 1999, 66)

After Mandela's speech, jets and helicopters flew over the crowd, trailing the colors of the new flag to the tune of a new national anthem. Emotions ran high as the world witnessed a rare peaceful transition from authoritarian to democratic regime.

Fifteen years have passed since that momentous event, and many report cards have been written about the Mandela period. First and foremost, he is given high marks for carrying out a peaceful and orderly change of government, particularly given the risks involved. He bent over backward to accommodate white concerns, particularly by using a consensus approach to decision making during the two-year period of Government of National Unity, when all major parties had a seat in the cabinet. He introduced a moderate budget, limited social welfare programs (which required considerable fine-tuning) to alleviate black poverty, and worked to open South Africa's economy to the world along liberal principles (Brent 1996). Gone were the threats of large-scale nationalization and Marxist policies. Political violence came to a virtual standstill. With his introduction of a Truth and Reconciliation Commission under the leadership of Desmond Tutu, Mandela also moved to resolve long-standing grievances of blacks and whites alike. The commission's report, issued in late 1998, offered a mountain of evidence from those who confessed to human rights abuses in exchange for amnesty that the National Party was guilty of systematic atrocities and abuses. But the black parties also came under attack—which prompted ANC and Inkatha Freedom Party leaders to condemn the report. Perhaps the greatest victory came on June 16, 1999, when Mandela's appointed ANC successor, Thabo Mbeki, won the presidency with 66% of the vote—a margin even greater than Mandela's. Although he experienced a period of public disapproval in 2002, his popularity rose once again. Pik Botha, a former apartheid enforcer, even announced his intent to join the ANC in early 2000. He was reelected overwhelmingly in 2004 and was in a strong enough position politically to remove Buthelezi from the cabinet and later sack his deputy Jacob Zuma for corruption. This move, however, was rejected by numerous ANC members, culminating in Mbeki's defeat as leader of the ANC in December 2007 and his eventual resignation from the presidency in September 2008.

Although the political achievements of Mandela and the ANC are breathtaking, serious problems persist and new ones have emerged. South Africa's economy, slated to grow at 6% by 2000, has slipped into the doldrums, in part because of the global repercussions of the Asian financial crisis. Unemployment of blacks approaches 50% in some communities, and there is a growing feeling of despair as the gap between wealthy whites and poor blacks continues to widen. In the transition to a postapartheid regime, little attention was paid to structural problems in South African society (Statman 1997).

Visitors to South African black townships still see poverty, illiteracy, and poor living conditions, all compounded by dramatically increasing crime rates and the spread of the AIDS virus. In spite of broad efforts to combat the spread of HIV/AIDS, its prevalence has increased from 24.8% in 2001 to 29.5% in 2004—or 5.6 million people. In 2003, after years of ambivalence, the government announced a new initiative to bring generic versions of HIV-fighting drugs to far more patients. The policy is ambitious and has been delayed by a lack of trained physicians, but given the scale of the problem, an ambitious program is doubtless called for (AVERT 2004). By 2005, the government could announce that it had established an AIDS clinic in all fifty-three districts in the country.

Crime is in some ways a result of a combination of new freedom (drugs and guns now flow almost freely into South Africa thanks to reopened borders), poverty, and frustration, as well as a legacy of an apartheid-era police force that was trained to persecute rather than protect blacks (Gordon 1998). Murder rates in South Africa reached a peak in 1995, with nearly 27,000 cases reported countrywide. The figure has gradually receded since then, and came in at under 20,000 for 2005. "While crime rates are among the highest in the world, the conviction rate, estimated at eight percent, is among the lowest. The high level of crime is a disincentive for much-needed foreign investment. It also contributes to disillusionment with democracy among South Africans" (USAID 2004). As a result, solving crime and other similar problems will require a multipronged policy strategy, and it is even possible that some tactics will be mutually contradictory. For example, rapid growth probably requires opening the market more, which will result in weak companies going bankrupt and laying off their workers, most of whom are likely to be black.

CONCLUSION: PROMOTING HUMAN RIGHTS

For all their troubles, the vast majority of South Africans are willing to support Mbeki and wait for better times (his popularity ratings are very high). For the moment, at least, they can clearly remember the pains of oppression, so the taste of freedom is deliciously sweet. It is doubtful, however, whether this situation will continue much longer.

Perhaps even more serious is the AIDS epidemic, which has swelled in significance in recent years. Nearly five million South Africans are HIV-positive (one in nine), and most victims are ostracized and even attacked by their neighbors. Mbeki's reaction was somewhat puzzling, as he blamed multinational drug companies that refuse to offer low-cost AIDS drugs while simultaneously questioning the link between HIV and AIDS. The government, meanwhile, did not make antiretroviral drugs available to rape victims until mid-2002. As of 2005, Mbeki's policies seemed to be growing more coherent and promised a more effective program (BBC News April 24, 2002).

Overall, life is still filled with violence, poverty, and despair for the vast majority of South Africans. Children growing up in the townships are increasingly turning to gang culture for validation and survival. As put by Virginia Gamba of the

Institute of Security Studies, "In twelve years time [2014] you'll have at least a quarter of a million orphans, with no role models to guide them. They won't care less, because they themselves are infected with HIV. . . . The escalation of violence could be so great that it becomes the only determinant of whether life is worth living. Such a future threatens democracy itself" (BBC News April 10, 2002).

Who is to blame? Have the political and social freedoms that have been achieved by average South Africans been abused in some way? Are South Africans to blame for the increase in crime and disease, or are these merely normal social ills that afflict every advanced, liberal democracy? Is it possible that the white minority government would be facing the same challenges if it were still in office? Most South Africans seem to think so, because there is no talk of returning to the political "Stone Age" of apartheid.

This point leads us back to the original concept for this case—human rights. South Africa is posing an increasingly troubling question for observers: Are political freedom and social order somehow contradictory? The Universal Declaration provides for both civil and economic rights, after all. Most world leaders and human rights activists would find it disturbing to think that civil rights must necessarily bring social breakdown, although the precedent has already been set in Russia. Fascists have always claimed that freedom was antithetical to social order and economic progress, while liberals have pointed out repeatedly that liberty and the good society can coexist—and that they are mutually reinforcing.

At this point, South African leaders are working hard to achieve both social and economic progress and to consolidate democracy and civil rights. One can hope that they will soon turn a corner and be able to guarantee both for the average South African.

QUESTIONS TO CONSIDER

1. To what extent has nonviolence succeeded where violence has not? Have Mahatma Gandhi's theories been validated by the South African experience?

2. How have human rights been perceived by various groups in South Africa? How have South Africans responded to international standards of human rights?

3. To what extent did the international community succeed in changing the human rights policies of the South African government? Does the South African situation strengthen the case for economic sanctions?

KEY FIGURES
APARTHEID IN SOUTH AFRICA

Hendrik Verwoerd   Prime Minister of South Africa, 1958–1966. An avowed white supremacist, he was the principal architect of the apartheid laws.

P. W. Botha   Prime Minister of South Africa, 1979–1989. He began the process of dismantling the apartheid laws after imposing martial law.

(continued)

(*continued*)

F. W. de Klerk   Prime Minister of South Africa, 1989–1994. He ended apartheid.

Daniel Malan   Prime Minister of South Africa, 1948–1954, and former Dutch Reformed Church minister.

Sol Plaatje   Founder of the African National Congress in 1912.

Nelson Mandela   Leader of the African National Congress, he was imprisoned for 27 years under apartheid. He became the first president of postapartheid South Africa, 1994–1999.

Steve Biko   Black Consciousness activist and founder of SASO. He was arrested and died in prison in 1976.

Mangosuthu Buthelezi   Ruler of the KwaZulu nation and leader of the Inkatha Party.

Walter Sisulu   A leader of the ANC.

Allan Boesak   Founder of the United Democratic Front in 1983.

Jan Smuts   Afrikaner general in the Boer War, and later political leader and Prime Minister of the Union (later Republic) of South Africa, 1919–1924.

Desmond Tutu   Roman Catholic Archbishop in South Africa. He fought apartheid and led the Truth and Reconciliation Commission under Mandela.

CHRONOLOGY
APARTHEID IN SOUTH AFRICA

1652
South African area is claimed and settled by Dutch.

1815
The British purchase the Cape Colony and establish a governmental presence. They begin discriminating against native African tribes and Dutch-born Boer settlers. A dispute leads to the killing of British troops and the hanging of their Boer attackers at Slachter's Nek.

1837
Thousands of Boers migrate inland in the beginning of the Great Trek.

1838
Piet Retief's Boers defeat a large Zulu army. Afrikaners see it as a sign of God's protection.

1867
Diamonds and other minerals are discovered in Kimberly.

1875
The first apartheid laws exclude blacks from diamond mine ownership. Later, they would exclude blacks from gold-mining profits in Johannesburg in the 1880s.

1899
British settlers under Alfred Milner begin a war to displace Afrikaners. The Boer War lasts until 1902, when Afrikaners surrender.

1910
The Union of South Africa under British dominance is formed.

1912
The African National Congress is formed to protect fast-eroding rights for nonwhites.

1918
Black workers strike and are arrested en masse.

1922
Two hundred Afrikaner miners are killed in government attempts to quell labor unrest.

1924
Afrikaner politicians gain significant electoral victories, speeding up passage of antiblack legislation.

1936
Blacks are no longer allowed to vote.

1948
Afrikaners control the South African government for the first time. They issue a Declaration of Grand Apartheid.

1950s
The government of Prime Minister Daniel Malan passes a series of apartheid laws, including the Population Registration Act, the Separate Amenities Act, the Bantu Authorities Act, and the Prohibition of Mixed Marriages Act.

1952
The ANC leads a series of antiapartheid demonstrations that turn violent.

1955
The Freedom Charter is passed at the Congress of the People. Many ANC leaders are imprisoned.

1960
The ANC is outlawed. A Pan-African Congress demonstration is suppressed in what is known as the Sharpeville Massacre.

1968
The South African Student Organization is founded by Steve Biko.

1973
The UN General Assembly passes the International Convention on the Suppression and Punishment of the Crime of Apartheid.

1976
Soweto riots result in 600 deaths. Steve Biko is killed while in police custody.

1977
The Sullivan principles are articulated, urging multinational corporations operating in South Africa to promote racial justice in the workplace.

(*continued*)

(*continued*)

1983
Outdoor meetings of blacks are banned.

1984
Two nonwhite national assemblies are created under a new constitution. Unrest in Sharpeville prompts the government to declare a state of emergency in 1985.

1985
Struggling under international economic sanctions, South African business leaders openly support the black franchise.

1987
Liberal whites form the National Democratic Movement in response to the increasingly hard-line attitude of the Afrikaner Conservative Party.

1989
P. W. Botha resigns the prime minister's post. F. W. de Klerk becomes prime minister and begins dismantling the apartheid laws.

1990
Nelson Mandela is released from prison after 27 years.

1992
The ANC is fully legalized. CODESA begins planning a new constitution.

1993
CODESA produces a draft constitution that is accepted by the Parliament. Mandela and de Klerk win the Nobel Peace Prize.

1994
Nelson Mandela is elected president of South Africa.

1996
The New South African Constitution is formally signed into law by Nelson Mandela in Sharpeville.

1998
The Truth and Reconciliation Commission issues its final report.

1999
Thabo Mbeki is elected to succeed Mandela.

2002
South Africa hosts the United Nations Conference on Racism.

2008
September   Kgalema Motlanthe inaugurated President after Mbeki resigns following his rejection by ANC members.

WEBSITES

The South African government's official web site: www.gov.za

The ANC home page: www.anc.org.za

COSATU's home page: www.cosatu.org.za
South African politics Web site: www.polity.org.za/
The Universal Declaration of Human Rights: www.un.org/Overview/rights.html

REFERENCES

AVERT. "South Africa Statistics." October 2004. Available at: www.avert.org/aidssouthafrica.htm.
BBC News, April 24, 2002.
Brent, R. Stephen. "Tough Road to Prosperity." *Foreign Affairs* 75 #2 (March/April 1996): 113–126.
Brewer, John D. *After Soweto: An Unfinished Journey* (Oxford: Clarendon Press, 1986).
Brown, Godfrey N. *Apartheid: A Teacher's Guide* (New York: UNESCO, 1981).
Christian Science Monitor, October 1, 1993, 8.
Fatton, Robert, Jr. *Black Consciousness in South Africa: The Dialectics of Ideological Resistance to White Supremacy* (Albany: SUNY Press, 1986).
Gordon, Diana R. "Crime in the New South Africa." *The Nation* 267 #15 (November 9, 1998): 17–21.
Hobson, J. A. *Imperialism* (Ann Arbor: University of Michigan Press, 1965).
International Labor Organization. *Special Report of the Director-General on the Application of the Declaration Concerning Action Against Apartheid in South Africa and Namibia* (Geneva: ILO, 1990).
Lambley, Peter. *The Psychology of Apartheid* (Athens: University of Georgia Press, 1980).
Lapping, Brian. *Apartheid: A History* (New York: George Braziller, 1986).
Lawyers Committee for Human Rights. *The War Against Children: South Africa's Youngest Victims* (New York: Lawyers Committee, 1986).
Lemon, Anthony. *Apartheid in Transition* (Boulder, CO: Westview Press, 1987).
Magubane, Bernard Makhosezwe. *The Political Economy of Race and Class in South Africa* (New York: Monthly Review Press, 1979).
Mandela, Nelson. *The Struggle Is My Life* (New York: Pathfinder, 1990).
Mann, Michael. "The Giant Stirs: South African Business in the Age of Reform," in Philip Krankel, Noam Pines, and Mark Swilling, eds., *State Resistance and Change in South Africa* (London: Croom Helm, 1988): 52–86.
New York Times, September 24, 1993, A1.
Omond, Roger. *The Apartheid Handbook* (London: Penguin, 1985).
Payne, Richard J. *The Third World and South Africa: Post-Apartheid Challenges* (Westport, CT: Greenwood Press, 1992).
Republic of South Africa. *Progress Through Separate Development: South Africa in Peaceful Transition* (New York: Information Service of South Africa, 1973).
Sparks, Alision. "The Status of the Dream." *The Wilson Quarterly* 23 #12 (Spring 1999): 66–67.
St. Jorre, John de. "White South Africa Circles the Wagons," in Mark A. Uhlig, ed., *Apartheid in Crisis* (New York: Vintage Books, 1986): 61–84.
Statman, James M. "No More Miracle?" *ReVision* 20 #2 (Fall 1997): 32–38.
Treurnicht, Andries P. "Conservative Party Congress Speech," in Mark A. Uhlig, ed., *Apartheid in Crisis* (New York: Vintage Books, 1986): 100–102.
USAID. "USAID's strategy in South Africa." 2004. Available at:
http://www.usaid.gov/locations/sub-saharan_africa/countries/southafrica/.

20
■ ■ ■
Global Governance: The Asian Financial Crisis

INTRODUCTION

For all their formality, pomp, and ritual, international relations scholars understand that the United Nations today and the League of Nations before it are not international governments in any meaningful sense. They cannot impose their will unilaterally on the peoples of the world—even if they wanted to. They cannot regulate industries, collect taxes, arrest and prosecute law-breakers, or even print their own currency (let alone raise their own armies). The states that created these institutions saw to it that this would never be the case. So there is no world government.

But to infer from this that all is chaos and disorder would be an even more serious misconception. For thousands of years—but especially in the last hundred—international rules have existed and been respected and enforced. What is more, the formulation of these rules has often involved a systematic process of reasoning and debate between a wide variety of actors. Ancient Rome had to contend with various barbarian tribes, large corporations, maritime pirates, and political movements as it strove to bring order to the known world. In many cases, the rules that emerged were more guidelines that were left to local officials to interpret and enforce with more or less zeal. Sometimes the result was more "negotiated settlement" than government as we traditionally think of it. During the Middle Ages in Europe, most kings had to consult their various feudal lords before embarking on any foreign enterprise, not to mention the Pope, various semi-autonomous religious orders such as the Jesuits, and trade guilds and other economic compacts. It was an open question circa 1300 whether the Church, the state, or the guilds would emerge as the principal actor in world politics (Spruyt 1996). Even during the 19th century, when national sovereignty was the rule, governments created international bodies to address certain issues and often allowed non-state actors—such as multinational corporations, trading companies, international relief bodies, and professional groups—to provide advice, input, and even share in the responsibility of regulating international transactions. Lloyd's of London, for example, probably played a larger role in regulating maritime traffic than the Royal Navy (Zacher 1996, 50).

So when the League was created in 1919, it was not the first effort by governments to establish permanent institutions and arrangements to regulate their affairs more systematically. States had learned that although sovereignty and freedom were desirable above all else, they came with an often heavy price. Not only were states prone to attacking each other and starting wars, they were just as prone to raise barriers to exports from their neighbors, imposing bans on currency exchange, or seizing assets of foreigners working in their territory. Even with respect to warfare, governments wished to minimize its more brutal and reckless aspects by restricting what types of weapons could be used, how soldiers should conduct themselves among civilians, and how prisoners of war should be treated.

All of these and other issues were addressed in a variety of conferences during the latter part of the 19th century and carried over into the League of Nations and United Nations talks. So although neither organization was given its own army, they were given the power to hire lawyers and social workers who could draw up guidelines on the treatment of prisoners of war. Further, they were allowed to collaborate with organizations like the International Committee of the Red Cross to carry out prison camp inspections to make sure that the prisoners were being treated humanely. These were among the first instances of what has come to be known as "global governance," defined as follows:

> Global governance may be defined as an approach to politics and public policy that transcends the nation-state and its formal institutions of government. It is *global* because it recognizes that virtually all problems on the public agenda—environment, public health, crime, migration, etc.—transcend in their scope, source, and solution national boundaries. It is *governance* (rather than "government") because non-formal, non-state actors—nongovernmental organizations, interest groups, professional associations, and so forth—have increasingly been accorded legitimacy in rule-making and rule-enforcement. (POSCIR 2008)

Today, there are hundreds of international governmental organizations and thousands of non-governmental organizations that interact with each other and with roughly 200 nation-states to draw up regulations, laws, and aspirations to guide the conduct of states, businesses, social movements, and any other important actor in world affairs. They draft proposals, organize international workshops and conferences, facilitate treaty negotiations, and help ensure they will be taken seriously once approved. Consider, for example, international rules on anti-personnel landmines. In the 1970s, veterans of the Vietnam War were among the first, upon their return home to the United States, to publicize the dangers of landmines to civilians designed to kill individual soldiers. They soon organized a lobbying group to put pressure on the U.S. government to stop their use. By the early 1990s, they were joined by five other groups from across the globe and created the International Campaign to Ban Landmines (ICBL; http://www.icbl. org/). Before long, they were not only lobbying their own governments and educating their own publics, but they were also showing up at the United Nations headquarters to lobby diplomats and UN staff in the hope of getting a treaty to ban them. They found in Lester Pearson, Foreign Minister of Canada, a particularly sympathetic listener, and before long he persuaded his government to sponsor an international diplomatic conference to discuss the issue. Seventy-five countries were represented in Ottawa in October 1996 when initial meetings were held, followed by a meeting of 121 countries in Oslo in September 1997 that resulted in a treaty to ban the production and deployment of new landmines and to carry out de-mining on a quick schedule. Since then, the ICBL has been actively involved in pressuring more governments to sign the treaty and monitoring compliance by those who already signed it, being quick to criticize governments it believes are dragging their feet (ICBL 2008).

With respect to the business world, states and international institutions interact with business groups, bond-rating services, insurance adjusters, political risk consulting firms, and a wide array of private actors to discuss and draw up solutions to the world's most serious economic problems. Central among these is the flow of credit and capital across international boundaries. Although great strides have been made to prevent and avoid financial turmoil, the speed of international financial transactions is such that even the most alert and well-intentioned regulators are often overwhelmed by events. One such case was the Asian financial crisis of 1997–1998. Before addressing this, an introduction to the world of international finance is in order.

A PRIMER ON INTERNATIONAL FINANCE

One way to begin understanding what occurred in Asia in 1997–1998 is to understand the nature of currencies. Countries are in some ways like a household, with a total cash flow involving expenditures and revenues relative to the outside world. Where a country has a currency that is widely respected overseas, it can use that currency in these transactions and gain some advantages in the process. Where the country produces a currency that is not widely respected as a means of exchange, it must compensate. One way this is done is by "pegging" the currency to a "hard" currency, like the U.S. dollar. This means that, by government edict, the currency can be exchanged for a fixed number of dollars at a rate that does not change over long periods of time. This provides a way of signaling to foreign investors and creditors that their money is relatively safe, even after they trade their hard currencies for the less reliable local currency.

But international bills still have to be paid in hard currency, and if the country begins buying more imports or stashing its money abroad, it must make up for it with more sales of exports or more capital coming into the country. The goal is to have an international account ("balance of payments") that is basically zeroed out at the end of the year, with the money going being offset by money coming in. Even better: a little more coming in than going out can accumulate "reserves" of hard currency—countries like to have enough in reserve to cover the cost of at least six months' worth of imports.

Imagine a situation where a country begins buying more imports than it is exporting, or local businesses put more money in foreign banks and assets than is the case with foreigners. In such a situation, the country's balance of payments goes into deficit, and the country—often the government itself—must come up with extra hard currency. Most will do this by drawing down their reserves and/or borrowing—much like a household going into debt or depleting the savings when income dries up or a new purchase is made. So long as creditors are willing to lend or the reserves are ample, this situation can continue for a long time.

But in most cases the problems are more fundamental, and the rest of the world knows that the country must engage in some belt-tightening. A government may seek to attract more capital on a short-term basis by raising the core interest rates offered by the country's central bank. Doing so usually causes foreign investors to shift funds to the country's banks or to invest in bonds offered by the government, both of which will increase the demand for the currency and raise its price. But doing so also makes local borrowing more painful, causing business to stop expanding and possibly to contract and fail. Excessive public debt can under-mine confidence in the country's overall stability and cause investors and spec-ulators to sell off the currency. If this is the case, the government may feel compelled to raise taxes and cut spending to balance the budget—both of which are likely to cause pain to the citizenry, possibly provoking social unrest. Where the problem is corruption or lack of regulation, it may be necessary for the govern-ment to create whole new institutions and laws—many of which will probably cost both the taxpayers and the newly regulated firms a great deal. This approach is perhaps the most risky, since many countries with pegged systems also have weak law enforcement and various forms of cronyism—elites that prosper because their friends in government protect them. Finally, some countries—such as India (see Chapter 15)—may decide the problem is the long-term trajectory of the country's economy, concluding that the only real solution is investment in the nation's roads, train tracks, wireless Internet, educational system, and health care infrastructures. Such decisions are never taken lightly and go far beyond sim-ply dealing with a falling currency.

To avoid these unpopular measures, countries look to another alternative: devaluation. By devaluing the currency, the government automatically raises the price of all imports and lowers the price of all exports. Furthermore, foreign investors will be able to buy more local assets with less hard currency, prompting an infusion of investment and lending, while local businesses will get fewer for-eign assets for their local currency. This new currency value might be left in place until the next time the country sees the balance of payments in trouble. Or it may decide to "float" the currency and simply never set an official exchange rate.

Doing so, however, risks a currency free-fall, which would lead to inflation at home and loss of confidence abroad. Only mature economies have successfully floated their currencies.

What about these changes in practice? In fact, as Milton Friedman points out, once the international financial community gets wind of a country in balance of payments trouble, it is on a hair-trigger to react dramatically. After all, the worst-case scenario for a foreigner holding lots of a local currency is that he or she won't be able to pull them out and exchange them for hard currency at the fixed rate. Imagine, for example, that you are an American investor looking for opportunities in Outer Slobovia. You decide to buy a skyscraper in the capital city for a million dollars, which translate to 10 million *spakls*—the local currency, which trades at a fixed rate of $1 = 10 *spakls*. You hope to one day resell the building to a local Slobovian for a profit. But you learn that the country is experiencing balance of payments problems and has started spending its reserves in an attempt to meet its foreign obligations. You see the writing on the wall and start doing the math. If the country devalues its currency by, say, 10% ($1=11 *spakls*), your building, while still worth 10 million *spakls*, will only be worth $909,090—a loss of over 9%. You have an offer on the table to sell the building for a 5% loss and decide to take it (a bird in the hand . . .). It is even possible for a savvy speculator to sell the *spakl* short and make a killing if it actually gets devalued. Either way, foreigners are looking for ways to unload *spakls* and convert them into hard currency once they're convinced devaluation is imminent (Friedman 1998).

In such a situation, hard currency floods out of the country, leaving it even more unable to meet its foreign obligations. No country can endure such a run on the currency, and while some might put up a fight—buying back the local currency with hard currency reserves to give the impression that its value is legitimate, for example—devaluation is inevitable, as well as a visit to rich foreign governments and international public creditors like the International Monetary Fund (lenders of last resort). Because the country has no economic power at this point, it must take whatever terms it can get: there is no bankruptcy law in the international financial system.

The International Monetary Fund is an international public organization that also assesses state performance and creditworthiness, although it typically does so privately and for the benefit of its member-states. The IMF was also intended to help countries with their short-term currency crises by providing both advice and money. The money would be doled out in small increments, depending on the seriousness of the crisis (governments would often use the funds to buy back their currencies and stabilize them). The IMF would also provide advice—sometimes phrased as an ultimatum—to help governments "adjust" their policies to make the country more financially sound over the long term. Finally, the IMF and the various major creditor governments and banks would sometimes coordinate a joint strategy to buy and sell currencies to offset the collapse of one or another particular currency. This was particularly true when it was a hard currency that was in trouble.

ASIAN FINANCES IN THE 1990S

Thailand, Indonesia, Malaysia, and South Korea were among the darlings of the international financial community in the early 1990s. They were all experiencing impressive economic growth, led by very strong exports—a strategy recommended by the IMF and most Western economists. Together, these four countries averaged annual Gross Domestic Product (GDP) growth of approximately 8% from 1990 to 1996—a rate that far exceeded their population growth and led to significant increases in the GDP per capita (Desai 2003, 90). Their inflation rates were well below 10% per year and were in the same range as most European countries. Most governments had budget surpluses, high savings rates, and even higher investment rates.

Perhaps the only statistic that could have caused concern was the short-term borrowing trend (see Table 20.1). As put by Desai: "Foreign short-term borrowing facilitated extravagant private sector overspending in dubious ventures and real-estate expansion, exposing all these economies to sharp declines in their currencies

Table 20.1   Asian Debt Trends, 1995–1997

		1995	1996	1997
Indonesia	Total foreign debt (US$b.)	124.4	129.0	120.7
	Private non-guaranteed foreign debt (US$b.)	33.1	36.7	50.8
	Bank claims on private sector as % of GDP	53.0	55.0	116.0
Malaysia	Total debt (US$b.)	34.3	39.8	42.9
	Private non-guaranteed foreign debt (US$b.)	11.0	13.0	25.9
	Bank claims on private sector as % of GDP	85.0	93.0	108.0
South Korea	Total debt (US$b.)	78.4	104.7	157.0
	Private non-guaranteed foreign debt (US$b.)	***	***	***
	Bank claims on private sector as % of GDP	137.0	141.0	145.0
Thailand	Total debt (US$b.)	83.2	90.8	95.9
	Private non-guaranteed foreign debt (US$b.)	25.1	36.2	66.8
	Bank claims on private sector as % of GDP	98.0	102.0	97.0

***Not available.

Sources: Adapted from Bird, Graham, and Alistair Milne. "Miracle to Meltdown: A Pathology of the East Asian Financial Crisis." *Third World Quarterly* 20 #2 (April 1999): 425; and Winters, Jeffrey A. "The Determinant of Financial Crisis in Asia," in T.J. Pempel, ed., *The Politics of the Asian Economic Crisis* (Ithaca: Cornell University Press, 1999): 82.

as speculators withdrew funds following bank and business failures" (2003, 89). Their foreign debt in 1996 was roughly half of their GDP, of which short-term debt made up between a quarter and half of the total. In South Korea, private borrowing from local banks totaled roughly one and a half times the GDP (Bird & Milne 1999, 425).

Foreign creditors, especially new players like mutual funds, were in a position to quickly move billions into the region.

High levels of short-term borrowing would not have been inherently problematic if not for several other conditions that did not always reveal themselves in the statistics. To begin, Asia had deregulated much of its financial sector, largely in response to pressure from foreign creditors (Winters 1999, 80). Banks were permitted to lend well beyond levels recommended by international regulatory agencies, and the collateral they demanded was often in highly overvalued real estate (Noble & Ravenhill 2000, 7; Kahler 2000, 244). They did not even provide depositor insurance. The situation was similar to the United States in the 1920s prior to the stock market crash.

Add to this important structural problems in the sociopolitical arrangements in several of these countries: crony capitalism. In Indonesia in particular, the wealthy elite often had personal and even family ties to President Raden Suharto (Hamilton-Hart 2000, 110). They were able to get government assurances that risky lending and borrowing would be protected in the event of failure. As of 1999, as many as 90% of Indonesian firms listed on the country's stock market were insolvent (Bird & Milne 1999, 432). In Thailand, pork barrel politics was the norm, with the result that many policies were adopted to keep certain constituents happy rather than working for the collective good (Haggard & MacIntyre 2000, 59). In South Korea, large family-run conglomerates called "chaebols" were able to protect themselves from regulation and economic reversals through their connections to the country's political elite (Desai 2003, 103, 113). As put by Winters:

> Liberal banking rules (or, when rules were tighter, the absence of strong enforcement) allowed [foreign] currency traders and hedge funds to borrow massive amounts of local money; this money would first be used to buy foreign exchange from dwindling reserves and, once the currency collapsed, could be traded back into local funds to pay off outstanding loans at a steep discount, leaving a tidy profit for the trader. (1999, 84)

Perhaps most problematic for these countries (except South Korea) was a pegged currency. In Thailand in particular, the baht was pegged to the dollar. This served to reassure foreign investors that they could collect on their money without worrying about wild exchange rate fluctuations. But it also meant that to a large extent the fate of the Thai economy was linked to conditions in the United States. As the dollar appreciated in value relative to the Japanese yen during the mid-1990s, so did the baht (Bird & Milne 1999, 427). This meant that products exported by Thailand were 50% more expensive in 1997 than in 1995 (in yen terms), and they were no longer able to compete with similar exports from Taiwan and Hong Kong (Bird & Milne 1999, 427). This began a series of economic reversals that culminated in the collapse of the baht, the Indonesian rupiah, and several other currencies and a half-decade long recession (Sachs & Woo 1999, 17). As put by Bird and Milne:

> The weak link in terms of macroeconomic policy, particularly in Thailand but elsewhere in East Asia as well, related to exchange rate policy. Thailand maintained a pegged value for the baht against the dollar. But . . . the baht became overvalued in real terms. This seriously weakened the current account balance of payments. However, Thailand did not take timely measures to eliminate currency over-valuation. (1999, 427)

None of the experts were issuing warnings about the precariousness of the situation. Standard & Poor's and Moody's continued to tout the creditworthiness of the countries, and the IMF's public statements were upbeat. This is not to say they did not know there were problems. The bond-rating agencies were simply giving their judgment about whether a creditor would get his money back, and since so many firms were implicitly backed by the state, the answer was yes. The IMF for its part wrote up its concerns in the form of confidential internal memos (Winters 1999, 95).

THE CRISIS ERUPTS

In early 1997, a few major firms in Asia found themselves unable to keep up payments on several very large loans, largely because their currencies were overvalued relative to the yen—and Japan was a major market. Efforts were made by several governments to regulate future loans as a way of signaling to creditors and speculators overseas that they were getting the situation under control (Desai 2003, 121). The measures failed, especially in Thailand, where foreigners began selling the baht and making it more difficult for Thailand to keep up its overseas payments in hard currency. There were also moves by local firms and banks to hedge against a future drop in the baht. At this point the government could have simply dropped the value of the currency and taken its lumps, but instead it chose to use its hard currency reserves—as much as $10 billion—to buttress it (Sachs & Woo 1999, 17).

It was likely this action—seen by some as desperate—that prompted the real run on the baht. After all, everyone knew the country lacked the resources to take on the entire financial community (it had less than six months' import costs on reserve). Foreigners began calling in their loans, exchanging baht for hard currency, and denying new cash. Locals who could converted their baht into hard currency and stashed it in overseas banks and assets to ride out the storm—something the government tried to outlaw (Desai 2003, 121). A few sold the baht short in the hope of scooping up easy profits.

It became clear to the government that it would never be able to shore up the currency through direct intervention, and so on July 2, 1997, the government decided to stop protecting the baht and allow it to fall as far as the markets would let it—then went to the IMF for assistance.

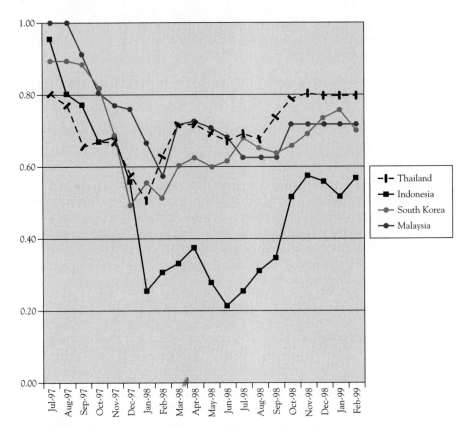

Figure 20.1 Real Currency Exchange Rates for Selected Asian Countries, 1997–1999 (1995=1.00)

Source: Adapted from Desai 2003, 205.

As we see in Figure 20.1, the fall of the baht was quickly followed by the fall of other currencies in the region. Much has been said about the "herd mentality" of foreign creditors. As we have seen, much of the investing that was taking place in Asia was of the portfolio variety, meaning that foreigners were looking only to buy portions of companies—stocks and bonds—not controlling interest (known as direct investment). As a result, their commitment to these countries' economies was very shallow, and it was a very simple thing to simply sell. Lenders could also call short-term loans due and not renew the contracts. Faced with relatively low exit costs, investors required little incentive to leave. They also lacked sophisticated knowledge of the markets and societies with which they were dealing and tended to lump all neighboring countries into the same financial category (Noble & Ravenhill 2000, 2). This was a new development in international finance: short-term private creditors funding large-scale private debt. Few understood the speed with which circumstances could change. One could compare the phenomenon to a driver drifting into another lane, then over-correcting and causing the car to flip. Many decisions lacked sound financial analysis to back them up. As explained by Pempel:

> Just as an optimistic "Asian contagion" involved the failure of many lenders to differentiate among individual Asian borrowers, when the crisis began, the contagion of pessimism was often insensitive to national borders. The first whiff of economic problems in one country led outside investors to question the economic underpinnings of its neighbors. (1999, 9)

The "contagion" spread for other reasons as well. Thanks to a cheaper baht, Thai exports were now very competitive. The only way Asian countries could keep their exports up was to follow suit (Bird & Milne 1999, 429). Indonesia took its currency off the peg a few weeks later. The rupiah lost nearly 80% of its value within six months. Even a year later, the currencies of Thailand, South Korea, and Malaysia had still not recovered and were worth less than half of what they were. In otherwise financially strong Singapore and Hong Kong, currencies moved only slightly, albeit thanks largely to a $1 billion intervention by the latter (Desai 2003, 121).

Japanese banks, fearful that Asian firms would not be able to pay in the near future, called in many loans as soon as the trouble appeared. Other banks followed suit, as well as institutional investors holding mutual funds that included shares in Asian corporations. A massive sell-off of Asian debt and assets began as investors moved their money to "safe havens"—countries with solid economies and strong regulatory regimes. Stocks fell dramatically in each of the four countries in currency crisis. The Indonesian, Korean, and Thai stock market indices fell by more than half, whereas Malaysia's fell by two thirds (Desai 2003, 133).

This loss of capital, combined with the drying up of credit from foreign banks, translated into serious economic contractions for these countries. Business closed shop, leaving workers on the streets. The savings of both the wealthy and the ordinary disappeared, and poverty increased—even for those who felt sheltered from such downturns. The 1998 GDP per capita in Thailand fell by one quarter from 1997 levels, whereas in Malaysia that drop was 30%, in South Korea 33%, and in Indonesia, 57%. To put this in perspective, the U.S. GDP per capita fell by roughly 28% during the Great Depression of the 1930s when the world was in economic and political chaos.

RUSSIA NEXT

The next three targets of divestment were Russia, Brazil, and Turkey. Russia was in the throws of radical economic liberalization by 1998 after the collapse of Communism ten years earlier. But although business was booming and inflation was down, the Russian economy was, to say the least, poorly regulated. Many large state-run firms had been sold to insiders who made a killing buying undervalued assets and then exploited the markets with ruthless abandon. Economic power was quickly concentrated in the hands of a few "oligarchs" who were able to dominate the economy without regard for rule of law. In part because of the direction the country was moving, opposition Communists in the parliament began to resist efforts by President Boris Yeltsin to liberalize even more. The result was policy paralysis and a deepening of the economy's troubles. Tax revenues were extremely low, largely because of very low collection rates, and the budget was bleeding red ink (Desai 2003, 142). Already fragile, Russia was hit by lowering oil prices—a key component of its export earnings—and rising interest rates on its short-term foreign debt. An IMF program of dramatic financial retrenchment was unsustainable, and in August 1998 the government found it could not keep up payments on public loans or secure additional lines of credit, and so it simply announced it would cease payment for a time. There was a run on the ruble, which the government allowed, and its value fell by about half within six months.

BRAZIL AND OTHERS

President Fernando Henrique Cardoso began his professional life as a leftist intellectual expounding dependency theory and advocating self-reliance and even revolution against global capitalism (Cardoso & Faletto 1979). By the time the Asian financial crisis hit in 1997, he found himself the President of Brazil, leading a program of economic liberalization. He changed the currency to reflect economic realities, helped keep inflation low, and maintained steady, if lackluster, overall growth. At the same time, he failed to bring the federal budget deficit or the international account deficit under control or increase savings by Brazilians (Desai 2003, 164).

In the summer of 1998, a year after the Thai baht collapse, speculators and investors began unloading Brazilian reals out of fear the country was going bankrupt. After spending roughly $30 billion in a failed attempt to shore up the currency, the government of Brazil let the markets have full sway and watched helplessly as the real lost half its value in January 1999 (Desai 2003, 162).

After Brazil's crisis, Argentina experienced a run on the currency in 2000, mostly due to fears that the government was about to default on its foreign debt. In Turkey, the government also faced a debt crisis, although here the problem was too little money in the banking sector rather than too much as in Asia.

MANAGEMENT OF THE CRISIS

Global governance involves numerous different agencies and actors, each of which is endowed with different resources and guided by different interests. In the case of the Asian financial crisis, we've already seen the role of private investors and creditors who, in the quest for high yields and low risk (a contradiction, to be sure), move their billions from place to place at a moment's notice. Although they respond to economic indicators and policy statements from various countries, they also watch each other. After all, they are usually in search of their own customers—stockholders, depositors, investors—and they care very much about whether some other firm has found a new place to make a profit—or lose one. Especially where risks are extremely high, it is not surprising that a herd can get "spooked" and quickly run away from a threat even where the evidence is weak.

The result, noted by economists as far back as John Maynard Keynes in the 1930s, is that market forces can result in volatility—dramatic fluctuations in prices and currency values—that in itself can create deeper economic problems than were really there. On August 27, 1998, after the collapse of the ruble, stock markets across the world lost billions in assets. In percentage terms, the one-day loss in the United States, Germany, France, and Spain were, respectively, 4.2%, 4.3%, 4.5%, and 5.9%. This occurred in spite of the fact that over the course of the entire year the value of these stock markets increased dramatically (in France, stocks rose by nearly 25%). There was obviously nothing fundamentally wrong with these stocks, and yet investors bid them down in a moment of collective panic prompted by an event on the periphery of the world economy (Desai 2003, 199).

Ultimately, although markets can work extremely well to set prices and values over the long term, they may become part of the problem in the short term. This is one of the reasons why governments seek to organize themselves to regulate international financial markets. They have agreed in most cases to serve as the "lender of last resort," providing capital when the market won't. In so doing, they may or may not ask for something in return—typically either the repayment of the loan over time, substantial changes in policies and practices, or both. The IMF has been the "tip of the spear" of such international intervention since the 1970s when it was asked to help provide funds to several indebted countries in crisis in exchange for dramatic policy reforms on their part. The World Bank has also played an active role, along with the Asian Development Bank and the central banks of certain major creditor states (the United States, Japan, Germany, and the United Kingdom—more recently, the European Union as well).

Because most of the countries the IMF has helped had put themselves in jeopardy through a series of inefficient and short-sighted policies (high tariffs on imports, low tax rates, high government spending—especially on unproductive activities like inefficient state-run firms, loose monetary policies, and excessive international borrowing), resulting in a credit crisis for the state, its role has primarily been to pressure governments into adopting strict financial discipline. Typically, it requires states to devalue the currency, raise taxes, raise interest rates, lower spending, stop borrowing, privatize state-owned assets, and lower trade and investment restrictions (see Chapter 15 on India). And in many cases these remedies, although painful in the short run, often help the country in the long run. Once a deal has been struck, the World Bank and major creditor states step in with their own capital—sometimes followed by large private banks and investors. The IMF's measures (especially in the opinion of IMF staff) does for indebted countries what a strict rehab program does for addicts.

But the Asian countries that experienced a financial crisis in 1997–1998 were not typical. The problems they experienced stemmed from an unregulated and hyperactive banking system that relied too heavily on short-term credit. Otherwise, the "fundamentals" of their economies were generally sound. Most had relatively low public sector deficits, low inflation, high export levels, few restrictions on imports or foreign investment, and stable currencies (until they crashed). In many respects, these countries had already put into practice the kind of policies the IMF and most creditors had been recommending. What they needed, more than shrinking the state through fiscal discipline and liberalization, was an expansion of state powers to regulate short-term capital flows—that, and lots of fresh capital to keep the economic engine running (Desai 2003, 214).

The IMF was generally unable to appreciate the new situation, however. Instead, it applied very similar fiscal disciplines on the Asian countries and later on the other states that were affected by the "contagion." It assumed that if there was a currency crisis, there must be fundamental problems (Bird & Milne 1999, 424). The IMF demanded tighter monetary policy (meaning higher interest rates in particular), and controls on the outflow of capital, as well as much stricter fiscal policy aimed at turning budget deficits into surpluses (Eichengreen 2000, 178). It later softened the fiscal targets when it realized the states needed to spend far more on public services since the recession proved to be much deeper than expected. The IMF also pressured states to adopt more state regulation of capital markets, a move that, although useful in the long term, could not be implemented in the short term (Desai 2003, 218). The measures simply cut too close to deep-seated cultural, political, and economic interests and practices to be quickly put in place. It would take many years of negotiation, pressure, and re-learning how to act. As put by Eichengreen:

> In Asia (and in its other recent programs), the IMF has become more deeply enmeshed in countries' internal affairs. It has sought to encourage authorities to improve prudential supervision, root out corruption, eliminate subsidies, break up monopolies and strengthen competition policy. In virtually every program country this has incited a backlash against the IMF, which is resented for its intrusiveness. (2000, 183)

Even the funds that the IMF mobilized ($36 billion of its own and $82 billion of others' money) proved woefully inadequate for economies which were among the world's largest.

The IMF was criticized from many angles. Japan, Australia, and several European countries felt the IMF was too preoccupied with liberalization, whereas liberal economists worried that the IMF's provision of funds for countries they felt were economically irresponsible amounted to a blank check—also known as moral hazard (actors behave more recklessly in the assurance they will be protected from their mistakes) (Noble & Ravenhill 2000, 24; Eichengreen 2000, 170). Still others expressed concern that the IMF did little to punish reckless creditors who both entered and exited the market—and made a killing. As put by Noble and Ravenhill:

> . . . [P]rivate sector actors, particularly those responsible for short-term capital movements, were not bearing their share of the adjustment costs that the crisis generated. Private sector actors were perceived to have benefited from an internationalization of moral hazard—as beneficiaries of official bailouts they did not suffer negative consequences when risky investments soured. (2000, 29)

CONCLUSION: GLOBAL GOVERNANCE?

Three years after the currency crisis, Asian states had mostly recovered. While the GDP per capita was nearly 80% of its pre-crisis level in South Korea and Malaysia, it was at only three quarters and two thirds in Indonesia and Thailand, respectively. Thailand's overall economic growth rate did not top 5% for three years (compared with 6% in 1996), although South Korea grew at over 10% in 1999— a new record. In fact, ten years after the crash, the South Korean economy was booming, with per capita income twice what it was in 1998 and nearly two thirds higher than before. With exception of Argentina, all of the countries directly affected by the currency crisis of 1997–1998 experienced dramatic growth beginning in 2002 (see Figure 20.2). But it would take until 2004 before most had returned to their pre-crisis wealth (Argentina has yet to recover). The same applied to the key problem during the crisis: access to foreign credit. Taken together, over $40 billion left the Asian crisis countries in 1998, 1999, and 2000 combined (Desai 2003, 134). But their economies were sound and attractive enough that in time, capital inflows picked up again, exceeding pre-crisis levels by 2006 (World Bank 2007).

The international community was engaged in the Asian financial crisis from the beginning, although this includes the synchronized withdrawal of capital, which helped create the crisis in the first place. International organizations and major creditors' central banks were also focused on providing what they considered to be the best policy advice and adequate funding to shore up the region's economies.

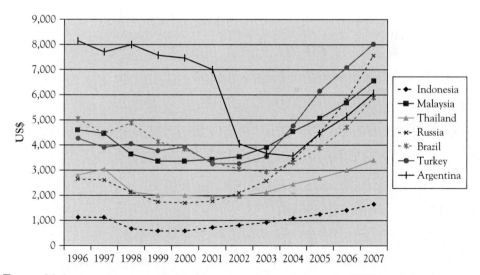

Figure 20.2 Post-crisis Economic Performance of Selected Countries (GNI/cap.), 1996–2007 GNI/capita Atlas method Source: World Bank 2007.

It is interesting to note the degree to which international actors worked at cross-purposes in this case. To a large extent, international public actors intervened to undo the behavior of international private actors. This is not particularly unusual. Most environmental regimes have been created to undo the damage by private industry. Likewise, many air traffic and shipping safety regulations were instituted because private actors were cutting corners and having preventable accidents.

Generally, public actors often work in tandem to bring about common objectives, and they often wield considerable power and authority. In fact, the IMF had enough power and leverage to pressure states into adopting policies that proved excessively severe and inappropriate. Even the IMF was forced to concede that its programs were too harsh and offered a more moderate, amended one a few months later. Global governance need not be successful or even fair to be significant, of course.

QUESTIONS TO CONSIDER

1. Compare the financial crisis of late 2008 with that of 1997. What started the crises? What were their key characteristics? How did governments respond? Is there any indication that lessons were learned from 1997?

2. Given the nature of the international financial system and what is at stake, who should be in charge of it? Should it be left to markets? Should a powerful international organization be created to manage it? Something in between?

3. Do feel you have a vested interest in global governance? How might international mismanagement affect you?

CHRONOLOGY
THE ASIAN FINANCIAL CRISIS

1997

May 14   Thailand spends billions of dollars of its foreign reserves to defend the Thai baht.

July 2   Thailand devalues the baht. News of the devaluation drops the value of the baht by 20%.

July 8   Malaysia's central bank intervenes to defend its currency.

July 11   The Philippine peso is devalued.

July 18   The IMF makes a billion dollars available to the Philippines.

July 24   The Singapore dollar starts a gradual decline.

August 5   Thailand agrees to adopt tough economic measures proposed by the IMF in return for a $17 billion.

August 14   Indonesia allows the currency to float freely.

October 8   Indonesian rupiah falls more than 30% in two months.

October 23   Hong Kong's stock index falls 10.4%.

October 27   The Dow Jones Industrial Average plummets 554.

October 31   The IMF agrees to a loan package for Indonesia.

November 17   The Korean won falls.

December 3   The IMF approves a $57 billion bailout package to South Korea.

December 12   The IMF restarts its loan disbursement to Russia.

December 18   Kim Dae Jung becomes South Korea's president.

December 23   The World Bank crafts an emergency loan of $10 billion to South Korea.

1998

January 15   Indonesian President Suharto signs a new loan deal with the IMF.

January 22   Indonesia's currency plunges to a new all-time low.

May 12   In Indonesia, troops fire into a peaceful protest at a Jakarta university, killing six students and sparking a week of riots.

May 21   Suharto resigns after 32 years in power. Vice President Habibie succeeds as president.

June 1   Russia's stock market crashes.

July 13   The IMF announces a package of $23 billion of emergency loans for Russia.

July 28   The IMF announces that it will ease conditions on its $57 billion aid package to South Korea, which had been blamed for rising unemployment and overburdened welfare programs.

September 24   Stocks on Wall Street and in Europe fall dramatically.

October 27   Brazil announces an austerity plan.

November 5   Russia strikes an agreement with foreign investors, but says it will not be able to repay $17.5 billion of debts due in 1999.

November 13   The IMF, World Bank and leading industrial nations announce a $41.5 billion rescue package for Brazil.

1999

January 15   The Brazilian government allows its currency, the real, to float freely.

March 25   The IMF approves a $1 billion increase in its emergency loan package for Indonesia.

REFERENCES

Bird, Graham, and Alistair Milne. "Miracle to Meltdown: A Pathology of the East Asian Financial Crisis." *Third World Quarterly* 20 #2 (April 1999): 421–437.

Cardoso, Fernando Henrique, and Enzo Faletto. *Dependency and Development in Latin America* (Berkeley: University of California Press, 1979).

Desai, Padma. *Financial Crisis, Contagion, and Containment: From Asia to Argentina* (Princeton: Princeton University Press, 2003).

Friedman, Milton. "A Primer on Exchange Rates," *Forbes* November 2, 1998. Available at: http://www.geocities.com/Eureka/Concourse/8751/versib/fb-mf-er.htm. Accessed on September 25, 2008.

Eichengreen, Barry. "The International Monetary Fund in the Wake of the Asian Crisis," in Gregory W. Noble and John Ravenhill, eds., *The Asian Financial Crisis and the Architecture of Global Finance* (Cambridge: Cambridge University Press, 2000): 170–191.

Haggard, Stephen, and Andrew MacIntyre. "The Political Economy of the Asian Financial Crisis," in Gregory W. Noble and John Ravenhill, eds., *The Asian Financial Crisis and the Architecture of Global Finance* (Cambridge: Cambridge University Press, 2000): 57–79.

Hamilton-Hart, Natasha. "Indonesia: Reforming the Institutions of Financial Governance?" in Gregory W. Noble and John Ravenhill, eds., *The Asian Financial Crisis and the Architecture of Global Finance* (Cambridge: Cambridge University Press, 2000): 108–131.

International Campaign to Ban Landmines (ICBL). "Campaign History." Available at http://www.icbl.org/campaign/history. Accessed on September 19, 2008.

Kahler, Miles. "The New International Financial Architecture and its Limits," in Gregory W. Noble and John Ravenhill, eds., *The Asian Financial Crisis and the Architecture of Global Finance* (Cambridge: Cambridge University Press, 2000): 235–260.

Noble, Gregory W., and John Ravenhill. "Causes and Consequences of the Asian Financial Crisis," in Gregory W. Noble and John Ravenhill, eds., *The Asian Financial Crisis and the Architecture of Global Finance* (Cambridge: Cambridge University Press, 2000): 1–35.

Pempel, T.J. "Introduction," in T.J. Pempel, ed. (1999) *The Politics of the Asian Economic Crisis* (Ithaca: Cornell University Press, 1999): 1–16.

POSCIR–The University of Delaware Department of Political Science and International Relations. The Global Governance Portal: A One Stop Shop on Global Governance. Available at http://www.globalgovernance.udel.edu/. Accessed on September 19, 2008.

Sachs, Jeffrey D., and Wing Thye Woo. "Understanding the Asian Financial Crisis," in Wing Thye Woo, Jeffrey D. Sachs, and Klaus Schwab, eds. *The Asian Financial Crisis: Lessons for a Resilient Asia* (Cambridge: MIT Press, 1999): 13–44.

Spruyt, Hendrick. *The Sovereign State and its Competitors* (Princeton: Princeton University Press, 1996).

Winters, Jeffrey A. "The Determinant of Financial Crisis in Asia," in T.J. Pempel, ed., *The Politics of the Asian Economic Crisis* (Ithaca: Cornell University Press, 1999): 79–99.

World Bank. World Development Indicators, 2007. Available at http://ddp-ext.worldbank.org/ext/DDPQQ/member.do?method=getMembers. Accessed on September 24, 2008.

Zacher, Mark (with Brent A. Sutton). *Governing Global Networks: International Regimes for Transportation and Communications* (New York: Cambridge University Press, 1996).

Index

A

Abbas, Mahmoud, 18, 23
Abdulaev, Nabi, 104
Abu Ghraib, 136, 313
Abyssinia, 33–36, 37
Acheson, Dean, 206, 214
ACT UP, 230
Advice and Reformation
    Committee, 148
Afghanistan, 50, 75, 146–147
Africa, HIV/AIDS in, 224–225
African National Congress
    (ANC), 318, 321–322,
    325–326, 328, 329,
    330–331, 335
Afrikaner Resistance
    Movement, 328
Aggressive war, 303
Agriculture
    Green Revolution in India,
        259–260, 263
    subsidies, 243–247
    trade trends in, 244
AIDS. *See* HIV/AIDS
Akhmadov, Hussein, 100
al-Aqsa intifadah, 18
Albanians, 168, 177
Albright, Madeleine, 17, 66
Alexander of Yugoslavia
Al Fatah, 19
Alkhanov, Alu, 108
Allawi, Iyad, 136, 139
Al Qaeda
    after September 11, 154–156
    Chechnya and, 103
    chronology, 158–160
    describing, 148–154
    finances, 153–154
    founding, 146–148
    geographic spread, 152
    global network, 151
    goals, 148–150

Islamic fundamentalism
    and, 144–146
Islamic teachings and, 149
key figures, 157–158
organization, 150–153
threat reports of, 67, 69, 70
al-Sadr, Moqtada, 141
American Express, 265
American National Institutes
    of Health, 226
Amnesty International, 229
Anarchy, 24–25, 232. *See also*
    League of Nations
    defined, 24
    peace and, 24
    power of, 37–38
ANC. *See* African National
    Congress (ANC)
Annan, Kofi, 138
Anti-Ballistic Missile Treaty, 53
Anti-sweatshop movement,
    270, 271, 275, 277, 279
Anti-war movement, 205–206,
    209–211
Apartheid
    1965-1988, 326–329
    dismantling, 329–330
    establishment and
        consolidation of, 321–326
    origins of South Africa
        and, 318–321
    postapartheid South Africa,
        331–332
Apparel Industry Partnership,
    279
Appeasement, 37
Arafat, Yasser, 17, 18, 19, 20, 22
Aramco, 253
Arbour, Louise, 179, 181
Argentina, 348, 351
Ashcroft, John, 67, 70, 72–73, 78
Asia, HIV/AIDS in, 225
Asian Development Bank, 349

Asian financial crisis
    Asian finances in 1990s,
        343–345
    chronology, 352–353
    eruption of, 345–347
    management of, 348–350
    post-crisis economic
        performance, 351
    spread to Russia, 347–348
    spread to South America, 348
Aslakhanov, Aslambek, 105
Assad, Hafez al, 7–8
Assertive multilateralism, 66
Atef, Mohammed, 147, 159
Atlantic Charter, 187
Atta, Mohammed, 78, 79, 152
Australia, Kyoto Protocol and,
    115, 116, 117, 118, 123
Austria, 293
Autonomous republic, 100
Avon, 272
Avturkhanov, Umar, 107
Axis of evil, 132
Aziz, Tariq, 138
Aziz al Omari, Abdul, 79
AZT (zidovudine), 226, 227,
    230, 233, 332
Azzam, Abdullah, 146–147,
    157, 158

B

Back-door draft, 126
Baker, James, 17, 76, 77, 128,
    172
Balance of payments, 341
Balance of power, 24, 36,
    41–42, 54–56. *See also*
    Sino-Soviet-American
    relations
    intervention and preserving,
        162–163
    tripolarity, 54–56

Balkans. *See also* Yugoslavia; *individual countries*
    map of, 166
Ball, George, 88, 93, 162–163, 203
Bangladesh, 252, 255, 267, 277
al-Banna, Hasan, 146, 157, 158
Banshiri, Abu Ubaidah al, 159
Bantu Authorities Act, 323
Barak, Ehud, 17, 18, 21
Baruch Plan, 44
Basayev, Shamil, 101, 102, 105, 107
Bay of Pigs, 47, 93
Beard, Charles, 188
Begin, Menachem, 3, 19, 20, 21
    Camp David accords and, 9–16
Belgian Congo, 252
Belgium, 236
Benelux countries, 284, 286
Bergsten, Fred, 66
Berisha, Sali, 178
Berlin Wall, 47, 59
Bernays, Murray, 303, 315
Bhagwati, Jagdish, 258
Biddle, Francis, 307, 314
Biden, Joseph, 180
Biko, Steve, 327, 334, 335
bin Laden, Osama, 78, 97, 146, 157, 159, 160, 235. *See also* Al Qaeda
    bomb materials, 152
    current position, 155
    discipline of, 148–149
    fortune of, 153, 271
    founding of al Qaeda and, 146–148
    U.S. intelligence on, 67, 68, 69, 70, 73
Birkett, Norman, 307
Black, Cofer, 68, 72
Black Consciousness movement, 327, 328
Black widows, 103, 107–108
Blair, Tony, 19, 138
Blair House Accords, 246
Blank, Margaret, 309
Blix, Hans, 133
Blockade of Cuba, 84–86
Boers, 319, 320–321, 334
Boer War, 320–321, 335
Boesak, Allan, 328, 334
Bolivia, 30
Bolshakov, Georgi, 85
Bormann, Martin, 310

Bosnia-Herzegovina, 53, 165, 167, 311, 312
    elections in, 171
    map 1391 A.D., 166
    warfare in, 173–176
Botha, Louis, 321
Botha, p. W., 327, 329, 333, 336
Botha, Pik, 331
Boutros Ghali, Boutros, 138, 173–174, 181
Boycotts, of South Africa, 330
Brandt, Willy, 50
Braudel, Fernand, 277
Brazil, 230–231, 347, 348, 351, 353
Bremer, Paul, 134
Bretton Woods, 237, 248, 284
Brezhnev, Leonid, 48, 57
Brinkmanship, 46
Britain. *See* United Kingdom
Broder, Samuel, 226
Brussels Treaty Organization, 285
Brzezinski, Zbigniew, 12
Bubonic plague, 221
Buchanan, Patrick, 78, 273
Bulgaria, 165
Bundy, McGeorge, 83, 87, 88, 93
Bundy, William, 209
Burroghs Wellcome Company, 226
Bush, George H. W., 77, 181
    Cold War activism and, 63
    global warming and, 115
    Gulf War and, 51, 127, 128, 130, 138, 139
    Yugoslavia and, 172
Bush, George W., 77, 122, 138, 310
    Chechnya and, 103
    global warming and, 114, 123
    HIV/AIDS and, 228, 233
    intervention and, 163
    invasion of Iraq and, 132–137
    Iraq War and, 140, 141, 213
    Israel and, 18, 19
    Kyoto Protocol and, 120
    terrorism and, 143
    terrorist threats and, 71, 76
    Vulcans and, 65, 68, 132–133
Bush Doctrine, 75–76, 133, 140
Buthelezi, Mangasuthu, 330, 331, 334

C

Cairns Group of Fair Trading Nations, 245–246
Calley, William, 212, 218, 313
Cambodia, 211, 212, 215, 217, 218, 311
Camp David accords, 9–16
    chronology, 21–23
    key figures, 20–21
    Middle East peace since, 16–17
Camp David II, 17–18, 22
Canada, 115, 117, 118, 123, 252
CAP. *See* Common Agricultural Program (CAP)
Carbon sinks, 118
Cardoso, Fernando Henrique, 348
Carter, Jimmy, 20, 58
    Camp David accords and, 3, 9–16, 19, 21, 22
    Nobel Peace Prize, 18
    Russian invasion of Afghanistan and, 50
Carter Doctrine, 51
Castro, Fidel, 47, 82, 91, 92, 93, 144, 253
Caucasus region, ethnolinguistic groups of, 98
Cells, al Qaeda, 150, 152–153
Center of Budget and Policy Priorities, 274
Centers for Disease Control and Prevention, 226, 227
Central Intelligence Agency (CIA), 67, 70, 72, 185
CFCs. *See* Chlorofluorocarbons (CFCs)
Chamberlain, Neville, 38
Charter of Fundamental Rights, 295
Chauvinism, 96
Chechen War, 1990–1996. *See also* Russian-Chechen conflict
    1817-1864, 99
    1997-2000, 102
Cheney, Dick, 65, 68, 77, 78, 132, 134, 138
Child labor, 269, 272, 276, 278
China. *See also* Sino-Soviet-American relations
    Manchuria and, 30–31
    wage competition and, 275

Chlorofluorocarbons (CFCs), 110–111
Chou En-Lai, 49
Christopher, Warren, 176, 181
Churchill, Stephen, 293
Churchill, Winston, 27, 187, 198, 284, 302
CIA. *See* Central Intelligence Agency (CIA)
Civil disobedience, 255
Civilization, as international relations concept, 97–98
Clark, Ramsey, 132
Clarke, Richard, 67, 69, 70, 71, 72, 78
Clean Development Mechanism, 118
Clifford, Clark, 206, 214
Clinton, Bill, 17, 18, 21, 65, 77, 122, 151, 163, 181, 227
CODESA. *See* Convention for a Democratic South Africa (CODESA)
Cold War
1949-1962, 45–48
1979-1985, 50–51
détente, 48–50, 51–52
outbreak of, 43–45
post-Cold War era, 52–54
Collective goods, 110–111
challenge of providing, 121–122
defined, 110
global warming and, 111–121
Committee on Trade and Development, 240
Common Agricultural Program (CAP), 287, 288–289, 298
Common Market. *See also* European Union
1957-1973, 286–288, 298
emergence of, 283–286, 298
under stress (1973-1985), 288–290
Communitarian perspective on globalization, 273
Complex interdependence, 54
Concert of Europe, 283
Congress of Berlin, 165
Congress of the People, 325, 335
Conservatives, 64
Constructive conciliation, 188
Containment strategy, 44, 45
Convention for a Democratic South Africa (CODESA), 330
Cooper, Richard, 64

Corporations, HIV/AIDS and, 225–226
Council of Europe, 298
Counter-Intelligence Security Group (CSG), 67, 70, 72
Countries, roles played in international system, 3
Cressy, Roger, 71
Crime, in South Africa, 332
Crime against humanity, 304–305
Crisis, defined, 82, 83
Croatia
1070 A.D., 166
elections in, 171
history, 165, 167, 181
nationalism in, 170
warfare in, 171–173
Croat nationalism, 165, 167
Croats
experience in World War II, 169
in Yugoslavia, 168
Cronkite, Walter, 207–208, 215
CSG. *See* Counter-Intelligence Security Group (CSG)
Cuban Missile Crisis, 47–48
analysis of decision of blockade Cuba, 86–89
blockade aftermath, 85–86
chronology, 93–94
eruption of, 83–85
key figures, 92–93
negotiating resolution, 86
precursors, 83
rationality and, 82, 91–92
response to Soviet offers, 89–91
Culture, defining, 98
Currencies, 340–342
Customs union, 282, 284, 286
Cyprus, 293, 294
Czech Republic, 294

D

Danzig, 32–33, 37
Dayan, Moshe, 5, 11, 16
Dayton Accords, 176, 177, 182
Debt bondage, 271
Declaration of Commitment on HIV/AIDS, 229, 233
Declaration on the Rights of the Child, 311
Decolonization, 251–252
of India, 255–257, 266
DEFCON, 4

Defense Planning Guidance, 76
de Gaulle, Charles, 287, 298
de Klerk, F. W., 329, 330, 334, 336
Delors, Jacques, 291, 297
Delors Plan, 291–292, 298
Democracy, 98, 163
Democratic convention (1968), 210–211, 217
Democratic peace theory, 202–204
mutual dependence and, 236
Vietnam War and, 212–213
Democratization, 294
Deng Hsaio Ping, 50, 52
Deng Hsiao Ping, 58
Denmark, 287
Dependency, decolonization and, 252
Dependency theory, 239
Détente
1963-1979, 48–50
1985-1991, 51–52
Cuban Missile Crisis and, 92
de Vabres, Donnedieu, 307, 314
Devaluation of currency, 341–432
Developing countries. *See also* North-South trade
agriculture subsidies and, 244
GATT and, 239–240
Group of 77 and, 241, 242–243
Kyoto Protocol and, 116, 118
Development, 251–253
in India, 257–267
Developmental perspective on globalization, 276–277
Diamonds, in South Africa, 319–320
Dicker, Richard, 179
Diem, Ngo Dinh, 204, 214, 215, 216
Dillon, Douglas, 86
Disney, 272
Displacement, worker, 274
Djindjic, Zoran, 180, 183
Dobrynin, Anatoly, 85, 89, 90, 92
Doenitz, Karl, 304, 309
Doha Round, 247, 248
Downsizing, 274
Dubai Islamic Bank, 153
Dudayev, Dzhokar, 100, 101, 102, 105, 106, 107
Dulles, John Foster, 47
Dutch Reformed Church, 321

E

Eagleburger, Lawrence, 175
East India Company, 254
Ebola, 149
Economic factors, democratic
  peace theory and, 203
Economic integration, 282
Economic interdependence,
  235–236, 247
  basic concepts, 236–237
  North-South trade, 237–248
Economic interest,
  intervention and, 164
Economic liberalization, in
  India, 260–263
Economic Policy Institute, 274
Economic regionalism,
  282–283
  Common Market (1957-
    1973), 286–288, 298
  Common Market emergence,
    283–286, 298
  Common Market under
    stress, 288–290, 298
  enlargement of EU, 293–294
  Euro, 291–292, 299
  European Constitution,
    294–296
  Europe and, 296–297
  Maastricht Treaty, 292–293,
    299
  security cooperation, 296
  Single European Act,
    290–291
Economics, international law
  and, 122
Economies in transition, Kyoto
  Protocol and, 116, 117, 118
Economist, The, 292
ECSC. *See* European Coal and
  Steel Community (ECSC)
ECU, 290
Eden, Anthony, 37, 38
Egypt
  Camp David accords, 9–16
  1973 war with Israel, 3–9
Eichmann, Adolf, 311, 314
Eisenhower Doctrine, 47
Electronic intelligence, 185
Ellsberg, Daniel, 215, 218
Emissions
  baselines for Kyoto Protocol
    signatories, 117
  market for, 117
EMS. *See* European Monetary
  System (EMS)

Enabling Clause, 240
ERDF. *See* European
  Regional Development
  Fund (ERDF)
ERM. *See* Exchange Rate
  Mechanism (ERM)
ESCB. *See* European System of
  Central Banks (ESCB)
Estonia, 294
Estrada, Raul, 119, 123
ETA (Euskadi Ta Askatusuna),
  144, 149–150, 156
Ethiopia, Abyssinia and, 33–36
Ethnic cleansing, 173, 174–175
Euratom, 286
Euro, 291–292
Europe. *See* Common Market;
  European Union;
  individual countries
European Coal and Steel
  Community (ECSC),
  285–286, 298
European Constitution,
  294–295
European Court of Justice, 295
European Economic Commu-
  nity. *See* Common Market
European Monetary System
  (EMS), 289–290
European Movement, 284, 298
European Regional Development
  Fund (ERDF), 289
European System of Central
  Banks (ESCB), 291
European Union. *See also*
  Common Market
  agricultural tariffs, 245,
    246–247
  Croatia warfare and, 172
  enlargement of, 293–294
  Euro, 291–292, 299
  European Constitution,
    294–296
  Kyoto Protocol and, 117,
    118
  Maastricht Treaty, 292–293,
    299
  security cooperation, 296
  Single European Act,
    290–291
Evening News, 37
Exchange Rate Mechanism
  (ERM), 290
ExComm (Executive
  Committee of the
  National Security
  Council), 84, 85–88, 93

F

Falco, Robert, 307
Fatwa, 148
FBI. *See* Federal Bureau of
  Investigation (FBI)
FCCC. *See* UN Framework
  Convention on Climate
  Change (FCCC)
Federal Aviation Administration,
  68, 72
Federal Bureau of Investigation
  (FBI)
  terrorist threat reports and,
    67, 69, 70, 72–74
Federalization, 283
Feklisov, Aleksandr, 85, 89, 92
Ferdinand, Archduke, 167, 182
Finances, al Qaeda, 153–154
Finland, 39, 293
FISA. *See* Foreign Intelligence
  Surveillance Act (FISA)
Floating currency, 341–342
FluNet, 226
Fomin, Alexander (Aleksandr
  Feklisov), 85, 89, 92
Food and Drug Administration,
  226
Ford, Gerald, 9, 212
Foreign Intelligence
  Surveillance Act (FISA), 74
Foreign investment, 253
  in India, 262, 264
France
  Abyssinia and, 33, 35, 36
  Asian financial crisis and,
    349
  Bosnia and, 176
  Common Market and, 286
  Kyoto Protocol and, 115,
    117, 118
  League of Nations and,
    27–29, 36–37
Frank, Hans, 304, 308, 309
Franks, Tommy, 132, 134, 138
Freedom Charter, 325, 335
Freedoms, four European,
  290–291
Free market perspective on
  globalization, 273–274
Free market theory, 239
Free riders, 111
Free trade, 236
Free trade zone, 282
Friedman, Milton, 342
Friedman, Thomas, 235
Fritzsche, Hans, 304, 309, 310

Fuchida, Mitsuo, 186
Fukuyama, Francis, 98
Fulbright, William, 204, 206, 214
Funk, Walter, 304, 309

G

Gaidar, Yegor, 105
Gam'a Islamiya (Islamic Group), 146
Gamba, Virginia, 332–333
Game theory, 81
Gandhi, Indira, 257, 259–260, 266, 267
Gandhi, Mohandas (Mahatma), 255, 256, 266, 322
Gandhi, Rajiv, 257, 260–261, 266, 267
Gandhi, Sanjay, 260
Gandhi, Sonia, 265, 266
Gap, the, 272
Garner, Jay, 134
GATT. *See* General Agreement on Tariffs and Trade (GATT)
Gelb, Leslie, 205
General Agreement on Tariffs and Trade (GATT), 66, 237, 238–241, 248
    Doha Round, 247, 248
    Tokyo Round, 242, 248
    Uruguay Round, 243–247
Generalized System of Preferences (GSP), 240–241, 248
Geneva Convention, 302, 303, 304, 311, 315
Genocide, 304
Genocide Convention, 311, 312
Georgia, Russian conflict with, 104, 108
Germany
    Abyssinia and, 35
    Asian financial crisis and, 349
    Common Market and, 286, 288–289
    Danzig and, 32–33
    exports flowing with Belgium and Netherlands, 236
    Kyoto Protocol and, 117, 118
    League of Nations and, 27–28, 29, 39
Gerow, Leonard, 192
Ghailani, Ahmed Khalfan, 155, 160
Gifford, Kathie Lee, 269–270

Gilpatrick, Roswell, 88
Gilpin, Robert, 273
Glaspie, April, 127
GlaxoSmithKline, 226, 227
Global factory, 270, 278
Global free market perspective on globalization, 275–276
Global Fund for AIDS, 228
Global governance, 338–340, 351–352. *See also* Asian financial crisis
    defined, 339
    international finance, 340–342
    management of Asian financial crisis and, 348–350
Globalization, 98, 269–271, 279
    competing perspectives on, 273–279
    developmental perspective on, 276–277
    global free market perspective on, 275–276
    humanitarian perspective on, 278–279
    labor perspective on, 274–275
    outsourcing and, 272–273, 276, 277
    structural Marxist perspective on, 277–278
    sweatshops and, 269–270, 271–272, 275, 276–277, 278, 279
Global level of analysis, 3
Global Public Health Intelligence Network, 226
Global warming, 111–114. *See also* Kyoto Protocol
    creating rules on gases, 114–119
Global weather patterns, global warming and, 113
Goering, Hermann, 303, 305, 307, 308, 309, 310, 314
Gold mining, in South Africa, 320
Goldwater, Barry, 205, 214
Gorbachev, Mikhail, 56, 58, 60, 100, 138
Gorbal, Ashraf, 16
Gore, Al, 66, 114, 116, 119, 120, 122
Government agencies, HIV/AIDS and, 225–226
Governmental level of analysis, 2
Grachev, Pavel, 105

Great Britain. *See* United Kingdom
Great Trek, 319
Greece, 289, 294
Greenhouse gas intensity, 121
Green Revolution, in India, 259–260, 263
Green Zone, 135
Grew, Joseph, 188, 193, 198
Group of 77, 241, 242–243
GSP. *See* Generalized System of Preferences (GSP)
Guerrillas, 144

H

Haass, Richard, 75
Habibie, B. J., 353
Hadley, Stephen, 68, 69, 70–71, 78
Hague Convention, 301–302, 304, 315
Haig, Alexander, 64
Hamas party, 19, 23
Hani, Chris, 330
Hapsburg Empire, 165–166
Harkin, Tom, 272
Harris, Lou, 211–212
Hayden, Tom, 215
Heath, Edward, 288
Hegemon, 111, 121–122
Hegemonic imperative approach, 64–65
Helms, Jesse, 64, 78
Helsinki Accords, 50
Hermann, Charles, 82
Hess, Rudolf, 303, 304, 309, 314
Hezbollah Party, 146
Hindus, 255
Hirohito, 38, 199
Hitler, Adolf, 28, 37, 38, 43, 303, 305, 309
Hitler Youth, 307
HIV/AIDS, 223–225
    chronology of pandemic, 233
    global view of infection, 224
    human rights advocates and, 229–231
    international response, 225–227
    North-South perspective on, 231–232
    security implications of, 228
    in South Africa, 332–333
    U.S. government response, 227–229
    Western spending on, 231–232

Ho Chi Minh, 49, 204, 214
Hoffman, Abby, 215
Holbrooke, Richard, 178, 181
Holocaust, 304
Homelands, 323–324
Hong Kong, 347, 353
Hopkins, Harry, 187
Horowitz, Jerome, 226
Hu Jintao, 53, 58
Hull, Cordell, 188, 194, 197, 198, 199
Human development index, 252
Humanitarian aid, to Bosnia, 174
Humanitarian intervention, 163–164
Humanitarian perspective on globalization, 278–279
Human rights, 317–318. *See also* Apartheid
promoting, 332–333
Human rights advocates, HIV/AIDS and, 229–231
Human Rights Watch, 104, 179
Human security, 220–221
HIV/AIDS and, 223–232, 233
pandemics and, 221–223
Humphrey, Hubert, 214
Hungary, 294
Huntington, Samuel, 97, 98
Hussein, Saddam, 138, 145
capture of, 136
first Persian Gulf War and, 126–127, 131
as part of axis of evil, 132
second Persian Gulf War, 76, 137

I

ICTY. *See* International Criminal Tribunal for the former Yugoslavia (ICTY)
IMF. *See* International Monetary Fund (IMF)
Inalienable rights, 317
India
birth and death rates, 263, 264
chronology, 266–268
current situation, 264–265
economic liberalization, 260–263
before independence, 253–256
under Indira Gandhi, 259–260
key figures, 266
languages, 256

under Nehru, 256–259
prime ministers, 257
trade and, 243
Individual level of analysis, 2
Indonesia, Asian financial crisis and, 343, 344, 346, 347, 351, 353
INF. *See* Intermediate-Range Nuclear Forces (INF) Treaty
Inkatha Freedom party, 331
Inkatha Party, 330
Insurgent groups, in Iraq, 135–136
Intelligence. *See also* Pearl Harbor
defined, 185
sources of, 185–186
Interdependence. *See* Economic interdependence
Intergovernmental Panel on Climate Change (IPCC), 115, 123
Intermediate-Range Nuclear Forces (INF) Treaty, 51, 60
International Action Center, 132
International Campaign to Ban Landmines, 340
International Committee of the Red Cross, 339
International Court of Justice, 27, 301, 306
International Covenant on Civil and Political Rights, 312
International crime, terrorism *vs.*, 144
International Criminal Court, 164, 302, 316
International Criminal Tribunal for the former Yugoslavia (ICTY), 178–179, 182, 316
International finance, 340–342
International Labour Organization, 27, 227, 272, 278
International law, 301–302, 312–314. *See also* Nuremberg trials
economics and, 122
United States and, 121
International Law Commission, 311
International Monetary Fund (IMF), 52, 66, 243, 253, 261, 284, 342

Asian financial crisis and, 345, 349–350, 352–353
International rules, 338–339
International Terrorism Operations Section (ITOS), 74
International Trade Organization, 238
Intervention, 162–164, 179–180
desire to spread democracy and, 163
economic interest and, 164
humanitarian, 163–164
preserving balance of power, 162–163
strategic, 162–163
war crimes tribunal, 178–179
warfare in Bosnia, 173–176
warfare in Kosovo, 177–178
warfare in Slovenia and Croatia, 171–173
Yugoslavia and, 179–180
Intifada, 16, 22
al-Aqsa, 18
IRA. *See* Irish Republican Army (IRA)
Iraq
invasion of Kuwait, 126–130
sanctions against, 131–132
war with United States, 76–77, 134–137, 213
Iraq Action Coalition, 131
Ireland, 287
Irish Republican Army (IRA), 149, 156
ISI, 147, 155
Islam. *See also* Muslims
al Qaeda and teachings of, 149
in Balkans, 165
Chechen people and, 99
Islamic fundamentalism, 144–146
Islamic Salvation Front, 152
Israel
Camp David accords, 9–16
Iraqi attack on, 129
peace agreement with Jordan, 17
PLO recognition and, 17
1973 war, 3–9
Italy
Abyssinia and, 33–36
Common Market and, 286
Kyoto Protocol and, 117, 118
League of Nations and, 27–28, 29, 39

ITOS. *See* International Terrorism Operations Section (ITOS)
Itzbegovic, Alija, 173, 176, 181
Ivins, Molly, 277

J

Jaafari, Ibrahim, 141
Jackson, John, 314
Jackson, Robert, 304, 306, 308, 309, 310, 312
Japan
   agricultural tariffs in, 245
   Asian financial crisis and, 347, 350
   Kyoto Protocol and, 115, 117, 118
   League of Nations and, 27–28, 29
   Manchuria and, 30–31
   Pearl Harbor and, 186–199
Jenner, Edward, 222
Jihad, 149
Jodl, Alfred, 304, 308, 309
Johannesburg Summit on Sustainable Development, 121
Johnson, Lyndon, 48, 49, 86, 92, 163, 204, 205, 209, 211, 214, 216
Jordan, peace agreement with Israel, 17
Juan Carlos, 150

K

Kadijevec, Veljko, 172
Kadyrov, Akhmad, 102, 103, 105, 107, 108
Kaltenbrunner, Ernst, 304, 309, 314
Karadzic, Radovan, 173, 175, 181
Karnow, Stanley, 207
Kashmir, 255, 266
Kasyanov, Mikhail, 123
Kay, David, 140
Keitel, Wilhelm, 304, 308, 309
Kellogg-Briand Pact, 305, 310, 315
Kennan, George, 44
Kennedy, John F., 57, 92, 214. *See also* Cuban Missile Crisis
   Vietnam and, 204
Kennedy, Robert F., 83, 85, 86, 87, 88, 89, 90, 93, 208–209, 210, 215

Kent State University, 211, 218
Keohane, Robert, 54
Kernaghan, Charles, 269
Kerry, John, 270
Keynes, John Maynard, 349
Khanh, Nguyen, 216
Khasbutalov, Ruslan, 101
Khattab, 105
Khomeini, Ruhollah, 127, 146, 157, 158
Khrushchev, Nikita, 57
   Cuban Missile Crisis and, 47, 48, 82, 83, 85–86, 89–91, 92, 93–94
   Sino-Soviet alliance and, 49
Kim Dae Jung, 353
Kimmel, Husband E., 186, 187, 188, 190, 191, 192, 197
King, Martin Luther, Jr., 208, 215
Kissinger, Henry, 20, 58, 214
   Camp David and, 16, 19
   Vietnam War diplomacy and, 49–50, 218
   1973 war and, 3–9
KLA. *See* Kosovo Liberation Army (KLA)
Knight, Phil, 275
Kohl, Helmut, 51, 288, 292, 297
Konoye, Fumimaro, 188, 189, 197, 198
Korean War, 45–46, 59
Kosovo, 53
   under Tito, 170
   warfare in, 177–178
Kosovo Liberation Army (KLA), 177–178, 182
Kostunica, Vojislav, 179, 181, 183, 312
Krauthammer, Charles, 64, 65, 78
Kreuger, Anne, 239
Kristol, William, 65
Kruger, Paul, 320
Kurds, 127, 131
Kurusu, Saburo, 188, 199
Kuwait, 126, 127, 128–130
Ky, Nguyan Cao, 217
Kyoto Protocol
   assessment of, 121–122
   chronology, 123
   current situation, 120–121
   getting to, 114–116
   impasse at Hague, 119–120
   key figures, 122–123
   pollution trading and, 116–119

L

Labor perspective on globalization, 274–275
Labor standards, national, 278–279
Landmines, rules on, 339–340
Latvia, 294
Laval, Pierre, 35, 38
Lawrence, Geoffrey, 307, 314
League of Nations, 283, 315, 338, 339
   Abyssinia and, 33–36
   Danzig and, 32–33
   decision-making structures, 26–27
   League politics, 27–30
   Manchuria and, 30–31
   origins of, 25–26
   World War II and, 36–37
Legitimacy, 246
Lembede, Anton, 322
Lenin, Vladimir, 277
Lennon, John, 232
Lester, Sean, 37, 38
Levels of analysis, 2–3
   assessing approach, 17–20
   Camp David accords, 9–16, 20–23
   Henry Kissinger and 1973 war, 3–9
   Middle East peace since Camp David, 16–19
Levi Strauss, 276
Lewis, Stephen, 231
Liberalization, 237
Liberal neoisolationists, 64
Life magazine, 269
Lithuania, 294
Lloyd's of London, 339
Lomé Convention, 244
Louis XIV, 62
Luthuli, Albert, 325, 326

M

Maastricht Treaty, 292–293, 296, 298
MacArthur, Douglas, 46
Macedonia, 163, 165–167, 170, 171
Macedonians in Yugoslavia, 168
Machiavelli, 42
Mad cow disease, 293, 298
Madrid terrorist attacks, 155
Magdoff, Harry, 164

MAGIC, 194
Mahfouz, Khalid bin, 153
MAK (Afghan Service
    Bureau), 146, 157, 158
Malan, Daniel F., 318, 321,
    322, 334, 335
Malaysia, Asian financial
    crisis and, 343, 346,
    347, 351, 352
al-Maliki, Nouri, 136, 139, 141
Malta, 293, 294
Manchuria, 30–31, 39
Mandel, Ernst, 277
Mandela, Nelson, 144, 322,
    325, 326, 329, 330–331,
    334, 336
Mankiw, Greg, 276
Mansfield, Mike, 206
Mansur, Sheik, 99, 106
Mao Zedong, 44–45, 49, 57,
    59, 144
Maquiladoras, 275
March, James, 88
Marriage (tripolar
    arrangement), 55
Marshall, George, 192, 199
Marshall Plan, 44, 283, 284, 298
Marx, Karl, 232, 277
Maskhadov, Aslan, 101, 102,
    105, 107, 108
Mattel, 272
Mbeki, Thabo, 331, 336
McCain, John, 2, 156
McCarthy, Eugene, 208, 210, 215
McCone, John, 84, 93
McGovern, George, 215
McNamara, Robert, 84, 86,
    87–88, 91, 93, 206, 214,
    216, 217
Media, public opinion on
    Vietnam War and,
    207–208
Medvedev, Dmitrij, 106
Meir, Golda, 5, 7, 20
Ménage à trois, 55
Mexico, 253, 275
Middle East. See also Camp
    David accords
    peace since Camp David,
    16–19
    political realignments, 17
Military power, 125–126
    first Persian Gulf war,
    126–130, 138–140
    inter- Persian Gulf war
    period, 131–132
    limits of, 137

second Persian Gulf war,
    134–137, 138–139,
    140–141
    Vulcans, 132–133
Military success, factors in,
    125–126
Milner, Alfred, 320, 335
Milosevic, Slobodan, 170–171,
    175, 176, 178, 179, 181,
    183, 312, 314, 316
Minh, Duong Van, 216
Minimum Age Convention, 272
Mitsuya, Hiroaki, 226
Mitterand, François, 174, 292
Mladic, Ratko, 180
Mohammed, Khalid Sheikh, 68
Monetary reform, European,
    289–290
Monnet, Jean, 283, 284, 285,
    288, 297
Monroe Doctrine, 162
Montenegrins, 168
Montenegro, 165, 171, 174, 180
Montreal Protocol, 122
Moody's, 345
Morgenthau, Henry, 302
Morillon, Phillippe, 174
Most-favored nation status, 237
Motlanthe, Kgalema, 336
Moussaoui, Zacarias, 73–75,
    78, 79
Mubarak, Hosni, 19, 21, 148, 151
Mujahaddin, 146
Multilateralist approach,
    65–66, 180
Musharraf, Pervez, 155
Muslim Brotherhood, 152,
    157, 158
Muslims. See also Islam
    Indian, 253, 255–256
    in Yugoslavia, 168
Mussolini, Benito, 27, 28,
    37, 38
Mutual dependence, 235–236
My Lai massacre, 212, 218, 313

N

Nagumo, Chuichi, 186
Nasser, Gamal Abdel, 47, 146
Nation, defined, 96
National Democratic
    movement, 329
National interest, 62–66
    debate over, 75–77
    hegemonic imperative
    approach, 64–65

multilateralist position,
    65–66
    national interest approach,
    63–64, 76–77
    September 11 attacks and,
    67–75
Nationalism, 96–97
    civilization as an
    international relations
    concept, 97–98
    defined, 96
    Russian-Chechen conflict,
    98–104, 105–108
    sovereignty vs., 104–105
National labor standards,
    278–279
National Mobilization
    Committee to End
    the War, 210
National Peace Action
    Coalition, 210
National Security Agency,
    185, 186
National Security Council,
    70, 72
Native Lands Act, 321–322
NATO. See North Atlantic
    Treaty Organization
    (NATO)
Nazi regime, Danzig and,
    32–33
Nehru, Jawaharlal, 255,
    256–259, 266
Neoconservatives, 64
Netanyahu, Benjamin, 17, 21
Netherlands, 236
Neurath, 309
Neutrality Acts, 187, 197
New International Economic
    Order, 241, 248
Newly industrializing countries
    (NICs), 241, 242, 243
Newsweek, 2
New York Times, 185, 306
NGOs. See Non-governmental
    organizations (NGOs)
NICs. See Newly industrializing
    countries (NICs)
NIEO, 242–243, 248
Nike, 272, 275, 279
Nikitchenko, I. T., 304, 307, 314
Nixon, Richard, 4, 49, 50,
    56, 57, 92, 211–212,
    214, 217
Nokhchii, 98–99
Nomura, Kichisaburo, 188, 197,
    198, 199

Non-governmental organizations (NGOs), 223
HIV/AIDS and, 225–226, 229–231
North American Free Trade Agreement, 275
North Atlantic Treaty Organization (NATO)
Croatia and, 172
Cuban Missile Crisis and, 87
expansion of, 53, 60, 285
founding, 44, 59
International Criminal Tribunal and, 179
interventions in former Yugoslavia, 176, 178, 180, 182–183
North-South trade
agriculture in Uruguay Round and beyond, 243–427
chronology, 248
collapse of G-77 and NIEO, 242–243
conditions after World War II, 237–238
creation of UNCTAD and NIEO, 238–242
Norton, Anne, 65
Norway, 287
NSC-68, 45
Nuremberg Principles, 311, 312
Nuremberg trials
chronology, 315–316
implications of, 310–312
judgment, 309–310
key figures, 314
organizing, 302–307
proceedings, 307–309
Nye, Joseph, 54, 64
Nyerere, Julius, 241

O

OAS. See Organization of American States (OAS)
Obama, Barack, 2, 136, 235
OEEC. See Organization for European Economic Cooperation (OEEC)
Olmert, Ehud, 19, 23
Omar, Mohammed, 147, 158
OPEC, 241, 243, 248, 288
Operation Enduring Freedom, 75
Orange Free State, 319, 321

Organization for European Economic Cooperation (OEEC), 284
Organization for Security and Cooperation in Europe, 296
Organization of African Unity, 282
Organization of American States (OAS), 85
Oslo Accords, 18, 22
Ottoman Empire, 165, 167, 181, 182
Outsourcing, 265, 270, 272–273, 276, 277

P

Pacific Fleet, Pearl Harbor and, 186, 188–189
Pahlavi, Reza, 146
Pakistan, 255, 272
Palau, 252
Palestine Liberation Organization (PLO), 7, 8, 16–17, 22, 149
Palestinian Authority, 18
Palestinian rights and self-determination, 5, 16
Palestinization, 104
Pandemics, 221–223. See also HIV/AIDS
Panic, Milan, 175–176
Parker, John, 307
Pass laws, 319
Pasteur Institute, 226
Patents, HIV/AIDS drugs and, 230–231
Patraeus, David, 136, 139
Peace, anarchy and, 24
Peace movement, 209–211
Pearl Harbor
attack, 186
chronology, 197–199
controversy over, 186–196
key figures, 196–197
lessons of, 196
Pearson, Lester, 340
Pease, Donald, 272
Penn, William, 283
Pentagon, attack on, 148
Pentagon Papers, 212, 215, 218
Peres, Shimon, 20, 22
Perimeter containment strategy, 47
Perle, Richard, 65, 76, 132

Permanent Court of International Justice, 27
Perot, Ross, 78, 273
Persian Gulf wars
1990-1991, 51
first, 126–130
Middle East political realignments and, 17
second, 134–137
Vietnam Syndrome and, 213
Personal responsibility, 311
Peru, 30
Peruvian Shining Path, 144
Pfaff, William, 64
PHARE, 294
Phoenix memo, 73, 79
Pickard, Thomas, 72–73, 74, 78
Piot, Peter, 231
Plaatje, Sol, 321, 334
PLO. See Palestine Liberation Organization (PLO)
Poland, 36–37, 117, 118, 294
Political integration, 282
Pollution trading, 116–119
Polo, Marco, 235
Population Registration Act, 322, 329, 335
Populist perspective on globalization, 273
Portugal, 289
Pottern Barn rule, 133
Poverty
globalization and, 274
Indian development and, 257, 258, 262, 264, 267
pandemics and, 222
Powell, Colin, 71, 77, 78, 132, 133, 134, 138, 140, 228
PRD-13, 66
Prébish, Raúl, 239
Preemption strategy, 132, 133, 140
Prescott, John, 122
Price guarantees, 287
Program of Action on the Establishment of a New International Economic Order, 241, 248
Prohibition of Mixed Marriages Act, 322, 335
Project for a New American Century, 65
Public opinion
Vietnam War and, 204–213
war and, 202–204
Putin, Vladimir, 53, 102, 103, 105, 106, 107

Q

Quat, Phan Huy, 216

R

Rabin, Yitzhak, 8, 17, 20, 22
Raduyev, Salman, 106
Raeder, Erich, 304, 309
Rahman, Omar Abdul, 67–68,
    146, 152, 157, 159
Ramos, Fidel, 151
Rao, p. V. Narasimha, 257, 261,
    266, 267
Rappard, William, 31
Rationality, 81–82. *See also*
    Cuban Missile Crisis
    test of, 91–92
Reagan, Ronald, 16, 50–51, 56,
    58, 60, 163
Reebok, 272, 279
Reich, Robert, 274
Reserves, of hard currency, 341
Ressam, Ahmed, 70, 71
Retief, Piet, 319, 334
Rhodes, Cecil, 320
Rhodes, James, 211
Ribbentrop, 309
Rice, Condoleezza, 67, 68, 69,
    71, 72, 78, 132, 134
Richardson, James, 187, 188
Rideout, Janet, 226
Rightful heritage concept,
    165, 167
Right to health, 229
Rogers, Warren, 91
Rolince, Michael, 74
Romantic triangle (tripolar
    arrangement), 55
Rome Statute for an
    International Criminal
    Court, 312
Roosevelt, Eleanor, 317
Roosevelt, Franklin D., 163,
    186–189, 196, 198, 199,
    302, 303, 315
Roosevelt, Teddy, 65
Roosevelt Corollary, 162
Rosenberg, Alfred, 304, 308,
    309
Rosenberg, Tina, 312
Rostow, Walt, 216
Rugova, Ibrahim, 177
Rules of origin, 240–241
Rumsfeld, Donald, 71, 77, 133,
    134, 135, 138
Rusk, Dean, 85, 93, 94, 216

Russett, Bruce, 98
Russia. *See also* Soviet Union
    conflict with Georgia,
        104, 108
    financial crisis, 347–348,
        351, 353
    involvement in Balkans, 165
    Kyoto Protocol and, 117,
        118, 123
Russian-Chechen conflict
    chronology, 106–108
    first Chechen war, 100–102
    history of since 2000,
        102–104
    history of to 1990, 99–100
    key figures, 105–106
    second Chechen war, 102
    sketch of Chechen
        people, 98–99
Rwanda, 311, 312, 316

S

Saakashvili, Mikhail, 106
Sadat, Anwar, 20
    assassination of, 148
    Camp David accords and,
        3, 9–16, 19, 21
    negotiations during 1973
        war, 4, 5, 7
    Society of Muslim Brothers
        and, 146
    Soviets and, 50
al-Sadr, Moqtada, 135, 138
Saint-Pierre, Abbe de, 283
Salinger, Pierre, 86
SALT. *See* Strategic Arms
    Limitation Talks (SALT)
Sanctions, against Iraq,
    131–132
Sarkozy, Nicolas, 104, 106, 108
SARS epidemic, 222
Satisficing, 88–89
Satyagraha, 255
Saudi Arabia, 145–146, 147,
    159, 253
Saukel, Fritz, 304, 308, 309, 314
Scali, John, 85, 89, 92
Schacht, Hjalmar, 304, 310
Schanberg, Sydney, 269
Schevardnadze, Eduard, 17,
    128, 138
Schirach, Baldur von,
    308, 309
Schuman, Robert, 285, 297
Schwarzkopf, Norman, 126,
    129, 138

SDI. *See* Strategic Defense
    Initiative (SDI)
SEA. *See* Single European Act
    (SEA)
SEATO. *See* South-East Asian
    Treaty Organization
    (SEATO)
Security, 220, 296
Selassie, Haile, 33, 34, 36, 38
Self-determination, 96
Sen, Amartya, 252
Separate Amenities Act,
    324, 329, 335
September 11, 2001 attacks, 160
    aftermath and debate
        over, 75–77
    al Qaeda after, 154–156
    al Qaeda and, 148
    chronology, 79
    government response to
        threat reports, 71–73
    Phoenix memo, 73
    threat reports, 67–71
    Zacarias Moussaoui and,
        73–75
Serbia, 165, 181–183
    1355 A.D., 166
    elections in, 171
    history, 165, 167
    warfare in Bosnia and,
        173–176
    warfare in Kosovo and,
        177–178
Serbs
    experience in World War II,
        169
    nationalism of, 170, 171, 180
    in Yugoslavia, 168
Serwadda, David, 226
Sese Seko, Mobutu, 252
Seyss-Inquart, Arthur, 304,
    309, 314
Shaka Zulu, 319
Shakhrai, Sergei, 106, 107
Shamil, Sheik, 99
Shamir, Yitzhak, 17, 20
Shanghai Communiqué, 50
Sharon, Ariel, 18, 19, 21, 23
Sharpeville Massacre, 326,
    328, 335
Shawcross, Hartley, 305
Shia Islam, 145
Shia Moslem rebellion, 131
Shipgun, Gennadi, 102
Short, Walter, 190, 192, 197
Shuttle diplomacy, 5
Simon, Herbert, 88

Singapore, 347, 352
Singh, F. M., 262
Singh, Manmohan, 257,
    261–262, 265, 266, 267
Single European Act (SEA),
    290–291, 298
Sino-Soviet alliance, 48–49
Sino-Soviet-American
    relations, 42–43, 56–57
    chronology, 58–60
    Cold War (1949-1962),
        45–48
    Cold War (1979-1985),
        50–51
    détente (1963-1979), 48–50
    détente (1985-1991), 51–52
    key figures, 57–58
    outbreak of Cold War,
        43–45
    post-Cold War era, 52–54
al-Sistani, Ali, 135, 139
Sisulu, Walter, 322, 326,
    329, 334
Slavery, 271–272, 278
Slovakia, 294
Slovenes, 168
Slovenia, 171–173, 294
Smallpox, 221, 222–223, 233
Smith, Bradley, 309
Smuts, Jan, 321, 322, 334
Sobukwe, Robert, 326
Social Accountability 8000
    code, 272, 279
Societal level of analysis, 3
Society of Muslim Brothers,
    146, 157, 158
Socioeconomic changes, global
    warming and, 113
Solar radiation, 112
Sorenson, Theodore, 86–87
South Africa
    apartheid in (1965-1988),
        326–329
    AZT and, 230
    dismantling apartheid,
        329–330
    establishment/consolidation
        of apartheid, 312–326
    origins of, 318–321
    postapartheid, 331–332
South African Student
    Organization, 327, 335
South-East Asian Treaty
    Organization (SEATO), 46
South Korea, Asian financial
    crisis and, 343, 344, 346,
    347, 351

Sovereignty, nationalism *vs.*,
    104–105
Soviet Union. *See also* Russia;
    Sino-Soviet-American
    relations
    first Persian Gulf War and,
        128, 131
    invasion of Afghanistan,
        50, 146–147
    League of Nations and, 27,
        28, 29, 39
    Manchuria and, 30
Soweto riots, 327, 335
Spaak, Paul-Henri, 283, 286,
    297
Spain, 289, 349
Speer, Albert, 304, 309, 314
Spoilers, 111
Stalin, Josef, 28, 29, 38, 47, 57,
    100, 302
Standard&Poor's, 345
Stark, Harold, 192, 199
START. *See* Strategic Arms
    Reduction Talks (START)
Stevenson, Adlai, 93, 133
Stiglitz, Joseph, 253
Stimson, Henry, 190, 192, 197,
    302–303
Stoessinger, John, 42
Strategic Arms Limitation
    Talks II, 10, 51
Strategic Arms Limitation
    Talks (SALT), 50, 60
Strategic Arms Reduction Talks
    (START), 51, 53
Strategic Defense Initiative
    (SDI), 51, 60
Strategic intervention,
    162–163
Strauss, Leo, 65
Streicher, Julius, 304, 309
Structural Marxist perspective
    on globalization, 277–278
Students for a Democratic
    Society, 210
Sudan, al Qaeda in, 147
Sufi, 145
Suharto, Raden, 344, 353
Suicide bombings, Chechen,
    103, 108
Sullivan Principles, 327, 335
Sunni Islam, 145
Sweatshops, 269–270, 271–272,
    275, 276–277, 278, 279
Sweden, 293
Syria, 1973 war with Israel,
    3, 5, 7–8

T

Tadic, Dusko, 179
Taiwan, 46
Taliban, 147, 148
Talibani, Jalal, 141
Tambo, Oliver, 322, 326, 329
Tamil Tigers, 144, 267
Tariff escalation, 244–245
Tariffs, 237, 240, 241
    agricultural, 244–245, 246
    India, 264
Tata Group, 258
Taylor, Maxwell, 86, 216
TEC. *See* Transitional
    executive council (TEC)
Tenet, George, 68, 70–71, 74,
    75, 78, 134, 138
Terrorism, 143–144. *See also*
    Al Qaeda; September 11,
    2001 attacks
    defined, 143
    international law and, 313
    lessons of war on, 156–157
    in Madrid, 155
    purpose of, 154
Test Ban Treaty, 48, 49
Tet Offensive, 207–209, 217
Thailand, Asian financial crisis
    and, 343, 344–345, 346,
    347, 351, 352–353
Thatcher, Margaret, 51, 288,
    292, 297, 298
Thieu, Nguyen Van, 214, 217
Third World debt crisis, 243
Thompson, Llewellyn, 86,
    90, 93
Tienanmen Square
    massacres, 52
Tito, Josip Broz, 169–170, 181,
    182
Tojo, Hideki, 188, 197, 198
Tokyo War Crimes Trials, 311
Tonelson, Alan, 64
Tonkin Gulf Resolution,
    204–205, 212, 216
Toyko Round, 242, 248
Toys R Us, 272
Trade. *See* North-South trade
Transitional executive council
    (TEC), 330
Treatment Action Campaign,
    230
Treaty of Amsterdam, 296
Treaty of Paris, 285
Treaty of Rome, 286, 287, 290,
    291, 298

Treaty of San Stefano, 165,
181, 182
Treurnicht, Andries, 328–329, 330
Tripartite Pact, 187, 198
Tripolarity, 54–56
Triumphalism, 64
Trollope Play, 86, 94
Troop withdrawal agreements,
Egyptian-Israeli, 6, 8, 14
Truman, Harry, 43, 46, 57,
58, 163
Truman Doctrine, 58
Truth and Reconciliation
Commission, 331, 336
Tudjman, Franjo, 176, 181
al-Turabi, Hasan, 157
Turkey, 293, 294, 347, 348, 351
Tutu, Desmond, 331, 334

U

Union republic, 100
United Democratic Front, 328
United Kingdom
Abyssinia and, 33, 35, 36
Bosnia and, 176
Common Market and, 287,
288–289
India and, 253–255
Kyoto Protocol and, 117, 118
League of Nations and,
27–29, 36–37
Manchuria and, 30–31
second Gulf war and, 134
South Africa and, 320–321
trade exemptions, 238
United Nations
anarchy and rule of
law and, 24
Commission on Human
Security, 221
global governance and, 338,
339, 340
League of Nations and
founding of, 37–38
national interest position
and, 64–65, 76–77
Nuremberg Principles, 311
Soviet attitudes toward, 44
UNAIDS, 226, 229, 230,
231, 233
UN Conference on the
Environment and
Development, 115
UN Conference on Trade and
Development (UNCTAD),
239–240, 248

UN Development Program, 227
UN Environmental
Programme, 114, 123
UNESCO, 227
UN Food and Agriculture
Organization, 132
UN Framework Convention on
Climate Change (FCCC),
115, 121, 123
UNICEF, 132, 226
UN Office on Drugs and
Crime, 227
UN Population Fund, 227
UN Security Council
AIDS and, 228, 233
anarchy and, 24–25
Bosnia and, 175
Croatia and, 172, 173
Cuban Missile Crisis and,
85, 88
first Persian Gulf War and,
127–128
Iraqi elections and, 136
Resolution 242, 4, 10
resolutions on Iraq,
127–128, 133
war crimes tribunal, 311
United States. *See also*
Sino-Soviet-American
relations; Vietnam War
agricultural tariffs,
246–247
Asian financial crisis
and, 349
Bosnia and, 176
Camp David accords, 9–16
diplomacy during
Arab-Israeli 1973 war, 3–9
entrance into World War II
(*See* Pearl Harbor)
farm subsidies, 238,
245, 247
first Persian Gulf War,
127–130
government response to
HIV/AIDS pandemic,
227–229
hegemonic imperative
approach to national
interest and, 64–65
income disparity in, 274
international law and, 121
intervention and, 162–163
Kyoto Protocol and,
115–116, 117–122
leadership role of, 3
League of Nations and, 27

multilateralist approach
to national interest and,
65–66
political integration of, 282,
283
sanctions against Iraq,
131–132
sweatshops in, 272
view on national interest,
62–64
United Students Against
Sweatshops, 270
Unit veto, 55
Universal Declaration of
Human Rights, 311,
317, 318, 333
Urbanization, pandemics
and, 222
Uruguay Round, 243–247
U.S.-Taiwan Mutual Defense
Assistance Agreement, 46
USS Cole, 147, 152, 159
Ustase movement, 169, 182

V

Vajpayee, A. B., 257, 265,
266, 267
Value added tax (VAT), 290
Vance, Cyrus, 10, 12, 13,
16, 174
Vance-Owen plan, 176
van Riebeeck, Jan, 318–319
Versailles Treaty, 28, 32, 39
Verwoerd, Hendrik F., 322, 323,
324, 326, 333
Vietnam Moratorium
Committee, 210
Vietnam Syndrome, 213
Vietnam War, 46, 49–50
chronology, 215–218
democratic peace theory
and, 212–213
international law and,
312–313
key figures, 214–215
Nixon and, 211–212
peace movement, 209–211
public opinion and, 204,
206–207
skepticism of, 205–207
Tet Offensive and,
207–209
Tonkin Gulf, 204–205
Vojvodina, 171
Volvchov, A. F., 307
von Neurath, Konstantin, 304

von Papen, Franz, 304,
   309–310
von Schirach, Baldur, 304
Vulcans, 132–133

W

Wage competition, 274–275,
   276
Wahhab, Muhammad Ibn
   Abdul, 145, 158
Wahhabis, 145–146, 148
Wallerstein, Immanuel, 277
Walmart, 269–270
War, aggressive, 303
War crimes, 175
War crimes tribunals, 178,
   311, 316
Warfare, terrorism *vs.*, 144
War Powers Act, 212
Warsaw Pact, 44, 59, 60
Washington, George, 63, 144
Washington Consensus, 243
Washington Post, 128
Watson, Dale, 72, 74
Weapons inspectors, 133
Weathermen, 210
Weizman, Ezer, 11
Werner Report, 289
Western European Union, 296
Westmoreland, William,
   215, 217

White-collar outsourcing,
   270, 273
Whitman, Christine Todd, 120
Wilson, Woodrow, 25, 38, 39,
   41–42, 163
Wirth, Timothy, 123
Wolfowitz, Paul, 65, 76, 78,
   132, 138, 139
Woodward, Bob, 128
World Bank, 226, 237, 284, 349
   Global Environmental
      Facility, 118
World Health Organization,
   222–223, 226–227, 233
World Meteorological
   Organization, 114, 123
World Trade Center, attack on,
   148. *See also* September
   11, 2001 attacks
World Trade Organization,
   52, 54, 248, 270, 275
World War I, 203
World War II, 187
   economic conditions after,
      237–238
   League of Nations and, 36–37
   Yugoslavia and, 169
Wye River Accords, 22

X

Xenophobia, 96

Y

Yarchoan, Robert, 226
Yeltsin, Boris, 51, 53, 60, 100,
   101, 102, 106–107
Yermolov, Aleksei, 99
Yousef, Ramsi, 152, 159
Youth League, 322
Yugoslavia, 53, 164
   1918-1980, 167–170
   after Dayton Accords, 177
   after Tito, 170–171
   chronology of
      dismemberment, 181–183
   current situation, 179–180
   history to 1918, 164–167
   key figures in
      dismemberment, 181
   nationalities of, 168
   in World War II, 169

Z

al-Zarqawi, Abu Musab, 132,
   139, 140, 153, 157
Zavgayev, Duko, 100
al-Zawahiri, Ayman Mohammed
   Rabi', 147, 148, 157
Zeitz, Paul, 228
Zimmern, Alfred, 26
Zubaydah, Abu, 68, 78, 150,
   155, 160
Zuma, Jacob, 331